LIFE WRITING IN THE LONG RUN

LIFE WRITING IN THE LONG RUN

A Smith & Watson Autobiography Studies Reader

Sidonie Smith and Julia Watson

Copyright © 2016 by Sidonie Smith and Julia Watson
Some rights reserved

This work is licensed under the Creative Commons Attribution-NonCommercial-NoDerivatives 4.0 International License. To view a copy of this license, visit http://creativecommons.org/licenses/by-nc-nd/4.0/ or send a letter to Creative Commons, PO Box 1866, Mountain View, California 94042, USA.

Paula Modersohn-Becker, "Self-Portrait," 1906-07. Oil tempera on cardboard and paper. 10.4 × 7.3 in. Private collection, Dortmund, Germany.

Published in the United States of America by
Michigan Publishing
Manufactured in the United States of America

DOI: http://dx.doi.org/10.3998/mpub.7133795

ISBN (print): 978-1-60785-409-8
ISBN (e-book): 978-1-60785-410-4

An imprint of Michigan Publishing, Maize Books serves the publishing needs of the University of Michigan community by making high-quality scholarship widely available in print and online. It represents a new model for authors seeking to share their work within and beyond the academy, offering streamlined selection, production, and distribution processes. Maize Books is intended as a complement to more formal modes of publication in a wide range of disciplinary areas.

http://www.maizebooks.org

*To the graduate students who, over this long run,
have inspired our thinking and kept us current.*

Contents

Acknowledgments and Permissions   xiii
A Personal Introduction to *Life Writing in the Long Run*   xix

Part I: Theoretical Frameworks

1. Introduction: Situating Subjectivity in Women's Autobiographical Practices, from *Women, Autobiography, Theory: A Reader* (1998)   3
2. The Rumpled Bed of Autobiography: Extravagant Lives, Extravagant Questions (2001)   89
3. Witness or False Witness? Metrics of Authenticity, I-Formations, and the Ethic of Verification in Testimony (2012)   111

Part II: Everyday Lives and Autobiographical Storytelling

4. Introduction to *Getting a Life: Everyday Uses of Autobiography* (1996)   165
5. Ordering the Family: Genealogy as Autobiographical Pedigree (Watson 1996)   191
6. Virtually Me: A Toolkit about Online Self-Presentation (2014)   225

Part III: Enabling Concepts

7. Performativity, Autobiographical Practice, Resistance (Smith 1995)   261
8. The Spaces of Autobiographical Narrative (Watson 2007)   283
9. The Autobiographical Manifesto: Identities, Temporalities, Politics (Smith 1991) *Print and e-book only*   305

Part IV: Visualized Lives

10. Introduction: Mapping Women's Self-Representation at Visual/Textual Interfaces, from *Interfaces: Women, Autobiography, Image, Performance* (2002) — 345
11. Autographic Disclosures and Genealogies of Desire in Alison Bechdel's *Fun Home* (Watson 2008) — 393
12. Re-citing, Re-siting, and Re-sighting Likeness: Reading the Family Archive in Drucilla Modjeska's *Poppy* and Sally Morgan's *My Place* (Smith 1994) — 435
13. Human Rights and Comics: Autobiographical Avatars, Crisis Witnessing, and Transnational Rescue Networks (Smith 2011) — 467

Part V: Women's Life Writing in the United States

14. Introduction: Living in Public, from *Before They Could Vote: American Women's Autobiographical Writing, 1819–1919* (2006) — 485
15. Cheesecake, Nymphs, and 'We the People': About 1900 in America (Smith 1994) *Print and e-book only* — 517
16. Strategic Autoethnography and American Ethnicity Debates: The Metrics of Authenticity in *When I Was Puerto Rican* (Watson 2013) *Print and e-book only* — 545
17. "America's Exhibit A": Hillary Rodham Clinton's *Living History* and the Genres of Political Authenticity (Smith 2012) — 577

Part VI: Global Circuits, Political Formations

18. Introduction: De/Colonization and the Politics of Discourse in Women's Autobiographical Practices, from *De/Colonizing the Subject: The Politics of Gender in Women's Autobiography* (1992) — 605
19. Memory, Narrative, and the Discourses of Identity in *Abeng* and *No Telephone to Heaven* (Smith 1999) — 629

20. Narratives and Rights: *Zlata's Diary* and the Circulation of Stories of Suffering Ethnicity (Smith 2006)   657
21. Parsua Bashi's *Nylon Road*: The Visual Dialogics of Witnessing in Iranian Women's Graphic Memoir (Watson 2016)   679

LIFE WRITING IN THE LONG RUN FOR THE CLASSROOM: COORDINATING THE ESSAYS WITH 20 SPECIFIC TOPICS

Authenticity and agency 1, 3, 16, 17, 20
Autobiography theories 1, 2, 3, 6, 7, 8, 9, 10, 14, 18
Autoethnography 5, 14, 15, 16
Biography 5, 11, 14, 17
Body, gender, and sexuality 1, 2, 8, 10, 11, 19
Diary 2, 7, 10, 11, 14, 19
Diaspora and migration 5, 8, 12, 15, 16, 18, 19, 21
Digital life narrative 3, 6
Ethnicity and hybridity 4, 9, 10, 14, 15, 16, 18, 19, 20
Genealogy, family narrative 4, 5, 11, 12
Genres of life writing 3, 4, 9, 10, 15, 16, 17, 20
Graphic memoir 11, 13, 21
Human rights and witnessing 3, 13, 20, 21
Manifesto 9, 13, 20, 21
Memory and subjectivity 1, 7, 8, 9, 10, 11, 12, 15, 19, 21
Paratexts and circulation 2, 3, 4, 6, 13, 14, 20, 21
Performativity 1, 7, 9, 10, 17
Post/colonial narrative, testimony 3, 12, 13, 14, 18
Relationality 1, 5, 11, 19
Visual portraiture, photography 2, 10, 11, 12, 20, 21

Acknowledgments and Permissions

We gratefully acknowledge the help of the professional staff at Michigan Publishing Services, particularly our editor savant, Jason Colman; our key idea-person Meredith Kahn; our editor Amanda Karby; and the production staff who facilitated the communication of our work in multiple-format platforms, including print and open-access versions. We depended on the research assistance of two doctoral students at the University of Michigan, Jina Kim and Tiffany Ball, who, while completing their dissertations, helped produce final versions of our previously published essays. Sidonie thanks Sheri Sytsema-Geiger, Key Administrator at the Institute for the Humanities at the University of Michigan, for her attention to permissions obligations. Julia thanks Professor Lesley Ferris for consultation and conversation about autobiographical theatre.

With two exception the essays included in this volume have previously appeared in our collections or journals. We thank the following publishers for permission to include our work here.

a/b:Auto/Biography Studies for the following permissions:

Smith, Sidonie. "Performativity, Autobiographical Practice, Resistance." *a/b: Auto/Biography Studies* 10.1 (January 1995), 17–33.

Biography for the following permissions:

Watson, Julia. "Autographic Disclosures and Genealogies of Desire in Alison Bechdel's *Fun Home*." *Biography* 31:1 (Winter 2008), 27–56; Smith, Sidonie and Julia Watson. "The Rumpled Bed of Autobiography: Extravagant Lives, Extravagant Questions." *Biography* 24.1. (Winter 2001): 1–14; Smith, Sidonie and Julia Watson. "Witnessing or False Witnessing? Metrics of Authenticity, I-Formations, and the Ethic of Verification in Testimony," *Biography*, 35:4 (Fall 2012), 590–626.

Böhlau Verlag for the following permission: Watson, Julia. "The Spaces of Autobiographical Narrative." In *Räume des Selbst. Selbstzeugnisforschung transkulturell*. (Selbstzeugnisse der Neuzeit 19), ed. Andreas Bähr/Peter Burschel/Gabriele Jancke. Köln/Weimar/Wien: Böhlau, 2007, 13–25.

Brill Publishing for the following permission: Smith, Sidonie. Reprint of "Memory, Narrative, and the Discourses of Identity in *Abeng* and *No Telephone to Heaven*." In *Postcolonialism and Autobiography: Michelle Cliff, David Dabydeen, Opal Palmer Adisa*, eds. Alfred Hornung and Ernstpeter Ruhe. Amsterdam: Editions Rodopi (Brill), 1999, 37–59. By permission of Brill Publications.

mfs: Modern Fiction Studies for the following permission: Sidonie Smith. Adapted from "Re-citing, Re-siting, and Re-sighting Likeness: Reading the Family Archive in Drucilla Modjeska's *Poppy* and Sally Morgan's *My Place*," *mfs* 40 (Fall 1994): 509–542.

Oxford University Press for permission to reuse: Smith, Sidonie. "'America's Exhibit A': Hillary Rodham Clinton's *Living History* and the Genres of Political Authenticity." *American Literary History*, Fall 2012, 523–42.

The Permissions Company for permission to reuse: Smith, Sidonie. Adapted from "Narratives and Rights: *Zlata's Diary* and the Circulation of Stories of Suffering Ethnicity." In *WSQ: Women's Studies Quarterly* 34, Nos. 1/2 (Spring/Summer 2006): 133–152.

© 2006 by the Feminist Press at the City University of New York. Used by permission of The Permissions Company, Inc., on behalf of the publishers, www.feministpress.org. All rights reserved.

The University of Michigan Press for the following permission: Smith, Sidonie, and Julia Watson. "Introduction: Mapping Women's Self-Representation at Visual/Textual Interfaces," adapted from *Interfaces: Women, Autobiography, Image, Performance*. Ed. Sidonie Smith and Julia Watson. Ann Arbor: University of Michigan Press, 2002, 3–22.

The University of Minnesota Press for the following permissions: Smith, Sidonie and Julia Watson. "Introduction: De/Colonization and the Politics of Discourse in Women's Autobiographical Practices," adapted from *De/Colonizing the Subject: The Politics of Gender in Women's Autobiography*, eds. Sidonie Smith and Julia Watson. 1992, xiii-xxxi; Smith, Sidonie, and Julia Watson. "Introduction." From *Getting a Life: Everyday Uses of Autobiography*, eds. Sidonie Smith and Julia Watson. 1996, 1–24; Watson, Julia. "Ordering the Family: Genealogy as Autobiographical Pedigree," adapted from *Getting a Life: Everyday Uses of Autobiography*. Ed. Sidonie Smith and Julia Watson. 1996, 297–323.

The University of Wisconsin Press for the following permissions: Smith, Sidonie. "Human Rights and Comics: Autobiographical Avatars, Crisis Witnessing, and Transnational Rescue Networks." From Chaney, Michael A., ed., *Graphic Subjects*. © 2011 by the Board of Regents of the University of Wisconsin System. Reprinted by permission of University of Wisconsin Press; Smith, Sidonie, and Julia Watson. "Introduction: Living in Public." From *Before They Could Vote: American Women's Autobiographical Writing, 1819–1919*. © 2006 by the Board of Regents of the University of Wisconsin System. Reprinted by permission of University of Wisconsin Press; Smith, Sidonie, and Julia Watson. "Introduction: Situating Subjectivity in Women's Autobiographical Practices." Adapted from Smith, Sidonie, and Julia Watson. *Women, Autobiography, Theory: A Reader*. © 1998 by the Board of Regents of the University of Wisconsin System. Reprinted by permission of the University of Wisconsin Press. While we hold copyright to the following essay, we acknowledge the role of the University of Wisconsin Press in bringing this work to the public: Smith, Sidonie, and Julia Watson. Adapted from "Virtually Me: A Toolkit about Online Self-Presentation," in *Identity Technologies: Constructing the Self Online*. Eds. Anna Poletti and Julie Rak. Madison: University of Wisconsin Press, 2014. 70–94.

This essay was developed specifically for this volume: "A Personal Introduction to Life Writing in the Long Run." It is copyrighted by Sidonie Smith and Julia Watson.

Though this essay is in preprint form, we acknowledge the role of *Lifewriting Annual* in preparing it for publication: Watson, Julia. "Parsua Bashi's *Nylon Road*: The Visual Dialogics of Witnessing in Iranian Women's Graphic Memoir." Copyright Julia Watson. Preprint for *Lifewriting Annual: Biographical and Autobiographical Studies*. Forthcoming, New York: AMS Press, 2017.

Taylor & Francis granted permission to reuse the following essays in the print and e-book versions of this book but not the open-access electronic version: Smith, Sidonie. "The Autobiographical Manifesto: Identities, Temporalities, Politics." *Prose Studies* 14.2 (September 1991), 186–212; Smith, Sidonie. "Cheesecake, Nymphs, and 'We the People': Un/National Subjects about 1900." *Prose Studies* 17.1 (April 1994), 120–40; Watson, Julia. "Strategic Autoethnography and American Ethnicity Debates: The Metrics of Authenticity in *When I Was Puerto Rican*." *Life Writing*, 10:2 (June 2013), 129–50.

We also thank the following for permission to use images:

> Images from Parsua Bashi: *Nylon Road*. Copyright 2006 by Parsua Bashi. Reprinted by permission of Parsua Bashi and Kein & Aber AG, Zürich. All rights reserved.
> Renée Cox and Lyle Ashton Harris: *Venus Hottentot 2000*, 1995. Courtesy Renée Cox.
> Images from *Fun Home: A Family Tragicomedy* by Alison Bechdel. Copyright © 2006 by Alison Bechdel. Reprinted by

permission of Houghton Mifflin Harcourt Publishing Company. All rights reserved.

Tracey Emin: "My Bed" 1999. 2016 Tracey Emin. All rights reserved, DACS, London / Artists Rights Society (ARS), New York.

Audrey Flack: *Marilyn (Vanitas)* 1977. Courtesy of the artist.

Mary Kelly: Detail of "Menace" from "Interim, Part I: Corpus" 1984–1985.

Laminated photo positive, silkscreen, acrylic on Plexiglas 30 panels: 36" H x 48" W x 2" D each. Courtesy of the artist, Susanne Vielmetter Los Angeles Projects, and Mitchell-Innes & Nash, New York.

Annette Messager: *Les Lignes de la main,* 1987–88. Overpainted black and white photograph with handwriting on the wall. Courtesy of the Artist and Marian Goodman Gallery.

Alice Neel: "Self-Portrait" 1980, Oil on canvas. Courtesy of National Portrait Gallery, Smithsonian Institution and © Estate of Alice Neel, 1980.

May Stevens: *Rosa Luxemburg and Alice Stevens*. From "*Rosa, Alice*: Ordinary/Extraordinary," artist's book, 1988. Courtesy of the artist and RYAN LEE Gallery, New York, New York.

Yong Soon Min: *deColonization*, 1991. Courtesy of the artist.

A Personal Introduction to *Life Writing in the Long Run*

I have never considered writing fiction. Life is much more interesting.
    Svetlana Alexievitch (Nobel Laureate in Literature, 2015)

[The author] believes sincerely in the truth of what [he] is writing at the same time that [he] knows it is not the truth.
    J. M. Coetzee, *The Good Story*

I'm imaginatively freer the further I get from myself.
    Richard Ford, "Afterword," *Let Me Be Frank with You*

If you don't look back, the future never happens.
    Rita Dove, "Dawn Revisited"

On the loftiest throne in the world we are still sitting only on our own rump.
    Michel de Montaigne, "Of Experience"

Now, when the "future" seems more the past, we take a retrospective look at the essays we authored over nearly three decades of scholarship on life writing. In assembling what we see as a wide-ranging and eclectic exploration, we seek to capture the range of issues that engaged us at the time of first publication, when they were at the forefront of discussion. All but one of the essays included here have already "gotten a life" in print. Here, we hope to give them another life, to insert them once again into conversations and debates around the globe about the formal, definitional, sociocultural, political, and practical features of all that is now construed as life writing, and that we've often termed autobiographical acts and practices.

Inevitably there is a component of hubris in assembling a retrospective, but it is not our only motivation. We hope to engage scholars new to the field of life writing studies, lest they think that the field's history begins with their own engagement or that the thorny issues they identify have not already been energizing three decades of debate. Occasionally we have been surprised to discover that emerging scholars or those in other fields reference predominantly the work of de Man, Barthes, and Lejeune, as if that triumvirate of theorists in the nineteen-seventies summed up the parameters of theorizing the autobiographical. In reprinting here the Introductions to our past five collections, what we then considered provocative interventions, we hope to bequeath the legacy of a past history of scholarly writing, not just our own but that of the many scholars whose work came before or alongside ours and who helped shape the arenas across disciplines in which the study of self-presentation, and the narration of lived lives, have been and might be constructed. We also hope that this collection reminds readers of the numerous scholars of autobiography studies, in the US, England, Germany, Canada, Australia, Canada, the Caribbean, Argentina, and elsewhere, who have worked to bring stature to a field long considered "sub-literary," "marginal," and "untheorized."

We have a further motivation, to reach curious scholars around the globe who have written to us requesting copies or summaries of our work by return message. This collection takes the bold step of being published simultaneously by Michigan Publishing in on-demand print and online open access versions, taking advantage of technological platforms that are transforming scholarly communication in the humanities. We aim to make *Life Writing in the Long Run* easily accessible to interested scholars and graduate students without access to comprehensive libraries and bookstores but with access to smart phones, tablets, computers or terminals for searching the Internet. As life-writing scholars seek to reach a wider readership, to encourage and mentor the next generation of scholars, and to help transform humanities scholarship into an interactive knowledge commons, open access is an increasingly attractive option.

From "Autobiography" to Life Writing

The earliest essay in this volume, Sidonie's on "The Autobiographical Manifesto," was written around 1990; the most recent, Julia's on Parsua Bashi's graphic memoir *Nylon Road* as an Iranian counter-history, has not yet been published. We followed one rule: No matter how tempted we were to "fix" parts of the essays, we have left them as they appeared when published, with the exception of minor changes for grammar and clarity. We therefore generally resisted inserting current terminology into our earlier essays. Although reliance on the term "autobiography" in essays from the 1990s now makes us cringe, we refrained from substituting either the phrase "autobiographical acts and practices" that we shifted to in the late nineties, or the terms "life writing" and "life narrative" that entered the field with the new millennium.

Since 2000 in North American scholarship "life writing" has been a preferred umbrella term for the heterogeneous genres, modes, and media of autobiographically-inflected storytelling and self-presentation. At the same time there is wider recognition that differing national histories and traditions infer quite different connotations with "autobiography." It is still considered a pejorative term in French,[1] does not align well with usage in German such as "self-documents" (*Selbstzeugnisse*), and may confusingly refer to both a specific mode of retrospective self-narration in prose and a whole range of discursive styles.

We shifted our terminology from "autobiography" as we were completing the final version of the first edition of *Reading*

Autobiography (2001). In a chance conversation, Mary Louise Pratt asked why we were still using that term, which for her signified the master narrative of the great Western "individual" as a product of modernity. By contrast, forms such as the *testimonio*, which her *Imperial Eyes* discusses as alternative, and other cultural formations in the contact zones of colonial and postcolonial encounter and violence were also, but quite differently, autobiographical. Mary's query was a salutary challenge for us to divest from the master's house, though we had long critiqued the tradition of "autobiography" as a legacy of the Enlightenment privileging of the "individual," the white, western man of property. But terminology remains a difficult question, as "autobiography" still drives search engines and cataloging. Now, of course, even the terms "life narrative" and "life writing" seem too limited for the ever-increasing modes of presenting, performing, imaging, and circulating a "life" in the multimedia of graphic memoir, performance art, visual art, and online platforms.

Readers will note the shift in terms throughout this collection. Essays and introductions published before 2001 generally rely on the term "autobiography"; those published since then carefully negotiate a cluster of terms and specify genres of the autobiographical, with the traditional mode of "autobiography" as only one of dozens of genres. Terminology may seem a small point, but we emphasize it because the critique of "autobiography" as insufficient to new modes of life writing or memoir seems a ghost that refuses to die. Both emergent scholars in the field and those in other disciplines making forays into life writing studies often ground their analyses in that critique and propose new coinages. But observing that not all modes of self-presentation are in the form of "traditional" autobiography, with its retrospective narrative of individualist becoming, is a cornerstone of over three decades of critique, signaled in neologisms such as Domna Stanton's "autogynography" (1984), J.M. Coetzee's "autrebiography" (1992), Leigh Gilmore's "autobiographics" (1994), and many more.[2]

While neologisms and the models they propose are often enabling in their historical moment, they can obscure a more complex factor, namely, how the expansion of the canon from "autobiography" to life writing was enabled by retrieval from the archives of many previously unrecognized genres of life writing: the slave narrative and the immigrant genealogical story, the rise of feminist "coming to voice" stories, the narration of illness or disability as a mode of gaining agency, the comics autographic, and many more. These expansive templates of self-presentation reside not so much within the official terrain of a genre of "autobiography" but rather can be positioned as its "outlaws" (in Caren Kaplan's 1992 term), outliers that have long subverted the notion of the autonomous, sovereign self often asserted as definitive of "autobiography." Acknowledging a fuller history of the field seems an indispensable first step, if scholars are not to recirculate arguments made one or two or even three decades ago when the term "autobiography"—not life writing—was the operative referent.

Autobiographically Speaking

Looking back on these essays is itself a kind of autobiographical journey, both to the moments of researching and writing them and to what was then known, assumed, or theorized about their topics. We want to speak personally, for a moment, with autobiographically inflected meditations on writing our essays.

Julia on the Unpredictable Consequences of Working on Genealogy

Julia composed her essay on genealogy, "Ordering the Family: Genealogy as Autobiographical Pedigree," in 1992–3 while a visiting Fulbright professor in Dakar, Senegal. There she often visited Gorée Island, the former detainment station for West Africans being shipped to enslavement in the Americas in the early nineteenth century.

Witnessing the evidence of systematic, brutal enslavement in the barred windows and chains of Gorée's fortress changed how I thought about claims to genealogical pedigree—the legacy of the victors—and the meanings of migration. My memories of writing in Dakar are inescapably material. I cannot return to that essay without recalling, re-feeling, the texture of daily life at my desk by a window that looked out onto mango trees, where I heard the cries of children at play and the screams of wild birds, and where I had to dust my Mac cube on the desk every day because the fine sand of desertification drifted through the window onto everything. Living in the partly oral culture that Senegal then still was, made clear the colonial inflection of genealogical practice, as it is understood in the West.

Now, however, I also wince at some points on rereading the essay's certainty about the codified practices of genealogy because of how my own thoughts on that process have changed. In 2004 I became very interested in my Irish family's genealogy and decided to trace the histories of my two Irish grandmothers, both of whom left for North America at the end of the nineteenth century. The strictures and structures of genealogical research served as guideposts and the Mormon researcher at my local Family History Center was a miracle-worker in locating manifests for ships and clarifying census details. More largely, I am now surprised to see how there has been a revolution in researching and writing family lives as a combination of autobiographical and biographical detail relying on genealogy in collective family stories such as Nancy K. Miller's intriguing *What They Saved: Pieces of a Jewish Past* and Shirlee Taylor Haizlip's wry *The Sweeter the Juice: A Family Memoir in Black and White*. With digital access the preservation and sharing of family archives has also profoundly changed genealogical practices. And the American public's interest in television shows about unearthing the genealogies of prominent people, such as Henry Louis Gates' *Finding Your Roots*, indicates how accessible not just a sense of the past but the evidence of one has become for everyday users. My 1996 essay underestimated the emotional satisfaction of finding historical information about my ancestors and inventing fuller stories of the lives they might have lived, let alone the possibility of meeting a distant relative still in the birthplace of one of my grandmothers. These satisfactions of developing autobiographical consciousness depended on learning the exacting if imperfect tools of genealogical method that now, through the wonders of DNA research, have become available to those of African, American, and Asian, as well as European, descent.

There were larger implications to thinking about genealogy from Dakar's locus of slavery and colonization than I foresaw at the time. The question of who speaks for and as whom became a thread guiding many of the texts and topics I chose, not only in essays about some of the first women's published autobiographical works in Senegal (Nafissatou Diallo's *A Dakar Childhood* and Ken Bugul's *The Abandoned Baobab*) but also in spurring curiosity about those marginalized by American imperialism, particularly Native Americans. I have never written the book on autoethnography that thinking about genealogy stirred me to, as the political sensitivities around a woman of privilege discussing "others" make for fraught conversations. But I am now persuaded that it is important to begin with a concept of "counter-ethnography" and address the exclusionary ethnographic norms and strictures that prevailed at the moment of "interviewer-informant" encounters.

When I look back, I also note my fatal curiosity about the work of "lesser" women writers—forgotten ones like Mary Arnold and Mabel Reed, Montana women writers not known beyond the Rockies like Mary MacLane and Janet Campbell Hale, quirky visual artists like Bobby Baker and Parsua Bashi, and well-known but idiosyncratic ones like Charlotte Salomon and Patti Smith. Engaging with outliers has been a sustaining pleasure for me.

Sidonie on Rereading Her Past Writing

In reading over these essays I am taken back to their places of composition. There was the office in the Department of Gender Studies and Social Analysis of the University of Adelaide in Australia, where I wrote the essay included here on Sally Morgan's

My Place and Drusilla Modjeska's *Poppy*, two very different life writing texts published in 1987 and 1990 respectively. I began reading Australian life writing in a haphazard manner to familiarize myself with works that were part of the burgeoning canon of settler literary culture in Australian life writing. A favorite of mine was Albert Facey's *A Fortunate Life* (1981); I also read numerous works of oral history, autoethnography, and testimony written by Australia's indigenous peoples, survivors of what has become known as The Stolen Generation. When I returned home I carried a memento of those months spent reading, exploring, and composing: a large lithograph print of a mother and child by Sally Morgan, who was a graphic artist as well as a writer. It now hangs in my living room, a constant reminder of my time in Australia—the literature I read, the friends I made, and the ongoing struggles of indigenous peoples in the long, sordid histories of settler societies.

At times I also recall the conditions of an essay's composition. While rereading an essay we decided not to include, I found myself captured by the illness that had kept me in bed as I composed and sent off that essay to be read by a generous volunteer at a conference on "material selves." Having the idea for an intriguing essay was the easy part; the hard part involved trying to sit up and write with as much polish as I could muster while my body endured five days of fever. The thought of that moment makes me feel queasy all over again.

At other times, how unfamiliar my scholarly voice seems. It isn't that I don't recognize the shape of the sentences, the particular idioms of theorizing, the points toward which I was driving. It is the certainty in the argument, a certainty that belies the labor of essay writing and the sense of despondency in trying to find a point of repose at the end of a piece. It is also the sense that, at that point in time, I knew something about a set of issues or a constellation of texts or a theoretical conundrum that now entirely eludes my memory.

Returning to particular essays also conveyed me backwards in time to sites of sociality that punctuate my history in the field of autobiography studies. Rereading essays returned me to the scenes of the conferences at which I presented them. Those conferences were consistently conversational occasions, opportunities to meet writers and scholars of life writing from around the world. I returned three times to Mainz, Germany, at the invitation of Alfred Hornung, literally the German "dean" of American Studies and the mentor to several generations of scholars now working in life writing studies throughout Germany. I have similarly warm memories of the biennial meetings of the International Auto/Biography Studies Association in Beijing, Melbourne, Sussex, Honolulu, Canberra, Banff, and other global locations. Given the hard slog of carving out a place for the purposeful study of life writing in academia, these meetings of a generous, welcoming community composed of established and emerging scholars forged networks, spawned three regional associations—for Europe, the Pacific, the Americas—, and provided generous mentors for graduate students. I am thankful for all of them.

The Essays Included in This Anthology

Introductions to Our Collections

The pleasure of revisiting our co-written introductions to four collections of essays and an anthology of short autobiographical essays by nineteenth-century American women writers is of a different sort. Our first co-edited volume, *De/Colonizing the Subject: The Politics of Gender in Women's Autobiography* (1992) had the excitement of a project that was at the time without precedent because so little autobiographical writing by women had been accorded international recognition. Ironically it would now be an impossibly large project to revisit, given the explosion of women's postcolonial life writing around the world and the need to more fully stipulate specific colonial histories in regions of the world where neocolonial practices stubbornly persist or fundamentalist regimes have been installed.

Our second edited collection, *Getting a Life: Everyday Uses of Autobiography* (1996), ranged wildly and widely. Yet the argument of its introduction, that we move in and out of multiple versions of our life scripts on a regular basis, now seems prescient for theorizing everyday life and the uses of social media. Its essays came from contributors in fields ranging from communication to political science, and took up topics such as Alcoholics Anonymous narratives and personal ads that have become a staple of cultural studies.

Our third introduction, to *Women, Autobiography, Theory: A Reader* (1998), was the compression of a book, which we did not have the time or occasion to write, concerning the retrieval and production of women's autobiographical writing since the inception of Second Wave feminism. We both came of age in the late sixties and, like many women graduate students, wondered why there were not models and theories that aligned with our own experience. At the same time, by the nineties we wanted to critique the notion of "women's experience" as an essentialist simplification. The thirty-nine previously published essays that we gathered chart a kind of dialectical history on topics in feminist theory that influenced not only the field of women's, but of all, autobiography studies. Its scope included concepts such as memory, experience, performativity, displacement, ethnic- and class-based self-construction, collectivized subjectivities, alternative genres, voices, and sexualities, and the pedagogy and practice of autobiographical writing—topics that now signal the wide range of our field.

For our fourth collection, *Interfaces: Women, Autobiography, Image, Performance* (2002), we wrote an introduction that involved a disciplinary stretch into life narratives that were not, or not only, in writing: self-portraits in painting, installation, sculpture, or performance. A challenging task both to organize and to theorize, the book taught us much about the frames of disciplinary parameters and modes of inquiry at a time when women artists were actively breaching those boundaries. We aimed to develop a systematic model for reading at what we call the visual-verbal interface of autobiographical acts and apply its lens to a wide range of women's strategies for self-presentation: as parallel or interrogatory, documentary or ethnographic, paratextual or palimpsestic, telescoped or serial. While such autobiographical acts cannot be fully schematized, the model suggests that they are by no means just transparent "expressions"; rather, they are complex and inventive projects engaging both the materiality of the body and the affordances or limits of various media.

Before They Could Vote: American Women's Autobiographical Writing, 1819–1919 (2006), our only venture into assembling a collection of autobiographical texts, involved lesser-known women's writing from the American "long nineteenth century" to the advent of women's suffrage in the United States. As we discovered how little we knew about everyday life writers of the past, the book became a conversation with some formerly excluded margins of autobiography studies.

Our collaborative collections would not have been possible without the active support of many editors, above all William L. Andrews and Craig Howes. Bill's encouragement over these decades, as he listened to the many possible projects we cooked up, was contagious and sustaining; and his passion for recovering the buried past of life writing, coupled with his encyclopedic knowledge of African American slave narratives evidenced in *To Tell a Free Story*, was inspiring. Craig's energy for organizing *Biography*, the preeminent journal in the field, as well as the IABA listserv, and the Center for Biographical Research at the University of Hawaii, has helped transform life writing into a global field and generated many occasions where we found inspiration for our own new projects. Our co-authored book, *Reading Autobiography: A Guide to Interpreting Life Narratives*, one hundred and fifty pages longer in its second edition (2010) than its first (2001), depended on the conversancy we gained over the years with a wide range of texts, scholars, and issues. In retrospect, our collections were a kind of autodidactic exercise. Like many others, we had to discover and excavate the field before we could map it—and, as we know, maps are temporally contingent and always incomplete and inadequate to the terrain.

Collaborative Essays

The story was somewhat different with our collaborative essays, a form that we have turned to in recent years when the sheer demands of time and energy required to produce a book across two states and in competition with our other interests and the demands of our jobs led us to compress Big Ideas into essay-length discussions that we hoped would be informative and provocative. Indeed, in recent years one of the most important contributions that scholars of life writing can make has seemed to be raising questions—about the settled canons of literature departments, the schemes and structures of narrative methodologies, the hierarchy of cultural modes for negotiating issues in the world.

The first non-introductory essay we co-authored, "The Rumpled Bed of Autobiography" (2001), was occasioned by an unsettling experience that we shared in London while viewing Tracey Emin's "My Bed," a finalist for the distinguished Turner Prize. To see a "life" presented as the material detritus of an actual body moving through a decade of experience that had obsessed her brought home a sense of the contradictory stakes of autobiographical work—as both careful self-scrutiny and, at times with Emin, flagrant narcissism. "My Bed" seemed a metaphor for a field of study that, in the wake of the "memoir boom," could no longer be contained within the neat critical prescriptions of earlier generations of life writing scholars. Assertions of the personal were exploding across multiple media and wreaking havoc with the norms of what retrospective self-study was supposed to be, and do. (As this suggests, part of our pleasure in over three decades of studying life writing has been the excitement of seeing new possibilities emerge.)

"Witnessing or False Witnessing? Metrics of Authenticity, I-Formations, and the Ethic of Verification in Testimony" (2012) was a different kind of collaborative venture, one that attempted to engage with the phenomenon of hoaxes that have rarely been absent from autobiographical practice but have acquired new energy and global scope with the memoir boom and the ease of online research. While we initially wanted to chart the varieties of hoax memoir, we came to realize that producing a taxonomy of imposture could suggest that these were aberrations in need of policing—an abhorrent thought. What was happening was far more interesting as a manifestation of the complex politics of witnessing in an age when testimony has both new currency and new problems. That we would come to see "authenticity" as a troubling claim in autobiographical presentation was a measure of how far the field has come in complicating simple notions of the rhetoric of self-presentation.

We vowed that "Virtually Me: A Toolkit about Online Self-Presentation" (2014), our tentative foray into digital media of self-presentation, would be a "one and done," as the field of online life narrative belongs to younger generations more adept with Instagram and Snapchat. But it was uncanny to discover the applicability of not just the terminology but also the concerns of autobiographical theory for aspects of new social media. We were also intrigued by how these concerns can break down as automedia propose and compose new formations that depend on digital affordances and demand new theories of algorithms and platforms. Our essay's "toolkit" offers readers a means to arm themselves against the seductive slide into reading digital self-presentation as transparent, identical with the biography of the author. Rather, the pleasures of the "toolkit" questions may provide points of departure for provocative conversations with virtual others, looking at a subject now through this lens, now that one.

Solo Essays

Of course each of us also developed our own projects and lines of inquiry, at times diverging into quite different areas, which we loosely group in the rubrics below.

Autoethnography

A shared and enduring—if frustrating—interest has been in autoethnographic narratives that tell stories of emergent cultures through I's that speak representatively yet against stereotypes of native informants. Indeed, the life writing of subjects in indigenous or developing-world contexts, be they in Africa, the Caribbean, Asia, Australia or on American Indian reservations, is among the most challenging to contextualize and "hear." In this area we have included Julia's essays on "Strategic Autoethnography and American Ethnicity Debates: The Metrics of Authenticity in *When I Was Puerto Rican*" (2013) and Sidonie's on "Memory, Narrative, and the Discourses of Identity in *Abeng* and *No Telephone to Heaven*" (1999), "Cheesecake, Nymphs, and 'We the People': About 1900 in America" (1994), and "Re-citing, Re-siting, and Re-sighting Likeness: Reading the Family Archive in Drucilla Modjeska's *Poppy* and Sally Morgan's *My Place*" (1994). While each of these essays addresses specific texts, they also work exemplarily. That is, their attention to particular narratives intends to raise larger questions about issues of migration, transculturation, and the complexities of identity in multicultural societies as well as the cultural norms of telling lives in moments of displacement.

Theories and Concepts
Other solo essays that we selected aim to define particular concepts and explore their usefulness for the analysis of life-writing texts. Clearly, issues in memory, the archive, rhetorical stances, and the expansive contours of the "I" loom large for life writing studies. Several of Sidonie's essays have applied new concepts to theorizing life writing. In "Performativity, Autobiographical Practice, Resistance" (1995), she reworks Judith Butler's reconceptualization of gender as a performance of identity for the specifics of autobiographical texts. In "The Autobiographical Manifesto: Identities, Temporalities, Politics" (1991), she probes how life writing can use the personal to advocate for change, be it feminist, political, or ecological. Turning to another kind of concept in "The Spaces of Autobiographical Narrative" (2007), Julia explores the multiple resonances of "space" as those are differently parsed in German, French, and Anglo-American languages and literary traditions, and calls for opening up its connotations for regions, cultures, and scenes of writing.

Genres

On issues of genre our selections may seem idiosyncratic. Sidonie's "'America's Exhibit A': Hillary Rodham Clinton's *Living History* and the Genres of Political Authenticity" (2012) explores the panoply of genres that Hillary Clinton juggles in narrating a version of her public life as an American story for a global public and a political launch for a presidential campaign. Its generic modulations offer a lens through which to read many kinds of life writing.

Both of us are intrigued by the possibilities that the autographic form of comics affords for new and unsettling modes of self-presentation. Julia became hooked on them when teaching *Maus* and *Persepolis* to undergraduates, and wrote "Autographic Disclosures and Genealogies of Desire in Alison Bechdel's *Fun Home*" (2008) as a way to think through the range of autobiographical prospects and perplexes posed by that intriguing comic. Sidonie's extensive work on human rights narratives and acts of witnessing led her to explore an often-ignored dimension of comics in "Human Rights and Comics: Autobiographical Avatars, Crisis Witnessing, and Transnational Rescue Networks" (2011). In a field where the west has focused on a few graphic memoirs as iconic, it seemed appropriate to include an example of graphic memoir offering alternative possibilities of narration and visualization; hence, our inclusion of Julia's essay on "Parsua Bashi's *Nylon Road*: The Visual Dialogics of Witnessing in Iranian Women's Graphic Memoir" before its journal publication. Our larger aim with these choices is to underscore the explosion of graphic memoir worldwide and highlight how global reading publics are intervening in debates about ideologically conflicted histories, issues, and subject formations at this time.

Two Notes on Using This Collection
1) To facilitate the use of this collection in courses, we have included a chart after the Table of Contents that lists several genres and concepts and correlates each to the essays in the collection that explore it in some detail.

2) Readers should bear in mind that the three essays published by journals that are now owned by Taylor & Francis, Ltd., are only available in the print and e-book versions of this collection. As Taylor & Francis refused to give permission for open access to them online, readers must access the Taylor & Francis website and pay its fee for access to each essay. We regret the inconvenience that this causes.

Prospects for Further Research

Working with our past essays in preparation for publishing this volume, we became aware of how our essays were embedded in the discourses of particular moments of theorizing. A long view of life writing studies over decades suggests that many projects still remain nascent and compelling:

Autoethnography

Although the term "autoethonography" has been employed for decades, there is surprisingly little concurrence on defining its practices and audiences, and a paucity of scholarship directly engaging it as a form. The term may seem transparent: *autos* signals the individual I; *ethnos* the group or socius; and *graphein* the act of writing. But just as with autobiography, the apparently prescriptive Greek words are subject to differing and controversial interpretations.

A focus on the role of ethnography has characterized debates about qualitative ethnography that have stimulated—and vexed—the social science disciplines since the 1980s. From the perspective of anthropology, it is a practice that inscribes the participant observer in the scene of field research and observation, making the autoethnographic possible. But by the mid-nineteen-eighties the concept of participant observation had become deeply problematic and paradoxical for scholars such as James Clifford, George Marcus, and Clifford Geertz, who critiqued the notion of "objective" observation of a group and challenged the transparency of the information given by "informants." In different ways, their provocative challenges implicate debates about the nature of anthropology, the project of fieldwork and field notes, and the site and perspective of observation. While taking autoethnography as a viable category has generated some engaging studies in the social sciences, such as those edited by Deborah Reed-Danahay, the concept is in our view still inadequately theorized as a reflexive praxis. Locating autoethnography as a practice of life writing spanning the social sciences and the humanities—and arguably the arts—promises to shift the focus of past debates.

From the point of view of life-writing studies, many narratives of the developing world are autoethnographic texts in which writers narrate their development of an interior consciousness in cultures shifting from an oral, group-based formation that place less value on interiority and introspection to written—print and digital—texts that "discipline" the subject's self-study in a Foucauldian sense. In such moments of transition, narrating "I"s may link the story of their growth as individuals to the changes in their social groups at moments of sociopolitical transformation, thereby complicating or undermining the *Bildungsroman* narrative on which so many western coming-of-age autobiographies rely. Understandably, writers in nonwestern countries and the global South have contended that ethnography often serves as a site or practice of the "master's house" of western scholarship that should be rejected or parodied. In autoethnographic narratives the categories for representing social organization that may have derived from anthropologists, missionaries, political scientists, or colonial governments become rubrics for describing a local world and critiques of cultural domination. In this sense, such narratives might more appropriately be considered counter-ethnographic. That focus—on how the autobiographical *Bildungsroman* is revised when personal narrators situate themselves in ethnographic surrounds in the afterlife of colonial regimes—could drive new investigations in life writing of the developing world.

Autofiction
Autofiction has long been regarded as a distinct genre of the autobiographical in the Franco-Belgian-Quebecois tradition, and has gained traction in Germanic contexts.

It is usually understood as a genre working the boundary of "fact" and "fiction" by eliding distinctions between the authorial narrator and the fictional character, while engaging non-fictional elements such as references to contemporaneous historical events.

French author-scholar Serge Doubrovsky, who has written both autofictional works and theoretical studies, coined the term in 1977, in a challenge to Philippe Lejeune's foundational work on demarcating the autobiographical pact and Gerard Genette's genre-mapping narratological studies. To situate autofiction as a boundary-crossing form, however, Doubrovsky defines autobiography narrowly as a kind of total and coherent factual reportage about its author. The concept of a deeper, intersubjective "truth" is reserved for what he regards as the transgressive mode of autofiction, which, he asserts, requires a different reconstruction of events than autobiography's: "Unlike autobiography, which explains and unifies... autofiction doesn't perceive someone's life to be a whole. It is only concerned with separate fragments, with broken-up chunks of existence, and a divided subject who doesn't coincide with him- or herself" (Doubrovsky, cited in Jones 176).

But critics of life writing might well ask in what sense autofiction's "fictionality" differs from the many genres of the autobiographical that engage with referentiality yet do not claim to be identical with "fact," and may emphasize their use of fictional techniques such as dialogue, characterization, and metaphor to problematize the factual and thematize indeterminacy. In France since the mid-twentieth century many works have been read as autofiction, including the novellas of Marguerite Duras and the narratives of Sophie Calle and Annie Ernaux, all of whose works in English translation have been discussed as autobiographical. In the American tradition much work with autobiographical allusions has been dubbed "metafiction," including novels by such writers as Philip Roth, Norman Mailer, and Bret Easton Ellis, and what Truman Capote called his "faction," *In Cold Blood*, strategically deploying the third person. But the work of, for example, Dave Eggers suggests that the concept of "autofiction" may be insufficient for the encounters of biographical fact, historical events, and personal narration that he stages in such works as *What Is the What: The Autobiography of Valentino Achak Deng* and *A Heartbreaking Work of Staggering Genius*. (See our discussion of the first in "Witness or False Witness?" and the second in "The Rumpled Bed" in this volume.) Similarly "autofiction" is an inadequate concept for the six volumes of Norwegian Karl Ove Knausgaard's *My Struggle*, which astonishingly seems to exhibit total recall of details of the past yet is also a sustained meditation on the meaning of events by an authorial figure writing a book that shuttles between present and past times of narration.[3]

In practice, critics of the autobiographical engage with a wide range of life writing genres, some of which take up texts and practices that involve pseudonymous characters, such as Michelle Cliff's *Abeng* and *No Telephone to Heaven*, Tim O'Brien's *The Things They Carried*, and the narratives of Paul Auster and Ruth Ozeki. In so doing they are responding to the proliferating modes of self-narration since the later twentieth century that directly engage the autobiographical, both its affordances and its seeming limitations. Whether a concept of "autofiction" enhances this discussion, or merely blurs it, remains to be seen. It may be helpful for scholars to put various definitions of "autofiction" from different national literary traditions into conversation to explore how the wide-ranging enactments of life writing discussed by scholars in the Anglo-American tradition over the past two decades play out in other contexts.

Such discussions could open up more extensive conversations between narrative theorists and autobiography scholars than currently occur. Certainly, using concepts from narratology such as focalization, diegesis, and homodiegetic narration could enhance our understanding of texts. But we have found that the taxonomy of narratology does not map seamlessly onto the dynamics of acts and practices in life writing. The heterogeneous modes and media of the autobiographical require recognition of its different limits and audiences, as well as attention to issues of referentiality and verification that have rarely been theorized in narrative studies. But is propounding a special meta-category of "autofiction," with its focus on the blurring or disruption of ontological and illocutionary boundaries between narrative worlds, the way to accomplish this? Will it enable new readings of autobiographical narratives as characterized by a radically different pact between narrators and readers than the pact of verisimilitude mobilized in fiction?[4] Determining whether "autofiction" enables, or disables, the theorizing of life writing remains in dispute.

Automedial Lives

An immense world of online life writing has developed in the wake of Web 2.0, as special issues of the journal *Biography* and the recent collection, *Identity Technologies: Constructing the Self Online*, attest. Indeed, Julie Rak argues that scholars need to rethink what happens to "life" and "writing" in automedia, "the enactment of a life story in a new media environment" (155). Grounding the analysis of life writing only in print forms is no longer adequate for mapping the different circuits, platforms, algorithms, paratexts, and seductive solicitations of online forms. At a moment when some scholars continue to discuss selves presented online as transparent and fixed entities, those of us versed in life writing theory can offer tools for a more nuanced understanding of the terms, processes, practices, and stakes of self-presentation.

Of course there are many modes of automediality besides the digital. The rich intersection of what Timothy Dow Adams memorably called "light writing" with life writing continues to be intriguing and vexing in a new generation of photo-memoirs. More generally, visual-verbal collages in their palimpsestic density invite reading practices that meld the methods of several disciplines, as Sarah Brophy and Janice Hladki suggest in considering how visualizations of the autobiographical emphasize the politics of embodiment. Indeed, flexible, heterogeneous theoretical frames are required to engage with the multimodal reflexivity of artists as challenging and politically engaged as William Kentridge, Ai Weiwei, Kerry James Marshall, and South African sculptor Jane Alexander.

The role of the autobiographical in live performance, and its video afterlife, is another rich area for theorizing. The work of such early twentieth-century performers as Valeska Gert, Baroness Elsa von Freytag-Loringhoven, and the Dadaists has been "rediscovered" as innovatively autobiographical. The increasing scholarship on performance art in the latter twentieth and twenty-first centuries by such artists as Carolee Schneeman, Marina Abramovic, Chris Burden, Spalding Gray, Joseph Beuys, Laurie Anderson, Stelarc, Bobby Baker, Deb Margolin, Peggy Shaw, and Robbie McCauley offers new arenas for thinking about "live" self-presentation, both solo and ensemble. In *Lives in Play: Autobiography and Biography on the Feminist Stage* (2014), for instance, Ryan Claycomb, takes up the formalist and narratological strands related to the performer's body and the embodied version of the self performed in the work of feminist performance artists such as Holly Hughes and Karen Finley. Performance art has also become a means for the global circulation of self-presentation in China, Latin America, Russia, and Eastern Europe.

Autobiographical theater is another challenging arena for life writing scholarship and one that poses intriguing issues. Although the names of characters rarely coincide with that of the author, there may be striking biographical parallels. Theorizing how to discuss what comprises the autobiographical in drama, however, requires thinking about how production effects, physical settings, human voices, and audience interaction inflect the dramatist's self-presentation. The work of various playwrights, including Eugene O'Neill, Adrienne Kennedy, Sarah Kane, and Alice Childress, invites exploration, as would the work of many European and African dramatists, depending on how the staging of the autobiographical is theorized.

Empathy and Ethics

Work at the intersection of life writing and human rights has stirred up another set of issues: How to frame the concept of empathetic identification? What are the conditions and limits of the role of empathy and empathetic identification for an ethics of reading life stories? How do autobiographical acts, with their assertion of the call, compulsion, and power to speak construct the reader as a secondary witness to experiential histories of radical injury and harm? How do they solicit, compel, or interrupt particular kinds of reading? How do they enter global circuits of witnessing? What do they request of readers, or expect of them? How do readers feel as they read, hear, or view acts of witnessing? What do others expect them to feel?

Soliciting, recording, editing, translating, and publishing first-person witness accounts of the violent denial of rights, as defined through human rights protocols, instruments, and claims, is a fraught enterprise. Heterogeneous acts of witnessing are released into reading publics near and far, familiar or unfamiliar with the contexts of telling. The "trafficking" in memoir, as Gillian Whitlock provocatively observed in *Soft Weapons*, is troubled by the acute asymmetry between the subject positions of those who witness and those who read, a distance often stretching from the Global South to the Global North. These routes of memoir mobility affect whose stories get told and which story forms and plots are credited by readers and publics with "authenticity" or inauthenticity. And these trafficked texts and performances can be mobilized as "soft weapons" in the arena of geopolitics, as Whitlock argues for life writing from the Middle East circulated in the global North post-9/11. All these conditions contaminate the sense of what empathetic identification is and why we do or don't value it as an ethical responsibility. As G. Thomas Couser probingly asks, "how can we guarantee, or at least try to ensure, that representation serves the best interests of vulnerable subjects generally?" (19). Or, as one of Sidonie's students queried in an essay on empathy, what does it mean to theorize an ethics "with empathy, without empathy, and beyond empathy"?[5] Fundamentally, are particular story forms required to activate empathetic identification? Can witness projects expose systemic violence and degradation? Or are they always expected to tell stories of the individual grit of the survivor or play on the sentimentalizing of victimization to unloose readers' purses? What modes of posthuman witnessing may become compelling to future readers and publics?

Human Rights and Witnessing

Issues of memory, witnessing, and their psychic effects have been central to two decades of critical and theoretical exploration in Holocaust and genocide studies. Approaches to personal witnessing within trauma studies are often framed through a psychoanalytic lens of belatedness that is attentive to the temporal disjunction of repressed memory, ethically motivated by the recognition of the pain of telling as re-traumatization, and revealing about the position of the reader as secondary witness and the teller/witness as distanced in a postmemory moment (Hirsch). But how do such perspectives understand the stakes of the production, circulation, and reception of autobiographical acts attached to the project of witnessing histories of radical violence and harm and the setting forth of rights claims?

Much activity in the arena of human rights scholarship could be brought to bear specifically on both recent and older life writing. Since 2000, Holocaust scholars centrally invested in memory studies have joined other scholars exploring the intersection of cultural formations and human rights institutions, discourses, and politics. They explore how cultural forms circulate within a human rights regime constituted by the formal institutions of the United Nations, nation-state-based commissions, the extensive networks of Non-Governmental Organizations (NGOs), and the unpredictable activities of individuals and groups calling attention to sites, conditions, and the actors involved in human rights violations around the globe. Sidonie, with Kay Schaffer, has explored the intersection of human rights and literary forms including life writing in *Human Rights and Narrated Lives: The Ethics of Recognition*. Hillary L. Chute's recent *Disaster Drawn: Visual Witness, Comics, and the Documentary Form* examines how the form of comics, making its "marks" within frames and gutters, has potential to provocatively document, bear witness to, and engage readers in projects of secondary witnessing. Gillian Whitlock's current work, most recently in "Black Sites and Grey Zones: 21st Century Testimony," has turned attention to the "testimony of things," asylum seekers, and black sites. These new directions suggest avenues that might be opened up in further projects on human rights and witnessing.

Relationality

"Relationality" is a concept employed with increasing frequency in critical writing and as a conference theme in autobiography studies. But what is this apparently transparent concept—a practice, a disposition, a thematic, or something else? Although the concept has been invoked for over three decades, much in its usage remains slippery. One option is to see relationality as a separate genre, the strategy employed by feminist scholars in the seventies and eighties. The term was applied to accounts of women's experience and ego formation through what were termed "fluid boundaries," as our introduction, "Situating Subjectivity in Women's Autobiographical Practices," discusses in detail. While relationality became a cornerstone of feminist theorizing about women's difference that was enabling for the rise of critical work on women's autobiography, the distinction now seems essentialist, western-focused, and, in a time of gender fluidity, untenable.

As many have since observed, there is a relational aspect to most life writing. A second option, therefore, is to view relationality as a particular mode of autobiographical storytelling that is sometimes engaged throughout an entire narrative. In 1999 both Paul John Eakin and Susanna Egan published excellent books on autobiographical practice that introduced concepts of relationality as a specific formation of other-related life writing. Eakin asserted that relational life writing is "the autobiography of the self and the biography and the autobiography of the other" (58), while Egan focused on dual-authored or generated narratives that oscillated between subjects who were in some sense "mirror lives" to each other. A few years later Nancy K. Miller encapsulated that view in proposing that relationality is not itself a genre but a negotiation among genres: "The challenge that faces autobiographers is to invent themselves despite the weight of their family history, and autobiographical singularity emerges in negotiations with this legacy" ("Entangled" 543).

A third option is to view relationality as a mode of life writing that arose in the later twentieth century as an alternative to traditional "autobiography." German scholar Anne Rüggemeier's recent book proposes this view of relationality and details schema for its kinds, the communicative contexts in which it arises, and a set of recent Anglophone texts that exemplify different modes of the relational. Rüggemeier's study is provocative, if troubling for its postulation of a new universalist binary between "autobiography" and "relational" narrative.[6]

Self-translation

For decades there have been case studies and cultural studies of the politics of language and the networks, transits, and public imaginaries constituted in postcolonial and settler nations where former colonial languages dominate, sometimes intertwined with créoles. Indeed, the relationship of the language of self-presentation to acts of remembering, narrations of experiential history, and negotiations of culturally legible identities remains an important topic in life writing studies, foregrounded in the comparative work of such critics as Françoise Lionnet, Mary Besemeres, and Bella Brodzki. Now, with increased migration and the global circulation of memoirs and other genres of life writing, some multi-lingual writers are self-translating their autobiographical narratives. They thereby become agents who produce their self-presentations "in other words" and as a plurality of texts rather than a single text. As the meta-questions generated about acts and practices of self-translation are taken up by scholars in life writing studies from Europe, the Americas, the Middle East (especially Israel), and Asia, several journals have dedicated issues to this rapidly growing subfield of self-translation, its strategies and rationales, and its history in life writing.[7] Thorny questions arise: Can self-translating life writers be said to be writing the "same" text in different languages? Are they representing the "same" self? When the narrating "I" speaks and writes in at least two languages and represents a narrated "I" with a complex relationship to language shaped by experience of multiple cultures and, in some cases, geographies, what does her or his linguistic identity become? Self-translation involves doubled acts of writing: in the first text the narrating "I" may engage in meta-commentary on the pressures, effects, and efficacies of telling a life; in the translation of that first version, the narrating "I" is joined to—or shadowed by—a translating "I" who may remain implicit or become an explicit commentator on the text's multiple temporalities. While in one sense, self-translators narrate the same events at least twice, in another sense the lapse of time from the writing the first text to completing a self-translation suggests that these may be successive versions of a life rather than the same version.

Indeed, some self-translators pose this relationship as a linguistic conundrum. For such bi- or multi-lingual writers, contestations around identity are a given, as self-narration is inevitably shaped by the language in which it is presented. A preeminent example is Vladimir Nabokov's *Speak, Memory. An Autobiography Revisited*, which was, in his words, a "re-Englishing of a Russian re-version of what had been an English re-telling of Russian memories in the first place" ("Foreword," 12). Writers such as Samuel Beckett, Ariel Dorfman, Julien Green, Nancy Huston, Jorge Semprún, Esmeralda Santiago, and Eva Hoffmann have alluded to the conflicts that arose as they shuttled between cultures, experiencing different inflections of identity in different languages and locations. Questions of transnational memory, the relationship of self-reinvention to self-censorship, and the *métissage* of indigenous and colonial languages in self-translation are among the issues that future scholars might fruitfully explore.

On the Smith and Watson Collaboration

Working in life writing studies tends to rub off and, over the decades, we have both succumbed to the seductions of memoir-writing: Sidonie with a complex and so-far incomplete and elusive narrative of her grandmother; Julia with a memoir in progress on the grandmother she never knew, and short pieces on the idiosyncrasies of her life. As much as both of us have resisted seeing life writing as simply "a retrospective narrative in prose" (Lejeune *Pact* 14), it seems we are both busily engaged in some aspect of that process—though with the difference that our relatives were not famous or public people but others whose lives we can read in relation to our own.

People have often asked us to speak about our collaboration of twenty-eight years, but we have not responded, other than to appreciate the moniker that Tim Adams gave us decades ago: "the Smith and Wesson of autobiography studies." (For those unfamiliar with the brand, Smith and Wesson is a leading American gunmaker.) Our rationale has been like that of some sports teams: If it's working, why talk about it? Just enjoy the ride.

For the record, however, our process has rarely been to parcel out sections of a project for individual drafting. We typically write together, in one of our studies, with Sidonie at the computer and Julia on the couch, piles of books and papers heaped on a card table nearby. Perhaps that is why we have come to see the voice of our introductions and collaborative essays as a "third voice" not identical with either of ours in our solo work. Indeed, one of the discoveries in looking back over our work was the realization that neither of us alone could have produced our co-written essays or our book, *Reading Autobiography*.

Despite never having lived in the same state, we developed our books and essays in tandem—something that is easier now than when we began in 1988, relying then on long-distance calls, work during conferences, and meet-ups halfway between our homes, before the connectivity of e-mail and Skype. At times the geographic distances were formidable—from Perth, Australia, to Missoula, Montana; from Binghamton, New York, to Dakar, Senegal. But our shared passion to bring formerly unrecognized voices into the terrain of autobiography studies was as strong a motivation as our enjoyment of global travel.

And it has been a life-sustaining journey. If, in looking back over the essays in this book, we wonder how we had the energy to write those wide-ranging introductions to edited collections and bring off projects across several fields, we note that such interdisciplinarity has now become commonplace. In the minuscule field of life writing studies in past decades, most of our essays, both those done singly and together, would have been fortunate to have a hundred readers. Like many in the humanities, we labored in the shadows, without audiences for our essays and no sense that our work would outlive us. But the "perk" of collaboration is that we did so with pleasure. The rigors of writing are considerably lessened when there is a writing partner to grit it out with, and the rewards for making progress on a draft enhanced when we could participate in that pleasure together and syncopate periods of hard work with the pleasures of dancing along with Sidonie's ever-patient partner Greg, cooking, tag-saling, watching sports on TV or movies in darkened theaters, and traveling to far-flung sites.

Coda

For those of you new to the field of autobiography or life writing studies, we recommend two congenial groups. The International

Auto/Biography Association is a worldwide organization that has chapters in Europe, the Pacific, and the Americas; and The Auto/Biography Society, founded by Rebecca and Joseph Hogan in the 1980s, is a sustaining group of scholars in the Americas and Europe. These organizations hold biennial conferences at different times, which means that somewhere in the world there is a major conference on life writing taking place every year. IABA, monitored by the indefatigable Craig Howes at the Center for Biography of the University of Hawaii-Manóa, also has a robust listserv that publishes information about new publications and conferences and sustains ongoing conversations. The associations and their conferences comprise a supportive and energizing community of scholars who, like us, are motivated by the pleasurable camaraderie, the excellent mentoring, and the generous support that flows between early-career and later-career scholars across global networks. Further, there are several journals, including *Biography*, *a/b: Auto/Biography Studies*, and *Life Writing*, that are venues for putting one's work in the field into transnational circulation and conversation.

We hope that, as you hold this volume in your hands or scroll through it on a screen in its open access version, you'll be motivated to take up the challenge of further developing the field of life writing studies and giving a hearing to those who have told, or are now telling, their stories. If life writing was a "rumpled bed" in 2000, it is now a messy multi-sensorium, teeming with the potential—and the pitfalls—of vibrant self-presentations across media, geographies, and worlds.

Notes

1   See Philippe Lejeune's enlightening endnote on this point. His Note 2 asserts: "The problem is that, in France or Italy, the umbrella term ['autobiography'] is used at the same time as the name of one of the genres covered by the umbrella, whereas in English there is no such confusion, 'life-writing' not being used for any particular genre. In French, we have

also tried to find a really general term, but it never succeeded: we tried 'récit de vie' or 'histoire de vie', but are letters and diaries really 'récit' or 'histoire'? We tried 'écriture de soi', but testimonies are not always centered on the self. So we keep 'autobiography' as an umbrella term, which is a pity, as so far the word often has a negative connotation in French" ("Europe's Treasure Hunters").

2   See the glossary in *Reading Autobiography* for a fuller discussion of these and other terms.

3   See James Wood's insightful discussion of Knausgaard's *My Struggle*, shockingly titled "*Min Kamp*" in Norwegian, as both a conventional autobiography, "one of those highly personal modern or postmodern works, narrated by a writer, usually having the form if not the veracity of memoir," and a meta-meditation on authorship "concerned with the writing of a book that turns out to be the text we are reading," indebted to Proust and the Rilke of *The Notebooks of Malte Laurids Brigge*.

4   It is worth recalling that Lejeune's concept of the autobiographical pact accommodates many nuanced modes of relationship—for those who cannot write, for "ordinary" people, in self-portraiture, and in diaristic writing.

5   The phrase comes from Evan Radeen, a doctoral student in Sidonie's winter 2016 course entitled "Autobiography: Theorizing and Engaging Written, Graphic, and Online Life Writing."

6   See Julia Watson's online review of a recent book in German by Anne Rüggemeier for an extended discussion of issues in theorizing relationality. Rüggemeier's book, *Die relationale Autobiographie: Ein Beitrag zur Theorie, Poetik und Gattungsgeschichte eines neuen Genres in der englischsprachigen Erzählliteratur* [*Relational Autobiography: A Contribution to the Theory, Poetics, and Genre History of a New Genre in English-language Narrative Literature*] is in German but an essay from it is available in English in the *European Journal of Life Writing*, 2016, in the same issue as the Watson review.

7   *Ticontre*, an Italian journal, issued a call for papers on the IABA electronic mailing list on June 10, 2016. The call for papers asserts that self-translation studies is a rapidly growing subfield focused on specifying translation strategies and their rationales, as well as constructing a history of self-translation in life writing. We are indebted to that call for sparking our interest in the issues provocatively set forth and providing a framework for our incorporation of "self-translation" in this delineation of areas for further inquiry.

Works Cited

Adams, Timothy Dow Adams. *Light Writing and Life Writing: Photography in Autobiography*. Chapel Hill, NC: University of North Carolina Press, 1999.

Andrews, William L. *To Tell a Free Story: The First Century of Afro-American Autobiography, 1760–1865*. Urbana: University of Illinois Press, 1986.

Brophy, Sarah, and Janice Hladki. *Embodied Politics in Visual Autobiography*. Toronto: University of Toronto Press, 2014.

Ken Bugul (Mariètou M'Baye). *The Abandoned Baobab: The Autobiography of a Senegalese Woman. (Le Baobab fou, 1984.) Translated by Marjolijn de Jager*. Brooklyn: Lawrence Hill Books, 1991.

Capote, Truman. *In Cold Blood*. New York: Random House, 1965.

Chute, Hillary L. *Disaster Drawn: Visual Witness, Comics, and Documentary Form*. Boston, MA: Harvard University Press, 2016.

Coetzee, J. M. *Doubling the Point: Essays and Interviews*. Ed. David Attwell. Cambridge: Harvard University Press, 1992.

Claycomb, Ryan. *Lives in Play: Autobiography and Biography on the Feminist Stage*. Ann Arbor, MI: University of Michigan Press, 2012.

Cliff, Michelle. *Abeng*. Plume/Penguin Books, 1984.

———. *No Telephone to Heaven*. Dutton Adult, 1987.

Couser, G. Thomas. *Signifying Bodies: Disability in Contemporary Writing*. Ann Arbor, MI: University of Michigan Press, 2009.

Diallo, Nafissatou. *A Dakar Childhood. (De Tilène au Plateau, 1975)*. Translated by Dorothy S. Blair. Harlow, England: Longmano 1982.

Doubrovsky, Serge. *Laissé pour conte*. Paris: Éds. Grasse, 1999.

Eakin, Paul John. *How Our Lives Become Stories: Making Selves*. Ithaca, NY: Cornell University Press, 1999.

Egan, Susanna. *Mirror Talk: Genres of Crisis in Contemporary Autobiography*. Chapel Hill: University of North Carolina Press, 1999.

Eggers, Dave. *What Is the What?: The Autobiography of Valentino Achak Deng*. New York: Simon & Schuster, 2006.

———. *A Heartbreaking Work of Staggering Genius: A Memoir Based on a True Story*. New York: Simon & Schuster, 2000.

Facey, Albert. *A Fortunate Life*. Sydney: Penguin Books, 1985.

Gates, Henry Louis, Jr. *Finding Your Roots with Henry Louis Gates, Jr.* Public Broadcasting Service television series.

Gilmore, Leigh. *Autobiographics: A Feminist Theory of Women's Self-Representation*. Ithaca: Cornell University Press, 1994.

Haizlip, Shirlee Taylor. *The Sweeter the Juice: A Family Memoir in Black and White*. New York: Simon & Schuster, 1994.

1 | A PERSONAL INTRODUCTION

Hirsch, Marianne. *Family Frames: Photography, Narrative, and Postmemory.* Cambridge: Harvard University Press, 1997.

Jones, E. H. "Autofiction: A Brief History of a Neologism." In *Life Writing: Essays on Autobiography, Biography and Literature.* Ed. Richard Bradford. Houndsmill, UK: Palgrave, Macmillan, 2010, 174–84.

Kaplan, Caren. "Resisting Autobiography: Out-Law Genres and Transnational Feminist Subjects." In *De/Colonizing the Subject: The Politics of Gender in Women's Autobiography.* Ed. Sidonie Smith and Julia Watson. Minneapolis: University of Minnesota Press, 1992, 115–38.

Knausgaard, Karl Ove. *My Struggle.* Trans. Dan Bartlett. New York: Farrar, Straus and Giroux, 2013.

Lejeune, Philippe. "Europe's Treasure Hunters. The Founding of a Network of European Diary Archives and Collections." *European Journal of Life Writing,* Vol 4 (2015), R-16–18. http://ejlw.eu/article/view/172, accessed Jan 11, 2016.

———. "The Autobiographical Pact." In *On Autobiography,* ed. Paul John Eakin. Minneapolis: University of Minnesota Press, 1989. 3–30.

Miller, Nancy K. "The Entangled Self: Genre Bondage in the Age of the Memoir." *PMLA* 122.2 (Mar. 2007): 537–48.

———. *What They Saved: Pieces of a Jewish Past.* Lincoln, NB: University of Nebraska Press, 2011.

Nabokov, Vladimir. *Speak Memory. An Autobiography Revisited.* New York: G. P. Putnam's Sons, 1967.

O'Brien, Tim. *The Things They Carried.* Boston: Houghton Mifflin, 1990.

Poletti, Anna, and Julie Rak, eds. *Identity Technologies: Constructing the Self Online.* Madison: University of Wisconsin Press, 2014.

Pratt, Mary Louise. *Imperial Eyes: Travel Writing and Transculturation.* New York, NY: Routledge, 1992.

Rak, Julie. "Life Writing Versus Automedia: The Sims 3 Game as a Life Lab," *Biography* 38.2 155–80, 2015.

Reed-Danahay, Deborah. *Auto/ethnography: Rewriting and Self and the Social.* Oxford: Berg, 1997.

Rilke, Rainer Maria. *The Notebooks of Malte Laurids Brigge.* (*Die Aufzeichnungen des Malte Laurids Brigge,* 1910.) Trans. Michael Hulse. New York: Random House, 2009.

Rüggemeier, Anne. *Die relationale Autobiographie: Ein Beitrag zur Theorie, Poetik und Gattungsgeschichte eines neuen Genres in der englischsprachigen Erzählliteratur.* Trier, Germany: Wissenschaftlicher Verlag, 2014.

Schaffer, Kay, and Sidonie Smith. *Human Rights and Narrated Lives: The Ethics of Recognition.* New York: Palgrave, St. Martin's Press, 2004.

Smith, Sidonie, and Julia Watson. *Reading Autobiography: A Guide to Interpreting Personal Narratives*. Second edition. Minneapolis: University of Minnesota Press, 2001, rev. ed. 2010.

Stanton, Domna C. "Autogynography: Is the Subject Different?" In *The Female Autograph*, ed. Stanton. New York: New York Literary Forum, 1984. 3–20.

Watson, Julia. "Is Relationality a Genre? Review Essay on *Die relationale Autobiographie: Ein Beitrag zur Theorie, Poetik und Gattungsgeschichte eines neuen Genres in der englischsprachigen Erzählliteratur*," by Anne Rüggemeier. In *European Journal of Life Writing*, 2016. http://ejlw.eu/

Whitlock, Gillian. "Black sites and grey zones: 21st Century Testimony." Online Essay. 2015. http://www.inter-disciplinary.net/probing-the-boundaries/wp-content/uploads/2015/06/GWhitlock-testimony2-wpaper.pdf

———. *Soft Weapons: Autobiography in Transit*. Chicago: U of Chicago P, 2007. Print.

Wood, James. "Total Recall: Karl Ove Knausgaard's *My Struggle*." *The New Yorker*, Aug. 13, 2012. http://www.newyorker.com/magazine/2012/08/13/total-recall, accessed July 25, 2016.

Part I
Theoretical Frameworks

1
INTRODUCTION: SITUATING SUBJECTIVITY IN WOMEN'S AUTOBIOGRAPHICAL PRACTICES (1998)

From *Women, Autobiography, Theory: A Reader*

The subject . . .—female autobiographies, memoirs, letters and diaries—represents one of those cases of maddening neglect that have motivated feminist scholarship since 1970. This body of writing about the self has remained invisible, systematically ignored in the studies on autobiography that have proliferated in the past fifteen years.
 Domna C. Stanton, *The Female Autograph* (vii)

There are four ways to write a woman's life: the woman herself may tell it, in what she chooses to call an autobiography; she may tell it in what she chooses to call fiction; a biographer, woman or man, may write the woman's life in what is called a biography; or the woman may write her own life in advance of living it, unconsciously and without recognizing or naming the process. . . . Women of accomplishment, in unconsciously writing their future lived lives, or, more recently, in trying honestly to deal in written form with lived past lives, have

had to confront power and control. Because this has been declared unwomanly, and because many women would prefer (or think they would prefer) a world without evident power or control, women have been deprived of the narratives, or the texts, plots, or examples, by which they might assume power over—take control of—their own lives.
  Carolyn G. Heilbrun, Writing a Woman's Life (11, 16–17)

Authors' Note: References to the essays in our collection, *Women Autobiography, Theory: A Reader*, have been retained because their arguments are interwoven with the concepts and theoretical frameworks discussed here. A possible project for students would be to take one of these concepts and update the discussion of, and sources on, it during the last eighteen years. For example, the important concept of "intersectionality", implicit here, might be linked to the history of multiple, conflictual identifications traced in our discussion of gender, ethnicity, and sexuality.

After two decades of a ferment of activity in theorizing women's autobiography, it seems important to attempt, not an overview of, but a guide to the field as it has evolved. We propose a set of categories, however provisional, overlapping, and contingent, to focus key issues in scholarship. Some categories are formalist, such as genre and history; others indicate terrains of debate, such as experience, subjectivities, and sexualities. We foreground concepts and pose questions helpful for *practicing* the critical activity of theorizing women's autobiography by capturing the complex interplay of multiple theoretical critiques as they have motivated a discussion of women's autobiography. The history of women's autobiography studies is yet to be written—and the dust has nowhere near settled.

As a guide for mapping the field of women's autobiography, this introduction has several goals:

- to *locate parameters* in the theory of women's autobiography by identifying how critics have read it in relation to dominant autobiographical theory;

- to *order the field* by surveying the "stages" of critical activity in women's autobiography, from theories of gendered experience, to theories of difference, to the proliferation of differences that inform postmodern and postcolonial theorizing;
- to *identify significant theoretical interventions* that have helped reframe critical perspectives on women's autobiography;
- to *propose prospects for future inquiry* in feminist critical investigation.

Our aim is to identify a set of tools—or building blocks, guides, recipes—for enabling your own entry into the activity (and the self-reflexivity) of theorizing women's autobiography. As a map for the perplexed, the skeptical, the uninitiated, the jaded, we hope to aid readers in discovering and valuing the rich ferment of feminist critical activity that has excited and sustained scholars and contributed to the ever-increasing production, "rediscovery", and analysis of women's life writings.

Our introduction is in four interrelated parts: Part 1 discusses the emergence of theories of women's autobiography as a series of critical movements; Part 2 considers theoretical perspectives on subjectivity that have led to the reformulation of women's autobiographical acts and practices; Part 3 discusses prospects for theorizing; and Part 4 considers the future of women's autobiography as a field.

Part 1: The Emergence of Theories of Women's Autobiography

> *The problem for the female autobiographer is, on the one hand, to resist masculine autobiography as the only literary genre available for her enterprise, and, on the other, to describe a difficulty in conforming to a female ideal which is largely a fantasy of the masculine, not the feminine, imagination.*
>
> Barbara Johnson, A World of Difference (154)

Prehistory—Laying the Groundwork of a Women's Tradition
It is remarkable that, although women have written autobiographically for many centuries and published autobiographies throughout the twentieth century that are widely read, advertised by book clubs, and taught in university courses, the criticism *of* women's autobiography as a genre is barely three decades old. Women's autobiographical writing, seldom taken seriously as a focus of study before the seventies, was not deemed appropriately complex for academic dissertations, criticism, or the literary canon. The phrase "Read this only to yourself," used by one of the diarists discussed by Elizabeth Hampsten, named the "bind" that readers confronted in discovering their "bond" to women's autobiography. Academic and popular historians alike regarded it as at best a mine of biographical information and salty citations and deemed it too windy and unreliable—since life stories "stretch" the truth—to be worthy of critical investigation. Those who took autobiography seriously, critics such as Georg Misch, Georges Gusdorf, and William Spengemann, restricted their focus to the lives of great men—Augustine, Rousseau, Franklin, Goethe, Carlyle, Henry Adams—whose accomplished lives and literary tomes assured their value as cultural capital.

The status of autobiography has changed dramatically in the intervening decades, both within and outside the academy. Women's autobiography is now a privileged site for thinking about issues of writing at the intersection of feminist, postcolonial, and postmodern critical theories. Processes of subject formation and agency occupy theorists of narrative and, indeed, of culture as never before. If feminism has revolutionized literary and social theory, the texts and theory of women's autobiography have been pivotal for revising our concepts of women's life issues—growing up female, coming to voice, affiliation, sexuality and textuality, the life cycle. Crucially, the writing and theorizing of women's lives has often occurred in texts that place an emphasis on collective processes while questioning the sovereignty and universality of the solitary self. Autobiography has been employed by many women writers to write themselves into history. Not only feminism but also literary and cultural theory have felt the impact of women's autobiography as a previously unacknowledged mode of making visible formerly invisible subjects.

The growing academic interest in women's autobiography may be the result of an interplay of political, economic, and aesthetic factors. The growth of gender, ethnic, and area studies programs to address the interests of new educational constituencies has created a demand for texts that speak to diverse experiences and issues. Too, publishers have discovered that recovering and publishing women's life stories is a profitable enterprise. Autobiographies by women and people of color introduce stirring narratives of self-discovery that authorize new subjects who claim kinship in a literature of possibility. Most centrally, women reading other women's autobiographical writings have experienced them as "mirrors" of their own unvoiced aspirations. Critic Barbara Christian, for example, wrote of her excitement when, as a graduate student in 1967, she first read the autobiographical novel *Brown Girl, Brownstones* by Paule Marshall: "[It] was not just a text; it was an accurate and dynamic embodiment both of the possibilities and improbabilities of my own life. In it I as subject encountered myself as object.... It was crucial to a deeper understanding of my own life" (197).

This interest in women's autobiographical practices as both an articulation of women's life experience and a source for articulating feminist theory has grown over several decades and was acknowledged as a field around 1980. Activity was evident on three interrelated fronts that we will explore: building the archive of women's writing, claiming models of heroic identity, and revising dominant theories of autobiography.

Building the Archive of Women's Writing
In the fifties and sixties, several women's memoirs became best-sellers; some were by prominent or "notorious" women, others by unknown writers who treated compelling life stories.

Critic Carolyn Heilbrun, author of the best-selling *Writing a Woman's Life*, noted, "Only in the last third of the twentieth century have women broken through to a realization of the narratives that have been controlling their lives. Women poets of one generation—those born between 1923 and 1932—can now be seen to have transformed the autobiographies of women's lives, to have expressed, and suffered for expressing, what women had not earlier been allowed to say" (60). By incorporating hitherto unspoken female experience in telling their own stories, women revised the content and purposes of autobiography and insisted on alternative stories.

Simone de Beauvoir's multivolume autobiography (in translation)—*Memoirs of a Dutiful Daughter*, *The Prime of Life*, and others—was important for its interrogation of the category of "woman" in the making of self-consciousness. Anais Nin's multivolume *Diaries* combined self-exposure and literary experimentation. A generation of girls grew up reading *The Diary of Anne Frank* and *I Never Promised You a Rose Garden* (Joanne Greenberg). Mary McCarthy's *Memories of a Catholic Girlhood*, first serialized in magazines in the fifties, was acclaimed as life writing of high seriousness by the eastern establishment. Lillian Hellman's three memoirs, *An Unfinished Woman, Pentimento*, and *Scoundrel Time*, were lionized as best sellers and incorporated in films. And the McCarthy-Hellman feud, aired on the Dick Cavett talk show in January 1980, in which McCarthy remarked of Hellman's autobiographical texts that "Every word she writes is a lie, including 'and' and 'the'", not only nurtured popular interest in famous lives but also exposed knotty issues of truth and lying in self-representation. An emerging generation of African American women, coming of age during the years of the civil rights movement and the later Black Power movement, published autobiographical narratives through which they staked out a place within political or artistic movements and explored the complex legacies of racial and sexual exploitation. Anne Moody's *Coming of Age in Mississippi* and Maya Angelou's *I Know*

Why the Caged Bird Sings were among many writings that introduced African American women autobiographers to a broader United States audience.

By the seventies the bravado self-assertions of some feminist critics were widely heard. Germaine Greer in *The Female Eunuch* and Shulamith Firestone in *The Dialectic of Sex* interwove autobiographical and theoretical writing to demonstrate that the personal is political; Kate Millett, in *Sexual Politics* and in her later autobiographical works *Flying* and *Sita*, took this posture to a limit in claiming experience as the foundation of theory. And Angela Davis used her life story, *An Autobiography*, not only to expose the reach of racism in the United States, but also to make her case for the necessity of a radical politics that included a critique of misogyny within the writings of Black Power activists.

Influential early feminist literary critics focused on the intersection of women's lives and their writing in studies that sought to map a women's tradition and to legitimate feminist scholarship. Widely available books such as Mary Ellmann's *Thinking about Women*, Ellen Moers' *Literary Women*, and Elaine Showalter's *A Literature of Their Own* interrogated the history of patriarchy and the invisibility of women's texts and voices in dominant literary and academic culture. These early feminist critics pointed out that an extensive women's literary tradition had existed for centuries, especially if one turned to supposedly "marginal" genres—memoir, journal, diary, the many modes of private autobiographical writing. Moers' fifty-page list of women writers and their works mapped a female tradition that generated innumerable studies. In recovering the long out-of-print writings of women over centuries and framing them as a tradition rather than as marginal or failed efforts to write master narratives for male audiences, these pioneering critics cracked literary history wide open.

The archive of women's writing was also built through the recovery of earlier women's texts, above all by historians and bibliographers. In numerous ways women historians redirected the attention of their discipline from large-scale political events to the social history of everyday subjects and practices. Historians such as Mary Beth Norton, Rayna Rapp, Ann Douglas, Nancy Cott, Mary C. Kelley, and Carroll Smith-Rosenberg used archival materials such as diaries, journals, and unpublished autobiographical narratives to rethink a rich record of women's histories. Bibliographies of women's writing were genuinely a work of cultural excavation. In addition to Ellen Moers' annotated list of women's published writings, women could turn to Louis Kaplan's *A Bibliography of American Autobiographies*, listing over six thousand works before 1945 and, in the eighties, to its extension to contemporary times that included many writings by women, *American Autobiography, 1945–1980*, edited by Mary Louise Briscoe, Lynn Z. Bloom, and Barbara Tobias. Though a bibliography of American women's autobiography would not appear until 1983, in Patricia K. Addis' *Through a Woman's "I,"* the groundwork was laid for exploring the vast and neglected storehouse of women's personal writing and revaluing women's place.

Claiming Models of Heroic Identity

As early feminist literary critics developed courses on "Women in Literature" and "Images of Women," autobiographical texts often supplemented fictionalized accounts of women's lives. Critic Patricia Meyer Spacks in *The Female Imagination* read life writing analytically rather than as simply a mirror of women writers' lives. Exploring what she called the "characteristic patterns of self-perception" that "shape the creative expression of women," Spacks used autobiographies to probe what shapes the "female imagination" (1). Spacks's influential book historicized a tradition encompassing four centuries and many genres, including diaries, journals, and autobiographies. Her rubrics suggested a history of gradual artistic and personal liberation for "selves in hiding": "Finger Posts," "The Artist as Woman," and "Free Women" discovering creative spaces for female self-expression. Spacks emphasized women's struggle to assert a "positive" identity and focused on self-mastery and the dangers of "relational" female self-definition, although she largely omitted texts by women of color, which now limits the usefulness of her study (267).

Germaine Brée was also an influential critic of women's autobiography. Her 1976 essay "George Sand: The Fictions of Autobiography" made an early call for reading a woman's personal narrative as a separate genre and a means for a writer to autobiographically "think back through her mothers" (441). In women's autobiographies students found models of heroic womanhood absent from their own education, as suggested by the title of Lynn Z. Bloom's 1978 essay "Promises Fulfilled: Positive Images of Women." To develop a feminist pedagogy teachers sought these positive models of women who had creatively talked back to patriarchs, defied, resisted, in short, been empowered through writing their lives. In a literary canon and a Western tradition that had "othered" women, whether as goddesses or demons, on pedestals or in back rooms, this effort to reclaim women's lives and discover how women would speak "in their own words" was an essential initiatory gesture. Without excavating and revaluing the buried texts of women's autobiography, the critical ferment of the last thirty years could not have occurred.

Revising Theories of Autobiography
With the loosening of formalist New Criticism's hold on literary scholarship, several critics began reading autobiographies as literary texts, rather than documentary histories. But the typologies, accounts, and theories of autobiography continued to dismiss, erase, and misidentify women's autobiographical texts. For example, Georges Gusdorf's seminal essay "Conditions and Limits of Autobiography," published in French in 1956 (and widely known through its publication in English in the Olney collection, 1980), defended autobiography as an "art" and "representative" of the best minds of its time because it "recomposes and interprets a life in its totality" (38).[1] But, like Georg Misch in his earlier three-volume *History of Autobiography*, Gusdorf configured autobiography as unquestionably white, male, and Western: "the artist and

the model coincide, the historian tackles himself as object ... he considers himself a great person" (31).[2] Wayne Shumaker in 1954 discussed some women's autobiographical texts in his history of autobiography in England, but ascribed to them "feminine" qualities that marginalized their contributions to the development of the genre. By the end of the seventies the growing critical interest in autobiography studies was evidenced by several texts that would remain influential throughout the decade for theorizing autobiography, notably the dissemination of French critic Philippe Lejeune's theory of the autobiographical pact, James Olney's collection of essays, *Autobiography: Essays Theoretical and Critical*, and studies of American autobiography by William Spengemann and Albert Stone. In the Olney anthology one essay, by Mary G. Mason, focused on women's autobiography and another, by Louis Renza, discussed the significance of a woman's autobiographical text (*The Life of Saint Teresa of Avila*) without foregrounding gender issues. In Spengemann, women were absent from the tradition of autobiography mapped. Only Stone made a sustained attempt to address the intersection of race, class, and gender in the American tradition by focusing on many women's and ethnic, notably African American, autobiographies.

Around 1980: First Forays—
Theories Based on Women's Experience

Around 1980 the criticism of women's autobiography necessarily came of age. It was clear that new theories and generic definitions were required to describe the women's writing that had been recovered and was being produced. Why? Gradually, it became clear to many feminist critics that academic scholars were complicit in broader cultural practices that valued women's writing only in terms of, and as the "other" of, men's writing. In publication, at conferences, in scholarly overviews, references to women's writing were often uninformed or condescending. Throughout the 1980s feminist critics intervened in what they saw as traditional reading practices that assumed the autobiographer to be male and reproduced cultural stereotypes of differences between men and women.

The 1979 collection of excerpts from British and American women's autobiographies *Journeys: Autobiographical Writings by Women*, edited by Mary G. Mason and Carol Hurd Green, mapped a skeletal canon. Mason's introduction proposed a women's autobiographical tradition rooted in four texts, the late-medieval life writings of Margery Kempe and Julian of Norwich and the self-effacing histories of others penned by Margaret Cavendish and Anne Bradstreet. Mason's essay, expanded as "The Other Voice" in Olney's collection, became the basis for much later theorizing of women's autobiography. It argued that women's alterity informs their establishment of identity as a relational, rather than individuating, process: "[T]he self-discovery of female identity seems to acknowledge the real presence and recognition of another consciousness, and the disclosure of female self is linked to the identification of some 'other'" (Olney, 210). Mason used an essentialized "woman" as an internally coherent gender distinction. And she contrasted the flamboyant self-staging of "the drama of the self" (210) in a male text, Rousseau's *Confessions*, with the relational self-presentations of these four women writing "radically the story of a woman" (235). Later critics, notably Susan Stanford Friedman, would productively expand Mason's argument for relationality by appeal to psychoanalytic theory and multicultural texts.

Even more influential in 1980 was the first anthology of essays in the field, *Women's Autobiography: Essays in Criticism*, edited by Estelle C. Jelinek. The fourteen essays, most on white twentieth-century literary autobiographers in the British and American traditions, inaugurated sustained critical inquiry into women's experience as the basis of their autobiographical practice. Several essays called for either expanding the literary canon of autobiography or establishing an alternative canon of women's writing (Suzanne Juhasz, Annette Kolodny, Sidonie Smith and Marcus Billson). Jelinek's introduction called for diverse kinds of analysis to be brought to reading women's autobiography: "the historical, the social, the psychological, and the ethnic," as well as "rhetorical, poststructuralist, and Jungian" analyses (x). Jelinek primarily used gender, uninflected by class, ethnicity, genres, or life cycle, to define women's autobiography, and paid little attention to geographic or political locations. She argued that differences between the sexes are manifest in both the content and the style of autobiography (xi) and may be ascribed to the long-term restriction of women to the private, personal world and the prevailing view that women's lives are too "insignificant" to be of literary interest (4).

Jelinek contrasted the autobiographies of women and men on several points: At the level of content, she argued, men distance themselves in autobiographies that are "success stories and histories of their eras" focused on their professional lives (10), while women's life writings emphasize personal and domestic details and describe connections to other people (10). At the level of life scripts, men aggrandize themselves in autobiographies that "idealize their lives or cast them into heroic molds to project their universal import" (14–15). Women, by contrast, seek to authenticate themselves in stories that reveal "a self-consciousness and a need to sift through their lives for explanation and understanding," employing understatement to mask their feelings and play down public aspects of their lives (15). At the level of temporality, men shape the events of their lives into coherent wholes characterized by linearity, harmony, and orderliness (16). Irregularity, however, characterizes the lives of women and their texts, which have a "disconnected, fragmentary . . . pattern of diffusion and diversity" in discontinuous forms because "the multidimensionality of women's socially conditioned roles seems to have established a pattern of diffusion and diversity when they write" (17). For Jelinek, women's narratives mime the everyday quality of their lives—their life writings are "analogous to the fragmentary, interrupted, and formless nature of their lives" (19). That is, a pattern of discontinuity consistently characterizes women's autobiography just as it marks their lives.

Jelinek's argument about women's discontinuous narrative textuality asserted a model of coherence for men's autobiographies that, from the perspective of the late nineties, seems difficult to maintain for the autobiographical writings of, say, Richard Wright and James Baldwin, as well as Augustine, Rousseau, and Franklin. Not only was this model of women's autobiography mimetic in form and expressive in content for women's lives, it also assumed that "experience" is unproblematically "real" and "readable," and can be captured transparently in language expressing the truth of experience. Jelinek's "Introduction" had a manifesto quality in its essentializing of gendered experience to the exclusion of other differences in women's autobiographies and its sweeping analogy between lives and texts.

Several critics in the Jelinek collection, however, gestured toward a more temperately theorized view of writing and analyzed texts such as *The Woman Warrior* that became crucial for exploring women's autobiography. The most significant impact of the Jelinek collection was that a vigorous group of feminist critics *claimed* women's autobiography as a field of cultural study and went on to extended studies of the field or of particular autobiographers.

A focus on women's experience as the true feminist "content" of women's autobiography and the transparent "expression" of their lives enabled critics' intervention in autobiography, but it essentialized woman. The approaches to women's autobiography that we have discussed tend to be based on experiential models that are vertical and foreground certain moments in the life cycle—childhood, adolescence, marriage/career, aging (for example, Spacks's analysis of "the female imagination" in the life cycle). Such models oppose all women to all men and set up a structure of resistance and self-authorization through collective critique and political action based on assumed universal subordination.

Clearly, the analysis of Second Wave feminism, which read women's lives as inextricably embedded in patriarchy—understood as a general, ahistorical, transcultural system of social organization through which men maintained domination over women—informed the experiential model of women's autobiography. Another foundational tenet of Second Wave feminism, the egalitarian sisterhood of all women as a collectivity undifferentiated in its subordination, is also evident in early analyses of women's autobiography, where the "we" of women was asserted unproblematically.[3] That assumption was being severely critiqued in autobiographical writings by women of color who had been rendered invisible in these accounts and who would write autobiographically to announce their differences in an irreducible plurality of voices.

Nonetheless, certain provocative questions were posed by first-stage theorists of women's autobiography: To what extent is women's autobiography characterized by the frequency of nonlinear or "oral" narrative strategies, unlike the master narratives of autobiography that seem to pose stable, coherent self-narratives? To what extent is it characterized by frequent digression, giving readers the impression of a fragmentary, shifting narrative voice, or indeed a plurality of voices in dialogue? Is the subject in women's autobiography less firmly bounded, more fluid? If in women's autobiography writers often authorize their texts by appeal to the authority of experience rather than by public achievement or historical significance, should this privileging of the personal and domestic be gendered female? To what extent can it be ascribed to class and cultural moment or to an alternative rhetoric of the familiar style within the essay tradition?

Second Stage—Theorizing Beyond the Experiential in Women's Autobiography

In the wake of Jelinek's 1980 collection, several influential books appeared throughout the eighties that, in offering readings of particular texts and laying the groundwork for a women's countercanon, gradually revised and expanded the conceptual terms she had laid out. By the end of the decade none of Jelinek's definitional parameters remained uncontested.[4]

Two American critics well-versed in French feminism and the French literary tradition, Nancy K. Miller and Domna C. Stanton, drawing on the early work of Germaine Brée, laid important groundwork for revising gender essentialism in the light of Second Wave theories of difference. They argued, in different ways, that theorizing in women's autobiography should not simply invert the exclusionary logic of the dominant tradition, but, instead, map women's dialectical negotiations with a history of their own representation as idealized or invisible. In "Toward a Dialectics of Difference" Miller critiqued the universalization of maleness as humankind in the literary canon and called for a gendered reading of genre. Refusing the "fiction" of a de-gendered reading, she urged critics to "read for difference," in a "diacritical gesture," and argued for reading as "a movement of oscillation which locates difference in the negotiation between writer and reader" (56).

Domna C. Stanton's collection *The Female Autograph* (1984), which announced itself as "a 'conversation' between writers and critics across cultural and temporal boundaries," cast a wide net for women's autobiography, with essays on women autobiographers from tenth-century Heian Japan to twentieth-century Palestine. Its spirit of inclusionary breadth indicated the expansion of boundaries, historically, generically, and in media, that critics of women's autobiography were pursuing in the decade. Stanton's lead essay, "Autogynography: Is the Subject Different?" critiqued the essentialism of first-stage criticism and theorized in terms of multiple differences of the subject. Stanton rehearsed with droll rapidity dozens of denunciatory comments by male critics about women's autobiographical texts and female textuality, positioning herself like Woolf's narrator in *A Room of One's Own*, at the margin of the literary world. Stanton's "I" asked why women's lives are suppressed in literary history and proposed a new nomenclature of "autogynography" for the separate genre of women's autobiography. In mapping a textual tradition of women's life writing, Stanton tried both to circumvent gender essentialism and to resist appropriation by the dominant tradition of autobiographical theory.

One of the emerging and enduring debates in theorizing women's autobiography, as Marjanne E. Goozé pointed out, is how narrowly or broadly to construct the field of autobiographical texts. Some early essays and collections argued strongly for an inclusionary scope of "women's personal literature of the self," in Margo Culley's phrase ("Women's," 13). The Hoffmann and Culley collection, *Women's Personal Narratives* (1985), included women's letters, diaries, journals, and oral histories to expand the canon of women's writing. Culley's title, "Women's Vernacular Literature: Teaching the Mother Tongue," announced the essay's agenda. Likewise, Hoffmann called for reading the writings of nonprofessional women to discover "the modes of verbal art practiced by most women who use language to give shape and meaning to their experiences" (1). These essayists asserted that the interrelational and conversational purposes of women's writing distinguish it from men's "rhetorical" purposes (Elouise Bell, 168).

An inclusionary view of women's personal writing was also emphasized in *Interpreting Women's Lives: Feminist Theory and Personal Narratives* by the Personal Narratives Group (1989). The group, including ten scholars in the literary and social sciences, gathered together essays that offered multidisciplinary perspectives—from anthropology, sociology, history, political science, as well as literary disciplines—on a wide range of women's personal narratives drawn from everyday life venues such as abortion activism and from developing as well as developed countries. Electing to speak of narrative forms rather than the genre of autobiography, the Group called for exploring women's narratives as sources for our understanding of gendered identity: "Women's personal narratives embody and reflect the reality of difference and complexity and stress the centrality of gender to human life . . . (they) provide immediate, diverse, and rich sources for feminist revisions of knowledge" (263). While it is beyond the scope of this Introduction to survey the ever-growing literature on women's personal narratives in the social sciences, clearly work on personal writing has become increasingly interdisciplinary. For example, the collection *Investigating Subjectivity: Research on Lived Experience*, edited by Carolyn Ellis and Michael G. Flaherty (1992), explored personal stories as a mode of incorporating the investigator's reflexivity.

Other theorists of women's autobiography called for a primary focus on the genre of autobiography, in order to read women's writing within, and against, the master narratives of the West. In 1986, in *The Tradition of Women's Autobiography*, Jelinek proposed to set forth a two-thousand-year-old tradition. But unfortunately this book, in its sparse documentation and focus on the white Euro-American tradition, demonstrated the limits of first-stage theorizing as surely as her 1980 collection had shown its strengths.

The late eighties saw a breakthrough in numerous studies of women's autobiography. Two books in particular proposed theories centered in women's textuality and the history of women's cultural production rather than simply a gendered identity. In 1987 Sidonie Smith's *A Poetics of Women's Autobiography* argued that, in an androcentric tradition, autobiographical authorization was unavailable to most women. Historically absent from both the public sphere and modes of written narrative, women were compelled to tell their stories differently, and had done so, at least since medieval autobiographer Margery Kempe (*Poetics*, 50). Smith asserted that any theory of female textuality must recognize how patriarchal culture has fictionalized "woman" and how, in response, women autobiographers had challenged the gender ideologies surrounding them in order to script their life narratives. Smith posed key questions for reading a woman's autobiography: How does she authorize her claim to writing? How does she negotiate the gendered fictions of self-representation? How is her literary authority marked by the presence or absence of her sexuality as subject of her story? Smith was particularly interested in the historical specificity of the double-voiced structure of women's narratives as it reveals the tensions between their desire for narrative authority and their concern about excessive self-exposure.

In *Autobiographical Voices: Race, Gender, Self-Portraiture* (1989), Françoise Lionnet staked out an intercultural territory of writing by women of color and proposed a theory of *métissage* to articulate how marginalized subjects voice their lives. Lionnet argued that as historically silenced subjects, women and colonized peoples create "braided" texts of many voices that speak their cultural locations dialogically. *Métissage,* viewing autobiography as a multi-voiced act, emphasized orality and the irreducible hybridity of identity. In privileging difference, plurality, and voices, Lionnet asserted that not only new subjects but new kinds of subjects were emerging, and that traditional autobiographies could be read differently as well.

In many ways Smith's and Lionnet's theories shared an interest in the rhetoric of women's self-presentation. Centering their investigations on histories of women's subjectivities in dialogue with one another, rather than as adjunct to a tradition of "high" literature, their books set forth frameworks to assert women's autobiography as a legitimate field of analysis and practice.

The year 1988 saw the publication of two collections that were also influential for women's autobiography. In *Life/Lines: Theorizing Women's Autobiography*, Bella Brodzki and Celeste Schenck gathered essays that read First World traditions of autobiography against postcolonial forms such as the *testimonio* (Doris Sommer), and diverse sexualities in the coming out story (Biddy Martin), as well as expanded the concept of autobiographical textuality to women's films, painted self-portraits, and poetry. Insisting on a more globalized concept of women's writing that ranged from Native American to Egyptian to Québecois texts, Brodzki and Schenck theorized explicitly as well as editorially. They reasserted the *bios* that Stanton had excised in her notion of autogynography, and called for a revision of poststructuralist theory, to assert "the imperative situating of the female subject in spite of the postmodernist campaign against the sovereign self" (14). Urging attention to female specificity against both feminist essentialism and "pure textuality," Brodzki and Schenck argued for a kind of theorizing that allows the female reader the "emotional satisfaction" of a referential world of women's lives (14).

Another 1988 collection, *The Private Self*, edited by Shari Benstock, with essays examining a wide range of women's narrative forms, includes two influential essays that contextualized female subjectivity in very different ways. Susan Stanford Friedman, in "Women's Autobiographical Selves: Theory and Practice," focused on relationality in women's autobiography as an expression of the "fluid boundaries" they experience psychologically. Shari Benstock, in "Authorizing the Autobiographical," offered a Lacanian reading of women's textuality as "fissures of female discontinuity" exemplified in the writing of Virginia Woolf. (These theorizings of subjectivity are explored in part 2 of this Introduction.)

Carolyn Heilbrun's *Writing a Woman's Life* (1988) was an important milestone in women's autobiographical criticism because it called the attention of a larger public to the field. On the one hand, because it was advertised by book clubs, taught in many women's studies courses, and used as a reference by readers uneasy with more "academic" feminist theory, Heilbrun's study was both inclusionary and deliberately nontheoretical. On the other hand, in analyzing women's coming to voice for a wide female readership, she focused on women's *lives* rather than their texts; for "we are in danger of refining the theory and scholarship at the expense of the lives of women who need to experience the fruits of research" (Heilbrun, 20). Heilbrun explored the recent past when women had begun to assert power and control—"only in the last third of the twentieth century have women broken through to a realization of the narratives that have been controlling their lives" (Heilbrun, 60)—rather than previous centuries of silencing in a patriarchal literary tradition, when this realization was encoded, often obliquely, in the long and rich history of women's self-representations. *Writing a Woman's Life* is a valuable resource for examining the lives of women in the

West who have written autobiography in the twentieth century, and its focus has been complimented by many theorists in this decade writing on the lives and autobiographies of women writers throughout the world.

If Heilbrun sought to find an autobiographical thread in many kinds of women's writing, Rita Felski's *Beyond Feminist Aesthetics* (1989) provided an alternative model for exploring women's personal narratives broadly in a European, notably Germanic, frame. Critiquing the gender essentialism of much feminist writing, Felski foregrounded the social contexts of a wide range of women's confessional narratives that enforce gender-based identifications and examined their discursive practices. Revisionist in intent and focused on the intersection of politics and personal narrative, Felski's book helpfully extended the text-based focus of such work in German women's autobiography as Katherine Goodman's *Dis/Closures: Women's Autobiography in Germany between 1790 and 1914* (1986) and anticipated the ambitious reading of women's autobiographical practices sketched by Barbara Kosta in *Recasting Autobiography: Women's Counterfictions in Contemporary German Literature and Film* (1994). Similarly, for French and francophone women's autobiography Leah D. Hewitt, in *Autobiographical Tightropes* (1990), mapped concerns that yoke writers of personal narrative such as Nathalie Sarraute, Monique Wittig, and Maryse Condé, who had not previously been linked as generic practitioners, and argued that "they all openly adopt dialogic patterns to sustain the figure of an interactive subject" (194).

Specifying Location—Materialist and Difference Theorists

While many theorists of women's autobiography worked primarily in generic terms, important explorations of women's writing were also grounded in analyses of specific historical periods. Notably Felicity Nussbaum's *The Autobiographical Subject* (1989) on eighteenth-century women's writing and Regenia Gagnier's *Subjectivities* (1991) on nineteenth-century British working-class writing performed close readings of neglected texts of women's writing and provided materialist analyses of culture to situate forgotten women's traditions within established periods of literary history, thereby revising the terms of subjectivity. In-depth analysis of Victorian women's autobiography by critics such as Mary Jean Corbett, in *Representing Femininity: Middle-Class Subjectivity and Victorian and Edwardian Women's Autobiography*, and Linda H. Peterson, in "Institutionalizing Women's Autobiography: Nineteenth-Century Editors and the Shaping of an Autobiographical Tradition," called attention to the multiplicity and variety of women's autobiographical writings during a period when most were supposed to be outside public life.

The important work of reclaiming African American autobiography also contributed to amplifying the canon and honing the critical lens of women's autobiography theory. Jean Fagan Yellin's revival of Harriet Jacobs' *Incidents in the Life of a Slave Girl*, long ascribed to Lydia Maria Child, and the restoration of Zora Neale Hurston's *Dust Tracks on a Road* and her other writings under the aegis of Alice Walker[5] are two cases in point; the current range and status of the field are unthinkable without these texts. Searching analyses by, among others, William L. Andrews, Joanne M. Braxton, Hazel V. Carby, Frances Smith Foster, and Nellie Y. McKay, of Jacobs', Hurston's, and other African American women's autobiographical writing, have reframed the foundations of American women's autobiography. Braxton's *Black Woman Writing Autobiography: A Tradition within a Tradition* mapped interrelationships among texts that, ten years earlier, had been out of print and known to few scholars.

Similarly, for Asian American writing, the proliferating critical scholarship on Maxine Hong Kingston's *The Woman Warrior* inspired examination of narratives of immigration and theorizing of specific national identities, hybridity, and generationally distinct histories. Studies of Asian American women's writing by Shirley Geok-lin Lim, Amy Ling, and Sau-ling Cynthia Wong, among others, have insightfully explored both the reception of Hong Kingston and the renegotiation of immigrant autobiography in second-generation Asian American women's writing.

The anthologizing, disseminating, and theorizing of ethnic identity in women's autobiography continue in a productive ferment, led by such critics as Tey Diana Rebolledo and Lourdes Torres on U.S. Latina women's autobiographies, Hertha D. Wong on Native American oral narratives and autobiographies, and Anne E. Goldman on working-class writing. Many other critics have contributed as well to the study of ethnic women's autobiographies. This critical explosion has rewritten the terms of American autobiography and arguably dislodged the novel as the master narrative of American literature. We call readers' attention to the pivotal role of such critics as William L. Andrews, Henry Louis Gates, Jr., Houston Baker, Ramon Saldívar, Genaro Padilla, John Beverley, Greg Sarris, and Arnold Krupat, whose theoretical interventions in autobiographies of women of color have made major contributions to revising the canon and the methods of literary history in the Americas.

Both American literature and autobiography studies have long existed in a state of willed ignorance about Canadian writing, but in women's autobiography valuable resources now exist for textual and comparative study. *Essays on Life Writing*, the collection of essays edited by Marlene Kadar (1992), Helen Buss's *Mapping Our Selves: Canadian Women's Autobiography in English* (1993), and the special issue on Canadian autobiography edited by Shirley C. Neuman for *Essays on Canadian Writing* (1997) have addressed this need in recent years. Julia V. Emberley's *Thresholds of Difference* (1993) foregrounded ethnographic issues in oral histories and written narratives of indigenous Canadian women writers. These studies of Canadian women's autobiographical writing helpfully complicate notions of "American" autobiography.

While many American critics lack the linguistic skill to engage the wealth of women's autobiographical writing being produced or revived in Mexico and the countries of Latin America and the Caribbean, feminist critics of autobiography including Doris Sommer, Debra Castillo, Amy Katz Kaminsky, Cynthia Steele, and Sylvia Molloy for writing in Spanish and Portuguese, and Françoise Lionnet,

Elisabeth Mudimbe Boyi, and VéVé Clark for French Caribbean, attest to a vigorous and nuanced tradition that includes collective histories and *testimonios*, as well as other genres of self-reflexivity.

The number and variety of collections on women's autobiography have increased during the nineties. *American Women's Autobiography: Fea(s)ts of Memory*, edited by Margo Culley (1992), assessed four centuries of women's personal narratives and, in her extensive bibliographical essay, proposed an eclectic view of women's self-reflexive writing. The University of Wisconsin Press series on American autobiography, notably in *American Autobiography: Retrospect and Prospect*, edited by Paul John Eakin (1992), has provided overviews in wide-ranging critical essays with extensive bibliographies. In that volume, critics Blanche H. Gelfant, on autobiographies of twentieth-century public women, and Carol Holly, on women's nineteenth-century autobiographies of affiliation, identified important subgenres of women's life writing. The essays in Susan Groag Bell and Marilyn Yalom's collection, *Revealing Lives* (1990), claimed that autobiographical texts are historical lenses through which readers may seek "evocations" of human beings and the mythologizing they do as they shape their life stories. Several of the essays selected by the editors deliberately blurred the distinction between biography and autobiography in employing gender as a lens for investigating life writing as a strategic response. An extreme and suggestive case is that of Charlotte Salomon, German painter-autobiographer and Holocaust victim, discussed by Mary Lowenthal Felstiner, who subsequently published a gripping biography of the artist in 1994.

Theorizing Women's Autobiography in the Wake of Postcolonialism and Postmodernism

For many new scholarly explorations, however, postcolonialism and postmodernism have become the dual focus, as the intellectual turn toward postcolonial studies in the eighties provoked serious engagement with women's status as multiply colonized in many parts of the world. Sidonie Smith and Julia Watson in *De/Colonizing the*

Subject: The Politics of Gender in Women's Autobiography (1992) and Françoise Lionnet and Ronnie Scharfman in *Post/Colonial Conditions: Exiles, Migrations, and Nomadisms* (1993, two volumes) gathered essays that mapped emergent literatures and reframed women's issues and subjectivities at diasporic sites on the Asian, African, Australian, and American continents. Along with Lionnet's *Postcolonial Representations* (1995) and Barbara Harlow's earlier *Resistance Literature* (1987), these studies proposed issues and examined practices that relate subjectivity to the material and economic conditions of women's lives, recasting the terms of theories rooted in Anglo-American autobiography. Similarly, the publication and translation of women's autobiographies on a global scale have given new impetus to international and indigenous feminist movements.

Postmodernist theorizing has also stimulated new analytical tools and generated collections, such as Kathleen Ashley, Leigh Gilmore, and Gerald Peters' *Autobiography and Postmodernism* (1994), that dedicate considerable attention to women's autobiography. Some postmodernist critics have proposed new rubrics—for example, Leigh Gilmore's "autobiographics" or Jeanne Perreault's "autography"—to subvert the hold of the term "autobiography" and renegotiate the definition of "woman" as a writing subject. Similarly, Sidonie Smith, in *Subjectivity, Identity, and the Body* (1993), explored the relationship between subjectivity and autobiographical practice by posing questions about how women, excluded from official discourse, use autobiography to "talk back," to embody subjectivity, and to inhabit and inflect a range of subjective "I's." Such critiques of women's autobiography, informed by the theoretical discourses of feminism and postmodernism, have strategically opened new doors for the articulation and analysis of women's autobiographical practices in a global framework.

Before 1980 James Olney could sum up the activity in women's autobiography thus: "As several recent bibliographical publications attest, Women's Studies courses have a sizeable autobiographical literature to draw on, but theoretical and critical writing is for the most part yet to come" ("Autobiography," 16). And come it did, with an extensive body of critical writing that would lead Paul John Eakin to state in 1993: "[T]he serious and sustained study of women's autobiography ... is the single most important achievement of autobiography studies in the last decade" ("Relational," 7)

Part 2: Theorizing Subjectivity

The gender balance of autobiographical history cannot be corrected simply by adding more women to the list; basic suppositions about subjectivity and identity underlying autobiographical theories have to be shifted.
      Laura Marcus, Auto/Biographical Discourses (220)

In this section we map various theoretical approaches to women's autobiography. To do so, we recast the history we have just sketched and, in this part, present a set of responses by theorists of women's autobiography to major theoretical currents of the eighties that changed the terms of the field. We want to emphasize here that feminist critics do not slavishly adhere to a particular theoretical line. They actively engage, critique, and modify theoretical models even as they import certain ideas and vocabularies into their reading practices. They also change their theoretical minds, so to speak. As they reflect upon responses to their analyses or as they read the work of other theorists and critics working in the field or in related—or even unrelated—fields, they formulate new ways of approaching the texts they take up.

Theories of Difference: Ego Psychology

By the early eighties the ferment of feminist and poststructuralist critical theory had brought a range of influences to bear upon women's autobiography. Above all, the psychological or psychoanalytical category of "sexual difference" elicited reformulations of what it meant to be "woman." In the United States the work of Nancy Chodorow was influential in rethinking the early dynamics of the mother-daughter relationship and their implications for creatively reframing the discussion of women interdisciplinarily. Chodorow, a psychologist specializing in ego psychology, took existing analyses of the "basic sex differences in personality" between girls and boys and postulated that "feminine personality comes to define itself in relation and connection to other people more than masculine personality does. That is, in psychoanalytic terms, women are less individuated than men and have more flexible ego boundaries" (44). This notion of "relationality" would have long-term implications for theorizing female subjectivity in autobiography.

Chodorow pursued the differentiating process of ego development before the oedipal stage that Sigmund Freud had described as formative of the (male) autonomous individual. She argued that the mother identifies differently with her boy and girl children. Because she is "a person who is a woman and not simply the performer of a formally defined role" (47) the mother "identif[ies] anticipatorily" with her daughter and therefore confounds for the daughter the process of separation and individuation. By contrast, the boy child turns away from the mother to the father in an identification that is positional rather than personal. In that process a boy learns to define himself as "that which is not feminine or involved with women . . . by repressing whatever he takes to be feminine inside himself, and importantly, by denigrating and devaluing whatever he considers to be feminine in the outside world" (50). As the boy turns away from the mother to identify with his father, he must enforce an emotional break, a rupture in identification, and impose a scheme of difference. A girl, by contrast, comes to develop more fluid ego boundaries than a boy because she does not have to resist her early identification with the mother or undergo a rupture. Therefore, she develops less of a desire to sense her difference from the mother. "Feminine identification is based not on fantasied or externally defined characteristics and negative identification," wrote Chodorow, "but on the gradual learning of a way of being familiar in everyday life, and exemplified by the person . . . with whom she has been more involved. It is continuous with her early childhood identifications and attachments" (51). That is, rather than a firm, differentiated boundary the girl child develops a fluid interface between self and others.

For literary critics reading avidly in the burgeoning interdisciplinary field of women's studies, Chodorow's theory of difference was attractive. Eventually a critique of her theory would emerge: that she hypostasized the difference between a universal boy and a universal girl, ignoring differences within communities; that she universalized the developmental process by giving only superficial attention to cultural practices not located in the twentieth-century West; that, consequently, her call for a political solution was naive. But in the early eighties Chodorow's psychoanalytic framing of difference was persuasive for scholars trying to define perceived differences in men's and women's narratives because it offered a foundational category informed by depth psychology and language acquisition theories. Her discussion of women's developmental difference also accounted for the formation of women's social roles within patriarchy. Linking vertical (psychological) and horizontal (social) axes, Chodorow's hypothesis moved beyond observed particulars of adult experience and roles.

Chodorow's emphasis on women's relationality informed thinking about women's difference among many early theorists. Although her argument was not specifically linked to Chodorow's work, Mary G. Mason, in "The Other Voice: Autobiographies by Women Writers," stressed that female identity is grounded in relationship and produces textual self-presentations that contrast with masculine self-representations. Mason's "set of paradigms" for women's life writing involved the postulation of an "other" toward, through, and by whom women come to write themselves, whether that other is God, for instance, or a husband. The work of Chodorow was also important in encouraging literary critics to shift their focus from how daughters relate to patriarchal fathers to how they are connected to their mothers and the larger community of women.

Susan Stanford Friedman, in "Women's Autobiographical Selves: Theory and Practice," incorporated Chodorow's hypothesis to postulate that women have more permeable ego boundaries. Friedman fused her emphasis on the interconnectedness of women's interpersonal relationships with an analysis drawn from Sheila Rowbotham's politically grounded focus on the importance of female community for women's self-definition. She compellingly summarized the significance of her argument for a difference theory of women's autobiography: "[a woman's] autobiographical self often does not oppose herself to all others, does not feel herself to exist outside of others, and still less against others, but very much *with* others in an interdependent existence that asserts its rhythms everywhere in the community" (35). By invoking examples from African American and lesbian women autobiographers, Friedman expanded not only the theoretical framework of the field but also its repertoire of exemplary texts. Her essay's emphasis on women's relationality and community has remained pivotal.

If terms such as female relationality and fluidity promised theorists of women's autobiography a more enlightened model for exploring and revaluing women's experiential histories, some have since cautioned against privileging these characteristics as innate to women's experience rather than as culturally conditioned responses. Considering theories of maternal identification, Jessica Benjamin warns of the dangers of a "one-sided revaluing of women's position; freedom and desire might remain an unchallenged male domain, leaving us to be righteous and de-eroticized, intimate, caring, and self-sacrificing" (Benjamin, 85; quoted in Marcus, 220).

Theories of Difference: Lacan and French Feminisms

Theoretical models based on the authority of experience assume the transparency of language. But this assumption of transparency has long been challenged by groups of theorists who, influenced by structural linguistics, problematize the relationship of the signifier to the signified and the relationship of the subject to language. In the early eighties feminist theorists began to draw upon the work of the French psychoanalyst Jacques Lacan in order to sort through the particular dynamics of the young girl's entry into language and thus of woman's relationship to the symbolic order of words. Rethinking the Freudian psychoanalytic paradigm, Lacan redirected attention to what he described as the "mirror stage," critical to the subject's entry into language.

In the mirror stage the child comes to recognize its image in the looking glass; but as it looks in the glass it sees its image as another. On the one hand, this image as other gives back to the child the semblance of a coherent identity. On the other hand, through acknowledgment of its image, the child mis/recognizes itself as a unified subject. This moment of mis/recognition is precisely the moment when the divided subject comes into being. As Elizabeth Grosz notes in discussing Lacan, "the subject recognizes itself at the moment it loses itself in /as the other. The other is the foundation and support of its identity, as well as what destabilizes or annihilates it" ("Contemporary," 44). This "loss" is the mark of "lack"—the incomplete identification of subject and other. "That," the child says to itself, is "me"! And thus the "I" becomes split. The split in the subject inaugurated by the entrance into language generates the sense of an ever elusive grasping toward self-presence that is forever unachievable. For the split in the subject can never be sutured. Thus, Lacan proposes, the coherent, autonomous self is indeed a fictive construct, a fantasy of the fully present subject in language.

The Lacanian "subject," established under and through the entry into the symbolic realm of language (what Lacan called the Law of the Father), is a masculine subject. Claiming the phallus as the transcendental signifier, Lacan rewrote the Freudian drama of castration by assigning to the phallus the compensatory promise of dominance in the symbolic realm. For the phallus is signifier for the intervention of the father and his laws in the desire of the child. With the entry into language—the realm of the law, what Susan Sellers described as "the pre-established order within which the child must take up its appointed place" (46)—the subject takes up a sexed position as either male or female. In this process "woman" becomes a reified cultural Other to the phallic masculine Subject—"the fantasised object (Other) that makes it possible for man to exchange and function" (Sellers, 47). Sexual difference is foundational, implicated in the entry into language.

Lacan's theorizing of the split subject, the privileged phallus, sexual difference, the function of the capital-O Other, and the Law of the Father has had a profound impact on feminist theories of the subject. For instance, the old notion of self has been redefined as an illusory ego construct (a fiction, a phantasm) and displaced by the new concept of the subject, always split, always in the process of constituting itself through its others. As a result the fundamental terms invoked in discussions of autobiography have shifted as attention has been directed to the etiology of sexual difference, the relationship of the subject to its constitutive others, and the rhetorics of the self.

Lacanian theory has been refracted by a host of subsequent theorists who in turn have influenced the reading of women's autobiographies. From France came the work of the French feminists, among them Luce Irigaray, Hélène Cixous, and Julia Kristeva, three theorists who have responded in markedly different ways to Lacan. In her militant manifesto "Laugh of the Medusa," Hélène Cixous urged women to resist their silencing within the Law of the Father and to "steal" the language in order to write *toward* their difference, difference that has been mis/identified in the Law of the Father. This new language would be, according to Cixous, a writing of and from the body.

For Luce Irigaray, representation is always representation within the "logic of the same" precisely because the subject is constitutively masculine. If the history of metaphysics and of representation in the West has been a history of the violent mis/representation of woman in "phallogocentrism," or what she labeled metaphorically a logic of solids, then what is required is a sustained critique of the "logic of the same"—the specular logic through which "man" projects onto the surface of "woman" her "lack" and his fullness in alterity. What is also required is the creation of a language alternative to specularity through which women can articulate their difference, their desire. This non-phallogocentric language she metaphorizes as the logic of fluids, a logic emergent from women's different sexuality. It is a sexuality transgressive of stable boundaries, unity, sameness.

Julia Kristeva, rethinking Lacan's notion of the symbolic realm, proposed a presymbolic realm she calls "the semiotic." For Kristeva the realm of the semiotic is the space of *jouissance*, the nonverbal effluence of subjectivity that lies outside the Law of the Father, outside logocentric thinking and practices of representation. The eruptions of the semiotic signal the eruption of the irrational, that which must be suppressed in order for the subject to imagine itself as coherent, unified, autonomous. Because the self is a fiction sustained by the very practices of representation, its fictiveness can be glimpsed in the shadows of the semiotic, in the gaps, in nonsense, in puns, in pleasurable rhythms, all of which erupt from the unconscious (or preconscious) to disrupt meaning. As a strategy for resisting the Law of the Father, Kristeva thus proposes a politics of negativity. In response to the force of identifications, the subject can resist by insisting "I am not this and I am not this." Critically, Kristeva locates the figure of the preoedipal mother in the domain of the semiotic. Hers is the powerful mother not yet diminished and denigrated by association with castration.

There have been significant critiques of psychoanalytically-based approaches to sexual difference. An unnuanced psychoanalytic logic is a universalizing, indeed essentializing logic, despite claims to the contrary, since it assumes the sexual difference of two oppositional sexes as foundational, implicated in the entry into language. For some as well, psychoanalytic logic has the effect of hypostasizing temporality because it proposes a "tragic" narrative paradigm of human psychosexual development that reinforces the impossibility of change and of communication, thus begging the question of the subject's agency.

The rereadings of Lacan (and Freud) enacted by Cixous, Irigaray, and Kristeva have had tremendous importance for the reading of women's autobiography. They provide a way to confront the entrenched hold of patriarchal structures by locating them deep within the unconscious and the subject's foundational relationship to language. They provide a way of understanding the complexity of female positioning as a split subject within the symbolic order and its logic of representation. They provide terms for understanding how the female subject mis/recognizes herself as a coherent subject. They encourage readers to look for gaps and silences in texts, to read away from coherence—in fact, to become skeptical about such previously accepted notions in autobiography theory as the linearity of narrative and a unified concept of selfhood. They provide a vocabulary for exploring the relationship of women to language, to systems of representation, to the mother, to the body. Since the intervention of the French feminists in psychoanalytic theories, critics have discovered in women's autobiographical texts strategies for writing the subject "other"-wise. Finally, all three theorists explored, in poetic and playful engagements with theory, possibilities for alternative languages. Their appeal to writing the body and to exploring diverse writing practices has prompted others to develop alternative critical styles. In fact, we might trace the current interest in personal criticism in part to the experimental texts of Irigaray, Cixous, and Kristeva.

Thus in the eighties, several theorists of autobiography adapted the work of Lacan and the French feminist theorists even as they remained skeptical of the extremist pronouncements issuing from France regarding the erasure of the author-function in the text. In "Writing Fictions: Women's Autobiography in France," Nancy K. Miller approached the issue of women's self-writing by asking: "Who is speaking? And in whose name?" (46). In "Autogynography: Is the Subject Different?" Domna C. Stanton asked a series of sophisticated questions about the writing woman and her autobiographical practices, proposing that the splitting of woman's subjectivity must be understood in the context of her "different status in the symbolic order": "Autogynography," concluded Stanton, "dramatized the fundamental alterity and non-presence of the subject, even as it asserts itself discursively and strives toward an always impossible self-possession. This gendered narrative involved a different plotting and configuration of the split subject" (15). In "Authorizing the Autobiographical," Shari Benstock looked to Lacan's "mirror stage" as a figure through which to trace how the definition of writing is loosened from self-consciousness toward the *un*conscious. Even as the autobiographical act gestures toward a desire for the "self" and "self-image" to "coincide," the act, especially for women who question the authority of the Law of the Father, leads not to the inscription of a unitary self but to the self decentered or elided by "the fissures of female discontinuity" (20). And in "Mothers, Displacement, and Language in the Autobiographies of Nathalie Sarraute and Christa Wolf," Bella Brodzki worked to reframe a Chodorovian focus on the mother/daughter dyad through the psychoanalytic notion of displacement. For Brodzki the compelling figure haunting the texts of women autobiographers is the figure of the lost mother. The daughter's representation (already a displacement) of the past loss involves her in a complex struggle with this loss that "initiates the metonymic chain of substitute objects of desire, some more productive than others" (246).

Subject Matters: Althusser and Foucault
For many critics, psychoanalytic claims about female subjectivity, whether made in the wake of the ego psychology of Chodorow or the split subject of Lacan, too quickly and thoroughly erased the very real imprint of history itself. For materialist historians, subjectivist psychoanalysis universalized sexual difference and ignored the very different material circumstances of people's lives over time.

Concurrently, then, throughout the eighties important work was done by scholars concerned about situating the autobiographical subject in her historical specificity. Some critics turned to the work of French political theorist Louis Althusser, whose concept of ideology attempted to infuse Marxist economic determinism with the dynamic imprint of cultural formations. Althusser understood the social subject as a subject of ideology—not ideology in the narrow sense of propaganda but ideology in a broad sense of the pervasive and inescapable cultural formations of the dominant class (what he termed "state apparati"). As a way of understanding how ideology works to conform the subject, Althusser differentiated "Repressive State Apparatuses" (RSAs) from "Ideological State Apparatuses" (ISAs). RSAs are more coercive state institutions such as the military, the police, the judicial system. ISAs are less overtly coercive institutions—social services, educational institutions, the family, and cultural formations, such as the institution of "literature" and modes of popular culture. Both RSAs and ISAs "hail" the subject who enters them, calling her to a certain subject position. In this sense she is "interpellated" as a certain kind of subject through the ideology that informs and reproduces the institution. Critically, the "individual" understands herself as "naturally" self-produced precisely because the processes of interpellation are hidden, obscured by the practices of institutions. The subject, then, is invested in and fundamentally mystified by her own production. An ideological critique of her engagement in the state apparati is required to understand her own social formation, though such a critique will not undo it.

Althusser's analysis of ideology and interpellation contributed to feminist critiques of the West's romance with the free, autonomous individual. For the Althusserian critique understood that individual to be a function of ideology. Students of Althusser directed attention to the ways in which historically specific cultural institutions provide ready-made identities to subjects. "Autobiography" becomes one such literary institution in the West. It has its traditions (or history); it participates in the economics of production and circulation; and it has its effects—that is, it functions as a powerful cultural site through which the "individual" materializes. Althusser's theory of ideology and subject formation sets the stage for political readings and for the politicization of subjectivity; that is, for readings that attend to the ways in which literary genres are complicit in reproducing dominant ideologies.

Michel Foucault was also influential for feminist theorists concerned with developing a materialist praxis. Unlike Althusser, Foucault came to understand power not as monolithic or centripetally concentrated in official and unofficial institutions; rather power (with a small *p*) is culturally pervasive, centrifugally dispersed, localized. For Foucault there is no "outside" of power; power is everywhere and inescapable. And it is "discursive," that is, it is embedded in all the languages of everyday life and the knowledges produced at everyday sites. Discourses function as so many "technologies of self" through which the subject materializes. To understand the technologies of self the theorist must attend to several aspects of historical practice: the historical specificity of discourses, historically situated ways of knowing and figuring the world, historically specific regimes of truth. And "history" itself must be redefined as a "genealogical" investigation into the historical emergence of concepts about persons through which knowledge claims are produced. Genealogical inquiry thus becomes what Lee Quinby termed "desacralization," the exposure of local disruptions, contradictions, and inconsistencies in the production of regimes of truth (xii-xiii).

Foucault's emphases on the discursivity of texts, on historically specific regimes of truth/knowledge, and on genealogy have had a profound impact on scholars studying women's autobiographical practices. They have used Foucauldian analyses to critique the notion of women's experience, the romance of the "authentic" woman's voice, and the recourse to transparent notions of the "truth" of autobiographical experience and the "truth teller" status of the autobiographer. In her essay "Experience," for example, Joan W. Scott challenged the foundational status of experience as a ground of analysis. She called for the historicizing of "experience" and for reading experiential categories of identity as "contextual, contested, and contingent" if we are to analyze productively how individuals think of, come to know, and represent themselves in its terms (37). "Experience," she writes, "is at once always already an interpretation *and* is in need of interpretation" (38).

As neither Althusser nor Foucault addressed issues of gender, however, scholars of women's autobiography have had to critique their theories even as they use them to ground their analyses. To read women's autobiographical texts is to attend to the historically and culturally specific discourses of identity through which women become speaking subjects. Scholars have explored which discursive practices determine the kind of subject who speaks, the forms of self-representation available to women at particular historical moments, the meaning they make of their experiential histories. Such readings encourage us to think about women's texts—as we do about any texts—as sites of the re/production of knowledge.

Leigh Gilmore, in *Autobiographics*, examined autobiography as a Foucauldian technology of the self-engaged with the discourses of truth telling and lying as it has authorized some "individual" identities and reproduced gendered identity. Focusing on noncanonical women's texts of self-representation, Gilmore argued for a counter practice of "autobiographics" that would emphasize the writing of multiple, contradictory experimental identities as a means to locate the autobiographical as a "point of resistance" (42). And Felicity A. Nussbaum's reading of eighteenth-century British autobiographical writing (in "The Ideology of Genre" and "The Politics of Subjectivity") emphasized, á la Althusser and Foucault, "the materiality of ideology" and explored "the way in which conflictual discourses are yoked together within ideology to encourage bourgeois subjects to (mis)recognize themselves" (*Autobiographical*, 10). At the scene of autobiographical writing, Nussbaum argued, conflicting concepts of identity are played out as writing subjects, among them variously marginalized women of the eighteenth century, negotiate the politics of subjectivity through generic expectations and contradictions.

In a quite different manner but one also informed by Foucault's interrogation of the confession as a technology of self, Rita Felski's "On Confession" interrogated the "sincerity" and transparency of confessional discourse, particularly recent feminist confessional discourses, to think about how autobiographies accommodate new or counter-knowledges. For Felski, a feminist recourse to confessional narrative signals a conscious mix of the personal and the political, which are held in tension out of a "concern with the representative and intersubjective elements of women's experience" (93). Confession thus becomes a means of creating a new feminist audience to perform the impossible—a validation of the female experience narrated in the text.

As they have invoked Foucault and Althusser with a difference, scholars of autobiography have had to tackle head-on the issue of human agency. Althusser made a space for the agency of the subject through "science," the development of an objective analysis of the effects of ideological interpellation. The earlier work of Foucault seemed to make no space for the agency of the subject; discursive subjection was total; power was all. Dissatisfied with a problematic scientific objectivity, on the one hand, or total subjection on the other, critics began to pose questions aimed at probing the agency of the subject. How can the subject come to know itself differently? Under what conditions can the subject exercise any kind of freedom, find the means to change? Scott, in a sense speaking for many feminist historians theorizing women's everyday and social history, offered a way of making space for agency by insisting that subjects, simultaneously implicated in contradictory and conflicting discursive calls, discover or glimpse spaces through which to maneuver, spaces through which to resist, spaces for change.

Questions of agency became central to discussions of women's autobiography. How does the woman autobiographer negotiate a discursive terrain—autobiography—that has been until recently a primarily masculine domain? How do discourses of identity differentiate the narrative scripts of normative masculinity and femininity? How does the narrator take up and put off contradictory discourses of identity? How does she understand herself as a subject of discursive practices? How does she come to any new knowledge about herself? What has been "repressed" in the narrative, which dis/identifications erased? By locating autobiographical subjects in a historically embedded context and probing the conditions for gaining agency, critics have reframed the discussion of women's "experience" as nonessentialized.

A thick materialist analysis offers yet another line of inquiry. In "A Feminist Revision of New Historicism to Give Fuller Readings of Women's Private Writing," Helen M. Buss turned to the reading strategies of New Historicist theory and practice, specifically thick description, to render more complex her approach to the personal diaries of a nineteenth-century British Canadian woman, Isabel West. Revising New Historicism for a feminist project, Buss locates her diarist among conflicting ideologies and the silence at the limits of patriarchal language in a way that renovates West for new readers.

Feminist theorists attentive to the material circumstances of women's lives also look at the production and circulation of texts, that is, at the commodification of narrative genres and the ways in which women's literary production is part of economic systems of exchange. British scholars have been especially concerned with the class status of the autobiographer. For these scholars the following questions are motivating: Who is writing? Where is she positioned within the socioeconomic field? How does her class status affect the way she negotiates autobiographical discourses? Who are her readers? How do autobiographical narratives function in the context of class politics and consciousness?

Regenia Gagnier, in "The Literary Standard, Working-Class Autobiography, and Gender," discussed the importance of socioeconomic status and mobility in her analysis of gender in nineteenth-century working-class autobiographies. Many women's working-class autobiographies, Gagnier argues, employ middle-class narratives of self, with their norms of familial, romantic, and financial success, at great psychic cost to the writer. The clash of enfranchised middle-class norms and disenfranchised working-class circumstances produces "narratives of disintegrated personality" that tell a counternarrative of the cost of the ideology of individualism for those positioned at its margin. Employing a class analysis to read Victorian women's autobiography, Mary Jean Corbett, in "Literary Domesticity and Women Writers' Subjectivities," explored how women autobiographers "master their anxiety about being circulated, read, and interpreted by carefully shaping the personae they present and by subordinating their histories of themselves to others' histories" (159). As they do so these women writers, who achieved public celebrity through work, forge "new concepts of history and subjectivity" as emergent "in and through all individuals" rather than in the "great man." The popular idiom of memoir enabled them to position themselves as astute observers of the familial and social scenes even if they sometimes chafed under the contradictions of publicity.

In "Stories," by contrast, Carolyn Kay Steedman positions subjects as "classed" in a complex way that informs her materialist reading of her own and her mother's lives. The personal interpretations of the past that autobiographical stories tell are often in conflict with a culture's ideology because "class and gender, and their articulations, are the bits and pieces from which psychological selfhood is made" (7). Locating herself and her mother in a problematic relationship to the particulars of mid-twentieth-century London, she reads their lives *against* the norms of British working-class autobiography and refuses any straightforward act of historical interpretation.

We have traced separate trajectories for psychoanalytic and materialist theories of the female subject, but ever more frequently theorists have sought to bridge the gap between them. Teresa de Lauretis, for example, has made a productive intervention for theorists of women's writing practices by reading materialist and psychoanalytic critiques through one another.

De Lauretis claimed that the psychoanalytic concept of the unconscious (the repressed) can be reconceptualized as a site of cultural dis/identifications (the repository of culturally unsanctioned identifications). As a result, she radically revised psychoanalytic theory, without jettisoning it, through attention to cultural and historical specificity.

Interrogating "Woman," Multiplying Differences

To historicize experience is to erode the holding power of the concept of the universal "woman" of psychoanalytic modes of analysis. But the most urgent and invested critique of universal woman came from those women of color who focused attention on the cultural productions of subjects marginalized by virtue of their race and/or ethnicity. As they established a communal tradition and proposed countertexts to the canon, women of color argued the instrumental role of autobiographical writing in giving voice to formerly silenced subjects. Thus another set of motivating questions generated new ways of approaching autobiographical texts: What alternative traditions of women's autobiographical writing are there? How is the canon of (predominantly white) women's writing disrupted and revised by a focus on texts by women of color?

Numerous scholars of women's autobiography, in the United States and throughout the world, have been engaged in exploring a range of texts and theorizing the difference of their differences. Some of those critics are included in *Women, Autobiography, Theory*, and their work gestures toward the work of other critics as well. In "The Narrative Self: Race, Politics, and Culture in Black American Women's Autobiography," Nellie Y. McKay suggested that African American women's writing needs to be read within a historically inflected paradigm attentive to the imbrication of gender and race. In nineteenth-century slave and spiritual narratives, McKay argued, African American women asserted models of selfhood distinct from those of both middle-class white women and African American men. In the twentieth century, however, their autobiographical practice has valued variously the experience of growing up black in a racist world, as writers both chart and resist victimization while moving beyond protest narrative to autobiographically bear witness to the costs of their psychic and political survival.

Reading Asian women's autobiographical texts in "Semiotics, Experience, and the Material Self: An Inquiry into the Subject of the Contemporary Asian Woman Writer," Shirley Geok-lin Lim pointed to the importance of multiple marginalities, of gender, ethnicity, nationality, and linguistic community, that continue to characterize the Asian woman writer's cultural status. But she mined this positionality through her engagement with her own experiential history and the cultural expectations of passivity—which she approached through Julia Kristeva's notion of the semiotic, secured as it is in the materiality of the body.

In "Immigrant Autobiography: Some Questions of Definition and Approach," Sau-ling Cynthia Wong called for a more historicized and ethnically specific approach to reading the genre, pointing out that the norms of autobiographies of Americanization are Eurocentric. In contrast, the narratives of many Chinese immigrants emphasize pre-American experience and assign non-utopian meanings to an America in which the autobiographer is "more a guide than an adventurer." Hertha D. Wong argues, in "First-Person Plural: Identity and Community in Native American Women's Autobiography," that relationality and community signify different practices and values in Native American and feminist contexts. Wong maps an inquiry into the possible "double relationality" of Native women and proposes terms for reading their autobiographical writing as something other than a foreclosed narrative of tragic loss.

Scholars writing on Chicana and Latina women's writing address a rich autobiographical tradition that encompasses nineteenth-century histories as well as a proliferation of contemporary voices. In "The Construction of the Self in U.S. Latina Autobiographies," Lourdes Torres read Latina autobiographical writing as both revolutionary and subversive. Latina autobiographers, appropriating a new literary space in which they can assert mestiza identity and theorize a politics of language and experience, write the contradictions of their multiple identities in ways that enable other women of color to reshape the paradigms and politics of identity in narrative.

In rethinking autobiographical narratives in terms of the politics of difference, scholars have necessarily developed a critique of Western individualism and the expectation that narrative lives conform to dominant cultural models of identity. They have also challenged theories that posit a universal woman—implicitly white, bourgeois, and Western—and that presume to speak on her behalf. This challenge has been aggressively directed at white feminists who complacently assume the white woman as normative; but it gestures as well to the need for collective affiliation with women of many and diverse differences. In *This Bridge Called My Back,* for instance, editors Cherríe Moraga and Gloria Anzaldúa brought over fifty voices together to insist on the inextricability of multiple differences. In doing so, the writers in *Bridge* challenged the white academic feminist establishment's allegiance to a privileged sexual difference and a white Western woman. They exposed as well the untheorized access to power of white academic feminists.

In proposing accounts and countercanons of women's autobiography, theorists of difference have explored alternative notions of subjectivity based not on the unique individual but rather on complex collective identifications. That collective identity may be an indigenous one or the kind of diasporic, "pan"-collectivity posited by such critics as Gayatri Spivak and Chandra Talpade Mohanty. Theorists of difference foreground such questions as the following: Who is speaking? How are they already spoken for through dominant cultural representations? What must they do to be heard? By focusing on such questions, theorists of difference provide the terms to articulate how dominant cultural values have been internalized by oppressed subjects. Major explorations of difference occur in autobiographies by North American women of color, such as *Borderlands/La Frontera* by Gloria Anzaldúa, *Loving in the War Years* by Cherríe Moraga, *Bloodlines* by Janet Campbell Hale, *Among the White Moon Faces* by Shirley Geok-lin Lim, and *The Sweeter the Juice* by Shirlee Taylor Haizlip.

These challenges by women of color to a white feminist theory of autobiography were launched as identity claims and from collective practices located outside the academy—in urban centers, among collectives and movements. Because critique is inseparable from resistance to dominant modes, new modes of writing were necessary to ground theory in experience, including reading experience. The language of *Loving in the War Years*, for instance, or of *Borderlands/La Frontera*, is language engaged with the meanings, mythologies, conflicts, and contradictions of experiential history. At work to give voice and words to personal history and to map the intersection of personal and public spheres of meaning, writers such as Moraga and Anzaldúa revise the meaning of "theorizing" about subjectivity. They make explorations of what Sidonie Smith has termed the "Autobiographical Manifesto" in her piece of the same name. Their theorizing does not announce itself as theory—high, dry, and hermetically sealed. It is theory at the bone and in the flesh. Autobiographical manifestos issue hopeful calls for new subjects even as they look back through critical lenses at the sources of oppression and conflictual identifications.

Women writing about multicultural practices repeatedly caution against reifying any simple model of difference as adequate to explore the complexity of lived or narrative lives. As Marianne Hirsch suggested, "Subjects are constituted and differentiated in relation to a variety of screens—class, race, gender, sexuality, age, nationality, and familiality—and they can attempt to manipulate and modify the functions of the image/screen" (120). This call to complexity in theorizing of difference multiplies these differences and raises a new issue of priority among heterogeneous differences. If differences are multiple and asymmetrical, who bears the difference? "It was a while before we came to realize that our place was the very house of difference rather than the security of any one particular difference," wrote Audre Lorde in her autobiographical "biomythography" *Zami*.

But how are all these differences held in some kind of dynamic tension? How does one understand the multiplication of identity vectors? Sexual difference is one of several differences mobilized at different moments—differences with histories, and with social and cultural effects. Responding to this thorny question, theorists continue to rethink the relationship between various positions of marginality, between those of gender and those of race, or those of sexuality, or those of class. If there has been a proliferation of categories of difference, there has also been an insistence upon their inextricable linkage to one another, upon the necessity of an intersectional analysis. Yet the question remains: How do we specify productively, rather than reductively, the triad of race/ethnicity, class, and sexuality?

For some theorists of women's autobiography, postmodern critiques of the subject have encouraged a rethinking of the terms of identity politics itself. They argue that "race" and "ethnicity" are not things in themselves but historically specific social constructs, materially realized in the discursive practices of everyday life. So too is "woman." Judith Butler argued that identity is always produced and sustained by cultural norms, and she pointed to the limits of identity politics by noting "tacit cruelties that sustain coherent identity" (*Bodies*, 115). If subjects are irreducibly multiple, as Butler observed, prioritizing one identification, such as gender, at the expense of others is not only reductive but paralyzing. Butler stated: "What appear within such an enumerative framework as separable categories are, rather, the conditions of articulation for each other" (117). Identities, imbricated in and constituted by one another, need to contribute to a politics rather than a policing. This politics would be aimed not only at empowering subjects but at overcoming cultural imperatives that sustain fictions of coherence.

Post/Colonial Moves

In the late eighties the influence of postcolonial theory also began to be felt in studies of women's writing, especially women's writing from global locations outside the United States. Through their critiques of Western imperialism and the asymmetries of power emergent in diverse contexts of colonization and decolonization, theorists of postcoloniality registered and assessed the continuing legacies of colonial histories and the contemporary, or neocolonial, reorganization of global capitalism. More precisely, in the wake of Frantz Fanon, Aimé Césaire, and Edouard Glissant, they pondered how the subjectivity of colonized peoples has been constituted through the processes of colonial conquest and the consequent bureaucratization of imperial power. Attention to "the colonized subject" and to what has been termed marginal or minoritized discourse has spurred rethinking of the paradigms of subjectivity. And a central site in that revisionary struggle has been autobiographical discourse, the coming to voice of previously silenced subjects.

Since "autobiography" in the West has a particular history, what we have understood as the autobiographical "I" has been an "I" with a historical attitude—a sign of the Enlightenment subject, unified, rational, coherent, autonomous, free, but also white, male, Western. This subject has been variously called "the individual" or "the universal human subject" or "the transcendent subject" or "man." Cultural attachment to this sovereign "I" signals an investment in the subject of "history" and "progress," for this "man" is the subject who traveled across the globe, surveyed what he saw, claimed it, organized it, and thereby asserted his superiority over the less civilized "other" whom he denigrated, exploited, and "civilized" at once. Theorists of postcoloniality have thus recognized autobiography as one of the cultural formations in the West implicated in and complicit with processes of colonization.

This critique has had a profound effect on our approach to women's autobiographical practices. If this autobiographical "I" is a Western "I," an "I" of the colonizer, then what happens when the colonized subject takes up a generic-practice forged in the West and complicit in the West's romance with individualism? Gayatri Chakravorty Spivak asked whether the "subaltern" can speak at all, given her assignment to a marginal status in colonial and patriarchal discourses. Can a colonized subject speak in or through cultural formations other than those of the colonial master? Is she always already spoken for? This becomes a particularly vexed question in engaging collaborative text, those narratives that emerge from the joint project of an informant lacking literacy and/or access to public outlets and an interlocutor or editor interested in bringing the informant's story to a broad audience. In such texts issues of power, trust, and narrative authority become critical to the politics of collaboration. Such texts also require that we acknowledge the importance of oral cultural forms and attend to the speakerly text, rather than remain preoccupied with the writerly effects of narrative.

Spivak's provocative question about the un-speakability of the subaltern has elicited countertheories that intend to account for possibilities of resistance and agency. Theorists of postcolonial agency ask the following kinds of questions: How might processes of decolonization take place through, against, and in spite of the cultural dominance of this "I"? How might subjects come to voice outside, or despite, the constraints of Western models of identity? What alternative possibilities of identity have been overwritten by Western models?

Postcolonial theorists also consider how processes of decolonization might be affected through alternative cultural practices. Some call for narrative modes that are neither linear nor developmental but that attend to specificities of indigenous cultural practices and how those are reformed within histories of colonization. Barbara Harlow attended to collective voicings of resistance by imprisoned women in "From the Women's Prison: Third World Women's Narratives of Prison." The autobiographical writings of imprisoned women at many sites—Palestinian, Egyptian, South African, Latin American, and other—are transforming narrative paradigms as they assert the textual authority of subjects repressed by authoritarian structures. Their narratives of detainment not only propose resistance but call for global social reorganization.

Caren Kaplan, in "Resisting Autobiography: Out-law Genres and Transnational Feminist Subjects," extended Harlow's analysis to sketch several alternative or "out-law" narrative practices through which women negotiate and reform such generic modes as ethnography, bio-mythography, and psychobiography. Similarly, both Doris Sommer and John Beverley have argued that the *Testimonio* challenges the norms of autobiography as the narrative of an irreducibly collective subject whose acts of witnessing address the hegemony of Western individualism. In "Sacred Secrets: A Strategy for Survival," Sommer extended Harlow's and Kaplan's readings of women's autobiographies of resistance to the writer-reader relationship as complicated by the ethnographer-informant situation. Sommer explores what she calls a rhetoric of particularism in writers such as Rigoberta Menchú, whose narrative refuses intimacy to privileged readers and warns "against easy appropriations of Otherness into manageable universal categories" (133). That is, an autobiographical testimony such as Rigoberta's artfully manipulates its audience to perform a cautious reading and resists the autobiographical genre's illusions of narrator-reader intimacy. In tracking multiple sites of identity and emphasizing the collectivity of subjects who talk back to Western concepts of the autonomous individual, these and many other theorists of postcolonial writing make clear how postcolonial texts have intervened to reframe the terms of subjectivity.

New terms have emerged to capture the complex vectors of de/colonization and of multicultural subjectivity. A variety of adjectives designate subjects of the "in-between," such as hybrid, marginal, migratory, diasporic, multicultural, border, minoritized, mestiza, nomadic, third space. Each term carries its own historical and theoretical valences. All name aspects of the complex conditions of subjectivity in the late-twentieth-century world. As they ponder this complexity, postcolonial critics of autobiography draw attention to narrative practices in diverse global locations, from the writing practices of indigenous Australians to the narratives of African American women identifying themselves with the black diaspora; from the stories of the First Peoples of Canada to the narrative testimony of Bessie Head in South Africa; from the memoirs of postcolonial intellectuals living in the West to the resistance literature of the imprisoned, the institutionalized; from the narratives of the immigrants to the New Europe to the narratives of diasporic Chinese. Each of these instances of narrative voicing calls for a careful focus upon the site of de/colonization in its historical, material, and national specificity.

Developing reading practices attentive to these migratory subjects in all their diversity has led theorists to develop new models of transnationalism and transculturation. It has also spurred incisive critiques of readings framed by Western interpretive approaches. And it has led to a shift from the term "women's autobiography" to terms such as "women's autobiographical practices," "women's personal narratives," "women's lifewriting." This shift away from the word *autobiography* marks a shift away from an uncritical Western understanding of the subject of autobiography.

Postcolonial theory remains contentious and fractured; it is not monolithic. There are critiques coming from within of the problematic basis upon which postcolonial theorists found their analyses. There are critiques of the very term "postcolonial." For the idea of time as separated into precolonial, colonial, and postcolonial periods is itself caught in a teleological framing of history that always privileges the moment of Western encounter. The critique of Western values as purely Western takes away the transformative agency of cultures as well as their *active* transformation of inherited Western values as those values are incorporated through indigenous traditions.

And the reification of the voice of the "authentic" indigenous subject can promote a new form of nativism, as Sara Suleri cautioned in "Woman Skin Deep: Feminism and the Postcolonial

Condition." Concerned to "dismantle the iconic status of postcolonial feminism" with its recourse to identity politics, Suleri cautioned that the invocation of the "postcolonial Woman" has the effect of erasing the specific historical contexts in which subjects are forced to understand their experience. She distrusted such identity politics because of its embrace of an unproblematized experience and the "local voice" of the autobiographical "as a substitute for any theoretical agenda that can make more than a cursory connection between the condition of postcolonialism and the question of gendered race" (764).

Françoise Lionnet argued, however, that it remains crucial for critics to analyze and represent "the subjective experience of muted groups within social structures that rarely allow them to speak as subjects and agents of knowledge," and to retain an "awareness of the multicultural, multiracial dimensions of various strands of feminism inside and outside the academy" (*Postcolonial*, 188). To that end, it is illuminating to recall Assia Djebar's *Women of Algiers in Their Apartment*. The noted Algerian novelist wrote her identity as a subject under erasure, colonized by the politics of imperialism, the practices of the harem, and the métissage of languages, in "Forbidden Gaze, Severed Sound." Speaking the silences of Algerian women's lives, she gave voice to collective "fragments of ancient murmuring" (151) to "embody" future conversations among women.

Theories of Heteroglossia and Heterogeneity

Theorists in the late seventies and early eighties argued the difference of women's voices. Notably, Carol Gilligan's influential *In a Different Voice* distinguished a "woman's" voice from a "man's" voice in an effort to better understand the differential ethical development of girls and boys. Boys' values she describes as rule-oriented, agonistic, goal directed; girls' values as communal, contextual, relational. The effect of Gilligan's theory of different voices was to assign to women an ethical high ground by appeal to a standard drawn from their own experience, not derived from the "universal" experience of men. Subsequent feminist theorists, suspicious of feminist metanarratives, pointed to the essentializing and universalizing effects of this way of understanding difference in voice (Butler and Nicholson, 33). Gilligan's notion of a different voice for women was thus fraught with problems for theorizing women's autobiographical practices; but theorizing women's voices—without recourse to a universalizing metanarrative—continued to be an issue.

Throughout the eighties critics employing the familiar metaphors "coming to voice" and "voicing female subjectivity" looked to the resonant theoretical framework provided by Mikhail Bakhtin, who elaborated the concepts of dialogism and heteroglossia. Arguing that "every word is directed towards an answer," Bakhtin claimed the internal dialogism of the word. Words, that is, are argumentative. They are also always full of play, "plung[ing]," as he says, "into the inexhaustible wealth and contradictory multiplicity" of meanings. For Bakhtin language is the medium for consciousness; thus he understands subjectivity as dialogical in that it is always implicated in "the process of social interaction." Since social groups have their languages, each member of the group becomes conscious in and through that language. But because of what he calls heteroglossia, the proliferation of languages, words, meanings that "mutually supplement one another, contradict one another and [are] interrelated dialogically" (qtd. in Henderson 121), the subject speaks through multiple voices. The utterance of the subject is irreducibly dialogic, contestatory, heteroglossic.

According to Mae Gwendolyn Henderson, Bakhtin's theory links "psyche, language, and social interaction" (121). The concept of heteroglossia provides a means to join theories of consciousness to theories of culture and to refocus questions of textuality. The individual's language is always language permeated by the voices of others, voices out of the sociocultural field. Dialogism supports the claim that there are always other voices in the text, that even the most monologic of texts can be read for heteroglossia and that the autobiographical subject is a subject of the play of voices.

Dialogism has been particularly illuminating for discussions of women's autobiographical voices. Thinking about heteroglossia and about the social constitution of consciousness enables theorists to get away from the naive notion of the primary text and its hidden or "latent" subtext. Heteroglossia assumes a pervasive and fundamental heterogeneity to human subjectivity. The text is multivocal because it is a site for the contestation of meaning. Numerous critics have argued for the multivoicedness of women's autobiographical texts as a crucial way to reframe issues of agency and ideological interpellation. By this tactic they avoid the paralyzing polarization of the total determination of the subject, on the one hand, or the total freedom of the subject to make meaning, on the other.

The heteroglossia of language and consciousness is not specific to women's texts as opposed to men's texts, nor is it specific to a particular genre. Thus the notion of the dialogism of the word precludes theorizing any essential or universal difference. It becomes problematic to speak of an authentic voice of some universal "woman." The voice of the narrator is a dialogical voice through which heterogeneous discourses of identity cross the tongue. To paraphrase Bakhtin, the word in one's mouth is always somebody else's word. Therefore the reader must be careful not to discredit certain texts as somehow inauthentic, or in a different (read "not right") voice.

The theorizing of Lionnet and Henderson, in different ways, demonstrates the enabling potential of theories of heteroglossia in discussions of women's autobiography. Lionnet's concept of *métissage*, put forth in "The Politics and Aesthetics of Métissage," has been influential for reading a wide variety of women's personal narratives. This "braiding" of voices addresses such issues as the agency of postcolonial francophone and anglophone women writers mixing indigenous and colonial languages. Lionnet reframed writing as voice, privileging orality and the incorporation of extra-(Euro)literary forms in women's texts as she reflected on the "muted" cultural status of women in many traditional cultures.

Similarly, Henderson, in "Speaking in Tongues: Dialogics, Dialectics, and the Black Woman Writer's Literary Tradition," emphasized "glossalalia" and the multiple voices in which black women writers enunciate a complex subjectivity that employs the discourse of the other(s), and as Other contests dominant discourses. For these critics women's "coming to voice" has taken on new theoretical potential that need not be essentializing.

Theorizing the Everyday and Cultural Studies

Everyday kinds of writing in personal venues such as the diary and the journal have long fascinated literary critics interested in women's autobiographical writing and in the relationship of texts to women's material lives. In their inclusionary and democratizing projects, these theorists of dailiness focus on differentiating the kinds of subjects who speak in letters, diaries, journals, and memoirs. And they rethink issues of temporality, noting the apparent discontinuity in diurnal forms.

In her "Introduction" to *A Day at a Time,* Margo Culley attended to the critical importance of the audience, either real or implied, addressed by the diary writer. For Culley the pages of the diary become "a kind of mirror before which the diarist stands assuming this posture or that" (12). Moreover, the ongoing effect of time in the diary means that the outcome of time is unknown by both diarist and reader, so that self-positioning is always in flux. Similarly, using the letters of eighteenth-century women to explore "Female Rhetorics," Patricia Meyer Spacks emphasized the ways in which self-revelation, assumed in the writing of personal forms, conflicts with the ideology of normative femininity as self-effacing. Thus, women letter writers develop strategies of deflection, preoccupation with others, protestations of insignificance, or identification with women as a collectivity, that enable them to engage in the self-assertion of epistolary correspondence.

Up until the 1990s, feminist critics who focused on forms of dailiness confronted criticism that these modes had a secondary or marginal status as literature. But since the end of the eighties, the methods and models of cultural studies have been brought to bear on forms of dailiness and generated theories of the everyday constructions of experience. The variety of approaches to women's inscriptions of dailiness is evident in the collection *Inscribing the Daily: Critical Essays on Women's Diaries*, coedited by Suzanne L. Bunkers and Cynthia A. Huff. Contributors to this collection considered the different audiences for diaries; the diary as fragments; the broadened textual boundaries of diaries into which women insert various materials; and the intertextualities of diaries by family members.

As Jerome Bruner has argued persuasively, everyday life can be understood as an ongoing narrative negotiation. Life narratives are articulated in collaborative everyday projects, such as family stories and interactions. Or, as the contributors to our collection *Getting a Life: Everyday Uses of Autobiography* suggested, people "get a life" that conforms them to particular institutions (medical institutions, social services, the academy, etc.) and practices (such as narrating the self-help or intimate pre-sexual or "Personals" version of one's life) in diverse social contexts. Michel de Certeau has theorized the significance of everyday negotiations as tactics of social groups and noted how self-signification proliferates in an era of advanced capitalism.

The projects of cultural studies are diverse; but in general they signal a move away from privileging "high" literary forms and toward the reading of all kinds of cultural production as textual. Culture is, in its broadest sense, understood as an ever-negotiated site of conflict. And so popular forms become endlessly productive venues for the social constitution of subjects and for their everyday resistances. Thus cultural studies, opening flexible spaces for the serious explorations of alternative modes of self-writing, has revitalized discussions of many kinds of women's textual practices.

The implications of cultural studies approaches for women's autobiography are only beginning to be realized. Linda Martin Alcoff and Laura Gray-Rosendale have explored the conservative and the liberatory effects of what they call "survivor discourse," a discourse emergent in popular culture venues such as television talk shows and self-help groups. Biddy Martin has pointed to the social uses and the everyday politics of coming-out narratives. Other cultural critics have become fascinated with contemporary visual practices, performance art, talk show confessions. Asking us to read all kinds of texts as autobiographical, cultural critics require us to refine our mode of reading.

Concerned with the rush to privilege women's collective "we" as an alternative to the reification of the singular individual, Anne E. Goldman, in "Autobiography, Ethnography, and History: A Model for Reading," attended to "those impulses toward self-presencing which I believe remain an essential characteristic of life writings" (xxiv). She looked particularly at the autobiographical writings of working-class white women and women of color in order to understand how autobiographical narrators negotiate the pressures of the "I" and the "we," how they "maneuver between autobiographical and political-cultural texts," how they pursue self-presence as they "represent" a collectivity (xxvii).

The autobiographical thus becomes an aspect of textuality rather than a narrowly defined generic practice about lives lived chronologically.

Personal Criticism

In 1988 Jane Tompkins issued a manifesto of sorts to literary critics and theorists in her essay entitled "Me and My Shadow"—get real and get personal. Nancy K. Miller has theorized the need for and the significance of "Getting Personal." "Personal criticism," she explained on her opening page, "entails an explicitly autobiographical performance within the act of criticism. Indeed, getting personal in criticism typically involves a deliberate move toward self-figuration, although the degree and form of self-disclosure of course vary widely" (1). Miller, who distinguished personal from autobiographical criticism, acknowledged its "internal signature" as self-authorizing while criticizing Tompkins' essay as finally turning its back on theory (2–4).

Personal criticism is widely practiced by women, in homage to the textual practices they work on but also as integral to their efforts to reframe the critical act through feminist pedagogy and praxis. It is in part a response to the sterile evacuation of the personal voice in what has by now become institutionalized as theoretical discourse. The critic who gets personal may critique the claim to universal judgment and the objectivity of any universal critical "I." Getting personal also becomes an occasion for the critic/theorist to examine her relationship to the object of study, for a white critic to examine her vexed relationship to issues of unequal power as they affect her reading of texts by women of color, for the psychoanalytic critic to turn the lens of psychoanalytic praxis upon her own critical enterprise. For some it becomes a means to theorize personal experience, or, in the words of Joan Scott, to see experience not only as an interpretation but as in need of interpretation. Thus personal criticism facilitates the reading of personal experience and theory through each other.

As a critical gesture personal criticism aims to bridge the troubling gap between academic feminists and feminist activists. It is a search for a wider audience, a broader conversation, ideally on more honest and equal terms. Thus, as Gayle Green noted, such writing works toward "a clearer sense of responsibility to a social movement... to revitalize some important connections—between ourselves and our audience, our writing and its effects" (20). For some, asserting the importance of engaged writing becomes a way of assuming certain characteristics of what Antonio Gramsci called the "organic intellectual" within the academy (normally a site of critical disengagement).

One of the most productive and widely circulated practitioners of personal criticism has, of course, been bell hooks. In several volumes of autobiographical essays and in the essay in *Interfaces*, "writing autobiography," hooks made essay writing a way of both "talking back" and "talking to myself." Moving between a personal "I" and a collective "we," hooks infused cultural critique with her own responses and politics. The directness of her writing has won her a wide and enthusiastic following, but also sharp criticism, from, for example, Sara Suleri in "Woman Skin Deep."

In redirecting attention from the object of inquiry to the critic's responses to the object, personal criticism can overwrite the subject of inquiry as the theorist's textual preoccupation becomes herself. At its worst it can resort to willful abandoning of theory for a simplistic identity politics. In a—personally narrated—dissent from personal criticism as critical practice, Linda S. Kauffman asserted: "Writing about yourself does not liberate you, it just shows how engrained the ideology of freedom through self-expression is in our thinking" ("Long," 133). But for the autobiographer, contextualizing her life narrative as personal criticism attentive to the norms of narrative self-disclosure may enable a more nuanced space for writing the self. Nancy Mairs, in *Remembering the Bone House*, insisted on an integration and eroticization of body and mind precisely in inscribing her experience of disability in the "house" of her past, of memory, to address the commonality of experience. "Our stories utter one another" (11).

Queering the Scene, Undoing "Woman"

In 1980 Adrienne Rich's influential essay "On Compulsory Heterosexuality and Lesbian Existence" appeared, challenging the norm of heterosexuality as natural or chosen. Throughout the seventies Monique Wittig articulated her reading of the lesbian as the third sex, neither the one nor the other, in essays such as "The Straight Mind" and "The Mark of Gender" and novels including *Les Guerilleres* and *The Lesbian Body*. Women in particular were called by these authors to reexamine their unreflective assumption of heterosexuality as normative and homosexuality as perverse or diminished sexuality. Coming-out narratives proliferated, and autobiographies of sexual experimentation became more explicit, as autobiographers investigated the relationship of personal and social experience. In "Lesbian Identity and Autobiographical Difference(s)," Biddy Martin argued that lesbianism must no longer be theorized as "an identity with predictable contents." Rather it should be understood as "a position from which to speak" that "works to unsettle rather than to consolidate the boundaries around identity" (83).

While many postcolonial autobiographers, according to Julia Watson in "Unspeakable Differences: The Politics of Gender in Lesbian and Heterosexual Women's Autobiographies," would resist placing sexuality at the center of women's affiliations, contestations around sexuality have emerged as a crucial ground for theory. Watson interrogated the unspeakable as a category "used to designate sexual differences that remain unspoken, and therefore invisible" (140). While lesbian desire has until recently been one potent cultural unspoken, so too, suggested Watson, has heterosexual desire remained unspoken. Assumed as normative, that unspeakable desire has functioned to block intercultural affiliations among women.

If difference theorists reinterpreted sexual orientation as relational positionality rather than fixed identity marker, the nineties have brought a retheorizing of debates on sexuality. Queer studies erupted on the academic scene to shift the terms of debate from sexual difference to issues of "performativity." Theorists such as Judith Butler argued against any simplistic recourse to the essentialized differences of identity politics. In an attempt to retain the "explanatory force" of psychoanalysis, Butler, in the "Introduction" to *Bodies That Matter*, used the term performativity to capture the provisional and political nature, the "gender trouble," of identity formation. She defined performativity as the "power of discourse to produce effects through reiteration" (20). For Butler, an "I" does not precede the social construction of gender identity; the "I" comes into being through that social construction: "The subject is produced in and as a gendered matrix of relations" (7). Social construction is always a process of "reiterated acting" (9). Thus bodies "materialize," but the body is not "site or surface"; rather the body is "*a process of materialization that stabilizes over time to produce the effect of boundary, fixity, and surface we call matter*" (9). Identity is always coming into being through reiteration and being unfixed through the "gaps and fissures" that emerge "as the constitutive instabilities in such constructions, as that which escapes or exceeds the norm" (10).

If gender identity, and identity more generally, is a reiterative process of coming into being and simultaneously failing to cohere, then masculinity and femininity are not fixed attributes of the "self." "Woman" is effectively a style of the flesh, a materialization, that can also be dematerialized, in unconscious and conscious iterations. For queer theorists challenging the notion that there are any differences that are "natural," man, woman—the most "natural" of human categories—are styles of the body. Nor are femininity and masculinity monolithic differences, coherent and unified. There are many styles of masculinity and femininity, specific to different times, places, and sociocultural locations.

In queer theory the very materiality of the body becomes a site of social construction and conflict. Thus queer theorists challenge any recourse to the body or to the direction of desire as the ground of essential difference. Once again, we find the critique of identity politics—signified by the shift from "lesbian" identity to "queer" identity, the former rooted in a theory of essential sexual difference, the latter in a theory of the performativity of difference. Queer theory proposes a thoroughgoing rhetorical sense of self, a notion of self that has influenced theorists of subjectivity more generally. Sidonie Smith, for example, drew upon theories of performativity in her essay on "Performativity, Autobiographical Practice, Resistance." Queer theory unfixes the relationship of gender identity to sexed body, and gender performance to gender identity. Yvonne Yarbro-Bejarano has, however, cautioned that queer theory's emphasis on performative gender "does not actively factor in how racial formations shape the 'performance' of gender and sexual identity" (129), thus pointing to an ongoing debate.

Deconstructing concepts of gendered voices, gendered bodies, and gendered texts, queer theory has influenced the ways in which women's autobiographical texts are currently being read. The terms of analysis now focus on autobiographical identity as performative. Such an approach undercuts earlier theoretical investments in certain kinds of autobiographical fixities. For instance, claims based on the binary opposition of man/woman are put into question as multiple gender positions are made available. Kate Bornstein's 1995 book *Gender Outlaw: On Men, Women, and the Rest of Us* captured this resistance to any fixed style of the body. A transgender performance artist, Bornstein intertwined a personal narrative with a journey through theories of sexual identity in order to challenge the reader to resist the notion of any essential concept of masculinity and femininity. In Bornstein's hybrid text the usual meanings of identity are evacuated: "My identity becomes my body which becomes my fashion which becomes my writing style. Then I perform what I've written in an effort to integrate my life, and that becomes my identity, after a fashion" (1).

Bodies and Desire

Any theorizing of the body in the West takes up the history of the polarization of thought and feeling that assigned the "natural" and "feeling" body to women and the higher capacities of reason to man, a polarization especially, pronounced in Enlightenment thinking and its philosophical legacies. The materiality of bodies was erased by the Cartesian identification of being with consciousness, rationality with a disembodied self-consciousness. Man thus projects onto what Irigaray called the "flat mirror" of woman a material groundedness from which he can launch into dematerialized speculation, the transcendental space of pure thought. Thoroughly saturated with her materiality, which is a sign of her diminished humanity, woman struggles to become bodiless as well, but for different reasons.

Theorists interested in the body seek to retrieve the body from its disembodied, denatured status and to relocate it in the subject. Some, influenced by psychoanalysis, do so by tracking the play of desire across the female body. Others seek to theorize female desire outside the model of psychoanalysis. Still others analyze how the materiality of the female body has been overwritten by—but also necessarily embedded in—social practices. In doing so they look to the histories of specific women's bodies. Still others challenge the notion of any unified body by exploring the multiplicity of embodiments. Indeed, Kauffman suggested that the late twentieth century is witnessing a paradigm shift from the specular body to the body staged as spectacle, its insides and outsides exhibited for consumption ("Bad").

Thus theorists interested in women's autobiography have begun to read for the ways in which the body emerges in, disrupts, redirects narrative practices. For if economic and political realities are played out quite literally on the bodies of women, the signature of the political is erased when the reader does not attend to the body in the text. Readers can resist being complicit in the denial of desire to women or the denigration of the body of women by attending to the ways in which narrative is about desire, embodiment, and the material conditions of women's experiential and narrated lives. But in theorizing the body, readers must discover strategies for taking back the (narrative) body in such a way as not to participate in the consignment of women to their bodies.

In *Interfaces*, Shirley C. Neuman's exploration of the phantasmatic male body, "Autobiography, Bodies, Manhood," insists that all, and not just women's, texts be read as sites of bodily inscription and desire. Fascinated by the erasure of the material body that characterizes so much of Western autobiography, Neuman considers an "anomalous moment in which a masculine body ruptures and exceeds the discursive effacement of the corporeal which is characteristic of autobiography" (140). Reading the body as simultaneously a material and cultural site on which the nonalignment of biological sex and gender is played out, Neuman looks at the autobiographical writings of Herculine Barbin, the nineteenth-century hermaphrodite about which so much has been written. She does so to tease out in that "rare autobiography which represents the body" the degree to which the narrating subject reproduces normative cultural meanings of sexed bodies and the degree to which s/he resists such cultural inscriptions (140). And in "Mystical Bodies and the Dialogics of Vision," Laurie Finke historicizes medieval mystical bodies to provide a framework for reading how women writers negotiate their constrained and devalued bodily status as they rewrite mystical experience to give themselves agency as visionaries.

Practical Theorizing

In this section we have been tracing the interplay between major theoretical interventions of the last two decades and theories of women's autobiography. But in fact women writing the autobiographical have always engaged in theorizing identity. This interplay between theory and autobiographical writing has intensified in recent years as women offer versions of theory in practice.

Feminist writers have used autobiographical forms, for example, to show how the personal is political. Adrienne Rich has mined the possibilities of poetry, the personal essay, and analysis in her explorations of lesbian identity and women's culture. Audre Lorde extended the mix of autobiography and critique toward the new form of "biomythography" to carve out a writing space expansive enough for her house of difference. Cherríe Moraga and Gloria Anzaldúa combined poetry and essay, Spanish and English, to probe and reimagine the cultural meanings of collective mythologies and the personal politics of border subjects. Related anthologies of women's writing, such as Anzaldúa and Moraga's *Making Face, Making Soul/Haciendo Caras*, reasserted the interweaving of personal narrative and the theorizing of difference. Other subjects of American multiculture, such as Maxine Hong Kingston, Janet Campbell Hale, and Meena Alexander, have written in quest of their voices within the vexed legacies of multiple cultural traditions. Shuttling the "black Atlantic," Michelle Cliff turned her experiential history as a subject of post/colonial education into the autobiographical novels *No Telephone to Heaven* and *Abeng*. Caroline Kay Steedman, in her "genealogical"

Landscape for a Good Woman, combined autobiographical remembering, biographical case study, and theoretical essay in order to retheorize the working-class subjectivity of her good-enough mother. In Portugal the three Marias engaged in a collaborative narrative of coming of age in a society that represses feminine assertion and denies women's voices. In Germany Christa Wolf repeatedly investigated her childhood as a site for exploring the collective German history of National Socialism and resisting arbitrary assignments of guilt based on political identification. Monique Wittig and Nathalie Sarraute in France, Oriana Falacci in Italy, Elena Poniatowska in Mexico, Bessie Head in Botswana, Nigerian-born Buchi Emecheta in London, Algerian-born Assia Djebar in France have all employed a blend of analytical critique and personal disclosure in shaping feminist voices that resist any easy ideological position. Authorizing their political critiques of women's subjection by appeal to personal experience, they show the resilience and persuasiveness of autobiographical writing as cultural critique.

Women's autobiography has also become a collection of generic possibilities. A wide and growing range of narrative projects have generated new or hybrid forms for addressing diverse audiences—forms such as autopathography, collective histories, collaborative life writing projects, testimonial and witnessing, manifesto, bilingual projects, survival narratives, performance art, ethnography, scriptotherapy, and legal testimony. In "Autography/Transformation /Asymmetry," for instance, Jeanne Perreault, mining the possibilities of hybrid writing practices, coined the term "autography" to call attention to the writing of the feminist self as an ongoing negotiation of the shifting boundaries of the "I" and the "we" of feminist collectivity. Through the negotiation of "I" and "we," the autographer resists "monadic" subjectivity to engage "in a (community of) discourse of which she is both product and producer" (7). These autobiographical occasions generate new reading practices, practices that refuse any simplistic notion of autobiography as a master narrative of the bourgeois subject. It is not surprising, then, that much of the energy devoted to theorizing subjectivity has come out of the practitioners and the readers who engage women's autobiographical texts.

In summary, we suggest that the real legacy of the last two decades of the 20th Century in theorizing women's autobiographical acts and practices has been the emergence of a heterogeneous welter of conflicting positions about subjectivity and the autobiographical. To the degree that autobiography studies is a contested field, it offers an enabling history through which students can gain confidence and flexibility as readers and can honor the richness of women's autobiographical practices.

Part 3: Prospects for Theorizing Women's Autobiography

Theorists of women's autobiography have occupied a special place in calling for new autobiographical practices and critiques adequate to the texts of women's lives while exposing the blind spots, aporias, complicities, and exclusions in dominant theorizing of the subject. This collection examines the alternatives proposed by theorists of women's autobiography. But the range of possibilities has by no means been exhausted. We foresee many options for scholars interested in autobiographical studies and in theories of women's autobiography to pursue—and our list is only partial.

Relationality, across genders and genres, deserves further exploration. The notion of "fluid boundaries" claimed in early theorizing by Friedman and Mason as characteristic of women's autobiography, in distinction to all others, and typical of all women's autobiography—across ethnicity, class, sexuality, age, historical periods—has been challenged by Hertha D. Wong, Nancy K. Miller, and Paul John Eakin, among others, in their inquiries about how *all* autobiography may be relational. What links exist between self-narrating and representation of an autobiography's others? How, and in what terms, should relationality be redirected and re-appropriated for feminist theory? How else might gendered aspects of women's subjectivity be described?

Autobiographical ethics includes a host of issues about how and what subjects and audiences know of each other, and how they comport themselves. The ethics of self- and family revelation within autobiographical texts, the positioning of audiences during and after the subject's lifetime, the subject's relation to biographical accounts and extratextual evidence are areas that deserve further scrutiny. What would a feminist ethics of autobiography look like? As Doris Sommer suggested in an essay on Elena Poniatowska and the testimonial novel, the relationship between (woman) informant and (woman) narrator, like that between writer and reader, may be neither symmetrical nor unmanipulated. Indeed, an informant may resist being "consumed" by an interlocutor's mediation. A writer attentive to issues of difference can acknowledge ethical problems in conversations of social unequals, can write so as to resist the "complicity between narrator and reader," acknowledging the social inequities of lives and the privilege of her own authority as author ("Taking," 914).

Narratology, or the telling of a life as a semiotic encoding and a transaction between writer and readers, has as yet been insufficiently theorized in women's autobiography. Perhaps this is due in part to the current interest in voice and the body, or the cachet of psychoanalytic and Foucauldian readings. Moreover, issues of performativity now obscure issues of narratology. But we might think more carefully about the textual features that distinguish autobiography from the novel or other forms of nonfiction, especially in light of the tendency of people to use "novel" and "autobiography" interchangeably when they discuss personal narratives. What does it mean for readers to blur the distinction, to read novelistically? The work of Philippe Lejeune on the autobiographical pact can be helpful here; but we would have to consider how Lejeune's concept of the pact might need to be modified in feminist practices.

The relationship of national identity formation and autobiographical narrative deserves sustained examination. As

Benedict Anderson aptly noted, nations are "imagined communities." Communities of people create and sustain narratives about the bases for their existence as distinct collectivities, and autobiography, at least in the West, has functioned as a potent vehicle for forging and reproducing such narratives. For theorists of multiculture and of postcoloniality, "national" identity is a deeply problematic category of meaning because national myths are founded upon the discourses of the "other," "the alien." This logic of alterity becomes the means through which national borders are established, policed, and breached. The gendered aspects of this logic are everywhere in evidence in debates about the nation and national identity. Readings of women's autobiographical texts need to attend to the complex ways in which narrators engage myths of national identity and represent themselves as national and/or unnational subjects.

The building of archives and documentary collections needs to continue. The archive of women's autobiographical history already recovered in the last four decades has transformed the field, establishing a rich legacy. Expanding the archive by incorporating works formerly regarded as "merely personal" and extraliterary will make available to scholars and students a broader range of corpora—including diaries, letters, journals, memoirs, travel narratives, meditations, cookbooks, family histories, spiritual records, collages, art books, and others. And in the last two decades the archive has expanded to digital environments, and to various platforms for social media, blogs, journaling websites, and other modes of online life writing.

Memory, the project for the millennium, has now come to preoccupy scholars from all areas of the academy—from philosophers to neuroscientists, from cultural critics to psychologists, from quantum theorists to poets. Increasingly, scholars are studying the making and unmaking of memory—personal, collective, biochemical. Since autobiography unfolds in the folds of memory, there are projects to be found in probing the limits of remembering, the politics of remembering, the communal effects of remembering, and the ways in which remembering confuses our expectations of linearity and spatiality, of poetics and thematics in narrative. Moreover, commitment to the imperatives of testimony, as Shoshana Felman argued in her work on testimony, requires us, as teachers and scholars, to develop radical pedagogies that can facilitate encounters between readers and the texts of unspeakable horror.

In the 1990s the project of recovering and validating memories of sexual abuse and psychic trauma through writing, which authorized much women's autobiographical narrative, was being vigorously debated on several fronts. Feminist therapist and theorist Janice Haaken, in "The Recovery of Memory, Fantasy, and Desire: Feminist Approaches to Sexual Abuse and Psychic Trauma," offered a critique of the stakes involved in debates on recovered memory and considered the implications of theories of memory for reading women's narratives of victimization and survival. Her project is directed at the "recovery" of conflictual discourses and fantasies in women's stories.

Theorizing travel turns our attention to issues of mobility, location, and zones of transit. We might argue that all theory is in transit, or that all subjects are in transit, shifting from one identity to another. This is to say that mobility is the condition for the stabilities of identification. To approach autobiographical texts with this focus on travel and mobility stimulates a provocative set of questions. What is subjectivity in transit? How do different kinds of mobility affect self-representational practices—the mobility of forced displacement, for example, or of emigration, immigration, asylum seeking, and exile? What are the personal and political costs to the autobiographer of homesteading and of homelessness? How do autobiographical subjects negotiate strangeness—whether the strangeness of language, behaviors, cultures, histories, gender differentiation, sexualities? And how does interest in mobility stimulate attention to borders—between places, spaces, identities, destinies—and to the crossings and re-crossings of those borders?

Spatiality, rather than temporality, as a focus of critical reading practices has been proposed by Susan Stanford Friedman as particularly appropriate to women's texts. "Spatialization emphasizes the psychodynamic, interactive, and situational nature of narrative processes; it also provides a fluid, relational approach that connects text and context, writer and reader" ("Spatialization," 82). For Friedman, drawing on Kristeva's notion of a text as an "'intersection of textual surfaces,'" spatialized readings allow readers to construct a "story" of the interactive play between narrative surface and a text's palimpsestic depths (83). Bringing a spatialized reading strategy to analyses of women's autobiography may bring new attention to their texture and new interpretations of apparent incoherences.

Interdisciplinary studies of personal narratives that draw analytical frameworks from sociology, history, psychology, anthropology, religion, medicine, and many other disciplines will produce more nuanced readings of autobiographical texts. The separate studies of first-person narratives that have gone on within fields such as ethnography, oral history, communications, and performance studies offer revolutionary possibilities for recontextualizing autobiographical writing in specific contexts.

Theorizing a new episteme implicated in the technological revolution will reform concepts of the subject and of narrative practices, as Donna Haraway's "A Manifesto for Cyborgs" has suggested. Cyborg identity, embodying both nature and "other," belongs neither wholly to nature nor to culture and subverts all certainties (Balsamo, 33). The mode of production of modernity elicited "identities as autonomous and (instrumentally) rational", but new communications technologies form subjects as "unstable, multiple, and diffuse," with a revolutionary fluidity of identity (Poster, 87). What has been called the "explosion of narrativity" in cyberspace calls for new theories of the relationship between human and machines. As we are drawn further into technology, we may find ourselves revising our notions of the autobiographical subject and of narrativity itself (Poster, 91, 93–94).

The therapeutics of writing autobiography has engaged feminist critics and generated calls for further theorizing. Writing and reading autobiography have long been regarded by psychoanalytic practitioners as instruments of healing, in the ongoing search to find and recognize one's story. Similarly, pathography, the writing of illness narratives as both "cure" and consolation, has created a body of literature that is only beginning to be read by such critics as Anne Hunsaker Hawkins, Mary Elene Wood, Suzette Henke, and Rita Charon.

New modes of women's self-representation invite revision of models of women's subjectivity. For example, to read Generation X writer Elizabeth Wurtzel's *Prozac Nation*, we need to attend to the modulation of consciousness by psychotropic drugs. In the case of the oral collaborative narratives of *taasu* among nonliterate Wolof West African village women discussed by Lisa McNee, the autobiographical involves neither the solitary individual writing, nor a "life" in the usual Western sense. This proliferation of autobiographical genres is not simply additive, for forms such as these confuse how we have understood the terms "woman'" and "autobiography."

Part 4: The Future of Women's Autobiography

At this historical moment, little can be asserted about women's autobiography without qualification. Whether to read the "women" in women's autobiography as referring to writers, subjects, readers, communities, performances, or other entities and processes is under debate. Indeed, as Jeanne Perreault suggested, an alternate concept such as "autography" may be desirable to designate a kind of life writing practiced by women that continually calls its own boundaries and activity into question. Virtually every critic of women's autobiography has challenged or modified its perceived definitional parameters to fit an evolving feminist sense of subjects and theories in process.

Given the directions that much recent feminist and postfeminist theorizing has taken, the subject of study here, women's autobiography, may itself have become suspect. All of the features once claimed as hallmarks of women's autobiography—nonlinear narrative, fragmented textuality, relationality, the authority of experience—have been challenged as gender essentialism, from within feminist theory and from outside it. For example, Nancy K. Miller suggested that the model of identity through alterity associated with women's autobiography by some early theorists operates in the autobiographical performances of some recent male authors as well. She asked if "we might not more usefully expand the vision of the autobiographical self as connection to a significant other and bound to a community rather than restrict it through mutually exclusive models.... When we return to male-authored texts in the light of patterns found in female-authored texts—reading for connection, for the relation to the other—we may want to revise the canonical views of male autobiographical identity altogether" ("Representing," 4, 5). That is, to what extent and in what ways does the category of women's autobiography continue to be a useful generic descriptor for women's autobiographical texts and for the *experience* of reading them? Reading other autobiographical texts or genres of life writing? As certain postfeminists also argue, isn't it time to move beyond this preoccupation with woman, women, and women's "this" or "that"? And hasn't the continuing proliferation of theoretical accounts of "difference" undermined any solid ground for focusing separately on women's texts?

While we recognize the need to continually critique cultural constructions of "woman" and of "difference," we also recognize the utility and the importance of continuing to focus on the cultural production of women. As Denise Riley advised, we have to act as if "women" exist even as we continue to resist the fixedness of particular forms of "woman" and "femininity" (Riley, 112). Or, as Friedman pointed out in a recent essay, the new geography of identity insists that we think about women writers in relation to a fluid matrix instead of a fixed binary of male/female or masculine/feminine ("Beyond," 13). A more flexible critical practice will not regard gender difference as a priori and immutable. It will "guard against using male writers or masculinity as fixed foils, as categorical Others whose static nature allows for the identification of female diversity and difference" ("Beyond," 22).

Rather, feminist criticism needs to consider how gender intersects with other components that comprise identity. Such a focus permits us to locate ourselves even as the theoretical grounds underneath us continue to shift. As we pursue a feminist theory of women's autobiographical practices, we might simultaneously pursue a critique of autobiographical practice generally. We hope that this collection offers a set of ideas for engaging in such projects.

Notes

1. See "Autobiography and the Cultural Moment" by James Olney for a more complete history of autobiography studies prior to 1980.
2. It is worth noting that early literary critic Anna Robeson Burr, unlike her male compatriots, took women's autobiography seriously and listed numerous works by women in her bibliography, but she did not attend to issues of gender.
3. Although the first efforts to theorize women's autobiography occurred in the seventies and early eighties, they should not be confused with First Wave feminism, which usually refers to movements for women's suffrage between 1890 and 1920. Second Wave feminism dates from the early 1970s. In *The Dictionary of Feminist Theory* Maggie Humm notes such hallmarks of the Second Wave as the slogan "The personal is political," the celebration of a women-centered perspective, and declarations of a feminist movement aimed at radical transformation of patriarchy and the creation of a feminized world (198). For an introduction to and readings in Second Wave feminist analyses, see Linda Nicholson, ed., *The Second Wave: A Reader in Feminist Theories*.
4. For a helpful discussion of ten major books on theorizing women's autobiography between 1980 and 1990, see Marjanne E. Goozé, "The Definitions of Self and Form in Feminist Autobiography Theory." The texts Goozé explores are discussed here, along with some she overlooks (Felski, Nussbaum, Hewitt). Goozé argues that these eighties critiques share a concern with the interrelation of self and form in women's writing (414). She reads women's autobiography theory as theorizing the female subject between French and American feminisms

and between two male traditions, the humanist view of autonomous unified selves, and the postmodern view of de-centered, split selves. Goozé's reservation about theorizing of women's autobiography in the eighties, namely that much of it equates "the de-centered self of postmodernism" with "a woman's self which defines itself in terms of interconnectedness to others and mutual interdependence," is a provocative one for theorists (425). Our discussion is indebted to Goozé's careful readings and helpful distinctions among theorists as we incorporate her observations and carry them forward to critiques in the nineties.

5 Novelist and critic Alice Walker was also an important force in the recognition of multiple women's textualities. In *In Our Mothers' Gardens* she distinguished herself from white feminists as a "womanist" who, in autobiographical essays such as "When the Other Dancer Is the Self," asserted the inextricability of her experience of political marginalization and personhood.

Works Cited

Addis, Patricia K. *Through a Woman's 'I': An Annotated Bibliography of American Women's Autobiographical Writings, 1946–1976*. Metuchen, NJ: Scarecrow, 1983.

Alcoff, Linda Martin, and Laura Gray-Rosendale. "Survivor Discourse." In *Getting a Life: Everyday Uses of Autobiography*, eds. Sidonie Smith and Julia Watson. Minneapolis: University of Minnesota Press, 1996. 198–225.

Allen, Paula Gunn. *Sacred Hoop: Recovering the Feminine in American Indian Traditions*. Boston: Beacon Press, 1986.

Althusser, Louis. *Essays on Ideology*. London: Verso, 1984.

Anderson, Benedict. *Imagined Communities: Reflections on the Origin and Spread of Nationalism*. London: Verso, 1983.

Andrews, William L. *To Tell a Free Story: The First Century of Afro-American Autobiography, 1760–1865*. Urbana: University of Illinois Press, 1986.

Anzaldúa, Gloria, and Cherríe Moraga, eds. *Making Face, Making Soul/Hacienda Caras: Creative and Critical Perspectives by Women of Color*. San Francisco: Aunt Lute Foundation Books, 1990.

Ashley, Kathleen, Leigh Gilmore, and Gerald Peters, eds. *Autobiography and Postmodernism*. Amherst: University of Massachusetts Press, 1994.

Baker, Houston A., Jr. *Workings of the Spirit: The Poetics of Afro-American Women Writing*. Chicago: University of Chicago Press, 1991.

Bakhtin, M. M. *The Dialogic Imagination: Four Essays*. Ed. Michael Holquist. Trans. Caryl Emerson and Michael Holquist. Austin: University of Texas Press, 1981.

Balsamo, Anne. *Technologies of the Gendered Body: Reading Cyborg Women*. Durham: Duke University Press, 1995.

Bell, Elouise. "Telling One's Story: Women's Journals Then and Now." In *Women's Personal Narratives: Essays in Criticism and Pedagogy*, ed. Leonore Hoffmann and Margo Culley. New York: Modern Language Association, 1985. 167–76.

Bell, Susan Groag, and Marilyn Yalom, eds. *Revealing Lives: Autobiography, Biography, and Gender*. Albany: State University of New York Press, 1990.

Benjamin, Jessica. "A Desire of One's Own: Psychoanalytic Feminism and Intersubjective Space." In *Feminist Studies/Critical Studies*, ed. Teresa de Lauretis. London: Macmillan, 1988.

Bennett, Paula. "Lesbian Poetry in the United States, 1890–1990: A Brief Overview." In *Professions of Desire: Lesbian and Gay Studies in Literature*, ed. George E. Haggerty and Bonnie Zimmerman. New York: Modern Language Association, 1995. 98–112.

Benstock, Shari. *The Private Self: Theory and Practice of Women's Autobiographical Writings*, Chapel Hill: University of North Carolina Press, 1988.

Beverley, John. *Against Literature*. Minneapolis: University of Minneapolis Press, 1993.

Blodgett, Harriet. *Capacious Hold-All: An Anthology of Englishwomen's Diary Writings*. Charlottesville: University Press of Virginia, 1991.

Blodgett, Harriet. *Centuries of Female Days: Englishwomen's Private Diaries*. New Brunswick, NJ: Rutgers University Press, 1988.

Bloom, Lynn Z. "Promises Fulfilled: Positive Images of Women in Twentieth-Century Autobiography." In *Feminist Criticism: Essays on Theory, Poetry, and Prose*, ed. Cheryl Brown and Karen Olson. Metuchen, NJ: Scarecrow Press, 1978. 324–38.

Bornstein, Kate. *Gender Outlaw: On Men, Women, and the Rest of Us*. New York: Routledge, 1994.

Boyce Davies, Carole. *Black Women, Writing and Identity*. London and New York: Routledge, 1994.

Braxton, Joanne. *Black Women Writing Autobiography: A Tradition within a Tradition*. Philadelphia: Temple University Press, 1989.

Brée, Germaine. "George Sand: The Fictions of Autobiography." *Nineteenth-Century French Studies* 4 (1976): 438–49.

Brinker-Gabler, Gisela, and Sidonie Smith, eds. *Writing New Identities: Gender, Nation, and Immigration in Contemporary Europe.* Minneapolis: University of Minnesota Press, 1996.

Briscoe, Mary Louise, Lynn Z. Bloom, and Barbara Tobias. *American Autobiography, 1945–1980: A Bibliography.* Madison: University of Wisconsin Press, 1982.

Brodzki, Bella. "Mothers, Displacement, and Language in the Autobiographies of Nathalie Sarraute and Christa Wolf." In *Life/Lines: Theorizing Women's Autobiography,* ed. Bella Brodzki and Celeste Schenck. Ithaca: Cornell University Press, 1988. 243–59.

Brodzki, Bella and Celeste Schenck, eds. *Life/Lines: Theorizing Women's Autobiography,* Ithaca: Cornell University Press, 1988.

Bruner, Jerome. "Life as Narrative." *Social Research* 54 (1987): 11–32.

Bruss, Elizabeth W. *Autobiographical Acts: The Changing Situation of a Literary Genre.* Baltimore: Johns Hopkins University Press, 1976.

Bunkers, Suzanne L., and Cynthia A. Huff, eds. *Inscribing the Daily: Critical Essays on Women's Diaries.* Amherst: University of Massachusetts Press, 1996.

Burr, Anna Robeson Brown. *The Autobiography, A Critical and Comparative Study.* Boston: Houghton Mifflin, 1909.

Buss, Helen M. "A Feminist Revision of New Historicism to Give Fuller Readings of Women's Private Writing." In *Inscribing the Daily: Critical Essays on Women's Diaries,* ed. Suzanne L. Bunkers and Cynthia A. Huff. Amherst: University of Massachusetts Press, 1996. 86–103.

Buss, Helen M. *Mapping Ourselves: Canadian Women's Autobiography in English.* Montreal and Kingston: McGill-Queen's University Press, 1993.

Butler, Judith. *Bodies That Matter.* New York: Routledge, 1993.

Butler, Judith. *Gender Trouble: Feminism and the Subversion of Identity.* New York: Routledge, 1990.

Carby, Hazel V. *Reconstructing Womanhood: The Emergence of the Afro-American Woman Novelist.* New York: Oxford University Press, 1987.

Castillo, Debra A. *Talking Back: Toward a Latin American Feminist Literary Criticism.* Ithaca: Cornell University Press, 1992.

Castro-Klarén, Sara and Beatriz Sarlo, eds. *Women's Writing in Latin America: An Anthology.* Boulder: Westview Press, 1991.

Césaire, Aimé, *Discourse on Colonialism.* Trans. Joan Pinkham. New York: MR, 1972.

Chandler, Marilyn R. *Dwelling in the Text: Houses in American Fiction.* Berkeley: University of California Press, 1991.

Cheung, King-kok. *Articulate Silences: Hisaye Yamamoto, Maxine Hong Kingston, Joy Kogawa*. Ithaca: Cornell University Press, 1993.

Cheung, King-kok. *Asian American Literature: An Annotated Bibliography*. New York: Modern Language Association of America, 1988.

Chodorow, Nancy. *The Reproduction of Mothering: Psychoanalysis and the Sociology of Gender*. Berkeley: University of California Press, 1978.

Christian, Barbara. "Being the Subject and the Object: Reading African-American Women's Novels." In *Changing Subjects: The Making of Feminist Literary Criticism*, ed. Gayle Greene and Coppelia Kahn. New York: Routledge, 1993. 195–200.

Cixous, Hélène. "The Laugh of the Medusa." In *New French Feminisms*, ed. Elaine Marks and Isabelle De Courtivron. New York: Schocken Books, 1981. 245–64.

Corbett, Mary Jean. "Literary Domesticity and Women Writers' Subjectivities." In *Representing Femininity: Middle-Class Subjectivity and Victorian and Edwardian Women's Autobiography*. New York: Oxford University Press, 1992.

Cott, Nancy. *The Bonds of Womanhood: "Woman's Sphere" in New England, 1780–1835*. New Haven: Yale University Press, 1977.

Culley, Margo. "Women's Vernacular Literature: Teaching the Mother Tongue." In *Women's Personal Narratives: Essays in Criticism and Pedagogy*, ed. Leonore Hoffmann and Margo Culley. New York: Modern Language Association, 1985.

Culley, Margo. *American Women's Autobiography: Fea[s]ts of Memory*. Madison: University of Wisconsin Press, 1992.

Culley, Margo, ed. *A Day at a Time: The Diary Literature of American Women from 1764 to the Present*. New York: Feminist Press, 1985.

Davidson, Cathy N., and Linda Wagner-Martin, eds. *The Oxford Companion to Women's Writing in the United States*. New York: Oxford University Press, 1995.

De Certeau, Michel. *The Practice of Everyday Life*. Trans. Steven Rendall. Berkeley: University of California Press, 1984.

De Lauretis, Teresa. "Eccentric Subjects: Feminist Theory and Historical Consciousness." *Feminist Studies* 16, no. 1 (1990): 115–50.

Djebar, Assia. "Forbidden Gaze, Severed Sound." *Women of Algiers in Their Apartment*. Trans. Marjolijn de Jager. Charlottesville: University of Virginia Press, 1992. 133–54.

Douglas, Ann. *The Femininization of American Culture*. New York: Knopf, 1977.

Eakin, Paul John. *American Autobiography: Retrospect and Prospect*. Madison: University of Wisconsin Press, 1992.

Eakin, Paul John. "Relational Selves, Relational Lives: The Story of a Story." In *True Relations: Essays on Autobiography and the Postmodern*, ed. G. Thomas Couser and Joseph Fichtelberg. Westport, CT: Greenwood Press, 1998. 63–81.

Ellis, Carolyn, and Michael G. Flaherty, eds. *Investigating Subjectivity: Research on Lived Experience*. Newbury Park, CA: SAGE Publications, 1992.

Ellmann, Mary. *Thinking about Women*. New York: Harcourt, Brace & World, 1968.

Emberley, Julia V. *Thresholds of Difference: Feminist Critique, Native Women's Writings, Postcolonial Theory*. Toronto: University of Toronto Press, 1993.

Fanon, Frantz. *Black Skin, White Masks*. Trans. Charles Lam Markmann. New York: Grove Press, 1967.

Farwell, Marilyn R. "The Lesbian Narrative: 'The Pursuit of the Inedible by the Unspeakable.'" In *Professions of Desire: Lesbian and Gay Studies in Literature*, ed. George E. Haggerty and Bonnie Zimmerman. New York: Modern Language Association, 1995.

Felman, Shoshana, and Dori Laub. *Testimony: Crises in Witnessing in Literature*. New York: Routledge, 1992.

Felski, Rita. "On Confession." *Beyond Feminist Aesthetics: Feminist Literature and Social Change*. Cambridge: Harvard University Press, 1989. 86–121.

Finke, Laurie A. "Mystical Bodies and the Dialogics of Vision." In *Maps of Flesh and Light: The Religious Experience of Medieval Women Mystics*, ed. Ulrike Wiethaus. Syracuse: Syracuse University Press, 1993. 28–44.

Firestone, Shulamith. *The Dialectic of Sex: The Case for Feminist Revolution*. New York: Morrow, 1970.

Foster, Frances. *Witnessing Slavery: The Development of Ante-bellum Slave Narratives*. Westport, CT: Greenwood Press, 1979.

Foucault, Michel. *The History of Sexuality*. Trans. Robert Hurley. New York: Pantheon Books, 1978.

Foucault, Michel. *Language, Counter-Memory, Practice: Selected Essays and Interviews*. Ed. Donald F. Bouchard and Sherry Simon. Ithaca: Cornell University Press, 1977.

Foucault, Michel. *Technologies of the Self: A Seminar with Michel Foucault*. Ed. Luther H. Martin, Huck Gutman, and Patrick H. Hutton. Amherst: University of Massachusetts Press, 1988.

Frank, Anne. *The Diary of a Young Girl*. Garden City, NJ: Doubleday, 1952.

Fraser, Nancy, and Linda J. Nicholson, eds. *Social Criticism without Philosophy: An Encounter between Feminism and Postmodernism*. Minneapolis: University of Minnesota Press, 1988.

Friedman, Susan Stanford. "'Beyond' Gynocriticism and Gynesis: The Geographies of Identity and the Future of Feminist Criticism." *Tulsa Studies in Women's Literature* 15 (Spring 1996): 13–40.

Friedman, Susan Stanford. "Spatialization: A Strategy for Reading Narrative." *Narrative* (1993): 75–86.

Friedman, Susan Stanford. "Women's Autobiographical Selves: Theory and Practice." In *The Private Self: Theory and Practice of Women's Autobiographical Writings*, ed. Shari Benstock. Chapel Hill: University of North Carolina Press, 1988. 34–62.

Gagnier, Regenia. "The Literary Standard, WorkingClass Autobiography, and Gender." In *Revealing Lives: Autobiography, Biography, and Gender*, ed. Susan Groag Bell and Marilyn Yalom. Albany: State University of New York Press, 1990. 115–30.

Gagnier, Regenia. *Subjectivities*. New York: Oxford University Press, 1991.

Gates, Henry Louis, Jr. *Bearing Witness: Selections from African-American Autobiography in the Twentieth Century*. New York: Pantheon Books, 1991.

Gates, Henry Louis, Jr. *Reading Black, Reading Feminist: A Critical Anthology*. New York: Meridian Books, 1990.

Gates, Henry Louis, Jr. *The Signifying Monkey: A Theory of Afro-American Literary Criticism*. New York: Oxford University Press, 1988.

Gates, Henry Louis, Jr., and K. A. Appiah, eds. *Zora Neale Hurston: Critical Perspectives Past and Present*. New York: Amistad (Distributed by Penguin USA), 1993.

Gelfant, Blanche. "Speaking Her Own Piece: Emma Goldman and the Discursive Skeins of Autobiography." In *American Autobiography: Retrospect and Prospect*, ed. Paul John Eakin. Madison: University of Wisconsin Press, 1992. 253–66.

Gilligan, Carol. *In a Different Voice: Psychological Theory and Women's Development*. Cambridge: Harvard University Press, 1983.

Gilmore, Leigh. *Autobiographics: A Feminist Theory of Women's Self-Representation*. Ithaca: Cornell University Press, 1994.

Goldman, Anne E. "Autobiography, Ethnography, and History: A Model for Reading." *"Take My Word": Autobiographical Innovations by Ethnic American Working Women*. Berkeley: University of California Press, 1996. xv–xxxv.

Goodman, Katherine. *Dis/Closures: Women's Autobiography in Germany between 1790 and 1914*. New York, Bern: Peter Lang, 1986.

Goozé, Maryanne E. "The Definitions of Self and Form in Feminist Autobiography Theory." *Women's Studies* 21 (1992): 411–29.

Gramsci, Antonio. *A Gramsci Reader: Selected Writings, 1916–1935.* Ed. David Forgacs. London: Lawrence and Wishart, 1988.
Greenberg, Joanne. *I Never Promised You a Rose Garden.* Garden City, NY: Holt, Rinehart & Winston, 1964.
Greene, Gayle, and Coppelia Kahn, eds. *Changing Subjects: The Making of Feminist Literary Criticism.* New York: Routledge, 1993.
Greer, Germaine. *The Female Eunuch.* New York: McGraw-Hill, 1971.
Grosz, Elizabeth. "Contemporary Theories of Power and Subjectivity." In *Feminist Knowledge: Critique and Construct,* ed. Sneja Gunew. London: Routledge, 1990.
Grosz, Elizabeth. *Space, Time, and Perversions: Essays on the Politics of Bodies.* New York: Routledge, 1995.
Grosz, Elizabeth. *Volatile Bodies: Toward a Corporeal Feminism.* Bloomington: Indiana University Press, 1994.
Grosz, Elizabeth, and Elspeth Probyn, eds. *Sexy Bodies: The Strange Carnalities of Feminism.* London and New York: Routledge, 1995.
Gusdorf, Georges. "Conditions and Limits of Autobiography." In *Autobiography: Essays Theoretical and Critical,* ed. & trans. James Olney. Princeton: Princeton University Press, 1980. 28–48.
Haaken, Janice. "The Recovery of Memory, Fantasy, and Desire in Women's Trauma Stories: Feminist Approaches to Sexual Abuse and Psychotherapy." *Signs* 21, no. 4 (Summer 1996): 1069–94.
Hampsten, Elizabeth. *Read This Only to Yourself: Writings of Midwestern Women, 1880–1910.* Bloomington: Indiana University Press, 1982.
Haraway, Donna. "A Manifesto for Cyborgs: Science, Technology, and Socialist Feminism in the 1980s." In *Feminism/Postmodernism,* ed. Linda J. Nicholson. New York: Routledge, 1990. 190-233.
Harlow, Barbara. *Barred: Women, Writing, and Political Detention.* Middletown, CT: Wesleyan University Press, 1992.
Harlow, Barbara. "From a Women's Prison: Third World Women's Narratives of Prison." *Feminist Studies* 12 (Fall 1986): 502–24.
Hawkins, Anne Hunsaker. *Reconstructing Illness: Studies in Pathography.* West Lafayette, IN: Purdue University Press, 1993.
Heilbrun, Carolyn G. *Writing a Woman's Life.* New York: W.W. Norton, 1988.
Hellman, Lillian. *Pentimento.* Boston: Little, Brown, 1973.
Hellman, Lillian. *Scoundrel Time.* Boston: Little, Brown, 1976.
Hellman, Lillian. *An Unfinished Woman.* Boston: Little, Brown, 1969.
Henderson, Mae Gwendolyn. "Speaking in Tongues: Dialogics, Dialectics, and the Black Woman Writer's Literary Tradition." In *Changing Our Own Words: Essays on Criticism, Theory, and Writing by Black Women,* ed. Cheryl A. Wall. New Brunswick, NJ: Rutgers University Press, 1989. 116–42.

Hewitt, Leah D. *Autobiographical Tightropes*. Lincoln: University of Nebraska Press, 1990.

Hirsch, Marianne. "Masking the Subject: Practicing Theory." In *The Point of Theory: Practices in Cultural Analysis*, ed. Mieke Bal and Inge E. Boer. New York: Continuum, 1994. 109–24.

Hoffmann, Leonore, and Margo Culley, eds. *Women's Personal Narratives: Essays in Criticism and Pedagogy*. New York: Modern Language Association, 1985.

Hogan, Rebecca. "Diarists on Diaries." *a/b: Auto/Biography Studies* 2, no. 2 (1986): 9–14.

Holly, Carol. "Nineteenth-Century Autobiographies of Affiliation: The Case of Catharine Sedgwick and Lucy Larcom." In *American Autobiography: Retrospect and Prospect*, ed. Paul John Eakin. Madison: University of Wisconsin Press, 1992. 216–34.

hooks, bell [Gloria Watkins]. "An Interview with Bell Hooks by Gloria Watkins: No, Not Talking Back, Just Talking to Myself, January 1989." *Yearning: Race, Gender and Cultural Politics*. Boston: South End Press, 1990. 215–23.

hooks, bell [Gloria Watkins]. "Writing Autobiography." *Talking Back: Thinking Feminist, Thinking Black*. Boston: South End Press, 1989. 155–59.

Huff, Cynthia. *British Women's Diaries: A Descriptive Bibliography of Selected Nineteenth-Century Women's Manuscript Diaries*. New York: AMS Press, 1985.

Huff, Cynthia. "Textual Boundaries: Space in Nineteenth-Century Women's Manuscript Diaries." In *Inscribing the Daily: Critical Essays on Women's Diaries*, ed. Suzanne L. Bunkers and Cynthia A. Huff. Amherst: University of Massachusetts Press, 1996. 123–38.

Hull, Gloria T., et al. *All the Women Are White, All the Blacks are Men, but Some of Us Are Brave: Black Women's Studies*. Old Westbury, NY: Feminist Press, 1982.

Humm, Maggie. *The Dictionary of Feminist Theory*. Columbus; Ohio State University Press, 1990.

Hurston, Zora Neale. *Dust Tracks on a Road: An Autobiography*. Urbana: University of Illinois Press, 1970.

Irigaray, Luce. *Speculum of the Other Woman*. Trans. Gillian C. Gill. Ithaca: Cornell University Press, 1985.

Irigaray, Luce. *This Sex Which Is Not One*. Trans. Catherine Porter and Carolyn Burke. Ithaca: Cornell University Press, 1985.

Jelinek, Estelle C. *The Tradition of Women's Autobiography: From Antiquity to the Present*. New York: Twayne, 1986.

Jelinek, Estelle C. *Women's Autobiography: Essays in Criticism*. Bloomington: Indiana University Press, 1980.

Johnson, Barbara. *A World of Difference*. Baltimore: Johns Hopkins University Press, 1987.

Kadar, Marlene. *Essays on Life Writing: From Genre to Critical Practice*. Toronto: University of Toronto Press, 1992.

Kadar, Marlene. "Whose Life Is It Anyway? Out of the Bathtub and into the Narrative." In *Essays on Life Writing: From Genre to Critical Practice*, ed. Kadar. Toronto: University of Toronto Press, 1992. 152–61

Kaminsky, Amy Katz. *Reading the Body Politic: Feminist Criticism and Latin American Women Writers*. Minneapolis: University of Minnesota Press, 1993.

Kaplan, Caren. "Resisting Autobiography: Out-Law Genres and Transnational Feminist Subjects." In *De/Colonizing the Subject: The Politics of Gender in Women's Autobiography*, ed. Sidonie Smith and Julia Watson. Minneapolis: University of Minnesota Press, 1992. 115–38.

Kaplan, Louis, et al. *A Bibliography of American Autobiographies*. Madison: University of Wisconsin Press, 1962.

Kauffman, Linda S. "Bad Girls and Sick Boys: Inside the Body of Fiction, Film, and Performance Art." In *Getting a Life: Everyday Uses of Autobiography*, ed. Sidonie Smith and Julia Watson. Minneapolis: University of Minnesota Press, 1996. 27–46.

Kauffman, Linda S. "The Long Goodbye: Against Personal Testimony, or An Infant Grifter Grows Up." In *American Feminist Thought at Century's End: A Reader*, ed. Linda S. Kauffman. Cambridge and Oxford: Blackwell, 1993. 258–78.

Kosta, Barbara. *Recasting Autobiography: Women's Counterfictions in Contemporary German Literature and Film*. Ithaca: Cornell University Press, 1994.

Kristeva, Julia. *The Kristeva Reader*. Ed. Toril Moi. New York: Columbia University Press, 1986.

Kristeva, Julia. "My Memory's Hyperbole." In *The Female Autograph*, ed. Domna C. Stanton. New York: New York Literary Forum, 1984. 219–35.

Krupat, Arnold. *For Those Who Come After: A Study of Native American Autobiography*. Berkeley: University of California Press, 1985.

Krupat, Arnold. *Native American Autobiography: An Anthology*. Madison: University of Wisconsin Press, 1994.

Lacan, Jacques. *Feminine Sexuality*. Ed. Juliet Mitchell and Jacqueline Rose. Trans. Jacqueline Rose. London: Macmillan, 1982.

Lacan, Jacques. *The Language of the Self: The Function of Language in Psychoanalysis*. Trans. Anthony Wilden. Baltimore: Johns Hopkins University Press, 1968.

Lacan, Jacques. *The Seminar of Jacques Lacan*. Ed. Jacques-Alain Miller. New York: W.W. Norton, 1988.

Lejeune, Philippe. "The Autobiographical Pact." In *On Autobiography*, ed. Paul John Eakin. Minneapolis: University of Minnesota Press, 1989. 3–30.

Lim, Shirley Geok-lin. "Semiotics, Experience, and the Material Self: An Inquiry into the Subject of the Contemporary Asian Woman Writer." *Writing S.E./Asia in English: Against the Grain, Focus on Asian English-Language Literature*. London: Skoob Books, 1994. 3–39.

Ling, Amy. *Between Worlds: Women Writers of Chinese Ancestry*. New York: Pergamon Press, 1990.

Ling, Amy, and Wesley Brown, eds. *Visions of America: Personal Narratives from the Promised Land*. New York: Persea Books, 1993.

Lionnet, Françoise. "The Politics and Aesthetics of Métíssage." *Autobiographical Voices: Race, Gender, Self-Portraiture*. Ithaca: Cornell University Press, 1989. 1–30.

Lionnet, Françoise. *Postcolonial Representations*. Ithaca: Cornell University Press, 1995.

Lionnet, Françoise, and Ronnie Scharfman, eds. *Post/Colonial Conditions: Exiles, Migrations, and Nomadisms*. New Haven: *Yale French Studies* 82, 83, 1993.

Lorde, Audre. *Zami: A New Spelling of My Name*. Trumansberg, NY: Crossing Press, 1982.

Mairs, Nancy. "The Way In." *Remembering the Bone House: An Erotics of Place and Space*. New York: Harper and Row, 1989. 1–11.

Marcus, Laura. *Auto/Biographical Discourses*. Manchester: Manchester University Press, 1994.

Martin, Biddy. "Lesbian Identity and Autobiographical Difference(s)." In *Life/Lines: Theorizing Women's Autobiography*, ed. Bella Brodzki and Celeste Schenck. Ithaca: Cornell University Press, 1988. 77–103.

Mason, Mary G. "The Other Voice: Autobiographies by Women Writers." In *Autobiography: Essays Theoretical and Critical*, ed. James Olney. Princeton: Princeton University Press, 1980. 207–35.

Mason, Mary G., and Carol Hurd Green, eds. *Journeys: Autobiographical Writings by Women*. Boston: G. K. Hall, 1979.

McCarthy, Mary. *Memories of a Catholic Girlhood*. New York: Harcourt Brace, 1957.

McKay, Nellie Y. "The Journals of Charlotte L. Forten-Grimké: Les Lieux de Mémoire in African-American Women's Autobiography." In *History and Memory in African-American Culture*, ed. Genevieve Fabré and Robert O'Meally. Oxford: Oxford University Press, 1994. 261–71.

McKay, Nellie Y. "The Narrative Self: Race, Politics, and Culture in Black American Women's Autobiography." In *Feminisms in the Academy*, ed. Domna C. Stanton and Abigail J. Stewart. Ann Arbor: University of Michigan Press, 1995. 74–94.

McNee, Lisa. "Autobiographical Subjects." *Research in African Literatures* 28, no. 2 (1997): 83–101.

Milani, Farzaneh. "Veiled Voices: Women's Autobiography in Contemporary Iran." In *Women's Autobiography in Contemporary Iran*, ed. Afsaneh Najmabadi. Cambridge: Harvard University Press, 1990. 2–17.

Miller, Nancy K. "Representing Others: Gender and the Subjects of Autobiography." *Differences* 6, no. 1 (1994): 1–27.

Miller, Nancy K. "Teaching Autobiography." *Getting Personal*. New York: Routledge, 1991. 121–42.

Miller, Nancy K. "Toward a Dialectics of Difference." In *Women and Language in Literature and Society*, ed. Sally McConnell-Ginet, Ruth Borker, and Nelly Furman. New York: Praeger, 1980. 258–73.

Miller, Nancy K. "Writing Fictions: Women's Autobiography in France." In *Life/Lines: Theorizing Women's Autobiography*, ed. Bella Brodzki and Celeste Schenck. Ithaca: Cornell University Press, 1988. 45–61.

Millett, Kate. *Flying*. New York: Knopf, 1974.

Millett, Kate. *Sexual Politics*. Boston: New England Free Press, 1968.

Millett, Kate. *Sita*. New York: Farrar, Straus & Giroux, 1977.

Misch, Georg. *History of Autobiography*. Trans. E. W. Dickes. 2 vols. 1907. Rpt. London: Routledge and Kegan Paul, 1950.

Moers, Ellen. *Literary Women*. Garden City, NY: Doubleday, 1976.

Mohanty, Chandra Talpade, Ann Russo, and Lourdes Torres, eds. *Third World Women and the Politics of Feminism*. Bloomington: Indiana University Press, 1991.

Moody, Anne, *Coming of Age in Mississippi*. New York: Dial Press, 1968.

Moraga, Cherríe. *Loving in the War Years*. Boston: South End Press, 1983.

Moraga, Cherríe, and Gloria Anzaldúa, eds. *This Bridge Called My Back: Writing by Radical Women of Color*. New York: Kitchen Table Press, 1981.

Neuman, Shirley. "Autobiography, Bodies, Manhood." In *Autobiography and Questions of Gender*, ed. Neuman. London: Frank Cass, 1991. 137–65.

Neuman, Shirley, ed. *Essays on Canadian Writing* 60 (Winter 1996). Special issue on Canadian autobiography.

Nicholson, Linda, ed. *The Second Wave: A Reader in Feminist Theories*. New York: Routledge, 1997.

Nin, Anaïs. *The Diary of Anaïs Nin*. New York: Swallow Press, 1966–80.

Norton, Mary Beth, and Carol Ruth Berkin, eds. *Women of America: A History*. Boston: Houghton Mifflin, 1979.

Nussbaum, Felicity A. *The Autobiographical Subject*. 2d ed. 1989; Baltimore: John Hopkins University Press, 1995.

Olney, James. "Autobiography and the Cultural Moment." In *Autobiography: Essays Theoretical and Critical*, ed. James Olney. Princeton: Princeton University Press, 1980. 3–27.

Olney, James. *Autobiography: Essays Theoretical and Critical*. Princeton: Princeton University Press, 1980.

Padilla, Genaro M. *My History, Not Yours: The Formation of Mexican American Autobiography*. Madison: University of Wisconsin Press, 1993.

Pascal, Roy. *Design and Truth in Autobiography*. Cambridge: Harvard University Press, 1960.

Perreault, Jeanne. "Autography/Transformation/Asymmetry." *Writing Selves: Contemporary Feminist Autography*. Minneapolis: University of Minnesota Press, 1995. 1–30.

Personal Narratives Group. *Interpreting Women's Lives: Feminist Theory and Personal Narratives*. Bloomington: Indiana University Press, 1989.

Peterson, Linda. "Victorian Autobiography." In *The Culture of Autobiography: Constructions of SelfRepresentation*, ed. Robert Folkenflik. Stanford: Stanford University Press, 1993. 80–103.

Poster, Mark. "Postmodern Virtualities." *SAGE* 1, nos. 3-4 (1995): 79–95.

Quinby, Lee, ed. *Genealogy and Literature*. Minneapolis: University of Minnesota Press, 1995.

Raiskin, Judith L. *Snow on the Cane Fields: Women's Writing and Creole Subjectivity*. Minneapolis: University of Minnesota Press, 1996.

Raoul, Valerie. "Women and Diaries: Gender and Genre." *Mosaic* 22.3 (1989): 57–65.

Rebolledo, Tey Diana. *Women Singing in the Snow: A Cultural Analysis of Chicana Literature*. Tucson: University of Arizona Press, 1995.

Renza, Louis. "The Veto of the Imagination: A Theory of Autobiography." In *Autobiography: Essays Theoretical and Critical*, ed. James Olney. Princeton: Princeton University Press, 1980. 268–95.

Riley, Denise. *"Am I That Name?": Feminism and the Category of "Women" in History*. Minneapolis: University of Minnesota Press, 1988.

Saldivar, Ramón. *Chicano Narrative: The Dialectics of Difference*. Madison: University of Wisconsin Press, 1990.

Sarris, Greg. *Keeping Slug Woman Alive: A Holistic Approach to American Indian Texts*. Berkeley: University of California Press, 1993.

Sarris, Greg. *Mabel McKay: Weaving the Dream*. Berkeley: University of California Press, 1994.

Scott, Joan C. "Experience." In *Feminists Theorize the Political*. Ed. Judith Butler and Joan C. Scott. New York: Routledge, 1993. 22–40.

Sellers, Susan. *Language and Sexual Difference*. New York: St. Martin's Press, 1991.

Showalter, Elaine. *A Literature of Their Own: English Women Novelists from Brontë to Lessing*. Princeton: Princeton University Press, 1977.

Shumaker, Wayne. *English Autobiography: Its Emergence, Materials, and Forms*. Berkeley: University of California Press, 1954.

Smith, Sidonie. *A Poetics of Women's Autobiography: Marginality and the Fictions of Self-Representation*. Bloomington: Indiana University Press, 1987.

Smith, Sidonie. "Autobiographical Manifestos." *Subjectivity, Identity, and the Body*. Bloomington: Indiana University Press, 1993. 154–82.

Smith, Sidonie. "Performativity, Autobiographical Practice, Resistance." *a/b: Auto/ Biography Studies* 10, no. 1 (1995): 17–31.

Smith, Sidonie, and Julia Watson, eds. *De/Colonizing the Subject: The Politics of Gender in Women's Autobiography*. Minneapolis: University of Minnesota Press, 1992.

Smith, Sidonie, and Julia Watson, eds. *Getting a Life: Everyday Uses of Autobiography*. Minneapolis: University of Minnesota Press, 1996.

Smith-Rosenberg, Carroll. *Disorderly Conduct: Visions of Gender in Victorian America*. New York: Knopf, 1985.

Sommer, Doris. "No Secrets." *The Real Thing: Testimonial Discourse and Latin America*, ed. Georg M. Gugelberger. Durham: Duke University Press, 1995. 130–159.

Sommer, Doris. "'Not Just a Personal Story': Women's Testimonios and the Plural Self." In *Life/Lines: Theorizing Women's Autobiography*, ed. Bella Brodzki and Celeste Schenck. Ithaca: Cornell University Press, 1988. 107–30.

Sommer, Doris. "Taking a Life: Hot Pursuit and Cold Rewards in a Mexican Testimonial Novel." *Signs* 20, no. 4 (1995): 913–40.

Spacks, Patricia Meyer. *The Female Imagination*. New York: Avon Books [Knopf], 1972.

Spacks, Patricia Meyer. "Female Rhetorics." In *The Private Self: Theory and Practice of Women's Autobiographical Writings*, ed. Shari Benstock. Chapel Hill: University of North Carolina Press, 1988. 177–91.

Spengemann, William C. *The Forms of Autobiography: Episodes in the History of a Literary Genre*. New Haven: Yale University Press, 1980.

Spivak, Gayatri Chakravorty. "Can the Subaltern Speak?" In *Marxism and the Interpretation of Culture,* ed. Cary Nelson and Lawrence Grossberg. Urbana and Chicago: University of Illinois Press, 1988. 271–313.

Stanton, Domna C. "Autogynography: Is the Subject Different?" In *The Female Autograph,* ed. Stanton. New York: New York Literary Forum, 1984. 3–20.

Stanton, Domna C., ed. *The Female Autograph.* New York: New York Literary Forum, 1984.

Steedman, Carolyn Kay. "Stories." *Landscape for a Good Woman: A Story of Two Lives.* New Brunswick: Rutgers University Press, 1987. 5–24.

Steele, Cynthia. *Politics, Gender, and the Mexican Novel, 1968–1988: Beyond the Pyramid.* Austin: University of Texas Press, 1992.

Stone, Albert E. *Autobiographical Occasions and Original Acts: Versions of American Identity from Henry Adams to Nate Shaw.* Philadelphia: University of Pennsylvania Press, 1982.

Suleri, Sara. "Woman Skin Deep: Feminism and the Postcolonial Condition." *Critical Inquiry* 18 (Summer 1992): 758–66.

Tompkins, Jane. "Me and My Shadow." In *Gender and Theory: Dialogues on Feminist Criticism,* ed. Linda S. Kauffman. New York: Basil Blackwell, 1989.

Torres, Lourdes. "The Construction of the Self in U.S. Latina Autobiographies." In *Third World Women and the Politics of Feminism,* ed. Chandra Talpade Mohanty, Ann Russo, and Lourdes Torres. Bloomington: Indiana University Press. 271–87.

Walker, Alice. "When the Other Dancer Is the Self." *In Search of Our Mother's Gardens: Womanist Prose.* San Diego: Harcourt Brace Jovanovich, 1983.

Warhol, Robyn, and Diane Price-Herndl, eds. *Feminisms.* New Brunswick, NJ: Rutgers University Press, 1991.

Watson, Julia. "Unspeakable Differences: The Politics of Gender in Lesbian and Heterosexual Women's Autobiographies." In *De/Colonizing the Subject: The Politics of Gender in Women's Autobiography,* ed. Sidonie Smith and Julia Watson. Minneapolis: University of Minnesota Press, 1992. 139–68.

Wittig, Monique. *The Straight Mind and Other Essays.* Ed. and foreword by Louise Turcotte. Boston: Beacon Press, 1992.

Wong, Hertha D. *Sending My Heart Back Across the Years: Tradition and Innovation in Native American Autobiography.* New York: Oxford University Press, 1992.

Wong, Sau-ling Cynthia. "Immigrant Autobiography: Some Questions of Definition and Approach." In *American Autobiography: Retrospect and Prospect.* Ed. Paul John Eakin. Madison: University of Wisconsin Press, 1992. 142–70.

Wong, Sau-ling Cynthia. *Reading Asian American Literature: From Necessity to Extravagance.* Princeton: Princeton University Press, 1993.

Wood, Mary Elene. *The Writing on the Wall: Women's Autobiography and the Asylum.* Urbana: University of Illinois Press, 1994. 142–70.

Wurtzel, Elizabeth. *Prozac Nation.* Boston: Houghton Mifflin, 1994.

Yarbro-Bejarano, Yvonne. "Expanding the Categories of Race and Sexuality in Lesbian and Gay Studies." In *Professions of Desire: Lesbian and Gay Studies in Literature,* ed. George E. Haggerty and Bonnie Zimmerman. New York: Modern Language Association, 1995. 124–35.

Yellin, Jean Fagan. Introduction. *Incidents in the Life of a Slave Girl,* by Harriet A. Jacobs. Cambridge: Harvard University Press, 1987.

2
THE RUMPLED BED OF AUTOBIOGRAPHY: EXTRAVAGANT LIVES, EXTRAVAGANT QUESTIONS (2001)

Preface

Our edited collection, *Interfaces: Women, Autobiography, Image, Performance*, responded to the remarkable outpouring of self-portraiture in contemporary painting, photography, artists' books, and mixed visual forms such as installations, collage, and quilting that marked autobiographical inquiry in the United States, Canada, Great Britain, Ireland, France, Germany, and elsewhere in the later twentieth century. In autobiography courses each of us began using slides of visual self-portraits to enliven discussion and dramatize difficult conceptual issues of self-representation in women's autobiographical narratives that were linked to the explosion of innovative work in visual and performance fields. Indeed, some aspects of gendered self-presentation, such as embodiment, are explored and resolved in strikingly different terms in visual and performance media than in written narratives.

The installation of a British performance artist, Tracey Emin, at the Tate Gallery in London caught our eyes because it both flaunted and troubled the question of autobiographical acts by probing the boundaries of "life" and art. Emin's work exemplifies several controversies about autobiography and raises provocative questions for both visual and verbal autobiographical narratives. But those questions are not restricted to the space of the museum, gallery, or video screen, as our subsequent discussion of a recent American memoir, Dave Eggers's *A Heartbreaking Work of Staggering Genius*, will suggest. Through reading an installation and a memoir side by side as examples of experiments in autobiography at this cultural moment, we want to foreground the gendered politics and ethics of life writing at the edge of life writing studies.

Although works such as Emin's and Eggers's, which dramatize and flaunt autobiographical conventions, may well be at the outer limits of the practice of memoir in the year 2000, they are important for autobiography scholars who wish to interrogate the limits of autobiography at a time when "the rule" is breaking the rule. Hence the suggestion in this essay's title that the procrustean bed of autobiography is now inescapably a rumpled one—much slept in; still warm, if soiled; and haunted by conspicuously absent bodies.

While Emin's performance piece evoked the metaphorics of the rumpled bed for us, the "bed" of autobiography has also been explored by Alison Donnell in an essay on women's contemporary autobiographical practices:

> The explosion of criticism surrounding autobiography, and particularly women's autobiography, over the last twenty years, has demonstrated that as a genre autobiography can be likened to a restless and unmade bed; a site on which discursive, intellectual and political practices can be remade; a ruffled surface on which the traces of previous occupants can be uncovered and/or smoothed over; a place for secrets to be whispered and to be buried; a place for fun, desire and deep worry to be expressed. Many of the most influential women writers of the twentieth century have chosen to make this bed and some to lie in it too. (124)

Rumpled, unmade, at this contemporary moment the bed is a generative metaphor for approaching contemporary experiments in self-presentation that mix a grab-bag of autobiographical modes, tropes, and histories. Paradoxically, the autobiographical is a conspicuous staging arena for the public world, if one with a foot lingering in the intimate bed of the personal.

Tracey Emin's "My Bed" and Autobiographical Performance

In 1999 Tracey Emin, a young working-class British artist, was one of four finalists for the prestigious Turner Prize awarded by the Tate Gallery in London.[1] Emin's submission to the Tate Gallery was explicit autobiographical memorabilia. It consisted of eight home videos, four miniature watercolor portraits, a wall of captioned drawings made during her adolescence, a quilt collage, and two assemblages, one of them evoking the memory of an uncle killed in an automobile crash. At the center was the installation "My Bed" (1998), a rumpled bed with stained, tossed sheets surrounded by overflowing ashtrays, used tissues and condoms, unwashed underwear, and medicine bottles—all the detritus of her intimate life in Berlin in 1992–93, as the caption made clear.

The photograph of the installation prominently displays a coiled rope hung from a gibbet-like hook in the background, giving the scene a sadomasochistic, if not suicidal, nuance. In fact, the rope was not part of the Tate installation when we saw it. After two young men, apparently confusing art and life, jumped on the bed, it had to be roped off from the public. Subsequently, the rope, as part of the history of exhibiting "My Bed," was included in the installation.

Emin's assemblage enacts multiple autobiographical performances in both visual and verbal media, and suggests their permeable interface. The bed becomes a memory museum to a specific time and place in Emin's past. Similarly, her labeled drawings comprise a kind of artist's diary on adolescent sexuality, with comments such as "I don't know what I want to do"; "What it

Figure 1. *My Bed*, 1999. 2016 Tracey Emin. All rights reserved, DACS, London / Artists Rights Society (ARS), New York.

looks like to be alone"; "I didn't say I wasn't scared. I said I'm not as scared as I used to be." With their misspellings and awkward phrasing, the doodles and childlike images create the sense of unedited and unpolished immediacy. Such immediacy accords a sense of "authenticity" to her lived experience of those moments in her past.

Emin's videos of summer vacations and high school days also catalog a young woman's self-representational possibilities as experiments in modes of self-chronicling. "My C.V. . . . (to 1995)," for instance, offers a deadpan recitation of sets of facts and yearly events, among them that she tried to commit suicide in 1982, and that she had two successive abortions in two years in the early nineties. Her C.V. entry for 1995 includes her reminder to herself to "Plan the Tracey Emin Museum." This voiceover recitation of a "curriculum vitae" is accompanied by a visual walkthrough of a "home" (with toilets, beds, a sitting room) that may be hers or her mother's. Another video presents a narrative of childhood, chronicling her adolescent sexual encounters, predominantly of a violent character, with working-class boys on the streets of her hometown, and her eventual escape from small-town hypocrisies and brutality. In another video, a seeming home movie captures the daughter and her father playing in the waves of a Cyprus beach. Yet another video, its title invoking Edvard Munch's painting "The Scream," shows a young woman drawn up into a fetal position clinging to a boardwalk. The image, shot from overhead, has as its soundtrack only a sustained scream. A traumatic memory, perhaps one linked to abortion or sexual abuse, is here visualized outside language. The sound of the scream punctures the silent image but gives no interpretive narrative of it. We are left to make our own surmises about the experiential pain expressed.

Deploying medium upon medium in this chronicling of moments in her life, Emin insists on the autobiographical as her artistic origin, performative identity, and preferred mode. For some viewers, her work exceeds self-portraiture in what they see as its narcissistic self-absorption, referring line, color, form, and sound back to the emotions of her experiential history. For others, including the many young people who thronged her installation day after day, Emin's work introduces, through the interweaving of images and written text, an autobiographical voice not previously heard or witnessed with such intensity. In that sense, her daring self-making as self-chronicling is an avant-garde gesture, expanding the modes of self-representation at a shifting matrix of publicly performed visuality and textuality. In this rumpled bed of autobiographical presentation, the material imprint seems to be at once monovocal, even solipsistic, and, at the same time, boldly inventive. Emin's work, balanced at the interstices of everyday life and an artistic avant-garde, is a convergence of anti-art and extreme artistic self-reference. No wonder that her work provoked controversy.

Emin's foregrounding and exploiting of the autobiographical suggests that it has been a foundational discourse for artistic production at the end of the twentieth century. But her insistence on palpable self-reference has annoyed many in the British art world, who for years have criticized her work as narcissistic, trivial, and unimaginative. "My Bed," following as it did upon her 1997 exhibition, a tent called "Everyone I Have Ever Slept With, 1963–95" (sold recently for £40,000), particularly provoked debate about the aesthetic value of a bed with soiled sheets surrounded by crumpled tissue and used condoms. David Lee, former editor of *Art Review*, summarizes this critique: "She can't paint, she can't draw and she can't sculpt. . . . 'My Bed' is stillborn artistically"; noted international collector Charles Saatchi, however, who paid £150,000 for "My Bed," stated "I was very slow to get the loopiness of Tracey's work, but I'm a helpless fan now" (both quoted in Brooks 7). Emin's provocative use of the *material* of her life, rather than an interpretation of it, as autobiographical suggests that the procrustean bed of self-reference is now being performed at a site of rumpled, disorderly, stubbornly literal artifacts that refuse remaking as "art." But it is simultaneously an extreme of the avant-garde.

In the practice of life narrative at this cultural moment, how much difference is there between the practice of citing one's past utterances and including memorabilia of the past, and performing that past as an experiential history? That is, how do we describe the difference between selected quotation of one's past moments in such memorabilia as objects and diaries, and the performance of that past as memory work? Does Emin's "art" reside in her pastiche of multiple modes that artifactually document her life? In her evocation, simultaneously, of many different moments of her experiential history? Does her making of art reside in framing moments that, when they occurred, were without self-consciousness? The single frozen moment of "My Bed" asks spectators to pose the question of "art" differently, to inquire about an absent subjectivity whose traces surround us. Does Emin's work require us to interrogate spectatorship, moving from consumption of the art object to uneasy speculation about subjectivity? If a rumpled bed asks to be read as an autobiographical signature, what could viewers do to make a pact between the covers with its author?

"Keeping It Real": Rumpling the Memoir

In performance and much visual art, the autobiographical bed is certainly a rumpled one. Emin's insistent, excessive self-referentiality troubles the "rules" of social decorum about the appropriate location of the materials, activities, and behaviors of a young woman's quotidian life. It threatens the boundaries that normally distinguish everyday life from "art." The rumpled bed of autobiography is not on display only in the visual arts, however. It is on display even when its narrators are resting—lying?—between the covers of a book. Like Emin, an inventive new group of Gen X writers schooled on zines and the Web frequently enmesh and deliberately confuse the boundaries of fiction and memoir, exploiting the terms of the "real." Under siege in such literary memoirs are what an earlier generation of critics regarded as the normative rules of autobiography. In this moment of a paradigm shift between analog and digital cultures, between the book and fluid hyperspace, the autobiographical has become a moving target of experimentation. Think of the airing of family "dirty linen" in memoirs by Mary Karr (*The Liars' Club*), Kathryn Harrison (*The Kiss*), Elizabeth Wurtzel (*Prozac*

Nation), Michael Ryan (*Secret Life*), and Lauren Slater (*Lying: A Metaphorical Memoir*), and of the autobiographical discourse embedded in the novels of Kathy Acker and Don DeLillo. These writers both depend on and undermine expectations of sincerity, authenticity, intimacy, and completeness long hailed by critics and readers as essential to the autobiographical pact.

Enter Dave Eggers with a memoir, *A Heartbreaking Work of Staggering Genius*, subtitled "based on a true story."[2] Eggers's (the writer's) narrative chronicles the lives and fortunes of a pair of brothers after the deaths, several years earlier, of both parents, within thirty-two days of each other. A narrative of trauma, then? Or perhaps not. Dave (the narrating I), then twenty-one and unwilling to surrender the familial structure and make his seven-year-old brother, Toph, a ward of the state after the catastrophe, resolves to raise him himself, with the help of other grown siblings. In effect, Dave and Toph refuse to be defined as orphans, and recompose themselves instead as a new-model family with Dave, in his version, assuming the roles of both maternal nurturance and paternal authority.[3] They thereby implicitly dispute the conservative model of the two-parent family as necessary to prevent the breakdown of moral values. Eggers's narrative reflects not only on the constraints of normative family life in contemporary America—drawn from experiences in Chicago and Berkeley—but on the complexity of roles that Dave must take up as brother and son, parent and child, lusty young male and moral arbiter, would-be artist and postmodern cynic.

Eggers is acutely aware that the contradictions of his multiple identities pose a dilemma for the tidy memoirist. In his hands the narrative becomes an occasion to both flaunt and test autobiographical conventions of the boy's-coming-of-age story. Celebrated in the memoirs of Tobias Wolff (*This Boy's Life*) and Geoffrey Wolff (*The Dukes of Deception*), this American tradition stretches back through Richard Rodriguez (*Hunger of Memory*), N. Scott Momaday (*House Made of Dawn*), Richard Wright (*Black Boy/An American Hunger*), and Thomas Wolfe (*You Can't*

Go Home Again) to Mark Twain (*Days on the Mississippi*), Frederick Douglass (*Narrative of the Life of Frederick Douglass*), and Benjamin Franklin (*Autobiography*). Like Emin's installation of her intimate history, Eggers's rumpling and remaking of autobiographical convention is a bold intervention in coming-of-age narratives, although their gendered histories, particularly as sexually licentious "boy" versus sexually victimized "girl," are differently inflected. But whereas Emin's memorabilia are presented without a present-tense critical narrative to frame them, Eggers calls attention to his "messing" with the memoir by prefacing his narrative of the new-model family with an elaborate apparatus of explanation and justification. We focus on that set of introductory texts.

Like a Cervantes novel, *A Heartbreaking Work* includes nearly forty pages of advice on how to read its narrative of loss and survival. Its introduction is divided into "Rules," a Preface, Contents, extensive Acknowledgements, and an Incomplete Guide to Symbols and Metaphors; there are also "outtakes" printed on the book's front end flap. In other words, the analytic conventions of the scholarly book are assembled to self-consciously frame a first-person narrative that announces itself as "a work of pure non-fiction" (ix), "a memoir-y kind of thing" (xx).[4] In these prefatory sections Eggers situates his narrative as autobiographical in ways more reminiscent of the metafiction of Sterne's *Tristram Shandy* and the stories of Cortázar and Borges. This elaborate set of introductions both draws readers in and warns about the traps of sincerity and authenticity in personal narrative.

The book is complexly framed, beginning with its cover and end flaps. The cover, with its outrageously egotistical title, a calculated oxymoron of shattering trauma and arrogant genius, signals its staging of an exceptional "I," as does the jacket illustration of a red theatrical curtain half-drawn back to reveal the last rays of the setting sun, a worn cliché of Romantic genius. The book, then, announces itself as a hyperbolic performance of egotism rather than the assumed modesty of the memoirist's self-presentation. Similarly, in the hardback edition the front jacket flap defies readers' expectations by offering not an overview of the book, but a section "removed" from chapter five, without beginning or ending. Although the back flap seems more conventional in its snapshot of the T-shirted Eggers with dog, a brief paragraph identifies "the author" as the editor of a zine now living in Brooklyn with his brother, but adds "And this is not their dog." In this gaming with the self-referentiality of the memoir, Eggers reproduces *and* violates its conventions of sincerity.

In the book's first pages, readers are advised that it is possible, and probably a good idea, to skip the lengthy sections of prose and the elaborate Table of Contents that preface the narrative. This warning not to read the book, familiar from Rabelais, Montaigne, and a host of other meta-autobiographers, both teases and provokes. The next section, "Rules and Suggestions for Enjoyment of This Book" (vi), couched in the royal "we," contains six numbered items listing what readers may skip, ultimately most of the book. But the "rules" also make clear the dilemma of self-interested autobiographers whose readers don't share their enthusiasm for their lives. Suggesting that readers skip a hundred pages on Dave and his twenty-something friends, the Preface notes, "those lives are very difficult to make interesting, even when they seemed interesting to those living them at the time" (vii).

The "Preface to This Edition" (this edition being the first and only) confesses to several kinds of fictionalization within a "nonfictional" memoir, and points up the arbitrariness of the genre's conventions. Although particular to Eggers's narrative, these warnings about autobiography's fictions suggest contradictions in the autobiographical pact itself. Dialogue, above all, is suspect. Eggers asserts that his dialogue has been almost entirely reconstructed so as to "manufacture" the true-to-life quality it has in the book (ix). He notes that characters' names have been altered and their qualities changed because they, as living subjects, for the most part demanded some concealment. When, occasionally, no fabrication has been made, he calls attention to it directly, as in "You can ask her. She lives in Southern California" (x). The narrator, then, in emphasizing the text's verisimilitude, also troubles it. Eggers notes that locations and dates or times have been switched; that no relationship to subsequently occurring "real" events, such as the Columbine shootings, was intended; and that what the narrator cut from the manuscript can be recouped in the section on the front jacket flap. By highlighting its rearrangements and masking of experiential history, the narrator asserts the "truth" of his tale. The apparent lack of contrivance in most memoirs, by contrast, is implied to be a deeper kind of contrivance.

Similarly, Eggers's elaborate Table of Contents is a two-page Shandy-esque mixing of the substantive with the cryptic, irreverent, irrelevant, and inconsequential. The Acknowledgements, dedicated to NASA, the Marine Corps, the United States Armed Forces, and the United States Postal Service—large, anonymous groups—are also a send-up of the memoir genre. "The author, and those behind the making of this book," the narrator announces,

> wish to acknowledge that yes, there are perhaps too many memoir-sorts of books being written at this juncture, and that such books, about real things and real people, as opposed to kind-of made-up things and people, are inherently vile and corrupt and wrong and evil and bad, but would like to remind everyone that we could all do worse, as readers and as writers. (xix)

While Eggers here makes readers exhaustively aware of bothersome questions of the "real" in autobiography's imperfect miming of it, his advice for readers with memoir trouble is equally ironic: "Pretend it's fiction" (xxi).

If autobiography imperfectly stages experience between the covers of a book that embeds his narrator Dave, Eggers steps forth to address the reader outside the memoir's illusion of a coherent past, inviting readers unhappy with the memoir to return it to the publisher in exchange for a floppy disk of same. In an ultimate send-up of autobiographical self-interest, readers are assured that the disk will function interactively, so they can search-and-replace the names in the book with their own and those of their friends: "This can be about you! You and your pals!" (xxii).[5]

Eggers also exploits self-advertisement as an aspect of autobiographical writing. He makes an immodest case for Dave's appeal with an extensive list of his personal characteristics, assuring readers that he is someone "like" you. There follows a list, in twenty-two exhaustive descriptions, of the memoir's themes, above all, "the painfully, endlessly self-conscious book aspect." In this labyrinth of self-assertion he claims that he is "clearly, obviously aware of his knowingness about his self-consciousness of self-referentiality" (xxvi-xxvii). But lest the verbal fireworks seem celebratory, Eggers reminds us of the memoir's theme of "weirdly terrible" deaths as a way of being "chosen" and its relation to "the search for support, a sense of community" (xxvii). The book's themes are concisely summarized in a graph published on one page and available in large format for five dollars through the mail. Not only does Eggers elaborately gloss his narrative, but he generates, graphs, and meta-critiques the range of possible critical approaches to it.

But this elaborate critical apparatus for seemingly controlling the reading of his memoir and proving his encyclopedic awareness of autobiographical convention is, Eggers asserts, in fact "gimmickry." It is in the service of obscuring "the black, blinding, murderous rage and sorrow at the core of the whole story," a story whose center is the stricken heart of childhood loss and trauma (xxvii). Assuming the other privileges of the memoirist, Eggers confesses and therapeutically exorcises his pain by the practice of testimony: "Telling as many people as possible about it helps" (xxvii). In such an ironic set of prefaces, how are we to value this assertion of a central self shattered by trauma? Eggers acknowledges the paradox of telling the heartbreaking story of a childhood riven by illness and death in order to exploit it for fame and profit and to "receive . . . a thousand tidal waves of sympathy and support" (xxvii). Publishing a memoir, Eggers acknowledges, is finally an "act of self-destruction," much like an emetic or the shedding of a skin (xxx). Yet self-revelation is also "endlessly renewable," an act of feeding solipsism but justified by the desire, through writing, to create an enduring relationship with his brother Toph, who has been both "inspiration for and impediment to writing of memoir" (xxxi). Posing "self-aggrandizement" against "self-flagellation" as the motives of autobiographical writing and its search for "self-canonization," Eggers's performance of memoir-writing is profoundly ambivalent. It suggests, finally, that being suspicious about the ethics of autobiographical writing may be the one ethical act available to it.

The Acknowledgments conclude with that most mystified, yet essential, aspect of autobiographical writing in our postmodern times, the material specifics of Eggers's financial arrangements with his publisher. Provocatively he invites the reader to participate in profiting from the pain of his memoir. Listing his relatively low costs and high profits (over $60,000 in advance for the book, before sales), Eggers promises a five-dollar check to the first 200 readers who "write with proof that they have read and absorbed the many lessons herein," and includes his editor's name and address (xxxv). Instructions are included on how to provide credible photographic proof that one has read the book.

Bringing this elaborate foreplay of almost forty pages to an end, Eggers provides "an Incomplete Guide to Symbols and Metaphors" in the narrative "to save you some trouble" and get on with the reader's desire for "uninterrupted, unself-conscious prose," for the pleasure of reading (xxxvi-xxxvii). As he summarizes the range of autobiographical excesses that have haunted the genre's practitioners—a propensity for exaggeration and lying, a lack of unique experience—we are reminded that he also has the good fortune to be under contract for what others must suffer silently.

In so elaborately sketching the rules of the memoir game, Eggers simultaneously underscores and undermines them. Claiming to tell a true story in a genre about whose maneuvers he is acutely, endlessly self-conscious, he invites readers to confront the undecidability of autobiographical acts. Is Eggers's calculated miming of memoir merely a bid for readerly sympathy? Or is his conceptual apparatus intended to distance and defer the inconsolable pain of traumatic familial experience? Like Emin's rumpled bed, Eggers's rumpled memoir gestures toward the excesses of embodied experience, now past but still palpable, that refuse containment by the disciplining power of autobiographical conventions.

And the controversy continues, after the publication of *A Heartbreaking Work of Staggering Genius*, in e-mail and zine wars about the status of the "real" and the sincerity of Eggers's ethos. A recent *Harper's Magazine* excerpted Eggers's elaborate "Addendum" to one of these dialogues, in response to a question from *The Harvard Advocate* (Summer 2000), which, concerned about his success and willingness to write for major magazines, asked "Are you taking any steps . . . to keep shit real?" In a long rant about "selloutitude," Eggers explains that the book's success and the other writing work it has netted him, as well as the prospect of its becoming a major motion picture, are not sellouts but indications of his lack of calculation in response to his own success. "I really like saying yes. . . . The keeping real of shit . . . [i]t's fashion, and . . . fashion doesn't matter" ("Too Legit" 24). Again he attempts to expose the audience's perceived demand for uncalculated sincerity as posturing, a false pose. He has gained media attention, he argues, because he is unself-consciously alive and in the moment, not because he works at being authentic. "Keeping it real" in an age of simulacra is, he suggests, at best an anachronistic naturalism. Eggers's "real," by contrast, is interested in play and engagement, inhabiting what's happening now. Like Emin,

Eggers keeps moving into a new "now" in which past memories are cited, staged, as the material for present ways of making visible an evanescent subject.

Extravagant Lives, Urgent Questions

Placing Emin's and Eggers's extravagant performances of the conventions, limits, and apparatus of autobiographical acts side by side suggests several questions about the uses of autobiography at this cultural moment. First, there are issues about experimental life writing. How may the autobiographical be a style of avant-garde experimentation? And how is autobiographical avant-gardism differently enacted in alphabetic, visual, and performance modes? What are the particular terms of avant-garde experimentation in autobiographical writing at this juncture? To what extent is the confounding of experiential history and its representation as the "real," or a "life," more compelling in this time of simulated realities—on television, in everyday life, and in cyberspace? How does the embodied materiality of visual and performance media reframe "art" as a site of lived experience, and turn daily life into material for performance?

A second issue concerns the gendered ethics of autobiographical acts. The autobiographical pact implies that writers seek to maintain a sincere and responsible relationship to their audiences and to the ethical imperatives of that relationship. But these artists probe the limits of sincerity through extravagant performances that flaunt the norms of modesty about self-disclosure, self-presentation, and experiential history. In Emin's work, the seemingly excessive disclosure of her personal past presented through installations, diaries, and videos could be read as both exploiting and flaunting gendered norms of female decorum. Nice girls, well-brought-up-girls, simply do not rehearse their intimate lives in public, let alone display the sordid leavings of them. Emin's public presentation of intimacy seems to mimic the stereotype that those of working-class origin are less concerned about decorum than the middle class. Similarly, Eggers's narrative seems to violate norms of masculinity by remaking the post-traumatic family as an all-male world of nurturance and bonding, resituated in the private domain of home and family, yet exploiting conventional norms of gendered roles to retain male authority. But if Eggers's narrative marks out a public-private boundary, his flamboyant framing and publication clearly transgress it.

In different ways, then, both of these works are extravagant performances of experiential history that interrogate gendered norms and redefine the spaces and roles normally assigned to men and women. And they adduce confusion on the part of audiences about how to respond. In Emin's case public outrage at the scandal of her extravagant performance was perhaps intensified by her working-class frankness in the bourgeois public sphere of the Tate gallery. Eggers's extravagant claim to remake the form of the memoir as a work of "genius" in the service of the family memoir is a similarly hyperbolic bid for readership.

A third issue concerns the autobiographical pact, that "contract of identity . . . [between writer and reader] sealed by the proper name" (Lejeune 19). What effect do such extravagant performances of the asserted "real" have upon our conception of an autobiographical pact in which, in Lejeune's terms, the "essence of [a] being is registered" (21)? The pact implies a kind of decorum in the writer's limiting of self-exposure before readers, as a guarantee of the narrator's reliability. In different ways, Emin and Eggers both maintain and breach these terms in order to renegotiate what is permissible in the name of public presentation of one's past. As a result, both autobiographical actors are seen by some as shameless self-advertisers, excessively and flagrantly exposing themselves, selling out and betraying the presumed desire of their works to capture the "real." Precisely because the work of both Emin and Eggers has been widely acclaimed and they have become *causes célèbres*, they may be mobilizing something in audiences that more discreet autobiographers have not tapped. People flocked to Emin's spectacle. Readers acclaim Eggers's memoir. Both artists have become financially successful. Autobiographical exploiters and sell-outs? Or avant-garde experimenters pushing the limits of disclosure in the form, and tweaking the cultural establishment all the way to the bank? The popularity, in the last few years, of these works reminds us that the autobiographical has historically consisted of popular forms consumed by reading publics hungry for intimacy and vicarious adventure. If academic critics want to say "no" to excessive and repeated self-display, the enthusiastic public response to these extravagant presentations of "lives" has been "yes."

Finally, consider the stakes of these autobiographical acts. What is Emin's extravagant multimedia autobiographical performance interested in achieving with such public exposure? Is it clearing a space in the bourgeois public sphere for an unattractive, working-class female bad-girl artist? Is this visual excess the equivalent of obsessive confession in the talk show, or of disclosure on the psychiatrist's couch? Is it, as her critics allege, the calculated act of a woman poor in imagination ransacking her private life for titillating details to be packaged and marketed as a new avant-garde, solely because of their anti-art rawness? Is Emin, then, the kind of performance autobiographer Linda S. Kauffman has termed a "bad girl" for the unflinching exploration of her own archive (56)? For Kauffman, such artists "stage their own bodies as sites of contestation through parody, defamiliarization, and incongruous juxtaposition" (60). Emin, however, is staging—if indeed she is staging, not just citing—something other than her adult take on public uses of and responses to women's bodies in the fantasies of contemporary culture. Rather, she presents the idiosyncratic particularity of her own past, one often at odds with both decorum and parody. In including her bed, her childhood diaries, her vacation videos, family news clippings, and other artifacts of her experience as art, Emin seems to undermine the notion that the autobiographical selects, edits, chooses, and rearranges the stuff of life into meaningful narrative, reworked by memory's intervention, for public scrutiny. And yet, in presenting these fragments of the past *as* art, Emin invites us to remake her in the present, to compose interpretive narratives, to collaborate in constructing the indisputable authenticity and flagrant excess of her autobiographical acts.

By contrast, what is Eggers's autobiographical narrative, with its elaborately self-conscious glosses and extravagant literary parodies, interested in making of autobiographical disclosure? If his elaborate apparatus encloses the pathos of a "heartbreaking" narrative that makes a bid for high literary seriousness, is it simultaneously the practice and the send-up of the genre? Is his narrative a call for a new version of white middle-class masculinity that undermines the masculine/feminine binary within heterosexuality? How does that reorganizing of the nurturing role in a "nuclear family" reconcile its displacement of woman from the center of the family? If Eggers's narrative both revises gender stereotypes and, in its assault on readers, revives a Maileresque stance of autobiographical machismo, it also invites readers to collaborate in reconstructing the authority of life writing as a site of "keeping it real" precisely by exposing its contrivances.

In discussing these two works, we have raised several questions about autobiographical acts in this cultural moment. In brief: What is the relationship of avant-garde practice to issues of gender and the ethics of narration? What is the impact of differences of class, gender, ethnicity, and national identity? What modes of self-representation extend across a visual/textual interface? We close not with a definitive statement, but with an observation about the fluidity of contemporary acts of self-representation. As distinct boundaries between and among all of the above categories are fading, to what extent are literary, or narratively based, theories of the autobiographical useful for inquiring into self-reflexive narratives that interweave presentations of self across multiple media, including virtual reality? To what extent does our theorizing itself need to be remade by contemporary practice at these "rumpled" sites of the experimental, so that we may take account of changing autobiographer-audience relations, shifting limits of personal disclosure, and changing technologies of self that revise how we understand the autobiographical? As, in different ways, self-representational acts such as those of Emin and Eggers test the limits of the autobiographical as act, discourse, and visual/verbal interface, their extravagant "lives" may remake the critical locus of our own theories.

Notes

1 Although Emin was not awarded the Turner Prize, her controversial entry provoked a raging discussion among British art critics about the autobiographical as art. In June 2000, "My Bed" was purchased by Charles Saatchi for £150,000 (Brooks 7). We are indebted to Suzanne Bunkers for bringing notice of the sale of "My Bed" to our attention at the "Autobiography and Changing Identities" conference.
2 Our thanks to William Chaloupka, cultural critic and co-editor of the online journal *Theory and Event*, for suggesting Eggers's memoir as a provocative case of contemporary Gen X memoir that includes a meta-critique of its own practice of memorialization.
3 The August 2000 *Harper's Magazine* includes an "Apologia," first run in *The Harvard Advocate* (Summer 2000) as an e-mail interview with Dave Eggers, in which he responds extensively to the charge that he has sold out to big-time publishing. Eggers responds to the charge: "We just don't care. We care about doing what we want to do creatively" ("Too Legit" 23). A sidebar, "Corrections," from Beth Eggers, Dave's older sister, however, tells a different story. It reprints selections from a correspondence between Beth and Gary Baum in the April 17, 2000, column of his webzine, *My Manifesto* (www.aphrodigitaliac.com), on the Dave Eggers phenomenon. Beth questions Dave's characterization in the memoir that she "helped out," describing how substantial her own contribution was to raising Chris(toph)er, her care of their dying parents, her oversight of housing and financial arrangements, her status as Chris's legal guardian, and, most damningly for Dave, her assertion that "Dave used my journal to refresh his recollection about many things—that's why he thanked me in the acknowledgments and probably also because he felt guilty for misrepresenting things" (23). The questions she raises about misappropriation of both life and writing are unresolved as this essay goes to press.

4 We do not take up distinctions between autobiography and memoir here, but refer readers to *Reading Autobiography: A Guide for Interpreting Life Narrative*. Eggers uses "nonfiction" and "memoir" interchangeably, and does not use the term "autobiography." As his text focuses on one part of his past during his parents' dying, and after their deaths, it does not encompass the whole of his or his brother's lives, though it draws on a range of autobiographical strategies.

5 This interchangeability of pronouns characterizes the mirror relationship of writer and reader, as well as that of memoir and fiction, often solicited by contemporary autobiographers, as Susanna Egan has pointed out in *Mirror Talk*. Egan discusses the "crisis-driven autobiography," especially of "autothanatographers," a genre to which Eggers's memoir, originating in his parents' deaths, is linked (225–26). Egan observes that such writers "create the life of the moment over and over, preferring to mark time as present, liminal space rather than in terms of past or future" (225). By being "multifaceted, mirror talk reflects the very indeterminacy of life in crisis," and calls on readers to engage in collaborative acts of interpretation (226). Egan's emphasis on narrative co-construction in an ongoing present moment is suggestive for the innovative autobiographical mode engaged by both Eggers and Emin.

Works Cited

Brooks, Richard. "Saatchi pays 150,000 for Emin's soiled bed." *The Sunday Times* [Vancouver, British Columbia]: 16 July 2000: 7.

Donnell, Alison. "When Writing the Other Is Being True to the Self: Jamaica Kincaid's *The Autobiography of My Mother*." *Women's Lives into Print: The Theory, Practice and Writing of Feminist Auto/Biography*. Ed. Pauline Polkey. London: MacMillan/New York: St. Martin's, 1999. 123–36.

Egan, Susanna. *Mirror Talk: Genres of Crisis in Contemporary Autobiography*. Chapel Hill: University of North Carolina Press, 1999.

Eggers, Dave. *A Heartbreaking Work of Staggering Genius: Based on a True Story*. New York: Simon & Schuster, 2000.

Gilmore, Leigh. "Limit Cases: Trauma, Self-Representation, and the Jurisdictions of Identity." *Biography: An Interdisciplinary Quarterly* 24.1 (Winter 2001): 128–39.

Kauffman, Linda S. *Bad Girls and Sick Boys: Fantasies in Contemporary Art and Culture*. Berkeley: University of California Press, 1998.

Lejeune, Philippe. "The Autobiographical Pact." *On Autobiography.* Ed. Paul John Eakin. Trans. Katherine M. Leary. Minneapolis: University of Minnesota Press, 1989. 3–30.

Poster, Mark. *What's the Matter with the Internet?* Minneapolis: University of Minnesota Press, 2000.

Smith, Sidonie, and Julia Watson. *Reading Autobiography: A Guide for Interpreting Life Narratives.* Minneapolis: University of Minnesota Press, 2001, expanded 2nd edition 2010.

——, eds. *Interfaces: Women's Visual and Performance Autobiography.* Ann Arbor: University of Michigan Press, 2002.

"Too Legit to Quit." *Harper's Magazine* Aug. 2000: 19–24.

3
Witness or False Witness?: Metrics of Authenticity, Collective I-Formations, and the Ethic of Verification in First-Person Testimony (2012)

Witness narratives educate and bind readers to the degree that they convince them of two things: that the story is the "real" story of a "real" survivor—that a narrative is joined to an embodied person; and that the reading experience constitutes a cross-cultural encounter through which readers are positioned as ethical subjects within the global imaginary of human rights advocacy. In this high-stakes, high-demand convergence of witnessing, reading, and rights activism, a genre of life writing so pervasive in the political field and so compelling in affective appeal becomes increasingly vulnerable, a magnet for suspicious reading.

Journalists and other readers, in increasing numbers, have become detectives of authenticity, publicly alleging in offline and online venues that such-and-such a book is a case of false witnessing. Some allegations are supported by evidence and stick to a narrative. Binjamin Wilkomirski's *Fragments: Memories of a Wartime Childhood*, a narrative of surviving the Holocaust, was withdrawn from bookstores when exposed as a fabrication in 1996, and later reissued as a novel. The charges of false witnessing have stuck to Norma Khouri's *Forbidden Love: A Harrowing True Story of Love and Revenge in Jordan*, published in Australia and in the United States in 2003/2004 (Whitlock, "Remediating"). While this harrowing narrative of honor killing gained Khouri readers and celebrity in Australia, in Jordan feminist activists discovered that places and businesses cited in *Forbidden Love* could not be verified, and posted online charges of fabrication. In early 2011, readers in the West were intrigued by the eyewitness blog posts of "Gay Girl in Damascus," celebrated as a critical voice of the Syrian revolutionary movement and a witness to violence against gays and lesbians under the al-Assad regime. By the summer of 2011, "Gay Girl" had been exposed as Tom MacMaster, a married American student writing under the pseudonym of "Amina," a Syrian-American lesbian (Mackey). In the same spring, *Three Cups of Tea* and *Stones into Schools*, Greg Mortenson's as-told-to autobiographical accounts of one man's efforts to redress gender discrimination in Afghanistan and Pakistan by building schools for girls, came under scrutiny by Jon Krakauer for the television news show *60 Minutes* and subsequently by the courts.[1] There are other cases in which allegations of hoaxing do not quite stick, though they may attach a taint of fabrication to the narrative that captures the attention of skeptical cosmopolitan audiences and fact-seeking journalists, even if the charges fail to deter local publics or rights advocates. Whether allegations stick or not, though, the scandal of the hoax shadows contemporary witness narratives as what Leigh Gilmore has called "the parasite that rides on testimony."[2]

The scandals and controversies that ensue from allegations of false witnessing unsettle relations among witnesses, publishers, activists, and readers, forcing us to confront the vulnerability of life writing and our attachments to its premise of truth-telling. Exposés of hoaxing and allegations of false witnessing in narratives of suffering do harm in the world, though it is important to note that not all hoaxes are harmful in the same way, nor are all hoaxes the same kind of hoax. Which narratives do or don't get tarred with the hoax brush, and under what circumstances do these charges stick? These questions vex any simple understanding of the truth status of narratives witnessing to atrocity and suffering as they foreground the potential limitations of readerly desires for cross-cultural en\gagement, and expose how thoroughly narratives of suffering have been commodified, fueling the markets publishers chase for profits.

This essay seeks to assess, if not redress, the crisis of suspicion surrounding narratives of witness in contemporary human rights campaigns by engaging with the cultural politics of the hoax that haunts acts of testimony. Our focus in what follows is not on whether the truth or falsity of witness narratives can be definitively determined. Rather, we have several seemingly disparate but ultimately interrelated aims. First, we specify the metrics of authenticity that have come to be associated with testimony as guarantors of the subject position of first-person witness and its credibility. Second, we track the currents of suspicious reading that so often trouble reception of witness narratives at this time. Third, we complicate the "I"-witness position of narration by disaggregating four distinctive "I"-formations. With reference to four published narratives—"Souad"'s *Burned Alive*, Ishmael Beah's *A Long Way Gone*, the Sangtin Collective's *Playing with Fire*, and Dave Eggers's *What Is the What: The Autobiography of Valentino Achak Deng, A Novel*—we tease out how particular "I"-formations produce, refuse, thematize, or circumvent the politics of authenticity. These forays into the metrics of authenticity, suspicious reading, and configurations of the "I" in first-person testimony bear on the practices and politics of reading witness narratives at this moment when allegations of hoaxing abound, and the neoliberal "management of difference" (Hanneken 49) so thoroughly organizes cross-cultural engagement.

Our ultimate aim is to rethink the ethics of reading testimonial narratives of suffering and harm. The capacities of digital data and archives, in combination with human rights protocols and cultures of rescue, have unleashed a powerful ethic of verification that expands the number and kinds of fact-checkers. To be sure, responsible verification is important to the advancement of rights arguments and activism on the ground. But the ethic of verification can be a problematic one. Its practice of "outing" false witnessing can serve to discredit testimonial acts that contribute to the exposure of rights violations, violence, and conditions of radical injury and degradation. Thus, we need to develop a more sophisticated understanding of the ethical work of testimony, one that does not rely on an over-investment in "authenticity." To this end, we ask the question: What protocols of reading might we, as readers both attentive and sympathetic, knowing but not credulous, bring to textual acts of first-person witnessing in the service of an ethics distinct from the ethic of verification and attentive both to the vulnerability of witnesses and to the commodification of narratives of suffering in the global market?

The Metrics of Authenticity

In the wake of three decades of personal witnessing to conditions of extremity, activists, publishers, and readers now identify several distinguishing features of first-person testimony. Such narratives chronicle conditions of oppression, assemble experiential histories of psychic degradation and bodily assault, register the aftereffects of survival and mourning, and commemorate victims who cannot give testimony. Circulating as "transnational artefacts" (Hesford 105) en route to reading publics around the globe, they lodge charges of rights violations and stake claims to recognition and redress.

It is imperative that people intervene in global asymmetries of power and privilege by bearing witness to their experiential histories of violence and suffering. Their narratives are mobilized as potent political weapons to wield against agents of a state, political factions, and the threat of national forgetting. As acts of witnessing, such narratives generate an archive of suffering that is critical to the efforts of activists and rights lawyers to document conditions of extremity before human rights institutions (see Cvetkovich 8). Such acts also call larger publics to attention and enlist them in the project of redressing harms. Witness narratives thus intensify the stakes of reading in the circuits of production, circulation, and reception through which they travel the globe.

To understand fully why the taint of the hoax haunts witness narratives, and how controversies and scandals regularly erupt around them, we need to recognize how authenticity effects are projected by and attached to them. If an "I"'s narration is to serve the purposes of testimonial life writing, it must promote an identity whose authenticity is sufficiently persuasive, compelling, and transformative to make its truth manifest and credible to readers. Unlike in the novel, in the referential world of written or filmic autobiographical testimony, questions of reliability are linked to two issues: whether the speaker's factual claims are documentable; and whether his or her asserted identity can be verified as what is called "authentic." Indeed, "authenticity" is often invoked in evaluating witness narratives as both a criterion and a test of their transparency, validity, and efficacy in campaigns for redress of injustice. But how does a narrative convince readers of its authenticity? How does it "communicate" authenticity?

Derived in part from the past narrative practices of ethnography, and in part from conventions of accuracy, validity, and propriety that have gained consensus in extra-legal jurisdictions as discourses of witnessing, several features have come to typify witness narratives circulating in the context of human rights campaigns. Adopting Hua Hsu's phrase, we call these features "the metrics of authenticity" (42). These metrics are produced internally at the intersection of the witness's singular experiential history and the shared communal discourses and narrative rhetorics through which that experiential history unfolds, and externally through the production, marketing, and circulation of witness narratives for transnational publics.

The following five metrics through which witness narratives project an aura of authenticity will be recognizable to many readers of first-person testimony.

The "you-are-there" sense of immediacy. Witness narratives communicate the immediacy and urgency of a conflict or situation to the reader. Through discursive positioning as a first-person witness, the narrator speaks as a first-hand actor in and observer of disastrous, violent, and degrading conditions of existence. He or she often speaks as a subject in danger, emphasizing a harmed self and body while chronicling a narrow escape from greater danger and death. In other words, the narrator adopts the subject position of both the victim of human rights violations and the survivor. As readers imaginatively share the vulnerable protagonist's struggle to survive, their empathetic identification is awakened. They are transported "there" by a narrator's rhetorical shifts into the simple present tense.

The invocation of rights discourse. The narrating "I," and/or an editorial commentator or advocate on the narrator's behalf, makes explicit reference to a recognized, violated identity that is compelling and shocking, such as "child soldier" or "comfort woman," and/or to human rights violations such as honor killing, persecution of indigenous groups, or the practice of torture or genocide. The narrator challenges established authority by naming powerful adversaries or, in the discourse of rights, positioning such people or institutions as "perpetrators." (The formations represented as reviled in rights discourse over the past decade have included "Islam," "Islamic patriarchy," "Socialist authoritarianism," and practices labeled as devastating to entire groups, such as "apartheid," "genocide," and "honor killing.") In so doing, the narrative functions ideologically as a kind of manifesto for the rights of the subordinated. By establishing conversancy in an arena of human rights activism, the witness links an individual story to available scripts of injustice circulating in the global flows of rights advocacy. Through the moral grammar of rights discourse, the witness experience is rendered more readily comprehensible, and the terms of judgment regarding innocence and culpability made seemingly unproblematic.

The affirmation of the duty to narrate a collective story. The narrator positions her- or himself as a representative subject, affirming the urgency of telling an experiential history that stands in for the unspoken narratives of other victims of the same rights violation. The obligation to narrate involves several rhetorical acts: documenting the fates of the dead, speaking for those who cannot speak, registering the difficulty of remembering a traumatic past, and memorializing the dead by producing a counter-history to official narratives of an event or everyday conditions of life.

The normative shape of victim experience and identity. Witness narratives differ according to the particular rights abuse referenced, but within a category of narrative a consensus emerges as individual iterations of the experience common to a group accumulate. It forms around the normative shape of a victim experience and the normative identity of the rights victim (as "sex prisoner," "child soldier," "stolen child," for instance). These stereotypical characterizations and typicalized experiences conform the story of the witness to a legible model of a particular violation. Actors are positioned as victims, perpetrators, and, sometimes, beneficiaries (Schaffer and Smith), and differences within a collectivity of victimized people are eliminated or harmonized.

The ethno-documentation of cultural specificity. The narrative projects a voice steeped in specific cultural practices and memories associated with the community of endangered people and attentive to the need to explain cultural contexts and political circumstances to readers. That is, the narrating "I" asserts and marks his or her locality and its difference from the locations of a predominantly Western readership. Often the narrative foregrounds markers of alternative and culturally specific forms of storytelling—for example, by incorporating cultural myths, or by shifting to the language of an oral storytelling tradition. In other words, the narrative's authenticity is asserted and marked as "local" and thus different from the reader's frame of reference.

To sum up, the aura of authenticity projected by first-person testimony to violence, atrocity, and degradation is the cumulative effect of several features internal to witness narratives. Witness narratives consolidate a composite figure of "the victim" with iconic features of vulnerability: for instance, a child, a woman under patriarchy, a persecuted ethnic or religious or sexual group, or most often, a lone individual mounting a heroic struggle against pervasive obstacles or powerful oppressors. The narrative of an event or conditions of duress evolves into a kind of "official" story employing a recognizable template accepted within local, national, or international communities as credible and retroactively binding. Finally, the narrative projects the witness as representative not of personal, idiosyncratic experience, but of the larger community of those who remain silent, but whose silence calls out for ethical redress. Cumulatively, these metrics generate the contours of, and project the truth effects of, a coherent and intelligible story of witness, and an "I" witness whose reliability seems guaranteed as "authentic."

Authentification: Paratexts and Epitexts

Additional features of the production and circulation of narratives of witness contribute to their aura of authenticity. Activists who organize to gain attention to and redress for people victimized by particular histories of violence invest in the authenticity of the witness and the story. Such activists seek to ensure that the cause is not jeopardized or undermined, as do the editors and publishers responsible for publishing, marketing, and selling the narrative. Through various means, these activists attempt to mediate troubling aspects of a narrative or its conditions of production, forestall potential resistance to the credibility of the witness and the narrative, and shore up the kinds of authenticity valued as evidentiary corroboration by Western readers, to whom witness narratives are most frequently addressed and marketed.

Paratexts, including forewords, introductions, and afterwords, are often attached to witness narratives, providing sites for activists and representatives with professional bona fides to attest to the veracity of the story and the integrity of the witness. As acts of secondary witnessing, these paratexts embed the individual story in the larger story of a group or movement, linking personal experience to known historical events. Professionals may also address absences, lacunae, or incoherence in the narration by providing an explanatory framework to guide reader response.

Introductions, which may explain the genesis of the story and offer "first readings," not only project an ideal reader, but seek to route the response of flesh-and-blood readers in particular ways. The sympathetic reader is asked to suspend critical judgment and instead respond with uncritical empathy, as he or she identifies with those positioned as victims. In such paratexts, reading itself becomes preparation for an act of rescue, and readers become potential rescuers—if not in fact, then vicariously, and often financially. Similarly, afterwords often provide information on how to become an activist in response to a rights violation, and how to donate to a cause. Such summative words return readers to the larger project of human rights campaigns, often by attaching the authority of a recognized United Nations, national, or nongovernmental organization. In effect, afterwords insert the individual story into the larger story of the group, affirming the intersection of personal experience with known historical events.

Witness narratives thus circulate in a global field where metrics of authenticity, modes of appeal, and paratextual cues to interpretation have been encoded in print, online, and oral venues. The work of affirming the authenticity of the witness and the narrative can continue in post-publication activities such as book tours and interviews—what Whitlock terms "the epitextual conditions" of a witness narrative's circulation and reception (*Soft Weapons* 61–62). In the United States, cultural brokers such as Oprah Winfrey add their imprimatur to a narrative, increasing both readership and publisher profits. Receiving the Nobel Peace

Prize may enhance world knowledge about the cause, the status of the activist witness, and international sales of the book, as it did for Aung San Sui Kyi in 1991, Rigoberta Menchú in 1992, Shirin Ebadi in 2003, Wangari Maathai in 2004, Liu Xiaobo in 2010, and Leymah Gbowee in 2011. The multiple roles of commentators as secondary witnesses and readers as agents of rescue in vouching for authenticity in testimonial narrative suggest that this process is now a transnational one, requiring that many agents work on behalf of an apparently singular "I." These secondary witnesses manage the reputation of the witness and try to negotiate effectively the "*doxa* of globalization" (Whitlock, *Soft Weapons* 7): they are the neoliberal discourses, transactions, and transnational entities that distribute world views, subject positions, funds, influence, and benefits across the world.

Suspicious Reading

For activists, survivors, publishers, and readers, the current appeal of narratives of witness is bound up with forces that make them vulnerable to suspicious readings. But on what grounds do readers become suspicious? How does the authenticity of a testimonial narrative come under suspicion and the taint of the hoax get attached to a particular witness narrative? And who are the suspicious readers?

Testimonial narratives share several vulnerabilities with autobiographical discourse generally—vulnerabilities that prompt suspicion. The use of dialogue as verbatim recall of experience inevitably invites skepticism because of its improbability. And, most acutely in testimony, the status of recalled or recovered memory is psychologically complicated, both because of the difficulty of recounting horrific repressed experience and because, in the meantime, another narrative has become dominant as the "official" version of an experience, as with some Holocaust and child soldier narratives. When a testimony is written or recorded long after the event, the memory may be shaped by the "prosthetic memory" that a nation or group constructs around the past, or the postmemory of a generation born after the event. Additional complications may arise when a paratextual commentator, attempting to flesh out the narrator's vagaries of memory and to acknowledge the difficult struggle to tell a story, introduces material that raises concerns about "interested" remembering and false memory.

Features internal to witness narratives may also catch the attention of skeptics whose critiques undermine confidence in a narrative's truth claims and the narrator's authenticity. For example, evidentiary referents and signposts such as dates and place names may be sketchy at best, sometimes nonexistent. Often absent too are independent sources documenting the kinds and extent of harm done, such as footnotes to historical accounts; referenced archives of notes, letters, or journals; and the visual evidence of photographs and maps. In such first-person testimony, the voices of corroborating witnesses who persuasively attest to a history of violence through verbatim stories, photos, and other narratives are rare or absent. As the story of harm unfolds, conflicting or contradictory plot strands, which introduce jarring or distracting details that could invite alternative interpretations, can be suppressed because they would project a less coherent past of victimization. As the narrative focalization is on victim experience, it is also unusual to find an unheroic portrayal of the survivor-subject that would disrupt the story template of victimization.

As a subject position, the survivor/witness is itself vulnerable. In both juridical and alternative venues, the status of the witness has long been crucial for the credibility of the narrative. If the witness speaks from a marginalized position as "uneducated," "poor," "indigenous," or a "child," the credibility of the testimony is more easily called into question, however unjustifiably. Witnesses who cannot draw on expertise and knowledge gained by education, social position, and elite status, or who do not have the literacy to tell their narratives in a dominant world language, may be subject to dismissal or heightened suspicion. Furthermore, for some readers, the relative homogeneity of plots, rhetorical conventions, and audience appeals in testifying to particular rights violations can make testimonial accounts seem formulaic rather than individually inflected. Suspicions thus arise that the witness may be reproducing an expected narration of events at the behest of activists or sponsors who are in control of shaping the story and making it public. In effect, precisely because they are regarded as subalterns, rights claimants are often held to exacting standards of verification by commentators and scholars.

In some instances, witness accounts may come across to readers as too literary because they incorporate language, tropes, plots, and characterizations identified with literary fiction. As Anne Cubilié observes, "approaches to collecting, analyzing, and performing testimony all rely on the 'knowability,' if not transparency, of what is being said: plain language conveying 'the truth' of horrific experience is one of the authenticating aspects of testimonial in whatever form." When those witnessing to experiences of extremity and atrocity incorporate metaphorical language, or organize the narrative through ready-made plots of quest, conversion, or collective empowerment, or stage scenes in dialogue, or reflect too often on the process of composing the testimony itself, readers become "uncomfortable" to the degree that "these literary devices seem to contravene and destabilize the authenticity of the bodily experience being recounted through the embodied vehicles of text and speech" (222). Literary rhetoric, the craft of shaping a story, can make readers suspicious about the "authentic" expression of pain, as so often happened with the narratives of American slaves.

The environment of suspicion in which witness narratives circulate and detectives of verification lodge their claims intensifies with every scandal that occurs after a fabricated act of witnessing is exposed. The convergence of global crises, expanded global markets, and the capacious appetite for "real" stories about "real" people creates conditions ripe for exploitation that digital media rapidly convey. In this context, the set of rhetorical and generic conventions associated with narratives of witness and the paratextual apparatuses that surround many of them can be mobilized regardless of whether the experience has been lived or imagined.

Hoaxes thrive on the markets that publishing houses pursue in their efforts to find stories that will generate large profits. Such currents bear the hoax commingled with testimonies and other kinds of life writing to reading publics hungry for the next story. Such first-person narratives of harm and violation promise readers gripping affective attachments: fantasies of identification, opportunities to feel good, or promises of cross-cultural exchange in a dangerous, fast-transforming world. The myriad routes of print, visual, and digital circulation that carry stories to new reading publics also increase the potential that a hoax may be exposed in the circuits of surveillance and information-exchange that spark readers' demands for authenticity, sincerity, and truthfulness. When we consider this accelerated circulation through multiple media, we may begin to grasp why a fascinating and varied array of autobiographical hoaxes—the fabrications of Gay Girl and Khouri, the exaggerations of Mortenson, among others—have rippled across markets to command attention in the last decade, creating crises within reading publics, the publishing world, and communities of writers.

In this contemporary environment of suspicion, digital technologies turn archives, documents, and data into sites to mine for those with an investigatory drive justified by an ethic of verification. And social media enable such detectives of authenticity to communicate suspicious readings to transnational networks of readers like never before. Who are these agents of suspicion turning a desire to "out" false witnessing into a demand for verification?

As witness narratives lodge rights claims through the discourse of "victim" and "perpetrator" to enlist reader sympathy and call for international intervention, they are situated within the contemporary politics of naming, shaming, redress, and reconciliation. Some in positions of authority and power—for example, heads of governments, their militaries, and police—have considerable investments in defending their nations against the shaming force of human rights narratives in the court of public opinion. Three groups of people stand out among the interested parties raising suspicion: those who would deny or deflect charges of rights violations that identify them or their group as "perpetrators"; those who have refused to acknowledge particular conditions of rights violations in the past—the "deniers"; and those beneficiaries who profit, financially or in reputation, from conditions of exploitation. These challengers can and do allege that witness narratives are self-interested, self-deluded, and/or manipulated by activists. They raise suspicions about the reliability of the story and the authenticity of the teller to discredit testimonial acts, deflect attention away from questions of perpetrator culpability, repulse international censure, counter media images, and effectively justify inaction.

Suspicious readings can also be generated by parties without a direct investment in a rights campaign, or by journalists and lay people, including rights activists, professional debunkers, cultural commentators, and culture warriors. All these parties can mobilize the vast archives of the internet to fact-check details such as dates, place names, and chronologies, and may assemble an inventory of inaccurate or problematic details to discredit the truth claims of a narrative. For example, interested parties can seize on a few lapses in accuracy in a text as synecdochic evidence that undermines the entire narrative, as occurred with David Stoll's attack on *I, Rigoberta Menchú*.[3] Readers may assert an ethic of verification in a virtual public sphere, as a motive for launching their own online investigations by comparing sources and writing or contributing to blogs on which they question the veracity of a particular text, as Janice Harayda does in her "Review" blog on Ishmael Beah's *A Long Way Gone*.

When testimonial narratives incorporating metrics of authenticity encounter the suspicions of inauthenticity and false witnessing that their use gives rise to, their truth status often becomes, and remains, indeterminate: potent for some, tainted for others, and ambiguous for more than a few. Ultimately, the uneasy equilibrium between attestations to the authenticity of witness narratives and denunciations alleging false witness plays out across networks of invested advocacy that focus on the use of such narratives in redressing situations of harm.

Configurations of the "I" Witness: Who Speaks as "I" in Testimony?

We have explored a set of metrics that ground the aura of authenticity in contemporary narratives of witness, and inquired into how the ethic of verification and detectives of reference may intervene to challenge the reception of these narratives as credible. We turn now to the kinds of "I"s that often occupy the subject position of witness, and consider what implications certain I-formations have for the politics of authenticity. Although the witnessing "I" is normally understood as a singular, if internally conflicted subject, testimonial "I"s, to a greater or lesser extent, claim to represent larger groups in order to tell stories of collective injury or suffering. While testimonies may not use a "we," they speak on behalf of, and at times through, multiple voices. Thus, as G. Thomas Couser and Mark Sanders have observed, the witness "I" is rightly understood as collaborative. But not all collective "I"s are generated through the same kind of interaction with the groups they represent. We need, therefore, to parse further the practices of collective I-witnessing.

Though more may well exist, four rhetorical configurations of witness narratives are prominent in currently circulating texts: the composite "I", the coalitional "I", the translated "I", and the negotiable "I". In the remainder of this essay we explore these "I"-formations through readings of exemplary texts, and consider the implications of how each situates its "I" in acts of witnessing.

The composite "I" is a figure often conflated with the genre of testimony itself, because the speaking subject is often collectively produced by numerous actors positioned across asymmetries of power. These include the witness and the witness's community of affiliation; the intended audience within the narrative; the coaxer or interlocutor, if there is one, usually with another affiliation and access to some means of redress; a group of others including the editor, publisher, and translator of the text; and activist groups, marketers, and the persons, organizations, and forums who have solicited, facilitated, and circulated the act of witnessing. Within this ensemble production, the narrating "I" at once occupies, and is assigned, the subject position of a victim to be rescued. Because this "I"'s apparently coherent narration is often in fact produced by collective "manufacture," it is vulnerable to suspicion, and has frequently been denounced in this digital age as a performance of false witnessing. In *Burned Alive* by "Souad," the story of a subaltern Middle Eastern woman abused in a harshly patriarchal system is narrated in such a way that the consolidation of a composite "I" becomes visible.

Not all witness narratives, however, claim to create a unified subject. Not all are edited and circulated through comparable processes by their publishers. And indeed, not all collective "I"s seek to insert themselves within existing frameworks of testimony and the asymmetrical social relations it establishes. Some radically revise the norms and templates of testimony to forge new genres and structures of witnessing that configure subject positions and discursive strategies differently. When performing these alternative modes of witnessing, they often harness authenticating practices to other ends: they set up complex texts that challenge rescue reading, and they invite readers to engage in structural analysis of the larger conditions that underlie violence, oppression, and suffering. When we turn to the other three formations—the coalitional "I," the translated "I," and the negotiable "I"—further alternative versions of the witnessing "I" emerge signaling that different relationships have been set up between the subject of the story and those positioned as "rescuers" and professionals bringing it to a transnational public.

In this discussion of four kinds of "I"-witnessing, we foreground the range of possible subject positions that first-person collaborative narratives establish, and the range of cross cultural relations that join the subjects of storytelling to those engaged in producing and circulating the story. These subject positions affect how acts of witnessing attempt to forestall suspicious readings, incorporate various metrics of authenticity, and solicit readerly expectations of identification and empathy.

1. The Composite "I" of "Souad"'s Burned Alive

Narratives witnessing to the conditions of women's lives in Islamic nations, including the persistence of honor killing and other repressive cultural and legal practices, have found ready audiences in the Global North over the last decades. Among the best-known of these witness-to-Islamic-oppression memoirs is *Burned Alive*, originally entitled *Brûlée Vive*, published by the French publishing house Oh! Editions in 2003 under the signature of "Souad." The American translation (2004), with the subtitle *A Victim of the Law of Men*, has a striking cover, depicting a woman encased in a white mask that reveals only her glowing eyes. A spectacular success, *Burned Alive* has sold over a hundred thousand copies.

The narrator, "Souad," is a Palestinian woman who recounts growing up in a rural village as one of several daughters constricted by a patriarchal Islamic tradition, embodied in her father and brother. After a liaison with a neighbor who awakens her romantic fantasies, she becomes pregnant. Her father and brother, enraged at the assault on family honor, set her on fire for this transgression. She tells how she was taken to a West Bank hospital where social workers and doctors allegedly refused to help her because the Islamic honor code forbids mercy in such cases. In interspersed chapters, a Swiss social worker, Jacqueline Thibault, narrates how she discovered "Souad" and the baby she gave birth to in squalor, and helped them escape to Lausanne. "Souad" is eventually relocated to France, under an assumed name. Over the course of two decades, "Souad"'s physical health and repressed memories are restored. Her emotional rehabilitation follows, and her narrative concludes with her reunion with the son she had abandoned. Metaphorically, she is reborn with a new European sense of self. "Souad" becomes motivated to speak out against Islamic patriarchal violence on behalf of a Swiss aid organization Fondation SURGIR (dedicated to tracking, rescuing, and advocating for women and child victims of violence worldwide[4]), which, in an afterword, appeals to readers for financial support.

As a witness narrative, *Burned Alive* observes many of the protocols of authenticity. The present-tense narration gives "Souad"'s story a sense of urgency. Her harrowing tale of narrowly escaping death at the hands of her father and brother extends into the narrative present. She states: "I put my life at risk in telling this love story" (75). "Souad" speaks as a representative "victim" of honor killing on behalf of women threatened by death and mutilation at the hands of patriarchal "perpetrators," employing the binary moral grammar of human rights claims. What Whitlock describes as "the tainted conditions for testimony" are reflected in the trauma of her experience and the slippages of memory, both of which are, according to Whitlock, "marks of the interiority and belatedness of trauma that is highly valued in subaltern stories of abuse elicited in human rights activism" (*Soft* 127). *Burned Alive*'s combination of conventional ethnographic details about rural Palestine and its lack of "literariness" contribute to its aura of authenticity.

A peritextual apparatus attests to and produces the authenticity of "Souad"'s witness narrative. Secondary witnessing is incorporated in the narrative through the social worker Jacqueline, who takes over the narrative of the burned and traumatized woman in later chapters of the book (119–50). A western rescuer, she attests to the conditions of "Souad"'s victimization, but also informs readers about the work of the Fondation SURGIR. Her interspersed narrative supplements "Souad"'s inability to remember and witnesses to the aftereffects of trauma, affirming the truth of an often-incoherent narrative by incorporating a psychoanalytic explanation of repressed memory. Epitextual occasions following the publication of *Burned Alive* further enhanced the narrative's aura of authenticity for readers. "Souad'" presented her story on several occasions to live audiences in France. In these performances, a masked "Souad" would expose her scarred hands and recount those parts of the story she could recall, given her loss of memory. Her testimony as an embodied honor-killing victim with the generic name "Souad" intensified the intimacy of the storytelling. Witnessing before live audiences, she literalized the danger associated with the violent story of the memoir.

Both despite, and because of, its layers of authenticating effects, *Burned Alive* has drawn suspicious readings and charges of fabrication. A searing critique was made by historian Thérèse Taylor, who describes it as a sensationalized "drama of endless death," and catalogs its documentary inconsistencies. For example, her research into medical practices in the Palestinian territories suggests that "Souad'"s charge of inhumane medical care cannot be corroborated. For Taylor, *Burned Alive* reproduces in exaggerated fashion the stereotypes of Muslims and of Islamic patriarchy in the Middle East that have increasingly circulated in the Global North over the last two decades.

In addition to the narrative's stereotypic projection of culpable perpetrators, *Burned Alive*'s problematic "authorship" raises troubling questions about who is actually telling this story that the jacket blurb proclaims as "the first true account ever published by the victim of an honor killing." We would argue that the unified "I" called "Souad" is temporally, geographically, and ideologically a composite of several voices that share a specific purpose. The name on the cover, "Souad," promises to bind the autobiographical subject and reader in Philippe Lejeune's pact of the proper name. Yet, that name projects an indeterminate identity of a woman living "somewhere in Europe" (225) who is without a visible "face," anonymous. In this respect she functions as a generalized figure, a stereotypical amalgam of the "Middle Eastern woman." Likewise, the narrative is a storytelling composite, produced by two kinds of collaboration.

Thibault, the rights worker, serves as the agent of rescue, simultaneously an actor, voice for the silenced subject, and NGO mediator. But an unvoiced collaborator is signaled on the title page: Marie-Thérese Cuny, the French editor of and ghostwriter for Oh! Editions, which has published several testimonies of women of North African descent in France, and women from other developing countries.[5] Cuny has acknowledged her hand in coaxing, shaping, and conforming the narrative to a recognizable template of suffering and victimization. Various websites note Cuny's collaboration on different Oh! publications. One states that "[h]er name seldom features on the covers of these books. She prefers to work with unknowns rather than with celebrities" (Hargreaves 53 n.4). The underlying implication is that survivors orally narrate the stories she scripts in the co-production of an "I" that finesses the boundary between oral and written testimony.[6] Asymmetries of power in the process of narrating the experience are obscured, making the question of authorship indeterminate. Thus, this composite testimonial "I" of *Burned Alive* blends the highly stylized victim-voice with those of the social worker, the editor-ghost-writer, the publishing house more generally, and the rescue mission of the Fondation SURGIR.

Alec G. Hargreaves suggests that the Oh! Editions testimonies, and others like them, are "a veritable industry trading on hyped-up negative stereotypes of the Islamic world and its diaspora" (48). Employing professional co-writers and sensationalist marketing tactics, the presses of these popular testimonies generate a composite "I" through a now-familiar script. Their titles boldly reference violations such as gang rape, forced marriage, scapegoating, or honor killing. They are marketed with eye-catching red bands. Many have been widely translated from the French. Charting the "dynamic of dispossession" through which women's stories are brought to the public with the assistance of such intermediaries, Hargreaves observes the ironic relationship of these intermediaries to European readerships. Persuasive precisely because their lack of literariness seems "true," memoirs such as *Burned Alive* capture and feed what Charles Bonn has described as the "sympathetic and unconsciously voyeuristic attention" of reading publics in the Global North (qtd. in Hargreaves 46).

The multiplication of *Burned Alive*'s "authors"—survivor, NGO social worker, editorial ghostwriter, and publishing house—suggests that much "management" has gone into producing its aura of authenticity, raising suspicions about the complicity of the publisher and collaborator in cashing in on the voyeuristic desires of readers for sensationalized narratives of beset womanhood "over there." *Burned Alive*'s status as a witness narrative, emblematic of the many memoirs of Oh! Editions, is troubling, and for some, fatally compromised. The narrative discloses to a skeptical reader an Islamophobic bent that celebrates liberatory compassion in Western Europe, contributing to the global traffic in stereotypes that juxtapose innocent victims to culpable perpetrators of gendered violence.[7]

2. The Coalitional "I" in the Sangtin Collective's *Playing With Fire*[8]
Its claim to an urgent situation of honor-killing in Palestine and to rehabilitation of self and family in the welcoming climate of France marks the composite "I" of *Burned Alive* as a "soft weapon" of testimony, seeking reader rescue through empathy and financial contributions. Its appeal is less to literary audiences than to those seeking rapprochement across geographic, religious, and ideological differences without having to reflect on their own investment in global asymmetry and gender-based subordination. The composite "I" producing "Souad"'s seemingly coherent narrative is a version of what Chimamanda Ngozi Adichie has called "the danger of a single story," a dominant version of the past and a people that homogenizes multiple inconsistent stories. In contrast, the I-formation we call "coalitional" navigates the desire for authentication in testimony while moving beyond rescue reading. In this "I" formation, collaborative production is not suppressed but foregrounded; and the multiple voices of the collaborative "I" are both distinguished and, at times, blended. Our example is

Playing with Fire: Feminist Thought and Activism through Seven Lives in India (2006) by the Sangtin Writers and Richa Nagar.

The Sangtin Yatra (yatra is "a term of solidarity, of reciprocity, of enduring friendship among women" [23]) is comprised of seven women who, at the time of composition, were employed as rural field workers for an NGO in Uttar Pradesh, India, focused on domestic violence and the rights of women in local communities. Over three years, the collective, in collaboration with Richa Singh and Richa Nagar, wrote and shared diary entries, engaged in extended discussions that produced collective reflection, and generated a multilayered text addressing diverse publics.[9] Across their differences of caste and religion, the Sangtin women share and comment on one another's experiences of growing up female, and articulate an analysis of the experience of being female in the family, community, and nation that voices their sense of "woman" as disempowered, unvalued, and suspect, as the following extended citation about their process of conversation and composition clarifies: "When we started reading our diaries to one another," the Sangtin Writers observe,

> we felt that the suffering we endured in our childhoods formed the most critical link that connected all of our lives. But as our conversations deepened, we realized that much more remained to be said and shared. So much of the discussion inside women's NGOs is focused on gender-based violence, but the thoroughness and completeness with which that violence is entangled with and stuck in the violence of casteism, communalism, and class politics is something that we have hardly paid attention to in our past meetings, workshops, and fieldwork. The way all these forms of violence get mingled, blended, and roped into one another; the degree to which these entangled structures of violence are rooted in our histories and present contexts; and the ways in which these understandings of our violent pasts and present must inform our future battles—these are the issues in which we have decided to immerse ourselves. (30)

Thus, the Sangtin analysis is intersectional, linking their gendered position to the experiential axes of economics, politics, sexuality, religion, caste, and class, and tying them relationally to one another. In this process over a few years, the Sangtin women become knowledge-makers and assert authority to "talk back" to the elite women running their NGO.

As their complex narration refuses a "raw" feminized subject position of victimage and emphasizes the survival and strength the Sangtin Writers gained through one another, it projects a degree of collective agency. *Playing with Fire* incorporates multiple layers of text that work to destabilize the priority of an original victim narrative, as it layers several forms: traces of the original diaries, fragments of which introduce each chapter and appear throughout the text; the edited transcripts or discussion about them prepared by editor Richa Nagar; and redrafted overlays. The first completed version, published in Hindi to national controversy, and the translation published by an American university press, with a Foreword by Chandra Talpade Mohanty and an Introduction and Postscript by Nagar, further contextualize the project. These multiple voices and levels of narration move the familiar testimony of abuse based on gender and caste privilege into a new kind of witnessing that does not emanate from a single speaker or experience. Rather, the focus, chapter by chapter, on particular moments that each woman experienced is modified and temporalized by the successive overlays as they revise their stories and blend them into one another's. Furthermore, the assertion expected within the metrics of authenticity that guarantees "truth to experience" is refracted through the conflicting experiences of the text's multiple interwoven "I"s. The Sangtin become a coalition in the process of articulating and constructing their textual voice as they navigate their differences into stories that can address multiple differences among Indian women.

Playing with Fire's coalitional subject, then, emanates from its dispersed focalization and generates a hybrid text that forestalls easy empathy or identification. Its multiple voices and narrators displace the singular narrative center of victimization that affectively binds readers in conventional first-person witnessing. Instead, we encounter a "blended but fractured we" (xxxiv), that, with its slippery personal pronouns, textual layers, and discursive disjunctions, unsettles identification. Sometimes the "blended we" is the seven field worker-diary writers, as in this passage: "Once the words started pouring from our pens and hearts, it was impossible to check their flow" (9). Sometimes it is a collective of nine women, the seven field workers and the two professional women with scholarly skills and credentials, as in the passage cited above. And sometimes it is the collective biographical composer of the narrative of individual field workers, differentiated by their social location and religion, as in the following passage: "For Chaandni, a Muslim working in an organization with a heavy Hindu presence, this matter was slightly different and more complicated. She knew that as soon as they had an opportunity, her people would accuse her of betraying the community" (75).

This fractured "we" resists the asymmetrical power relations that in testimony often join victim to rescuer. The Sangtin "interrogate pre-given notions of what constitutes an expert" (xxxvii), and evade the singularizing of suffering by requiring readers to engage in a larger structural analysis. In sum, *Playing with Fire* short-circuits the feel-good sentimentality of rescue reading by requiring readers to confront the coalition's resistance both to the NGO professionals who reproduce a hierarchy of authority and to conventional expectations of the coherent, unilateral "I" of testimony.

The activist project that produced *Playing with Fire* complicates the metrics of authenticity observed in first-person witness narratives in several ways. The sense of you-are-there immediacy is here mediated by the process of drafts and collaborative revisions in the layered text. Excerpts from the participants' diaries offer glimpses of the intimate voice of each woman, but they are in part overwritten by the coalitional analysis that the women produce in reading and sharing their diary entries. Throughout, the duty to narrate is acknowledged, but the narration, while producing a collective story, persistently attends to and thematizes differences of experience and of religious and caste orientation among the women. While the chapters, organized as topics in their life-cycle experience, confer a unified shape on the story of marginalization, the disaggregation into individual vignettes and analyses in each interrupts the drive toward a representative "subaltern woman's" story of otherness. *Playing with Fire* thus forestalls both transnational identification and speaking for others. The Sangtin women cannot simply be appropriated as victims because their "I"s participate in an action-oriented coalition.

Implicitly, *Playing with Fire*'s strategic, coalitional "I" mounts a critique of how a culture of rescue informs the human rights regime and feminist NGOs active in rights work. As this local project circulates in metropolitan centers and classrooms, it contributes to unsettling the affect of sentiment attached to victim storytelling by challenging readers, workers, and scholars in the Global North to imagine and participate in ethical justice-making without reproducing the justificatory tropes of neediness and victimization.

3. The Translated "I" of the African Child-Soldier Narrative

In the composite "I" and the coalitional "I," a first-person narrator is produced by an ensemble of actors that includes addressees within the narrative who contribute to shaping it either for a specific human rights cause or as a critique of the agents and aims of international rescue work. Further, editors take an active role, covertly ("Souad") or overtly (Sangtin), in determining the ultimate narrative structure of the testimony, as well as its uses with targeted audiences of rescue (though transnational reading publics may bend the narrative to unanticipated purposes and lodge unanticipated critiques). Other models of witness narratives that have widely circulated in the last decade among reading publics marshal different kinds of collective "I"s to navigate and innovate on the strictures of testimonial discourse that have made it vulnerable to suspicions of embellishment or fabrication as hoaxing. We here restrict our focus to one subgenre of testimony, the

African child soldier narrative, and to two foremost exemplars, *A Long Way Gone: Memoirs of a Boy Soldier* by Ishmael Beah (2007) and *What Is the What: The Autobiography of Valentino Achak Deng, a Novel* by Dave Eggers (2008); however, this model is not solely restricted to masculine narratives of immersion in the brutal violence of internecine civil wars.[10] We turn first to *A Long Way Gone*.

In the midst of the civil war in Sierra Leone (1991–2002), which pitted the All People's Congress of the government against the insurgency of the Revolutionary United Front, the adolescent Beah and friends of his who had escaped the devastation of their village and become a band of nomads were, by his account, forced to become child soldiers. In 1996, through the auspices of UNICEF, he was relocated to a rehabilitation center for former child soldiers in Freetown. In 1998 he was again relocated to the United States and placed under the supervision of a rights worker and storyteller, Laura Simms, with whom he subsequently lived. Simms, a cultural historian of folklore, embraced Beah as "my heart's son" (Minzesheimer). While a student at Oberlin College, in a fiction-writing class Beah developed a witness narrative that his professor, David Chaon, helped him bring to Farrar, Straus, and Giroux, a foremost American literary publisher. The narrative was hailed as a groundbreaking story about brutality toward children that the long arm of human rights organizations in the Global North could redress. When it was published, Beah was celebrated in multiple media as an eloquent survivor. His engaging presence helped promote *A Long Way Gone* in bookstores, on college campuses, on many television and radio talk shows, and in YouTube videos, and he became a celebrity spokesperson for Human Rights Watch. The narrative and its gracious author, struggling to communicate his horrifying experience, were showcased on Oprah's "Book Club." The book was marketed as the first book choice at Starbuck's coffee houses, which led to skyrocketing sales and its translation into several languages. With the profits, Beah established the Ishmael Beah Foundation, dedicated to the rehabilitation of children in Sierra Leone,[11] and he continues to work as an advocate on behalf of children's rights, calling for, in his words, "strengthen[ing] international legal standards by . . . prosecuting people who use children in war" (Denton).

In its structure the narrative seems organized to finesse the pitfalls that have dogged victim testimonies. Its "I" is translated from local to international contexts to distill the experience of a collective subject engaged in a process of immersion in conflict and dehumanization of self and others that is doubly mediated by narrative processes. The story itself is told as a kind of conversion narrative, with a moment of enlightened affirmation of shared community following the "dark night of the soul" of participation in brutal acts as a soldier; and the process of telling is presented as an act of self-examination that goes beyond the confession of victimage to the creation of a subject with a degree of agency over his story. Beah's acts of self-translation take place at multiple levels. At a literal level, the narrative translates memories and idioms of retrospection from his childhood language Krio, as well as other tribal languages of Sierra Leone, to communicate in his adopted English. At the metaphorical level, he converts idiomatic figures and tropes of West African traditional storytelling to reshape oral conventions that predominated in his childhood into a linked string of story vignettes crafted for a reading public (see Besemeres, Watson). At the level of reflexive self-presentation, Beah reworks the subject position of victim-narrator through a temporalized narrative voice that reflects on its own history and acknowledges the subjective processes of memory: "These days I live in three worlds: my dreams, and the experiences of my new life, which trigger memories from the past" (20). At the collective level, he speaks as a representative "I" on behalf of his compatriots, friends, and other child soldiers, who either did not survive or were not rescued in the Kenyan refugee camp, as he was. In contextualizing his story as a collective one, he "translates" particulars of experience into a seamless amalgam for the figure of the child soldier, giving voice to a troubled and troubling figure. These multiple and different acts of translation obscure any clear understanding of how this story of an individualized "I" has been managed.

Even as *A Long Way Gone* weaves details into a compelling literary voice, many of its features project an aura of authenticity: the you-are-there intensity of its I-witness narration of constant and inescapable danger; the narrator's commitment to commemorating the dead among his family and friends; the geographic and ethnographic detail of his home village, Yele, and the region; and the self-positioning of the narrator and his friends as "boys" conversant with the styles and attitudes of global youth culture, such as rap music. Incorporated paratexts locate and authenticate the story geographically, with a map at the beginning of the book, and historically, with a timeline of the civil war at its end. In documenting its authenticity, the narrative also thematizes traumatic remembering as a condition of its telling: how memory was repressed by the combination of drugs such as heroin and crack cocaine and the shock of violence; how memory returned in the UNICEF camp with detoxification; and how the horrific events persist in the narrator's current consciousness despite his relocation to the United States. The powerful prose style and reflective voice of *A Long Way Gone* remain persuasive for the narrative's authenticity, as does Beah's own fresh and candid affect in photographs and interviews.

But Beah's translated "I" encountered skepticism of various sorts as *A Long Way Gone* circulated internationally among reading publics. As a double narrator recollecting both his innocent childhood and the brutally awakened, narcotized soldier, as well as the Western-educated narrating adult, he sought to project a transnational ethical appeal on behalf of victims of horrific civil wars. The paradoxical position he spoke from, however, as both a West African perpetrator of bloody civil war and a subject reformed through a Western education in storytelling, formally at Oberlin and informally with Simms, created a complex ethical stance. Given these internal tensions around narration, it is hardly surprising that allegations of false witnessing began to emerge.

In late 2007 and early 2008, *The Weekend Australian* investigated the validity of claims in Beah's story of participating in the civil war, after an Australian couple raised questions about the accuracy of some of its information. *The Australian*'s research and interviews led to the allegation that Beah may have been fifteen rather than thirteen when he was forced into child soldiering; that he may have spent not three years in the Sierra Leone army, but two or three months; and that the battle narrated at the beginning of his book took place two years later than he claimed. In Sierra Leone a local official, Sylvester Basopan Goba, challenged the veracity of Beah's claim that he was conscripted into the military at Yele, implying he went voluntarily, and casting doubt on some of the other events reported. Beah vigorously responded to these allegations of false witnessing in a 2008 press release, as did his publisher and his supporters ("Ishmael"). In an ends-justifies-means argument, Simms, his American sponsor, defended the narrative's alleged discrepancies in chronology by saying: "If you were a kid in a war would you have a calendar with you after you had lost everything and were running through the bush? This young man has literally changed the world and how human beings look at children in war" ("Ishmael").

What is at stake in challenges to the veracity of *A Long Way Gone* is not simply a dispute about the dates and extent of Beah's conscription and similar unverified or incorrect details within the narrative that provoked suspicious readers. One could easily argue that the trauma of forced soldiering can account for warping and compressing a vulnerable child's sense of time. The more serious implication of challenging Beah's age at the time of his conscription is that it would undercut his claim to the identity of child soldier as a victim. We noted earlier that certain kinds of victim identities gain cultural saliency and political force, as stories about particular rights violations circulating transnationally are documented by activists, and the discourse of an authenticated rights identity travels through rights organizations. Perhaps the most potent of these victim identities is "the child," constructed in such documents as the United Nations Convention on the Rights of the Child. As Alexandra Schultheiss observes, in much rights discourse, "the child" is universally recognized as naturally innocent, undeveloped, and emotionally immature, hence incapable of agency in conditions of extremity such as soldiering and thus impossible to position as a perpetrator.[12] This child of humanitarian discourse is in need of rescue, as is childhood itself (32–33). With so much invested in the authenticity of a rights identity, the question becomes: Was Beah in fact a "child" soldier, authentically innocent despite his participation as an agent of violence in the civil war? If so, then Global Northern readers can unproblematically invest, affectively and financially, in this story and herald this witness as an authentic victim deserving humanitarian empathy. But if he is understood as a less innocent adolescent capable of leading others in murderous acts, questions arise that trouble the text, even as it remains widely read and taught as a memoir.

Beah's alleged inconsistencies have not been definitively stigmatized as false witness, in part because, in the absence of official birth records, his age is unfixable, and in the absence of irrefutable documentation, his dates of participation in the war are unverifiable. While his rights identity cannot be irrefutably determined, the taint of the hoax is forestalled because the narrated literariness of *A Long Way Gone* subordinates the metrics of authenticity we have been exploring to the construction of a meditative and self-querying voice. We would argue that the narrating "I" does not take refuge solely in the subject position of child victim. In chapter two, using the present tense, the narrator situates us at once in a scene of violent carnage and in his traumatic nightmare of that scene. By linking the present to the past, he acknowledges his culpability as a soldier in wounding and killing his captives in cold blood (18–20). That is, Beah problematizes for the reader the notion of a fixed subject position for the child victim.

Epitextual conditions may also have worked to mediate charges of falsifying the documentary record. In the intervening years, other child soldier narratives and videos have circulated versions of that experience that, by contrast, confer credence on *A Long Way Gone* despite its possible inconsistencies of fact.[13] More importantly, allegations may not have stuck because Beah's *A Long Way Gone* testifies eloquently to the importance and power of stories and storytelling itself. It opens with a scene, set at his school in the United States, in which he is asked for his story of leaving Sierra Leone. The book that follows is his response to his high school friends' query. Practices of storytelling structure the narrative as a mode of visualizing the traumatic past, recovering cultural and familial traditions, and surviving into the present. There is, then, a double narrative—the personal and collective story of war's devastation, and the story of the efficacy of storytelling. This latter story is not open to allegations of falsification because it does not make truth claims; rather, it relies on the reader's concurrence about the power of stories to imagine possible worlds and effect change.

A Long Way Gone continues to draw and move readers, despite or because of the questionable status of its "truth." In fact, the skepticism expressed about the authenticity of Beah's narrative serves to shore up the universalized identity upon which humanitarian law's assertion of the rights of the child is founded, and implicitly, readers' belief in the legitimacy of Beah's claim to a rights identity. For, there is much at stake in the humanitarian agenda of neoliberalism in this figure of the authentic child soldier. As Schultheiss observes, witnessing by former child soldiers implicitly projects the need for some kind of—usually Northern—global intervention. Romanticizing child soldiers as "wayward products of technological advances in light weaponry, faulty family structures, and postcolonial statehood" positions them, like Africa itself, as wretched and victimized figures in need of rescue (Schultheiss 33). What remains occluded in valorizing this story of a translated "I" resuscitated by the reader's vicarious "rescue effort" is an interrogation of two things: international aid agencies and the politics of civil wars. The marketing of Beah's narrative as a story of lost, violated childhood, but with a "redemptive" ending, and the positioning of Beah as a child "just like" a western child, collapse the real differences between developed nations and war-ravaged ones like Sierra Leone recently created from colonial territories. The individual narrative of loss and redemption also obscures the histories of violence that ensue when international conglomerates extract natural resources and labor, notoriously the "blood diamonds" of Sierra Leone, in a globalized economy.

In sum, because of its translation of oral storytelling into a polished literary memoir, crafted in the individualized voice of the translated "I"'s position, the narrative does not allow access to its compositional process. That is, Beah's narrator is not equipped to resolve the dilemmas that his own witnessing of violence has introduced. Nor is the reader equipped by details that the narrative makes available to form a judgment about the contribution of various hands—village storytellers, creative writing professor, expert folklorist adoptive "mother," editors—in the process of composing the story. Similarly, readers do not have sufficient access to the conditions of its production to distinguish between past experience and the duty to narrate that is imposed by witnessing violence toward the text's unvoiced others. Finally, an examination of details such as dates and ages will not uncover the grounds of truth of the narrative; given its setup, they are undecidable, because the details for their verification are erased from the narrative.

The resilience of *A Long Way Gone* against charges of false witnessing is grounded not primarily in questions of fact, but in a recognition that it navigates complexities of experience and situated memory. Yet, it is important to note that resilience may be more or less potent for different reading publics. Contexts and conditions for narrating testimony vary widely, and what engages a metropolitan audience in the Global North may be suspicious to local readers on the ground. As some West African forums signal, readers in Sierra Leone expressed skepticism, perhaps because some of them actively shared the experience, but also because they are resistant to hegemonic interpretations of specific regional conflicts and suffering that expose cracks in the translated story, and well aware of how the export of locally based stories can be mobilized to enhance Western assertions of ethical superiority.

4. The Negotiable "I" in Dave Eggers's *What Is the What*

While Beah's I, the individualized representative of vulnerable boys, seeks to reach across political conflicts, geographical regions, and differing narrative models and subject positions as a "translated I," Dave Eggers constructs a double subject across the autobiography-novel boundary that as a "negotiable I" traverses problems and contradictions built into the mode of testimonial discourse itself. For this project of witness, Valentino Achak Deng, a "lost boy of Sudan," collaborated with the American writer to inform the public about the fate of the "walking boys" (21). Eggers presents Deng's story, as told to him over the phone and in person, as a novel with the paradoxical subtitle: *The Autobiography of Valentino Achak Deng, a Novel*. The survivor "I" of Deng in the text is thus at once an autobiographical and a fictive "I." By referring to this "I" as a negotiable "I," we focus on how the project emerged out of the back and forth movement between two parallel and relational, but distinct, acts of storytelling. In this ongoing and unfinished collaboration, the two parties are differently situated in the text's mix of autobiographical and fictive discourses. The survivor Deng and the writer Eggers come together across asymmetries of location and access to power, as well as discursive universes of reference, to create a narrative that neither could credibly construct alone. In this negotiable co-construction of testimony, Deng the survivor assigns the work of storytelling to an author, but neither claims exclusive ownership of the story.

The distinctiveness of *What Is the What* is its negotiation with first-person witnessing itself. True, its fictive strategies reproduce the metrics of authenticity common to witness narratives: the "you are there" sense of immediacy; the urgency of telling a collective story of violence and suffering, referenced when Deng as narrator observes, "Written words are rare in small villages like mine, and it is my right and obligation to send my stories into the world, even if silently, even if utterly powerless" (29); the struggle for survival and witnessing of death; the compelling voice of the narrating "I"; and the credibility of the victim position as a "lost boy of Sudan." As narrator, Deng also expresses concern about the difficulty of representing traumatic events: "But thinking, bringing forth any memory at all, causes such searing pain in the back of my skull that I close my eyes and soon lose consciousness again" (27). In reproducing these metrics of authenticity, *What Is the What* intensifies the aura of truth-telling critical to the work of witness narratives in human rights campaigns.

While the use of such metrics seems designed to obscure the doubleness of the "I" by enhancing the illusion of a transparently referential subject of witness, the complex narrative set-up of *What Is the What* both reshapes and undermines the aura of authenticity that the conventions and rhetoric of witnessing seek to secure. As readers, we are addressed directly by Deng in his "Foreword": "The book is historically accurate, and the world I have known is not different from the one depicted within these pages" (xiv). Deng's paratextual commentary confounds the normative relationship of typical witness narratives, in which someone with cultural authority attests to the credibility of the witnessing subject and the truth of the story that follows. Here, in contrast, the survivor of violence and extremity attests to the verisimilitude of the fictional version of the life story presented. As a consequence, *What Is the What* stakes its claim to authenticity in fiction and troubles the ground upon which authenticity is secured. In it, the question of autobiographical truth-telling in testimony to atrocity is aesthetically problematized at the same time as it is ethically resolved (as we will discuss).

The co-production of the collaborative "I" in *What Is the What* is a process of discursive negotiation that informs the entire narrative structure. Its "I" combines the historical experience of Deng's recorded story and the fictive "I" of Eggers's character "Deng" as if they could be collapsed into a singular act of witnessing, yet its title keeps the fictive and the autobiographical modes of narration in constant play. And it highlights that both Deng and Eggers are historical actors as well as storytellers. Importantly, there are two "I"s speaking in the text, at moments distinguishable from each other: the "I" of Deng, with his stories of surviving murder, displacement, hunger, and plans for transformation into a Child Soldier; and the "I" of "Deng," the fictional protagonist of Dave Eggers's novel based on another's "true story." In effect, the focalizing intensity of the singular "I" is simultaneously doubled and displaced, and the location and authority of the speaking subject are fractured and dispersed. As a result, both the witness narrative as a form and the experiential life testified to become ambiguous within current conventions of first-person testimony.

Throughout, *What Is the What* also thematizes the narrative politics of witnessing to histories of violence and suffering. Early in the novel, "Deng" offers a meta-comment on the formulaic quality of narratives of Lost Boys:

> [T]he tales of the Lost Boys have become remarkably similar over the years. Everyone's account includes attacks by lions, hyenas, crocodiles. All have borne witness to attacks by the murahaleen—government-sponsored militias on horseback—to Antonov bombings, to slave-raiding. But we did not all see the same things. . . . But now, sponsors and newspaper reporters and the like expect the stories

> to have certain elements, and the Lost Boys have been consistent in their willingness to oblige. Survivors tell the stories the sympathetic want, and that means making them as shocking as possible. My own story includes enough small embellishments that I cannot criticize the accounts of others. (21)

While referencing the templates of suffering that readers now expect of witnesses to violence, and that advocates, the press, and publishers rely on for international circulation, "Deng" ironically signals his own unavoidable implication in the process.

Later returning to the trope of boys lost to lions, the narrator meditates on how the trope of encounters with lions served to enhance interest in the story of the Sudanese civil war, and yet how "the strangest thing about these accounts is that they were in most cases true" (30). At another point, he highlights storytelling for effect, referencing "the broad strokes of the story of the civil war in Sudan, a story perpetuated by us Lost Boys, in the interest of drama and expediency" (56). Elsewhere, "Deng" makes a parallel between witnessing to the condition of the Lost Boys in Africa and in the United States: as a witness and storyteller he and other young men like him are treated as celebrity victims, yet when they "prove to be a nuisance" they are "ignored" (239). Throughout, Eggers's "Deng" attests to the problematic aspects of cultures of witness and rescue, while Deng's "Deng" recalls the fates of those who did not survive to tell their stories.

The "I" of Eggers's novel and the "I" of Deng's oral account tell stories of "lost" boys and "found" cultures of rescue that are both different and dissonant. As a narrative strategy, Eggers interweaves two distinct temporalities throughout the novel: the time of Deng's experience as a Lost Boy in the Sudan and Kenya, and the later time of Deng's life as an immigrant living precariously in Atlanta after his "rescue" from the Kenyan refugee camp. The experience of violence, survival, and rescue is co-located in seemingly opposed worlds, the United States and the Sudan. The narrative begins in Atlanta, where the immigrant Deng is being held prisoner in his home by burglars; it then shifts to Deng's earlier experience as a "lost boy" in Sudan. The Atlanta story is condensed into several days, while the Sudanese story expands in scope to include many characters and plots, and spans years of wandering. Yet the narratives are structured to highlight parallels in many ways. The invasion of Deng's apartment in Atlanta by burglars is mirrored in the earlier invasion of his home in southern Sudan by rebel troops. The African-American thieves in Atlanta have left a gun-wielding child behind to watch him; in the Sudan, child soldiers, recruited and trained to kill by both northern and southern forces, constantly threaten the wandering children. After Deng survives the burglary, he goes to the emergency room for treatment. Similarly, as refugees in Ethiopia, the roaming children and adults seek medical help to treat injuries, illness, and starvation. Deng's long wait in the Atlanta hospital for treatment and restless wandering after leaving the hospital parallel his lengthy sojourn in refugee camps waiting for something to happen. Just as the police fail to investigate the crime against him in Atlanta, activists struggle without success (at the time of the novel's writing) to have human rights violations in Sudan investigated (471).

Contrary to narratives of rescue and redemption in the Global North, such as those of "Souad" or Beah, *What Is the What* does not conclude with the resolution or relief of rescue in the United States. Rather, it ends with Deng's loss of his defining rights identity. On the one hand, "the Lost Boys of Sudan" fractures as a category of victim identity and identification once the survivors have immigrated to the United States. "Deng" the narrator often remarks on how pathetic the Sudanese lost boys are in the United States, and asks whether these people can be the future of South Sudan: "We are pathetic, I decide. [His friend] is still working in a furniture store, and I am attending three remedial classes at a community college. Are we the future of Sudan? This seems unlikely. . . . Our peripheral vision is poor, I think; in the U.S., we do not see trouble coming" (236). On the other hand, lost boys are everywhere, including in Atlanta the figure of Michael, to whom "Deng" often addresses his narrative. As an African American child caught in urban warfare, Michael is, in fact, a mirror image of Deng in this hall of mirrors.

What Is the What, as a project of negotiation between Valentino Achak Deng and Dave Eggers, both incorporates and interrogates child soldier testimony, and complicates the polarizing of global north and south into static positions. In resituating the informant-interlocutor relationship as an open and dialogic one, it effectively frames first-person testimony within a metanarrative that undoes "America" as a place of rescue. The negotiable "I" of the Eggers-Deng collaboration, in all its asymmetries and reversals, calls for a new way of reading in which "authenticity" is interrogated on multiple levels, and rescue must begin at home. This project of negotiation in constructing a powerful fictional voice for Deng involves what Elizabeth Twitchell terms "Eggers's process of authorial self-annihilation and imaginative becoming" (639). It thus performs for the reader a situated ethics of recognition involving "careful listening, imaginative interpretation, and re-creation" that situates its "truth" not in verifiable accuracy but in "faith in the possibility of Valentino/Deng's truth" (639, 641).

In its attentiveness to storytelling processes as at once experientially based and incorporating fictional strategies, *What Is the What* reframes assumptions about the features of witness narratives and the work they do. In addition to "matching," rather than blending, Deng's and the narrator's versions of the "lost boy" experience, it extends their collaboration into the historical world by dedicating the book's profits to supporting the educational foundation the two men created to improve children's education in South Sudan.[14] It thus both complicates and remediates the framing of global suffering within the narrative, and addresses it as an ethical issue, if one that admits of no easy resolution.

Conclusion: Reader Responses and Responsible Reading

As we have seen, questions of false witnessing need to be contextualized and complicated at this moment when the acts, practices, and production of testimonial narration circulate in contemporary cultures of suspicion. There is no question that fabricated narratives of witness can do harm in the world: they may undermine campaigns for social justice, commodify suffering for personal gain, or contribute to compassion fatigue among readers that fuels skepticism about the claims of victims. But, like testimony itself, the interrogation of false witnessing can also do important work in campaigns for human rights and social justice. As our introduction noted, in cases such as those of Khouri, Gay Girl, or Mortensen, allegations by advocacy groups or journalists of false identity or embellished experience became persuasive enough to undermine the validity, and the moral suasion, of those testimonial projects. Yet they did so in ways that served to validate the necessity of, respectively, women's rights struggles in the Middle East, the rights of gays and lesbians, and the need to educate girls in Afghanistan. We could conclude that scandals around such hoax narratives can affirm that reader-consumers, the marketplace, and the media are alternative jurisdictions (Gilmore) for adjudicating autobiographical testimony, as they intervene on media forums to differentiate legitimate acts of witness and discredit false ones. In other words, an ethic of verification can serve to support the goal of social justice and work potently with the technologies that put vast resources at readers' fingertips, and, through social media, connect communities of readers hunting for the verifiably factual.

We would argue, however, that reading through the lens of verification is ultimately inadequate to adjudicate the truth claims made in heterogeneous cultures and specific contexts of witness. In the name of verification, interested parties can mobilize campaigns that undermine the credibility and authority of witnesses, and thereby undermine urgent claims to expose conditions and experiences of violence and suffering. Furthermore, the tactical use of an ethics of verification to "police" first-person testimony is insufficient to account for the long-term reception of hoaxes, be they addiction narratives, fantasized Holocaust testimony, or rights claims.[15] Despite the protests of a Jordanian human rights group that her story was faked and was hurting their efforts, Khouri's false witness narrative has gotten an afterlife in Australian filmmaker Anna Broinowski's documentary *Forbidden Lies* that both interrogates and refuses to dismiss its claims (see Whitlock, "Remediating"). That is, a paradox at the heart of testimony is that surveilling the "truth" of first-person witness narratives to allay cultural anxieties can in turn exacerbate anxieties—referential, epistemological, and affective. As Jamie Hanneken argues of "minority literature" more broadly, "scandal offers a productive place to examine the economy of minority literature, not only for the starkness but also for the frequency with which it lays bare the expectations behind technologies of recognition and other First-World rituals of recognition" (50). What a call for an ethic of verification does not take into account is that scandals are productive, and not only of profits for their inventors, publishers, and distributors. They also stir public discussion, in forums from rights campaigns to media talk shows and weblogs to college classrooms; that is, they may enhance democratic discussion of complex issues in parts of the developing world, even as they may breed cynicism and propound stereotypes in the Global North.

In the economy and politics of reading, rescue, and rights, controversies about outright fabrication and questions of fact and reference in first-person witnessing can more usefully be approached as complicating our understanding of authenticity, truth claims, and the strategic conventions of first-person witness. As we have seen, the scandals that arise around hoaxes can be salutary in disrupting comfortable protocols of reading. If we consider why certain authenticity effects or metrics aimed at shoring up the demonstrably factual are so persuasive for readers, we can begin to think about the indeterminate status of subjective discourse differently. As our discussions of the "I" in several kinds of first-person testimony suggest, ethical reading practices need not be based primarily on verifying claims of authenticity. Rather, these complex examples deploy various kinds of "I"s that provoke a larger analysis of the intricate locales of production and routes of circulation in contemporary markets, and the asymmetries of power, privilege, and access to reading publics that literary and "non-literary" (ethnographic, formulaic) testimonies travel.[16]

How, then, can we as readers adjust our orientations and assumptions to become responsible and ethical, as well as empathetic, in engaging with first-person witness narrative? As we have seen, specific witness narratives are instructive precisely because witnesses and their advocates must anticipate self-interested and suspicious readings when they enlist readers in what become transnational transactions of recognition. The example of *Burned Alive* suggests that the asserted authenticity of victim experience can be managed and processed by practices of editing and circulation on behalf of multiple parties interested in co-composing a lucrative composite "I." This narration of witness solicits sympathetic readers who are coaxed into suspending critical judgment, and invited instead to respond with uncritical empathy through cross-cultural identification with the subject positioned as victim. While the witness in *Burned Alive* emerges as an individualized center of storytelling dependent upon rescue by and collaboration with professionals, by contrast, the Sangtin collective creates a coalitional "I" in an ensemble production of multilayered storytelling. No one woman's story is situated as representative of a particular rights violation. Far from being just the victims of patriarchal social relations, the women coproduce an analysis of their gendered condition and relations in a narrative resistant to the analytical framing of advocacy professionals.

The "I" that is produced in *Playing with Fire* troubles the notion that those positioned as victims in need of rescue can only be silenced bearers of authentic suffering without agency.

While in these first two examples, the witnesses to conditions of oppression and violence are women engaged with agencies or businesses working on behalf of women's human rights, Beah's *A Long Way Gone* and Eggers's *What Is the What* are testimonial narratives more consciously focused on constructing a literary "I" for international readerships. In both of these cases, testimonial discourse to validate claims to a rights identity is employed in the service of storytelling aimed at credibly engaging transnational audiences. Although the translated "I" of *A Long Way Gone* seems seamlessly sutured, interrogating its amalgamation of languages, locations, political affiliations, subject positions, and ethical identifications reveals slippages as it attempts to weld these positions to both invoke and rescue the "innocent child." The negotiable "I" of *What Is the What* productively disrupts reading habits by requiring us to rethink the formation and location of a narrating "I," as well as who is speaking for whom at various axes of indeterminacy. The Eggers-Deng negotiable "I" thus finds a structure of authorship less vulnerable to charges of fabrication than first-person testimony because it turns on a paradox of fictive truth that unsettles the metrics of authenticity. All of these examples complicate the assumption that a singular "I" either does or does not speak authentically in ways that prompt readers to trouble the notion of authenticity itself.

Why is it important to rethink the position of the witness in relation to authenticity claims, suspicious reading, transnational cultures of rescue, and the ethic of verification? Like Bhaskar Sarker and Janet Walker, we observe the emergence of a new paradigm for framing testimony in life narrative. In this new formation, the subject's position as victim is abated by emphasis on survivors' potential for agency, a focus on geopolitical contexts and constraints, and possibilities for productive narrative intervention. This new paradigm foregrounds more nuanced distinctions among different kinds of collective "I" witnesses, and aims to resolve some of the binds of verification and avowals of authenticity in first-person testimony that have entrapped it in both documentary film and life writing.

As Sarker and Walker suggest about the indeterminacy of testimony as a form, "its power derives more from a pledge of truthfulness and a performance of good faith than from a strict, conclusive evidentiary reliability" (21). New reading frameworks might foreground survivor witnessing and questions of agency in ways that an earlier trauma paradigm relying on the singularity of the "I" and its claim to authentic experience could not account for. They can also enable a reading practice that seeks recognition beyond identification with the individualized story of a "victim," thereby resisting the demand for unquestioning belief that has been complicit in the culture of rescue as a neo-imperial formation supporting Global Northern hegemony. Finally, a new paradigm for reading texts of first-person witness may invite us as readers to acknowledge that we confront a tension, if not an impasse, between our desire for cross-cultural communication to remedy harms and the limitations of our interpretive standpoints, not just locationally but ideologically. Our suggestion is to treat such frameworks and practices as a situated ethic of reading that resists the either-or pull of detection only in the service of verifying the status of "facts."

As this new model of accountability generated by both the achievements and the limits of testimony emerges, we anticipate that the norms and expectations of rhetorical reliability will also shift from the demand for, and the production of, authenticity in acts of witnessing to a focus on formations of first-person testimony that productively exploit its constraints. Similarly, new modes of mobilizing activist campaigns are emerging that may well qualify or even displace the reliance of advocates primarily on first-person witnessing to advance social justice (Muller). Alternative modes and sites of address such as social networking technologies, online and PDA video, and graffiti art now solicit groups of individuals and communities for transnational networks and meshworks around ideas and hopes for change—both taking up and transforming the terms of the work that personal testimony has historically done. As narrators of first-person witness increasingly engage with multiple online forums and media in presenting stories of suffering and violence to international publics, they will surely encounter other obstacles, but also new possibilities for communicating urgent testimony to engaged, judiciously empathic, informed, and proactive reading publics.

Acknowledgements

We are grateful to Gillian Whitlock and Leigh Gilmore for sustained conversations over three years about the impasses and the new possibilities of "hoax" narratives. This essay could not have been generated without both their generous critiques and their perceptive insights.

An early, quite different version of this discussion was published as: "Say It Isn't So: Autobiographical Hoaxes and the Ethics of Life Narrative," in *Life Writing: Autobiography, Biography, and Travel Writing in Contemporary Literature.* The essay's perspectives and positions are extensively informed by Sidonie Smith's coauthored work with Kay Schaffer: *Human Rights and Narrated Lives: The Ethics of Recognition* (2004); and "Human Rights, Narrated Lives and the Position of the Beneficiary" (2006).

We are also indebted to the responsive audiences at conferences where versions of this paper were presented. Venues included the American Comparative Literature Association annual meeting, Brown University, 2012; Franklin College, Lugano, Switzerland, 2011; Department of English, University of Buffalo, 2011; Conference on Life Writing and Human Rights: Genres of Testimony, University of Kingston, United Kingdom, 2011; Symposium on Feminist and Queer Narrative Theories, The Ohio State University, 2011; British Sociological Association Study Group on Auto/Biography, University of Leicester, 2010; International Autobiography and Biography Association conference, Honolulu, 2008;

Department of English, University of Illinois, Urbana-Champaign, 2008; "Writing Life: Truth or Fiction?" conference, University of Lisbon, 2006; Ludwig Boltzmann Institut für Geschichte und Theorie der Biographie, Vienna, 2006; Institute for Ethnology and Folklore, University of Zagreb, Croatia, 2006; "The Theory and Practice of Life Writing: Autobiography, Memoir and Travel Writing in Post/modern Literature" Conference, Halic University, Istanbul, Turkey, 2006; and "Contemporary Narrative Theory: The State of the Field," The Ohio State University, 2003.

We are indebted to the generosity of our home institutions, for Sidonie the University of Michigan and for Julia The Ohio State University, in funding our attendance for some of these presentations. We thank Emily Lind for her support in preparing this essay for publication. And finally, we thank the three reviewers who gave the essay so thorough a reading and who made incisive suggestions that can be seen throughout this final version.

Notes

1 The exposé led to two lawsuits accusing Mortensen of "being involved in a racketeering scheme to turn him into a false hero, defraud millions of people out of the prices of the books, and raise millions in donations to the charity." Other defendants included in the class action suit are his co-author, publisher, and Montana-based charity (Volz).

2 Hoax narratives are by no means peculiar to the present moment of memoir-writing. Indeed, as Susanna Egan discusses, the history of hoaxes stretches as far back as early Christianity. In contemporary, as in older, forms of personal narrative, she observes, "the very concept of imposture depends on readers' concerns with authenticity, sincerity, and intent" (38). For us, autobiographical fabrications and embellishments characterize moments of shift within post-modernity that are marked by mobility, migration, encounter, and changes in the composition of nation-states.

3 Stoll's charge that Rigoberta Menchú fabricated parts of her *testimonio* about the systematic oppression of the Quiché Indians in Guatemala stirred controversy that continues to engage advocates and detractors to this day.

4   Thérèse Taylor provocatively suggests that Fondation SURGIR has links to a right-wing Israeli organization (para 4).
5   Others include *Marieé de force*, by the anonymous "Léila" (2004); *Vivre libre* by Loubna Meliane (2003); *J'ai commencé avec par un joint* (2006) by "Hélène"; *Mutilée* (2005) by Khady; and *Déshonorée* (2006) by Mukhtar Mai, all co-authored by Cuny.
6   Oh! Editions also has an English-language website. One of its recent best-sellers is *Blasphemy!* (2011), a witness narrative by Asia Bibi, a Christian Pakistani woman who was condemned to death for blaspheming Islam by drinking from the Muslim women's cup at the village well.
7   This tropic figuring of "victim" and "perpetrator" can be mobilized as a "soft weapon" in ideological and geopolitical confrontations that pit "rescuing" cultures and nations against rights-violating cultures and nations (Whitlock, *Soft*). And indeed, *Burned Alive* can be seen as a kind of "soft weapon" mobilized in an ideological war in the West against what it regards as "radical" Islam.
8   This discussion of *Playing with Fire* is adapted and expanded from Smith and Watson, *Reading Autobiography* (159–60, 284) and from Smith, "Cultures of Rescue and the Global Transit in Human Rights Narratives" (631–33).
9   Sociologist Nagar revised the collaborative texts, appended an explanatory introduction and conclusion that situates the stories within global conversations about gender, and oversaw the American publication.
10 See, for example, China Keitetsi's *Child Soldier: Fighting for My Life*. Keitetsi's witness narrative has retained its status as credible for several reasons: it contributed to her celebrity as a survivor of radical suffering, and it launched her career as an international spokesperson for the rights of the child—a podium from which she could both counter her critics and establish her own authority as an informant, buttressed by the approval of human rights giants such as Nelson Mandela. The book found reading audiences throughout Europe. It raised awareness and mobilized other activists on behalf of children forced into military service at a moment of critical need. It reconfirmed faith in human rights advocacy and "fit" the model for popular consumption in the West.
11 The US Internal Revenue Service asserts that taxes on the income netted by the Ishmael Beah Foundation have not been paid for several years.
12 Julia Emberley also discusses the "complicities of innocence" that narratives in film, theatre, and literature exploit to circumscribe and

overdetermine the subject position opened up by this discursive construction of childhood (380–81).

13 These include Dave Eggers's *What Is the What*; YouTube videos such as "Kony 2012" (Halliday); films such as *Blood Diamond* that represent child soldiers as drugged puppets brutalized by warlords and mercenaries; and African novels, including Uzodinma Iweala's *Beasts of No Nation* (which won the 2006 John Llewellyn Rhys prize) and Chris Abani's *Song for Night*. Other events and activist projects include the Invisible Children campaign to end violence in Uganda. This project is a collaborative effort of youth from around the world: "We are story tellers. We make documentaries about war-affected children in east Africa and tour them around the world" ("Invisible Children").

14 According to the foundation website, the Marial Bai Secondary School opened in Deng's hometown in 2009, although the Sudan-South Sudan conflict may make its future uncertain.

15 Consider that Frey's *A Million Little Pieces* saw increased sales and reader enthusiasm after it was exposed as invented, Wilkomirski's narrative was reissued as a novel, and decades ago, Jerzy Kosinski's *The Painted Bird*, also alleged to be embellished, was one of the most widely read early narratives of suffering in the death camps. Readers of such texts repeatedly attest to the powerful affect of such stories, and profess that they changed their behaviors.

16 We recognize that there is an essay to be written on the differences in the conditions of production of witness narratives; the degree of intervention in the telling of the story by multiple players such as editors and publishers and activists; and the erasure or foregrounding of that metanarrative process.

Works Cited

Abani, Christopher. *Song for Night: A Novella*. New York: Akashic, 2006. Print.

Adichie, Chimamanda. "The Danger of a Single Story." *TED Talk*. July 2009; posted 2009. Web. 4 Jan. 2013.

Beah, Ishmael. "Ishmael Beah's Statement to the Press, January 2008." Farrar, Straus, and Giroux. 22 Jan. 2008. Web. 22 June 2012.

———. *A Long Way Gone: Memoirs of a Boy Soldier*. New York: Farrar, Straus, and Giroux, 2007. Print.

Besemeres, Mary. *Translating One's Self: Language and Selfhood in Cross-Cultural Autobiography*. New York: Peter Lang, 2002. Print.

Bibi, Asia. *Blasphemy: The True, Heart-Breaking Story of the Bibi Woman Sentenced to Death Over a Cup of Water*. Paris: Oh! Editions, 2011. Print.

Blood Diamond. Dir. Edward Zwick. Perf. Leonardo DiCaprio, Djimon Hounsou, and Jennifer Connelly. Warner Bros., 2006. Film.

Couser, G. Thomas. "Making, Taking, and Faking Lives: The Ethics of Collaborative Autobiography." *Literary Ethics*. Spec. issue of *Style* 32.2 (Summer 1998): 334–50 Print.

Cubilié, Anne. *Women Witnessing Terror: Testimony and the Cultural Politics of Human Rights*. New York: Fordham University Press, 2005. Print.

Cvetkovich, Ann. *An Archive of Feelings: Trauma, Sexuality, and Lesbian Public Cultures*. Chapel Hill: Duke University Press, 2003. Print.

Denton, Andrew. "Ishmael Beah." *Enough Rope with Andrew Denton*. ABC. 12 Nov. 2009. Web. 17 June 2012.

Ebadi, Shirin, with Azadeh Moaveni. *Iran Awakening: A Memoir of Revolution and Hope*. New York: Random House, 2006. Print.

Egan, Susanna. *Burdens of Proof: Faith, Doubt, and Identity in Autobiography*. Waterloo, ONT: Wilfred Laurier University Press, 2011. Print.

Eggers, Dave. *What Is the What: The Autobiography of Valentino Achak Deng: A Novel*. San Francisco: McSweeney's, 2006. Print.

Emberley, Julia V. "A Child Is Testifying: Testimony and the Cultural Construction of Childhood in a Trans/National Frame." *Journal of Postcolonial Writing* 45.4 (Dec. 2009): 378–88. Print.

Frey, James. *A Million Little Pieces*. New York: Doubleday, 2003. Print.

Gbowee, Leymah with Carol Mithers. *Mighty Be Our Powers: How Sisterhood, Prayer, and Sex Changed a Nation at War*. New York: Beast, 2011. Print.

Gilmore, Leigh. "Jurisdictions: *I, Rigoberta Menchú*, *The Kiss*, and Scandalous Self-Representation in the Age of Memoir and Trauma." *Signs* 28.2 (Winter 2003): 695–718. Print.

Halliday, Josh. "Kony 2012 Documentary on Ugandan Warlord is Unlikely Viral Phenomenon." *The Guardian* 8 Mar. 2012. Web. 18 June 2012.

Hanneken, Jaime. "Scandal, Choice and the Economy of Minority Literature." *Paragraph* 34.1 (2011): 48–65. Print.

Harayda, Janice. "Ishmael Beah's 'A Long Way Gone' Is 'A Long Way From Truth,' Sierra Leonean Magazine Says in a Report That Raises 'Serious Doubts' About Its Story." *One-Minute Book Reviews* 16 July 2009. Web. 17 June 2012.

———. "Ishmael Beah Foundation Didn't File Tax Returns for 3 Years, IRS Says / Revokes Exemption for 'A Long Way Gone' Author's Group." *One-Minute Book Reviews* 8 Apr. 2012. Web. 17 June 2012.

Hargreaves, Alec. "Testimony, Co-Authorship, and Dispossession among Women of Maghrebi Origin in France." *Research in African Literatures* 37.1 (2006): 42–54. Print.
Hélène. *J'ai commencé par un joint*. Paris: Oh! Editions, 2006. Print.
Hesford, Wendy S. "Documenting Violations: Rhetorical Witnessing and the Spectacle of Distant Suffering." *Biography* 27.1 (Winter 2004): 104–144. Print.
Hsu, Hua. "The Fraud Squad." *BookForum* Feb/Mar 2009. Web. 22 June 2012.
Invisible Children. *Invisible Children*. nd. Web. 22 Mar. 2011.
Iweala, Uzodinma. *Beasts of No Nation: A Novel*. New York: HarperCollins, 2005. Print.
Keitetsi, China. *Child Soldier: Fighting for My Life*. Johannesburg: Jacana Media, 2002. Print.
Khady. *Mutilée*. Paris: Oh! Editions, 2005. Print.
Khouri, Norma. *Forbidden Love: A Harrowing True Story of Love and Revenge in Jordan*. London: Doubleday, 2003. Print.
"Kony 2012." *YouTube*. 5 May 2012. Web. 22 Jun 2012.
Kosinski, Jerzy. *The Painted Bird*. Boston: Houghton Mifflin, 1964. Print.
Kyi, Aung San Suu. *Letters From Burma*. London: Penguin, 2010. Print.
Léila. *Marieé de Force*. Paris: Oh! Editions, 2004. Print.
Liu Xiabo. *No Enemies, No Hatred: Selected Essays and Poems*. Cambridge, MA: Harvard University Press, 2012. Print.
Maathai, Wangari. *Unbowed: A Memoir*. New York: Anchor, 2007. Print.
Mackey, Robert. "Gay Girl in Damascus Blogger Admits Writing Fiction Disguised as Fact." The Lede. *New York Times* 13 June 2011. Web. 17 June 2011.
Mai, Mukhtar. *Déshonorée*. Paris: Oh! Editions, 2006. Print.
Méliane, Loubna. *Vivre libre*. Paris: Oh! Editions, 2003. Print.
Menchú, Rigoberta. *I, Rigoberta Menchú: An Indian Woman in Guatamala*. Ed. Elisabeth Burgos-Debray. Trans. Ann Wright. London: Verso, 1984. Print.
Minzesheimer, Bob. "War-torn Childhood 'A Long Way Gone,' But Not Forgotten." *USA Today* 14 Feb. 2007. Web. 17 June 2012.
Mortenson, Greg. *Stones into Schools: Promoting Peace with Education in Afghanistan and Pakistan*. New York: Viking, 2009. Print.
Mortenson, Greg, and David Oliver Relin. *Three Cups of Tea: One Man's Mission to Promote Peace . . . One School at a Time*. New York: Penguin, 2006. Print.
Muller, Mark. "The Importance of Taking and Bearing Witness: Reflections on Twenty Years as a Human Rights Lawyer." *We Shall Bear Witness*. Madison, WI: University of Wisconsin Press, 2014, 257–64.
Sanders, Mark. "Theorizing the Collaborative Self: The Dynamics of Contour and the Contour and Content in the Dictated Autobiography." *New Literary History* 25 (1994): 445–58. Print.

Sangtin Writers and Richa Nagar. *Playing with Fire: Feminist Thought and Activism through Seven Lives in India*. Minneapolis: University of Minnesota Press, 2006. Print.

Sarker, Bhaskar, and Janet Walker. *Documentary Testimonies: Global Archives of Suffering*. New York: Routledge, 2009. Print.

Schaffer, Kay, and Sidonie Smith. *Human Rights and Narrated Lives: The Ethics of Recognition*. New York: Palgrave Macmillan, 2004.

———. "Human Rights, Storytelling, and the Position of the Beneficiary: Antjie Krog's *Country of My Skull*." *PMLA* 121.3 (2006): 1577–1584. Print.

Schultheis, Alexandra. "African Child Soldiers and Humanitarian Consumption." *Peace Review* 20.1 (2008): 31–40. Print.

Smith, Sidonie. "Cultures of Rescue and the Global Transit in Human Rights Narratives." *Handbook of Human Rights*. Ed. Thomas Cashman. London: Routledge, Taylor and Francis Group, 2012. 631–33. Print.

Smith, Sidonie, and Julia Watson. *Reading Autobiography: A Guide for Interpreting Life Narratives*. 2nd ed. Minneapolis: University of Minnesota Press, 2010. Print.

———. "Say It Isn't So: Autobiographical Hoaxes and the Ethics of Life Narrative." *Life Writing: Autobiography, Biography, and Travel Writing in Contemporary Literature*. Ed. Koray Melikoğlu. Stuttgart: Ibidem Verlag, 2007. 15–34.

Souad. *Brûlée Vive*. Paris: Oh! Editions, 2003. Print.

———. *Burned Alive: A Victim of the Law of Men*. Trans. Judith Armbruster. New York: Warner, 2004. Print.

Stoll, David. *Rigoberta Menchú and the Story of All Poor Guatemalans*. Boulder, CO: Westview, 1999. Print.

Taylor, Thérèse. "Truth, History, and Honor Killing: A Review of *Burned Alive*." AntiWar.com 2 May 2005. Web. 17 June 2012.

Twitchell, Elizabeth. "Dave Eggers's *What Is the What*: Fictionalizing Trauma in the Era of Misery Lit." *American Literature* 83.3 (Sept. 2011): 622–47. Print.

Valentino Achak Deng Foundation. *The Valentino Achak Deng Foundation*. nd. Web. 22 June 2012.

Volz, Matt. "Greg Mortenson Scandal Over 'Three Cups Of Tea' Bears Resemblance To James Frey Scandal." *Huffington Post* 9 Feb. 2012. Web. 21 June 2012.

Watson, Julia. "Autoethnography, Performance, and the Metrics of Authenticity in Trans-American Ethnicity Debates: The Case of *When I Was Puerto Rican*." *Life Writing* 10:2 (June 2013), 129–50. Print.

Whitlock, Gillian. "Remediating the Hoax." *Australian Feminist Studies* 26.69 (2011): 349–67. Print.

———. *Soft Weapons: Autobiography in Transit*. Chicago: University of Chicago Press, 2007. Print.

Wilkomirski, Binjamin. *Fragments: Memories of a Wartime Childhood*. Trans. Carol Brown Janeway. New York: Schocken, 1996. Print.

Part II
Everyday Lives and Autobiographical Storytelling

4
INTRODUCTION TO *GETTING A LIFE: THE EVERYDAY USES OF AUTOBIOGRAPHY* (1996)

Social life multiplies the gestures and modes of behavior (im)printed by narrative models; it ceasely [sic] reproduces and accumulates "copies" of stories. Our society has become a recited society, in three senses: it is defined by stories (récits, the fables constituted by our advertising and informational media), by citations of stories, and by the interminable recitation of stories.
      Michel de Certeau, The Practice of Everyday Life[1]

[Identity] is found in all the properties—and property—with which individuals and groups surround themselves, houses, furniture, paintings, books, cars, spirits, cigarettes, perfume, clothes, and in the practices with which they manifest their distinction, sports, games, entertainments, only because it is in the synthetic unity of the habitus, the unifying generative principle of all practices. Taste, the propensity and capacity to appropriate (materially or symbolically) a given class of classified, classifying objects or practices, is the generative formula of a life-style.
      Pierre Bourdieu, Distinction[2]

> *The opacity of the everyday, then, is crucial. It reflects the poststructural recognition that all anyone can do is gesture to the real; subjects cannot experience it unmediated and untransformed by expectation, by representation, or by their own attention to it. In resisting definition, the everyday becomes a category that foregrounds those mediations and, in that sense, becomes a position or marker rather than a stable referent.*
>
> Laurie Langbauer, "Cultural Studies and the Politics of the Everyday"[3]

Reciting Postmodern Lives

In a column for the *New York Times*, William Safire, exploring, as is his wont, language usage in the contemporary United States, discussed a glib and sometimes dismissive phrase from the 1980s and early 1990s, "Get a life." "Get a life" functions as a corrective to someone's excessive complaining, or their failure to extract themselves from repetitive takes on the world, or their self-absorbed preoccupations. In effect, it is simultaneously an indictment of the interlocutor's everyday life, a testimony of the speaker's belief in a realizable agenda for change, and a self-validating gesture.[4] After all, in their use of the phrase speakers imply that they know what a viable life is and that they have gotten one.

The casualness of the directive suggests that there is a broader cultural phenomenon that charges the phrase with its potent, if flip, meanings. Not only do autobiographical narratives permeate capitalism's marketplace, in our time they overflow our everyday life. On a daily basis we all act as if we're getting a life.

Americans are, to invoke the epigraph above from Michel de Certeau, a "recited" community in all three senses of his term. We are habitual authenticators of our own lives.[5] Every day we are confessing and constructing personal narratives in every possible format: on the body, on the air, in music, in print, on video, at meetings.

Political candidates work up compelling personal narratives that project "character" and "values." Some, like Ross Perot, rely on them.

Daytime television talk shows spill over with confessional obsessions.

In every community the formulaic confessions of participants in self-help groups fill the halls of churches and the meeting rooms of numerous communal buildings.

Rock singers chant the lyrics of self-promotion.

People don identity clothing in the morning to signify status, origin, occupation, political consciousness, availability.

Family members assemble stories through family albums.

Some respond to queries about their medical histories.

Others fill out innumerable forms for social service benefits.

Many advertise their desires in personal ads.

If we are not telling our stories, we are consuming other people's lives. Consuming personal narratives on an everyday basis, we imbibe the heterogeneous "lives" authorized by and authenticated in the institutions through which we negotiate daily existence. Media, for instance, offer a dazzling display of possible lives through daytime television, the movies, the news, and social media. The news frames its selected fragments of autobiographies of political candidates that are shaped by the institutions of official politics as permissible life stories.

Through our consuming habits we circulate our own personal narratives, even by the cars we drive, the beverages we drink, and the furnishings with which we surround ourselves, as Bourdieu has observed. By wearing particular items, by wearing them in particular ways, or by making a pastiche of recognizable identity gear, we telegraph "probable" autobiographical stories. We make icons of ourselves through identification with consumer brands that constitute ready-made, wholesale identities. Women, men, children, grandparents, environmental activists elect recognizable identities and circulate the probable histories they suggest.

In postmodern America we are culturally obsessed with getting a life—and not just getting it, but sharing it with and advertising it to others. We are, as well, obsessed with consuming the lives that other people have gotten. The lives we consume are translated through our own lives into story. Getting a life is a necessary negotiation in the everyday practice of American culture/s.[6]

A word of clarification: the term *postmodern* here is used not to define a set of aesthetic practices and effects as distinct from modernist practices and effects (as implied in the term *cultural postmodernism*) or to define a set of practices to be deployed in what Nelly Richard terms "a critical rereading of modernity."[7] Rather, we use it to acknowledge what Inderpal Grewal and Caren Kaplan term "the historical situation of postmodernity."[8] This historical situation is characterized by the global reach of late commodity capitalism, the widespread bureaucratization of all aspects of corporate life, the digital communications networks that are altering notions of time and space, the condition of "cultural asymmetries,"[9] and the interrogation of received concepts of a universal, rational, and autonomous humanist self.

"America" and Me

> *They live it and I see it and I hear it. They repeat it and I hear it and I see it, sometimes then always I understand it, sometime then always there is a completed history of each one by it, sometime then I will tell the completed history of each one by it, sometime then I will tell the completed history of each one as by repeating it I come to know it.*
>
> *Every one always is repeating the whole of them.*
>
> Gertrude Stein, *The Making of Americans*[10]

> *All profound changes in consciousness, by their very nature, bring with them characteristic amnesias. Out of such oblivions, in specific historical circumstances, spring narratives. . . . Out of this estrangement comes a conception of personhood,* identity . . . *which, because it cannot be "remembered," must be narrated.*

Against biology's demonstration that every single cell in a human body is replaced over seven years, the narratives of autobiography and biography flood print-capitalism's markets year by year.
   Benedict Anderson, Imagined Communities[11]

Autobiographical narratives, their citation, and their recitation have historically been one means through which the imagined community that was and is America constitutes itself on a daily basis as American.[12] As one potent means of testimony through which identities are constituted and critiqued, autobiographical storytelling has played a major role in the making of Americans and the making, unmaking, and remaking of "America." For several centuries, America has been a desirable destination for certain groups of people, a promising place where people have come to get a new life, to re/form and to remake themselves as social subjects "free" of a variety of constraints they experienced in the cultures and locations they left behind. For some people the promise proved a dismal disappointment. For many it proved a problematic achievement for themselves even as it proved a palpable if complex achievement for their children. For others, however, the journey was a radical rupture of unmaking. For African slaves, transportation to the New World brought diasporan dispersal and a long, arduous, and violent struggle for inclusion in the American promise. And for the peoples who inhabited the American landscape before settlement, the making of America and Americans was tantamount to cultural, even literal, genocide.

America became a nation as those preconditions Benedict Anderson has identified as prerequisites of the imagining of nation and national identity in the West coalesced:

the proliferation of print capitalism's reproductions of vernacular texts;

the new notion of time as a vacuum to be filled with evolutionary history;

the Enlightenment concept of the universal human subject; and

the imagination of a social community constituted of individuals who do not know one another, live far from one another, but are joined in an imagined society.[13]

All of these conditions also characterize the imagining of "autobiographical" lives as possessions of "individuals" and of individual lives as "representative" of a community of lives. Autobiographical storytelling, therefore, functioned personally and publicly in related but distinct ways. The private and unique individual proclaimed representative status through a life worthy of inspection, summation, and print. But the very gesture of proclamation became one means by which national mythologies produced the conformity of individuals to new notions of identity and normative concepts of national subjectivity. Writing autobiography testified to arrival in "America" and the achievement of an "American" identity.[14]

Yet if autobiographical storytelling has functioned as a means to assert identification with the idea of "America" and what it means to be an "American" subject, it has also exposed what Donald Pease calls the "postnational" and what we would call the "unnational" subject.[15] Think, for instance, of Crèvecoeur's celebration of the American character as a moral enlightenment universally accessible to those who immigrated.[16] This very articulation of the "American" character also exposed a set of differences between such a subject and all its self-constituting others. That exposure opened a gap between the ideology of subjectivity assigned the new Republican subject and the cultural erasure of those assigned nonsubject or noncitizen status, including, early on, the African slave, the Native American, the white woman, the white man of no property, the child.[17] For such persons, autobiographical narrative provided an opportunity to negotiate their complex positioning within and without the corporate sphere.

Autobiographical discourse continues, to a considerable extent, to be a palpable means through which Americans know themselves to be American and not-American in all the complexities and contradictions of that identity. Its forms, both those officially endorsed and those at times sought by individuals apparently as subversive personal versions, are means to align the privatized consciousness with identities credited in the public sphere and to glimpse and critique the misidentifications of that alignment. Some of those narratives get identified as "high cultural achievements" and subsequently are canonized in educational curricula as "the best" or "most representative" or "most American." Others, the more popular or "low" forms, such as the plethora of narratives by the rich and variously famous and infamous, circulate through lending libraries, publishers' lists, and book-of-the-month clubs, e-books, providing everyday "dreams," everyday eavesdroppings.[18] Personal histories—in all their varieties—serve as individualized testimonies to getting a "successful" life together (however success is defined) and/or to the failure of self-remaking in terms of the dream.

Modern Subjects and Bad Faith in "Democracy"

Another side of the deficiency of general historical life is that individual life as yet has no history. The pseudo-events which rush by in spectacular dramatizations have not been lived by those informed of them. . . . What is really lived has no relation to the official irreversible time of society and is in direct opposition to the pseudo-cyclical rhythm of the consumable by-product of this time. This individual experience of separate daily life remains without language, without concept, without critical access to its own past which has been recorded nowhere. It is not communicated. It is not understood and is forgotten to the profit of the false spectacular memory of the unmemorable.
                            Guy Debord, *Society of the Spectacle*[19]

This brief history characterizes several centuries of "modern" narrative in America, particularly as it has contributed to the formation of an idea of "American" character. But the obsessive desire to create and authenticate individual identity characteristic of our times is a peculiar preoccupation at this historical moment, for our "postmodern" culture everywhere offers evidence of two contradictory dispositions: on the one hand, modern democratic culture continues to privilege individuality and the sovereignty of a human subject with certain inalienable rights; on the other, many who share this modern culture profoundly distrust traditional autobiography, one of the narrative forms through which the West sustains its romance with individualism and promotes a universal, representative subject.

The paradox of radical individualism haunts the contemporary United States. We mistrust it, yet want to believe in it. Democracy as a political ideal is one that even ardent postmodernists finally confess to admiring, whether romantically or radically. Yet the paradoxes of the "American character" and of bourgeois individualism require us to ask questions that strike at the heart of democratic individualism:

What does the right to privacy mean in a world of fragmented and dispersed subjects?

What does it mean to insist on a culture of individuals whose very individuality must be authenticated again and again?

What kind of autobiographical subjects are produced and verified in a culture that commodifies self-authentication?

How does commodification operate at a time when the bases of authentication seem unstable?

How do we account for the simultaneous promise and corrosion of identity and identity politics? For the promise of subject formation and the disillusion of deformation?

How can we account for the obsessive desire to find a "true" self in the midst of a culture that fetishizes what we might call touristic identities, throwaways?

Michel de Certeau argues that we are members of "a society in which the disappearance of subjects is everywhere compensated for and camouflaged by the multiplication of the tasks to be performed."[20] We might paraphrase his remark by suggesting that *we are a postmodern society in which the disappearance of an unproblematic belief in the idea of true selves is everywhere compensated for and camouflaged by the multiplication of recitations of autobiographical stories.* As social relations undergo major realignment, as indigenous communalisms contest the notion of a corporate "We the People," as bureaucracies gather and organize information about an increasing proportion of our lives, as telecommunications networks and social media broadcast ready-made identities, *this telling and consuming of autobiographical stories, this announcing, performing, composing of identity becomes a defining condition of postmodernity in America.*

Because of this intimate relationship of America with the remaking of lives, with a proliferation of heterogeneous autobiographical narratives, with, that is, the romance of democratic individualism, we want to look more closely at the ways in which people in America today negotiate everyday lives through the recitation of everyday "lives."

Composing and Decomposing

As pieces of our stories are regularly and anonymously dispersed to the files and archives of various institutions, we may feel less confident about both our privacy and the protection of governmental and corporate institutions. Decentralization and dispersion of autobiographical subjects attends the bureaucratization of life stories in postmodern culture/s. Our personal histories are

> dismembered into zeroes and ones;
> passed through electrons;
> stored on microchips;
> channeled throughout the local community, the nation, even the world;
> and stored on paper in file drawers and in files in the cloud.

And they are there for the taking by a host of unknown entities, including computer hackers.

Such fragments of our personal narratives become bits and bytes of a proliferating number of data banks. Each data bank parcels out pieces of our personal histories, converts them to different forms, aligns various subsets of fragments into different "stories" or recitations. Consider the languages of the "profile": the medical history, the work history, the credit history, the educational history, the testing history, the psychological profile. All these profiles provide various occasions and versions of our story/ies. As a consequence, a profile becomes a form of otherness; the collection and dispersal of the profile, a form of othering. *Collecting autobiographical data is, perversely, a central instrument in the othering machinery of modern technological culture.*

The Myth of Fingerprints and Imposed Systems

> *The notion of essence, character, structure, is, one might argue, social . . . expression in the main is not instinctive but socially learned and socially patterned; it is a socially defined category which employs a particular expression, and a socially established schedule which determines when these expressions will occur. . . .*

We are socialized to confirm our own hypotheses about our natures.
Erving Goffman, *Gender Advertisements*[21]

The myth of autobiography is

>that the story is singularly formative,
>that the gesture is coherent and monologic,
>that the subject is articulate and the story articulable, and
>that the narrative lies there waiting to be spoken.

But autobiographical storytelling, and by this we mean broadly the practices through which people assemble narratives out of their own experiential histories, cannot escape being dialogical, although its central myths resist that recognition. Autobiography is contextually marked, collaboratively mediated, provisional. Acknowledging the dialogical nature of autobiographical telling, we confront the ways in which autobiographical telling is implicated in the microbial operations of power in contemporary everyday life.

In telling their stories, narrators take up models of identity that are culturally available. And by adopting ready-made narrative templates to structure experiential history, they take up culturally designated subjectivities. Their recitations of personal narrative thereby attest to and verify their participation in corporate culture. Becoming a social subject paradoxically sustains the articulation of the "private" individual in our time, when all forms of privacy are so extensively mediated. In getting a life, then, whose life are we getting?

Everyday autobiographical practices are enmeshed in the technologies of selfhood dispersed across a heterogeneous field of institutional locations, all with their own pressures to regulate subjects through reforming them—in both senses of the word—in specific ways.²² There are state-sponsored bureaucracies designed to manage people and facilitate their movement through state institutions. There are numerous non-state organizations, such as churches and self-help groups, hospitals and talk shows, which provide localized sites through which certain kinds of subjects are recognized and misrecognized. There are the intimate spaces of the family and of sexual exchange. On a daily basis individuals move into, through, and out of these disparate social spaces, and participate in specific, yet different, narrative practices through which we become subjects in and of our stories.

Recitations of our personal narratives, that is, are embedded in specific organizational settings and in the midst of specific institutional routines or operations:

Religious confession goes to church.
Psychological trauma goes to the counselor's office or the analyst's couch.
Social victimization and economic impoverishment go to social service agencies.
Medical history goes to the hospital.
Political oppression goes to the immigration bureau.

But in taking our stories into various venues, we enter what de Certeau terms an "imposed system." Each location manages a specific piece of our lives and calls for specific kinds of personal recitations.

The hospital manages health and illness.
The immigration bureau manages the selection and orderly entry of immigrants and refugees into the country.
Religious organizations designate the saved and manage the orderly pursuit of spiritual health.

The classified section of the newspaper manages the telescoping of salable information to the customer.

A therapeutic community such as Alcoholics Anonymous manages the (re)habilitation of an alcohol-free body.

Only certain kinds of stories need be told in each narrative locale. *Only certain kinds of stories become intelligible as they fit the managed framework, the imposed system. The recitation is, in effect, prepackaged, prerecited.* In this way, the institution writes the personal profile, so to speak, before the person enacts and experiences it as "personal."

It is a familiar fact of contemporary life that institutions—as opposed to specific individuals working in the institutions—are less concerned with persons who enter their locales than with their own inerrant stability, with maintaining efficient performance of designated tasks. The institution can work efficiently only if it imposes structures of legible subjectivity, and that work can be done only on particular kinds of subjects. Institutional needs frame the specific "reading" of the disparate details and facts of the life recited by the subject; in so doing, they frame information selectively. The process works synecdochally, substituting the part for the whole and claiming that they are interchangeable. Those acting on behalf of the institution promote an official reading of the life to fit their institutional parameters. *Thus, in everyday life, autobiographical narratives are part of a frame-up.*

When we interact with these institutions we engage their already provided narratives of identity, their already mapped-out subject positions.

Men and women seeking divorce enter courts in which they have to create macronarratives of their marriages that are recognizable in terms of a particular state's codes of intelligibility.

People will be represented differently if "irreconcilable differences" constitutes permissible grounds for divorce than if only "mental cruelty" is admissible.

Rape victims present their personal narratives of the body in specific ways before the law and the courts. Engagement in sexual conduct in the past may contaminate the profile of the ravished maiden necessary for vigorous prosecution.

People seeking social service benefits have to present themselves as victims. This requires arranging one's life history so as to appear impoverished enough to make a convincing appeal.

In these and other social situations people assume positions as actors within known scripts. Successful achievement of their goals and interests depends on the right alignment of many kinds of evidence, including that of the body itself. Erving Goffman elaborates this evidentiary nature of display (linguistic, bodily, gestural) when he writes that "displays . . . provide evidence of the actor's *alignment* in a gathering, the position he seems prepared to take up in what is about to happen in the social situation."[23] *Autobiographical narrative is one such performative display.*

These everyday occasions, and the practices attached to them, function as one form of "discipline" in the Foucauldian sense. They are among the many means by which models of acceptable identity are circulated and renewed in society, the many means by which subjects are conformed. Through them the state, the church, the school, the corporation, the government, the advertising industry secure normative subjects in acceptable social relationships. Such everyday practices also function to establish cultural conditions determining

> who can speak,
> what can be spoken,

what narrative forms can be understood, and
to whom personal narrative can be addressed.

By these means, everyday practices determine not only the spoken but the unspoken:

what subject cannot speak,
what part of a personal story cannot be spoken, and
what kind of story cannot be understood or credited.

But we too participate in and represent various institutions. We too are advocates of known scripts, even as we are imbricated in them. In everyday life we negotiate the terms in which others will present their lives to us—be it as our students, employers, or, more complexly, our friends, families, and lovers. In this way we not only act out our alignment but solicit alignments as well.

Everyday Agents of Resistance

One of the rules of my game is to echo back his words to an unexpected din or simply let them bounce around to yield most of what is being and has been said through them and despite them.
    Trinh T. Minh-ha, "The Language of Nativism"[24]

The more insidious and effective strategy, it seems, is a thoroughgoing appropriation and redeployment of the categories of identity themselves, not merely to contest "sex," but to articulate the convergence of multiple sexual discourses at the site of "identity" in order to render that category, in whatever form, permanently problematic.
    Judith Butler, *Gender Trouble*[25]

The commodification of everyday life in late consumer capitalism may seem virtually total, but there are possibilities for agency in spite of the technologies of commodification elaborated above. The everyday uses of autobiography are not merely disciplining occasions through which pervasive manifestations of decentralized power operate to conform persons through imposed autobiographical narratives. In looking at the "ways of operating" that "constitute the innumerable practices by means of which users reappropriate the space organized by techniques of sociocultural production," de Certeau cautions that we must not attend only to "the microbe-like operations proliferating within technocratic structures and deflecting their functioning by means of a multitude of 'tactics' articulated in the details of everyday life," but also and critically to "the clandestine forms taken by the dispersed, tactical, and makeshift creativity of groups or individuals already caught in the nets of 'discipline.'"[26] The nets of "discipline" are unevenly distributed, the knowledges of subjects are generated in heterogeneous sites and productive of contradictory positions, and the tactics of resistance are regenerative.

In specific situations, people may choose not to narrate the stories that are prescribed for them. They may remain silent. Their refusal may be rooted in the stories' unspeakability. (Refusal may also have dire consequences: they may not receive the benefits they need; they may be punished, even executed.) Or they can tell narratives appropriate to one situation in another, thereby confounding the grounds of the credible (but risking dismissal as "confused" or "mad" or "naive"). They can invoke, or dissociate themselves from, the values of the institution prescribing their narratives. Or they can tell their stories so as to disrupt the normative relationship between story and speaker. They can narrate their prescribed lives "too well," with excessive earnestness or flamboyance, and disrupt or "camp up" the scene of narration.

The complexities of postmodern life require individuals to negotiate multiple locations of identity on a daily basis. Such potentially dissonant negotiations undermine any complacent belief in consistent, transparent, and noncontradictory subjects. And so it is important to emphasize that the everyday occasions for autobiographical storytelling are multiple. The context of the autobiographical occasion varies with the participant, the historical moment, the site, the others participating in the dialogue, and the uses to which the life is being put. That is,

   autobiographical occasions are not congruent;
   each is differently structured, differently mediated, differently experienced;
   the lives they call for and forth are differently configured;
   in each context there are different forms of knowledges and of ignorances put into play.[27]

On a daily basis, then, personal narrators assume the role of the bricoleur *who takes up bits and pieces of the identities and narrative forms available and, by disjoining and joining them in excessive ways, creates a history of the subject at a precise point in time and space.* Such tactics of autobiographical storytelling become one of the means by which the narrating subject "constantly manipulate[s] events in order to turn them into 'opportunities.'"[28] Through assembling autobiographical memories one more time, personal narrators can turn an interpretation of and judgment about the past, however inflected by previous knowledge, into a countermemory. That is, they can remake their understanding of the "truth" of the past and reframe the present by bringing it into a new alignment of meaning with the past.

In this way, autobiographical narrators become agents in and of the story, momentarily and not uncontradictorily agents of their own ordering imperative. Seizing the occasion and telling the story turn speakers into subjects of narrative who can exercise some control over the meaning of their "lives." This assertion of agency is particularly compelling for those whose personal histories include stories that have been culturally unspeakable, for instance, histories of

> child abuse and spouse battering,
> interracial marriage,
> homosexuality,
> alcoholism,
> mental illness, and
> disability.

These have been among the unrecited narratives of American cultures. The very conditions of their unrecitability sustain the citations and recitations of privileged cultural narratives and privileged cultural identities. In citing new, formerly unspeakable stories, narrators become cultural witnesses insisting on memory as agency in its power to intervene in imposed systems of meaning. These witnesses also participate in the cultural work of reframing the meanings of the speakable, of voicing the speakable differently.

Then, too, telling what was formerly unspeakable builds communal identification. As Erving Goffman says of social situations generally:

> It is here in these small, local places that |people| can arrange themselves microecologically to depict what is taken as their place in the wider social frame, allowing them, in turn, to celebrate what has been depicted. It is here, in social situations, that the individual can signify what he takes to be his social identity and here indicate his feelings and intent—all of which information the others in the gathering will need in order to manage their own courses of action—which knowledgeability he in turn must count on in carrying out his own designs.[29]

In everyday occasions autobiographical narrators move out of isolation and loneliness into a social context in which their stories resonate with the stories of others in a group. And even if the story remains unspeakable in the larger community, narrators can find ways to convey the unspeakable to a community of secret knowers. The narrative can be coded, signaling certain meanings while masking others before those not sharing the secret knowledge. Phrases or intonations or certain rhetorical gestures become veiled signals to other participants in the unspeakable.

Thus the everyday uses of autobiography can produce changes in the subject, for narratives are generatively excessive as well as reconstitutive. That is, narratives afford a means of intervention into postmodern life. Autobiographical subjects can facilitate changes in the mapping of knowledge and ignorance, of what is speakable or unspeakable, disclosed or masked, alienating or communally bonding. They can force changes in the story by moving into new arenas of self-narrative—people immigrate, they join self-help groups, they exchange stories in peer counseling. In this way they attempt to "escape from older narratives to a new beginning."[30] In this way they create the past as "the undesirable other" in order to change the story.[31]

Yet new narratives can become confining and conforming with time. Individuals may experience a sense of exhilaration and empowerment in telling their new personal histories, in speaking the unspeakable; but exhilaration and empowerment are neither guaranteed by the telling of their life stories nor necessarily and reliably liberating. Storytelling occurs in a dialogical, social context. A person's efforts to make a gesture of tactical resistance to a stereotypic communal notion of the unspeakable can be co-opted and reordered into the community's normative patterns of speakability. We see this clearly in the case of self-help groups. If telling one's story is a way to exercise control over one's life, the people in self-help groups have to tell the same story again and again in order to get control over their loss of control. The narrative is reworked and performed—if not preformed—until the teller experiences healing. But participating in the collective autobiographical narrative of a self-help group, this "taking control," can be a way of capitulating to another's control of one's life. Thus the very institution of "self-help" can enforce the normative telling of life stories. Many institutions established to help people change their stories impose specific new stories. *The negotiation of everyday narratives is an ongoing process rather than a certain achievement.*

Autobiographical Stories and Backyard Ethnography

> *What illusion to believe that we can tell the truth, and to believe that each of us has an individual and autonomous existence! How can we think that in autobiography it is the lived life that produces the text, when it is the text that produces the life!*
> Philippe Lejeune, "The Autobiographical Pact (bis)"[32]

Whether the story is ever one's own is a question that can perhaps no longer be posed in terms of individualism and ownership in a postmodern world where concepts of self are negotiated socially and dialogically. "Individualism" has been commodified; the personal contents of the "personal" have been largely evacuated. But owning the stories that shape us as subjects is a different, more political issue, and an act of collective consciousness informing newer notions of what is at stake in autobiography. As Jana Sawicki argues, certain practices are not inherently or universally complicitous or resisting. "Neither wholly a source of domination nor of resistance," she writes, "sexuality"—to which we would add autobiographical practice—"is also neither outside power nor wholly circumscribed by it. Instead, it is itself an arena of struggle. There are no inherently liberatory or repressive [narrative] practices, for any practice is co-optable and is capable of becoming a source of resistance."[33]

Of course, we are not autobiographical subjects at every moment of the day, but we are called on to become autobiographical subjects in a variety of situations, a range of temporalities. Thus we move in and out of autobiographical subjectivity, sometimes by our own desire and purposes, sometimes through the exertions or coercion of others. *Getting a Life*, our collection of essays, explores the ways in which we move in and out of autobiographical subjectivity in daily ways, thereby contributing to what is currently called "backyard ethnography," with its focus on the everyday practices of autobiographical narrating in America rather than the "high culture" of published, "artful" autobiography.

We thus argue that the "others" of the American "self" need to be examined in the mirror of our own habitual practices, those situations of self-presentation and composition that are largely unreflective but that structure our narratives of subjectivity. Not just in remote times and countries, recondite theories, or complex performances, but in our own collective backyard, attending to the "others" uncovers strategies and codes bracketed out in historical celebrations of "the American character."

Autobiographical Acts as Everyday Occasions

Waiting to be collected, published, and interpreted are unnumbered autobiographical texts created daily in the social, commercial, educational, religious, and therapeutic transactions of everyday life.
    Albert E. Stone, "Modern American Autobiography"[34]

Rather than viewing the autobiographical production of identity as a solitary and introspective process of articulating individual difference, we read the production of identity as generated by encounters that are social, collaborative, contestatory. "Who" one is, is necessarily framed by interrogation of the institutional discourses that converge at a specific historical moment in the macro-processes of shaping the lives we want to call "individual" in postmodern America.[35] And those institutions are multitudinous and overlapping, as formal as the law and as idiosyncratic as the family. The essays in our collection frame sites or media where the negotiation of identity takes place, moving from the most direct experience of the body as a context of subjectivity through the social sites, mediations, and family-centered processes of ordering identity, to some macro-institutional frames whose attempts to regulate the forms of identity may trigger subversion by resistant subjects. Almost everything, from bumper stickers to clothing to reshaping personal stories with migration, could be regarded as implicated in the choosing, imposing, evading, or negotiating of an identity. Fingerprints are everywhere.

Autobiographical acts, thus, can be everyday occasions for rehearsing, performing, circulating, and consuming carefully fashioned and rapidly interspersed identity fragments. In attending to them, we examine not only how we intend to compose ourselves, but how in daily negotiations "we" and its "I's" are proposed, supposed, disposed. In conducting theoretical forays into everyday practices that structure subjectivity and designate the "individual," autobiography studies can be a repository of imposed subjectivities but also a means of resisting complicity in their operations. Its speculations on "the myth of fingerprints" can offer templates of possible subjectivities. Finally, in examining how everyday life compels ordinary Americans to order themselves in myriad ways, we conduct a postmodern investigation into the mystique of autobiography. What and where is the "truth" of the autobiographical subject, and what is invested in maintaining that "truth"? How and to what effect do autobiographical subjects oscillate between the narratives that write them and those they reconfigure in their local and strategic interventions? Constructed as social actors in multiple, overlapping communities, making and unmaking provisional identities, we are located as both subjects and witnesses—to our own proliferating and regulated identities, and to their internal dissonance. People may tell us to "get a life," but that is never simple.

Notes

1. Michel de Certeau, *The Practice of Everyday Life*, trans. Steven Rendall (Berkeley: University of California Press, 1984), 186.
2. Pierre Bourdieu, *Distinction: A Social Critique of the Judgment of Taste*, trans. Richard Nice (Cambridge: Harvard University Press, 1984), 173.
3. Laurie Langbauer, "Cultural Studies and the Politics of the Everyday," *diacritics* 22 (Spring 1992), 49.
4. Safire traces early media usage of the phrase to 1989 and speculates: "The expression originated as 'Get on with your life,' influenced by a comment like 'You call that a life?'" Safire suggests that "Get a life" is a call to stop imitating celebrity lives or adopting social roles and to "get real," a bracing piece of "constructive" advice. William Safire, "Get a Life!" *New York Times Sunday Magazine*, May 16, 1993.
5. We use the terms *America* and *Americans* in this essay to refer to the United States of America and the citizens of that nation. We are aware of the contested usages and meanings of these terms. The historical construct *America* originally signified what was termed in Europe the *New World*, and what is now two continents of many countries. Although the continuing use of the term *America* by people who live in the United States may be seen as a gesture of cultural imperialism, the phrase *the United States of America* at every reference is awkward. We therefore follow the usage of American studies.
6. We are indebted to Laurie Langbauer's probing discussion of "the everyday" as a foundational category of cultural studies that is usefully problematized through feminist theory as "a site of irresolvable difference, of conflict whose resolution is not simply delayed, but theoretically impossible." See Langbauer, "Cultural Studies and the Politics of the Everyday," 48.
7. Nelly Richard, "Postmodernism and Periphery," *Third Text* 1 (Winter 1987/88): 11.
8. Inderpal Grewal and Caren Kaplan, "Transnational Feminist Practices and Questions of Postmodernity," in *Scattered Hegemonies: Postmodernity and Transnational Feminist Practices*, ed. Inderpal Grewal and Caren Kaplan (Minneapolis: University of Minnesota Press, 1994), 4.
9. Ibid., 3.
10. Gertrude Stein, *The Making of Americans* (1925), in *Selected Writings of Gertrude Stein* (New York: Random House, 1962), 267.
11. Benedict Anderson, *Imagined Communities*, rev. ed. (London: Verso, 1991), 204.

12 We use this term in its broadest meaning, as a variety of practices through which people assemble narratives out of their own experiential histories. Other phrases that might be used to designate these practices are *autobiographical discourse, personal narrative,* and *life storytelling*. We have chosen to use the term *autobiographical narrative* at the same time we caution that the word *autobiography* has a specific "history of debatable origins, ambiguous parameters, and disputed subject matter" that has to do with the Western privileging of individuality and the concept of the universal, autonomous "self," as Caren Kaplan notes in "Resisting Autobiography: Out-Law Genres and Transnational Feminist Subjects," in *De/Colonizing the Subject: The Politics of Gender in Women's Autobiography,* ed. Sidonie Smith and Julia Watson (Minneapolis: University of Minnesota Press, 1992), 115–19.

13 Anderson, *Imagined Communities,* especially chaps. 2 and 3.

14 William Boelhower interestingly discusses the Americanization of immigrants through their writing of autobiography. See, for example, "The Making of Ethnic Autobiography in the United States," in *American Autobiography: Retrospect and Prospect,* ed. Paul John Eakin (Madison: University of Wisconsin Press, 1991), 123–41. But, for an important challenge to Boelhower's thesis from the perspective of Asian immigrants in a multigenerational context, see, in the same volume, Sau-Ling Cynthia Wong, "Immigrant Autobiography: Some Questions of Definition and Approach," 142–70.

15 Donald Pease used this term in analyzing the disruptive claim of the postnational subject in texts of the American Renaissance in a paper delivered at Binghamton University, October 1992.

16 In Michel-Guillaume-Jean de Crevecoeur, Letter III ("What Is an American?"), in *Letters from an American Farmer,* in *Anthology of American Literature,* ed. George McMichael et al. (New York: Macmillan, 1985).

17 Toni Morrison persuasively argues for the construction of American identity around a central repressed darkness of racial difference: "What seemed to be on the 'mind' of the literature of the United States was the conscious but highly problematic construction of the American as a new white man." *Playing in the Dark: Whiteness and the Literary Imagination* (New York: Random House, 1992), 39; see also chap. 2, passim.

18 This distinction between high and low forms derives from the binarism of high and low discourses explored by Peter Stallybrass and Allon White in *The Politics and Poetics of Transgression* (Ithaca, N.Y.: Cornell University Press, 1986), especially 3–5. Whereas their interest is in "the system of extremes which encoded the body, the social order,

psychic form, and spatial location" (3) in the formation of modernity, our location of the everyday is in a postmodern New World Order that, although antithetical to the "high" discourses, is not debased and degraded, or assigned by class status to the peasantry, the urban poor, or the colonized. Discourses of the everyday pose a conglomerate view of history that contrasts with the "high" emphasis on the singular representative "man."

19 Guy Debord, *Society of the Spectacle* (1967), trans. Ken Sanborn (Detroit: Black and Red, 1983), unpaged.
20 de Certeau, *The Practice of Everyday Life*, 190–91.
21 Irving Goffman, *Gender Advertisements* (New York: Harper & Row, 1976), 7.
22 The work of Michel Foucault on technologies of the self informs our discussion. See his "Technologies of the Self," in *Technologies of the Self: A Seminar with Michel Foucault*, ed. Luther H. Martin, Huck Gutman, and Patrick H. Hutton (Amherst: University of Massachusetts Press, 1988). Foucault distinguishes techniques by which individuals perform operations on their own bodies and minds with the goal of self-transformation (18). He argues that writing about oneself is not a recent but an ancient practice that developed a new attention to self-experience in the first and second centuries, and, with Marcus Aurelius, evolved a focus on personal experience of everyday life (28–29). The discussion of the significance of the emergence of confession in Foucault's *The History of Sexuality*, vol. 1, trans. Robert Hurley (New York: Vintage, 1980), has, of course, also informed our argument about the ability of the listener to exercise silent power over the speaker in autobiographical discourse.
23 Goffman, *Gender Advertisements*, 1.
24 Trinh T Minh-ha, "The Language of Nativism," in *Woman, Native, Other: Writing Postcoloniality and Feminism* (Bloomington: Indiana University Press, 1989), 49.
25 Judith Butler, *Gender Trouble: Feminism and the Subversion of Identity* (New York: Routledge, 1990), 128.
26 de Certeau, *The Practice of Everyday Life*, xiv-xv. See also his description of a "tactic" (xiv).
27 See Eve Kosofsky Sedgwick, *Epistemology of the Closet* (Berkeley: University of California Press, 1990), especially chap. 1, for a discussion of the relationship of ignorances to knowledges.
28 de Certeau, *The Practice of Everyday Life*, xix.
29 Goffman, *Gender Advertisements*, 6.

30 Keya Ganguly, "Migrant Identities: Personal Memory and the Construction of Selfhood," *Cultural Studies* 6, no. 1 (1992): 37.
31 Ibid., 38.
32 Philippe Lejeune, "The Autobiographical Pact (bis)," in *On Autobiography*, ed. Paul John Eakin, trans. Katherine Leary (Minneapolis: University of Minnesota Press, 1989), 131.
33 Jana Sawicki, "Identity Politics and Sexual Freedom: Foucault and Feminism," in *Feminism and Foucault*, ed. Irene Diamond and Lee Quinby (Boston: Northeastern University Press, 1988), 185.
34 Albert E. Stone, "Modern American Autobiography," in *American Autobiography: Retrospect and Prospect*, ed. Paul John Eakin (Madison: University of Wisconsin Press, 1991), 114.
35 Consider the claim by James "Bo" Gritz, leader of the "Almost Heaven" Christian Covenant Community established near Kamiah, Idaho, that he is an "Identity Christian" seeking others "just like you" who *know* the centrality of their Christian identity (by which he means the region's whites but not its original Nez Perce inhabitants). *Missoulian*, May 25, 1994, B-3.

5
Ordering the Family: Genealogy as Autobiographical Pedigree (Watson 1996)

All those dumb generations back of me, are crying in every breath of every word that itself is struggling out of me.
                        Anzia Yezierska, *Children of Loneliness*[1]

The unconscious is not deciphered only in dreams and lapses, but in the texture of family history, if only one takes an interest in its secrets.
           Phillippe Lejeune, "The Autobiographical Pact (bis)"[2]

Documented or not, biographical and historical materials are intersubjective through and through.
                Louis Renza, "The Veto of the Imagination"[3]

Genealogy is an abiding passion and a big industry in the United States. It establishes the family's collective biography as a rooted network that has legitimately and verifiably inhabited the past. Tracing one's ancestors is a hedge against mortality in an increasingly mobile, global world. Genealogy specifies origin. Its fundamental assumption is categorical: Humans are defined by who and where we are "from" in terms such as stock, blood, class, race. Books of genealogy refer to the "pedigree," the validated evidence documenting ancestral identity, transactions, and events. A family genealogical project often involves producing a book of the pedigree—with documents, lists, a family tree charting generational history. Unlike the ancient Romans, we no longer carry the *lares* or household gods with us in urns, as Aeneas did from burning Troy. But genealogy offers the book and, increasingly, the digital archive as a collective record that establishes a vital connection to a personal past. Through establishing their genealogy, family members are assured that their everyday lives have transpersonal significance and are embedded in a historical chain. Genealogy is an extended "life" that, in principle, we all can "get," because we all descend from parents somewhere; in practice there are of course many obstacles to becoming life tracers, and those are connected not only with circumstances (for example, being orphaned, adopted, or descended from slaves) but with the institution of genealogy itself.

Genealogy is a vast and complex practice, with a methodology and apparatuses—journals, archives, societies, certified professional researchers, how-to books, indexes—for establishing pedigreed origin. The Church of Jesus Christ of Latter-day Saints alone lists the births, baptisms, and marriages of more than 220 million deceased persons throughout the world in its *International Genealogical Index*, the largest microfiche genealogical record in the world.[4] In American culture, though the myth of the melting pot has afforded the opportunity to become someone else and leave the past behind, tracing one's roots is a countervailing impetus that has preserved both power elites and the descent records of ordinary citizens. Knowing one's roots signifies being *someone*; it reaffirms old values of hierarchy and origin that are arguably at odds with the egalitarian ideology of democracy.

In American culture the pedigree impulse of genealogy works against Crevecoeur's vision of ethnic intermixture as a hallmark of the "American" character.[5] Genealogy's emphasis on fixity of "descent" contradicts the democratic and egalitarian "melting pot" as a figure for erasing originary differences in a culture of "consent," as Werner Sollors has argued in characterizing these two dominant, opposed facets of American culture.[6] William Boelhower elaborates on Sollors's culture of descent for American ethnic autobiographies by observing how it encodes a "genealogical narrative program" that sets the immigrant's cultural tradition in a problematically perspectival relationship to the experience of Americanization. That is, genealogical ordering, as a given of many traditional cultures, is deployed by displaced immigrants to make narrative sense of the radical discontinuity of their American experience and impose on it a frame of narrative coherence. Genealogy values origin, stock, race, blood, in an increasingly heterogeneous world. Boelhower's provocative discussion of this "politics of memory" suggests that genealogical ordering is a necessary fiction for displaced subjects who can no longer map their ancestry onto a geography of origins; it establishes "descent" where it is most in question.[7] The "melting pot" culture of America, he suggests, needs both the methods and the fictions of genealogy to contain and counteract the pluralistic character of the lives its members have gotten.

Genealogy as a highly organized and codified set of practices for recording family history claims the disinterested objectivity of a science. It mistrusts "family secrets" as a subjective record that contaminates the preservation and transmission of accurate family history. The life it confers is teleological, ordering the particulars of family into a coherent, demonstrable chart. Each generation of a family is connected to its "tree" and assigned a "pedigree" that commemorates its origin and—overtly in Mormon practice—provides a means of election for its members among the true believers destined for salvation. But genealogy does more than give the family a life—it installs particular families in the privileged world of those who can trace their origins and attest to the coherence of their stock.

The "life" conferred on a family by establishing its genealogical pedigree is, however, a strange one. Genealogy makes truth claims about the knowability of family history and its power to authorize the individual while actively resisting the incursions of autobiographical storytelling. Tracing one's genealogy requires verifying biographical detail as documentable fact and suppressing "subjective" autobiographical detail. Yet the "life" it confers invites at every point the "autographing" that its discourse seeks to repress. Analyzing the uses of genealogy in everyday life uncovers contradictions in how the family is constituted and validated, in descent and election as applied to "polyglot" American origins, and in constructions of subjectivity itself.

A closer look at how genealogical research is conducted also suggests that, despite the objectivity it claims, it has functioned as an exclusionary practice, providing a network of connection for some, but an impermeable boundary to others. Ambivalent when not silent about the historically dispossessed (African Americans, Native Americans) and invisible (women, rootless adventurers, orphans, the adopted), genealogical narrative, in graphing the history of some, literally de-faces many others. Thus, though genealogy has enabled some to "get" lives, those lives have been ordered in ways that can suppress *stories* of enslavement, colonization, and appropriation that underlie American history.

The impulse of genealogy, in every sense conservative, reinforces ethnic claims but contests another kind of identity politics: we are not who we think we are, or who we create or imagine ourselves to be. Though some of the same motives drive both autobiographical writing and genealogical charting, and comparable "information" may be used in both, as practices they have little in common. Identifying origin by class and ethnicity implies a history of domination and struggle that profoundly influences a group's view of and access to history. If we turn to justifications in genealogical manuals for "how" and "why" genealogy is done, a rationale about how American life is ordered and socially inscribed emerges.

The "How" of Doing Genealogy

The methods of genealogy need to be described in some detail, as the high seriousness of the enterprise and its remarkable resources are not well known to non-practitioners. One is published by the Church of Jesus Christ of Latter-day Saints (Mormon Church), which regularly updates its *United States Research Outline* as a "how-to" for laymen. It presents genealogy as a compilation and consolidation of kinds of evidence, asserting:[8] "The term genealogy is used in this outline and in the FHLC (Family History Library Catalog) to describe a variety of records containing family information previously gathered by other researchers, societies, or archives. These records can include pedigree charts, compiled data on families, correspondence, ancestor lists, research exchange files, record abstracts, and collections of original or copied documents" (USRO 21). The purpose of doing genealogical work, then, is to verify an established past. It is impermissible to add or invent; rather, the project is to discover historical connections and bring the record together for future generations. A personal story is subordinated to the history of the family, and that story tolerates no embroidery. For the genealogist, the introduction of a personal perspective would undermine the validity of history.

Genealogy requires expertise in research methodology and the use of many kinds of historical documents. The USRO refers to levels of expertise—beginning, intermediate, and proficient—in handling resources. The casual researcher wondering about charting her family history discovers an entire section in the bookstore or library of how-to's, a labyrinth of documentary sources, and official bibles of various societies detailing their authorized methods. Extensive bibliographies, many organized by ethnicity, others by place, kind of archive, or source, can provide information. There are pages of guides and reference books on ancestry and much to be learned—about summaries, immigration and refugee settlements, organizing a family tree, and so forth.

And that is only the beginning. The United States has extensive archival resources. The National Archives and Records Administration in Washington, D.C. has regional branches in every state. Their holdings, complemented by those of state offices, include vital statistics, offices of town and county records, and other private archives. Libraries include the major holdings of the Library of Congress, the Newberry Library, the New York Public Library, the National Society of the Daughters of the American Revolution, the New England Historical and Genealogical Society, and others. There are more than nine thousand historical and genealogical societies, two of the largest and most influential of which are the American Society of Genealogists and the National Genealogical Society (USRO 45). Major journals published in this field include *American Genealogist, Genealogical Journal, National Genealogical Society Quarterly,* and several regional journals. Among archives, the Family History Library of the Church of Latter-day Saints towers, literally and figuratively. Its new facility, opened in Salt Lake City in 1985, now serves more than three thousand researchers daily and is being greatly enlarged to accommodate more who make pilgrimages to use its holdings, which are vast and comprehensive and include a wealth of technological equipment, such as microfilm, CD-ROM, and digital networks, to manage access to millions of pages of sources.[9] The unwary beginner may be overwhelmed by the elaborateness of the genealogical apparatus, though "user-friendly" computers stand ready to assist. For those who cannot travel to the Family History Library, the church has more than fifteen hundred centers for family history throughout the United States and the world.

The researcher can also use many kinds of civil records, including birth records, marriage certificates and registrations, divorce decrees, and death records, and religious records on baptism, marriage, and death. Censuses—federal, state, and local—are available since statehood, as early as 1790, but are not entirely accurate because they often do not list slaves, women, or children by name, do not itemize household information until 1850 (SYA 205), and involve personal reporting. Census records may be unreliable, the USRO advises, because of incorrect information (11). At several points, invisible human agents threaten genealogical ordering.

The genealogical research process is straightforward and ordered to minimize human intervention. Users are advised that personal judgments are inappropriate. Documents should be gathered and discussed with a member of the family who clearly remembers the family's history; copies assembled of the records for birth, marriage, and death for the family within the United States; religious documentation and cemetery records checked; immigration and naturalization information sought. The genealogical researcher may also consult federal census and military records and review documents such as the passenger lists of ships, city telephone directories, and obituaries (SYA 211). In this welter of documents, the researcher is invariably advised to maintain disinterested objectivity and to validate the accuracy of all evidence.

Doane and Bell, in *Searching for Your Ancestors*, explore another side of genealogy, namely, how doing research "remakes" the genealogist as someone who can assume several roles: tactician, detective, archaeologist, psychologist. Objectivity is crucial; personal connection to the "object" of study, those who can talk back, hold back, or, worst of all, distort and fantasize, is discouraged. The researcher must be committed to detection, to uncovering plain fact by using good timing and relentless curiosity. The sources of investigation are vulnerable to forgetfulness and mortality. Indeed, an archaeological discourse of recovery characterizes much genealogical discourse: "In digging for ancestors, no stone is too small or too insignificant to be left unturned" (55).[10] The genealogist also needs to develop psychological skill and tact with older relatives who have trouble remembering or focusing. The guide recommends mnemonic strategies that can elicit familial data while evacuating its personal content, the residue of autobiographical contamination. Researchers are urged to develop a set of tactics: interview personally where possible to maximize chance remarks, or write questions on a sheet of paper with space for respondents to answer (29); learn the art of "getting along with irascible people" by becoming sympathetic and "roundabout" (27); defuse suspicion and reassure relatives that the project is honorable for the family, who "may suspect, however far it may be from the truth, that you are getting ready to claim some mythical estate" (42); show an artifact of the past—"Sometimes the sight of an old letter or a bit of silver recalls to an aging mind the story back of it or relationships that have been forgotten" (55); visit a cemetery with the relative and ask him or her to explain the relationships among those buried there (30). The budding genealogist develops a host of investigative skills for helping subjects to "get a life," to talk of a historical past that will speak through them if their conscious or unconscious impediments to it are removed.

With these how-to's, the researcher can resist autobiography's grip by stripping information of its narrative elements and distilling the "facts" about the reliability of older relatives. "Beware of fantasy," we are warned (SYA 37). The investigator must keep in mind the pursuit of verifiable objective truth. The "story" mapped by genealogy permits no narrative elaboration of data that are considered totalizing and transparent. Sources are notoriously unreliable, Doane and Bell insist, because of the tendency of the human mind to construct events using narrative techniques familiar to readers of both fiction and autobiography:

> Don't accept as gospel truth all that [you are told] about the history of the family. People do not always realize that they have confused two different episodes and *telescoped* them into one, and sometimes they *do not discriminate between fact and fiction*. Some are *natural-born storytellers* and quite unconsciously *embroider the facts a little* here and there to make the tale more *dramatic*. (SYA 32; my emphasis)

"Fiction," the elaboration and deviation of historical "fact," contaminates. To resist it, the researcher is urged to verify details and avoid what is "hearsay, not bona fide evidence" (SYA 34). Narrative accounts are not facts, and human subjects are unreliable.[11] They distort or report inaccurately, especially about events before their own times. Autobiographical fantasy invariably erodes historical fact.

Even individual memories of an event in which several participated can be unreliable: "It is sometimes very difficult to reconcile statements made by different members of the family" (SYA 28). What autobiography celebrates as the fruitful diversity of human memories of events is suspect to the genealogist. Where, for example, Mary McCarthy in *Memories of a Catholic Girlhood* contrasted various family members' memories of a photographed moment, for the genealogist the truth must be unitary, verifiable, and charted in the family pedigree.[12]

Most dangerous to the genealogist, then, is human imagination, which willfully corrupts memory. Discussing the potential of diaries as sources of genealogical information, Doane and Bell warn that the writer's personality may taint historical accuracy: "Unfortunately, sometimes the keeper of the diary was more interested in the affairs that were going on about him or her than in the details for which the genealogist is looking. In that case, however interesting it may be, the diary is a disappointment" (SYA 49). Wayward impressions threaten an orderly pedigree. Similarly, the Family History Library is deeply mistrustful of narrated family history. The USRO section on biography warns: "A biography is a history of a person's life . . . [with] birth, marriage, and death information . . . [including] photographs, family traditions and stories, clues about an ancestor's place of origin. . . . *The information must be used carefully, however, because there may be inaccuracies*" (9; my emphasis). No distinction is made between biography and autobiography; both can be contaminated by personal motives and subjective points of view, which contribute, however well-meaningly, to errors and inaccuracy. Research methodology demands careful evaluation of evidence: reliable sources, eyewitness or proximate accounts, internal consistency, and assessment of potential contradiction (USRO 4). Only impersonality and task orientation in the investigation can protect against the temptation to autobiographical fantasy.

The researcher's quest is challenging. Record keepers may be "jealous" of records in public offices and "guard them from 'alien hands'" (SYA 73). Access to personal history is for initiates, those with credentials attesting to their legitimate interest in their own past. The "detective" may also encounter state laws that prohibit use of personal records by those who are not provably genealogists or members of historical societies. But if the quest is riddled with obstacles, the investigator can also develop appropriate skills to navigate it. The genealogist learns to play hunches, to home in on clues, in order to enjoy the payoff of developing latent skills for detecting, unearthing, connecting to other times. In performing genealogical research correctly, the investigator becomes the family's validated "life-giver."

The "Why" of Doing Genealogy

Motives for doing genealogical research vary with the searcher and range from legitimating the tacitly certain to re-creating an unknown, inaccessible family history. They include validating and authorizing descendancy for membership purposes (especially in the Church of the Latter-day Saints), inserting the researcher into an insufficiently known past to be enriched by it, and uncovering and articulating an eradicated past as a means of gaining individual and transpersonal identity (e.g., in Alex Haley's *Roots*).

The Family History Library materials that I have examined say little about the "why" of genealogy, but it is in fact a central Mormon practice. Within the belief structure of the Church, members seek to preserve genealogical records for family ancestors and establish generational connections in order to ensure they are saved. The practice by which deceased family members are saved is called "baptism of the dead." According to *Mormon Doctrine*, "Genealogical research may be performed for those who have died without a knowledge of the gospel, but who presumably would have received it had the opportunity come to them."[13] Through genealogical tracing, then, a family can not only discover, but *save* the lives of its ancestors; they get a second and eternal life through baptism and other rituals that bring them into what Mormons see as the true Church of Jesus Christ. Temple ordinances, necessary for salvation, are provided for deceased family members upon presentation of information about them to enable their inclusion among the elect (USRO 4). Families sharing common ancestors are urged to form "family organizations" for the purpose of keeping genealogical data current, as well as "to create family solidarity and honor the patriarchal system."[14] The Family History Library also invites non-Mormon families to be recorded within its worldwide genealogical project by registering a documented family in the "Family Registry™," which holds a nationwide collection of such records (USRO 22). Researchers are assured that these resources make one's family history sharable with others, including possible "lost" relatives, and accessible to other genealogical searchers. No matter how fragmented the family may become in these postmodern times, its orderly contours will be mapped online for posterity.

What is not said, however, is that users may be "baptized" in a genealogical project more radically inclusive than the Family History Library indicates. According to Mormon theology, everyone who ever lived should have an opportunity to accept baptism and become a Mormon; whether they are dead or alive is inconsequential because all wait in the "spirit world" for the Millennium yet to come. Genealogical research identifies potential converts and establishes records of their baptism in church temples. Indeed, dozens of Roman Catholic saints have been baptized, Joan of Arc fourteen times.[15] Movie stars and famous statesmen have also been inducted, including all the signers of the Declaration of Independence.[16] This genealogical labor is vast in scope, given the estimate that nearly seventy billion have lived in the history of the world, and identification documents exist for only about 10 percent of them.[17] The church has now registered more than two billion names and has incorporated computer systems to allow quicker access to ancestral records. Anyone who chooses to research his or her genealogy through the Family History Library may eventually also get a second life as a Mormon—like it or not.

Searching for Your Ancestors, by contrast, has a secular, eclectic approach to the why of genealogy that is less compelling than salvation but also potentially transformative—the thrill of learning history with a personal connection: "You don't dig merely to accumulate a lot of dry bones . . . you simply cannot back-trail your progenitors without becoming interested in the times in which they lived and in the various phases of their lives and activities" (SYA 5–6). History "assumes an intimate meaning" when the researcher discovers an ancestor who took part in a national event (SYA 6). The past becomes "fact rather than hearsay" (SYA 8). The imagination is stimulated as one becomes able to "picture" one's ancestors as historical actors. Researching your genealogy promises that "history will become part of your blood" (SYA 8). Connecting to a generational family gives access to the nation itself and reactivates patriotic feeling as the individual invests in historical significance and experiences an intimate "blood" connection to events that were formerly only dates in history books. Studying family history becomes "an engrossing occupation, a new vocation for an active and inquisitive mind" (SYA 5).

Other more tangible rewards may also accrue if one can produce a verified genealogical pedigree: namely, membership in societies that require a family past documented as worthy. In addition to membership in churches requiring proof of origin, these include such groups as the Daughters of the American Revolution, the Society of Mayflower Descendants, and the Society of Colonial Wars. These societies are hereditary, have a patriotic orientation, and are by definition highly exclusionary. Testifying to one's commitment to the goals of the organization will not suffice; either the bloodline is there or it is not. A similarity of surname is also insufficient, as experienced genealogists know that "claiming relationship because of identity of family names [is] treacherous" (SYA 276). Names do not necessarily signify descent from a common progenitor or even a shared nationality. Only researched family trees document historical claims to membership privilege among the historically elite, those who know who—that is, *from whom*—they are.

Another kind of motivation no doubt impels genealogists: to recreate symbolically the sense of familial connection that has been in fact displaced by geographic mobility and identity-shifting. The current popularity of tracing one's family genealogy may relate to changes within the family itself: smaller number of children (on average fewer than two among Caucasian Americans); frequent divorce and remarriage, or serial monogamy as partnership; and changes in the life cycle that make parenthood in the home less than one-third of adult life experience and grandparenting an extended period. The family, shrunken to its nucleus, is expanded vertically through the family tree. Part of the lure of genealogy is that it charts a linear history foregrounding lineage as pedigree. It emphasizes the family's sense of the stability and the "cleanness" of its ethnic composition, its maintenance of or "improvement" in social class, and the perpetuation from generation to generation of identified social institutions—religion, profession, the production of heirs.[18] Who begat whom, where, and in what line is knowledge that secures a patriarchal mooring in an increasingly destabilized world.

Immigrant and "Minority" Genealogy

Clearly, tracing a genealogical connection is most pleasurable for those with long, free histories in the United States. Recent immigrants and descendants of slaves may find their "intimate" connection to history more ambivalent and the quest more difficult. How-to's focus on the documents associated with immigration and slavery, while avoiding or minimizing remarks concerning the oppressive histories that occasioned them. In an American context the right of equal access to documents, however unlikely, is assumed in genealogical method to normalize past inequities and abuses. The difficulties in the how-to's are technical: records of immigrants before they have crossed an ocean or a border to enter the United States are kept by a wide variety of systems, if at all, in other countries. Typically, such records are in various languages and widely scattered regions that may have changed national identities several times. If we turn to accounts of how to map genealogy for historical "others," it becomes clear that its practices have been formed around the normative WASP subjects who first invaded and ordered the Americas.

Personal and family histories negotiate the terms of identity informed by social categories, but also need to articulate what is compressed or subsumed in them. Mae Gwendolyn Henderson makes this point in a succinct summary of Bakhtin's categories of identity, to which she makes crucial additions: "Bakhtin's social groups are designated according to class, religion, generation, region, and profession. The interpretive model I propose extends and rereads Bakhtin's theory from the standpoint of race and gender, categories absent in Bakhtin's original system of social and linguistic stratification."[19] Categories of race and gender are briefly touched on in many genealogical how-to's, but they are usually addressed to a universal "he." Typically, non-Europeans are treated as ethnically marked "others" and this marginal treatment justified by the course of European histories. The rationale given is that it is difficult to do research for non-Europeans, as for women, orphans, and the adopted, because census data often have not recorded them. Before 1850, for example, census records gave the name only for the head of the household; date of immigration is not listed until 1900 (USRO 12); cemetery records are helpful for "children who died young or women who were not recorded in family or government documents" (USRO 10). Genealogy's reliance on pedigrees lacks a means of historical authorization for those without public social status or agency.

The Family History Library is particularly evasive, treating "minorities" as an elastic, apolitical concept. The *United States Research Outline* includes the following as examples: "the Irish in New York," "Huguenot immigration," "*The Swedish-American Historical Quarterly*," "the American Historical Society of Germans from Russia in Lincoln, Nebraska" (USRO 36). Examples for the subject section of the library catalog cited are "BLACKS, AFRO

AMERICANS, JEWS, and QUAKERS" (USRO 36). Thus the basis for the designation "minority" mixes ethnicities, religious identities, and historical examples of persecuted sects. The history sections of the Family History state research outlines I have examined are equally noncommittal on distinctions by ethnicity; they refrain from comment on crucial historical moments such as the Emancipation Proclamation, which politically legitimated ex-slaves. In the documentary "objectivity" of the *United States Research Outline,* "minority" expands to a category of all-embracing otherness that erases distinctions of persecution. Questions about historical agency, guilt, and blame are carefully avoided. But its construction of the family is implicitly Caucasian and European in origin, and it has difficulty accounting for others, especially those whose immigration was forced through slavery.

The umbrella categorization of "minority" thus hides a world of cultural differences. The category of "American" is presented neutrally and without allusion to central events of human history in the past five hundred years, such as the enslavement of African Americans and the genocide of millions of Jews. Certainly there is not comparable access to historical documentation of family ancestry for all the groups listed as examples of "minorities." For would-be historians of Jewish family history, the *United States Research Outline* notes only, "The ancestors of most American Jewish families arrived in the late nineteenth and early twentieth centuries" (14). The recourse to immigration data evades the question of Jewish immigrants since the 1930s who fled persecution in Germany, the Soviet Union, and elsewhere. Nor does the Family History Library research outline give advice to survivor children of families that disappeared in the Holocaust. Where and how should they search for records? The treatment of ancestral history by the Family History Library as personalized and apolitical renders much and many unspeakable; those whose ancestors escaped persecution are the research norm.

Searching for Your Ancestors, on the other hand, makes an effort to address research issues concerning the diversity of cultural origins and difficulties in finding ancestors. The impact of historical events on compiling a family history for some groups is evident; for example, "the turbulent course of Irish history, crowned by the burning of the Public Record Office in Dublin" in 1922 destroyed many records that are needed by ancestral hunters (SYA 221). Difficulties that Jewish Americans may encounter in compiling family histories because of

Idiosyncratic naming practices, lack of surnames before the nineteenth century, and frequent modification of names as a result of migration between countries are noted. A history of persecution is recalled: the Diaspora from the twelfth century onward, the persecutions of the fifteenth and twentieth centuries, extensive emigration during the nineteenth century. Resources are recommended, such as the *yizkor* (memory books) kept for many Eastern European towns. There is an implicit acknowledgment that genealogical tracing is a complicated process for those not of the dominant culture.

Genealogy, as an institution, has universalized written records to legitimate family lineage and authorize identity, as becomes clear with two main categories of historical "others" in the United States, Native Americans and "free blacks," who were often lumped together without ethnic distinction. (Slave schedules were prepared separately until 1860, with slaves listed under their owners' names; SYA 205.)[20] Yet the procedures for tracing their genealogies are quite different.

In contrast to the historical authorization that genealogy books celebrate for subjects of European origin, emergence into its official written history coincided with diminished autonomy for Native Americans. Oral genealogies were devalued and family ties broken by missionary schools and the reservation system. Native American tribes, consisting of many interrelated families, are traditionally organized into clans; the network of relationships, which is preserved and known, may be large.[21] But from the perspective of genealogy, as an instrument of the American "civilizing mission," this familial richness was regarded as a "heathen" lack of history that needed reorganizing under Christian auspices. Not only was the traditional clan system devalued and broken; written record keeping was in several respects driven by greed and ideological zeal. Colonial conquest in the New World naturalized the right and descent lines of the conquerors, a fact that the how-to manuals do not acknowledge.

The treatment of Native American history depends to a significant extent on the ideological persuasion of the genealogical group or author. The Mormon Family History Library, which still uses genealogical research actively as a means of proselytizing, states blandly that "before 1830, Indians living among non-Indians were generally encouraged to accept Christianity and adopt western customs" (USRO 36).[22] Similarly, Family History Library publications characterize federal government intervention as benign "civilizing." They note the concern of the Bureau of Indian Affairs (BIA) for "educating the Indians" and land allotment trusts that registered an individual and his heirs until he "demonstrated his competency to administer the land" as required, which they observe that most Indians did not succeed in doing; hence the persistence of reservations (USRO 38).

Searching for Your Ancestors, in contrast, discusses how to investigate Native American heritage by implicitly acknowledging native peoples' dispossession and domination by Europeans, "a heritage eroded by three-and-a-half centuries of mistreatment and injustice" (SYA 183). Its how-to acknowledges the use of genealogical recording as a justificatory mechanism for conversion, though it stops short of critiquing the use of genealogy as a means of domination in the New World. Doane and Bell provide background on Native American history, as the Church of Latter-day Saints manual does not, that traces the simultaneous recording and erasure of Native Americans. Their mini-history of encounters with religious and civil bureaucracy recounts the dispossession of Native Americans through the manipulation of documents. The main record keepers, Christian churches (notably the Franciscan and Jesuit missionaries of Roman Catholicism) and the federal government, especially the BIA, from 1850 to 1952, are identified as prime forces of colonization, along with the military. The full or partial omission of Indians in federal censuses until 1890 is noted (SYA 185). The special censuses of the Creek and Cherokee nations (made in 1832 and 1835, respectively) prior to removing them from their lands for the westward march along the "Trail of Tears" are cited as evidence of the marginalization of native peoples in American documentary life.

Indeed, Doane and Bell are revealing on how the evidentiary documents required to do genealogy were prohibited. Native Americans could not file wills until 1910, and then only with approval by the commissioner of Indian affairs (SYA 187). Starting in 1885, when most Indians had been forced onto reservations, the federal government took annual rolls of them for taxation purposes (see Indian census rolls, 1885–1940; SYA 186); these were not done alphabetically and could include several different names for given individuals. Identities became unstable, contingent. The National Archive of Tribal Records (in Washington, D.C., and regional branches) contains much documentary information, but the searcher is warned to consult a guide and learn the labyrinthine administrative structure of the BIA before embarking on a project (SYA 185). Indeed, the subtext of this discussion is a sober and cautionary one: European migration to the New World established some American dynasties at the cost of dislodging the collective identities of native peoples, miring them in a bureaucratic apparatus of imposed regulations, geographically, politically, and genealogically.

The situation of African Americans also poses problems for genealogical how-to books and exposes their normatively European assumptions. The Family History Library's advice is scarce, unspecific, and noncommittal; mixed racial ancestry is not a category in the Family History Library research outlines. Its reticence needs to be read in light of beliefs encoded in the Book of Mormon, which, according to its critics, refers to a dark skin as a "curse" (p. 201, verse 6), signifying transgression and inferior status, a valuation of normative whiteness that has strongly racist overtones, though the recent (1978) granting of the Mormon priesthood to "blacks" may suggest a renegotiation of traditional prejudices.[23]

Searching for Your Ancestors, by contrast, devotes a subsection to "African-American ancestors" in which the impact of historical events is sympathetically, if ineffectually, acknowledged (202–10). Americanization is a traumatic process:

> Recall too that black people had been captured in Africa, transported in bondage across the Atlantic, and sold into slavery in America. Families had been broken forever, husbands and wives, parents and children, children and children, never to see each other again.... The search for African ancestors can be very difficult due to the abruptness of the rupture between Africa and America (203).

The authors note the disruption of family life for slaves, the paucity of family records because marriages were not legally binding, and the late date of constitutional amendments mandating equality. They list sources for African Americans to consult[24] and suggest methods for using vital records, lists of beneficial societies, and African American newspapers. But the implication is clear: the degree of historical accuracy in one's genealogical pedigree depends to a significant extent on one's ancestors' cultural status before 1850. White male Western Europeans will be more successful than others in verifying their ancestral pedigrees.

Unlike the Family History Library, *Searching for Your Ancestors* acknowledges the difficulty of providing "proof of a family's past" for African Americans (207). Descendants confront the historical fact that slaves were regarded as property and included in estates that were passed from generation to generation. Information is more available in wills, tax records, and manumission statements than in plantation accounts, many of which were lost or destroyed (207). Although mixed ancestry is acknowledged in the heritage of many African Americans—"liaisons were a feature of plantation life until the end of the Civil War" (208)—its origin in practices such as rape is omitted; the work of tracing erased networks of descendancy falls to fictional texts such as Toni Morrison's *Beloved*.

Doane and Bell's how-to book thus neutralizes the transgressive character of power relationships under slavery. The African American reader is offered sanguine, Disney-like advice on finding African ancestors: "Your search should focus on the nations and tribes of that region" (SYA 208); "A trip to Africa may be necessary" (SYA 208); "Griots... are really walking and talking libraries" (SYA 209). But for West Africa, an area larger than the entire United States and populated by hundreds of "tribes" or ethnic groups with several unrelated language families, such advice is delusive. Its bland generalizations gloss over differences of language and ethnicity and ignore problems of time, access to griots, language differences, and the money necessary for extended research. Hypothetically, one can find one's black ancestors—with the resources of, say, Bill Cosby.[25] The reader is gently encouraged to seek "inspiration" in *Roots*.

What use are African American descendants of slaves to make of genealogy as familial authorization? How may they lay claim to a generational family history, the legitimating basis of white American culture? Though how-to books can offer little, strategic intervention in the documents-driven impulse of genealogy has been posed by the alternative of creation and recovery of the family in myth.

Roots: Genealogy as Cultural Quest

> To the best of my knowledge and of my effort, *every lineage statement* within *Roots* is from either my African or American families' carefully preserved oral history, much of which I have been able *conventionally to corroborate with documents*... from years of *intensive research in fifty-odd libraries, archives, and other repositories* on three continents.

> My own ancestors' [book] would automatically also be a *symbolic saga of all African-descent people—who* are *without exception t*he seeds of someone like Kunta who was born and grew up in some black African village, someone who was captured and chained down in one of those slave ships that sailed them across the same ocean, into some succession of plantations, and since then a struggle for freedom.[26] (Italics are my emphasis.)

In these two passages Alex Haley suggests the genealogical methods that *Roots* applies and its mythic cross-purposes. *Roots* links two narratives: the imagined saga of Kunta Kinte of Juffure (a river village now in The Gambia), who comes to the United States in a slave ship and begets heirs whom Haley can, with increasing accuracy, document as his forebears; and Haley's own saga of a twelve-year search for pre-slavery origins in the Old World as a transforming personal pilgrimage. The language of mythic saga moving from an indefinite ur-past toward the present generation in Kunta Kinte's family line is counterpointed by the language of genealogical method as a process of detection for Haley's own quest. Placing his "frame" story of how he wrote *Roots* after the six-hundred-page ancestral saga, Haley makes a tree of oral history to negotiate a collective African American entry into genealogical record. By relying on the oral transmission of griots, he utilizes genealogical method yet subverts its Western dependence on writing. In this way *Roots* offers a mode of historical authentication replacing the traditional practice of genealogy with an older, oral tradition that is unverifiable in written documents but functions nonetheless as collective autobiography.

Roots's success as a bestseller of genealogy has not been lost on its practitioners; Doane and Bell note that is has sold more than twelve million copies and been translated into thirty-seven languages (SYA xi). *Roots* is a cultural phenomenon that speaks to a widespread need to mobilize the authority of genealogy in redressing American familial and social relations.[27] It meditates on the centrality of ancestral "rooting" to self-understanding and values family as a repository of generational memory that is ultimately oral and pre-documentary. *Roots* insists on the primacy of the griot, the oral rememberer with scriptural authority.[28] "Throughout the whole of black Africa such oral chronicles had been handed down since the time of the ancient forefathers" (674). Oral history is revalued as a means of self-discovery in the search for "our ancestral tribe" (671). The narrative begins with the birth of Kunta Kinte and concludes with the death and burial of Haley's father as the sons, "members of the seventh generation from Kunta Kinte," eulogize his life, their individual memories now embedded in mythic history (688). That moment coincides with the completion of Haley's twelve-year project and his own emergence into ancestrally located self-consciousness.

In his account of how he came to research and write *Roots*, Haley spins a tale that reinterprets genealogical objectivity and points to an unstable narrative core lurking at the heart of its method. *Roots* is finally circular in giving its author-questor a resonant familial identity and cultural heritage. Haley voyages in space as well as time, traversing West Africa and archival and maritime sites up and down the Atlantic coast. His voyage to Juffure fuses the language of revelation and dream: going forward in time to return to an originary place in which griots still recite hundreds of years of genealogical descent. The locus of *Roots* is itself ambivalent, with one pole in the village of Juffure and the other on Gorée Island, about one hundred miles away, off Dakar, Senegal, where thousands of slaves were detained after captivity for inspection, shackling, and chained export to the Americas. Genealogical research is impossible in Gorée's historical museum, which contains no written records. As Haley wryly concludes, "Preponderantly the histories have been written by the winners" (688).

Haley's own genealogical quest is a detective story, in which he becomes a detective on a breathless and at times reckless quest for clues in the stages of the investigation: "If any black American could be so blessed as I had been to know only a few ancestral clues—could he or she know *who* was either the paternal or maternal African ancestor or ancestors, and about *where* that ancestor lived when taken, and finally about *when* the ancestor was taken—then only those few clues might well see that black American able to locate some wizened old black *griot* whose narrative could reveal the black American's ancestral clan, perhaps even the very village" (680).

Detection mingles with the discourse of quasi-religious election as Haley comes to see himself as the scribe designated to write the Word and unravel the history of the Kinte clan "as if a scroll were being read" (678). Genealogy as cultural quest can inscribe an authorized African American history by revalidating the oral and everyday erased in the writing of official history. Haley mobilizes the tools of the scriptural historian: the name fragment of "Kintay" lingers in his memory until curiosity activates it as his own "Rosetta Stone" to be decoded (669). Haley's narrative is teleological, moving toward the final "fulfillment" chapters, where he is revealed as both the narrator who has been in the background and the inheritor and bearer of a genealogical tradition. Implicitly his mission offers African Americans a way of "getting a life" that is generationally resonant in providing symbolic tools for social mobility and familial consolidation.

Roots opens an alternative context for potent family history in the oral culture of a Mandinke village and enlivens genealogical detail with the biographical richness of narrative. Mimicking the griot, Haley makes genealogical record into a "talking book."[29] He reforms the detached objectivity of the genealogist into an instrument for reinventing the family as a transformative experience for the reader-searcher. In so doing, he uncovers in genealogy a transparently autobiographical impetus that it abhors yet secretes as familial "glue." The pointed mistrust of genealogists for autobiography may be read against its covert narrative "itch." *Roots* both calls on and confounds documentary evidence in exposing the speculative character and mythic power of genealogical legitimation for historically invisible subjects.

Autobiography and Genealogy: Incompatible Frames of Reference?

I first became aware of the immensity of the genealogical enterprise in the United States when I attended the yearly convention of the Montana State Genealogical Society, along with more than a hundred people who journeyed for as long as ten hours to convene, appropriately, in Great Falls to discuss their descendancy. There were two speakers, a professor of history expert in genealogy from Brigham Young University, who had worked extensively with the Family History Library in Salt Lake City; and myself, a displaced Midwesterner defending the usefulness of autobiography for family history. We had virtually no assumptions in common. The expert focused on records: how to track down, gain access to, verify, and possess acceptable copies of them. For him, family history was a matter of irrefutable documentation and unambiguous attribution. I, on the other hand, was interested in family history as a means of collective self-creation giving voice to the past, be it in attic diaries or fragments of memory or silent, inherited things. This experience led me to wonder whether autobiography and genealogy have anything to say to each other. Are they mutually informing, sustainable activities, or unrelated, incompatible impulses?

These questions are not idle ones, because the issues of the autobiographical referent, the relationship of the one who writes to the one who speaks, and the verification of that identity in a "pact" with the reader have been at the heart of debates about autobiography since Philippe Lejeune theorized the autobiographical pact. Critics have disputed whether the subject of autobiography is referential or in some sense deconstructed, always already de-faced. Paul John Eakin argues for relocating the referentiality of autobiography to its mode of representing the subject's inscription in history. He notes that theoreticians of autobiography have moved from "a documentary view of autobiography as a record of referential fact to a performative view of autobiography centered on the act of composition" as a revised way of conceiving "the reality of the past."[30]

Unwilling to surrender the referential dimension of autobiography yet concerned with "the agency of the imagination" and "the individual's constructed relation to history," Eakin proposes two projects: (1) reconceiving the work of history phenomenologically as "the individual's experience of 'historicity,'" and (2) expanding our awareness of the kinds of historical reference that autobiography may make (144–45). Eakin's analysis suggests that autobiography can furnish a more extensive account of lived history than can the documented historical record. In that sense the autobiographical story of the family is a "truer" account than the genealogical pedigree, precisely because it incorporates several modes of rendering lived experience. Haley's project in *Roots*, the genealogical quest subsumed in a mythic history impossible to verify through documents, has resonated as a collective authorization, or what Eakin terms a "sustaining structure of relation" to the past through autobiographical writing (157).

Autobiography and genealogy address personal history from different locations and for different ends. Whereas documenting historical "fact" is at the heart of genealogy, autobiography does not rely on the verifiability of the information given, but on something else that has been variously described as the sincerity of the writer-reader pact (Lejeune), belief in the writer's credible ethos (Beaujour), and multiple modes of representing lived history (Eakin).[31] Autobiography is located at an uneasy nexus of past—the retrospective record of one's life—and future—the wishes, dreams, and aspirations of the subject-in-process. Autobiography's multi-directionality is inflected by eruptions of the present, its "present-ification" in Louis Renza's term, that repeatedly destabilize the linear narrative with the complexity of self-experience in the moment of writing.[32] Subject-ification, autobiography as the liberation of possible identities from past fixity, is a coming to voice inimical to the descent-oriented project of genealogy. Although autobiography does not create stable, autonomous, free subjects that endure, it proposes the liberatory possibility of human agency—for future readers, if not for the writer. Genealogy's use of life history retrospectively, by contrast, embeds legitimate subjects in an extended historical chain.

Genealogy and autobiography can be contrasted on several counts:

> Genealogy detects the recorded past; autobiography pursues the desire for the creation of a free, agentified subjectivity.
>
> Genealogy is a chronicle that can be verified through documents and records; autobiography depends on memory to dislodge the writing subject from the norms, traditions, and constraints that governed past generations.
>
> Genealogy justifies and legitimates social status, through both genealogical record and the ability to produce a pedigree; autobiography can dispute and revise the inherited past through the different, even contradictory, memories of family members at different historical moments.

In this comparison autobiography emerges, in Sollors's sense, as consent-driven, if not fully consensual.

Genealogical pedigrees are inadequate and even misleading schemata for explaining the multi-referentiality of autobiography. The force of ancestry may be strong in an autobiography such as *The Education of Henry Adams*, where descent from a family of British subjects who became American presidents and statesmen and his father's autobiography cast a long shadow on the writer's own project. But the imbrication of autobiography and genealogy is unavailable to, say, fifth-generation ex-slaves in the mid-nineteenth century writing a narrative of liberation from the "hell" of slavery, who could not present ancestral records to legitimate themselves. In autobiography the desire for origin and rooting has to be relocated from the verifiable past to a sense of emergent and incomplete history existing in a productive tension between individual and public notions of experience. If genealogy is driven by an ideology of the durability of family and the significance of origins now being contested in postmodern America, does genealogy sustain a nostalgia for what, in some sense, never was? The pedigree that embeds the contemporary nuclear family in a network reaching several generations into the past suggests a yearning for verifiable historical connection. Autobiography both cultivates and resists a genealogical impulse in its inclination to "root" self-location and self-understanding in the experience of lived history. Getting an autobiographical life neither replicates models of selfhood uncritically nor appropriates the privileges of subjectivity recklessly. And yet the genealogical project, in another sense, has been revived as a critical method for reforming the imperial gesture of autobiographical selfhood, the claim to "have" a historically significant life.

"Genealogical" historicization, as distinct from the institution of tracing family origins, is used by recent theorists uneasy about the imperializing and ethnocentric claims of identity discourses. Following Foucault, Michael J. Shapiro has proposed the application of genealogical method as a critical apparatus for political analysis.[33] Shapiro's notion of "genealogical history loosens the hold of present arrangements by finding their points of emergence as practices and thus by opposing the forces tending to neutralize them."[34] Shapiro explicitly contrasts the genealogical and the (auto)biographical as opposed modes of cultural analysis: the (auto)biographical posits an individual, autonomous human subject that imposes its view of the world as the mode of interpretation and naturalizes its others. The genealogical, in contrast, is a method that attempts to evacuate subjectivity from the analysis of practices by making it critically, ironically self-conscious. A genealogical understanding makes a textually registered acknowledgment that what it represents are humanly constituted "peculiar acts of the imagination rather than ... outer structures of the world."[35]

Shapiro's argument for the genealogist as a figure of the postmodern critic radically reinterprets the practice of traditional genealogists that I have been tracing and suggests a model for rethinking the position of the autobiographer as well. If genealogy as a naturalized practice has forgotten its own contextual basis, ironically self-critical theorizing may correct the excesses of imposing subjects and the evacuation of othered subjects. The implications of this critical reinterpretation exceed the reach of this essay, but they suggest a possible redirection of the genealogical impulse to privilege descent and hierarchy. Genealogy as a liberatory method of relationality without pedigrees may become, for the reflective subject, a means of getting a new kind of life.

Notes

1. Anzia Yezierska, *Children of Loneliness* (New York: Funk & Wagnalls, 1923), 10. Quoted in William Boelhower, "The Making of Ethnic Autobiography in the United States," in *American Autobiography: Retrospect and Prospect*, ed. Paul John Eakin (Madison: University of Wisconsin Press, 1991), 137.
2. Philippe Lejeune, "The Autobiographical Pact (bis)," in *On Autobiography*, ed. Paul John Eakin, trans. Katherine Leary (Minneapolis: University of Minnesota Press 1989), 133.
3. Louis Renza, "The Veto of the Imagination: A Theory of Autobiography," in *Autobiography: Essays Theoretical and Critical*, ed. James Olney (Princeton, N.J.: Princeton University Press, 1980), 293.
4. This information is taken from a handout of the Lawrence Ward Family History Center. Another center handout notes that a worldwide index available on microfiche lists about 187 million names of deceased persons; living persons are not included. The church's Family History Library materials may be used at its centers throughout the world by persons of any faith.
5. Crèvecoeur idealistically states that genealogy will count for nothing in the New World: "the American . . . is neither an European nor the descendant of an European; hence that strange mixture of blood, which you will find in no other country . . . the American . . . leaving behind him all his ancient prejudices and manners, receives new ones from the new mode of life he has embraced." St. John de Crèvecoeur, "Letter III—What Is an American?" in *Letters from an American Farmer: An*

Early American Reader, ed. J. A. Leo Lemay (Washington, D.C.: U.S. Information Agency, 1985), 120.

6   Werner Sollors, *Beyond Ethnicity: Consent and Descent in American Culture* (New York: Oxford University Press, 1986). Sollors is critical of the emphasis on ethnic identity and roots: "In the present climate consent-conscious Americans are willing to perceive ethnic distinction—differentiation which they seemingly base exclusively on descent, no matter how far removed and how artificially selected and constructed—as powerful and as crucial. . . . Taken to its radical conclusion, such a position really assumes that there is no shared history and no human empathy, that you have your history and I have mine" (13). But as Sau-Ling Cynthia Wong has argued, it is impossible to go "beyond ethnicity" without engaging multiple differences both among ethnicities and *within* the generations of each, a complex discussion that she sees Sollors and Boelhower as unwilling to engage. See Wong, "Immigrant Autobiography: Some Questions of Definition and Approach," in *American Autobiography: Retrospect and Prospect*, ed. Paul John Eakin (Madison: University of Wisconsin Press, 1991), 142–70.

7   Boelhower, "The Making of Ethnic Autobiography," 137.

8   The *United States Research Outline* is officially titled *Research Outline: United States*, bur is usually referred to by the former name; I will henceforth refer to it as USRO, and page numbers will appear in the text. I will refer to the Church of Jesus Christ of Latter-day Saints by conventional usage as the Mormons or the Church of Latter-day Saints. The genealogical materials of the Family History Library that I used in preparing this essay include "Research Outline: Michigan," "Research Outline: Montana," and "Research Outline: United States" (Salt Lake City: Corporation of the President of the Church of Jesus Christ of Latter-day Saints, 1988).

9   The information on archives, libraries, journals, and bibliographies is drawn from both the *United States Research Outline* and from Gilbert H. Doane and James B. Bell, *Searching for Your Ancestors: The How and Why of Genealogy*, 6th ed. (Minneapolis: University of Minnesota Press, 1992), especially 309 (henceforth SYA). Page numbers for further citations of this work appear in text in parentheses. The enduring popularity of this how-to is attested to by its numerous editions and by its selection for the Quality Paperback Book Club in 1992, the marketing materials of which described it as "the most readable and reliable genealogical how-to book available."

10 Metaphors of detection and uncovering, so important for genealogy, are of course central to Freudian psychoanalysis. In Freud's *Gradiva*, the archaeological project of excavating forgotten layers of memory within the individual psyche is compared to a set of strata throughout the history of a culture. Similarly, genealogical inquiry is seen as access to the textured strata of national history.

11 Narrativization of life history is being interestingly investigated from several disciplinary approaches. Psychologists, for example, have used the observations of Jerome Bruner (see "Life as Narrative," *Social Research* 54 [1987]: 11–32) about narrative construction of life history to study "autobiographical memory": how oral narrators subdivide memories into episodes or "chapters," segments that they have analyzed and compared with written memories solicited in other studies. See David B. Pilmer, Lynne Krensky, Sandra N. Kleinman, Lynn R. Goldsmith, and Sheldon H. White, "Chapters on Narratives: Evidence from Oral Histories of the First Year in College," *Journal of Narrative and Life History* 1 (1991): 3–14, especially 3–5.

12 Mary McCarthy, *Memories of a Catholic Girlhood* (New York: Harcourt Brace 1957).

13 Bruce R. McConkie, *Mormon Doctrine*, 2d ed. (Salt Lake City: Bookcraft, 1966), 308–9.

14 Ibid., 274.

15 Vern Anderson, "Dead or Alive, Mormons Want Everyone Baptized" (Associated Press), in *Missoulian*, April 30, 1994, A-5. Baptized saints include Augustine, Thomas Aquinas, Francis of Assisi, and many others.

16 "Endless Genealogies," in *Mormonism: Shadow or Reality?* 5th ed., ed. Jerald Tanner and Sandra Tanner (Salt Lake City: Utah Lighthouse Ministry, 1987), 452. A testimonial entry by John Taylor, third president of the Mormon Church, states that the spirits of the signers "waited on me for two days and two nights" until he could be baptized for them, along with Christopher Columbus, John Wesley, and all U.S. presidents but three whose cause was not yet "just." Quoted in *Journal of Discourses* 19: 229.

17 Anderson, "Dead or Alive." Although duplications are a problem, during the Millennium mortal mistakes in record gathering and recording are to be rectified: "The Creator has the master list."

18 Tamara K. Hareven, "Continuity and Change in the American Family," in *Making America*, ed. Luther S. Luedtke (Washington, D.C.: U.S. Information Agency, 1987), 253–55. Hareven notes: "The historical evidence now shows that there has never been in American society an

era when co-residence of three generations in the same household was the dominant pattern. The 'great extended families' that have become part of the folklore of modern industrial society were rarely in existence" (241–42).

19 Mae Gwendolyn Henderson, "Speaking in Tongues: Dialogics, Dialectics, and the Black Woman Writer's Literary Tradition," in *Reading Black, Reading Feminist*, ed. Henry Louis Gates Jr. (New York: Penguin, 1990), 139, n. 6.

20 Note the carefully neutral language in which Doane and Bell describe historical "othering": "There was no special procedure for noting free blacks in the first census, so they were frequently recorded in the 'other' category, which also included American Indians. Furthermore, the census enumerators freely noted of some families that they were Negro, mulatto, or free, but some received no racial designation at all. Until 1850 only the heads of households were identified by name" (SYA 205).

21 For example, Gerard Baker, the first Native American superintendent of Little Big Horn National Monument (formerly Custer Battlefield), has noted that he has eighty-seven familial relationships, all of which are known. Lecture delivered at the University of Montana, September 15, 1994.

22 A prejudice against dark skin in some parts of the Book of Mormon notwithstanding. See the discussion below of African Americans and the Book of Mormon.

23 This information is taken from Jerald Tanner and Sandra Tanner, eds., *Mormonism: Shadow or Reality?* 5th ed. (Salt Lake City: Utah Lighthouse Ministry, 1987). The Tanners were excommunicated, at their request, from the Mormon Church in 1960 for challenging its doctrines, and they have waged a critique of Mormon doctrine in their books and newsletter, *Salt Lake City Messenger*, since that time. Their pre-1978 chapter, "The Negro in Mormon Theology," cites derogatory passages on the barbarism of dark-skinned peoples from several additional Mormon sources, notably *The Juvenile Instructor* (262–63). Unquestionably this critique is controversial, but it is supported by a sizable group of questioning and ex-Mormons. I am indebted to my colleague Judith Johnson at the University of Montana for the Tanner texts and the narrative of her firsthand experience.

24 Sources for material on Black life in both the United States and Africa include the bibliographical guide *Black Genesis* (James Rose and Alice Eicholz, 1978), the histories of free blacks by Carter G. Woodson,

Black military records, and the Schomburg Library in New York City (SYA 204–5).

25 See Johni Cerny, "From Maria to Bill Cosby: A Case Study in Tracing Black Slave Ancestry," *National Genealogical Society Quarterly* 75 (March 1987): 5–14 cited in SYA (207). Cerny is a noted genealogist who attempted to establish the family line of the Cosby family.

26 Alex Haley, *Roots: The Saga of an American Family* (Garden City, N.Y.: Doubleday, 1976), 686, 681. Page references for further citations of this work are included in the text in parentheses.

27 At this time discussion of Haley's project is complicated by the "discovery," after his death, that much of the "authenticated" material left in his estate and used for the television miniseries *Queen* was fictionalized rather than documented by research. This discovery has made less certain some of his statements about genealogical verification in *Roots*. See *New York Times*, March 3, 1993, C18:4. For this essay the "truth" question is not central, however, as Haley was demonstrably mobilizing a vast machinery of documentary verification to authorize, through an oral tradition, subjects for whom documents of written origin are largely absent.

28 The griot is a liminal figure because he or she spins tales and uses rhetoric in mediating; traditionally, griots are of the lowest social caste and are shunned by uncasted warriors. For an elegant and sophisticated discussion of the functions of griots in traditional West African cultures, see Christopher L. Miller, *Theories of Africans* (Chicago: University of Chicago Press, 1990), especially 79–87 and 114–80.

29 The trope of the talking book has been important for recent theorizing of African American autobiography. See especially Henry Louis Gates Jr., *The Signifying Monkey* (New York: Oxford University Press, 1988), 127–68.

30 Paul John Eakin, *Touching the World: Reference in Autobiography* (Princeton, N.J.: Princeton University Press, 1992), 143. Page references for further citations of this work are included in the text in parentheses.

31 The difference of autobiography from fiction is discussed by Philippe Lejeune in "The Autobiographical Pact," in *On Autobiography*, ed. Paul John Eakin, trans. Katherine Leary (Minneapolis: University of Minnesota Press, 1989), 3–30. Autobiography as *doxa*, received opinion, rather than biography, is explored in Michel Beaujour, *Miroirs d'encre* (Paris: Seuil, 1980). Autobiography as lived history is discussed in Eakin, *Touching the World*, 138–80.

32 Louis Renza, "The Veto of the Imagination: A Theory of Autobiography," in *Autobiography: Essays Theoretical and Critical*, ed. James Olney (Princeton, N.J.: Princeton University Press, 1980), 277–79.

33 See also Walter Benn Michaels, "Race into Culture: A Critical Genealogy of Cultural Identity," *Critical Inquiry* 18 (Summer 1992): 655–85. Benn Michaels applies the "objectivity" of genealogical tracing as a corrective to ethnicity-based identity claims and, in so doing, uses a "genealogical" method to subvert the discourse of descent by which such claims are privileged. Benn Michaels's position is, however, extreme; he views all claims to identity as "essentialist" (689 n. 39).

34 Michael J. Shapiro, *Reading the Postmodern Polity: Political Theory as Textual Practice* (Minneapolis: University of Minnesota Press, 1992), 12. Shapiro also conducts a sustained critique of biography in *The Politics of Representation: Writing Practice in Biography, Photography, and Policy Analysis* (Madison: University of Wisconsin Press, 1988). As his analysis does not make a distinction between autobiography and biography, I would argue that his critique applies primarily to biographical texts and acts, whereas the conditions of autobiographical selfhood require a critical self-analysis of self as simultaneously subject and object. Thus, much autobiographical reflexivity acknowledges its own constructed and unstable status, its distance from "outer structures of the world."

35 Shapiro, *Reading the Postmodern Polity*, 10.

6
VIRTUALLY ME: A TOOLBOX ABOUT ONLINE SELF-PRESENTATION (2014)

Opportunities for composing, assembling, and networking lives have expanded exponentially since the advent of Web 2.0. The sites and software of digital media provide occasions for young people to narrate moments in coming of age; for families to track and narrate their genealogical histories; for people seeking friends and lovers or those with similar hobbies to make connections; for political activists to organize around movements and causes. These everyday sites of self-presentation appear to be categorically different from what is understood as traditional life writing, be it published autobiography, memoir, or confession. And yet, as Nancy Baym (2006) observes, "online spaces are constructed and the activities that people do online are intimately interwoven with the construction of the offline world and the activities and structures in which we participate, whether we are using the Internet or not" (86, qtd. in Gray 2009, 1168). Thus, online lives exist in complicated relationship to offline lives and to what has been termed the "outernet" (Nakamura 2008, 1676). And "electronic persons" have multiple connections to "proximate individuals," as J. Schmitz (1997) has observed (qtd. in Kennedy 2006, 4). For these reasons, the analytical frames and theoretical positions of scholarship on life writing can provide helpful concepts and categories for thinking about the proliferation of online lives in varied media and across a wide range of sites.

Our contribution to understanding subjectivity and identities online, as well as the modes and media mobilized to present and perform lives, is this toolkit, organized alphabetically through rubrics derived from the framework we developed in *Reading Autobiography* (Smith and Watson 2010).[1] Studying the presentation of online lives makes clear that both the self and its presentation are only apparently autonomous, as many life-narrative theorists, as well as media theorists, argue. In fact, online lives are fundamentally relational or refracted through engagement with the lives of their significant others: the lives presented are often interactive; they are co-constructed; they are linked to others—family, friends, employers, causes, and affiliations. Many online lives profess attachments not to flesh-and-blood others but to media personages, consumer products, and works of art or music linked to online resources such as YouTube videos. As N. Katherine Hayles asserts for electronic literature, so for online relationships and subjectivities: they are re-described and re-presented "in terms of a networked environment in which individual selves blend into a collectivity, human boundaries blur as people merge with technological apparatus, and cultural formations are reconfigured to reflect and embody a cyborgian reality" (Hayles 2003).

Here we offer two preliminary comments. The first clarifies the key terms "self," "subject," and "subject position" as used in this toolkit. Throughout, we use the term "self" as a pronomial marker of reflexivity, the shorthand term for acts of self-reference. This sense of the term should not, however, be conflated with the liberal humanist concept of the self as a rational, autonomous, self-knowing, and coherent actor, which is a legacy of the Enlightenment. Indeed, this liberal humanist self, understood as essential, free, and agentic, has been a focus of critique for four decades. When constructing personal web pages or the like, users themselves often imagine that they are revealing their "real" or "true" essence, a person or "me" who is unique, singular, and outside social constructions and constraints.[2] Theorists of media and autobiography, however, approach the constructed self not as an essence but as a subject, a moving target, which provisionally conjoins memory, identity, experience, relationality, embodiment, affect, and limited agency.

In online self-presentation as in offline life narration, then, the "I" of reference is constructed and situated, and not identical with its flesh-and-blood maker.[3] Moreover, that "I" is constituted through discursive formations, which are heterogeneous, conflictual, and intersectional, and which allocate subject positions to those who are interpellated through their ideological frames, tropes, and language. Those subject positions in turn attach to salient cultural and historical identities. Both offline and online, the autobiographical subject can be approached as an ensemble or assemblage of subject positions through which self-understanding and self-positioning are negotiated.

Our second comment clarifies what the term "online lives" encompasses in this chapter.[4] Many media theorists invoke the term "digital storytelling" to refer to the transmission of personal stories in digital forms. Nick Couldry, for example, refers to "the whole range of personal stories now being told in potentially public form using digital media resources" (Couldry 2008, 347). We follow Couldry's lead in limiting online lives to "online personal narrative formats ... [now] prevalent: ... multimedia formats such as MySpace and Facebook, textual forms such as webblogs (blogs), the various story forms prevalent on more specialist digital storytelling sites or the many sites where images and videos, including material captured on personal mobile devices, can be collected for wider circulation (such as YouTube)" (381–82). We oscillate between the forms attached to particular sites, and the acts and practices of self-representation and self-performance employed by users on a range of standardized forms and templates.

Further, we do not take up oral storytelling such as co-produced stories told in offline workshops and then mounted online.

Others have focused on the contrast of online narrative forms to practices of oral storytelling and projects involving listening to others' stories, as does Joe Lambert (2012) and scholars and writers affiliated with the Center for Digital Storytelling in Berkeley, California. Nor do we consider the collective websites that make available collaboratively produced life stories of ordinary people, such as StoryCorps, Lifebio.com, or My Life Is True. While many kinds of online life stories use autobiographical templates for narration, not all are produced by the single subject/user telling, performing, and/or imaging a life, the focus of this chapter.

In our online toolkit of fifteen concepts presented in alphabetical order, each brief discussion is followed by questions to enable scholars and students to productively engage with the vast variety of sites presenting lives online. You might pose these questions as you produce or interact with online "life" presentations of many sorts: an opinion blog, a profile of a desirable self on a dating site, a webcam "reality" video, a Facebook profile or LiveJournal entry. The questions offer points of entry for analyzing online self-presentations and points of departure for constructing, and critiquing, your own online life and those of others.

Archives and Databases

Online sites gather, authorize, and conserve the version of self a user is assembling. Various kinds of documents become evidence capturing varied aspects of the presenter's life, habits, desires, and the like. That is, a site incorporates and organizes documents about a self as a personal archive, and that personal archive may become incorporated into other archives, official or unofficial, designed or accidental. Moreover, the algorithmic data generated by the site directs information about the self into online databases. The prodigious capacities of online archives have therefore shifted how we understand the relationship of archives to databases. Tara McPherson (2011) argues that today's database has supplanted the archive, and distinguishes the archive—which has an archivist of some kind, a principle of collection, and a design for storage and structure for categorization—from the database, which is an instrument of a governmentality that bureaucratizes and commodifies bits and pieces of information.

Neither the archive nor the database has a fail-safe delete button for past tidbits of the self. Code may break down, and the new service industry of reputation management may eventually delete substantial data archives. Nonetheless, online users are implicated in contributing user-generated content, which can return in digital afterlives, as online archives and databases become ever more searchable. Thus, the archival possibilities of the Web include deliberate efforts by users to store a profile that becomes an online version of the self; the random bits that are dispersed across the Internet that could be pulled in to construct, alter, or contest a user profile; accidental archives assembled by others such as Wikileaks, which disseminate personal data that has been kept out of public circulation; reassemblages of the data of the self, circulated by others with varied motivations; and the "digital character" (Noguchi 2011) that data aggregators assemble from user's buying habits, GPS locations, phone connections, and the like.

In examining an online site of self-presentation, consider the following questions related to archiving and producing data. What comprises a database through which "digital character" is constructed? Who benefits from the accumulation of data about users? What comprises an archive of self and how is it built? Are official documents scanned in, such as birth, marriage, or death certificates, or citizenship records? How are the documents authenticated, and is that certification persuasive? What kind of authority does the user seek to establish in assembling documentation to curate a life? Is a motive or purpose given for this documentation? Are the testimonies of others included or links made to them? Is there a link to evidence asserting the history and legitimacy of a larger group?

Over time, online presentation of embodiment creates an archive of the body. What kind of archive of embodiment can be observed on various sites? Does it make visible segments of the life cycle, or particular bodily forms, or particular conditions of the body? Which aspects of the body archive are drawn from history, and which are projected as fantasies of a future moment in the life cycle?

For what occasions, to what extent, and for whom is an archive or database being assembled? Which media of archiving have been employed and to what effects? Is the purpose of self-archiving to build a legacy, to mislead or deceive by creating a false identity, and/or to register a history of successfully overcoming a past identity? Has the user's life story been inserted into someone else's archive, for example in the collection of stories amassed by the StoryCorps project on National Public Radio, in sports histories, or in opposition research for political campaigns? What larger story does the archive produce? Does the site construct a history that aims to counteract or undermine other information available online about the user?

Digital archives are unlike print archives in several ways: the categories and hierarchies of information storage are leveled; the incidental and the characteristic seem of the same magnitude and significance. Careless users can lie and conflate people sharing a characteristic such as name or birthdate. What is involved in searching an archive for some part of one's story or history? How do the archives of such institutions as the Church of the Latter-day Saints or websites such as ancestry.com contribute to a user's story and how might their protocols co-construct that story?

Audiences

Online venues assume, invite, and depend on audiences, sometimes intimate, sometimes not. Both how a site appeals to an audience and the kind of response it solicits deserve attention. It may seek to enhance its authority with endorsements from, or links to, celebrities, experts, or an index of commercial success. It may invite a voyeuristic response by offering access to intimate details about the subject of the site or others. It may feed an appetite for the melancholic, sensational, morbid, or violent. Visitors also need to follow the money, evaluating who has funded and who is asked to contribute to the site. It may espouse a social need or cause, but users may want to determine who paid to mount the site or who ultimately profits from it.

What kind of audience does the site call for? Whom does the site explicitly address as its imagined audience? What verbal or visual rhetorics does the site deploy to engage visitors? How does the site attempt to bracket out potentially hostile users from its audience? What is the reach of the assumed or desired audience—local, national, transnational? Are issues of language or cultural difference foregrounded and are ways of translating those differences provided on the site?

What action does the site invite its audience to undertake or support? What affect does the site seek to produce in readers—for instance, shame, pity, anger, or melancholy? And how might actual users respond in ways aligned or unaligned with an affect? How is audience interaction incorporated into the self-presentation? Over a longer period of time, how much change or continuity can be observed in the self-presented?

In terms of actual users, who are the frequent users, and what are their demographics or characteristics as a group? What other audiences might use or interact with the site? Are there potentially hostile users, or user groups, that the site tries to bracket out? Has the demographic of the audience changed over time, and if so, in what ways? Is the audience a potential market, and what kind of a market?

Authenticity

Users find online environments potent sites for constructing and trying out versions of self. The availability of multiple and heterogeneous sites for self-presentation promises seemingly endless opportunities for conveying some "truth" about an "authentic" self for those with access to web technologies. The selves produced through various sites can convey to visitors and users a sense of intimacy—the intimacy of the quotidian details of daily life, the intimacy of shared confession and self-revelation, the intimacy of a unique voice or persona or virtual sensibility, contributory to the intimate public sphere theorized by Lauren Berlant (1997) and Poletti (2011).

Yet cultural commentators question the extent to which presenters can be "authentic" in virtual environments. If by authenticity, one means the unmediated access to some "essence" or "truth" of a subject, virtual environments only make clearer the critique of poststructural theorists that all self-presentation is performative, that authenticity is an effect, not an essence. Jeff Pooley (2011), for instance, observes that "authenticity today is more accurately described as 'calculated authenticity'—... stage management. The best way to sell yourself is to not appear to be selling yourself." David Graxian even more strongly emphasizes that authenticity is "manufactured." Graxian is exploring the ways in which authenticity is "manufactured" within the context of the Chicago blues club, but his observations on this offline environment are productive for thinking about digital authenticity: "Broadly speaking," he writes, "the notion of authenticity suggests two separate but related attributes. First, it can refer to the ability of a place or event to conform to an idealized representation of reality: that is, to a set of expectations regarding how such a thing ought to look, sound, and feel. At the same time, authenticity can refer to the credibility or sincerity of a performance and its ability to come off as natural and effortless" (Graxian 2003, 10–11; cited in Gray 2009, 1164).

If authenticity can be "manufactured," if it is an effect of features of self-performance, then credibility, veracity, and sincerity acquire a slipperiness that can prompt suspicious readings (see Smith and Watson 2012). And indeed, users themselves often read sites with a skeptical eye, assessing the presenter's degree of sincerity or speculating about whether he or she is posing as a false identity. Alternatively, authenticity can be rethought through the concept of "realness" proposed by Judith/Jack Halberstam. Halberstam shifts attention from questions of authenticity to the unpredictability of effects in the world. She/he defines "realness" as "not exactly performance, not exactly an imitation; it is the way that people, minorities, excluded from the domain of the real, appropriate the real and its effects" (Halberstam 2005, 51; cited in Gray 2009, 1163). Appropriations of realness in online environments may reinforce social norms and they may open a space for recognition of the constructedness of those norms.

In interacting with online performances of self, the following questions arise with regard to authenticity and realness. Is this a site where the authenticity of self-presentation matters and if so, for whom and for what reasons? What strategies for creating a situated, historical subject does the user or site mobilize? Does an aura of authenticity attach to a particular identity category on particular kinds of sites; for example, sites acknowledging victimization or transgression such as coming-out sites, weight sites, illness sites, or grief sites?

What strategies for winning belief are deployed? What are identified as guarantors of authenticity on a site? How convincing are those guarantors? Are there different kinds of guarantors for different kinds of sites? For example, webcam sites seem to guarantee the moment-to-moment authenticity of the subject of their surveillance, and yet "surveillance realism" can be manufactured as reality show. The web-based video series that began in June 2006 named LonelyGirl15, for instance, was unmasked in September 2006 as inauthentic, a bid to gain celebrity status for an aspiring nineteen-year-old American actor (Jessica Lee Rose as Bree Avery). The narration of personal histories on video sites such as YouTube appears to be a slice of life, but the production of a video is a collective project involving a camera person, a sound person, and sometimes a director other than the performing "I." How, then, is the aura of authenticity attached to an online performance constructed by a crew, which could include a camera person, sound person, director, and script-writer? Do you find this self-presentation to be sincere or to be calculated authenticity, a pose or "manufactured" pseudo-individuality?

How is "authenticity" surveilled online? How does the site try to convince visitors of its creator's "truthfulness"? What degree of fabrication or exaggeration do visitors tolerate and correct for in an online environment? For instance, on dating sites users may expect idealized representations of others as younger, thinner, and more attractive, and adjust for a vanity-driven profile. How does an aura of authenticity get attached to "anonymity" in sites where the user is not identified? Can a fabricated online identity contribute to a different kind of "truth" aimed at correcting a social harm or inequity? That is, to what extent does it matter that an online identity is inauthentic if the blogger or journal writer claims to speak on behalf of victims who cannot dare to risk speaking out publicly? What are the larger politics of authenticity in the global traffic in narratives of suffering? What is the relationship of authenticity to the ideological formations of global capitalism, to transnational activism, to online marketing, to reputation management?

Automediality

Scholars in media studies and autobiography studies invoke a set of related terms to illuminate the relationship of technologies and subjectivity: medium, mediation, mediatization, automediality, autobiomediality, and transmediality. Jay David Bolter and Richard Grusin (2000), for instance, describe the relation of medium and mediation in this way: "A medium is that which remediates. It is that which appropriates the techniques, forms, and social significance of other media and attempts to rival or refashion them in the name of the real" (65). British cultural studies theorists are concerned to distinguish mediatization generally from mediation. "Mediation," observes Nick Couldry, "emphasize[s] the heterogeneity of the transformations to which media give rise across a complex and divided social space" (Couldry 2008, 375). Mediatization, in contrast, "describes the transformation of many disparate social and cultural processes into forms or formats suitable for media representation" (377). His argument is that media cannot simply be conceptualized as "tools" for presenting a preexisting, essential self. Rather, the materiality of the medium constitutes and textures the subjectivity presented. Media technologies, that is, do not just transparently present the self. They constitute and expand it, and imagine new kinds of virtual sociality, which do not depend on direct or corporeal encounter. (See Smith and Watson 2010,168.)

The concept of automediality (or autobiomediality) directs the concept of mediation to the terrain of the autobiographical and the self-presentation of online sites. It provides a theoretical framework for conceptualizing the way subjectivity is constructed online across visual and verbal forms in new media. Brian Rotman (2009) places the concept of autobiomediality in the long history of encounters between modes of self-enunciation and locates the present moment in "a radically altered regime of space-time" in which there is "an emerging co-presence of mobile, networked selves with identities ... 'in perpetual formation and reformation at the moment of use'" (121). Scholars in Germany and France, among them Joerg Dünne and Christian Moser (2008), have focused on the concept of automediality as well. Ruth E. Page refers to transmediality and multimodality as forms of electronic literature that are gaining attention in narrative studies (2008). Automediality implies an aesthetics of collage, mosaic, pastiche. Subjectivity cannot be regarded as an entity or essence; it is a bricolage or set of disparate fragments, rather than a coherent, inborn unit of self. Automedial practices of digital life writing impact the prosthetic extension of self in networks, the reorientation of bodies in virtual space, the perspectival positioning of subjects, and alternative embodiments.

How does the choice of a medium or media contribute to the construction of subjectivity on a particular site? If you observe multiple media of self-presentation, where do you see them merging or conflicting in a self-presentation?

Avatars

Embodiment is a translation in various media of the experienced and sensed materiality of the self. While the body is always dematerialized in virtual representation, embodiment in many forms and media is a prominent feature of online self-presentation. The possibility of configuring oneself as an avatar with nonhuman features and capacities on sites such as *Second Life* or *World of Warcraft* offers new dimensions to the performance of the self. Bodily extensions and fantasies (e.g., of animals, cartoon heroes, or machines; enhanced, streamlined, or transformed human capacities) are enabled. And yet, while avatars are assumed to function as the erasure of identity markers such as race or ethnicity, gender, sexuality, and age, the choice of an avatar can be a form of what Lisa Nakamura (2008) labels "identity tourism." This troubling practice, according to Nakamura, "let users 'wear' racially stereotyped avatars without feeling racist, yet it also blamed users who reveal their real races and were victims of racism online" (1675). She argues that the Internet is not "a post-racial space" where users can "'choose' a race as an identity tourist" or withhold a racial identity (1676), and therefore that the avatar is not necessarily a medium for escaping identity.

What possibilities of avatar identity are generated by site templates and protocols? How is the avatar stylized—through, for instance, adornment of the contemporary or a historical period, body markings, prostheses, or amputation? What does the choice of an avatar suggest about the relationship among bodily systems and organs, visible bodily surfaces, and bodily histories and meaning? How might the codes or rules of a community affect the choice of an avatar?

What social boundaries are crossed or transgressed through self-presentation as an avatar? Are scenarios of desire or violence or mystical transformation enacted and to what end? Are fantasies of embodiment engaged through dreams, rituals, myths, or other projections? How is the avatar of the user related to other bodies? What are the effects of capturing the body in other ways than photos and video? If identity markers are referenced, is there evidence on the site for determining whether they are markers of race, ethnicity, gender, nationality, age? What contextualization in the form of chatting or blogging surrounds the avatar?

Branding

Online environments are fully corporatized, with sites ripe for data mining by aggregators and marketers. So, we can't be surprised that the discourse of corporate management has promoted "Brand Me" as the mode of online self-presentation. Or as William Deresiewicz (2011) observed, "The self today is an entrepreneurial self, a self that's packaged to be sold" (7). That is, the self is regarded as a commodity to be packaged for brokering in a variety of media sites, including videos such as YouTube, the personal websites of entrepreneurs, and product-related sites.

Online venues are preferred vehicles for composing, circulating, monitoring, and managing one's brand. Individual users adopt the methods of corporate marketers, simplifying and honing their self-images and presentational behaviors to project a desirable brand "Me"—digitally hip, successful, fully sociable, intriguing. Some identify what sets them apart in their quirky individuality; some emphasize achievements. Some turn themselves into a kind of "logo," which will consistently deliver a product and up-to-date status reports. As self-curators, users utilize the Web to create a multimedia CV that marks "you" as a brand. The brand is consolidated and marketed through narratives and images, especially those on social networking sites. Thus, telling personal stories or performing one's sense of one's personality is critical to the conveyance of the brand "you." Narrative, profiles, images all link aspects of your experience and your character into a coherent presentation.

With the imperative of branding, however, comes the necessity of managing the brand by managing online reputation. To do this, users may contract with any one of the many reputation managers advertising their services, such as www.reputationmanagement consultants.com and www.ironreputation.com. The message here is that the impulse to online self-disclosure can be reckless and can undermine the self-image or brand a creator wants to project.

Is the creator branding herself or himself on the site? How is the brand linked to autobiographical stories about experiences, character features, achievements? And how convincing is the assertion of brand coherence? How consistently and coherently is branding employed on various sites where the user appears?

Confession Online

Many consider confession a prime motivation for self-presentation in online environments. The sense of intimacy within anonymity that a virtual community of sharers experience in online sites provide may encourage users to disclose secrets but at potential risk to their privacy. Many online sites invite confessional disclosure and set out protocols for the degree and kinds of intimacy they invite. PostSecret, one of the most widespread and intriguing of these, combines the discourse of confession with the material traces of personal forms such as handwriting, photos and drawings, and small objects to secure the promise of authenticity for the secrets disclosed on the handmade postcards mailed or uploaded (which are in turn adjudicated by the site's manager, Frank Warren). As Anna Poletti (2011) observes, the "confessional meta-narrative" of PostSecret protects anonymity through the postal system while connecting the secret to both the body of the creator and to the intimate public who comes to possess it. "The secrets," she emphasizes, *"remain secrets"* (32). The technologies that mark the confession as such may be multiplied and focused in online environments to emphasize its special status for creators and to call site-users to an ethical response to it, though the boundaries of the genre seem more blurred than in its written form as practiced by, say, Augustine, Rousseau, or Joan Didion, Annie Ernaux, and Maya Angelou.

How does the site invite confession of secrets, self-doubts, or fantasies? What guarantees of protection does it offer users, and are those reliable? Does the site link confession to anonymity? What form does the confession take? Is it framed as a "sin" by a religious template? Told as a psychological disclosure? Acknowledged as a political transgression? To what extent does the confession seem "sincere," and why or why not? (Consider both internal evidence within the narrative and its reference to external data.) Is the confession a reference to an incident in the teller's past or to an ongoing habit pattern? In what ways is, or isn't, the narrating "I" distinct from the narrated actor who did the deed or had the thought? Are others implicated as victims or as beneficiaries? Has some form of retribution been made, and if so, how? In your view, was it sufficient to redress the harm? Is the confessor overly scrupulous about her or his actions or motivations? Who benefits from this act of confession? What politics does the confession seem to serve? What communities?

What risks and rewards of the online confession are observable? What role did or do site visitors play in pardoning the confessor? Do they remain a multiple, impersonal audience or are they personalized? Does the confession generate similar acts by visitors, and if so, to what effect?

Ethics

The Web seems to be a fluid environment in which "anything goes"; but increasingly, users, corporations, and managers are confronting difficult ethical issues related to online behaviors, borrowing, copyright, repurposing of gathered materials (such as video clips and images), surveillance, and data-mining. Ethical questions about appropriate online behavior, for instance, relate to the site and its management and to users.

Site management can be a form of self-care or a form of surveillance. Does the site articulate an ethics as a protocol for its use, and does it observe that ethics? How do the site and its management assert or delimit zones of privacy? How does the site address issues related to disclosure of intimate details? Does the site protect anonymity? Does the site propose a code of use relating to borrowing from other sites? Is some form of remedy available to users with respect to these ethical issues? What implicit dangers or risks to self-disclosure exist on this site? Does the site address the implications for vulnerable users such as children?

Users engaged in acts and practices of online self-presentation also confront pressing ethical issues. Does the user assert or imply an ethical code or practice on his or her site? What is the ethics of going public with intimate material about family and friends in the context of online self-presentation? What is the ethics of appropriating materials from other people's lives or sites? How can users manage their personal sites to care for their privacy and vulnerability while pursuing self-exploration or trying out versions of selves? How does a personal ethics of online self-performance intersect with a corporatized system for developing and managing one's public image? What is at stake in the conjunction of excessive attention to performing one's self and the increasing scope of surveillance enabled by the technology and by site monitors?

Global Circuits

The instantaneity and reach of Internet technologies join people together as what is considered a global community of users. But access to online technologies remains unevenly distributed across the globe. Moreover, the asymmetrical distribution of access and benefits; the differential treatment of the labor forces producing hardware, software, and cloudware; the differential degrees of technical literacy; the incommensurability of culturally specific idioms of self-presentation; and the persistence of larger formations of imperialism and neocolonialism all impact the lived realities of the digital divide and the digital future. At the same time, though, the increasing digital literacy and access to some kind of technology such as cell phones, the proliferation of translation sites, and the availability of nonlinguistic modes of communication mean that the possibilities for linking one's story and self-presentation across geographic, languages, and political borders have expanded.

To what extent does online self-presentation map onto transnational social identities, political movements, activist causes, or transnational formations such as global youth cultures, human rights movements, and transnational community-building among indigenous peoples across the globe? On sites that assemble an archive of life stories, such as those witnessing to histories of violence, how do paratexts around them, testimonials embedded in them, and their placement online affect the subject position of the witness, the form of story told, and the projected audience? What kinds of responses are invited from visitors to the site, for instance, a donation of money or a pledge of advocacy? To what extent is an online self-presentation implicated in programs and policies of a neoliberal nation-state or in efforts to subvert or challenge a neoliberal ideology? How might online acts and practices of self-presentation reassemble the textual legacies of one or diverse cultural traditions that extend back over centuries?

What means of self-translation are available to users addressing a global audience? How are photos and videos mobilized to translate a self across differences of language and culture? What kinds of online lives gain salience and why and how?

Identity Online

While identity is often regarded as a set of components of personhood, such as markers of gender, race, nationality, class, sexuality, generation, family genealogy, political belief, and religious affiliation, theorists have come to view identities as multiple, provisional, contextual, intersectional, and historically specific. That is, people are situated and situate themselves discursively in relation to context-specific social norms, which determine and constitute identities as subject positions. In the expanding array of virtual environments, identities become increasingly manipulable. Indeed, for some commentators, online identity, as virtual, seems unbounded, purely a matter of choice and invention among avatars, roles, and subject positions. Paul Longley Arthur (2009), for instance, observes that "online identities are easily manipulated at any time by the individual subject or by others" and this "ability to 'manage' online content at will is changing the way we see ourselves and each other" (76).

The malleability and interchangeability of identities online, however, is qualified offline in several ways by both the complexity of identity performance and the *Realpolitik* of situated subjects. Considering the performance of identity, the sociolinguist Ruth E. Page (2011) distinguishes between those aspects that are "transportable identities," traveling across several kinds of discursive situations, and those aspects that are "discourse- and situated-specific, . . . locally occasioned roles adopted in relation to a particular speech situation" (18). In RealLife (RL) social settings as well, Page observes that not all aspects of identity are intrinsic to a person's performed characteristics; some may be provisionally adopted for a particular occasion or context. While the origins and correlatives of virtual identities are not embodied as are those presented in RL social settings, distinguishing between transportable and role-based or assumed aspects of identity may enable more nuanced theorizing.

Furthermore, not all valences of identity are equalized and sharable online. New media scholars such as Lisa Nakamura, Helen Kennedy, and Mary L. Gray caution that the utopian vision of an Internet where the free play of identity is unbounded obscures the persistent asymmetries of power and access that attach to marginalized and normative identity positions on and offline, and to the labor of producing, circulating, and consuming lives in Web 2.0. Nakamura (2008, 1678), for instance, asserts that "the 'larger flows of labor, culture and power' that surround and shape digital media travel along unevenly distributed racial, gendered, and class channels" (see also her chapter [000]).

In this environment, at once fluid yet inflected by asymmetrical power relations, some artists have created meta-identity projects that reformulate identity as contingent and arbitrarily networked. The Australian painter Jennifer Mills (2009–11), for example, developed *What's in a Name?* Googling her own name, she found more than 325 women from across the globe, especially the English-speaking world—the United States, Australia, Canada, New Zealand—who shared it. She then used their websites or Facebook pages to make candid watercolor images of her avatars as intimate "secret sharers." Exhibited at the Queensland Art Gallery, *What's in a Name?* illustrates how self-representation through online avatars is an increasingly important aspect of contemporary self-identity, yet it fractures social identity. One of Mills's "Googlegängers," Australian *writer* Jennifer Mills, notes the compelling but dislocated intimacy of the Internet: "The idea that in the mass of difference and differentiation you might have something in common with a stranger has a kind of dizziness about it. . . . These Jennifers have traveled through the hyperreality of the network, and come back home."

What components of identity are presented in an online site, and which ones are assumed? How do site protocols and templates manage identity? Do discourses of a "true" self or an imaginary self inform the site? To what extent are distinctions of social identities blurred and dispersed in the online environment of self-presentation? To what extent are an individual's multiple or conflicting identities homogenized? Do you observe ways in which normative identities—as effects of racialization, heternormativity, or ableism, and the like—are invoked, sidetracked, queered, reformulated, rematerialized?

Some self-presenters consider themselves as primarily embedded within online collectivities; that is, they are part of a group of actors speaking as a homogenous "we." How would you describe the community or collective? How large is it? How connected in time and space? Is the community multigenerational? Does it make links across sexes, ages, national, ethnic, or linguistic boundaries? What shared characteristics make this "I" part of a larger "we," and which are inherited, which consciously chosen? Is there a set of beliefs or an ideology at the core of the group's formation? Does the site assume that visitors are members of a particular community or provide a way for them to claim or participate in an identity through membership and/or IRL (In Real Life) meetings, activities, and rituals?

Memory

Processes of individual and collective memory are both changed and enabled by the Internet. The encoding of memory is also technologically vulnerable in that data may be lost or corrupted. But, as scholars of life narrative have argued, memory was always more than the storage of impressions of past events. There are many processes of memory: retrieval, association over time, flashback and flashbulb, dreams, traumatic memory, postmemory, and prosthetic memory, to name some kinds (see Smith and Watson 2010, ch. 2). It is important to distinguish between the "stored" memory of an online archive or database and what is available as historical and collective memory through other sites and non-online sources.

The Internet also provides technologies for creating what might be called "future memory," which is prospectively retrospective. Consider an ongoing project by the multimedia artist Christian Boltanski. Titled "Storage Memory," it is a project he hopes to continue for the rest of his life. Each month he will film ten one-minute movies, which can be watched separately but, as a set, will be a "jigsaw puzzle" as a "self-portrait depicting his emotions and sensations . . . a record as time goes by, of the transformations in his life."[5] Boltanski has solicited online subscribers (for an annual fee) to reach beyond his fans to individuals around the world. He describes the project as "a work in progress of unknown duration which only death will put an end to." Here, future memory is enabled by technologies for recording, storing, and sharing what an artist becomes, on a regular basis throughout his life, merging past and future with the reflexivity of an ever-moving present.

What does memory become on online sites where entries can be made episodically, and where both the site and the Web itself serve as a kind of memory bank? In engaging a site, consider how it incorporates memory or practices of memory such as association, emplacements, or substitution? Are prompts to memory retrieval used, such as lists of "firsts" and genealogical trees? How is the emotional content or freight of a memory conveyed online? In authoring a self is there attention to forgetting or an effort to engage others in a search for lost memory? What sources of personal memory are mobilized online, such as genealogy, family albums, photos, and objects, and are they personal artifacts or public documents, events, or rituals?

How is individual memory linked to larger contexts, such as collective memory, historical record, and transnational processes of migration, exile, and diaspora? Does the user/creator highlight traumatic or belated memory as a self-authoring practice for telling about suffering or events that seem unrepresentable to him or her? Does the self-author use the site therapeutically for engaging, overcoming, and healing from painful memories?

Paratexts and Parasites

Paratext is the name given to material of several sorts, which supplements and mediates a written text, among them tables of contents, chapter headings, and endnotes; letters, documents, and endorsements; book covers, illustrations, and advertisements. Paratexts have various effects: they solicit specific audiences; they produce a certain "look" that brands a narrative for consumption; and they seek to influence reading publics (see Smith and Watson 2010, 99–102). In online environments, in addition to the kinds of paratexts associated with written texts, the screen content may include the visible features of the formal template, blog commentaries, hyperlinks, pop-up ads, associated inventories in sidebar suggestions, "I-like-this" options, and other algorithmically generated matter that mediates acts of self-presentation to contextualize an individual's self-presentation differently with a rapid shifts in the environment.[6] Constantly changing frames, driven by behind-the-scenes algorithms, contextualize self-presentation relationally and in ever-changing juxtapositions, affecting how site visitors and reading publics view, read, understand, and respond to the presented self. For instance, the paratextual box registering the constantly changing number of site visitors on a particular site informs viewers about its popularity and can even create celebrity. The sources, purposes, and effects of paratextual apparatuses are thus radically altered in virtual media. Most critically, online paratexts are not only part of author- and/or publisher-generated content; they are also effects of online environments, including site architectures and algorithms, and the economic transactions and business models based on Big Data.

There are also new and striking parasitical aspects of online paratexts. In online environments, as noted above, paratexts may have no intrinsic relationship to the autobiographical project of the user/author, in terms of values, beliefs, and intentions. Indeed, as uninvited occupiers of the screen, paratexts can establish symbiotic relationships with sites: the sites provide advertising space and Big Data for businesses while the paratexts net resources to support site owners. An effect of this symbiotic relationship is that paratexts also project readings of the life and self of site-users by imputing habits, values, and identifications to them. They make linkages unanticipated and unintended by site-authors, and these can inflect, in dramatic and subtle ways, how the presenter is interpreted. They produce "digital character" and project imagined desires, interests, and affiliations. As parasitic, online paratexts mobilize the transport of identities to unanticipated locations and stimulate surprising cohabitations.

Because paratexts can be modified over time, online authors may find their self-presentations framed differently whenever they return to their sites. For example, "thinspirational" songs and photos of stick-thin models might change the interpretation of disclosures on a site where users monitor their eating habits. Self-presentations surrounded by pornographic or political-advocacy paratexts might influence how visitors interpret the self-presenter's motives and beliefs. Then, too, because fragments of self-presentations can be, and often are, copied without user-authorization, online lives can be resituated on another site, such as Tumblr, and reinterpreted through new paratextual juxtapositions. The circulation and recombination of paratexts open any online life to multiple framings, some of which are chosen by the author, some of which are algorithmic and impersonal, and some of which are effects of ceaselessly shifting placement and juxtaposition.

Consider what kinds of paratexts accompany and situate an online self-presentation. In what larger narrative does a particular paratext situate this self-presentation? For example, on sites that gather oral histories into an archive, individual stories are often organized within an interpretive apparatus dedicated to projecting a collective overview and a counterhistory. Are there contradictory, dissonant, or competing narratives set in motion by different paratextual frames? How might paratextual frames call into question the reliability or accuracy that a self-presenter claims?

Consider, as well, how the inevitability of parasitic paratextual frames commodifies a self-presentation as a demonstration of products, buying habits, and projected desires, making a "life" into a practice of self-branding. Can you distinguish between paratextual frames that impose branding and those that are intentional self-branding? And are there paratexts that are not oriented to commodifying the subject but rather to the projection of values or the exploration of ethical issues, such as a commitment to social justice or human rights activism?

Self: Computational or Quantified

The shift from an alphabetical to a computational self has opened the way for individuals to become their own quantification engines. A case in point is the "loosely organized group known as the Quantified Self," centered in Boston. The Quantified Self is constituted of people who digitally self-monitor their bodily processes, intake, outgo, and activities. Gary Wolf (2010) has called this new dispensation of the computational self "the data-driven life." And he asks: "Does measuring what we eat and how much we sleep or how often we do the dishes change how we think about ourselves?" (38). In answering his own question, he observes that "almost imperceptibly, numbers are infiltrating the last redoubts of the personal" (40).

One might think of the self in this context as a site of time-stamped data. But what is interesting about the Quantified Self is the capacity of people to become contributors to Big Data; they can increasingly contribute their personal data to large databases, which will become a source of research in the biomedical sciences—through applications such as Foursquare and various weight-tracking programs and sites such as fitday.com or thedailyplate.com, as well as the online journals myfooddiary.com and weightwatchersonline.com. Emily Singer (2011) observes that "the most interesting consequences of the self-tracking movement will come when its adherents merge their findings into databases. The Zeo, for example, gives its users the option of making anonymized data available for research; the result is a database orders of magnitude larger than any other repository of information on sleep stages" (41). She also notes that "[p]atient groups formed around specific diseases have been among the first to recognize the benefits to be derived from aggregating such information and sharing it" (43). The quantified self, then, is more than a practice of self-monitoring; it suggests a shift to sharing such information for collectivized profiles of groups that serve as authorities on themselves.

Wolf recognizes that the Quantified Self, as an assemblage of data driven by the body and by habits, will reorient us to ourselves, even if the impetus to quantify remains attached to a logic of self-development, which is part of the cultural imaginary. "When we quantify ourselves," he observes, "there isn't the imperative to see through our daily existence into a truth buried at a deeper level. Instead, the self of our most trivial thoughts and actions, the self that, without technical help, we might barely notice or recall, is understood as the self we ought to get to know" (Wolf 2010, 44). Paradoxically, the Quantified Self is at once located as a singularity and made anonymous in numeric code.

Efforts to quantify the self, however, occur not just for the purpose of monitoring bodily functions. The Bangladeshi American media artist Hasan Elahi, for example, has created an ongoing project called Tracking Transience—The Orwell Project, which records his movements in multiple, specific ways on his website. He began in response to being detained by the FBI on September 12, 2001. Elahi, an American citizen with a Muslim name who does not speak Arabic, was repeatedly questioned, nine times over six months, and given lie-detector tests concerning his whereabouts during the terrorist attacks (Mihm 2007). Despite his protestations, he remains a "person of interest" to the FBI (which has never charged him); but because of his status he cannot be issued an official letter of clearance and therefore remains vulnerable to re-arrest.

As a response to his situation, Elahi has chosen to wear a GPS-positioning device and uses Google Earth to track his movements to and from airports and hotels, as well as his meals in restaurants and even use of public toilets. He regularly posts his movements, using a red arrow to show his location. As Siegel (2012) observes, the anonymous "eye" of the satellite camera acts as a kind of all-seeing, superhuman surveillance mechanism (94). In 2011 Elahi wrote an essay for the *New York Times Magazine*, "You want to watch me? Fine. But I can watch myself better than you can, and I can get a level of detail that you will never have." Elahi's website, which is open so that *all* can track his movements, contained more than 46,000 images in early 2012 and is regularly updated. He points out that continuous self-surveillance, exposing everyday details about oneself, can be a response to the misapplication and uncritical use of identity management technologies. Elahi's strategy is to show his location every day but never any part of his body. Elahi's self-tracking project, which uses uploaded photos to quantify locational aspects of himself, suggests that the Quantified Self concerns not simply measurement but may be employed in self-representations with aesthetic and political implications. His response to government surveillance in "quantifying" himself, yet not revealing his own body, reverses the logic of public disclosure as a means of "establishing the paradoxical condition of public privacy" and suggests an innovative means of intervention in the imperative of Big Data (Siegel 2012, 92).

Can aspects of the quantified self be observed on a personal website—data about the body, habits, or measurable achievements of the site creator? To what extent does quantified data dominate the self-portrayal? Is there much personal narrative or self-reflection? How does this quantification shape the kinds of interactions the site invites or permits? For example, on a weight-monitoring site, what informs your response?

Temporality

Self-presentation in online environments, unlike in analog life writing, does not have narrative beginnings and ends distinguishable by birth or death. Its structuring is primarily episodic rather than emplotted. In this way, online presentation is located in time and ever-changing. This mobility of selves in online environments complicates our notions of temporality: it is both an eternal present of moments of self-accretion and extensible across time through the archive. Online, the chronicle is one temporal mode of self-presentation. On sites such as Facebook and blogs, time is successive and accreted, a form of chronology ever changing through modification. Temporality can also be organized by associative memory, by dispersed status updates, or by larger frameworks of historical periods, such as the framework of music history implied in changing attachments to certain kinds of music. Moreover, users can "go backward" in time to delete or amend content. For example, bloggers time travel when they edit earlier posts, which have been criticized as slanderous or offensive.

What time or times, whether a specific moment or a more general time, does the site set up? Does it situate itself in an ongoing series of moments, as in a blog or online journal or webcam site? Are temporal moments signaled through dates or other chronological distinctions? If the site is interactive, how do other users temporally mark their engagements in time? To what extent is the site changed or added to over successive moments? Is there a pattern of self-modification? How are the temporalities of different archives of the self that are mounted at different sites interarticulated? To what other temporalities is the site linked? Is the self-presentation conscious of the subject's location in generational time, or national time, or a religious moment, or a collective time? Can there be said to be a temporal "end" to a site and the creator's self-presentation? How many temporal dimensions are observable on a site?

User-authored and/or Protocol-Driven Sites

It is helpful to distinguish between two kinds of online sites. *Protocol-driven sites* have elaborate formats, driven by algorithms that dictate how users organize what they tell or present themselves. The protocols of Facebook, for example, require that users enumerate themselves in established formats, which may suppress some aspects of individual difference. Users can, however, modify or disrupt some site formats, which seem constricting or incomplete, in order to create more nuanced and complex self-presentations. They might add photographs or mention distinctive features of tastes to customize a self-presentation, or they might add a link to another site of self that complicates or expands the limits of the protocol template.

While *user-authored sites* observe some protocols, they are looser and may be minimal. For example, personal websites, such as LiveJournal and collaborative diary sites, permit blogging of unspecified length without a narrowly scripted protocol and extensive commentary by site visitors. Blogs permit users to modify their entries in successive posts and invite interactive comments from others.

What are the norms and rules of the site? What does it allow users to include or require that they exclude? What kind of "life" does the site's format solicit? If it employs the ready-made templates of protocol-driven sites, how does the template shape the user's projection of identity and communal affiliation? How do more constricting formats normalize or typicalize or deindividualize a certain kind of subject as a general social type? What is excluded, obscured, or deformed in a life ready-made through a template? What kind of subject is rendered abnormal through a site format? Are there ways that users can intervene in or innovate upon the protocols?

Conclusion

We regard this toolkit as functional. The questions are intended to supply concepts and prompt analysis. They attend to new ways of presenting a self online, and new formations of subjectivity generated by combinations of media enabled by the Internet. We hope this assemblage of questions contributes to a better understanding of the transformations of subjectivities and lives that the revolutionary shift to digital environments has enabled.

Online self-presentation raises provocative questions for scholars of life narrative and cyber-environments alike. We might ask whether the formulas, protocols, and ready-made environments of online sites call the singularity and uniqueness of the authored self into question. Is this a new critical formation distinct from a postmodern view of subjectivity, such as Derrida's, that written selves are always already citational assemblages? Will the potential of online forms provoke new innovations in self-authoring to convey explorations of self-experience digitally in ways similar to the powerful innovations of Augustine and Rousseau in their *Confessions* and Montaigne in his *Essays*? Or will radically distinct models of prosthetic personhood emerge, as posthumanist theorists suggest?

Online environments can incorporate multiple media and juxtapose them in ways that produce new possibilities for self-representation. A site can configure the self of the user as, for example, a map, a puzzle, a portrait, an assemblage of tastes and habits, a genealogical chronology, a type representative of a group, an aficionado of particular celebrities, heroes, or sports figures. Users may choose to encode themselves through fantasies of being someone or something else, as avatars or alternative identities. The notion of "bricolage," assembling a profile from disparate parts and allowing other users to recombine it differently, is also a feature of some online sites.

Reflection on online self-presentation leads us to wonder what is added, what lost by the ease of assembling multiple versions of a self in disparate media, with different limits and emphases. And it provokes some concluding provocative questions:

- What consequences might the explosion of virtual self-authorship have for the de- or re-formation of subjectivities?
- How does the flattening of online lives into a successive chronicle of moments or an ongoing, updateable present alter expectations that the self in visual and written forms is a construct of depth, interiority, and reflexivity?
- Does the archival capacity for searchability among earlier entries on, or versions of, self-presentation foreclose or expand the prospect for complex self-representation?

- Do self-presentations and extensions through assemblages, links, and avatars signal the emergence of a new posthuman subjectivity? Or is the virtualization of the subject only a neoliberal manifestation of the mind-body split as a legacy of Enlightenment humanism?
- Do the archives and architecture of the Web transform the self into a "switching point" or "transit" or "node"? That is, should acts of self-composition that are nonverbal and in constant flux be conceptualized as the extension of a self into multiple relations, or its evacuation?
- What becomes of the concept of agency ascribed to the self constructed through autobiographical performances in writing or other media? Where does agency reside in the narrating and performing subject; as a co-construction in networked interactivity? in the ideological orientation of templates and protocols? or in their intersections? Or is agency delusory? Because of interactivity and transpersonal fluidity, are "virtual me's" post-agentic?
- To what extent are the risks of public disclosure balanced by the new possibilities of self-exploration and self-expression for generations of users who were formerly inhibited about constructing versions of themselves and making enduring multimedia portraits?
- How might the social work of life narrative—for instance, memorialization of family or nation, political activism, group identification—be modified by the archiving, storage, and communicative networks and rhetorics of online environments?
- How might disciplinary norms and practices of online environments for self-presentation contribute to increased commodification and surveillance of selves and life stories? And how might the protocols, politics, and frames of online sites prescribe and enforce ideological norms of identity, belonging, and communicative practice?

We do not have answers to these questions, but we regard online self-presentation as neither Huxley's "brave new world" nor REM's "the end of the world as we know it." The prospect of being simultaneously self-presenters, self-curators, consumers of others' lives, and bricoleurs of individual and collective subjectivities heralds a new age in which the old certainties no longer apply, but spaces of experimental combination are likely to provoke new formations of self, relation, and community. As we confront these transformations, we might recall Sherry Turkle's trenchant observation: "We have to love our technology enough to describe it accurately. And we have to love ourselves enough to confront technology's true effects on us" (2012 ch. 13).

Notes

We are grateful to Tony Smith-Grieco, James Hixon, Andrew Mayer, and Kate Black for consulting on online concepts and environments. In the United States, David Herman was a resource about work on narrative aspects of online storytelling. In Berlin, Steffen Siegel helpfully enhanced our knowledge of the work of Hasan Elahi; and Christian Moser and Regina Straetling organized the "Ludic Self-Fashioning" Conference at the Free University in October 2012, a productive forum for presenting and receiving feedback on a condensed version of this chapter. Julie Rak and Anna Poletti provided insightful editorial suggestions.

1. For a fuller toolkit of aspects of autobiographical subjectivity, such as memory, experience, identity, spatial location, embodiment, and agency, see *Reading Autobiography*, ch. 2 (2nd ed.).
2. We have not found the term "user" sufficiently distinctive for online self-representation but have not been able to come up with an alternative. Sometimes we use alternate words such as person, people, author, or individual.
3. In *Reading Autobiography*, we theorized the "I"s of autobiographical acts, distinguishing the flesh-and-blood historical "I" of the outernet, to whom others have no direct access, from the speaker or narrator or composer of the textual "I"; we also noted that that textual "I" is always composed of multiple narrated and narrating "I"s. (See Smith and Watson 2010, chs. 2–3).
4. We have not, by and large, pursued the burgeoning corpus of electronic autobiographical literature as such, that is, narratives composed

as literary creations conceived for the Internet. Dr. Ruth Page, who focuses on electronic "semi-autobiographical" narratives, trenchantly discusses new possibilities that consciously literary electronic self-presentation can achieve and the effect they may have: "By defamiliarizing the linear reading process through hypertextual fragmentation, electronic literature reminds us that self-representation is inevitably partial, and storytelling an illusory creation of coherence. In a parallel move, readers might then reconsider their own attempts to build mental profiles of narrative participants as similarly partial and open to reconfiguration" ("Stories of the Self").

5   See info@mariongoodman.com and www.christian-boltanski.com.
6   For a discussion of paratexts in online gaming, see Paul (2010).

Works Cited

Arthur, Paul Longley. 2009. "Digital Biography: Capturing Lives Online." *a/b: Auto/Biography Studies* 24, no. 1 (Summer): 74–92.

Baym, Nancy K. 2006. "Finding the Quality in Qualitative Research." In *Critical Cyberculture Studies*, edited by D. Silvery and A. Massanari, 79–87. New York: New York University Press.

Berlant, Lauren. 1997. "Introduction: The Intimate Public Sphere." In *The Queen of America Goes to Washington: Essays on Sex and Citizenship*, 1–24. Durham, NC: Duke University Press.

Boltanski, Christian. 2013. "Storage Memory." http://www.christian-boltanski.com/eng/2/presentatio-oeurvre and http://www.facebook.com/pages/Christian-Boltanski-Storage-Memory/258575834210811?sk=info. Accessed January 20, 2013.

Bolter, Jay David, and Richard Grusin. 2000. *Remediation: Understanding New Media*. Cambridge, MA: The MIT Press.

Couldry. Nick. 2008. "Mediatization or Mediation? Alternative Understandings of the Emergent Space of Digital Storytelling." *New Media and Society* 10:373–91.

Deresiewicz, William. 2011. "Generation Sell." *New York Times Magazine*, November 12. http://www.nytimes.com/2011/11/13/opinion/sunday/the-entrepreneurial-generation.html?pagewanted=all&_r=0. Accessed January 20, 2013.

Dünne, Jörg, and Christian Moser. 2008. "Allgemeine Einleitung. Automedialität." In *Automedialität: Subjektkonstitution in Schrift, Bild und neuen Medien*, 7–18. Munich: Wilhelm Fink Verlag.

Elahi, Hasan. http://trackingtransience.net/. Accessed March 21, 2012.
Graxian, David. 2003. *Blue Chicago: The Search for Authenticity in Urban Blues Clubs*. Chicago: University of Chicago Press.
Gray, Mary. 2009. "Negotiating Identities/Queering Desires: Coming Out Online and the Remediation of the Coming-Out Story." *Journal of Computer-Mediated Communication* 14:1162–89.
Halberstam, Judith/Jack. 2005. *In a Queer Time and Place: Transgender Bodies, Subcultural Lives*. New York: New York University Press.
Hayles, N. Katherine. 2003. "Deeper into the Machine: The Future of Electronic Literature." In *Culture Machine* 5. http://www.culturemachine.net/index.php/cm/article/viewArticle/245/241. Accessed June 15, 2012.
Jackson, Shelley. 1997. *My Body, A Wunderkammer*. Available at http://www.altx.com/thebody/, accessed by Ruth E. Page, November 20, 2007.
Kennedy, Helen. 2006. "Beyond Anonymity, or Future Directions for Internet Identity Research." *New Media and Society* 8, no. 6: 859–76.
Lambert, Joe. 2012. *Digital Storytelling: Capturing Lives, Creating Community*. 4th ed. New York: Routledge.
McPherson, Tara. 2011. "After the Archive: Scholarship in the Digital Era." Paper presented at the Institute for the Humanities, University of Michigan, November 29.
Nakamura, Lisa. 2008. "Cyberrace." *PMLA* 123, no. 5 (Winter): 1673–82.
Mihm, Stephen. 2007. "The 24/7 Alibi." *New York Times Magazine*, December 9. http://www.nytimes.com/2007/12/09/magazine/09247alibi.html?_r=0. Accessed January 20, 2013.
Mills, Jennifer. 2009–11. *What's in a Name?* Water color with pencil on paper. Queensland Art Gallery, Brisbane. http://www.qagoma.qld.gov.au/collection/contemporary_australian_art/jennifer_mills. Accessed January 20, 2013.
Noguchi, Yuki. 2011. "Following Digital Breadcrumbs To 'Big Data' Gold." National Public Radio, *Morning Edition*. November 29.
Page, Ruth E. 2008. "Stories of the Self on and off the Screen." In *Electronic Literature: New Horizons for the Literary*, edited by N. Katherine Hayles. http://newhorizons.eliterature.org/index.php. Accessed February 21, 2012.
———. 2011. *Stories and Social Media: Identities and Interaction*. London: Routledge.
Paul, Christopher A. 2010. "Process, Paratexts, and Texts: Rhetorical Analysis and Virtual Worlds." *Journal of Virtual Worlds Research* 3, no. 1 (November): 4–17. http://seattleu.academia.edu/ChristopherAPaul/Papers/1236770/Process_Paratexts_and_Texts_Rhetorical_Analysis_and_Virtual_Worlds. Accessed June 15, 2012.

Poletti, Anna. 2011. "Intimate Economies: PostSecret and the Affect of Confession." *Biography* 34–1 (Winter): 25–36.

Pooley, Jeff. 2011. "Authentic? Get Real." Quoted in the *New York Times* Sunday Style Section September 11, 1–2.

Rotman, Brian. 2009. "Gesture and the I Fold." *Parallax* 15, no. 4: 68–82.

Schmitz, J. 1997. "Structural Relations, Electronic Media, and Social Change: The Public Electronic Network and the Homeless." In *Virtual Culture: Technology, Consumption and Identity*, edited by S. G. Jones, 80–101. London: Routledge.

Siegel, Steffen. 2012. "Sich selbst im Auge behalten: Selbstüberwachung und die Bilderpolitik des Indiskreten." ("Keeping an Eye on Oneself: Self-surveillance and the Cultural Politics of Indiscretion.") In *Kultur-Poetik* 12, no. 1: 92–108.

Singer, Emily. 2011. "The Measured Life." *Technology Review*. July/August. 38–45.

Smith, Sidonie, and Julia Watson. 2010. *Reading Autobiography*. 2nd ed. Minneapolis: University of Minnesota Press.

———. 2012. "Witness or False Witness? Metrics of Authenticity, Collective I-Formations, and the Ethic of Verification in First-Person Testimony." *Biography* (Fall): 590–626.

Turkle, Sherry. 2012. *Alone Together: Why We Expect More from Technology and Less from Each Other*. New York: Basic Books.

Wolf, Gary. 2010. "The Data-Driven Life." *New York Times Magazine*, May 10, 38–45.

Wright, Tom. 2004. *In Search of Oldton*. Available at http://www.oldton.com/my_oldton.html. Accessed November 20, 2007.

Part III
Enabling Concepts

7
Performativity, Autobiographical Practice, Resistance (Smith 1995)

Performativity is thus not a singular "act," for it is always a reiteration of a norm or set of norms, and to the extent that it acquires an act-like status in the present, it conceals or dissimulates the conventions of which it is a repetition.
          Judith Butler, *Bodies that Matter*

Autobiography and Performativity

Every day, in disparate venues, in response to sundry occasions, in front of precise audiences (even if an audience of one), people assemble, if only temporarily, a "life" to which they assign narrative coherence and meaning and through which they position themselves in historically specific identities. Whatever that occasion or that audience, the autobiographical speaker becomes a performative subject.

This is another way of suggesting that autobiographical telling is not a "self-expressive" act. The theory of self-expression that has driven various strands of autobiography theory assumes that self-identity emerges from a psychic interiority, located somewhere "inside" the narrating subject. There it lies in a state most coherent, unified, evidentiary, even expectant, awaiting transmission to a surface, a tongue, a pen, a keyboard. Through such media the essence of this inner self can be translated into the metaphorical equivalence in language, into strings of words and narrative sequences. This theory of autobiography assumes an ontological and integumentary relationship of interiority to bodily surface and bodily surface to text as well as the identity (synonymity) of the "I" before the text, the "I" of the narrator, and the "I" of the narrated subject.

But the "self" so often invoked in self-expressive theories of autobiography is not a noun, a thing-in-itself, waiting to be materialized through the text. There is no essential, original, coherent autobiographical self before the moment of selfnarrating. Nor is the autobiographical self expressive in the sense that it is the manifestation of an interiority that is somehow ontologically whole, seamless, and "true." For the self is not a documentary repository of all experiential history running uninterruptedly from infancy to the contemporary moment, capacious, current, and accessible. The very sense of self as identity derives paradoxically from the loss to consciousness of fragments of experiential history. Benedict Anderson suggests that this "estrangement" from our experiential history necessitates "a conception of personhood, *identity* . . . which, because it cannot be 'remembered,' must be narrated" (204).

Autobiographical narration begins with amnesia, and once begun, the fragmentary nature of subjectivity intrudes. After all, the narrator is both the same and not the same as the autobiographer, and the narrator is both the same and not the same as the subject of narration. Moreover, there are many stories to be told and many different and divergent storytelling occasions that call for and forth contextually-marked and sometimes radically divergent narratives of identity.

In each instance, then, narrative performativity constitutes interiority. That is, the interiority or self that is said to be prior to the autobiographical expression or reflection is an effect of autobiographical storytelling. What Judith Butler says of gender performativity can be reframed in terms of autobiographical performativity: "Within the inherited discourse of the metaphysics of substance, gender proves to be performative—that is, constituting the identity it is purported to be.... There is no gender identity behind the expressions of gender; that identity is performatively constituted by the very 'expressions' that are said to be its results" (*Gender* 24–5). And those expressions of interiority are effects produced through the action of public discourses, among them the culturally pervasive discourses of identity and truth-telling that inform historically specific modes, contexts, and receptions of autobiographical narrating (see Gilmore, *Autobiographics* 1–15).

Such discourses might well be understood, à la Michel de Certeau, as hegemonic "strategies" for the cultural reproduction of normative selves (xviii-xx). They function as culturally credible means of making people "believers" in deep selves. For, as de Certeau recognizes,

> To make people believe is to make them act. But by a curious circularity, the ability to make people act—to write and to machine bodies—is precisely what makes people believe. Because the law is already applied with and on bodies, "incarnated" in physical practices, it can accredit itself and make people believe that it speaks in the name of the "real." It makes itself believable by saying: "This text has been dictated for you by Reality itself." (148)

Autobiographical storytelling becomes one means through which people in the West believe themselves to be "selves." In this way, autobiographical storytelling is always a performative occasion, an occasion through which, as Butler argues in theorizing performativity, the "power of discourse ... produce[s] effects through reiteration" (*Bodies* 20).

De Certeau and others trace this conjunction of bourgeois subjectivity and disciplined bodies to various effects of post-Enlightenment culture. Emergent capitalist economies and new republican nations encouraged and required persons to understand themselves to be equal, free, autonomous, and rational subjects, "individuals." But such free individuals in turn required disciplining through an internally generated program of self-scrutiny.¹ Thus the bourgeois reification of self-regulation assumed an interiorized self to be regulated. To this self was assigned depth beneath/inside the surface of the body, what was sometimes considered synonymous with "soul."

But the specificities of flesh determined the degree and kind of interiority assigned the self-regulating subject. Interiority became an effect, and not a cause, of the cultural regulation of always already identified bodies, bodies that were sexed and gendered, bodies that were racialized, bodies that were located in specific socioeconomic spaces, bodies that were deemed unruly or grotesque. Interiority, in complicated ways, became the effect of the surface politics of the body, its physical characteristics, gestures, behaviors, location. And the cultural affirmation of a normative "self" became an effect of the evacuation of unruly heterogeneity within the individual and within the body social and politic. Thus autobiographical storytelling emerged as one powerful means of constituting bourgeois subjects and thereby regulating both bodies and selves. Autobiographical storytelling also became a culturally potent means through which this Enlightenment self was situated in what the West understood as "historical time." As Dipesh Chakrabarty notes, historical time is understood as "a natural, homogeneous, secular calendrical time." It is time necessary to the modernist master narrative of development and progress, a time, citing Chakrabarty again, "without which the story of human evolution/civilization—a single human history, that is—cannot be told" (431).²

Autobiography and Disidentification

Consider, then, the "mîse en scene" of autobiographical performativity. The "scene" is at once a literal place, a location, but also a moment in history, a (sociopolitical) space in culture. Permeating the scene are all those many and non-identical discourses that comprise the sense of the "credible" and the "real." Then there is the "audience" or the implied reader. An audience implies a community of people for whom certain discourses of identity and truth make sense. The audience comes to expect a certain kind of performativity that conforms relatively comfortably to criteria of intelligibility. Thus a specific recitation of identity involves the inclusion of certain identity contents and the exclusion of others; the incorporation of certain narrative itineraries and intentionalities, the silencing of others; the adoption of certain autobiographical voices, the muting of others. But audiences are never simple, homogeneous communities. They are themselves heterogeneous collectives that can solicit conflicted effects in the autobiographical subject.

And so the cultural injunction to be a deep, unified, coherent, autonomous "self" produces necessary failure, for the autobiographical subject is amnesiac, incoherent, heterogeneous, interactive. In that very failure lies the fascination of autobiographical storytelling as performativity. For Butler the failure signals the "possibility of a variation on [the] repetition" of "the rules that govern intelligible identity." "The injunction *to be*" a particular kind of subject, she continues,

> produces necessary failures, a variety of incoherent configurations that in their multiplicity exceed and defy the injunction by which they are generated. Further, the very injunction to be a given [subject] takes place through discursive routes: to be a good mother, to be a heterosexually desirable object, to be a fit worker, in sum, to signify a multiplicity of guarantees in response to a variety of different demands all at once. The coexistence or convergence of such discursive injunctions produces the possibility of a complex reconfiguration and redeployment. (*Gender* 145)[3]

It is as if the autobiographical subject finds him/herself on multiple stages simultaneously, called to heterogeneous recitations of identity. These multiple calls never align perfectly. Rather they create spaces or gaps, ruptures, unstable boundaries, incursions, excursions, limits and their transgressions.

How might we understand these disruptions? Rethinking the role of the unconscious and its relationship to feminist consciousness, Teresa de Lauretis calls this disruptive space the space of *disidentification* (125–7). The unconscious might be understood as the repository of all the experiences and desires that cannot be identified with the symbolic realm and its laws of citationality, those calls to take up normative subject positions. And Butler reminds us that this power of the symbolic ("the domain of socially instituted norms" [*Bodies* 182]) to effect citationality is installed in what Freud referred to as the super-ego or the conscience ("the interiorized judge . . . the psychic agency of regulation" [*Bodies* 181]). The unconscious thus becomes the repository of surplus, of excess, of unbidden and forbidden performativity. The repository of that which is not speakable, not intelligible, not credible, the unconscious is an interiority of disidentifications nested inside the interiority of the identifying subject, an effect of an effect (or what Paul John Eakin describes as "a construct of a construct," "a story of a story" [102, 120]). This domain of the excluded, according to Butler, "haunt[s] signification as its abject borders or as that which is strictly foreclosed: the unlivable, the nonnarrativizable, the traumatic" (*Bodies* 188).

Yet this process of identification and disidentification is ongoing. As a result there can be no fixed or essential preconstitutive identity. Identifications become what Chantal Mouffe describes as "nodal points" or "fixations" which "limit the flux of the signified under the signifier" (371). This "dialectics of fixity/non-fixation" generates practices that can be unfixings of imposed systems of identification.

In the midst of the "strategies" of what de Certeau calls the "strong" ("whether the strength be that of powerful people or the violence of things or of an imposed order" [xix]), a specific autobiographical subject seizes the occasion to effect a timely adjustment of the norm. De Certeau calls such interventions the "tactic" of the weak through which habitable spaces are staked out, through which ruptures in disciplined interiority are effected. "The weak," he contends, "must continually turn to their own ends forces alien to them. This is achieved in the propitious moments when they are able to combine heterogeneous elements . . . ; the intellectual synthesis of these given elements takes the form, however, not of a discourse, but of the decision itself, the act and manner in which the opportunity is 'seized'" (xix). Through tactical dis/identifications, the autobiographical subject adjusts, redeploys, resists, transforms discourses of autobiographical identity.

The history of an autobiographical subject is the history of recitations of the self. But if the self does not exist prior to its recitations, then autobiographical storytelling is a recitation of a recitation. Ultimately, as Jerome Bruner has argued, the life as lived experientially is itself performative. The living of a life becomes the effect of the life as narrated.

Now I turn to performative moments in and performative aspects of a diverse set of autobiographical texts. I start with Benjamin Franklin's *Autobiography* because it has been such an influential text in the history of American national identity, autobiography, and bourgeois subjectivity. I follow with discussions of three texts written by people who take up autobiographical discourses from different cultural locations, but locations on the margins: Frederick Douglass's *My Bondage and My Freedom* (1855), Gertrude Stein's *The Autobiography of Alice B. Toklas* (1933), and Cherríe Moraga's *Loving in the War Years* (1983). My comments are not meant to be readings of the texts as such; they are meant to explore the textual implications of the autobiographical performativity mapped out in these opening comments.

Benjamin Franklin's Wheelbarrow

Franklin's *Autobiography* is a kind of "conduct book," a generic commonplace of the seventeenth and eighteenth centuries that offered formulas for living through normative discourses of gender/race/class. But Franklin's is a conduct book with a critical difference. English conduct books of the eighteenth century tended to describe the character and delineate the education of the aristocratic gentleman. Franklin's conduct book deconstructs these aristocratic notions of identity in service to a new bourgeois notion of identity.[4] Filled with maxims for living, instructional episodes, and "contrastive fables," the *Autobiography*, according to Malini Johar Schueller, "celebrate[s] the mythology of new America—the privatized individual's rise to success in the marketplace" (20).

Franklin deftly incorporates and effectively realigns various discourses of identity culturally available to him as he consolidates a new autobiographical subject out of the discourses of liberal humanism joined to capitalist entrepreneurship (Schueller 21–30). In this sense he takes up discursive tools where they lie, to invoke Butler. For instance, those discourses of Puritan antinomianism that rebuked the privileges of established authority were redeployed by Franklin in order to challenge any kind of received authority, from the authority of his own father or brother to that of any aristocratic privilege based on birth and social status. Those Calvinist discourses outlining the just pursuit of moral perfection he reformulated and redeployed in service to a secular ethics. If the bits and pieces of these discourses lay around for inclusion and refashioning, so did newer ones such as the Lockean discourse of egalitarian individualism and universal rights. He is both the conservator of provided identities and the active agent, the self-fashioner who adjusts to new interpretive possibilities.

But I want to look more closely at one commonly-cited passage revelatory of Franklin's self-fashioning as a particular kind of autobiographical subject:

> I began now gradually to pay off the debt I was under for the printinghouse. In order to secure my credit and character as a tradesman, I took care not only to be in reality industrious

and frugal, but to avoid all appearances to the contrary, I drest plainly; I was seen at no places of idle diversion. I never went out a fishing or shooting; a book, indeed, sometimes debauch'd me from my work, but that was seldom, snug, and gave no scandal; and, to show that I was not above my business, I sometimes brought home the paper I purchas'd at the stores thro' the streets on a wheel-barrow. (83)

On one level this autobiographical moment provides a meticulous description of Franklin's everyday presentation of self. On another it exposes the performative nature not only of his everyday self-presentation but also of his self-narrating project. Consequently, this narrative scene in the *Autobiography* resonates with the narrative scene of the *Autobiography*. Franklin is putting himself together ("secur[ing]" himself) narratively (in daily life, in autobiographical representation) in the coherence of a "character," the tradesman specifically and the capitalist entrepreneur in the broader sense.

In her study of autobiographical subjectivity in the personal writings of the eighteenth century, Felicity A. Nussbaum takes up the meaning of character in the century. On one hand, "character," à la the Theophrastian model, "is imagined to be a public construction, the material evidence of a private interior reality that reflects an individual's essence," a construction that is "expressive of a whole and unified personality" (107). On the other hand, there is an emerging emphasis in the century on the impact of education and experience on "character," that is, an acknowledgment of its socially-situated nature, its malleability and its inessentiality. Thus, the very word "character," Nussbaum argues, is charged with that tension so ripe in the century between the essentialist notion of a personal identity tied to birth and social status and the more flexible notion of an earnable identity, a notion central to the emerging ideology of the bourgeois republican subject.

Franklin's *Autobiography* negotiates this tension in a complex way. Averring that he is "in reality" a tradesman, he affirms the self-expressive capability of identity by affirming the interiorized self of the "self-made" man. The myth he promotes is that these behaviors might be said to express the character of the new bourgeois tradesman. Yet he simultaneously exposes the performative nature of the tradesman's identity, attesting to what Erving Goffman argues is the relationship between expressions of character and social contexts. According to Goffman, "expression in the main is not instinctive but socially learned and socially patterned; it is a socially defined category which employs a particular expression, and a socially established schedule which determines when these expressions will occur" (7). There would be no way of testifying to his character as someone not above his business but by attending to his business behaviors. Industriousness is the performance of industry, being frugal the performance of frugality. Validating the regulatory behaviors of frugality and industriousness (among other bourgeois behaviors), this passage reveals the ways in which the discourse of the "tradesman" enacts itself on and exacts the compliance of the body through bodily deportment, gestural display, actions, and placement. The interiorized character or identity of the tradesman is an *effect* of bodily acts and behaviors, the regulatory practices of emergent bourgeois identity formation.

Franklin's text reveals the ways in which the interiority of a privatized (individual) consciousness is an effect of a set of behaviors, gestures, actions in the world. The interior self of this "self-made man" is comprised of the behaviors and activities of the virtuous capitalist, an apparent oxymoron that Franklin strips of its oxymoronic status. If Franklin's affirmation is meant to suture the gap between the interiority of consciousness and the public self with its politics of the body, it in fact opens up that gap and reveals it as a space of performativity. And yet the performative nature of the "self-made man" is fundamentally a bourgeois opportunity. The emphasis on the reproducibility of virtuous behaviors supports Franklin's promotion of personal achievement. What one did and how one behaved led directly to what one owned, and what one owned, not one's birth or class origin, determined one's identity as a new American man. Further, it promotes the reproducibility of bourgeois subjects. Paradoxically, the bourgeois individual becomes a commodity, and autobiography itself a bourgeois enterprise, the production of a "life" reproducible and consumable. The *Autobiography* serves as a conduct book through which American men become "self-made men" by interiorizing the performativity of individualist masculinity.

Frederick Douglass's Amnesia

If in the Franklin passage we have performativity within consciousness, in the following passage from Frederick Douglass's second autobiography, *My Bondage and My Freedom*, we have performativity without consciousness. Douglass divides the narrative of *My Bondage and My Freedom* into two parts, life in slavery and life after escape. In the early pages of the second part he recounts his first speaking appearance at an anti-slavery convention held in Nantucket in 1841. After explaining that William C. Coffin "sought me out in the crowd and invited me to say a few words to the convention," he continues:

> Thus sought out, and thus invited, I was induced to speak out the feelings inspired by the occasion, and the fresh recollection of the scenes through which I had passed as a slave. My speech on this occasion is about the only one I ever made, of which I do not remember a single connected sentence. It was with the utmost difficulty that I could stand erect, or that I could command and articulate two words without hesitation and stammering. I trembled in every limb. I am not sure that my embarrassment was not the most effective part of my speech, if speech it could be called. At any rate, this is about the only part of my performance that I now distinctly remember. But excited and convulsed as I was, the audience, though remarkably quiet before, became as much excited as myself. (*Bondage* 357–8)[5]

In this scene, the ex-slave is summoned to speak for the first time before a white audience. In other words, he is put on display and asked to perform. But precisely "who" is doing the performing? A man? A free Negro? A former slave? A slave? If Franklin remembers his performance of industriousness, Douglass, suffering a precise amnesia, forgets his. If what Anderson suggests is the case, that "all profound changes of consciousness, by their very nature, bring with them characteristic amnesias", then what do we make of this memory of amnesia (204)? Douglass has recently gone through a change of "identity," from that of the "slave" to that of "free" man. And yet the Fugitive Slave Law ensures that even in the north, where he assumes the identity of a "free" man, he remains "a slave." As both/and, Douglass remains suspended in consciousness changes.

This amnesia signals the radical difference between the autobiographical projects of a Benjamin Franklin and a Frederick Douglass. Franklin's exuberant and optimistic narrative assumes his rights of ownership—as a tradesman in an emergent capitalist economy, as a person in the tenets of egalitarian liberalism, as an autobiographical subject with an autonomous interiority. The textual "Franklin" is a product/property of the narrating Franklin who has the rights to his own life and his own body. But Frederick Douglass has a different relationship to the location of the autobiographical subject because of the experiential history of slavery that has rendered him a non-subject and thus a non-"man." He has no history of property rights, including the right to his own body, person, and subjectivity.

What Douglass does remember of the speaking experience are activities, gestures, behaviors of his body: he can barely stand erect; he stammers; he speaks in discontinuous sentences; he trembles. The material of his body unconsciously "speaks" for/as "Frederick Douglass." The bent rather than upright body and the incoherent language create the effect of unconsciousness, the very unconsciousness that has been assigned him in the organized system of slavery. As a slave he has been assigned the identity of the beast of burden, irrational, less-than-fully-human. Ironically, the body speaks as the "slave," the non-human being objectified in the discourses of slavery. Douglass's amnesia evacuates the interiority of the bourgeois republican subject from this moment of public display.

If Douglass cannot remember his own, he can vividly recall Garrison's performance:

> Mr. Garrison followed me, taking me as his text; and now, whether I had made an eloquent speech in behalf of freedom or not, his was one never to be forgotten by those who heard it. . . . For a moment, he possessed that almost fabulous inspiration, often referred to but seldom attained, in which a public meeting is transformed, as it were, into a single individuality—the orator wielding a thousand heads and hearts at once, and by the simple majesty of his all controlling thought, converting his hearers into the express image of his own soul. (*Bondage* 358)

What Douglass vividly remembers here is being spoken for. Garrison, he says, "t[ook] me as his text," interpreting his life for him. That is, Douglass remembers that Garrison turned his life into the "other" of his (Garrison's) speaking performance.

In taking "Douglass" as his text the white abolitionist appropriates the other, an act that signals the differential relationship of the black speaker and the white speaker to the public occasion. "Douglass" disappears into the rhetorical art and artifice of Garrison's performance, his otherness apparently obliterated. He becomes a (rhetorical) effect of a (rhetorical) effect. It is almost as if Douglass's performance becomes the unconscious of Garrison's performance (Pease). In this sense Garrison also takes "Douglass" as his "pre-text" in two senses of the word. Not only is Douglass's object status the unconscious content of Garrison's subjectivity, but the autobiographical story of the escaped slave provides a pretext, an occasion for the white abolitionist to perform his power and his glory, the wielding of the audience into his single individuality. Douglass's amnesia reveals how the story of the escaped slave was neutralized: by incorporating the story of this cultural other into his proselytizing agenda, the white abolitionist makes it his own, effectively dis-owning Douglass. Douglass's subsequent experience, described in his narrative, suggests that again and again he failed to speak "as a slave" and was thus labeled an "imposter" or "impersonator." His speaking was unintelligible to an audience that expected an already written script.

Intriguingly, Garrison himself wrote of Douglass's speech in his "Preface" to Douglass's earlier narrative, the 1844 *Narrative of the Life of Frederick Douglass, An American Slave*:

> I shall never forget his first speech at the convention—the extraordinary emotion it excited in my own mind—the powerful impression it created upon a crowded auditory, completely taken by surprise—the applause which followed from the beginning to the end of his felicitous remarks. I think I never hated slavery so intensely as at that moment; certainly, my perception of the enormous outrage which is inflicted by it, on the godlike nature of its victims, was rendered far more clear than ever. There stood one, in physical proportions and stature commanding and exact—in intellect richly endowed—in natural eloquence a prodigy—in soul manifestly "created but a little lower than the angels"—yet a slave, ay, a fugitive slave,—trembling for his safety. (*Narrative* 4)

In this passage Garrison constructs Douglass as a perfect specimen of "man"—in body noble, in speech eloquent, in intelligence rich. He becomes more miracle than escaped slave, exceptional rather than representative. And like Douglass Garrison uses Douglass's body as a text to be read; what Douglass presents as nervous trembling, Garrison presents as "trembling for his safety," thereby heightening the effects of slavery in reducing someone so noble to such powerlessness. Garrison's projection of Douglass tames the otherness of the escaped slave by rendering him in the discourse of the same, that is, the discourse of liberal humanism. The political implications of such a biographical portrait are profound: The exceptional can be incorporated and neutralized; the representative remains more threatening to the discourses of republican identity.

At the close of the version of his life to which Garrison's comments are prefatory Douglass describes his first speech in this way: "The truth was, I felt myself a slave, and the idea of speaking to white people weighed me down. I spoke but a few moments, when I felt a degree of freedom, and said what I desired with considerable ease" (*Narrative* 153). There is no mention of Garrison's speech at all. There is no comparison of himself to Garrison. There is no lingering on his inability to remember. The difference in the 1855 version is therefore arresting. Certainly Douglass would have read the abolitionist's description of his first speech since Garrison's letter was included in the introduction to Douglass's 1844 narrative. The 1855 narrative in effect challenges the white man's account of Douglass's public appearance and challenges also the way in which Garrison rewrote him as a "text."

Douglass's narrative unconsciousness signals a variety of meanings within the context of his autobiographical text. He speaks before the white audience as someone who has been a "slave" and thus as someone who has been assigned a blank interiority. At this moment of crossing over from one system of discursive identities to another, he fittingly or ironically goes blank. Thus the unconsciousness might evidence the blank interiority projected by white Americans upon slaves and ex-slaves. Or it might evidence the blank interiority assumed by the slave who has been brutally cathected as the self-consolidating other. Or it might evidence the radical point of transformation. Simultaneously his refusal of consciousness at the moment of commanded public display might signal his refusal of identification with the stipulated posture of degraded "slave" or of the exceptional and noble "ex-slave," those contradictory identities he carries to the podium. This narrative staging of unconsciousness might then serve as a "tactic" of disidentification as well as a gesture of resistance to Garrison's appropriation of his "life," an appropriation that takes place in the "free" territory of the North. Here, then, is a narrative hesitation, a narrative interruption in the power of discourse (in this case, Garrison's abolitionist politics) to command an easy and easily intelligible citationality.

Gertrude's Alice (Being and Possessing)

If in the discussion of Franklin and Douglass I have looked precisely at particular moments of self-conscious performance, in turning to Gertrude Stein's *The Autobiography of Alice B. Toklas* I want to consider the performative nature of the entire autobiographical enterprise:

> About six weeks ago Gertrude Stein said, it does not look to me as if you were ever going to write that autobiography. You know what I am going to do. I am going to write it for you. I am going to write it as simply as Defoe did the autobiography of Robinson Crusoe. And she has and this is it. (252)

Quite simply, Stein undermines the basis upon which what Philippe Lejeune describes as the "autobiographical pact" is founded: the self-identity of the subject of the autobiographical narrative and the autobiographical speaker. We might call this a first-person biography or a second-person auto/biography or un/collaborative storytelling. The subversive nature of Stein's "camp" autobiography (Gilmore, "Signature") reveals the fantasy that sustains "traditional," or what Stein would call "paternal," autobiography. In the ruse of conclusion, Stein's tour de force confuses the differentiation of identities, roles, and performances.

Thus the trick in the ending becomes thick with meaning. As many have noted, in their long-term relationship, Stein assumed the role of "husband" to Toklas's "wife," the lesbian couple thereby reiterating the normative heterosexual model of domesticity. With this context in mind, we can unpack the implications of the autobiographical project. One woman, Stein, who assumes the positionality of "husband" in the heterosexual couple, speaks as another woman, "Toklas," who assumes the positionality of "wife." Stein, that is, puts on the identity of "wife." But something excessive happens when a woman performs femininity; as Mary Russo suggests: "To put on femininity with a vengeance suggests the power of taking it off" (224). Thus a disjunction occurs between the sexed body (Stein as biological female), gender identity (Stein as "husband"), and gender performance (Stein as "Toklas"/the culturally credible "wife"). Body/identity/gender are rendered non-identical.

Stein also camps up the performativity of gendered narrative expectations. The autobiography of Alice B. Toklas begins with the failure of Toklas to perform her "wifely" duty. In other words, the "wife" fails to enact the rituals of "wifehood." As a result, the husband takes on the "wife's" duty. As "Alice" then, Stein reiterates a conventional wife's tale, the narrative of the husband's public "life." In this sense the narrating Stein puts on "femininity" as she narrates a normative "feminine" story (a biography rather than an autobiography). But neither the "wife" nor the "husband" functions as a unified narrator. And so this narrative ventriloquism not only sustains the notion of a "feminine" narrative—the "wifely" tale is finally told, after all—but also subverts it—the "husband" tells it as a "wife," but the "husband" is "him"self a "her"self. "There is no there there," as Stein said of Oakland.

The very autobiographical recitation that promises to shore up gender identity becomes its undoing. And so the notion of autobiography as expressive of a gendered "self" is here undermined through Stein's emphasis on the performative nature of identity. Stein's ventriloquism disrupts the stabilities of "feminine" and "masculine" narratives as it disrupts the normative alignment of interiority to bodily surface to gender performance in the context of compulsory heterosexuality. Heterosexual coupling becomes here a fiction both re-sited and dis-located in the camped-up performance and the "compelled" performativity of heterosexual norms (Butler, *Bodies* 1).

Cherríe Moraga and Her Malinche

The last text I want to consider is Cherríe Moraga's *Loving in the War Years*. In this personal/political compendium of multiple genres,[6] Moraga explores through poetry, essays, memory fragments, myths, the complex relationship of the surface of bodies, the construction of interiority, and the specific inscription of history. As I have noted elsewhere the body moves through all the disparate forms intermixing in this text, fragmented into specific parts and pieces, crossed by desires, overwritten by cultural inscriptions and discourses, but most particularly the discourse of female treachery and betrayal signified by the body and the history of La Malinche (Smith 139–46). The Chicana lesbian is rendered as the cultural grotesque, assigned an "unnatural" body, a disruptive, corrupting body, and thus a traitorous interiority.

Moraga explores her experiential history of passing, passing across her racial identities, disappearing into the Anglo in her or returning to the Chicana in her. "I was 'la guera,'" she writes, "—fair-skinned. Born with the features of my Chicana mother, but the skin of my Anglo father, I had it made. . . . Everything about my upbringing (at least what occurred on a conscious level) attempted to bleed me of what color I did have" (51). The materiality of her specific body and the historical conditions of her experiential history enforce upon her the ways in which racial identity can be performative. But she also explores another kind of passing, the passing of the lesbian girl/woman as a heterosexual "woman." She discovers the ways in which she learned to perform as a heterosexual woman in a cultural context that joined treachery to lesbian desire. Moraga's incisive analysis reveals the complexities of identity formation and deformation. It isn't that identity is totally disjoined from the surface politics of the body; it is that identity, produced by complex cultural locations, is at once culturally overdetermined and manipulable. Paradoxically identity is dis/identity.

It is precisely the possibility of "passing" in double-time that unmasks the regulatory fictions disciplining the Chicana body. The internalization of cultural fantasies of gender identity (for instance, the cultural fantasy invoked by the very name La Malinche as a negative fantasy, as the "woman" not to be) creates a conflicted interiority that produces necessary failures. The discomforts of dis/identifications, the increasing gaps in stable identifications, prompt the increasing awareness, awareness gained through the very acts of writing, that interiority is an effect of social discourses: "But at the age of twenty-seven, it is frightening to acknowledge that I have internalized a racism and classism, where the object of oppression is not only someone *outside* my skin, but the someone *inside* my skin" (54). Refusing to remain in the "passing" lane, Moraga confronts the disabling judgments that had become what Butler terms "the psychic agency of regulation" (*Bodies* 181).

The experiential and cultural histories of the lesbian body provide Moraga with a means to confront the cultural injunctions that enforce a specific gender/racial/class interiority. This desire is an "excess" in the system, an excess de Lauretis describes as "a *resistance to* identification rather than unachieved identification" or "a *dis-identification* with femininity that does not necessarily revert or result in an identification with masculinity but, say, transfers to a form of female subjectivity that exceeds the phallic definition" (126). Moreover, this desire becomes a material window opening onto the social construction of a disempowered interiority as well as a point of view used to resist that disempowerment. This excessive space stretches open interiority and thereby motivates a changed consciousness, an awareness of the performative effects of the discourses of identity culturally provided her.

Speaking autobiographically as a Chicana lesbian is itself a "variation" on the repetition of "rules that govern intelligible identity, e.g., that enable and restrict the intelligible assertion of an 'I'" (Butler, *Gender* 145). For the very assertion of that identity signals a failure to be a "woman" within both Chicano and Anglo cultures. In making intelligible a culturally unintelligible subject, Moraga deconstructs the normative identity founding multiple communities. The diverse autobiographical writings incorporated in the text entitled *Loving in the War Years* mark the performativity of identity as differences.

Conclusion

I have tried in this eclectic reading of disparate texts to illuminate various aspects of autobiographical performativity and resistance. The moments signal the making and unmaking of identities and thus undermine the foundational myth of autobiographical storytelling as self-expressive of an autonomous individualism. The occasion of Benjamin Franklin offers us a monologic performance through which one individual works to consolidate a new notion of the American individual. Thus in Franklin's text we discover the mechanisms whereby the performativity of bourgeois subjectivity comes into being and is commodified as national myth. The examples of Douglass, Stein, and Moraga, each in their different ways, register the degrees to which the white Euro/American norm is recited by those persons it positions as self-consolidating others. Yet the performative interiority of the autobiographical subject can produce many and conflicted "effects" that also mark interventions in normative identifications with stagings of incommensurable differences that re-site those norms. Writing from eccentric cultural positions, Douglass, Stein, and Moraga take up autobiographical storytelling in order to critique the regulatory effects of the West's romance with bourgeois individualism. They occupy an "I" and in doing so scramble the boundary markers delimiting the sites of the included and the excluded. In effect, these narratives become sites where a complex and disruptive theorizing of autobiographical performativity takes place.

Notes

A version of this essay, presented as the keynote address at the 1994 University of Wollongong conference, entitled "Self, Life, Writing: Postcolonial Perspectives," was reprinted in *Self, Life, Writing*, ed. Anne Lear and Paul Sharrad (Sydney: Dangaroo Press, 2000).

1. For an incisive analysis of the construction of an interiorized female subjectivity in conduct books written at the end of the eighteenth and beginning of the nineteenth century, see Armstrong, esp. ch. 1.
2. Chakrabarty calls history "this gift of modernity to many peoples" (433).
3. Please note that I have substituted the word "subject" for "gender" in the original.
4. A literate American, Franklin writes his conduct book to and for other literate Americans. Through that community of literate Americans he binds together a newly literate middling class. See, for instance, Nussbaum (53–5). Also, with the reproduction of his *Autobiography*, his life circulated broadly through the newly literate bourgeois class, thereby binding together people in different locations. Anderson argues that this community of readers held together by print rather than proximity became the precondition for the emergence of nationalism. See Anderson, ch. 3 and 4.
5. I am indebted to Donald Pease for directing attention to this passage in Douglass's text. In his brilliant analysis of specific passages in works by Douglass, Harriet Beecher Stowe, and Walt Whitman, Pease explores the ways in which a post-national consciousness destabilizes the notion of American national identity. Pease himself wants to rethink the facile description of the literature of the 1850s and 1860s as part of an "American Renaissance."
6. On the intermixing of generic forms in writings by women of color, see Emberley (163).

Works Cited

Anderson, Benedict. *Imagined Communities: Reflections on the Origin and Spread of Nationalism*. London: Verso, 1991.

Armstrong, Nancy. *Desire and Domestic Fiction: A Political History of the Novel*. New York: Oxford University Press, 1987.

Bruner, Jerome. "Life As Narrative." *Social Research* 54 (1987): 11–32.

Butler, Judith. *Bodies That Matter*. New York: Routledge, 1993.

———. *Gender Trouble: Feminism and the Subversion of Identity*. New York: Routledge, 1990.

Chakrabarty, Dipesh. "Marx after Marxism: History, Subalternity and Difference." *Meanjean* 3 (Spring 1993): 429–45.

De Certeau, Michel. *The Practices of Everyday Life*. Trans. Steven F. Rendall. Berkeley: Universeity of California Press, 1984.

De Lauretis, Teresa. "Eccentric Subjects: Feminist Theory and Historical Consciousness." *Feminist Studies* 16 (Spring 1990): 115–50.

Douglass, Frederick. *My Bondage and My Freedom*. New York: Arno, 1969.

———. *Narrative of the Life of Frederick Douglass, An American Slave, Written by Himself*. Cambridge: Harvard University Press, 1960.

Eakin, Paul John. *Touching the World: Reference in Autobiography*. Princeton: Princeton University Press. 1993.

Emberley, Judith V. *Thresholds of Difference: Feminist Critique, Native Women's Writings, Postcolonial Theory*. Toronto: University of Toronto Press, 1993.

Franklin, Benjamin. *The Autobiography of Benjamin Franklin*. New York: Washington Square, 1967.

Gilmore, Leigh. *Autobiographies: A Feminist Theory of Autobiography*. Ithaca: Cornell University Press, 1994.

———. "A Signature of Lesbian Autobiography: 'Gertrice/Altrude.'" *Autobiography and Questions of Gender*. Ed. Shirley Neuman. London: Frank Cass, 1991. 56–75.

Goffman, Erving. *Gender Advertisements*. New York: Harper, 1976.

Lejeune, Philippe. "The Autobiographical Pact." *On Autobiography*. Ed. Paul John Eakin. Trans. Katherine Leary. Minneapolis: University of Minnesota Press, 1989. 3–30.

Moraga, Cherríe. *Loving in the War Years: lo que nunca pasó por sus labios*. Boston: South End, 1983.

Mouffe, Chantal. "Feminism, Citizenship, and Radical Democratic Politics." *Feminists Theorize the Political*. Ed. Judith Butler and Joan W. Scott. New York: Routledge, 1992. 369–84.

Nussbaum, Felicity A. *The Autobiographical Subject: Gender and Ideology in Eighteenth-Century England*. Baltimore: Johns Hopkins University Press, 1989.

Pease, Donald. Lecture. SUNY Binghamton. Binghamton, NY, Oct. 1992.

Russo, Mary. "Female Grotesques: Carnival and Theory." *Feminist Studies/Critical Studies*. Ed. Teresa de Lauretis. Bloomington: Indiana University Press, 1986. 213–29.

Schueller, Malini Johar. *The Politics of Voice: Liberalism and Social Criticism*. Albany: State U of New York P, 1992.

Smith, Sidonie. *Subjectivity, Identity, and the Body*. Bloomington: Indiana University Press, 1993.

Stein, Gertrude. *The Autobiography of Alice B. Toklas*. New York: Random, 1960.

8
THE SPACES OF AUTOBIOGRAPHICAL NARRATIVE (WATSON 2007)

Prologue: What Is "Space"?

I first thought about space in life writing when I participated in the research group "Self-Narratives in Transcultural Perspective" focused on "*Raum*" at the Free University in Berlin in 2006. I knew from years of study in Germany that the connotations of *Raum* differ from those of its English cognate "room" and are not identical with the general term "space"; *Raum*, with its focus on co-constructed social space, is more philosophical and metaphorical than related English concepts such as place and landscape. But thinking between languages and life writing traditions about what "space" connotes can be productive for reading life narratives.

Interestingly, space in Anglo-American autobiography has not been theorized in a systematic way.[1] The two-volume *Encyclopedia of Life Narrative* has no entry for "space" or "landscape," "site," or "zone"—and, of course, not for "*Raum*." American literary history, for example, focuses extensively on differentiating between the concepts of place and space in discussing locale or region, particularly in studies of the South and the West. Lawrence Buell argues that there is no unmediated access to place because "nature has been doubly otherized in modern thought," symbolically reinforcing the subservience of disempowered groups (21). Buell argues that the sense of place is necessarily always a social product and not simply a notion of unmarked space as what is there (77). Space, as the natural environment on its own terms, cannot be articulated outside the history of cartographies that have assigned it place-names and boundary markers. Place is "felt space, space humanized, rather than the material world taken on its own terms" (253). For Buell, space becomes place when one is conscious of where one lives and develops a "sense of place" through life of various sorts that inhabits a locale. Space, in American studies, then, is often the locus of place, landscape, and myths of a promised land.

Kathleen A. Boardman and Gioia Woods, in their introduction to a collection of women autobiographers' narratives of the American West, read place as spatial network, asserting: "One marker of autobiography produced in and about the North American West is a preoccupation with place, along with a focus on identity issues directly related to place: rootedness, anxiety, nostalgia, restlessness. . . . For some autobiographers, place is a problem to be solved; for others, it is the basis (or "ground") for a claim to authenticity" (3). Boardman and Woods assert that the performance of identity can be observed at the intersection of three kinds of location—physical, rhetorical, and political—and that it is never reducible simply to geography (19). Situating a life narrative in space, then, means specifying multiple coordinates that bring the discussion closer to the implications of *Raum* as co-constructed social space.

Ethnic American studies throughout the nineties interrogated the space of the border, the "borderlands" of identity, employing Gloria Anzaldúa's concept of *la frontera*. Anzaldúa stresses the ambiguity and anxiety of location along the border, which becomes a site of encounter between different cultures that may configure local inhabitants as "aliens" in both. Their acts of crossing, translation, and inventing new hybrid languages and practices, which Anzaldúa calls "linguistic terrorism," are ways of navigating a geopolitical space that can never be called "home" (58). Similarly, José David Saldivar's study of border writing discusses zones of encounter, contestation, and negotiation between subjects whose access to power and authority in one history—Mexican—are subordinated to colonial practices of a dominant American other. The rich conceptual vocabulary generated around thinking about space through its borders and zones of encounter thus offers critical terms for texturing the representation of place.

Essays in a special issue of *PMLA* on urban lives and the city assert that displacement is the other side of place. For multitudes of urban peoples in the twenty-first century—in post-Katrina New Orleans, in Beirut and Baghdad, Grozny and Mogadishu—Patricia Yaeger discerns a new formation, the "tragic mobility of space" in the wounded city. Traditionally viewed as both "shelter and economic flow," the city is now often a site of crisis, marked by migration and production zones that structure and complicate the experience of daily life (10). Thinking about the space of the city not as an autonomous metropolis, but as the intersection of multiple populations, redefines some connotations of space, although that discussion is beyond the purview of this essay.

Theorizing Location and Position in Life Narrative

Because the autobiographical is in part a retrospective act of narrating earlier moments of self-experience from the position of a present-time "I", it has been analyzed primarily in temporal terms. While this focus in some way informs nearly all thinking on self-representation, it is inescapably concerned with the problematics of experience in time. The self represented in narrative must in some sense be a moving target, since both the narrated "I" or I-then and the narrating "I" or I-now are embedded in a temporal sequence.[2] An autobiographical narrator, in telling a coming-of-age story, typically traces the movement of the I-then at different ages from the perspective of an adult I, which is constituted in the writing of the text. In such a process, temporal tropes of mobility and instability, and the marking of narrative junctures or "turning points" become critical tropes for autobiographical discourse.

Prior to the 1980s, the autobiographical self was often treated as a static monument that attested, by its achieved status, to the superiority and permanence of Western culture, a point of view articulated in Georges Gusdorf's 1956 definition of autobiography as the creation of an edifice of self. His tropes are architectural, emphasizing static monumentality. For example, when the writer adds consciousness to nature through autobiography, "The historic personage now appears, and biography, taking its place alongside monuments, inscriptions, statues, is one manifestation of his desire to endure in men's memory" (31). Creating an autobiography of the individuated life is seen as a transpersonal monument to life and humanity, the highest and distinctive achievement of Western civilization.

Needless to say, this concept of the static monument, predicated on the works of aristocratic, white "great men," is not the sense of autobiographical space I am tracing, and it has been redefined in recent critical thinking. Now critics emphasize mobile and flexible versions of subjectivity embedded in social relations that both individual and collectivized subjects take up in their autobiographical practices of self-narration. As Judith Butler asserts, "the 'I' has no story of its own that is not also the story of a relation—or set of relations—to a set of norms" (8). Theorists now assert that life narrators are situated in relation to others, often at cultural margins or intersections, and deploy autobiographical discourses for a wide range of purposes: to chronicle, to justify or exculpate, to negotiate communities of membership, to memorialize, to testify and to bear witness in ethical acts of disputing or reframing dominant narratives, and so on.

Thus, the focus on both the *location* and the *position* of an autobiographical narrator has importantly reshaped thinking about autobiography. The concept of location emphasizes not just the geographic, but the national, ethnic or racial, and gendered, sexual, social and life-cycle coordinates at which a narrator situates her- or himself. Location, expanded to include what Susan Stanford Friedman terms "the geopolitics of identity within differing communal spaces of being and becoming," has become central to debates in feminist, multicultural, postcolonial, and cultural studies (17).[3] The concept of position, by contrast, implies the ideological stances—multiple and heteroglossic rather than single and unified, despite the narrator's values—adopted by a narrator toward both self and others. Both concepts are inescapably *spatial* in their stress on emplacement, the juncture from which an articulation issues. Yet this spatial focus is often implied rather than explicitly specified in discussions of autobiographical texts.[4]

To return briefly to an American discussion of space, the extended borders north and south of both the United States and other nations in the Western hemisphere have generally led critics to emphasize the geographical aspect of spatial location over other coordinates of situated subjectivity. An exception to this is the work on avant-garde autobiography of William Boelhower, who draws on notions of spatial surround to emphasize the fluidity and fragmentation of modernist locations and to situate the self as a network of the functions of *habitare* and a desire for spatial fixity that is disrupted in the metropolis. Boelhower asserts, "the avant-garde autobiographer, in his attempt to create a coherent grammar of the self out of the spatial vocabulary of the metropolis, ends up with a loosely bound inventory of fragmented forms." In his view the life narrator is "both cause and structural effect of the system of constructed spaces to which he belongs" (275). Boelhower's rich analysis suggests that autobiographical writing serves as a map not so much of place as region or ground, but as the site of spatial dislocations that structure a deeper layer of "topological encoding" (277). Mapping the coordinates of particular cities as different systems for structuring the self, he suggests that the narratives of modernist figures—the artist, the immigrant, the architect, attempting to find an orientation to the city's dense grids—are cut loose from a former synthetic view of the self. Montage rather than chronology becomes the form taken by a modernist self that is fragmented and shattered, but available to the literary anthropologist reading for signs of "the crisis of *habitare*" (275).

The city, as a troubling and provocative site of self-representation, has provoked other speculations about shifting conceptions of the spaces of self as well. In the aftermath of September 11, 2001, the focus on borders as a means of making contested terrain visible takes on new significance in mapping historical contestations about ownership and citizenship. The attention to borders, as markers of translation and exchange between people who are unequally situated as social subjects, puts an emphasis on *negotiating* social space and the need to challenge or revise the codifications of identity that they legitimate. If in the United States autobiography studies has tended to privilege temporality and to fix on spatial binaries—such as urban-rural, north-south, or margin-center—that occlude the complexity of constructed intersubjective spaces, these binary tropes of location are now being reformulated in more nuanced ways.

While Anglo-American and Australian theorists of settler colonialism have emphasized encounters across borders, postcolonial theory has importantly emphasized another sense of the location of colonized subjects as a "third space," in Homi Bhabha's term. For Bhabha the third space is a zone or "place of hybridity" produced at the moment of colonial encounter, a site at which communication, negotiation, and cross-translation may occur. In the third space, "the construction of a political object that is new, *neither the one nor the other*," produces a changed form of recognition (25). Both colonizer and colonized are implicated in the dynamics of this encounter, which may enable the colonized to claim a new political identity through mimicry and innovation, if not always to produce change, at the site of in-between spaces. Situatedness in a "third space" is crucial for theorizing the postcolonial life narratives of writers such as Jamaica Kincaid, Maryse Condé, and Wole Soyinka. Similarly, Steven Pile and Michael Keith have suggested that locations of diaspora around the globe should be read as shifting political spaces: "Spatiality needs to be seen as the modality through which contradictions are normalized, naturalized and neutralized. . . . Spatialities represent both the spaces between multiple identities and the contradictions within identities" (224–5). Hence the geopolitical may be understood as a space both of negotiation and of cancellation.

That is, concepts of personhood are often directly tied to particulars of location and position. While my discussion cannot provide a comprehensive overview, I want to propose some categories based on spatial coordinates in order to suggest ways in which we might employ spatiality as a *reading practice* in life writing to examine the networks of social relations negotiated across differences of location and position.

What differing contexts and limits of space, place, and zone may be specified when reading in the Anglo-American intellectual tradition, given the slippage between "space" and "place" in American theorizing? Our critical practices might investigate some contexts of life narrative that invoke "space"; consider issues of genre, readership, and the ethics of self-presentation that are not obviously linked to place; and map some autobiographical sites at which, literally or metaphorically, a spatial vocabulary is mobilized. In the rich ferment of contemporary work on life narrative, cataloguing these terms, tropes, and contexts may serve as a space-clearing gesture, as Sidonie Smith and I suggested in calling for more study of spatiality.[5]

1. *Space as Material Surround*

First, there is a literal, geographic specificity of "place" as *region or immediate material surround*, which has been richly contextualized in national literature studies—for example, in narratives of immigrants writing within American, Canadian, Caribbean, and Australian contexts, as well as in the focus on region and the history of struggles waged by both indigenous peoples and settlers to claim the land as place, to become emplaced. This emphasis on place as conferring or shaping identity has been a defining characteristic of regional autobiographical narratives. For example, Mary Clearman Blew asserts in *All But the Waltz*, "I am bone-deep in landscape" and links her sense of space as formative of her subjectivity to particulars of the northwest Rocky Mountain region and the social interactions enabled or impeded among local Euro-Americans, Native Americans, and the Hutterite community of Montana (7). Similarly, another western American writer, Terry Tempest Williams, argues that our relationship to place must become subjective, a "Pansexual" one. Williams asserts, "we are lovers, engaged in an erotics of place . . . acknowledging, embracing the spirit of place" (84). Engaging space as place, these life narrators transform it into a resonant, responsive network called "the land."

If, for life narratives of the American West, the vast landscape becomes a horizon against and in terms of which subjectivity is defined, autobiographical writing may also be located on a small, even minuscule scale. Consider the centrality to the scene of narration of such domestic spaces as the writing desk or word processor, the intimate space of the bedroom or bath, the sociality of the dining room table, such gendered spaces as the kitchen and the garage or workroom, and that most prized space of postmodern self-reflection, the automobile. In a renowned essay on confession in autobiography, for example, Stephen Spender metaphorically described the reflexive situation of autobiographical discourse via the automobile: "We are seen from the outside by our neighbors; but we remain always at the back of our eyes and our senses, situated in our bodies, like a driver in the front seat of a car seeing the other cars coming toward him" (116).[6]

In travel narratives, the encounter with material space may occur via a mode of transportation—train, plane, an earlier form of conveyance. Sidonie Smith, in *Moving Lives*, observes that "Narrating travel . . . the travel narrator negotiates the dynamics of and contradictions in the drift of identity and reveals the ways in which modes of mobility—engines of temporality, spatiality, progression, and destination—are (un)defining" (27–8). This literal understanding of space as the site, emplaced or mobile, from which writing issues does not, however, exhaust the possibilities of conceptualizing it.

2. Spaces of Embodiment

There is also the subjective space of the life narrator's *embodiment*. The body is a site of autobiographical knowledge, a site at which memory recovers and reworks experience in constructing a sense of identity through processes that are felt, physiological, neurological, and biochemical, as well as resonant in the body politic. The subject is inescapably embodied, and located in culturally specific ways at a nexus of language, gender, class, sexuality, ethnicity, and historical moment. We have argued that the body may be understood complexly as four kinds of entities: a neurochemical system, an anatomical body, an "imaginary anatomy" that "reflects social and familial beliefs about the body more than . . . the body's organic nature", and a sociopolitical body of cultural attitudes and discourses which encode the public meanings of bodies in ways that underwrite relationships of power (*Reading* 38).

Because space is embodied, the cultural meanings attached to specific bodies at a given historical moment affect the kinds of stories life narrators can tell. For example, the narratives of "skin" that are prominent in multicultural life narratives in many parts of the world—not just the United States, Great Britain, and Australia, but India, Latin America, and many nations of Africa—both mark and contest class positions. In *When I Was Puerto Rican*, Esmeralda Santiago locates her family's status as rural and lower-class by positioning their skin color within the nation's hierarchy of European-inflected color values, and dramatizes the surprise of her own rise as an immigrant New Yorker, given that in childhood her family name was "Negi" because of her particularly dark skin. Similarly, Michelle Cliff in *Abeng* encodes the social spaces of Jamaica in terms of its colonial history. She situates her light-skinned protagonist Clare as aligned with British neocolonial rule yet awakened to her nascent desire and sexuality through discovering a history of indigenous resistance embodied in generations of native women in the remote highlands.

A different kind of example of embodied space is evident in the life writing of religious women of the European Early Modern period. They could not tell sexual stories of their bodies unless those stories were linked to a critique of the body's waywardness from the perspective of Christian conversion, as the narratives of Spanish women religious that had to be censored by their confessors indicate.[7] To narrate the sexualized body, as Charlotte Charke did in her *Narrative of the Life of Mrs. Charlotte Charke* in eighteenth-century England, was scandalous, as Felicity A. Nussbaum suggests, because a Christian discourse of the sexualized body underwrote belief in the corrupt nature of female sexuality and the lower-class status of acknowledged sexual activity (195–6). Similarly, until the later nineteenth century much male embodiment tended to be in repressed or encoded stories of the sexual body, sometimes figuring it as the non-rational "ground" to be dominated by the Cartesian mind. Indeed, the practice of reading autobiographies, particularly men's, as embodied sites of knowledge production about desire, danger, and disease deserves more critical attention. In examining spaces of embodiment we can uncover social norms about the proper uses of bodies, consider their relationship to cultural spaces and behaviors, and note how autobiographers define and situate the normative body in relation to the ab-normative or disabled body. As G. Thomas Couser asserts for "vulnerable bodies," those "who are customarily on the receiving end of life writing, those who get represented by others, often without their permission" are vulnerable to having their bodily abilities misrepresented and their stories appropriated in ways that life narrative should ethically guard against (198).

3. Social Spaces

Autobiographical narratives are also organized around *spaces of sociality*, as *"Raum"* suggests, spaces of relationships and actions that are formalized in communicative interaction and may be ritualized or identified by gesture and bodily positioning, as Erving Goffman explored in *Gender Advertisements*. In life writing, actors may be situated discursively vis à vis others who are present explicitly, as is the host to the traveler, or implicitly, the warden to prisoners, or a divinity to a religious community. In such narratives negotiations occur across boundaries—of rank, nation, ethnic, religious, and gendered difference—that are both constructed and redefined in the encounter. By articulating these spaces of the self, their dynamics, and the fluctuating positions actors take up within them, critics are able to specify what has often been characterized as "relationality" in life narrative, that is, how a subject's narration of her or his life is implicated in and impinges upon the lives of others, and may encapsulate their biographies. For example, John Edgar Wideman in *Brothers and Keepers* refracts the story of his brother Robby, who as a youth was convicted of murder on the streets of Pittsburgh and imprisoned for life, through his own quite different career trajectory as a writer, to create what he calls a "mix of memory, imagination, feeling, and fact" that characterizes the experience of urban American space for many African American men (1).

When collective stories are situated in a social surround, it is often at borders that may be heightened by entrenched asymmetries. Consider two examples. First, there are the narratives of colonized or newly postcolonial subjects, situated in a terrain of colonial encounter that may be understood as a transcultural space. In autoethnographic writing such narrators seek to redefine not only their own access to agency at sites of former dispossession, but to legitimate the subject status of the group to which they belong and on behalf of whom their insider-outsider narratives are shaped, even when they are addressed to international audiences. One might look to such overtly or covertly autobiographical texts as Nafissatou Diallo's *A Dakar Childhood*, which charts her coming of age in post-independence Dakar, Senegal, in the 1960s in tandem with the liberation of the city and the revitalization of its local practices and festivals. Or we could consider Manthia Diawara's *In Search of Africa*, which interrogates his experience growing up as an expatriate child in the Guinea of Sékou Touré and as a teenager in Bamako, Mali. In different ways both narratives are iconic for a generation of post-independence Africans seeking a "pan-African" connection to African American intellectuals and race theorists at that moment of liberation. Here the story of the "I" is both representative of a larger group's experience at a powerful moment of change and an articulation of their desire for social transformation.

Consider also the explicit use of "in-between spaces" that link artist and viewer—yet disrupt interaction—in the art installations of African American autobiographical artist Adrian Piper, who presents a range of official identity documents that contradictorily identify her as white and as black in her installation *Cornered* in order to confront the audience with the arbitrary nature of practices of racialization in the US.[8] Similarly, Carrie Mae Weems, in *The Jefferson Suite*, interrogates the histories generated by Thomas Jefferson's children with his black slave Sally Hemmings as indicative of the double legacy of slavery in the foundation of the American republic. These visualizations of social relations as a space of antagonistic difference inflected by the history of racial struggle have implications for both artist and viewers. They call us to self-reflection, often uncomfortably, about differentiated socio-cultural locations and the inequities that they sustain. More broadly, art historians Jennifer González and, later, Mieke Bal have argued that the spatialized concept of visual life narrative as "autotopography" crystallizes a practice of many contemporary installation artists. Defined as "a spatial, local and situational 'writing' of the self's life in visual art," autotopography situates an artist's—perhaps oblique—self-presentation within a surround of cultural objects that reference specific times, places, and networks of the past (Bal 163). In Bal's phrase, autotopographies such as the giant spiders of sculptor Louise Bourgeois "conceptualize metaphor in a hyperbolic materiality" (182).

4. Geopolitical Space

While social relations are situated within *geographic space*, sometimes geopolitical space is explicitly foregrounded, as transnational cultural studies demonstrates. For subjects located in complex spaces of citizenship, or multicultural spaces across nations with histories of conflict, questions of migration and the negotiation of borders or points of transition engage contradictions of geopolitical space. For example, to turn again to the narrative of Esmeralda Santiago, *When I Was Puerto Rican* not only contrasts her experience of coming of age in 1950s San Juan and its countryside with her teenaged years as an immigrant to working-class Brooklyn. The narrative also situates her family story as emblematic of the ambiguous status of Puerto Ricans in the United States, who are citizens for the purpose of military service and the rule of law but cannot vote; rather, they are racialized as a Spanglish-speaking, impoverished minority and stereotyped as an ethnic other in the dominant American narrative. Interrogating the space of the watery border between the island of Puerto Rico and the continental US, as well as the less palpable internal borders of her Brooklyn neighborhood, Santiago emphasizes the shifting valences of particular locations and the irreducibility of these heterogeneous sites to a monolithic place called "America."

In thinking about geopolitical space, Wendy S. Hesford has employed the concept of "spatial rhetorics" to discuss how human rights documentaries about rape in the Balkan conflicts of the 1990s created "a rhetorical space of intersubjectivity" that filmmakers used to engage visual texts bearing witness to violence and violation, and to elicit a situation of "transnational rhetorical witnessing" (121). Similarly, Theresa Kulbaga has employed the notion of "spatial rhetorics of memory" to discuss tropes that [represent] . . . memory as both temporally (historically) and geographically (politically) located" in, for example, Eva Hoffman's treatment of her Jewish family's post-Holocaust immigration, first to Canada and then to the United States, in *Lost in Translation*. In a different way, German filmmaker Ursula

Biemann's documentary film *Performing the Border* represents the US-Mexico border as a performative space constructed in embodied acts of crossing and constitutive of spatial surrounds that are unstable, conflictual, and vulnerable to manipulation by nations, by transnational corporations, and by violent outlaw practices (as in hundreds of unsolved Ciudad Juarez murders of young women). Spatial rhetorics, then, configure autobiographical subjects as migratory and transnationally situated, rather than as inhabiting a single national identity and citizenship. Reading for how life narratives foreground spatial dynamics across geographic borders and forge new alliances with readers understands geopolitical spaces as sites for transacting or contesting new hybrid identities and global practices.

5. Spatial Figurations

Space may also be invoked in *tropes* and *topoi* that represent self-relationship. The *Essays* of Montaigne, for example, are rife with figures in which he characterizes his self-experience through a metaphorics of space. To cite just a few examples, in the essay "Of Presumption" (II, 17) he uses the phrase, *"je me contreroulle"* (translated as "I roll around in myself") to describe the capaciousness and intensity of his self-study (ed. Saulnier 653; Frame 499). In the essay "Of Solitude" (I, 39) Montaigne presents his creative process as occurring in the "arrière boutique" or back room of his mind, a space for solitary self-contemplation that readers are invited to imagine.[9]

In a different way Virginia Woolf, in "A Sketch of the Past," characterizes the pre-linguistic dimension of relationship to her infant self through a spatial metaphor. She says she has "the feeling, as I describe it sometimes to myself, of lying in a grape and seeing through a film of semi-transparent yellow" (65). Further, "I am hardly aware of myself, but only of the sensation. I am only the container of the feeling of ecstasy, of the feeling of rapture" (67). Sidonie Smith, discussing Woolf's "grape" subjectivity in this passage, notes its fluidity, a state prior to the consolidation of the ego when the body is a locus of sensation in immediate contact with the world, in a sense an extension of its space (95–6).

Indeed, an entire autobiographical genre might be established around spatial metaphor, either explicit or implicit. Consider the centrality of the "interior landscape" to the spiritual autobiographies of mystics from Teresa of Avila to Thomas Merton, from Christianity to Buddhism.[10] Such narratives focus on processes of self-examination according to protocols for developing an internal spiritual space. This space of self is counter to and often at war with both the desires and limits of the material body and the social world's emphasis on wealth and status. The spiritual autobiographer retreats from a hostile external world by creating an imagined verbal landscape in which to express devotion to an otherworldly being or idea. In another genre of life narrative, the apology, the narrator may invoke tropes of the courtroom to create the imagined surround of a trial, and may rehearse opposing arguments pro and contra the speaker in inviting the reader to render judgment. Such implied spatial contexts also come into play in the confessional narratives of Augustine and Rousseau, which juxtapose sites of self-exposure and contrition with scenes of flagrant sinning in intimate or back rooms.

6. *Memory and the Spatialization of Temporal Distances*

It is possible to represent the temporal distance that one traverses in *memory* by recourse to spatial terms. A narrator may engage history, the surround in which one is located as both actor and acted upon, as the space of "the past." Memory is invoked spatially when narrators imagine themselves enshrining their personal and collective pasts in a kind of personal archive. Of course memory is itself unstable, tropological, and subject to interpretation. As Andreas Huyssen suggests, what it captures is never a "recovery" but an approximation: "The past . . . must be articulated to become memory. The fissure that opens up between experiencing an event and remembering it in representation is unavoidable. . . . This split should be understood as a powerful stimulant for cultural and artistic creativity" (2–3). If articulating the past stimulates creativity, it also reveals much about the remembering subject. Marita Sturken observes, "Memories are narratives that are told and retold, reenacted and reimaged. Memory is ontologically fluid and memories constantly subject to rescripting and fantasy. . . . What memories tell us, more than anything, is about the stakes held by individuals and institutions in what the past means" (689). Both critics suggest that the elusiveness of past experience can only be approximated. Narrative attempts to fix it by a focus on objects—photos, documents—or on personal testimony are scripts under ongoing revision.

The use of spatial practices for remembering is by no means recent. Renaissance mnemonic practices and memory logics, as Frances A. Yates long ago pointed out, were based on spatial practices. The places of memory were conceived in two senses—visualized as *loci*, as in memory theaters, and localized for recall by a process of assigning a particular meaning to each "place." This model of memory worked associatively by "emplacement," making the objects of memory touchable in imagination. And while the technologies of memory no longer invoke such logic, autobiographical narratives may still become repositories for preserving memory against the erosion of history. That is, a narrative may act as a space of commemoration and an archive for retrieving a vanished past.

Consider, for example, the linkage of the geopolitical space of national and ideological confrontation with the space of collective memory and desire that occurs in Jana Hensel's *Zonenkinder (After the Wall)*. For Hensel, writing over a decade after the demise of the German Democratic Republic (GDR), artifacts such as her Pioneer photos and membership cards, depicted in the book, and recollections of her "Ossie" clothing, holidays, and education, form a textured site for GDR readers' collective recall and association, despite the impossibility of verifying their accuracy in the reunified German nation. Her "Zone" is now only a zone of memory with artifacts preserved in a personal archive (and incompletely in Berlin's various GDR museums), a space of memory that will not be available to the next generation, born after the Wall came down in 1989. But Hensel writes as a member of a particular in-between "Ossie" collectivity, too young to have been fully formed subjects of the GDR state yet imprinted with its everyday practices and assumptions, even while experiencing conflicting "Wessie" desires. The location of her generation, Hensel suggests, is itself in a liminal zone that is a "nowhere" between the former East and a new nation that does not reflect their collective past. This in-between zone is a "nowhere" imagined as the material remains of personal and collective memory archives that may be activated by readers who bring their own memories to her story.

7. Peritextual Space—Life Narrative in the World

Finally, autobiographical texts can be situated in a *peritextual surround*, what we may think of as, collectively, the spaces of publication, reception, and circulation. As Gillian Whitlock's studies of life narrative have emphasized, the peritext concerns not only who reads whom, when, and to what effect; but also the kind of audience a text may construct at a given moment and the kinds of audiences that subsequently take it up for different occasions and purposes. Drawing on Gérard Genette's theorizing of paratexts, Whitlock considers how life writing circulates as a product that takes up space on a shelf or in a display addressed to the public, whether or not they become its readers. The material apparatus of the text begins with its book cover or jacket, which situates the narrative within potential markets and makes an appeal to be read in certain ways. Whitlock's focus on the outpouring of "burqa narratives" with explicit covers, after the New York World Trade Center attacks of September 11, 2001, observes how, in such stories, the cover "images, the titles, and the subtitles are designed to grab the Western eye with a glimpse of absolute difference, of the exotic" (59). As Whitlock provocatively suggests, these life narratives offer the Western reader the fantasy of explanatory stories about Islamic desires and rituals for voyeuristic consumption. In some texts the space of looking may also be constructed as an intersubjective one that establishes a relationship between an image and its viewers. As metropolitan subjects "we are invited to see ourselves seeing" the faces of those we call our "others" (61).

In digital space a narrative is also situated in the midst of epitexts, such as the publisher's advertising and the reviews posted by customers on Amazon.com, indicating how it was received by readers (Whitlock 61–2). That is, in the consumer culture of late capitalism, our encounters with autobiographical narratives are mediated, whether they occur in material spaces or in digital space. We are required to translate narratives across cultures and, in so doing, may understand our own complicity in the circulation of cultural fantasies that intersect with political realities of domination (Whitlock 67–8). By understanding life narratives as situated not only in the peritextual spaces that surround them, but also in the spaces they come to occupy in our daily lives over time, we begin to locate how we ourselves are addressed within the spaces of the autobiographical.

Conclusion

We encounter autobiographical space in multiple ways: as a site that encloses life writing, as a border of contact and contention, and as a presentation addressing readers and subjects engaged in the creation of narrative worlds. The German concept of "*Räume des Selbst*" implies spaces of intersubjectivity that may be mobilized in autobiographical encounters to reflect on the negotiation of communicative situations. While such an understanding may seem far from the notion of geographic place with which I began, "space" as a concept within Anglo-American theorizing of life narrative invites us to consider the social and cultural, interactively constructed, and differently localized borders, margins, and centers that mark zones of self-relation, of encounter, and of the discursive networks of the autobiographical.

Notes

1. As this book goes to press, a collection, *Life Writing and Space*, has appeared that explores how concepts of subjectivity draw on theories of place and space (ed. Eveline Kilian and Hope Wolf, Routledge 2016).
2. See our discussion of the production of the "I" in *Reading Autobiography*, first ed., 58–64.
3. Friedman asserts, "a locational approach to feminism incorporates diverse formations because its positional analysis requires a kind of geopolitical literacy built out of a recognition of how different times and places produce different and changing gender systems as these intersect with other different and changing societal stratifications and movements for social justice" (5). Her analysis draws on the definitions of locational feminism by such critics as Adrienne Rich in "Notes toward a Politics of Location" (*Blood, Bread, and Poetry*, 1986, 210–32); Inderpal Grewal and Caren Kaplan, "Introduction: Transnational Feminist Practices and the Question of Postmodernity" (in *Scattered Hegemonies*, 1994, 1–36); and Elspeth Probyn, "Travels in the Postmodern: Making Sense of the Local" (in Linda J. Nicholson, *Feminism/Postmodernism*, 1990, 176–89). Friedman's essay "Spatial Poetics and Arundhati Roy's *The God of Small Things*" productively emphasizes "a compensatory emphasis on space" interacting with time in the production of narrative, a return to Bakhtin's notion of the chronotope as "time space" (194).
4. For a discussion of space from a linguistic-cognitive point of view, see David Herman's treatment of spatialization as a "macrodesign" in *Story Logic: Problems and Possibilities of Narrative*. Lincoln: University of Nebraska Press, 2002.
5. See the discussion of spatiality in "Introduction: Situating Subjectivity in Women's Autobiographical Practices," *Women, Autobiography, Theory: A Reader*, 39.
6. Phenomenologists such as Jean Starobinski have distinguished the proprioceptive sense of being *in* one's body from the kinaesthetic sense of the body in motion, occupying space differently in successive temporal moments.
7. See Christine Cloud's dissertation for a discussion of "embodied authority."
8. A transcription of Piper's performance was published in *Voicing Today's Visions: Writings by Contemporary Women Artists*, ed. Mara Witzling. When I saw the Piper installation, the spectators, mostly white, were

distinctly uncomfortable. See also the discussion by Jennifer Drake of Piper's installation.

9   The sentence is worth citing: "Il se faut reserver une arrièreboutique toute nostre, toute franche, en laquelle nous éstablissons nostre vraye liberté et principale retraicte et solitude" (ed. Saulnier 241). It is translated by Frame as "We must reserve a back shop all our own, entirely free, in which to establish our real liberty and our principal retreat and solitude" (177).

10 For a memoir of conversion to Buddhist spirituality as a mental "space" of serenity, see Matthieu Ricard, *Happiness*, Little-Brown, 2006.

Works Cited

Anzaldúa, Gloria. *Borderlands / La Frontera: The New Mestiza*. San Francisco: Aunt Lute, 1987.

Blew, Mary Clearman. *All But the Waltz*. NY: Viking, 1991.

Bal, Mieke. "Autotopography: Louise Bourgeois as Builder." *Interfaces: Women, Autobiography, Image, Performance*, ed. Sidonie Smith and Julia Watson. Ann Arbor, MI: University of Michigan Press, 163–185.

Bhabha, Homi K. 1994. "Introduction: The Locations of Culture." In *The Location of Culture*. London and New York: Routledge, 1994, 19–44.

Biemann, Ursula. *Performing the Border*. Videotape: Women Make Movies, 1999, 42 min.

Boardman, Kathleen A. and Gioia Woods, eds. *Western Subjects: Autobiographical Writing in the North American West*. Salt Lake: University of Utah Press, 2004.

Boelhower, William. "Avant-Garde Autobiography: Deconstructing the Modernist Habitat." In *Literary Anthropology*. Ed. Fernando Poyatos. Amsterdam & Philadelphia: John Benjamins Co., 1988, 273–303.

Buell, Lawrence. *The Environmental Imagination*, Cambridge, MA. Harvard University Press, 1995.

Butler, Judith. *Giving an Account of Oneself*. New York: Fordham University Press, 2005.

Cliff, Michelle. *Abeng: A Novel*. Trumansburg, NY: Crossing Press, 1984.

Cloud, Christine. *Embodied Authority in the Spiritual Autobiographies of Four Early Modern Women from Spain and Mexico*. Dissertation: The Ohio State University, 2006.

Couser, G. Thomas. *Vulnerable Subjects. Ethics and Life Writing*. Ithaca, NY: Cornell University Press, 2004.

Diallo, Nafissatou. *A Dakar Childhood*, tr. Dorothy Blair. London: Longmans, 1982. (Translation of *De Tilène au Plateau: une enfance dakaroise*. Dakar: Les nouvelles editions africaines, 1975.)

Diawara, Manthia. *In Search of Africa*. Cambridge, MA: Harvard University Press, 1998.

Drake, Jennifer. "Variations on Negation: Breaking the Frame with Lorna Simpson and Adrian Piper." *Interfaces: Women, Autobiography, Image, Performance*, ed. Sidonie Smith and Julia Watson. Ann Arbor: University of Michigan Press, 211–39.

Friedman, Susan Stanford. *Mappings: Feminism and the Cultural Geographies of Encounter*. Princeton: Princeton University Press, 2001.

Friedman, Susan Stanford. "Spatial Poetics and Arundhati Roy's *The God of Small Things*." *A Companion to Narrative Theory*, ed. James Phelan and Peter J. Rabinowitz. Oxford, UK, and Malden, MA: Blackwell, 2005, 192–205.

Genette, Gérard. *Paratexts: Thresholds of Interpretation*, tr. Jane E. Lewin. Cambridge, England: Cambridge University Press, 1997.

Goffman, Erving. *Gender Advertisements*. New York: Harper & Row, 1976.

Gonzalez, Jennifer A. "Autotopographies." In *Prosthetic Territories: Politics and Hypertechnologies*, ed. Gabriel Brahm Jr. and Mark Driscoll. Boulder, CO: Westview Press, 1995, 133–50.

Gusdorf, Georges. "Conditions and Limits of Autobiography." In *Autobiography: Essays Theoretical and Critical*. Ed. James Olney. Princeton: Princeton University Press, 1980, 28–48.

Hensel, Jana. *Zonenkinder*. Reinbek bei Hamburg: Rowohlt, 2002.

Hesford, Wendy S. "Documenting Violations: Rhetorical Witnessing and the Spectacle of Distant Suffering." *Biography*, 27:1, Win. 2004, 104–44.

Hoffman, Eva. *Lost in Translation. A Life in a New Language*. NY: Penguin, 1989.

Huyssen, Andreas. *Twilight Memories: Marking Time in a Culture of Amnesia*. New York: Routledge, 1995.

Jolly, Margaretta, ed. *Encyclopedia of Life Narrative*. Two vols. Oxford and Chicago: Fitzroy Dearborn, 2001.

Kilian, Eveline, and Hope Wolf. *Life Writing and Space*. London: Routledge, 2016.

Kulbaga, Theresa. "Trans/National Feminist Lives." Dissertation: The Ohio State University, June 2006.

Montaigne, Michel de. *Essais*, three vols. Paris: Presses Universitaires Françaises, ed. V.-L. Saulnier, 1960. (Translated as *The Complete Essays of Montaigne*, Donald M. Frame. Stanford, CA: Stanford University Press, 1965.)

Nussbaum, Felicity A. *The Autobiographical Subject: Gender and Ideology in Eighteenth-Century England*. Baltimore: Johns Hopkins University Press, 1994.

Pile, Steven, and Keith, Michael. *Place and the Politics of Identity*. London: Routledge, 1993.

Piper, Adrian. *Cornered*. African Museum of New York City. November 2001.

Saldivar, José David. *Border Matters: Remapping American Cultural Studies*. Berkeley: University of California Press, 1997.

Santiago, Esmeralda. *When I Was Puerto Rican*. NY: Random House, 1993.

Smith, Sidonie. *Moving Lives: Twentieth-Century Women's Travel Writing*. Minneapolis: University of Minnesota Press, 2001.

Smith, Sidonie. "The Autobiographical Eye/I in Virginia Woolf's "Sketch." *Subjectivity, Identity, and the Body*. Bloomington, IN: Indiana University Press, 1993, 83–102.

Smith, Sidonie, and Julia Watson. "Introduction: Situating Subjectivity in Women's Autobiographical Practices," *Women, Autobiography, Theory: A Reader*. Madison: University of Wisconsin Press, 1998, 3–53.

Smith, Sidonie, and Julia Watson. *Reading Autobiography: A Guide for Interpreting Life Narratives*. Minneapolis: University of Minnesota Press, 2001.

Spender, Stephen. "Confessions and Autobiography." *Autobiography: Essays Theoretical and Critical*. Ed. James Olney. Princeton: Princeton University Press, 1980, 115–122.

Sturken, Marita. "The Absent Images of Memory: Remembering and Reenacting the Japanese Internment." *Positions: East Asia Cultures Critique* 5.3 (Winter 1997): 687–707.

Weems, Carrie Mae. *The Jefferson Suite*. Exhibition, International Center of Photography, New York City, June 2001.

Wideman, John Edgar. *Brothers and Keepers*. NY: Penguin, 1984.

Whitlock, Gillian. *Soft Weapons: Autobiography in Transit*. Chicago: University of Chicago Press, 2007.

Williams, Terry Tempest. "Yellowstone: The Erotics of Place." In *The Unspoken Hunger*. NY: Random House, 1994, 81–87.

Woolf, Virginia. "A Sketch of the Past." In *Moments of Being*. NY and London: Harcourt, Brace, Jovanovich, 1976, 61–137.

Yaeger, Patricia. "Introduction: Dreaming of Infrastructure." *Publications of the Modern Language Association* 122: 1 (January 2007), 9–26.

Yates, Frances A. *The Art of Memory*. Chicago: University of Chicago Press, 1966.

9
THE AUTOBIOGRAPHICAL MANIFESTO: IDENTITIES, TEMPORALITIES, POLITICS (SMITH 1991)

Decolonization never takes place unnoticed, for it influences individuals and modifies them fundamentally. It transforms spectators crushed with their inessentiality into privileged actors, with the grandiose glare of history's floodlights upon them. It brings a natural rhythm into existence, introduced by new men, and with it a new language and a new humanity. Decolonization is the veritable creation of new men. But this creation owes nothing of its legitimacy to any supernatural power; the 'thing' which has been colonized becomes man during the same process by which it frees itself.
                    Frantz Fanon, The Wretched of the Earth (28)

All "I"s are not equal. Nor are they conceptualized similarly. There is, for instance, the "we" that is sometimes an autobiographical "I." There is also the Rastafarian "I and I"; and the female "I" that, as Maxine Hong Kingston suggests, in Chinese is the same as "slave." Charged with history, representational imprints, and self-representational politics, "I"s are consolidated, naturalized, centralized or marginalized through certain cultural practices that effectively "regulate" the epistemological, ontological, and hermeneutical implications of autobiographical utterances (Butler, *Gender Trouble* 1–34).

In the postcolonial, global environment, the cultural hegemony of the West comes under question. Imperial gazes become *déclassé* as the old imperial "I" is revealed for what it has been: a locus of normative and exclusionary stabilizations of subjectivity that silence marginalized peoples, thereby occluding specific temporalities of identity and specific heterogeneous histories. Stripping the silver from the back of the mirror that reflects back the imperial gaze, revealing the palimpsistic lineaments of their status as subject rather than object, formerly "subject" peoples begin to resist the totalizing definitional politics of traditional autobiographical practice. But what kinds of autobiographical strategies lead to what kinds of empowerments? That is the issue I want to explore here, with particular attention to the autobiographical manifesto.

We might label one strategic move mimesis. In this move the autobiographer positions herself as the subject of traditional autobiography: that is, she mimes the subjectivity of universal man. Speaking from this location proffers authority, legitimacy, and readability. It proffers membership in the community of the fully human, the "brotherhood of metaphysical man." For oppressed peoples, such membership can be psychologically and politically expedient and potent. Unselfconsciously embraced, however, mimesis invites recuperation as well as the promise of power, the maintenance of subjection to the self-definitions that bind.

Yet there is another side to this mirroring, the nitrate of mimicry, for something may be exposed here: an unauthorized speaker positions herself in the locale of the universal subject, thereby introducing a menacing suspicion of inexact correlation between representations. "As incomplete mirrors, as the waste of the system that produced the identity of the white male," suggests

Linda Kintz, "[an unauthorized speaker] can only reflect back to the male subject a partial representation of himself, a reflection that is askew, flawed, not specular" (131). As a result, autobiographical mimicry may subtly contest the "natural," "commonsensical," "universal" categorizations of difference. In addition to mimesis's treacherous invitation to recuperation, then, comes its promise of escape from an exclusionary configuration of subjectivity.

A second strategy for a contestatory autobiographical practice looks to the politics of fragmentation as the means to counter the centrifugal power of the old unitary self of western rationalism. Promoting the endless possibilities of self-fragmentation, the politics of fragmentation reveals the cultural constructedness of any coherent, stable, and universal subject. It may also reveal how problematic it is to maintain a decisive, unified point of departure for identity as the ground of a liberatory autobiographical practice since the exclusions of unified points are legion. But shattering the old notion of the unitary individual in favor of the split and multiply fragmented subject may not always serve emancipatory objectives; rather, it may serve further oppressive agendas, as Judith Butler cautions: "If oppression is to be defined in terms of a loss of autonomy by the oppressed, as well as a fragmentation or alienation within the psyche of the oppressed, then a theory which insists upon the inevitable fragmentation of the subject appears to reproduce and valorize the very oppression that must be overcome" ("Gender" 327). Any autobiographical practice that promotes endless fragmentation and a reified multiplicity might be counterproductive since the autobiographical subject would have to split itself beyond usefulness to be truly nonexclusionary. And it is difficult to coalesce a call to political action founded upon some kind of communal identity around a constantly deferred point of departure.[1]

Other strategies for oppositional autobiographical practice are grounded in conceptions of "experiential" politics.

Difficulties negotiating the terrain of the "real" lead in fact to opposing orientations to experience. For some there is an experience outside representation to which the autobiographical text refers. And there is an ontological basis to identity in this experience. So a potentially emancipatory practice would be one that seeks to uncover the "true" self and the "truth" about that self's experience, the sources of oppression and strength, the essential difference in body, psyche, and modes of knowing and being in the world. For others such a positivist approach to experience neglects the relationship of experience to discourse, the artifactual nature of representation, the operations and apparati of cultural determinations. From this perspective, there is no subject outside language, as textuality displaces any transparent experience. And since language operates to fix subjects, the subject of resistance can only engage in a drama of negativity, to allude to Julia Kristeva's theoretical frame, a drama of the what-I-am-not (292–300). Perhaps we can linger in the space of negativity, consciously resisting the attempt to universalize any "us," "we," or "I," but once again we might be caught in an endless qualification of our individual positionalities that takes us further away from any community of interest and political action.

However problematic its strategies, autobiographical writing has played and continues to play a role in emancipatory politics. Autobiographical practices become occasions for restaging subjectivity, and autobiographical strategies become occasions for the staging of resistance. Thus within what Judith Butler calls "this conflicted cultural field" (*Gender Trouble* 145) the autobiographer can lay out an agenda for a changed relationship to subjectivity, identity, and the body. We see this agenda in recent texts by women who pursue self-consciously political autobiographical acts, who issue calls for new subjects, in texts I call autobiographical manifestos. Purposeful, bold, contentious, the autobiographical manifesto contests the old inscriptions, the old histories, the old politics, the *ancien régime*, by working to dislodge the hold of the universal subject through an expressly political collocation of a new "I." In service to a new "social reality," what Donna Haraway describes as "our most important political construction, a world-changing fiction" (191), the manifesto offers an arena in which the revolutionary subject can insist on identity in service to an emancipatory politics, even if, as Robert K. Martin argues, that identity is "assumed" (n.p.).

The Subject of Manifesto

Dictionary definitions suggest that a manifesto is a proof, a piece of evidence, a public declaration or proclamation, usually issued by or with the sanction of a sovereign prince or state, or by an individual or body of individuals whose proceedings are of public importance, for the purpose of announcing past actions and explaining the reasons or motives for actions announced as forthcoming (OED). Within this definitional context seven constituent aspects of manifesto inform this discussion.

To appropriate/to contest sovereignty

As noted in the introduction, the universal subject consolidates sovereignty through exclusionary practices. These practices figure "others" as "not-an-individualized-'I,'" persons whose humanity is opaque, and whose membership in the human community is negated by relegation to what Nancy Hartsock describes as "a chaotic, disorganized, and anonymous collectivity" (160–1). Autobiographical manifestos issue from persons assigned to this anonymous collectivity who vigorously reject the sovereignty of this specular *ancien régime* and the dominance of the universal subject. Through the manifesto, the autobiographical subject confronts the ghost of the identity assigned her by the old sovereign subject, what Paul Smith terms the ideological "I," a fixed object position representing culturally intelligible and authorized performances of identity. These fixed identifications (of "woman," "black," "lesbian," etc.) function as cultural templates for repetition. Repetition, however, breeds contempt; that is to say, repetition brings with it alterations precisely because, as Smith suggests, "imaginary identifications . . . are continually vulnerable to the registration of ever renewed and contradictory interpellations" (106). The autobiographical manifesto confronts this process directly: the tensions set in motion by contradictory identity assignments incite, to use revolutionary rhetoric, self-conscious encounters with the politics of identification and catalyze subjectivity around specific and oppositional contours of "I-ness." Resisting "the taken-for-granted ability of one small segment of the population to speak for all" (Hartsock 171), the autobiographer purposefully locates herself as a subject, leaving behind the object status to which cultural identities have confined her.

To bring to light, to make manifest (*literally, struck with the hand*)

Since awareness of the pressures to repeat certain cultural identifications is the ground of resistance to repetition, the difficult road to a liberatory autobiographical practice lies through the terrain of cultural critique. And so, when Cherrié Moraga comments in *Loving in the War Years* that "the Third World lesbian brings colored female sexuality with all its raggedy edges and oozing wounds—for better or for worse—into the light of day," she captures colloquially the political agenda of the autobiographical manifesto: to force issues "into the light of day" (138). Intent on bringing culturally marginalized experiences out from under the shadow of an undifferentiated otherness, the autobiographical manifesto anchors its narrative itinerary in the specificities and locales of time and space, the discursive surround, the material ground, the provenance of histories.

To bring things "into the light of day," to make manifest a perspective on identity and experience, affects an epistemological breakage of repetition. The legitimacy of a new or alternative knowledge located in the experience of the margins is affirmed.[2] The autobiographical manifesto thus attempts to develop what

Hartsock describes as "an account of the world as seen from the margins, an account which can expose the falseness of the view from the top and can transform the margins as well as the center . . . an account of the world which treats our perspectives not as subjugated or disruptive knowledges, but as primary and constitutive of a different world." The individual story becomes the occasion for what Hartsock calls "standpoint epistemologies," analyses of specific confluences of social, psychological, economic, and political forces of oppression (171–2). The trajectories, strategies, and tools of these analyses take various forms, some of which I will explore below as part of the enabling myths and motivating metaphors of resistance.

To announce publicly

Autobiographical writing is always a gesture toward publicity, displaying before an impersonal public an individual's interpretation of experience. The very impetus for contemporary autobiographical manifestos, however, lies in the recognition of a vexed relationship between what too easily becomes the binary opposition of the political and the personal. The early rallying cry of the white, middle-class feminist movement was "The personal is political." And through the last two decades the politics of personal relationships, the economics of reproduction, and the politics of psychosexual development have been central to feminist analyses in many fields. In challenging the hegemony of white middle-class feminism, however, theorists of multiple differences have differentiated the personal stakes and psychological impacts of systems of colonization, focusing on personal experiences of multiple oppressions—of class, caste, race, gender, sexuality, nationality. In this more heterogeneous context, "the private" requires reconceptualization, as Aida Hurtado suggests when she emphasizes that "the political consciousness of women of Color stems from an awareness that the public is *personally* political. . . . There is no such thing as a private sphere for people of Color except that which they manage to create and protect in an otherwise hostile environment" (849). And so a cautionary gesture is necessary here. Different autobiographers come at the private/public duality from different experiences of oppression, from different locales in discourse. As a result, the mapping of private/public politics may proceed to lay out different borderlines.

Hurtado argues that we need to attend to the relative positionality of specific women vis-à-vis the "middle-class white man," the prototype for the universal subject who stands centrally in the public space and whose standpoint determines the places of power, the margins of meaning, the geographies of knowledge. As a result, the cartography of private space takes its contours from multiple spaces of adjacency. For instance, the white middle-class woman exists alongside "public man," sharing his private spaces. But the woman of color exists separately from that man, generally at a distance from his private space. Different alignments toward the dominant private space condition different cultural constructions of "woman," different cultural practices for women.[3]

The autobiographical manifesto asserts unqualifiedly, even exuberantly, both the politicization of the private and the personalization of the public, effectively troubling the binary complacencies of the *ancien régime* of selfhood with its easy dichotomization of private and public (see Haraway 205). But the trajectory of its mappings must be considered in the specific cultural locations of the woman who issues the manifesto's call to action.

To perform publicly

While it might seem strange to repeat the former aspect of the autobiographical manifesto with a change of one word, it is important to note separately the performative aspect of the autobiographical manifesto. Expressly a public performance, the manifesto revels in the energetic display of a new kind of subject. The manifesto engages directly the cultural construction of identities and their sanctioned and legitimated performances, engaging the ideological systems pressing specific identities on specific persons. It takes a public stand on behalf of purposeful deflections, intervening in oppressive identity performances, troubling culturally authorized fictions.[4] Historicizing identity, the autobiographical manifesto implicitly, if not explicitly, insists on the temporalities and spatialities of identity and, in doing so, brings the everyday practices of identity directly into the floodlights of conscious display.

To speak as one of a group, to speak for a group

In the manifesto, group identification, rather than radical individuality, is the rhetorical ground of appeal. During her public performance the manifesto speaker positions herself expressly as a member of a group or community, an auto/ethnographer, so to speak (see Lionnet 99). The "I" anchored in collectivity is the "I" of what Rita Felski, à la Jurgen Habermas, labels a counter-public sphere (166). Counter-public spheres are multiple, invoking identification around various experiences of oppression and exclusions from the central or centrifugal bourgeois public sphere and its ideology of the universal subject. While Felski's particular interest focuses on the dynamics of the feminist counter-public sphere, which she says "does not claim a representative universality but rather offers a critique of cultural values from the standpoint of women as a marginalized group within society," for the purposes of this discussion we need to emphasize the existence of multiple counter-public spheres that operate along analogous lines and generate their specific critiques of universalizing spheres of influence (167).[5]

Critique in this instance is motivated by the autobiographical subject's desire to contest dominant discourses surrounding the subject, discourses through which the subject is objectified in strategic difference making and rendered abnormative. Moreover, the subject in this instance of the autobiographical manifesto speaks as a member of a non-hegemonic group or counter-public sphere, and that group too has what Mikhail Bakhtin suggests is its own "social dialect," its language/s. For Bakhtin it is through the conflictual, supplementary, consonant action of heteroglossia that consciousness emerges. Psyche, sociality, language converge to link consciousness to critique. But critique does not proceed univocally. Critique is accompanied by what Mae Gwendolyn Henderson describes as "testimony." According to Henderson, testimony derives from the subject's "dialectic of identity," that is, from her acknowledgment of a communality of "history, language, and culture" with others of the group (118–21).

In the manifesto communitarian auto/ethnography functions as a kind of "nationalism." Bernice Johnson Reagon captures the nationalism inherent in communitarian politics when she suggests that a liberatory space "should be a nurturing space where you sift out what people are saying about you and decide who you really are. And you take the time to try to construct within yourself and within your community who you would be if you were running society . . . [this is] nurturing, but it is also nationalism. At a certain stage, nationalism is crucial to a people if you are ever going to impact as a group in your own interest" (163). Nationalism determines the specific moves through which the manifesto negotiates the landscapes of identity and difference. Postulating a testimonial nationalism, the manifesto quarrels with "*competitive discourses*" (Henderson 121) and through its narrative itinerary stages a breakage in repetitions. As it does so it struggles to resist the totalizing agenda of the universal subject and proclaims the viability of a non-universal position.[6]

To speak to the future

The generic contracts of western literary practices promise something, but what exactly they promise is subject to various theoretical interpretations. Traditionally, western autobiography involves a contractual obligation in which the autobiographer engages in a narrative itinerary of self-disclosure, retrospective summation, self-justification. Thus scholars of autobiography, including such contemporary theorists as Philippe Lejeune, emphasize the retrospective aspect of autobiography. Postmodern theorists have shifted the trope to the autobiographical text as the site of a deadly specularity. Paul de Man, for instance, argues that "autobiography veils a defacement of the mind of which it is itself the cause" (930). As a result, "the autobiographical project" becomes, according to Paul Smith, "a privileged kind of impossibility, always given over to uncertainty, undecidability, and, finally, to death" (Smith 103). But other theorists resist what they consider the dead end of death in autobiography. For instance, Kathleen Woodward talks of the writing of autobiography as taking place not under the sign of death, defacement, or desire but under the sign of anxiety, "a state of expecting a danger and preparing oneself for it, although the danger may be unknown to oneself, that is, not consciously known." Attempting to suggest a difference between male and female narratives, Woodward suggests that where men may write under the sign of desire and its "emphasis ... on past loss," women write under the sign of anxiety for future loss (108–9).

The autobiographical manifesto offers another sign. Here the "I" does not write under the sign of desire or the sign of anxiety. Rather, the "I" writes under the sign of hope and what Hélène Cixous calls "the very possibility of change," emphasizing the generative and prospective thrust of autobiography (249). Calling the subject into the future, the manifesto attempts to actively position the subject in a potentially liberated future distanced from the constraining and oppressive identifications inherent in the everyday practices of the *ancien régime*. Thus while the manifesto looks back in what Teresa de Lauretis terms "the critical negativity" of theoretical critique, it also gestures forward in "the affirmative positivity of its politics" to new spaces for subjectivity (26).[7]

Since new interpretations and hopeful futures are "crucially bound up with power," the manifesto always foregrounds the relationship of subjectivity to power (Modleski 136). It insists on new interpretations as a means of wresting power, resisting universalized repetitions that essentialize and naturalize. In service to that political cause, the autobiographer issues the call for a new, revolutionary subject, offers an agenda for "I" transformations. Ultimately, then, the manifesto proffers a utopian vision, "a 'waking dream' of the possible," writes Françoise Lionnet, "which might inspire us to see beyond the constraints of the here and now to the idealized vision of a perfect future" (110).[8]

Hélène Cixous's "Medusa"

I have tried to elaborate some descriptive markers as a way of stimulating certain ways of reading the subject of the autobiographical manifesto. Like theory generally, they are meant not to rigidify and specify all the workings of the autobiographical manifesto but to suggest some lines of inquiry and some originating points for considering variations and problematics. I turn now to a consideration of three autobiographical manifestos.

With its vibrant, provocative, always troubling but never dull prose, Hélène Cixous's "The Laugh of the Medusa" offers a flamboyant and gutsy performance of gender, enacts what Friedrich Nietzsche describes in *The Will to Power* as "the magic of the extreme, the seduction that everything extreme exercises" (para 749; qtd. Lionnet 74). Cixous's provocative "Laugh" is certainly a manifesto. The language that establishes its tenor is the language of revolution—future oriented, explosive, subversive. Its expressed gesture is toward both the breaking up of the old and the positing of the new: "As there are no grounds for establishing a discourse, but rather an arid millennial ground to break," she proclaims, "what I say has at least two sides and two aims: to break up, to destroy; and to foresee the unforeseeable, to project." (245). The prose abounds in the terminology and metaphors of revolutionary warfare. There are "sovereigns" to fight, an "empire" to "seize" by a "militant" (253) who goes on "scouting mission[s]" (248). A freedom fighter, Cixous's woman recognizes that "there's no room for her if she's not a he. If she's a her-she, it's in order to smash everything, to shatter the framework of institutions, to blow up the law, to break up the 'truth' with laughter" (258).

For Cixous the revolutionary is a woman fighting for "Woman." Here she promotes a communitarian identity politics based on a foundationalist notion of woman. If the goal of her manifesto is to foster effective revolution, the means to victory may indeed be a "strategic" essentialism, a strategic universalization of Woman (although not biological woman) operating at a specific historical juncture with a "common or shared epistemological standpoint" (Butler 14). Cixous herself seems aware of the difference between strategic and ontological essentialism when she declares: "I do not deny that the effects of the past are still with us. But I refuse to strengthen them by repeating them, to confer upon them an irremovability the equivalent of destiny, to confuse the biological and the cultural" (245).

For Cixous the enemies are two: man the oppressor and woman without a body. The former is the entirety of patriarchal culture with its fantasy of the normative human/male. Thus she metaphorizes the male body as a state dick-tatorship (259). The latter enemy is "a woman without a body, dumb, blind," who can never be "a good fighter" because she functions only as a "servant of the militant male, his shadow" (250). Man is the sovereign to be deposed, woman without a body, the specular peasantry holding up the state dick-tatorship. To fight the war of liberation, Cixous's freedom fighter must capture the female body, the lost territory of subjectivity, releasing it from its status as lack, its relegated negativity.

In order to carry out a revolutionary plot, the speaking "I" must become an agent provocateur, infiltrating herself doubly, inside her body and inside history. The two agendas, the one individual and the other collective, are affected through the revolutionary medium of language since writing will "give her back her goods, her pleasures, her organs, her immense bodily territories which have been kept under seal" (250). It will also facilitate her "shattering entry into history, which has always been based *on her suppression*" (250). For Cixous only the writing "I" has the potential to become the revolutionary "I" since writing enables woman to come into agency and to escape the confinement of objectification.[9] The battleground for the freedom fighter is thus the battleground of state representationalism, of language itself. Since language is the revolutionary's arsenal, to be "a good fighter" (250) is to wield "the antilogos weapon" (250), "scoring [her] feats in written and oral language" (251). Hers is a revolutionary mouth, an oral insurgency: "If woman has always functioned 'within' the discourse of man, a signifier that has always referred back to the opposite signifier which annihilates its specific energy and diminishes or stifles its very different sounds, it is time for her to dislocate this 'within,' to explode it, turn it around, and seize it; to make it hers, containing it, taking it in her own mouth, biting that tongue with her very own teeth to invent for herself a language to get inside of" (257). Language must become the revolutionary palace, the symbolic (in the double sense of the term) bastille to be seized: "Writing is precisely *the very possibility of change*, the space that can serve as a springboard for subversive thought, the precursory movement of a transformation of social and cultural structures" (249). And this text, this instance of writing, this "laugh" is such a space of revolutionary seizure and transformation.

To explode the stabilities of phallic history and assassinate authoritarian historians, the revolutionary writing subject must deploy a "feminine practice of writing," a writing whose materiality derives from the recovery of the female body. The relationship between revolutionary practices and the female body coalesces in the manifesto around the two figures of Dora and the Medusa.

Cixous positions Dora as a heroic precursor of the new revolutionary woman, a figure of the formerly repressed woman of "the poetic body" (257), a woman who resisted the inscriptions of Freud's hystericization of her. In this way Dora is identified with Freud's later reference to female sexuality as "the Dark Continent." The manifesto's speaker then links the revolutionary agenda of her emancipatory psychosexual politics to the Black Nationalist movement pressing its anticolonial, anti-imperialist agenda during the late 1960s and 1970s. Like "the colonized peoples of yesterday, the workers, the nations, the species off whose backs the history of men has made its gold" (258), woman is positioned under the sign of oppression/repression. *"The Dark Continent is neither dark nor unexplorable,"* the speaker declares: "It is still unexplored only because we've been made to believe that it was too dark to be explorable. And because they want to make us believe that what interests us is the white continent, with its monuments to Lack" (255). In fact, the speaker goes so far as to identify women with black nationalists: "We the precocious, we the repressed of culture... we are black and we are beautiful" (248). Thus the revolutionary potential of woman is magnified by her positioning as surrogate black African: "You can incarcerate them, slow them down, get away with the old Apartheid routine, but for a time only" (247). Blurring the apparently stable boundaries between the personal/conjugal "subjective economy" (259) and the political economy, she links the psychosexual drama of the repressed to the political/economic exploitation of the oppressed: the personal is political, the political personal.[10]

If Dora is the foremother of the New Woman, then Medusa is her mythical mentor. While mythically Medusa figures as a deadly threat to male power and destiny, in the utopian space of new women she functions differently: "You only have to look at the Medusa straight on to see her. And she's not deadly. She's beautiful and she's laughing" (255). Literally laughter breaks up the assembled and calm planes of the face; and as the movement of laughter breaks up the consolidated features of the face, laughter aligns the human with the animal, with the grotesque body. The effect of laughter on the body elides the gap between species and gestures toward the instability of boundaries separating one species from another, unhinging secure placements in hierarchies of meaning. It also breaks up the elegant, cool, controlled planes of statuesque representationalism, forcing the irrational through the lucid planes of reason and control. The sound itself breaks through the language of phallocentrism, a call from beyond, from the body, from elsewhere. Ultimately laughter breaks up the consolidations of a universalized, rational, unifying truth, destabilizing foundational notions of truth by traducing the boundaries of binary opposites: control and abandon, reason and the irrational: body and mind.

As the vatic representative of the oppressed, the seer of the dark continent, the narrator both calls for and practices a revolutionary writing practice that "laughs." Of a feminine practice, she writes: "It is impossible to *define* a feminine practice of writing, and this is an impossibility that will remain, for this practice can never be theorized, enclosed, coded—which doesn't mean that it doesn't exist.... It will be conceived of only by subjects who are breakers of automatism, by peripheral figures that no authority can ever subjugate" (253). While definitions confine and delimit, writing can explode old practices, disrupt old patterns. Throughout, the narrator's analysis of the conditions of women's silence and her alienation from her body proceed by turns indirectly and directly. As Linda Singer suggests in her analysis of the comparative politics of the texts of Michel Foucault and Cixous, "to establish her differences from hegemonic forms of authority, Cixous dispenses with or conspicuously transgresses much of the textual etiquette and many of the conventions of academic discourse. Her texts are constructed eclectically.... By transgressing disciplinary and paradigmatic boundaries, Cixous positions her work within a different economy of legitimation. Dispensing with conventional footnotes and attributions, she constructs her authority as separate and apart from validation through the chain of fathers" (150). She also destabilizes the notion of narrative progression, moving forward through allusion and language rather than through idea, analysis, and development.

Moreover, in the flamboyant performance of this revolutionary "woman," certain stylistic strategies are deployed exuberantly. Iconoclastic statements common to the manifesto abound: "Let the priests tremble, we're going to show them our sexts!" (255). Excesses of language signal a revolutionary playfulness and cavalier rebellion against the automaticism of common coinage. Thus new words are formed—*erotogeneity* (246), *frigidified* (247), *sexts*. Forceful imperatives explode on the page: "Write your self, inscribe the breath of the whole woman" (250). Pronominal boundaries are breached as the narrator intermingles the interlocutor and the self, fluidly moving through the "I," "you," "she," and "who" as a way of disrupting the certain differentiations separating object and subject, the "I" and the "you." Further, the narrator often shifts her interlocutor—to the "you" of the other woman, to the "You" of the oppressor. Within a particular passage the narrator shifts perspectives, pronomial locations, and defies the boundaries between the "I" and the other so that the relative positioning of narrator and interlocutor seems undecidable. She dismantles the old pronomial relationships as part of her revolutionary agenda to explode the old engendering of language.[11] "Blaz[ing] *her* trail in the symbolic," the narrator destabilizes the old certainties separating pronouns and the old symbolic configurations of gender, creating what she herself calls "the chaosmos of the 'personal'" (258). She is herself "flying/stealing" in "the gesture that jams sociality" (258).

In jamming sociality with the language of the body, the narrator inaugurates the utopian regime of the New Woman, that newly coined sovereign. Cixous thus heralds the new age, one in which the New Woman's "libido will produce far more radical effects of political and social change than some might like to think" (252). The new subject is constituted of a "vatic" bisexuality that "doesn't annul differences but stirs them up, pursues them, increases their number" (254). In each of us reside "both sexes," which are "variously manifest and insistent according to each person, male or female," and in each is present the "nonexclusion either of the difference or of one sex," with the result that the new subject contains the "multiplication of the effects of the inscription of desire, over all parts of my body and the other body" (254). This newly constituted subject will join with others, men and women, "to render obsolete the former relationship and all its consequences, to consider the launching of a brand-new subject, alive, with defamilialization" (261). Radical change will occur in love as Cixous ends her revolutionary manifesto with an almost scriptural call to love: "In the beginning are our differences. The new love dares for the other. . . . She comes in, comes-in-between herself me and you, between the other me where one is always infinitely more than one and more than me, without the fear of ever reaching a limit" (263-4). With no limits, "she finds not her sum but her differences. I am for you what you want me to be at the moment you look at me in a way you've never seen me before: at every instant" (264). With the Law "blown up," violence, volcanic eruption, destruction subside into the aftermath of a pronomial revolution of new love. The nationalistic revolution with epistemological, psychosexual, ontological, and teleological implications finds its utopian conclusion by ushering in a new history.

Serpentine Subjects and Pastoral Manifesto

The rhetoric of Gloria Anzaldúa's autobiographical manifesto is not a rhetoric of revolutionary explosiveness and exuberant or excessive performance. Anzaldúa's manifesto progresses through the rhetorical focus on the geographical subject signaled in the title *Borderlands/La Frontera: The New Mestiza*. For Anzaldúa the topography of the borderland is simultaneously the suturing space of multiple oppressions and the potentially liberatory space through which to migrate toward a new subject position. The geographical trope is at once psychological, physical, metaphysical, and spiritual, since it functions as a space where cultures conflict, contest, and reconstitute one another. Like Cixous, Anzaldúa actively constitutes and projects a revolutionary subject through metaphor—here the *mestiza* who "has gone from being the sacrificial goat to becoming the officiating priestess at the crossroads" (80).

Because Anzaldúa's text so persistently invokes geography, I want to consider its pastoral qualities and their relationship to the subject of manifesto. I do not mean to imply here that Anzaldúa writes in the pastoral tradition, for that would be to define her manifesto through and contain it within the very history she challenges. I do want to consider what silenced history subtends western notions of the pastoral in order to explore the ways in which Anzaldúa's manifesto resists official histories.

The word *pastoral* invokes a long-lived western tradition, originating with the classical authors Theocritus and Virgil. It is a tradition self-conscious of itself, since later pastoral exercises often echo implicitly or explicitly Virgil and other classic pastoral texts. The speaker in pastoral evidences knowledge of and thus authorizes his participation in that tradition. Access to the pastoral speaking position is determined by cultural possessions—of specific educational, class, gender, and racial identities. The pastoral speaker tends to be a sophisticated speaker of the aristocratic or middling classes. Even if that speaker speaks as a shepherd, that is, as one of what is called in pastoral theory the "low," the use of literary language and formal rhetoric as well as the thick web of allusion identify the speaker as the sophisticated artist who assumes a place in the genealogy of high culture.[12] Obviously then only certain people can claim a pastoral speaking position. Most often, though not exclusively, the pastoral subject has been male, primarily a privileged male artist. Lowly people, people of color, women, peasants, may have been subjects in pastoral, objects of a pastoral lament, but they have not had the same access to pastoral's primary speaking position.

The term *pastoral* invokes the topography of bucolic spaces, broad landscapes, rural environments, environments that locate pastoral subjects close to nature. In this landscape a simpler, more direct, and less mediated and artificial relationship to experience plays out. Because of its antithesis to the urban environment, pastoral space seems to harken imaginatively if not specifically to an earlier time (in various pastoral visions the golden age, the arcadian scene, the innocent state of childhood), a kind of timeless moment. Pursuing a pastoral relationship to the land and experience, the pastoral speaker thus travels (literally or imaginatively) away from an urban center or metropolis to the rural or local scene. In this space the speaker finds a home-away-from-home, sometimes in the literal sense but most often in a metaphorical sense. The pastoral space (even if only the space of consciousness[13]) promises fullness, and in that fullness lies the possibility of reinvigoration, reorientation, respite from corruption, perhaps a new innocence, perhaps access to "truer" values and selves.

But the simplicity is part of the illusion of pastoral spaces, of that inviting home. In the pastoral mode some power beyond the rural space seems to press ineluctably upon the scene, if kept at uncertain bay. Call the nonpastoral space the metropolis, call it progress, call it urbanization, call it an imperial "civilization." That is, there is a sense of fragility about the pastoral way of life as the grip of the metropolis becomes stronger and stronger, insinuating itself into a simpler way of life that cannot forestall an inevitable transition to another way of life.[14] Or call it time, for there is an implied relationship between this space and time (Gridley 65). While pastoral spaces seem to be ahistoricized spaces, the time of history actually functions as a subterranean subtext of pastoral (see Garber). If the surface of pastoral promotes timeless spatiality, the subtext introduces historical specificity, the very history that undermines the pastoral vision, the very history from which the subject of pastoral would escape.

In that desire to escape the corruptions of the metropolitan center, the pastoral speaker often journeys to colonized territories, there to identify with indigenous peoples, those who seem to have maintained that close relationship to nature and to the essential core of being. And so there is a long history that conjoins pastoral visions and colonization. Virgil's *Eclogues* emerged at the cultural moment when Rome had consolidated its imperial power. The opening up of "new worlds" in the Renaissance renewed interest in pastoral narrative.[15] And throughout the centuries of exploration pastoral descriptions punctuated travel narratives of explorers and colonizers. The pastoral mode has often been complicit in imperial and colonial projects (see Weston 166–80) because even when they identify with the "low" or indigenous peoples against the "high culture" of the distant metropolis, subjects of pastoral journeys take a residue of representational violence with them into the countryside. After all, the lowly are projections of the universal subject's desire for innocence, integrity, and uncomplicated meaning. They are not assigned a subjectivity of their own.

With the emergence of national resistance movements and various postcolonial writing practices in the First World, critiques of the politics of pastoral emerge as the indigenous "shepherds" learn to speak and write, not just be spoken as and for. In America, slave narratives functioned as powerful antipastoral challenges to the myth of the southern way of life. Those narratives insisted on making vivid the price of pastoral visions, the exploitation of slaves whose labor underwrote the idyll of country life. Further, the narrative of Harriet Jacobs, as an instance, emphasized the price exacted on the body of the slave woman to make the pastoral environment thrive. Anzaldúa's autobiographical practice participates in this antipastoral tradition, but with the difference that she writes a new revolutionary subject into being.

Anzaldúa fights the collective amnesia that the colonial situation engenders in borderlands people by engaging in a project of anamnesis: a recollection or remembrance of a past efficiently erased by the forces of oppression and acculturation. But here the anamnesis is not so much personal, albeit the personal punctuates the analysis, as it is collective. The narrator looks through the opacities of colonization for the remnants of the traditions of multiple cultures. For the narrator's purposes, the mythic possibilities of the occluded cultural past are the provocative source of reinterpretation, the new nationalism of the *mestiza* that will encourage a breakage in the repetition of what Françoise Lionnet describes as "historically and Eurocentrically determined racial metaphors of the self" (Lionnet 116).

But the official histories are multiple, not monolithic. There are histories written upon the land, histories that situate the *mestiza* as a certain kind of subject. And so Anzaldúa works to debunk not only colonial history but the history of the colonized as well. It is not enough that she rediscovers the land as it was in precolonial days; she must explore the oppressions even within that precolonial landscape, for oftentimes Arcadian ideals, even if energized for revolutionary struggles, are patriarchally organized. Ketu Katrak has cautioned that "in nationalist movements 'traditions' tend to get glorified in order to counteract colonialist, racist attitudes that desecrate native culture. The dangers of reifying 'traditions,' of historicizing them as the transcendent emblems of a culture, are felt most negatively by women, particularly after independence when the rationale of justifying tradition against the enemy is no longer needed" (168). So as a woman, Anzaldúa must untangle the patriarchal web of precolonial history. And in order to counteract the trouble with gender in Aztecan culture, she posits another kind of Golden Age.

To pursue a new nationalism of transformative "hybridization," Anzaldúa's narrator elaborates an "empowering and enabling countermyth." (Lionnet 189). Pressing backward and ever backward through the history of the Mexican and Aztec people, she finds a source of inspiration and counter-mythology in the "complete" figure of the pre-Azteca-Mexica great goddess. Recovering a precolonial history, the narrator finds that the Goddess *Coatlicue*, "Lady of the Serpent Skirt, contained and balanced the dualities of male and female, light and dark, life and death" (32). Explicitly linked to the Medusa of Greek mythology and of Cixous's manifesto, Coatlicue is "a symbol of the fusion of opposites: the eagle and the serpent, heaven and the underworld, life and death, mobility and immobility, beauty and horror" (47). This serpent state refuses a dualistic ontology, captures imaginatively that "something more than mere duality," that "third perspective."

Inspired by the discovery of Coatlicue, the narrator proceeds to rewrite the history of the Azteca-Mexica nation. She refuses the common story of La Chingada's (Malinche's) culpability, setting forth instead another interpretation of Cortes's victory over the Aztecs: "the ruling elite had subverted the solidarity between men and women and between noble and commoner" (34). Once the Coatlicue "state," in both senses of the word, had been undermined and superseded by a hierarchical/dualistic state, defeat by colonizing armies followed inevitably. This cultural reorganization accounted for colonization, not a discrete moment of a woman's treachery. Adding greater complexity to the cultural history of her peoples, integrating an analysis of the oppressions of gender to those of class and race, the narrator multiplies the sources of colonization. Doing so, she begins to transform the experience of oppression into the call for a new consciousness, and the recovery of an alternative cultural myth empowers her to both critique the sovereign regime and to countervalorize an alternative nationalism. And so Anzaldúa does not linger in this Golden Age of Coatlicue. She carries the history forward and reconstitutes the Coatlicue state as the consciousness of a new kind of subject.

For the narrator, Coatlicue effectively becomes "in my psyche, the mental picture and symbol of the instinctual in its collective impersonal, prehuman. She, the symbol of the dark sexual drive, the chthonic (underworld), the feminine, the serpentine movement of sexuality, of creativity, the basis of all energy and life" (35). Consequently, the recovery of the Coatlicue state is the recovery of body and soul, spirit and matter, that "other mode of consciousness" which "facilitates images from the soul and the unconscious through dreams and the imagination" (37). The insinuating serpent is the figure for the animistic recovery of a larger consciousness, one fuller than the rational self of the universal subject. Such a state uproots the source of violence in the West, the specularization of things and people, and the consequent erasure of spirit from the physical realm (37). Thus the strategic significance of the "serpent skirt" individually and collectively derives from the intervention it encourages in the repeat performances of the "terrorized" self, a self that blames, hates, and divides into the "accusatory, persecutory, judgmental" on the one hand and "the object of contempt" on the other (45), a repressed self from which the body is banished.

Movement toward the new consciousness, the new nationalistic state, is a geographical move that becomes the "crossing," or *travesia*, into a "new territory" (48). Crossing to this "state" the old identities crack, shed and give way to a newly constitutive knowledge that exposes the "falseness of the view from the top":

> Every time she makes "sense" of something, she has to "cross over," kicking a hole out of the old boundaries of the self and slipping under or over, dragging the old skin along, stumbling over it. It hampers her movement in the new territory, dragging the ghost of the past with her. It is a dry birth, a breech birth, a screaming birth, one that fights her every inch of the way. It is only when she is on the other side and the shell cracks open and the lid from her eyes lifts that she sees things in a different perspective. It is only then that she makes the connections, formulates the insights. It is only then that her consciousness expands a tiny notch, another rattle appears on the rattlesnake tail and the added growth slightly alters the sounds she makes. Suddenly the repressed energy rises, makes decisions, connects with conscious energy and a new life begins. (49)

A new autobiographical practice dislodges the old practice of "autonomy," which the narrator describes as "a boulder on my path that I keep crashing into" (50). The old notion of the sovereign self of western autobiographical practice fades from consciousness as she surrenders her conscious "I" to the "power" of her "inner self, the entity that is the sum total of all my reincarnations, the godwoman in me" (50). Surrendering to her mythical and cultural inheritance, she recovers a new sense of subjectivity, a subjectivity multiplied in more than "one" person:

> And someone in me takes matters into our own hands, and eventually, takes dominion over serpents—over my own body, my sexual activity, my soul, my mind, my weaknesses and strengths. Mine. Ours. Not the heterosexual white man's or the colored man's or the state's or the culture's or the religion's or the parents'—just ours, mine. And suddenly I feel everything rushing to a center, a nucleus. All the lost pieces of myself come flying from the deserts and the mountains and the valleys, magnetized toward that center. *Completa.*

> Something pulsates in my body, a luminous thin thing that grows thicker every day. Its presence never leaves me. I am never alone. That which abides: my vigilance, my thousand sleepless serpent eyes blinking in the night, forever open. And I am not afraid. (51)

The new consciousness leads to a state of openness, not self-closure; it is not individual but transindividual, not unitary but multiple. Thus the narrator of *Borderlands/ La Frontera* configures the Coatlicue-state in its psychological and political dimensions as a space through which to negotiate ambivalence and heteroglossia.

The new state is achieved through the representational politics of language. In counter-pastoral as in pastoral spaces, the role of the artist is central, as creator of an alternative world. Like Cixous, the revolutionary subject of *Borderlands/ La Frontera* must constitute her new subjectivity from her languages. While Anzaldúa specifies three predominant cultural identities constitutive of her borderlands experience—Anglo, Mexican, Indian—she also multiplies the matrices of identifications, the serpent eyes, when she explores the multiplicity of languages spoken throughout her experiential domain. The tongue is the tongue of a linguistic borderland, a wet surface where multiple languages meet and mix, slip and slide. Thus at the beginning of her manifesto, Anzaldúa issues a challenge to the Anglo reader and to the sovereignty of English as the language of self-representation in the United States:

> The switching of "codes" in this book from English to Castillian Spanish to the North Mexican dialect to Tex-Mex to a sprinking of Nahuatl to a mixture of all of these, reflects my language, a new language—the language of the Borderlands. There, at the juncture of cultures, languages cross-pollinate and are revitalized; they die and are born. Presently this infant language, this bastard language Chicano Spanish, is not approved by any society. But we Chicanos no longer feel that we need to beg entrance, that we need always to make

the first overture—to translate to Anglos, Mexicans and Latinos, apology blurting out of our mouths with every step. Today we ask to be met halfway. This book is our invitation to you—from the new *mestizas*. (Preface)

In not apologizing for the agglomerative linguistic potpourri that is the language of her autobiographical project, in resisting the pressure to translate the Spanish passages for the Anglo reader, the manifesto's narrator refuses to reconcile her self-portraiture with the dominant forms of subjectivity in the West or with the call to univocity. Many languages intermingle with one another, in a state of nonhierarchical multiplicity, creating a hybrid language that captures the multiplicity within the speaking subject and resists the seductive call to recuperation into the power of the one and the same tongue. The narrator of *Borderlands/ La Frontera* embraces her multiple voices, multiple identities, multiple positionalities: Mexican, Anglo, Indian. "I will no longer be made to feel ashamed of existing. I will have my voice: Indian, Spanish, white. I will have my serpent's tongue—my woman's voice, my sexual voice, my poet's voice. I will overcome the tradition of silence" (59). Fighting the "linguistic terrorism" of the cultural position of Chicanas, she proclaims the nationalistic allegiance to her specific tongue/s.

The new mestiza works to transcend a dualism that inevitably hierarchizes everything and thereby determines what histories are recorded, what voices are heard; what epistemological projects succeed, what ontological status people bear. She does so through the autobiographical practice of *métissage*, to use a phrase from Lionnet's theoretical vocabulary. In the spaces of *métissage*, suggests Lionnet, "multiplicity and diversity are affirmed . . . . For it is only by imagining nonhierarchical modes of relation among cultures that we can address the crucial issues of indeterminacy and solidarity. . . . *Métissage* is such a concept and a practice: it is the site of undecidability and indeterminacy, where solidarity becomes the fundamental principle of political action against hegemonic languages" (5–6).

In fact, Anzaldúa seems determined to speak in tongues and to do so in the two senses of the phrase Henderson elaborates. She participates in both glossolalia and heteroglossia. Henderson reminds us that glossolalia usually connotes "the particular, private, closed, and privileged communication between the congregant and the divinity," while heteroglossia refers to "the ability to speak in the multiple languages of public discourse" (Henderson 122–3). Through her unique blend of multiple languages Anzaldúa finds a means to represent an ineffable serpent spirit. As tribal storytelling, her self-representational practice induces a "shamanic state" in which her "awakened dreams" (70) enable her to play with crossings of borderlands, with crossings between "my Self" and "the world's soul" in a great "dialogue." Through the great materiality of language she "writes the myths in me, the myths I am, the myths I want to become" and thus feels the power of transformation, the utopian power of re-creation, reconstitution, resistance: "My soul makes itself through the creative act. It is constantly remaking and giving birth to itself through my body. It is this learning to live with *la Coatlicue* that transforms living in the Borderlands from a nightmare into a numinous experience. It is always a path/state to something else" (73). But her practice is not only personal but political, as she captures the relationship of public discourses to consciousness. This is the discursive borderland where subjectivity emerges out of what Henderson calls the dialogue with difference and the dialectic of identity going on inside her. And the material changes of the written language on the page visualize for the reader the sinuosities of both dialogue and dialectic. This linguistic sinuosity is serpentine work.

The new subject is also the bodied rather than disembodied subject. And that is why the language of the text is replete with physical description and bodily metaphor. If the body is the source of an identity that leads to oppression, the sexed body, the racialized body, then the body must be taken back and honored on the way to speech and writing. "Only through the body, through the pulling of the flesh," the narrator writes, "can the human soul be transformed. And for images, words, stories to have this transformative power, they arise from the human body—flesh and bone—and from the Earth's body—stone, sky, liquid, soil. This work, these images, piercing tongue or ear lobes with cactus needles, are my offerings, are my Aztecan blood sacrifices" (75). Through the text the body is deployed in endless metaphors of movement, meaning, and metamorphosis, the most provocative of which is the metaphor of the serpent, privileged here against a western mythology that denigrated the serpent.

The serpent as female im/personation and as agent provocateur insinuates itself throughout the narrator's text in a "quickening serpent movement" (81). Like Cixous's, the rhetorical style and structural arrangement of Anzaldúa's manifesto reflect her new *mestiza* consciousness in a performance of the very discursive slippages and tongues she elaborates. Here too we find a pronominal fluidity as the "I" becomes a "she" and the "she" an "I" and both a "we." The narrator breaks the formal boundaries that characterize the *ancien régime*, that old structure of domination through hierarchization. Multiply voiced in its languages, the text does not work toward a totalized vision but celebrates the multiplicity of eyes, voices, and speaking positions that engage in dialogue with one another. Poems, critical essays, prose evocations, fragments from other poets and writers, fragments of street languages, all combine to capture the vitality of cultural politics, the interdependencies of identities, the collage of the new subject. Finally, they coalesce in a defiant call to communal action: "Stubborn, persevering, impenetrable as stone, yet possessing a malleability that renders us unbreakable, we, the *mestizas* and *mestizos*, will remain" (64).

Anzaldúa's invocation of borderlands and her call to the politics of a new subject refuses the traditional pastoral dualism of country and city spaces. Anzaldúa promotes borderlands, ones inscribed on her body and on her tongue as well as on the land. For borderlands are spaces in which history is intensified rather than escaped and where it can never be fixed. Her geography becomes fluid rather than fixed in its oppositional politics. Multiplying identities and histories creates a homelessness—a homelessness that undermines any secure anchorage in one history, even the history that becomes a national romance. The figure of the borderlands also foregrounds the constructed nature of boundaries, including the boundaries of the subject. And so unlike traditional pastoral speakers, Anzaldúa does not linger in the space of pastoral nostalgia. There is a sense of something that has been lost, but her autobiographical narrative takes us further than a whispering loss. As a counter-pastoral manifesto, *Borderlands/ La Frontera* interrupts the cycle of nostalgia—both the nostalgia of nativist history, which Edward W. Said has critiqued (69–95), and the nostalgia of personal homelessness. In fact, Anzaldúa creates an empowered subject out of language, the language through which she braids the various histories that cannot be escaped.

Beyond the Subject to the Cyborg

Donna Haraway's "A Manifesto for Cyborgs: Science, Technology, and Socialist Feminism in the 1980s" is not an autobiographical manifesto in the ways that Cixous's and Anzaldúa's texts are, but her essay provides a third point from which to consider the possibilities of revolutionary subjectivity. In her "ironic," or, as she suggests, "blasphemous," manifesto, Haraway argues "for the cyborg as a fiction mapping our social and bodily reality and as an imaginative resource suggesting some very fruitful couplings" (191). To celebrate the cyborg is to employ a "postmodern strategy" (194) through which to resist any unitary and therefore imperial subject secured by identitarian politics. Haraway would dislodge all sovereigns, not only the *ancien sovereign* of western discursive practices but the *nouveau sovereigns* of Marxism and feminism with their "dream of a common language" because any dream of a common language, any dream "of a perfectly faithful naming of experience is a totalizing and imperialist one" (215). Working to undo the old teleology of the western humanist tradition, including its psychoanalytical and Marxist agendas, Haraway deploys the cyborg metaphor in order to subvert the old story of origins, original wholeness, developmental individuation, paternal inheritance, engenderment: "The cyborg is a creature in a postgender world; it has no truck with bisexuality, pre-Oedipal symbiosis, unalienated labor, or other seductions to organic wholeness through a final appropriation of all the powers of the parts into a higher unity" (192). All these narratological templates for identity politics look backward to a natural point of origin, and for Haraway points of origin need to be exposed for the fictions they ultimately are. Points of origin are politically suspect precisely because they map a totalizing uniformity on diverse peoples and experiences through a specified locus of identification. And identity politics are exclusionary, fractured, partial (197). The problem with any "we" is that its deployment colludes in the colonizing naturalization of categories such as "woman." The contemporary project must be to make the category of woman and the category of man evaporate altogether.

The cyborg is a metaphor for its time. Recognizing the importance of historicizing epistemology, of accounting for the metaphorical specificities of particular moments in time, Haraway's manifesto is "rooted in claims about fundamental changes in the nature of class, race, and gender in an emerging system of world order analogous in its novelty and scope to that created by industrial capitalism; we are living through a movement from an organic, industrial society to a polymorphous, information system" (203). The scientific-technical world, governed by the "domination of informatics," renders obsolete the old epistemological certainties of a dualistic world, a world naturalized by the semiotics of dichotomies ("between mind and body, animal and human, organism and machine, public and private, nature and culture, men and women, primitive and civilized" [205]). In the current postmodern surround of a postcolonial global world, the old naturalized categories rearrange themselves into denaturalized categories of meaning. Now the operative organizational mode is that of "coding" at all levels—of the atom, the cell, the information circuit, the multinational economy. And so we must recognize that women live and operate in an "integrated circuit."[16] While the integrated circuit may be constraining and colonizing in new ways and render former oppressions nostalgically preferable, it can also provide "a source of power" through which "fresh sources of analysis and political action" can illuminate a "subtle understanding of emerging pleasures, experiences, and power with serious potential for changing the rules of the game" (215).

Thus the cyborg is "a kind of disassembled and reassembled, postmodern collective and personal self" (205). As an assemblage of "networks" in a surround of "structural rearrangements related to the social relations of science and technology" (214), cyborgs inhabit multiple spaces, presenting multiple identities that expose "the permeability of boundaries in the personal body and in the body politics" (212). In the "utopian tradition of imagining a world without gender, which is perhaps a world without genesis" (192), Haraway embraces the ironic possibilities presented by the cyborg. While, as she suggests, "the main trouble with cyborgs . . . is that they are the illegitimate offspring of militarism and patriarchal capitalism, not to mention state socialism," they nonetheless provide liberatory possibilities because "illegitimate offspring are often exceedingly unfaithful to their origins. Their fathers, after all, are inessential" (193). Imagining cyborg politics requires imagining unnatural borders. Thus, like Anzaldúa, Haraway explores a "border war," but the topography of her revolutionary skirmish is not originally geographical. Rather her border dispute, her border rearrangement takes place in the space "between organism and machine" (191). Multiple borderlands are breached by the cyborg: between human and animal, living organism and machine, the physical and nonphysical realms (195). Through the breaches, Haraway suggests, "perhaps, ironically, we can learn from our fusions with animals and machines how not to be Man, the embodiment of Western logos" (215).

Thus Haraway's manifesto calls for cyborg performances of "permanently partial identities and contradictory standpoints" upon which to build epistemologies. "Monstrous" and "illegitimate" collocations of animal, human, and machine, cyborgs promise a new kind of politics contestatory of identity politics. This new politics she calls "affinity" politics (196). Denaturalizing the old certainties of identity, the cyborg functions as a de/naturalized locus of affinity, and the politics of affinity promise an escape from the exclusionary impact of identitarian standpoints: "The theoretical and practical struggle against unity-through-domination or unity-through-incorporation ironically not only undermines the justifications for patriarchy, colonialism, humanism, positivism, essentialism, scientism, and other unlamented -isms, but all claims for an organic or natural standpoint" (198).

Finally, cyborgs—such affinity groups as "women of color" who represent "a potent subjectivity synthesized from fusions of outsider identities"—must seize the very technology of preference in the late twentieth century, that is, writing: "Cyborg politics is the struggle for language and the struggle against perfect communication, against the one code that translates all meaning perfectly, the central dogma of phallogocentrism. That is why cyborg politics insist on noise and advocate pollution, rejoicing in the illegitimate fusions of animal and machine" (218). Critically, the cyborg does not chase a dream of a common language but rather deploys "a powerful infidel heteroglossia," through which "she" "recod[es] communication and intelligence to subvert command and control" (217), through which she posits and deconstructs one boundary after another, through which she constantly crosses borders. Concluding with a call to a new revolutionary subject, Haraway places her utopian confidence in affinity with the cyborg: "Although both are bound in the spiral dance, I would rather be a cyborg than a goddess" (223). And she keeps insisting on the energy of a revolutionary "irony," which, she says, "is about contradictions that do not resolve into larger wholes, even dialectically, about the tension of holding incompatible things together because both or all are necessary and true" (190).

The autobiographical manifesto is a revolutionary gesture poised against amnesia and its compulsory repetitions. It is not anamnesis (or reminiscence) as much as a purposeful constitution of a future history, the projection of anamnesis into the future. Moreover, the manifesto offers a point of departure for the current generation (of women, of people from the borderlands, of cyborgs) to resist a former generation imposing its multifarious technologies of identity. Through compelling myths and metaphors, these three manifestos map alternative futures for the "I" in the late twentieth century. They point to blurred boundaries, crossed borderlands of multiplicity, differences and divergences, political possibilities and pitfalls, strategies for intervention. They offer fascinating performances of the revolutionary subject, performances that, as Frantz Fanon noted, effectively "transform spectators crushed with their inessentiality into privileged actors, with the grandiose glare of history's floodlights upon them." Whether we follow them or not, whether we pursue some other kind of alternative subjectivity, such performances hold out hope by insisting on the possibility of self-conscious and imaginative breaks in cultural repetitions of the universal subject.

Notes

1 For a critique of postmodern fragmentation, see Susan Bordo (133–56).
2 "Knowledge" is, as Edward W. Said argues in his study of Orientalism, "essentially the *making visible* of material" (127); see also Probyn (178).
3 Hurtado argues that "for white women, the first step in the search for identity is to confront the ways in which their personal, individual silence endorses the power of white men that has robbed them of their history. For women of Color, the challenge is to use their oral traditions for specific political goals" (848–9).

4 See Butler's discussion of the relationship of acts to ideas: "Because there is neither an 'essence' that gender expresses or externalizes nor an objective ideal to which gender aspires," argues Butler, "and because gender is not a fact, the various acts of gender create the idea of gender, and without those acts, there would be no gender at all. Gender is, thus, a construction that regularly conceals its genesis; the tacit collective agreement to perform, produce, and sustain discrete and polar genders as cultural fictions is obscured by the credibility of those productions—and the punishments that attend to agreeing to believe in them; the construction 'compels' our belief in its necessity and naturalness. The historical possibilities materialized through various corporeal styles are nothing other than those punitively regulated cultural fictions alternately embodied and deflected under duress" (*Gender Trouble* 140).

5 What Felski says of the internal and external dynamics of the feminist counter-public sphere applies to these multiple spheres: "*Internally*, it generates a gender specific identity grounded in a consciousness of community and solidarity among women; *externally*, it seeks to convince society as a whole of the validity of feminist claims, challenging existing structures of authority through political activity and theoretical critique" (168).

6 The collective identification of the manifesto's speaker is perhaps the most problematic aspect of this autobiographical form precisely because the postulation of a counter-public sphere, of "women" for instance, functions yet again as a gesture of universalization, if a universalization whose application is narrower than the hegemonic center's universalization. As recent theorists have argued, community is a problematic utopian ideal. (See Young; Felski, chap. 5; and Hartsock, 171.) Posited on exclusivities, or blindness to complex material realities, an idealized community erases differences and contradictory experiences. As Felski notes, "The ideal of a free discursive space that equalizes all participants is an enabling fiction which engenders a sense of collective identity but is achieved only by obscuring actual material inequalities and political antagonisms among its participants" (168). Thus, however attractive the ideal of "a unified collective subject" might be, we must constantly remind ourselves that the price we pay for celebrating collectivity may be "the actual activities and self-understanding of women, in which gender-based divisions frequently conflict with a whole range of other alliances, such as those based on race or class, and work against any unproblematic notion of harmonious consensus" (Felski 169).

7   De Lauretis calls these future spaces the "space off"—"those other spaces both discursive and social that exist . . . in the margins . . . of hegemonic discourse and in the interstices of institutions, in counter-practices and new forms of community" (26).
8   As Lionnet via Rèné Dumont has suggested, "utopian thinking is perhaps the only way out of the impasse created by the neocolonialist strangulation of nations and peoples" (247).
9   Linda Singer argues that for Cixous "the absence of a female-identified discourse adequate to representing women's sexuality in its difference is both a symptom of and instrumental to the continued subjugation of women within the patriarchal order" (139).
10 Of course, Cixous's invocation of "the dark continent" in the midst of this manifesto remains problematic.
11 See also Wittig, "The Mark of Gender."
12 The pastoral speaker is a figure of cultural authority, either conferred or self-identified. Pastoral speakers often refer to previous pastorals, invoking a specifically Western genealogy. The speaker joins in that genealogy of artist/intellectuals and assumes generic authority. Over the body of the pastoral, the tug and resistance of generational struggles is played. The pastoral can be invoked to establish genealogy, or it can be invoked to be rejected as an old worn-out form, no longer viable for the new artist. In its embrace and its dismissal it maintains a kind of privileged status.
13 With the romantics, for instance, the pastoral space became the space of an expanding consciousness, forged despite the onslaught of technology, industrialization, urbanization, etc. The pastoral space promised access to a "truer" consciousness.
14 Even in Virgil's *Eclogues,* the authority and power of Rome is pervasive.
15 With the opening of new territories around the globe, pastoral spaces were identified more with geographical space than with past time, with arcadian and golden ages.
16 Haraway acknowledges the phrase from Grossman.

Works Cited

Anzaldúa, Gloria. *Borderlands/La Frontera*. San Francisco: Spinsters/Aunt Lute Press, 1987.

Bordo, Susan. "Feminism, Postmodernism, and Gender-Skepticism," *Feminism/Postmodernism*. Ed. Linda J. Nicholson. New York: Routledge, 1990. 133–56.

Butler, Judith. *Gender Trouble: Feminism and the Subversion of Identity.* New York: Routledge, 1990.

———. "Gender Trouble, Feminist Theory, and Psychoanalytic Discourse." *Feminism/Postmodernism.* Ed. Linda J. Nicholson. New York: Routledge, 1990. 324–40.

Cixous, Hélène. "The Laugh of the Medusa." *New French Feminisms: An Anthology.* Eds. Elaine Marks and Isabelle de Courtivron. Amherst: University of Massachusetts Press, 1976. 245–64.

De Lauretis, Teresa. *The Technologies of Gender: Essays on Theory, Film, and Fiction.* Bloomington: Indiana University Press, 1987.

De Man, Paul. "Autobiography as Defacement." *Modern Language Notes* 94 (1979): 919–30.

Fanon, Frantz. *The Wretched of the Earth.* Trans. Constance Farrington. Harmondsworth: Penguin, 1967.

Felski, Rita. *Beyond Feminist Aesthetics: Feminist Literature and Social Change.* Cambridge: Harvard University Press, 1989.

Friedman, Susan Stanford. "Women's Autobiographical Selves: Theory and Practice." *The Private Self: Theory and Practice of Women's Autobiographical Writings.* Ed. Shari Benstock. Chapel Hill: University of North Carolina Press, 1988. 34–62.

Garber, Frederick. "Pastoral Spaces." *Texas Studies in Literature and Language* 30 (Fall 1988): 431–60.

Gridley, Roy E. "Some Versions of the Primitive and the Pastoral on the Great Plains of America." *Survivals of Pastoral.* Ed. Richard F. Hardin. Lawrence: University of Kansas Press, 1979.

Grossman, Rachael. "Women's Place in the Integrated Circuit." *Radical America* 14 (1980): 29–50.

Haraway, Donna. "A Manifesto for Cyborgs: Science, Technology and Socialist Feminism in the 1980s." *Feminism/Postmodernism.* Ed. Linda J. Nicholson. New York: Routledge, 1986/1991. 190–233.

Hartsock, Nancy. "Foucault on Power: A Theory for Women?" *Feminism/Postmodernism.* Ed. Linda J. Nicholson. New York: Routledge, 1990. 157–75.

Henderson, Mae Gwendolyn. "Speaking in Tongues: Dialogics, Dialectics, and the Black Woman's Literary Tradition." *Reading Black, Reading Feminist: A Critical Anthology.* Ed. Henry Louis Gates, Jr. New York: Meridian, 1990. 118–21

Hurtado, Aida. "Relating to Privilege: Seduction and Rejection in the Subordination of White Women and Women of Color." *Signs* 14 (1989): 833–55.

Kintz, Linda. "In-Different Criticism: The Deconstructive 'Parole.'" *The Thinking Muse: Feminism and Modern French Philosophy.* Eds. Jeffner Allen and Iris Marion Young. Bloomington: Indiana University Press, 1989. 113–35.

Kristeva, Julia. "A New Type of Intellectual." *The Kristeva Reader*. Ed. Toril Moi. Oxford: Basil Blackwell, 1986. 292–300.

Lionnet, Françoise. *Autobiographical Voices: Race, Gender, Self-Portraiture*. Ithaca: Cornell University Press, 1989.

Martin, Robert K. "Is Anybody There? Critical Practice and Minority Writing." Paper, Modern Language Association Convention. Washington, D.C., December, 1989.

Modleski, Tania. "Feminism and the Power of Interpretation: Some Critical Readings." *Feminist Studies/Critical Studies*. Ed. Teresa de Lauretis. Bloomington: Indiana UP, 1986. 121–38.

Moraga, Cherrie. *Loving in the War Years*. Boston: South End Press, 1983.

Nietzsche, Friedrich. *The Will to Power*. New York: Vintage Books, 1968.

Probyn, Elspeth. "Travels in the Postmodern: Making Sense of the Local." *Feminism/Postmodernism*. Ed. Linda J. Nicholson. New York: Routledge, 1990. 176–89.

Reagon, Bernice Johnson. "Coalition Politics: Turning the Century," in *Home Girls*. Ed. Barbara Smith. New York: Kitchen Table: Women of Color Press, 1983.

Said, Edward W. *Orientalism*. New York: Random House, 1979.

———. "Yeats and Colonization." *Nationalism, Colonialism and Literature*. Minneapolis: University of Minnesota Press, 1990. 69–95.

Singer, Linda. "True Confessions: Cixous and Foucault on Sexuality and Power." *The Thinking Muse: Feminism and Modern French Philosophy*. Eds. Jeffner Allen and Iris Marion Young. Bloomington: Indiana University Press, 1989. 136–55.

Smith, Paul. *Discerning the Subject*. Minneapolis: University of Minnesota Press, 1988.

Weston, Peter. "The Noble Primitive as Bourgeois Subject." *The Pastoral Mode*. Ed. Bryan Loughrey. London: Macmillan, 1984. 166–80.

Wittig, Monique. "The Mark of Gender." *The Poetics of Gender*. Ed. Nancy K. Miller. New York: Columbia University Press, 1986. 63–73.

Woodward, Kathleen. "Simone de Beauvoir: Aging and Its Discontents." *The Private Self: Theory and Practice of Women's Autobiographical Writings*. Ed. Shari Benstock. Chapel Hill: University of North Carolina Press, 1988. 91–113.

Young, Iris Marion. "The Ideal of Community and the Politics of Difference." *Feminism/Postmodernism*. Ed. Linda J. Nicholson. New York: Routledge, 1990. 300–23.

Part IV
Visualized Lives

10

INTRODUCTION: MAPPING WOMEN'S SELF-REPRESENTATION AT VISUAL/TEXTUAL INTERFACES

From *Interfaces: Women, Autobiography, Image, Performance* (2002)

Preface

The first section of this Introduction, which discusses Tracey Emin's installation *My Bed* (1998) at the Tate Gallery, London, appears separately in this volume as "The Rumpled Bed of Autobiography."[1] An assemblage of autobiographical memorabilia, Emin's installation enacted multiple autobiographical performances in both visual and verbal modes that, to us, "suggest that the procrustean bed of autobiographical self-reference is now being performed at an extreme of the avant-garde. [Emin's] "bed" is simultaneously a site of rumpled, disorderly, stubbornly literal artifacts that insist on their artifactual status as 'art'" (see Figure 1, p. 92 this volume).[2]

The twentieth century was an exciting moment for the increasingly "rumpled bed" of autobiography studies. In what follows we offer an overview of, and theorize, women's self-representation as a performative act, never transparent, that constitutes subjectivity in the interplay of memory, experience, identity, embodiment, and agency. We will address two suspicions that have informed traditional histories of art: on the one hand, that women's autobiographical representation in self-portrait, diary, and performance is "merely personal"; and that, on the other hand, it is "merely narcissistic." We will consider what is at stake when women remake practices of self-presentation to claim their authority as artists and to contest the history of artistic representations of woman. We will propose a grammar describing four modes of the visual/textual interface: as relational, contextual, spatial, and temporal. Finally, we will gesture toward the larger question of how women artists as makers of their own display are related to the history of woman as an object of speculation and specialization, and the kinds of intervention women artists have deployed to disrupt that specularity. The rumpled bed of autobiographical representation remains a site for productive investigation.

The Ubiquity of the Autobiographical

In visual/textual self-portraiture, the sign of the autobiographical is the identity of the name of the artist (on the painting, on the poster announcing an installation or performance) and the subject of the work. As Lucy Lippard aptly comments, "naming is the active tense of identity, the outward aspect of the self-representation process, acknowledging all the circumstances through which it must elbow its way" (19). During the twentieth- and twenty-first centuries women have named themselves by making art and performance from their own bodies, experiential histories, memories, and personal landscapes in myriad textual and visual modes and in multiple media. These autobiographical acts situate the body in some kind of material surround that functions as a theater of embodied self-representation. At times these materializations of autobiographical subjectivity function as self-portraiture in a traditional mode, such as painted or photographic representations of head and torso. Often, however, the likeness of the artist may be nowhere visible although the imprint of autobiographical subjectivity is registered in matter or light. Sometimes in performance art, voice and body register a heterogeneous or dispersed autobiographical subjectivity. In contemporary self-presentations women have expanded the concept of the self-portrait, once considered the definitive mode of visual autobiography. Modes of self-reference now include visual, textual, voiced, and material imprints of subjectivity, extending the possibilities for women to engage both "woman" and "artist" as "a social and cultural formation in the process of construction" (Nochlin 15) and reconstruction.

If we look beyond the conventions of painted self-portraiture that encode the likeness of the artist, we become aware of the proliferating sites of the autobiographical. In addition to the textual modes of autobiography, memoir, diaries, and journals, there are many visual modes—sculpture, quilting, painting, photography, collage, murals, installations, as well as films, artists' books, song lyrics, performance art, and websites in cyber-space—that have not yet been recognized as autobiographical acts. Consider the scope of autobiographical presentation in the following media and the artists associated with them (a list by no means exhaustive):

- The painted, drawn, photographic, or sculpted self-portraits of Käthe Kollwitz, Paula Modersohn-Becker, Suzanne Valadon, Claude Cahun, Frida Kahlo, Remedios Varo, Leonora Carrington, Alice Neel, Joan Semmel, Audrey Flack, Jenny Saville, Kiki Smith, Addela Khan, and Elvira Bach
- The artists' books of Joan Lyons, Susan King, May Stevens, and Kara Walker
- The photographic series of Tina Modotti, Cindy Sherman, Nan Goldin, Jo Spence, Eleanor Antin, Lorna Simpson, Carrie Mae Weems, Renee Cox, and Francesca Woodman
- The painted or collage memorials to family and childhood of Carmen Lomas Garza, Joanne Leonard, Rita Duffy, Aminah Robinson, and Jaune Quick-to See Smith

- The installations of Adrian Piper, Helen Chadwick, Annette Messager, Kiki Smith, Sophie Calle, Mariko Mori, Yong Soon Min, Ann Hamilton, and Nancy Spero
- The billboard interventions of Barbara Kruger, Jenny Holzer, and the Guerrilla Girls
- The performance pieces of Baroness Elsa von Freytag-Loringhoven, Carolee Schneemann, Orlan, Carmelita Tropicana, Laurie Anderson, Diamanda Galas, Annie Sprinkle, Karen Finley, Rachel Rosenthal, Bobby Baker, Blondell Cummings, Joanna Frueh, Coco Fusco, Anna Deavere Smith, and Hannah Wilke
- The sculptural formations of Betye Saar, Alison Saar, Janine Antoni, and Louise Bourgeois and the earthbound projections of Ana Mendieta
- The diaries and daybooks of Unica Zürn, Anne Truitt, and Frida Kahlo
- The feminist cartoons of Lynda Barry, Nicole Hollander, Mónica Palacios, and Erika Lopez
- The material femmages (fabric collage and acrylic painting) of Miriam Schapiro and Judy Chicago
- The murals of Judy Baca and of artists' collectives in New York, Los Angeles, Chicago, Vancouver, and San Francisco
- The cybersites of Lorie Novak
- The artist autobiographies of Charlotte Salomon, Beatrice Wood, Leonora Carrington, Howardena Pindell, Judy Chicago, and Faith Ringgold

This list—to which readers will assuredly add other names—suggests how intimately women's artistic production during the twentieth century has engaged the cultural politics of self-representation. And it indicates how frequently women's artistic production of the autobiographical occurs at the interface of the domains of visuality (image) and textuality (the aural and written word, the extended narrative, the dramatic script).[3] In these heterogeneous self-displays, textuality implicates visuality as, in different ways, the visual image engages components of textuality at material, voiced, and/or virtual sites.[4] Thus, it is essential to expand the concept of autobiography as self-portraiture to include visual, textual, voiced, and material modes of embodied self-representation. These self-referential displays at the visual/textual interface in hybrid or pastiche modes materialize self-inquiry and self-knowledge, not through a mirror for seeing and reproducing the artist's face and torso but as the artists' engagement with the history of seeing women's bodies.

We should point out that women artists have not only mined the visual/textual interface in many media for its autobiographical possibilities but also frequently used repetitive series of self-images to tell a story through sequencing and juxtaposition, as in Kahlo's, Varo's, or Kollwitz's self-portraits, or to perform successive versions of their lives, as in Wilke's and Orlan's performances. The fascination of many women artists with serial self-representation, intensified throughout the last century, is abetted by technologies of mechanical reproduction and dispersal and by the opportunity to repeatedly stage performance art on video and film. Thus, what began in the early twentieth century as an experimental engagement with serial self-presentation has become, by now, a frequent and multifaceted exploration of seriality itself, of self-representation in time.

Self-representational acts in all these media—singular, dual, serial, or hybrid—exceed the conventions of painting a head or torso to represent the artist, the traditional conception of self-portraiture. In their diversity and complexity, such acts call for a nuanced theorizing of the autobiographical and of the interface of textual and visual modes that enables self-imaging, auto-inquiry, and cultural critique

Theorizing the Autobiographical

In order to understand the ways in which modernist and contemporary women artists mine the innovative self-representational possibilities of visual and textual interfaces, we engage more systematically with the nature of "the autobiographical." First, two widely held suspicions about women's recourse to the autobiographical in visual and performance media need to be addressed—that it is a transparent mirroring and that it is narcissistic self-absorption.

Too often "the autobiographical" in visual and performance media is seen unproblematically as a transparent rendering of the "real" life. In visual self-representation, the autobiographical is assumed to be a mirror, a self-evident content to be "read," not a cultural practice whose limits, interests, and modes of presentation differ with the historical moment, the conventions invoked, and the medium or media employed. Thus art critics and feminist art historians have often used biographical material to elucidate the autobiographical contexts and practices of women's visual and performative self-representation in analyzing specific works (paintings, photographs, etc.). That is, they place the emphasis on *bios*, the biographical life, to "explain" the artist's history; conversely, the artist's life history is invoked to elucidate the work. In order to refute this assumption that self-referential works are transparent, we need to engage more systematically with the nature of the autobiographical.

The autobiographical is not a transparent practice. As we have argued elsewhere, "autobiography" is a term with a complex history (*Reading Autobiography* 1–4). While it has signified multiple practices of self-representation, it has come to be narrowly identified by many critics since the twentieth century with a particular mode of life storytelling, the retrospective narration of "great" public lives. This latter understanding of the term has often obscured the ways in which women, and other people not included in the category of "great men," have inscribed themselves textually, visually, or performatively. For us, the term "life narrative" better captures the diverse kinds of life stories and practices of telling one's life that occur in literary genres as different as diary, slave narrative, and collaborative life story, and that inform self-referential practice in much visual and performance art since the twentieth century. While we often use the adjective "autobiographical" to describe women's self-representation in various visual and performance modes, we prefer to think of the works not as "autobiography" but as enacted life narrative.

As a moving target, a set of shifting self-referential practices, autobiographical narration offers occasions for negotiating the past, reflecting on identity, and critiquing cultural norms and narratives. The life narrator selectively engages aspects of her lived experience through modes of personal "storytelling"—narratively, imagistically, in performance. That is, situated in a specific time and place, the autobiographical subject is in dialogue with her own processes and archives of memory. The past is not a static repository of experience but always engaged from a present moment, itself ever changing. Moreover, the autobiographical subject is also inescapably in dialogue with the culturally marked differences that inflect models of identity and underwrite the formation of autobiographical subjectivity. And she is in dialogue with multiple and disparate addressees or audiences. In effect, autobiographical telling is performative; it enacts the "self" that it claims has given rise to an "I." And that "I" is neither unified nor stable—it is fragmented, provisional, multiple, in process (Smith and Watson 74).[5]

To theorize the autobiographical we need an adequate critical vocabulary for describing how the components of subjectivity are implicated in self-presentational acts. In earlier explorations of autobiographical narratives, we have defined five constitutive processes of autobiographical subjectivity: memory, experience, identity, embodiment, and agency.[6] These five terms are foundational for an engagement with women's acts of self-representation in modern and postmodern narratives. In brief, we understand them as follows.

Memory. In the act of remembering, the autobiographical subject actively creates the meaning of the past. Thus, narrated memory is an interpretation of a past that can never be fully recovered. As psychologist Daniel Schachter has suggested, "Memories are records of how we have experienced events, not replicas of the events themselves" (6). He goes on to explore how "we construct our autobiographies from fragments of experience that change over time" (9). That is, we inevitably organize or form fragments of memory into complex constructions that become the stories of our lives. Memory, moreover, has a history: we learn how to remember, what to remember, and the uses of remembering, all of which are specific to our cultural and historical location. And that history is material. We locate memory and specific practices of remembering in our own bodies and in specific objects of our experiential histories.

Experience. "Experience" is the process through which a person becomes a certain kind of subject with certain kinds of identities in the social realm, identities constituted through material, cultural, economic, and interpsychic relations. "It is not individuals who have experience," Joan W. Scott claims, "but subjects who are constituted through experience" (60). Autobiographical subjects do not predate their experience. In effect, autobiographical subjects know themselves as subjects of particular kinds of experience attached to social statuses and identities.

Identity. Identities materialize within collectivities and out of the culturally marked differences that constitute symbolic interactions within and between collectivities. But social organizations and symbolic interactions are always in flux. Identities, therefore, are discursive, provisional, intersectional, and unfixed.

Embodiment. As a textual surface upon which a person's life is inscribed, the body is a site of autobiographical knowledge because memory itself is embodied. And life narrative is a site of embodied knowledge because autobiographical narrators are embodied subjects. Subjects narrating their lives, then, are multiply embodied. There is the body as a neurochemical system. There is the anatomical body. There is, as Elisabeth Grosz notes, the "imaginary anatomy," which "reflects social and familial beliefs about the body more than it does the body's organic nature" (86). And there is the sociopolitical body, a set of cultural attitudes and codes attached to the public meanings of bodies that underwrites relationships of power.

Agency. If selves and self-knowledge are constituted through discursive practices, then the process through which autobiographical subjects assume agency—that is, control over the representations they produce about themselves—becomes particularly complex. We need to consider how, within such constraints, people are able to change existing narratives and to write back to the cultural stories that have scripted them as particular kinds of subjects. Moreover, we need to consider how narrators negotiate cultural strictures about telling certain kinds of stories, visualizing kinds of embodiment. Recent theorizing on agency is extensive, locating the possibility of change in the autobiographical subject's oppositional consciousness as it emerges at cultural locations of marginality or in the contradictions of heterogeneous discourses of identity swirling around the autobiographical subject. In one rethinking of agency, political theorist Elizabeth Wingrove conjoins the agency of the subject and the system, arguing, in rereading Althusser, that "agents change, and change their world, by virtue of the systemic operation of multiple ideologies" that "expose both the subject and the system to perpetual reconfiguration" (871).

Given the processes that constitute autobiographical subjectivity, "the autobiographical" as a referent in narrative cannot be taken for granted. *Rather, autobiographical acts of narration, situated in historical time and cultural place, deploy discourses of identity to organize acts of remembering that are directed to multiple addressees or readers.* Therefore, it is possible for narrators to produce multiple, widely divergent stories from one experiential history, as many literary autobiographers writing "serial lives" have done—Maya Angelou, Lillian Hellman, bell hooks, and Buchi Emecheta, to name a few. Autobiographical narratives, then, do not affirm a "true self" or a coherent and stable identity. They are performative, situated addresses that invite their readers' collaboration in producing specific meanings for the "life."

Understanding the components of autobiographical acts enables us to think critically about the practice of reading the life of the artist in—and as—the work, in effect assuming a transparent or "mirror" relationship between the life and the visual and/or verbal text. In *Differencing the Canon*, feminist art historian Griselda Pollock mounts a critique similar to what we have sketched here for textual life narrative. Pollock contests the tendency of art historians to "index" works of art "directly to experience" and to offer "no problems for interpretation" (97). In the "popular" or "traditional" model of art history, which takes as its subject great artists and their works, she argues, "the artwork is a transparent screen through which you have only to look to see the artist as a psychologically coherent subject originating the meanings the work so perfectly reflects" (98). In effect, traditional models of art history read the work through a constructed biography of the artist as evidence for the biographical life. That is, the artwork becomes a body of mimetic evidence out of which the historian or critic forms a narrative for the artist. In so doing, the historian/critic assumes knowledge of and access to the artist's "true self." Pollock criticizes this traditional model for approaching the artwork as a transparent canvas upon which the autobiographical life of the artist is encoded, there to be read unproblematically by the viewer.

Both Pollock's and our own critiques suggest that in textual and visual regimes autobiographical acts are inescapably material and embodied. They cannot be understood as individualist acts of a sovereign subject, whole and entire unto itself. And the representation produced cannot be taken as a guarantee of a "true self," authentic, coherent, and fixed. The autobiographical is a performative site of self-referentiality where the psychic formations of subjectivity and culturally coded identities intersect and "interface" one another.

Self-Portraiture and the Question of Narcissism

Understanding autobiographical acts as performative interfaces enables us to address the second suspicion, that the autobiographical is excessively self-absorbed, particularly when *women* artists take themselves as their own subject. Women artists' self-portraiture and their repeated acts of self-representation have been alleged to be "narcissistic," evidence of a merely personal desire to keep looking in the mirror. This charge is rarely made about the serial self-portraiture or the practice of repeated self-portrayal of such male masters of painting as Dürer, Rembrandt, and Van Gogh. Why has the relation of women to the autobiographical been so vexed?

The identification of "woman" with "the autobiographical" calls up a history of reading practices that encode that relationship in specific ways in both literary and art-historical studies. As Domna C. Stanton eloquently argued three decades ago, invoking the descriptor "autobiographical" in literary histories "constituted a positive term when applied to Augustine and Montaigne, Rousseau and Goethe, Henry Adams and Henry Miller, but . . . had negative connotations when imposed on women's texts" (6). In their gendered reading practices, literary historians ascribed to male autobiographical writers the intellectual and aesthetic command to make their lives richly self-reflexive, to assess the problematic nature of self-knowing and self-telling. In contrast, the "autobiographical," when applied to women, was "used . . . to affirm that women could not transcend, but only record, the concerns of the private self; thus, it has effectively served to devalue their writing." "The autobiographical," Stanton concludes, was "wielded as a weapon to denigrate female texts and exclude them from the canon" (132). If "great" literature achieves canonical status because it "rises" to the level of the "universal," then the inability of the woman writer—and by extension the woman artist—to rise above "the personal" and achieve a "universal" vision condemns her to an inevitable second-rate status. Effectively, the descriptor "autobiographical" has functioned to exclude women from the cultural category of "writer" and to constitute literature as a masculine domain. From this masculinist perspective, women are considered unable to see beyond their own narrowly self-interested lives; they can only write the personal, the domestic, the private life; and that production cannot speak profound universal truths.[7]

Limiting the woman artist to the domain of the autobiographical —that is, seeing women's art as "merely" personal—is one way in which "the autobiographical" has signaled that women can only be self-interested, implying their diminished artistic capacities and vision. But since the 1970s, theoretical work within feminist art historical studies has taken this identification of "woman" with "the autobiographical" in productive directions and in different terms than in literary studies. A key concept has been narcissism, which traditional art histories have tended to understand as the self-absorbed identification of the female subject with her own alterity. In the spectatorial gaze of the male artist and constitutively male viewer, woman is defined as there-to-be-seen, all too visible; and yet she remains inscrutable, passive yet threateningly quiescent and untouchable. In this scopic regime, her passivity and remoteness signify her "inability to cathect with an external object" (Silverman 154). But if male representations of woman project her as the self-contented, arrested, and arresting Other, what might it mean for the woman artist to take herself narcissistically as subject?

Since the 1970s, some feminist critics have pointed out how traditional art historians and critics project this script of women's primary narcissism in reading women artists' cultural productions and how they fail to interrogate the terms of their essentialist projection of woman as narcissistic. Others, however, have used psychoanalytic theory to argue, quite differently than in literary studies, that narcissism, defined as "the exploration of and fixation on the self" (Jones 46), needs to be revalued. The obvious link between the artist and her body in visual and performance art is material and demands that both internal and external self, and self and other, be connected (Jones 46). The viewer, then, must confront the immediacy of the body or its pieces and debris. Redefining narcissism as a political and performative psychic mechanism for intervening in patriarchal social arrangements, these theorists have recuperated it as an enabling force for feminist projects. Kaja Silverman has done this by arguing that "female narcissism may represent a form of resistance to the positive Oedipus complex, with its inheritance of self-contempt and loathing." The very condition of femininity is a desire for and identification with the mother as the first love object, a love relocated as self-love, a self-love, according to Silverman, that "presupposes love of the object in whose image one 'finds' oneself" (154).

Jo Anna Isaak has also redefined narcissism as enabling. The strategic deployment of narcissism, for Isaak, offers a means of agency to the disenfranchised woman, an agency derived from laughter invading, at least temporarily, the paternal law of woman's nonexistence. As Isaak suggests, women artists of the autobiographical can explore "the possibility of women's strategic occupation of narcissism as a site of pleasure and a form of resistance to assigned sexual and social roles" ("In Praise" 54). Similarly, Amelia Jones recuperates narcissism as a strategy adapted by feminist artists in the 1970s to politicize their personal concerns by speaking them publicly, thus proclaiming their status as subjects of culture (Jones 47). Jones observes, "Narcissism, enacted through body art, turns the subject inexorably and paradoxically outward" (48). In late capitalism, she argues, the narcissistic projection of self becomes "a marker of the *instability* of both self and other" to be positively valued for its dislocation of a mythic transcendent Self (49).

Isaak's, Silverman's, and Jones's invocations of women's "strategic occupation of narcissism" illuminate one of the defining features of women's self-representational art practices in the last century. Turning their attention to their own bodies and subjectivities in diverse ways, women artists working in multiple media have used the bits and pieces, the debris and excesses, the constraints and effusions of their own embodiment to materialize self-referential displays. In this strategic self-preoccupation, they have engaged the codes and genres of masculinist self-portraiture and a tradition of modes of representing "woman" as other in art's histories.

The Stakes of the Autobiographical

Feminist art historians of the last three decades have extensively explored how the tradition of Western artistic practice often presents the female body, nude or clothed, at the center of a painting or sculpture, as situated through the specular gaze of the male artist and patron. It is through this gaze, and the regime of visuality encoded in and encoding that gaze, that "woman" has been figured in her difference.[8] What we would emphasize is that this figuration projects upon woman a subjectivity, an identity, and a life script—that is, a biography of a sort—of a different order from her intimate experience of herself. To paraphrase John Berger, women engaging this represented figure of woman become conscious of "watch[ing] themselves being looked at" (47).[9] Women become conscious of being biographically scripted in disabling ways, disciplined to a constraining script of femininity.

Thus, historically, women have encountered themselves as the objects of art and not as its makers. Those women who became artists before the late twentieth century, as well as many of those now making art, have had to confront the constitutive masculinity of the institutions of cultural production and their own cultural status as objects of the male gaze—that of the artist and that of the patron. To see themselves outside this history of representation requires coming to terms with the "woman" of art and art history as an idealized figure, an object of male desire, and an idealized or debased other to flesh-and-blood women with radically diverse experiential histories. In Peggy Phelan's terms, they have had to both engage "the ideology of the visible" and expose the blind spot within theoretical framing of who and what is visible or "marked" (7). Doing so, women artists acknowledge their shared status as interlopers in a masculinist tradition, a status derived from "women's subordination in difference" (Mouffe 382). Acknowledging and negotiating that status, they participate in a paradox—a tradition of persistent rupture.[10] "Positioned to collude in their objectification," observes Whitney Chadwick, "unable to differentiate their own subjectivity from the condition of being seen, women artists have struggled toward ways of framing the otherness of woman that direct attention to moments of rupture with—or resistance to—cultural constructions of femininity" (9).

Considering the "art of reflection" in women's self-portraiture, Marsha Meskimmon describes the dilemma for women artists linking self-portraiture and life narration: "There is, on the one hand, a need to show the 'self,' to rejoice in being able to come to representation in your own terms rather than as an object in another dominant schema which forces you into the margins. At the same time, there is a recognition that the models used most commonly cannot simply be appropriated without critical adaptation. The final products, therefore, express the multiplicity of identity and concepts of negotiating positions and voices" (95). Paradoxically located between appropriation and adaptation, women artists exercise what Susan Rubin Suleiman describes as a double allegiance to traditions of representation, affirming and critiquing the masculinist traditions they inherit (131).

This examination of the relationship of women artists to the traditions of art history, particularly self-portraiture, suggests that visual/textual interfaces are acute sites for engaging issues of gendered subjectivity and agency in self-representational acts. Contemporary histories of women's artistic production in the twentieth century often understand the motive for narrating one's life as politicizing the personal. And they read it as an originating point of, prime motive to, content of, and/or transformative site for women's self-representation and the problematizing of woman as artist. Many critical tropes or themes inform discussions of the autobiographical in women's visual/textual work and offer terms tor engaging their artistic production. They include:

- Woman's objectification, seeing herself as seen in the gaze of the male artist, particularly in the legacy of the "female nude"
- The commodification and fetishization of female beauty and bodies in art and advertising
- Women's visualized difference and the differencing of women (in ethnicity, race, sexuality, age, class)
- Women artists' vexed relationship to the canons, conventions, and visual vocabulary of art history as an institution
- Women artists' ambivalent relationship to the materials of production and their exploration of alternative materials, such as quilts, collages, and the earth
- The project of identifying genealogies and foremothers prior to an articulated tradition of women's art and issues of essentializing "woman" in that process
- The appropriation, through parody and critique, of the canonical work of the "masters"
- Remappings of identity as fragmented, unstable, alternative, hybrid, and/or collective
- The embodiment of subjectivity and the subject of embodiment
- Censorship and self-censorship

Of course, these recurrent themes can be understood as invocations of feminist issues and debates taking place more generally across humanistic disciplines since the 1970s. But, of more interest to us, they can be approached as localized engagements with the potential, the politics, and the privileges of the "autobiographical" as a mode of self-presentation and self-knowledge in women's visual and performance art.

Through these localized engagements, women artists have, according to Meskimmon, "challenged simple psychobiography in the form of serial self-portraiture, subverted easy 'historical' or 'biographical' accuracy, queried the significance of mimesis and revealed the ways in which their 'selves' were the products of shifting social constructs and definitions of 'woman'" (73). They have also, as Helaine Posner observes, situated the quest for self-knowledge in visual terms "somewhere between exposure and disguise." According to Posner, multiple self-representations both "reveal and conceal" the subject, enacting the tension between assertion and denial of self (158).

Consider an example of localized engagement in the painted self-portrait. In 1980, four years before her death, eighty-year-old Alice Neel completed *Self-Portrait*, one of her many wryly experimental self-portraits (Figure 1). Recollecting a career that spanned much of the twentieth century, this self-portrait alludes to her conversancy with its major art movements, suggested by the Matisse-like striped chair and the juxtaposition of bold green and orange diagonal planes of color on the lower half of the canvas. Although Neel has recently been commemorated, in a film and an exhibition, as a nurturer of the New York School of male poets and artists, this self-portrait suggests vigorous and audacious reflection on the emergence of women as artist-subjects in their own right.

In her naked *Self-Portrait*, Neel in one sense paints herself into a corner, leaning forward in a blue-striped chair near the angle where two rear walls of a white room meet. The subject's fleshy, naked body, framed by a penumbra of bluish shadow from an invisible source of light to her right, is the focus of the painting, her concealed vagina at its center. But in another sense Neel confronts the viewer as a woman artist who has found her way out of that marginalized space on her own terms. Her body, at a three-quarter angle, is neither idealized as a female nude nor made into the mythic crone of Western representations of aged women. Neel's body, with its sloped shoulders, its pendulous breasts over full belly, and fleshy legs, sags in every muscle except those of her agile right and left hands, one grasping a paint brush, the other a rag; her nimble feet; and her still, alert head. But as she offers her body for inspection, its

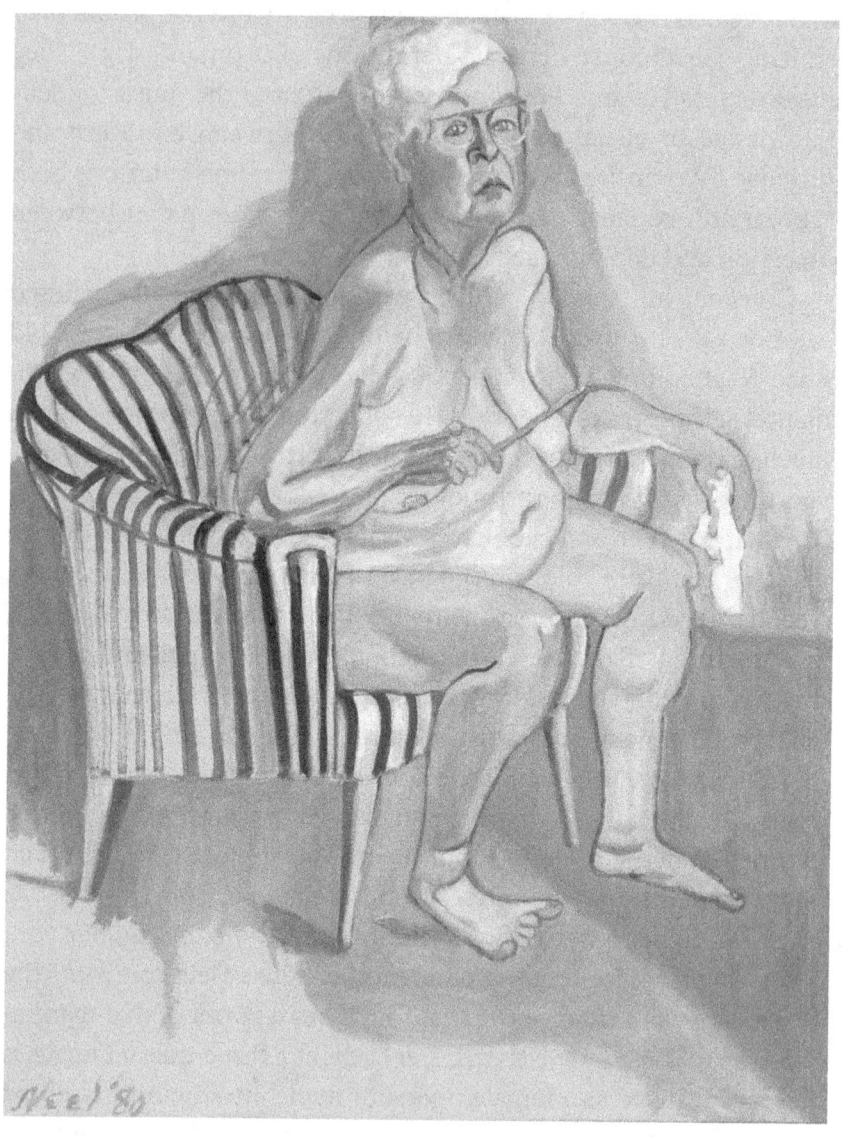

Figure 1. Alice Neel: *Self-Portrait*, 1980, oil on canvas. Courtesy of National Portrait Gallery, Smithsonian Institution, and Estate of Alice Neel, 1980.

sag is as much one of ease as of age. This body is not an object for spectatorial consumption. The artist's face, framed by long gray hair caught up in a knot, looks out at the viewer through top-rimmed glasses with calm, impassive scrutiny, like that of Käthe Kollwitz's sculpted, drawn, and etched self-portraits of the 1930s. There is an intimacy in this inspection by a calm, intelligent, naked woman. In this compelling and moving self-portrait, Neel's candid regard of the viewer invites our own self-assessment. As Frances Borzello suggests, "This is a manifesto self-portrait embodying Neel's belief that nudity brings the viewer closer to the subject" (161). In *Self-Portrait*, Neel, without either vanity or false modesty, invites the spectator's gaze as both an aged woman and an accomplished artist, with a body of work and a body at work.

As Neel's naked *Self-Portrait* suggests, a woman artist's self-portrait is often, by the end of the twentieth century, a complex site of negotiation, appropriation, and adaptation. It alludes to both a history of representations of "woman" that are critiqued and a history of artistic self-portraits of assumed masters of painting. Using Matisse's interiors, colors, and angles, Neel "ruptures" a modernist mode in which a nude woman, as an ideal of beauty, is an object to be viewed and presents herself instead as a creative agent. Her work is autobiographical in its engagement with the changing position of women artists in the twentieth century and with our habit of viewing naked women as nudes for spectatorial consumption and possession, rather than as actors whose work reflects on how art's histories fixed and immobilized them. Precisely in fusing representation of the female nude and the artist's self-portrait, Neel's naked self-portrait, like those of several other twentieth-century women artists, situates autobiographical subjectivity in and as embodiment.[11]

The Visual/Textual and Performative Interface

Philippe Lejeune has written of the self-portrait: "I see the self-portrait as a particular situation, somewhat irregular, in which in the middle of the most coded genre (the portrait) a spark abruptly bursts forth (which is at times only in the mind of the spectator), allowing the essence of the art to be seen in a staggering way: the self-representation of humans (and not the representation of the world), the self-portrait becoming the allegory of art itself" (114). If, indeed, the self-portrait might be read as an allegory of art, then we as viewers can view the sparks of women's acts of self-representation as they reread, and trope upon, their relationship to art's histories and to their status as subjects of and in representation.

In the fields of art history and performance studies, many critics, including Griselda Pollock, Whitney Chadwick, Marsha Meskimmon, Peggy Phelan, and Susan Suleiman, as well as Amelia Jones, Jo Anna Isaak, and Linda S. Kautfman, have significantly influenced the ways in which we read and understand women's visual and performance self-representations. In autobiography studies, Timothy Dow Adams, Linda Haverty Rugg, and Marianne Hirsch are among those who have directed attention to the ways in which the regime of visuality, particularly photography, has come to play an ever larger role in written autobiographical narratives, incorporated as another mode of telling within the text or described and thematized within the narrative. *Interfaces* seeks to complement this corpus of critical studies of women's autobiographical practice in visual and performance media by foregrounding the sparks or encounters or interfacings of different media.

The possible relationships between visuality and textuality at the interface have been theorized by scholars exploring the cultural construction of scopic regimes and historical cultures of visual practices. Some have mapped the complex relationships between pictorial and narrative aspects of paintings, as do Svetlana Alpers and Michael Baxandall (*Tiepolo and the Pictorial Intelligence*), who tease out the "twisted tale" of how Tiepolo's pictorial representations disrupt pictorial narrative. Other scholars look broadly at regimes of textuality and visuality. In *Iconology: Image, Text, Ideology*, W. J. T. Mitchell sets textuality up as a foil to visuality in order to explore how visual image and language or text have been defined as oppositional. Rather than accept that opposition as "real," Mitchell suggests that the opposition is saturated with the history of regimes of representation. At particular historical moments the opposition of image and text (or word) inscribes ideological forces that make certain differences "readable" and significant. Thus, "the dialectic of word and image seems to be a constant in the fabric of signs that a culture weaves around itself" (43). And the usual suspicion of image, as opposed to text, suggests that "every theory of imagery is some form of the fear of imagery" (159). Yet Mitchell's argument that visual images "are inevitably conventional and contaminated by language" (42) suggests that the relationship of the visual and the textual is intimate, inextricable, and multivalent. Visual modes encode histories of representation and invite viewers to read stories within them. Textual modes make their meanings through imagery and through such figures as ekphrasis. Mitchell helpfully calls not for a facile reconciliation between the imperatives of words and visual images but for historicizing that relationship and its cultural meanings.[12]

Other art critics and theorists have historicized the visual/textual matrix at particular historic conjunctures, as Hal Foster does in his two volumes on practices in the twentieth century. In *The Return of the Real*, for instance, Foster explores American art from the 1960s to the present, paying particular attention to the "textual turn" that gained ascendancy in the 1970s. In that turn artists experimented with postmodern interrogations of the sign, with proposing the evacuation of meaning of the sign, and with challenging the cultural coding of artistic institutions and settings. In many modes of the visual, the textual turn came to problematize referentiality itself, most centrally in the intimate mingling of the pictorial and the narrative in film, a medium not addressed in *Interfaces*.[13]

Critics of women's art have theorized more explicitly the gendered dimension of the visual/textual matrix. Rosalind Krauss, in numerous works and, most recently, *Bachelors*, considers how the gendered histories of image and text are negotiated by artists who, though women, position themselves as artistic innovators, deconstructing modernist and postmodernist framings of the relation of image and text. French modernist photographer Claude Cahun, Krauss argues, situates herself simultaneously as subject and object of representation, not to make an autobiographical narrative of reclaiming agency for the female subject but to "suspend the fixity of gender" (37). Such art made by women, Krauss concludes, "needs no special pleading" (50) because their disruption of fixed spectatorial positions mobilizes boundaries to create a continuing instability of masculine and feminine identifications, like, but more effectively than, say, Duchamp.

Feminist theorists of performance art have characterized the interplay among embodiment, visuality, and textuality somewhat differently. Many of them have drawn upon Judith Butler's theorizing of identity formation as performative, a concept that has profoundly influenced debates about performance art. For Butler, gendered identity is always already performative. "Within the inherited discourse of the metaphysics of substance," she argues, "gender proves to be performative—that is, constituting the identity it is purported to be.... There is no gender identity behind the expressions of gender; that identity is performatively constituted by the very 'expressions' that are said to be its result" (*Gender* 24–25). Performance art thus offers occasions for artists to deploy self-imaging, voice, gesture, and text in exposing the gendered features of what Butler calls "the domain of socially instituted norms" (*Bodies* 182) and interjecting traces of the excluded and abject.

RoseLee Goldberg notes the confrontational aspect of performance work, in painting as in theatrical modes, and emphasizes the viewer's active role in keeping it "live art." The fluid status of live art across various divides, not only of word and image but also of high and popular culture, theatrical space and cyberspace, the alternative and the mainstream, suggests how boundaries of visual and performance art have been, and continue to be, redrawn. Itself an unstable term with different connotations in different nations, *performance* is characteristically provocative, critical, and often unnerving (Goldberg 12–13). Similarly, Peggy Phelan's concept of the "unmarked" as "a configuration of subjectivity which exceeds, even while informing, both the gaze and language" makes of performance a disruptive mode of exposing difference and disappearance within regimes of cultural reproduction (27). As Amelia Jones argues for body art, the collapse of distinctions between subject and object, self and other, and public and private in performance makes corporeal display a means of "claiming the immanence and intersubjective contingency of *all* subjects," an exposure of the subject as both destabilized and irreducibly embodied (51).

The visual/textual interface of feminist performance art since the 1970s, then, has often made public display of personal convictions, interrogating ethnic and racial identities, diverse sexualities, and national affiliations through edgy material that confronts spectators with formerly unspoken notions about "woman," as discussions of performance artists make clear.

A Model for Reading the Gendered Interface

Given the multiple sites of the autobiographical not only *in* visual, aural, and textual media but *at* their intersections, no single-discipline model is sufficient to address the complex interweaving, explicitly or implicitly, of image, word, and voice in twentieth-century women artists' self-representation. We propose here an interdisciplinary model for interpreting diverse autobiographical practices, projects, and effects generated at visual/textual interfaces. This model draws upon autobiographical theory to discern rhetorics of self-presentation and narrative scripts of identity in women's visual and performance art. In our reading of particular works, the interface is a site at which visual and textual modes are interwoven but also confront and mutually interrogate each other. The textual component, either explicit or implicit, is configured differently as a "script" than is the visual mode; and these modes must be read against/through each other, in the varied ways detailed later, to elucidate the autobiographical presentation of a subject.

Directing attention to the interfaces of autobiographical acts illuminates how they affect or mobilize meanings: the textual can set in motion certain readings of the image; and the image can then revise, retard, or reactivate that text. In enumerating modes of the interface, we turn to many women artists and performers not elsewhere discussed in this collection of essays. Our brief explorations here may suggest how rich the work of innovative artists and performers is for further investigation by scholars working at the intersection of textual and visual studies.

There are four primary ways in which artists may texture the interface to mobilize visual and textual regimes: (A) *relationally*, through parallel or interrogatory juxtaposition of word and image; (B) *contextually*, through documentary or ethnographic juxtaposition of word and image; (C) *spatially*, through palimpsestic or paratextual juxtaposition of word and image; and (D) *temporally*, through telescoped or serial juxtaposition of word and image.

A. Relational Interfaces: Parallel, Interrogatory

In *relational* interfacing the visual and textual are set side by side, with neither subordinated to the other. They may, however, either complement (be parallel to) or interrogate each other. When visual and textual modes run parallel to each other, their different vocabularies overlay different versions of autobiographical subjectivity. As Mitchell suggests of the visual and textual composites in William Blake's art, "their relationship is more like an energetic rivalry, a dialogue or dialectic between vigorously independent modes of expression" (*Blake* 4). That is, the visual and textual are not iterations of the *same* but versions gesturing toward a subjectivity neither can exhaustively articulate; they are in dialogue. In illustrated daybooks and diaries, especially, the visual and textual modes may run along parallel axes as they "record," through the disparate means of words and images, responses to everyday occasions and fashion identity from the flux of dailiness.

Consider an example *of parallel* relationality at the interface. In her artist's book entitled *Alice, Rosa: Ordinary Extraordinary,* May Stevens juxtaposes photographs of her mother and of German socialist feminist Rosa Luxemburg (Figure 2). On the book's page, the image of Alice on the left and the image of Rosa on the right are side by side. Placed on two pages, one in white ink on black paper, the other in black ink on white paper, the pages form a mirror opposition. Each has three layerings of citations from Luxemburg and Stevens's mother, Alice, written in three languages (French, English, German). Here the words at once are commentary, referential signs, and visual image, a "sea of words."¹⁴ It is a feminist sea, a theoretical sea, as her painting *Sea of Words* explicitly suggests. Stevens states: "I love a page of text. Pages of text or writing are very, very beautiful" (lecture). The sea of words images how women's words can become, for the woman artist, an originary point of self-knowledge and artistic practice.

For Stevens, Luxemburg was a major intellectual figure and her mother a relatively uneducated housewife. Paralleling Luxemburg's extreme of activism to her mother's private domesticity, Stevens brackets the possibilities of women's lives in the early

Figure 2. May Stevens: *Rosa Luxemburg and Alice Stevens*. From *Rosa, Alice: Ordinary/Extraordinary*, artist's book, 1988. Courtesy of the artist and RYAN LEE Gallery, New York, New York.

twentieth century. For Stevens, both women were simultaneously ordinary and extraordinary. Joining their images and marking their differences with captions, Stevens brings the historical figure of Luxemburg closer and puts distance between herself and her mother. This series is autobiographical in showing Stevens's relationships to women who have "made" her. By juxtaposing a personal and a historical figure, she uses the interface of their biographies to evoke versions of her own story, which is not explicitly told. As she has indicated, this Rosa is not objectively biographical but is the idea of "Rosa Luxemburg" in her imagination, a construct; her mother, in contrast, is "real," known to her, but also a subjective presence, saturated by childhood memory. In the artist's imagination, twining them inextricably together produces their meaning for her life. Even as the particular figures of Alice, her biological mother, and Rosa, an activist foremother,

Figure 3. Mary Kelly: Detail of "Menace" from Interim, *Part I: Corpus*, 1984-1985. Laminated photo positive, silkscreen, acrylic on Plexiglas 30 panels: 36″ H x 48″ W x 2″ D each. Courtesy of the artist, Susanne Vielmetter Los Angeles Projects, and Mitchell-Innes & Nash, New York.

remain distinct, they are parallel. Relating and entwining their histories elicits the artist's own history.

The visual and textual components of a work may also be *interrogatory*, standing in a relation of inversion, telling radically different, even contradictory, stories. This is the case in Mary Kelly's *Interim, Part 1: Corpus* (1984–89), a visual diary (Figure 3).[15] In *Corpus*, Kelly presents texts incorporating her own and other middle-aged women's subjective voices as they negotiate a postmaternal identity no longer representable as idealized "femininity." This diaristic, confessional writing of women excluded, as woman, from cultural discourse, is juxtaposed to captioned photos of various women's garments. The photos present the five articles of clothing (in a triptych) as fetishes, substitutes for the women whose bodies they are designed to both shield and reveal.

In *Corpus*, the visual images of garments that syncopate with women's voicings of the experience of middle age are labeled with such words as "Menace," the caption attached to a black leather jacket. These labels mime the labeling of Charcot (the nineteenth-century French doctor and pioneer in the study of hysteria, which he gendered as female), who attached captions to his photographs of hysterical women taken at the Salpêtrière in Paris. Invoking Charcot's visual catalog of hysterical symptoms and attaching labels to three photographic images of the articles of clothing rather than to an embodied woman, Kelly reorients the viewer to the female body by reinterpreting hysteria through the discursive domains of fashion, medicine, and fiction. Doing so, she appropriates the photographic practices used in the production of female hysteria for her own purpose of calling the diagnosis into question. Kelly disentangles the Charcotian significr from its signified and assigns psychological states to the commodities (the clothing) that "make" the "woman," so that these conventional norms are interrogated by the voicings of women excluded from their discursive regimes.

Thus the images function as metonyms for the figure of objectified and commodified woman.[16] The textual voicings of the women and the visual images of the garments interrupt and contradict each other, making this self-presentation disjunctive and incoherent. Words and images are in irreducible tension. While such an inverse relationship may seem to foreclose autobiographical subjectivity, in fact it asks us, as viewers, to reexamine our assumptions about the knowability of any subject, unless we put the domains of language and image into sociohistorical context in order to "know" how they contradict each other and destabilize forms of identification.

In sum, at a relational interface, layerings of text and image interplay in ways that can seem either complementary or contradictory. Each elucidates the other, but is not reducible to it. The separateness of textual and visual media is maintained, not blurred. Working at this interface, women artists may conduct a dialogue that simultaneously sustains difference and distinction and enables connections across histories and cultures, as in Stevens's *Rosa Luxemburg and Alice Stevens*. At this interface, women artists can also disrupt the viewer's desire to resolve contradictions and tensions, as in Kelly's *Corpus*. The use of relational tactics disrupts the seeming coherence of an autobiographical subject and foregrounds women's disparate voices, discourses, identities, and desires.

B. Contextualized Interfaces: Documentary, Ethnographic

In a second mode of interfacing, the artist *contextualizes* her self-representation by explicitly citing sociohistorical sources that situate her individual "I" in a cultural surround. This may be done either through documentary or ethnographic means that embed the experiential history of the subject within texts and/or images of collectivized memory.

At a *documentary* interface, the textual is used to situate the visual—whether an image, installation, or performance—within a context of social and cultural meaning. That is, artists assemble and juxtapose such documents of everyday life as newspapers and official records to place the autobiographical subject in a sociocultural surround. These practices make visible the official, often stereotyped, histories through which women's lives have conventionally been "framed" in order to interrogate them. In her essay in *Interfaces*, for example, Jennifer Drake explores Adrian Piper's use of documents in her installation entitled *Cornered* (1988). In *Cornered*, two birth certificates hang on the wall near a monitor that plays a videotape of Piper addressing the visitors seated before it. Next to the monitor is a table turned on its side. The two historical documents provide evidence of the fluidity of the social category of "race" and thus racial identity: one registers her father's identity as "octaroon"; the other registers his identity as "white." This doubled documentation reveals cultural confusion about reading "color" visibly off the body. In her accompanying monologue, Piper explores this cultural confusion about the readability of her own identity, an indeterminate identity "inherited" from her father and played out in everyday life by her cultural position as an African American woman of white appearance. Piper's situating of birth certificates against her videotaped address deconstructs historical discourses of American racial difference and recontextualizes the conventional meanings of "whiteness" and "blackness" as arbitrary. As a contemporary racialized subject, Piper acknowledges that she's "cornered" by a normative interpretation of bodily difference. But her juxtaposition of textual and visual media offers a new "angle" or possibility for understanding the instability of seemingly fixed categories of identity, one that "corners" spectators in their assumptions of what constitutes "race." Using "authentic" historical documents and the public history they invoke, Piper calls into question their truth status and our naive conviction that an autobiographical identity must stay in the corner to which racial politics have assigned it.

Similarly, many life narratives juxtapose verbal stories and photographic histories that narrate multiple, culturally assigned, conflicting versions of racial or ethnic status. Through such juxtapositions, life narrators explore collective histories and the arbitrariness of fixed ethnic identities. For example, Norma Cantú's *Canícula*, Sheila Ortiz-Taylor's and Sandra Ortiz-Taylor's *Imaginary Parents,* and Shirlee Taylor Haizlip's *The Sweeter the Juice* in different ways interweave family stories with photographs from family albums and historical and familial documents or memorabilia to disrupt essentialist notions of identity. In such texts, photographs, rather than being stable visual markers of ethnic or racial identities, unsettle the fixedness of family history by depicting multiple, disparate, even contradictory versions of it.[17]

The *ethnographic* is another kind of social contextualization that draws primarily on remembered scenes of collective memory in creating an image or performance that commemorates or revalues a past moment and links the personal to a community, for instance a communal ethnic group. This collective history resituates an autobiographical "I" within a "we" that is indispensable for configuring an identity. That is, the "I"'s meaning is entwined with, read through, the "we" of collective memory and authorized by it. This interface is probed in a series of painted *recuerdos* by Carmen Lomas Garza. In paintings of what she calls "special events" and "unusual happenings," Lomas Garza captures the precise details of her childhood and young adulthood in images of collective everyday life in a Chicano community of South Texas to both locate and authenticate her individual experience as transpersonal and exemplary. "I felt I had to start with my earliest recollections of my life," she has stated, "and validate each event or incident by depicting it in a visual format" (13).

Tamalada (1987), for example, details a cultural milieu in which thirteen members from several generations of a family are shown in various stages of making tamales. Particulars of the room and the familial relationships autoethnographically frame the young artist as a participant in a process that is collective and ritualized. The pictures on the wall include one of the Catholic Last Supper as a folkloric event and a calendar with two silhouettes dancing a traditional Mexican dance. All members of the family, except the youngest girl and her caretaker, engage in tamale-making in the kitchen. Some mix the dough in a large pan; others in the seated assembly line cut out the triangular pieces, fill them with savory spices, tomato sauce, and meats, or wrap them in cornhusks and lay them in a baking pan. In this setting "home" is both a private and a social space, and the painting becomes a visual record of familial bonding. Lomas Garza's use of bright, unmodulated colors and lack of vanishing point perspective incorporate Mexican folkloric traditions of representation; and yet the painting's status as "art" also places it in the American art market. Enumerating details of a folk tradition, Lomas Garza understands her own life as implicated in communal life. By celebrating her roots in a collective "we" and telling a story of ethnic identification as foundational and enabling, she mobilizes art's power to "heal the wounds inflicted by discrimination and racism" (13).[18]

In sum, at the contextual interface of documentary or ethnographic practice, a dynamic relay between personal and communal memory reconfigures the relationship of forms of communal memory and reworks the nation's official memory of a group as devalued or invisible. Working at this interface enables women artists to foreground the experiential history of the identity statuses they bear, and bare. Their representations in various media embody and body forth in culturally specific settings their experiential histories. Particularly for postcolonial and multicultural women artists exploring the relationship of a colonized ethnic identity to a national identity that has, historically, dominated and effaced it, replacing that received history with collective histories of tradition and intimate bonds is a productive means of telling new autobiographical stories.

C. Spatial Interfaces: Palimpsestic, Paratextual

Third, the interface can be *spatialized* as a site that is permeable, infiltrated either from inside out as a *palimpsest* or outside in as a *paratext*. The apparent space of the surface is redefined by its surround; or, alternately, shown as masking a history of previous iterations that can be differently arranged. In either case, the act

Figure 4.1. Yong Soon Min. *deCOLONIZATION*. 1991. Courtesy Yong Soon Min.

INTRODUCTION: MAPPING WOMEN'S SELF-REPRESENTATION | 377

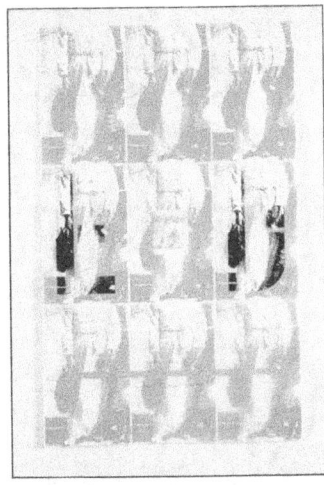
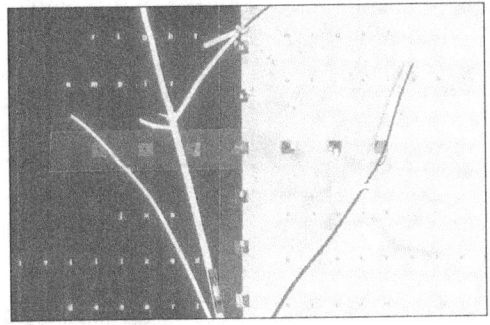

Figure 4.2. Yong Soon Min. *deCOLONIZATION*. 1991. Courtesy Yong Soon Min.

of putting a seemingly two-dimensional surface into the three-dimensionality of embodied space animates surfaces with cultural residue.

In a *palimpsest*, one image lies submerged, apparently erased or overwritten by a second image; but traces of what has been erased or overwritten leak through the overlaid surface. The layers underneath, as in an archeological site, house alternative narratives or images that compete with and contest the visible or apparent meaning. For example, the installation by Korean-American artist Yong Soon Min entitled *deCOLONIZATION* (1991) makes visible the multiple layers of a postcolonial, multicultural identity (Figures 4.1 & 4.2). The installation is punctuated with words, from the *"COLONIZE"* that adheres to the floor, to the black and white words on a vinyl sheet that capture the binary oppositions foundational to colonizing concepts and events, to the Plexiglas intersection of "NATURE" and "NURTURE," to a poem written upon the front and back of a dress in English and Korean, to a poem by Martinician writer Aimé Césaire, to the "OCCUPIED" layered over with frosted Mylar. Amid the words that constitute a complex history of discourses of colonialism stands a tree branch of

Figure 5. Audrey Flack: *Marilyn (Vanitas)* 1977. Courtesy of the artist.

knowledge. A traditional Korean dress hangs suspended from the ceiling. The layerings multiplied in the diverse contexts of *deCOL-ONIZATION* suggest the multiplicity of colonizations of Korea by China, Japan, and the United States as a nationalist bricolage. The physical layerings—the dress that hangs layered above the words on the floor, the layers of Plexiglas—combine with the metaphorical layers of the pages of the table of contents of an *Encyclopedia Americana* and the mirrored images of letters. Taken together, they situate the viewer in the internalized cacophony of external forms of gendered identity. Displaying fragmented objects and letters to evoke in pieces a culture that has been splintered through colonization, Yong Soon Min uncovers the differential effects on female

INTRODUCTION: MAPPING WOMEN'S SELF-REPRESENTATION | 379

subjectivity of the processes of de/colonization often occluded in official discourses of nation.

The relation of visuality to textuality may also be *paratextual*. Paratexts are apparatuses that surround or accompany a text. In textual life narrative, paratexts include epigraphs, prefaces, acknowledgments, letters of authentication, et cetera. But there are paratexts in visual and performance art as well. In *Marilyn (Vanitas)* (1977), Audrey Flack incorporates a long epigraph from a biography of Marilyn Monroe into her meditation on female commodification and artistry (Figure 5). The passage from the biography describes a scene in which Marilyn Monroe spoke of her childhood experience of being made visually beautiful by the application of powder instead of being punished for running away. The biographer's commentary suggests the importance of the scene in understanding that "one could paint oneself into an instrument of one's will." Flack places a childhood photo of herself and her brother between two images of "Marilyn," one reproduced as if on the opposite page of the biography, the other a reflection of it in a mirror set obliquely at a right angle to the book. In front of the representations of Marilyn—in biography, photo, and reflected mirror image—Flack paints a still life mixing traditional art-historical and contemporary graphic symbols of the vanity of human time as an inevitable process of decay and death: a calendar, a (compact) mirror, overripe fruit, a blue Delft mug, a wineglass filled with pearls that reflects a viewer's room outside the frame, a half-burnt candle, a timepiece, an hourglass, and an anamorphosic framed portrait to the left of the frontal image of Marilyn. Through her meditation on the fate of Marilyn as a popular icon of femininity, the artist alludes to her own struggle as a woman artist to forge the paintbrush into, in the painting's phrase, "an instrument of one's will." Thus, Flack embeds an autobiographical meditation on gendered difference in a narrative about the distorting effects of cultural representations on what became "Marilyn." Her portrait probes the production of "Marilyn" as a cultural icon of an impossible woman and the system of gender that celebrated yet destroyed her. This apparent focus on Marilyn also places her, via the "Vanitas" tradition, as a memento mori for Flack. The artist both forges the image and finds her own image as a culturally constructed subject through situating it in the spatial surround of the paratext.

In sum, the complex layerings of autobiographical subjectivity become visible when surfaces project through canny juxtapositions disparate histories, images, identities, all coexisting in the same space. As viewers move through three-dimensional space either literally, as in Yong Soon Min's installation, or metaphorically, as in the semiotic space of Flack's *Marilyn (Vanitas)*, they interact with and create the layered spaces of an artistic representation that is both personal and "about" woman. In the process, they inescapably enter into dialogue with the verbal fragments and images they encounter compressed in one space, on one surface.

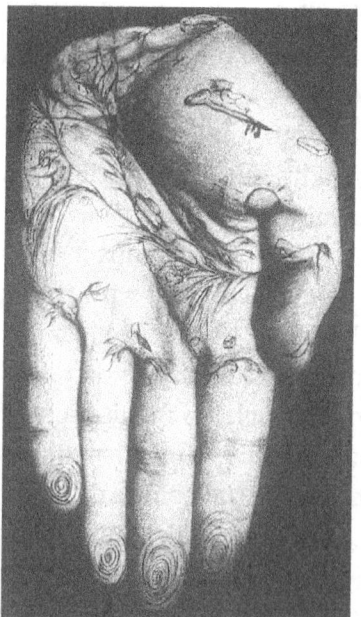
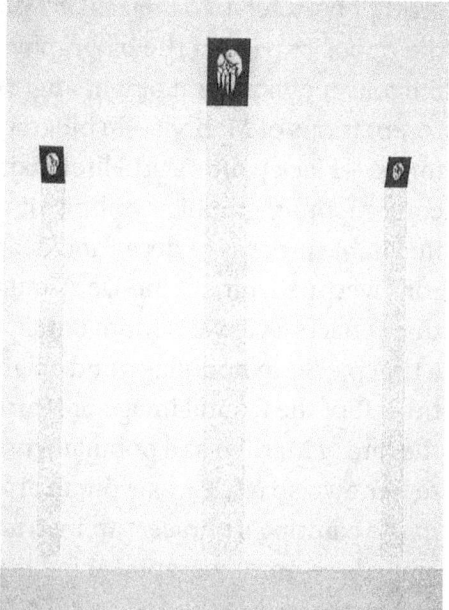

Figure 6. Annette Messager: *Les Lignes de la main*, 1987–8. Overpainted black-and-white photograph with handwriting on the wall. Courtesy of the artist and Marian Goodman Gallery.

D. Temporal Interfaces: Telescoped, Serial

A fourth mode of interfacing concerns the *temporal* contraction or expansion of the stages of an embodied action through which the artist engages in autobiographical storytelling.

When *telescoped,* distinct modes, the visual and the verbal, collapse into one another, confusing the viewer's expectation that their boundary or separation will be maintained. The textual, for instance, may be used as an image, even an architecture. In an installation she titled *Les l.ignes de la main* (Lines of the hand) (1987–88), French artist Annette Messager placed close-up photographs of hands on the gallery wall (Figure 6). The enlarged hands, overwritten by various lines and figurations, point downward. Underneath the hands, Messager has written single words directly onto the wall in colored pencil. The words, repeated again and again in narrow columns down the wall, signify particular emotional states, such as fear or confusion. The reiteration of a word, suggests Sheryl Conkelton, "drains meaning from it, reducing the words to mere form; they become instead elements of ritual architecture, visually supporting the images" (24). Yet the repeated words also function, we would argue, as the architectonic elements of autobiographical subjectivity. In their formal organization on the wall, they link the materiality of the body (the images of the body parts to which they are attached) to the unrepresentable somatic markers of internal, psychical states. In another of Messager's installations, entitled *Mes Ouvrages* (My Works) (1987), strings of words written on the walls in colored pencil become so many threads used to weave images together into what Conkelton describes as a "diagram" of emotion (24), with multiple emotions/words attached to the imaged objects. In this sense, words do what they seem unable to do—they visualize the autobiographical subject's private memory museum.[19] Collapsing the word-image distinction evokes a primal experiential core that could not be represented separately by either verbal narrative or single image.

The artistic medium may also become embodied as the subjectivity of the artist, so that performance and body are telescoped.

The artist Mona Hatoum, in her two-hour video performance entitled *Pull* (1995), placed herself in an area hidden from the visitor; only her long ponytail, hanging in a niche in the wall, was visible. Visitors confronted the "real" ponytail and above it a video of the artist, who seemed to be hanging upside down. Invited to "pull" the ponytail by the very title of the piece, they could watch the effect of their pulling on the artist. Assuming the video to be recorded, they saw no connection between pulling the hair and the facial expression on the monitor. In fact, they were pulling the hair of the artist present behind the wall. In other words, the artist was there in person, connected to her hair, not merely represented on the video. Her hair, as Desa Philippi suggests, is here materialized as fetish (369). Body and image, usually separated, were conjoined, compressed in this telescoping of medium and material body. As Guy Brett says of the piece, "at a certain moment the spectacle suddenly ceases to be a spectacle" (74) as visitors are confronted with their own role in causing pain to the artist whose art and body are telescoped.[20]

Hatoum's installations attach the processes of represented subjectivity to the very materiality of her body, forcing viewers to confront the conundrum of her presence in apparent absence. This absent presence is a central paradox of autobiographical acts and practices. In addition, her installations link "presence" to notions of female excess and women's embodied subjectivity. If Hatoum's installations are, in a sense, like Emin's rumpled bed, synecdoches of subjectivity, Messager's compressions of word and image are closer to metaphor. Telescoping body and artistic medium, word and image, past and present moments, these artists insist on the coextensiveness of body, language, and art.

Temporal succession may also create a *serial* relationship in which multiple instances of self-referencing unfold as process. Here wordless visual images are organized in a series that may be linear, geometric, or disjunctive, to tell a story through their sequence and juxtaposition. Many women have represented themselves in a series of related self-images, no one of which would be sufficient to tell the story. Hannah Wilke's self-images in *S.O.S.-Starification Object Series* are a series of thirty-five photographs in which she poses as cultural icons whose bodies are scarred/starred with wads of chewing gum shaped to suggest female genitalia. Similarly, Ann Hamilton presents herself, in photographs conceived as studies for her installation work, as a series of "body objects" (1988): sixteen disparate objects, such as a chair, a bush, a paddle, a stove, are shown intersecting her body. In one, for example, a shoe disappears into her face at the site of her mouth and nose (70–72).

Eleanor Antin's series on weight loss entitled *Carving: A Traditional Sculpture* presents another set of photographed poses that reiterate, with variation, the artist's playful shedding of weight as a gradual displacement of female embodiment by negative space on the photograph's surface. Sequential self-presentation enables women artists to propose subjectivity as processual rather than static and to insist that identity is performative, not essentialized. No single pose or frame of the sequence is the "definitive" or "truthful" self-portrait. In sequential self-portraiture, women artists may engage stages of the life cycle: for instance, performing the childhood past, enacting daughterhood, maternity, professional roles, bodily illness and disability, and aging. In serial self-representation, viewers witness the artist's body in parts, at angles, inside out, upside down, three-dimensionally, perspectivally. At once discrete and multiple, the embodied subject of serial self-representation stages life narrative as sequence with unpredictable variation. The serialized personal narrative thus enacts a larger story about women's relation to historical representations of woman and gendered sexuality.

Consider Renee Cox's *Yo Mama* series of photographic self-portraits. Through this narrative series Cox, performing the *Yo Mama* figure of Black street talk, places her own body in various cultural locations and in art-historical and ethnographic cultural intertexts. For instance, in *Yo Mama's Last Supper* (1996), Cox assumes the central space of the da Vinci painting, displacing the Christ figure with her own nude self-portrait to intervene in

Figure 7. Renée Cox and Lyle Ashton Harris. *Venus Hottentot 2000*. 1995. Courtesy Renée Cox.

its white, masculine tableau. In *Venus Hottentot 2000* (1995), she assumes the place of that fetishized African woman of nineteenth-century ethnography, the "Hottentot Venus" (Figure 7). Through this time-traveling play on place, space, and identity, Cox as an African American woman artist, critiques the history of cultural representations, and absences, of the Black female body. As she "looks" out from those sites of representation not created for her, she asserts autobiographical agency for the gendered and racially marked body (Myers 27).

In sum, women artists and performers, as they mine the possibilities of the temporal contraction or expansion of embodied feelings, actions, and statuses, ask to have their embodied subjectivity reseen in time through telescoped or serialized modes of self-presentation. Doing so, they explore and expose the dynamic processes through which women experience the materiality of a female subjectivity constituted through gendered and raced codes of cultural intelligibility. Often alluding to other cultural texts in a range of verbal and visual media, these artists renovate iconic stereotypes to create a composite subject of difference and resistance. At other times, they expose the disappearance of the subject into the gaps and absences of codes of cultural intelligibility; or they expose the tenuous differentiation of embodied materiality and imaged representation.

Conclusion

We do not claim that these four modes of the interface are the only possibilities for producing meaning at a visual/textual matrix. But we *do* see them as suggestive of the heterogeneity, ambiguity, and complex intersectionality of the visual/textual interface in autobiographical acts. While we have focused on the importance of gendered representations specific to women's art practices and tactics for subverting normative femininity, we suggest that these modes of visual/textual interfacing have been particularly productive for women artists and performers engaging the gendered politics of artistic production in the last century and the legacies of their own inheritance as embodied subjects. Ultimately, these autobiographical acts at the interface work intersubjectively. That is, they force us as viewers, who are addressed in and by the works, to participate actively, and oftentimes uncomfortably, in negotiating the politics of subjectivity. They invite us to confront our own participation in "othering" the text, the image, and the "woman" embodied before us. They prompt us to re-vision the spectacle of femininity and to remake women as cultural agents of the autobiographical interface.

Our model for reading the interface suggests one way of approaching women's visual and performance art through the lens of autobiography studies. It cannot, however, account for the complexity of diverse practices of self-representation staged by visual and performance artists that are the subject of the essays in *Interfaces*, which expand the repertoire of modes of women's self-portraiture and theorize more extensively the nature of autobiographical subjectivity at a visual/textual interface that has often been underread, overread, misread, or read exclusively as mimetic self-referentiality. These essays seek to capture the heterogeneity, complexity, and hybridity of women's self-representational practices at the visual/verbal interface. Such modernist artists as Baroness Elsa and Claude Cahun perform kinds of gender-bending transgression now commonly attributed to postmodern performance artists. And work such as Faith Ringgold's quilts is more productively read through an autoethnographic model attentive to new histories of racialized subjects than through an exclusively postmodernist frame.

We decided against organizing *Interfaces* by medium—photographs, painted self-portraits, installation, performances—because so many of the artists discussed work across media in a dynamic interplay among visual, textual, and aural media as sites of the autobiographical. The four sections of *Interfaces*, which map sites of visual/textual interfacing around, loosely, the body, space, diaristic lives, and visual storytelling. "Acting Out the Body" explores how the embodiment of subjectivity composes both material and metaphoric critiques. "Performing Spaces" gathers essays in which subjectivity is situated in a range of gendered spatio-temporal surrounds that are both visualized and interrogated. "Serial Lives/Imaged Diaries" takes up the juxtaposition of visual and performance diaries as distinct practices. "Visual Narratives" pursues multi-medial constellations that are simultaneously material, image, and text. The essays in *Interfaces* thus offer new readings that engage with the stakes of autobiographical self-portraiture and performance at the interface of regimes of visuality and textuality. Attentive to the materiality of self-presentation, they examine ways in which specific women artists engage a history of artistic or performance modes of representing "woman" and the woman artist's relationship to disciplines and institutions of subjectivity. The essays ask how the personal, as experienced and remembered, may be linked to the politics of gender and visibility and the norms of visual and discursive regimes through particular theoretical lenses—psychoanalytic, feminist, materialist, postcolonial, multicultural, rhetorical, or postmodern. As such, they illuminate issues of subjectivity, agency, embodiment, and identity that mark the self-presentation of autobiographical artists in the modern and postmodern world.

Notes

1 The discussion of Emin's installation is drawn from our keynote address presented on July 27, 2000, at the Autobiography and Changing Identities conference, held at the University of British Columbia, and subsequently published in *Biography*, Winter 2001.

2 In 1999, Emin was a finalist for the Turner Prize awarded by the Tate Gallery in London. Although Emin was not awarded the Turner Prize, her controversial entry provoked a raging discussion among British art critics about art and the autobiographical. In June 2000 *My Bed* was purchased by Charles Saatchi for 150,000 pounds (Brooks 7).

3 As the parenthetical aside indicates, it is difficult to choose the appropriate term for language and story in words. Adopting W. J. T. Mitchell's strategy in *Iconology*, we have decided to use the textual, or textuality,

as an umbrella term that refers to word, narrative, and verbal practice. Similarly, the word "visual" is used as an umbrella term for image, object, and bodily or gestural aspects of performance. Of course, contemporary theorists read the image as a text, which means that this distinction between image and text, the iconic and the alphabetic, is in a sense untenable, although many art historians have sustained it in practice. We adopt W. J. T. Mitchell's strategy in *Iconology* of using the term text in its broadest sense.

4 A wide range of positions on the methodological approaches to, theoretical assumptions about, and political history of visual studies as an academic discipline and cultural activity is set forth by diverse art historians and cultural studies scholars in *October* 77.

5 For a fuller discussion of the performativity of autobiographical acts, see Smith, "Performativity" (108–11).

6 This discussion is condensed from an extended analysis of the constitutive components of autobiographical subjectivity, and the situational contexts of individual autobiographical acts, in our *Reading Autobiography*.

7 Since 1980, however, feminist theorists and critics have turned their attention to the autobiographical writings of a broad range of women, from medieval religious to contemporary writers of color. Women's literary self-representation has become a field of study in itself, examining how, historically, in response to their invisibility, women have constituted themselves as subjects of discourse. In our introduction to *Women, Autobiography, Theory: A Reader* (included in this collection), we have traced this history.

8 For an exploration of diverse regimes of visuality, see the collection of essays edited by Teresa Brennan and Martin Jay.

9 John Berger offers an extended discussion of "seeing" and "being seen" as "ways of seeing" (45–47).

10 In our focus on women's art practices, we are not arguing for an "essentialist" reading of women's difference or an essentialist understanding of women's artistic practices. Rather, we are invoking a counter-tradition that does not necessarily assume an essentialist category of identity. This women's tradition is one invoked by women artists and authors as they articulate a relationship to past practices of other women artists, writers, and public figures.

11 For example, the nude self-portraits in the painting of Paula Modersohn-Becker, Suzanne Valadon, Frida Kahlo, Sylvia Sleigh, Joan Semmel, and Yolanda Lopez and the self-photographs of Imogen Cunningham, Jo Spence, Hannah Wilke, Carolee Schneemann, Helen Chadwick, and

Laura Aguilar all represent the woman artist performing acts of naked re-presentation that comment on embodied womanhood.

12. To the dialogue of visual and textual modes, Mary Ann Caws attributes the possibilities engendered by "interruption," the setting in motion of a dialogue that "works towards openness and struggles against the system as closure, undoing categories" (6).

13. Much has been written on the complex interface of pictorial and narrative practices in various genres of film, from film noir to western. Tom Conley, for instance, has investigated the relation between image and script, alphabetical and iconic writing in film in order to understand the "creative conflict between dialogue and pictorial narrative." Considering titles and credits, the captions of silent film, the allegorical gesture to literary references, filmic signatures, and filmic icons, Conley argues that these alphabetic and graphic components of narrative film are "foreign elements integral to the image" and therefore "define it by their own alterity within cinema" (xxxi).

14. Stevens says of the artist's book that its incorporation of text "situates, locates, and makes more potent, hopefully, the images" (lecture).

15. *Corpus* is one of four series of texts and photographs that make up *Interim*. The four series explore the body, money, history, and power.

16. See Jo Anna Isaak's discussion of Kelly's project in *Feminism and Contemporary Art: The Revolutionary Power of Women's Laughter* (40–41).

17. See Adams on Cantú's *Canícula*.

18. Similarly, collage artist Aminah Robinson has produced over twenty thousand works in her career, many of which combine her self-representation with the oral history of her African American family and community in Columbus, Ohio. Executed in painting, drawing, button-beading, fabric, stitching, and other media, these autoethnographic images connect the traditions and lore of Midwestern African America to her own experiential history in a communal visual ethnography (see Myers).

19. For an extended discussion of Messager's artist's books, see also Renée Riese Hubert and Judd D. Hubert (137–40).

20. For an extended discussion of Hatoum's project, see Phillipi.

Works Cited

Adams, Timothy Dow. "'Heightened by Life' vs. 'Paralyzed by Fact': Photography and Autobiography in Norma Cantú's *Canícula*." *Biography* 24, 1 (Winter 2001): 57–71.

———. *Light Writing and Life Writing: Photography in Autobiography*. Chapel Hill: University of North Carolina Press, 2000.

Alpers, Svetlana, and Michael Baxandall. *Tiepolo and the Pictorial Intelligence*. New Haven: Yale University Press, 1994.

Berger, John. *Ways of Seeing*. London: Penguin Books, 1972.

Borzello, Frances. *Seeing Ourselves: Women's Self-Portraits*. London: Thames and Hudson, 1998.

Brennan, Teresa, and Martin Jay, eds. *Vision in Context: Historical and Contemporary Perspectives on Sight*. New York: Routledge, 1996.

Brett, Guy. *Mona Hatoum*. Interview by Michael Archer; essays by Guy Brett, Catherine de Zegher. London: Phaidon Press, 1997.

Brooks, Richard. "Saatchi Pays 150,000 for Emin's Soiled Bed." *The Sunday Times*, Vancouver, July 16, 2000, 7.

Butler, Judith. *Bodies That Matter: On the Discursive Limits of "Sex."* New York: Routledge, 1993.

———. *Gender Trouble: Feminism and the Subversion of Identity*. New York: Routledge, 1990.

Cantú, Norma Elia. *Canícula: Snapshots of a Girlhood en la Frontera*. Albuquerque: University of New Mexico Press, 1995.

Chadwick, Whitney. *Mirror Images: Women, Surrealism, and Self-Representation*. Cambridge: MIT Press, 1998.

Conkelton, Sheryl, and Carol S. Eliel. *Annette Messager*. Los Angeles: Los Angeles County Museum of Art, Harry N. Abrams, 1995.

Conley, Tom. *Film Hieroglyphs: Ruptures in Classical Cinema*. Minneapolis: University of Minnesota Press, 1991.

Foster, Hal. *Compulsive Beauty*. Cambridge: MIT Press, 1993.

———. *The Return of the Real*. Cambridge: MIT Press, 1996.

Goldberg, RoseLee. *Performance: Live Art since 1960*. New York: Harry N. Abrams, 1998.

Grosz, Elisabeth. "Intolerable Ambiguity: Freaks as/at the Limit." In *Freakery: Cultural Spectacles of the Extraordinary Body*, ed. Rosemarie Garland Thomson, 55–66. New York: New York University Press, 1996.

Haizlip, Shirlee Taylor. *The Sweeter the Juice: A Family Memoir in Black and White*. New York: Touchstone, 1994

Hamilton, Ann. *The Body and the Object: Ann Hamilton 1984–1996*. Columbus: Wexner Center for the Arts, 1996.

Hirsch, Marianne. *Family Frames: Photography, Narrative, and Postmemory*. Cambridge: Harvard University Press, 1997.

Hubert, Renée Riese, and Judd D. Hubert. *The Cutting Edge of Reading*. New York: Granary Books, 1999.

Isaak, Jo Anna. *Feminism and Contemporary Art: The Revolutionary Power of Women's Laughter*. London: Routledge, 1996.

———. "In Praise of Primary Narcissism: The Last Laughs of Jo Spence and Hannah Wilke." In *Interfaces: Women, Autobiography, Image, Performance*, eds. Sidonie Smith and Julia Watson, 49–68. Ann Arbor: University of Michigan Press, 2001.

Jones, Amelia. *Body Art/Performing the Subject*. Minneapolis: University of Minnesota Press, 1998.

Krauss, Rosalind. *Bachelors*. Cambridge, MA: MIT Press, 1999.

Lejeune, Philippe. "Looking at a Self-Portrait." In *On Autobiography*, ed. Paul John Eakin, trans. Katherine Leary, 109–18. Minneapolis: University of Minnesota Press, 1989.

Lippard, Lucy. *Mixed Blessings: New Art in a Multicultural America*. New York: Pantheon Books, 1990.

Lomas Garza, Carmen. *Pedacito de mi corazon*. Austin, Tex.: Laguna Gloria Art Museum, 1991.

Meskimmon, Marsha. *The Art of Reflection: Women Artists' Self-Portraiture in the Twentieth Century*. New York: Columbia University Press, 1996.

Mitchell, W. J. T. *Blake's Composite Art: A Study of the Illuminated Poetry*. Princeton: Princeton University Press, 1978.

———. *Iconology: Image, Text, Ideology*. Chicago: University of Chicago Press, 1986.

Mouffe, Chantal. "Feminism, Citizenship, and Radical Democratic Politics." In *Feminists Theorize the Political*, ed. Judith Butler and Joan W. Scott, 369–84. New York: Routledge, 1992.

Myers, Susan. "Precious Moments." Gallery notes. Columbus, Ohio: Hammond Harkins Galleries (spring 2000).

Nochlin, Linda. *Representing Women*. New York: Thames and Hudson, 1999.

Ortiz Taylor, Sheila, and Sandra Ortiz Taylor. *Imaginary Parents*. Albuquerque: University of New Mexico Press, 1996.

Phelan, Peggy. *Unmarked: The Politics of Performance*. New York: Routledge, 1993.

Phillipi, Desa. "Mona Hatoum: Some Any No Every Body." In *Inside the Visible: An Elliptical Traverse of Twentieth-Century Art in, of, and from the Feminine*, ed. Catherine de Zegher, 363–70. Cambridge, MA: MIT Press, 1996.

Pollock, Griselda. *Differencing the Canon: Feminist Desire and the Writing of Art's Histories*. New York: Routledge, 1999.

Posner, Helaine. "The Self and the World: Negotiating Boundaries in the Art of Yayoi Kusama, Ana Mendieta, and Francesca Woodman." In *Mirror Images: Women, Surrealism, and Self-Representation*, ed. Whitney Chadwick, 156–71. Cambridge, MA: MIT Press, 1998.

Rugg, Linda Haverty. *Picturing Ourselves: Photography and Autobiography*. Chicago: University of Chicago Press, 1997.

Schacter, Daniel L. *Searching for Memory: The Brain, the Mind, and the Past*. New York: Basic Books, 1996.

Scott, Joan W. "Experience." In *Women, Autobiography, Theory: A Reader*, ed. Sidonie Smith and Julia Watson, 57–71. Madison: University of Wisconsin Press, 1998.

Silverman, Kaja. *The Acoustic Mirror: The Female Voice in Psychoanalysis and Cinema*. Bloomington: Indiana University Press, 1988.

Smith, Sidonie. "Performativity, Autobiographical Practice, Resistance." *a/b: Auto/Biography Studies* 10, no. 1 (Spring 1995): 17–33.

Smith, Sidonie, and Julia Watson. "The Rumpled Bed of Autobiography." *Biography* 24.1 (Winter 2001): 1–14.

———. *Reading Autobiography: A Guide for Interpreting Life Narratives*. Minneapolis: University of Minnesota Press, 2001.

———, eds. *Women, Autobiography, Theory: A Reader*. Madison: University of Wisconsin Press, 1998.

Stanton, Domna C. "Autogynography: Is the Subject Different?" In *The Female Autograph*. Ed. Domna C. Stanton. 5–22. New York: New York Literary Forum, 1984.

Stevens, May. *Rosa, Alice: Ordinary Extraordinary*. New York: Universe Books, 1988.

———. Lecture presented at the School of Art and Design, University of Michigan, November 12, 1999.

Suleiman, Susan Rubin. *Subversive Intent: Gender, Politics, and the Avant-Garde*. Cambridge, MA: Harvard University Press, 1990.

Wingrove, Elizabeth. "Interpellating Sex," *Signs* 24.4 (Summer 1999): 869–93.

11
AUTOGRAPHIC DISCLOSURES AND GENEALOGIES OF DESIRE IN ALISON BECHDEL'S *FUN HOME* (WATSON 2008)

Gillian Whitlock has observed the "potential of comics to open up new and troubled spaces" ("Autographics" 976). Alison Bechdel's autographic memoir *Fun Home: A Family Tragicomic* (2006) is such a text, a provocative exploration of sexuality, gendered relations in the American family, and Modernist versions of what she calls "erotic truth" (228). It both enacts and reflects on processes of autobiographical storytelling, and exploits the differences of autographic inscription in the art of cartooning. Bechdel is a well-known American feminist cartoonist who for over two decades has published the politically savvy lesbian-feminist syndicated comic strip "Dykes to Watch Out For."[1] In taking up the graphic memoir form, she composes *Fun Home* in seven extended chapters that are beautifully drawn in black line art and gray-green ink wash. It is a dazzlingly and dauntingly complex set of interconnected life stories, modes of print text, and panoply of visual styles. A memoir about memoirs, memory, and acts of storytelling, *Fun Home* is at all times an ironic and self-conscious life narrative. It hovers between the genres of tragedy and comedy, as its subtitle

"A Family Tragicomic" asserts and its project of affirming the family despite and because of her father's history avows.

Fun Home's title refers to the family's mid-century funeral home in the small town of Beech Creek, Pennsylvania, near the Allegheny front, where Alison is the eldest child and only daughter in a family with three children. Their father Bruce is the funeral home's director and mortician; additionally, both parents teach high-school English. "Fun Home" as a concept also evokes a fun-house of mirrors, which the family's restored Gothic Revival home proves to be as a psychic incubator for Alison's story. *Fun Home* reworks this experience in an autobiographical act of retrospective interpretation that is multiply embedded: in the familial network of other lives; in the psychic pull of deep identifications around gender and sexuality; in the commingling of literary and popular identity discourses that intersect in particular ways at a given historical moment; and in the interplay of views on and views of the artist-maker as a self-construction always in process, in the reflexive exchange of hand, eye, and thought. As Nancy K. Miller observes, "Autobiography's story is about the web of entanglement in which we find ourselves, one that we *sometimes* choose" ("Entangled" 44, my emphasis). By working on and working through several aspects of the generational, personal, psychosexual, and political entanglements of family life, *Fun Home* maps new ground in life narrative.

Fun Home is, however, fundamentally different from verbal autobiography. By engaging with and drawing a range of visual forms, Bechdel emphasizes that cartoon representation, as a genuinely hybrid form or "out-law" genre of autobiography in Caren Kaplan's term, is a multimodal form different from both written life narrative and visual or photographic self-portraiture.[2] At the same time it is intertextual, incorporating a wealth of Modernist literary references into comics that turns the form into a forum on the multi-textual pastiche of contemporary culture. As a result, *Fun Home* invites—and requires—readers to read differently, to attend to disjunctions between the cartoon panel and the verbal text, to disrupt the seeming forward motion of the cartoon sequence and adopt a reflexive and recursive reading practice. As Hillary Chute and Marianne DeKoven argue, "comics is constituted in verbal and visual narratives that do not merely synthesize. . . . The medium of comics is cross-discursive because it is composed of verbal and visual narratives that . . . remain distinct" (769).[3] Gillian Whitlock has coined the term "autographics" to call attention to the representational strategies of graphic memoirs and the vocabularies mobilized by the possibilities of cartooning. Whitlock observes, "I mean to draw attention to the specific conjunctions of visual and verbal text in this genre of autobiography, and also to the subject positions that narrators negotiate in and through comics" ("Autographics" 966). *Fun Home*'s improvisations upon the terms of autobiography in its graphic disclosures draw on the hybrid form of autographics to explore complex formations of gender and sexuality in the modern family.

The practice of composing autobiography implies doubling the self, as its practitioners, from Montaigne on, and critics, notably James Olney in *Metaphors of Self*, have long observed. That splitting of self into observer and observed is redoubled in autographics, where the dual media of words and drawing, and their segmentation into boxes, panels, and pages, offer multiple possibilities for interpreting experience, reworking memory, and staging self-reflection. Whitlock has proposed the provocative term "autobiographical avatars" to characterize the drawn personae of cartoonists in graphic memoirs, noting how their self-reflexive practices use cartoon drawing not only as a form of self-portraiture, but to "engage with the conventions of comics" ("Autographics" 971). The term "avatars" recalls the new popular media of unstructured virtual role-playing environments such as *Second Life*, where game players choose visual self-representatives (called avatars), often quite different from themselves, to play roles and interact in virtual space; as such, the avatar implies new possibilities for forging identity in autographics.[4]

The way we read cartoons, as a pleasurable alternative to high seriousness, also affords occasions for reader identification with characters and situations that solicit our autobiographical intimacy. In commenting on Scott McCloud's argument about the cartoon as a "vacuum into which our identity and awareness are pulled," so that instead of just observing the cartoon "we become it" (36), Whitlock suggests how differently autobiographical practices work in this verbal-visual medium (*Soft* 191). Representation of the artist's face in particular, she observes, may serve as an icon that elicits identifications with our own image, thereby changing the reader-viewer experience. And this process of recognition in cartooning assuredly resonates for the artist-autobiographer as well. As Jared Gardner observes, "comics do open up (inevitably and necessarily) a space for the reader to pause, between the panels, and make meaning out of what she sees and reads" ("Archives" 791), thereby serving as "collaborative texts between the imagination of the author/artist and the imagination of the reader who must complete the narrative" ("Archives" 800). *Fun Home* calls upon readers to be literate in many kinds of texts—not only comics and Modernist literature but feminist history and lesbian coming-out stories, as well as many modes of the decorative arts—as a sophisticated and politically impassioned community.

Notes Toward a Reading—Graphing the Split Subject of *Fun Home*

As a self-reflexive autographic, *Fun Home*'s narrative world is bisected by "splits" of several sorts. Some are enabled by two structural principles: the resonance between the autobiographical avatar Alison and her father Bruce, as the telling of her life is shadowed by the mysteries of his; and the autographic play between the graphics of Alison's and her family's story inside the comics' frame and the ironic detachment of the discursive narrator Bechdel's voiceover comments in boxes above. But Bechdel's elaborately constructed narrative framework goes beyond notions of what a "relational autographic" might imply. (Indeed, the notion of relational life narrative is both too capacious and too vague, as

Nancy K. Miller has suggested—a fuzzy concept we might abandon in order to think more precisely and creatively about how the autobiographical plays out in family stories.[5]) The narrative set-up of *Fun Home* depends on both the perception that characters occupy opposed positions and the eventual dissolution or reversal of these apparent binaries in a process that Bechdel, drawing on Proust, calls a "network of [narrative] transversals" (102). To chart a way through the intriguing complexity of *Fun Home*, I want to briefly suggest several sites of "splitting," before going on to discuss the autographic interplay between drawn photographs and cartoons that underwrites Bechdel's mapping of sexual legacies over generations. The following series may offer prospects for further theorizing.

The narrative is split between a solo story, Bechdel's child narrator Alison's development of an "I," and the domestic ethnography of the family, punningly presented as both artistic and autistic (Figure 1).[6] This "dysfunctional" unhappy family evokes a literary tradition of the modern novel, referenced in the copy of *Anna Karenina* lying on the floor on the first page of Chapter One. The family's oddity is not only experienced by young Alison, who at ten develops obsessive-compulsive disorder (OCD); it is also diagnosed by her, in her dual role as patient and therapist, trying to parent her parents via Dr. Spock's famed manual *Baby and Child Care*. In a further conflation of identities and intertexts, she situates her narrative as a reworking of the Icarus-Daedalus myth, telling a story of her relationship to her father in which the parental and child positions are complexly reversed, and the inheritor of the parental legacy—who, in an inversion of Icarus, survives—is a woman.

In a different sense the narrative acknowledges its origin as split between verbal and visual modes of diary-keeping, suggesting Bechdel's dual aspiration to become a writer and an artist. After Alison's father urges her to keep a journal when she is ten to help manage her OCD (initially on a wall calendar from a burial vault company, 140), she faithfully keeps a diary for years. It is initially

Figure 1. Excerpted from FUN HOME: A Family Tragicomic by Alison Bechdel (top: p. 134 bottom; bottom: p. 139 bottom). Copyright © 2006 by Alison Bechdel. Reprinted by permission of Houghton Mifflin Harcourt Publishing Company. All rights reserved.

a non-committal record of events, but with puberty, becomes a site to encode discoveries about her lesbian identity, aided by library books on coming out that open a new world to her. But the preteen notes she dutifully jots down are gradually engulfed by the emergence and persistence of a "curvy circumflex" (143), an upside-down "V" that marks moments of subjective doubt, as Jared Gardner discusses (*Biography* 3–5). As Alison's diary drawings, like a palimpsest, come to engulf her tentative verbal narrative, Bechdel's story of coming to artistic consciousness is visually mapped. *Fun Home*, as an autobiographical Künstlerroman, glosses Joyce's *Portrait of the Artist*, with Stephen Dedalus as one alter ego for Alison; but it also remakes the genre's emphasis on forging language in the smithy of the artist's soul by emphasizing Alison's fascination with the image, cartooning, and visual detail generally as a means of both perceiving and representing her world. We might ask how the current outpouring of comics about becoming an artist modifies our assumptions about the Künstlerroman as the story of the growth of artistic consciousness.[7] As a narrative form particularly widespread among women practitioners of the "New Comics," the artist's story can be reworked to tell ethnically specific stories, as Melinda Luisa de Jesús has observed.[8]

Furthermore, *Fun Home*, as an origin story, makes a genealogical connection between Alison's efforts at parental management and pleasure in visual record-keeping and her father's compulsive personality, shown in his archivist habits—his elaborately decorated personal library (drawn in exquisite detail with embossed wallpaper and busts of writers), his meticulous attention to personal records, his artistic bent expressed in fastidious house-decorating and gardening, and his precision as a mortician. The story of "blood" as the legacy of character and desire, linking the artistic and the psychosexual, is thematized as an explanatory myth that, when understood, enables Alison to incorporate a past she initially did not understand and could have feared or despised. And the genealogical narrative casts back speculatively through generations of her father's family to link land, immigration, and childhood experience to the formation of subjectivity.

Located at the "split" or juncture of disparate media, *Fun Home* also exploits, through multilayered visual play, the flatness of the page by introducing three-dimensional depth into the frame. Its dazzling textual collages of drawn objects often interact to form a kind of meta-commentary on the comic page as a site of intertexuality. The panels, gutters, and page, as bounded and delimited visual space, allow texturing of the two-dimensional image through collage, counterpoint, the superimposition of multiple media, and self-referential gestures (such as the drawn hands holding pages that I discuss below). Bechdel's rich exploitation of visual possibilities places *Fun Home* at an autobiographical interface where disparate modes of self-inscription intersect and comment upon one another.[9]

For example, at the start of Chapter Two (the bottom of page 27), a drawn cover of Camus's *A Happy Death*, the book her father was reading when he died, overlaps *The Express*, the local newspaper referencing the month of her father's death. Both lie on his desk with car keys and letters (Figure 2). A kind of still-life memento mori, it refers back to another copy of *The Express* at the top of the same page, dated two days later, whose headline proclaims her father's death after being hit by a truck. This texturing situates the memory of the everyday in its lived density and poignancy and registers it as a visual archive.[10] *Fun Home* is an encyclopedic display of visual modes, from detailed topological maps and schematic charts to drawings of notebooks, notably Alison's diary, incised within the frame on the page we are reading. Bechdel also adopts the tagging style of other cartoonists occasionally as a kind of intertextual riff. For example, a frame depicting the "fragrances" of Greenwich Village that the family encounters on a visit marks the odors with seven rectangular tags, referencing Julie Doucet's irreverent style of cataloging the urban scene (103).

Fun Home also provides a mirror for the reader's own engagement and complicity in its acts of self-reflection. Twice, Bechdel

Figure 2. Excerpted from FUN HOME: A Family Tragicomic by Alison Bechdel (p. 27 bottom). Copyright © 2006 by Alison Bechdel. Reprinted by permission of Houghton Mifflin Harcourt Publishing Company. All rights reserved.

uses near-life-sized drawings of a hand holding a sheaf of photographs to call readers' attentions to our voyeuristic looking at her intimately personal acts of investigating her father's hidden history and her own identification with it (100, 120). In the last part of this essay I discuss her graphing of spectatorial sites as a mode of metacritical autographics that Whitlock, referencing Scott McCloud, sees as offering readers a particular kind of autobiographical identification (*Soft* 191) (see Figure 6).

The play with mirroring and illusion is also taken up peritextually. There is a tension in *Fun Home* between its decorous cover and the graphic disclosures inside, much as a funeral home's display galleries mask the work done in its back rooms—or how the placid surface of small-town, middle-class, mid-century America hid seething tensions around gender and sexuality in the family. The book is dedicated to Bechdel's mother (who, she acknowledges, is troubled by its frank revelations) and two younger brothers, with the caption: "We did have a lot of fun in spite of everything."[11] The hardback's front cover, an elegant color scheme of teal and silver on black, frames themes of the memoir: a close-up drawing of a tabletop with an embossed silver tray for calling cards at a funeral home (with cut-outs on the tray's edges revealing the contrasting orange book binding) holds the book's title like a card, with an endorsement from autographic cartoonist Harvey Pekar ("She's one of the best") in small white letters at the top. On the back are other early review endorsements of the memoir, topped by a drawn photo inside an arch of the mother and three young children standing in a frame at the other edge of the table, a kind of funerary photo (which their father is shown taking on the bottom of page 16). The book's end papers, featuring green-shaded white chrysanthemums on a silvery teal background, imitate the wallpaper in the funeral home.[12] By contrast, the book-binding, in a vivid light orange, is a blowup of the panel depicting each family member inside a black-edged bubble in different parts of the house, in their paradoxically artistic/autistic self-focus (134). Thus *Fun Home*'s elegant presentation as an artifact invites readers inside its decorous exterior for an encounter with its graphic—in both senses—disclosures about life between the covers.

Fun Home also maps the splits in cultural views and practices that characterized the post-World War II US, torn between the norm of compulsory heterosexuality that had long coded same-sex desire as "inversion," a clinical term connoting perversion and moral decadence, and a repressed, smoldering consciousness of polymorphous sexuality that erupted in the "gay revolution" of the late sixties and early seventies, with the public protests of Stonewall (1969) and a flood of manifestoes and coming-out

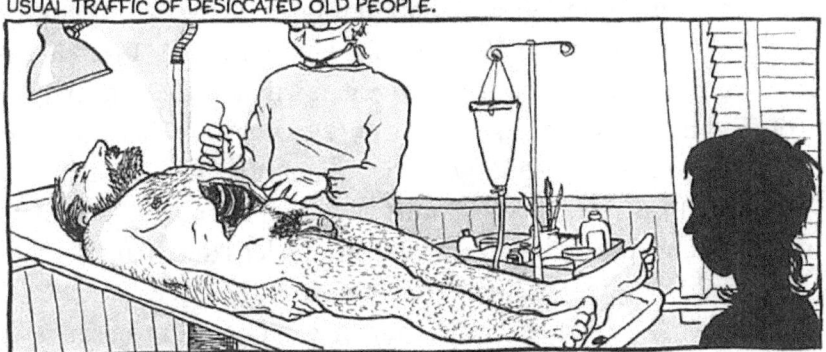

Figure 3. Excerpted from FUN HOME: A Family Tragicomic by Alison Bechdel (p. 44 top). Copyright © 2006 by Alison Bechdel. Reprinted by permission of Houghton Mifflin Harcourt Publishing Company. All rights reserved.

stories that comprise a counter-archive of modernist reading in the literary world of *Fun Home*.[13] This split between generations is marked in the contrast between her father's closeted homosexuality, with its elaborate denials and displacements, and Alison's coming-of-age story of discovering her own sexuality, awakened in early childhood by the sight of a "butch" woman and emerging through her experiments with a range of lesbian identity positions. The father's and daughter's contrasting stories anchor the narrative transversals through which Bechdel interprets the paradoxes of her family, which the form of an extended graphic memoir, unlike a weekly comic strip, enables her to track in multiple flashbacks and jagged temporalities. As readers, we are asked to trace the complex narrative arc of her coming of age and/as coming out, enacted in reverse by her father's covert, furtive liaisons and official heterosexuality.[14] Finally, at the memoir's end the balletic dance of their two narrated stories, in parallels and inversions of each other, sutures their sexual kinship—as a legacy both genealogical and chosen.

Perhaps the most dazzling visual display of *Fun Home* is its depiction of bodies, staged in the "theater" of the morgue.

Bechdel's drawings of newly dead bodies in the process of being embalmed or autopsied, in frontal and side views with cutaway sections, are a virtuoso Vesalian display (Figure 3). In counterpoint to the focus on bodies in rigor mortis are the drawings of erotic bodies in action, in scenes of her father's and her own sexual encounters. This begins with the originary scene of sexuality in Chapter 1, drawn from vertiginous angles, of a young Alison playing "airplane" hoisted aloft on her father's legs and hands—what she punningly refers to, in a circus term, as their acrobatic "Icarian games" (3). As their bodies mirror each other, the erotics of the father-daughter relationship are visually suggested, as well as the reverse of the Icarus-Daedalus myth, because it is Alison who will fly on the wings of homosexual desire that her father never trusted (3-4). The depiction of bodily erotics extends to graphic sexual depictions of herself—and, in drawn photographs, possibly her father—with lovers, as I will discuss. *Fun Home*'s interplay between the erotic and the necrotic generates meanings as incarnate—in bodies of desire, some positioned as "porn bodies" (viz. 214); bodies performing gender in costume or drag; bodies in the stillness of a photo or diagram, or the rigor mortis of death; and, not least, bodies connected to our own as we touch and turn the pages.

In sum, Bechdel's linkage of autographic modes and graphic disclosures creates a richly embodied subjectivity different, in its sustained semiotic cross-referencing, from the narrative consecutiveness of verbal autobiography. Like other autographic narrators (Spiegelman, Satrapi), Bechdel brilliantly deploys a wealth of autobiographical genres juxtaposed as alternative life possibilities. But the use of such templates also poses questions about life narrative in this autographic moment. How is the story of coming of age linked to or rewritten in the coming-out story (as a discovery of what was always already inherent)? How does the solitary story of the artist's growth intersect with or disrupt the family's domestic ethnography of reproducing itself? How is the melancholic process of dying and death reworked in its literary afterlife by acts of narrative reconstruction (in Bechdel, reworking the trauma of a tragic death as a literarily comic "happy ending")? How does the autobiographical meta-story, reading the experience of a youthful self against the family's official and unofficial or repressed stories, alter or improvise upon—as a chiasmic "network of transversals" or at times a kind of jazz riff—the novel-driven model of literary Modernism celebrated in the canon of Proust, Joyce, James, Wilde, Fitzgerald, Camus, and Colette's memoirs, all intertexts in *Fun Home*? And how is each autobiographical template changed by its translation into the vocabulary of cartooning? While I don't propose answers to these questions, they seem, to me, to signal the potential of this autographic moment in life narrative studies, and to invite new theorizing of subjectivity, genre, and readers' engagement with the autobiographical.

Reading between the (Ink) Lines in *Fun Home*

In its histories, both personal and political, visual and narrative, *Fun Home* offers an archival mine for new kinds of autographical readings. Jared Gardner productively explores the relationship of *Fun Home* to "autography," particularly in its relationship to the visual vocabulary of self-reference developed in cartooning practices since 1972 (*Biography* passim). Narrative theorists such as David Herman also consider Bechdel's use of visual tags or labels in the frame to mark different temporalities of experience for the narrating "I."[15] For feminist autobiography critics such as myself, Bechdel creates a richly complex storytelling world, grounded both in the everyday experience of mid-twentieth-century American small-town family life and in the feminist practice of making the personal political through hybrid forms of personal criticism.[16]

In the rest of this essay, I think about autographical practice as a visual and comparative act: by contrasting Bechdel's drawings of photographs (no actual photos are reproduced) as archival documents with the cartooned story of a remembered—and fantasized—past, we can observe how Bechdel reinterprets the authority that photos as "official histories" seem to hold, and opens them to subjective reinterpretation. In her focus on varying visual versions of her father and her wildly changing impressions of him (recorded in her diary) at different moments, Bechdel composes a textured autobiographical reflection that moves by an ongoing process of her own recursive reading. In these examples we also see Bechdel's contrast of Second-Wave feminist concepts of gendered subjectivity and sexuality (1970s) through which the teenaged Alison interprets her own experience (at times satirizing the movement's tendency to jargon-laced, dogmatic pronouncements), to a view, both performative and genealogical, that she constructs as an alternative way of reading her own sexuality in relation to—and against—her father's.

I focus on a few points in *Fun Home*—its middle, end, and beginning—to think about how its temporal sequence is punctuated by introspective acts that cast back into the past in spirals of reflection; thus the tendency of the page to impel us forward in reading the comic as a narrative sequence is repeatedly disrupted, spatialized. This itinerary for reading *Fun Home* may seem perverse, moving from the center of the book to its last page, which I take as an originary point that—in recursive fashion—returns us to a different reading of the drawn photograph with which the book's first chapter begins.[17] But in this narrative so concerned with *transversals*, the movement toward reversing characters' positions as a story develops, and *inversions*, the traditional term coding homosexuals as inverts of normative heterosexual identity, we are asked to read via this to-and-fro movement. Its arc traces the links Bechdel makes between Alison's narrative present and the memories of childhood that intrude, and the family's repressive past and her own liberatory future. We follow how her narrative sets up the possibility of both closure—on the traumatic past of her father's death, probably a suicide—and opening to her own adult life.

Who's Looking? Discursive Intersections at the Centerfold

In *Fun Home* drawings of photographs (no actual photo reproductions are used) play a central role. Photos from her family's past (some hidden from the children) serve not only as evocations of memory but as evidence of the material reality of what Bechdel investigates as her father's double life. But her work depends on photographs in a second, uniquely contemporary way. As she described to Hillary Chute, Bechdel created a reference photograph with her digital camera for each pose (there are nearly 1,000) in each panel of *Fun Home*, photographing *herself* as the actor for each subject (parent, child, etc.). Her acts of impersonation give a new resonance to the autographical, as she has in a sense literally "tried on" all of the subject positions she depicts—sometimes wryly, as when she notes on a promotional DVD that she had to pose for each parent when they had a fight (Chute, "Gothic" 3). We cannot know to what extent she also literally "inhabited," as a model, the realistically drawn photographs that figure importantly in her chapter heads, or the photos I discuss that document "secret" intimacies. But her practice suggests ways in which she empathically—and quite literally—could imagine the positions of her characters. And while using drawn photos would seem to guarantee the separate existence of others, Bechdel's technique unsettles that boundary. In a narrative interested in the permeability of categories of gender and sexuality, the potential for slipping into "all the poses" in acts of autographical identification is provocative.

Fun Home incorporates photographs in several ways: as the chapter head image for each chapter, and at key moments throughout the narrative, where the act of rereading them—some only discovered after her father's death—is the impetus to her own acts of recognition and autobiographical identification with her father's desire embedded in a complicated history of overt heterosexuality and closeted transgression with young boys. The chapter head photos are done in a meticulously drawn realistic style, with much shading and cross-hatching, that differs from her cartooning style. In using photos to frame its chapters, *Fun Home* is allied to the family album, but also marks a distance from its function as official history by reading photos for their transgressive content. At strategic moments, photos also offer Alison occasions for introspection, as she rereads her past to discover untold family stories. And our spectatorial complicity links us, as viewer-readers, with these acts of looking that raise questions about the nature of visual evidence and the possibility of viewers' empathic recognition.

Chapter 4, "In the Shadow of Young Girls in Flower," the middle of *Fun Home*'s seven chapters, is a key one for thinking about this interplay of family histories.[18] It narrates moments that link Alison's teenaged declaration of her lesbian sexuality with "secret"—at least to his family—moments from her father's young adulthood that she discovers only after his death in a box of photographs. And it offers, via linking their stories of transgressive sexual desire to Proust's novels, a framework for reading the narrative not as linear but as a recursively spiraling story along a "network of transversals." Referencing Proust's model of convergence as a structure for producing reader recognition of the desires that bond characters in seemingly oppositional social positions, Bechdel parallels their two lives as a gay father and daughter. Wittily she observes that they are linked not only as sexual "inverts," in the derogatory psychoanalytic term of the early century that Proust used (97), but also as inverted versions of each other in the family. That is, she presents Alison's rejection of femininity as a compensation for her father's lack of manliness, and his insistence on her dressing and acting "feminine" as a projection of his own desire to perform femininity (98).

This and subsequent chapters depict Alison's own adolescent coming of age as always a coming-out story, and provide a context for imagining the story her father did not, could not, tell his family, and that, she suggests, fueled his artistic obsession with order and design, as well as his authoritarian parenting. Recalling the several young men who floated through the family's life, culled from her father's high-school classes and cultivated "like orchids" (95) for future plucking, Alison recognizes an ideal of masculinity she herself aspires to. Called "Butch" by her cousins for her tomboy prowess (96), the young Alison—Al, she would prefer—is critical of her father as a "sissy," a version of the identity he attempts to enforce on her (90). Bechdel thus rereads the surface memoir of her childhood as an analysis of how gender binaries are sustained within the family. Her father's imposing of conventional feminine norms of dress and behavior in the effort to "make a girl of her" conceals his own story of discovering the feminine within himself and rejecting the masculine within her. The adult narrator thus frames the negotiations by which, within the constraints of the family, father and daughter displaced onto each other versions of conventional femininity and masculinity as a way of enacting their refusal of conventional heteronormative gender roles. In this version of the coming-out story, there is no simple narrative of rebellion against parental strictures by transgressive performance; rather, she and her father are linked in both a contest of wills and a deep affinity of desires.

The core of Bechdel's coming-of-age/coming-out story occurs in her recognition that she and her father could meet only at a phantom middle, a "slender demilitarized zone," in the appreciation of the pubescent male body as an epitome of androgynous beauty (99). At this evanescent point the family legacy of desire materializes across generations and genders. A double-page literal centerfold at the middle of the chapter, and the book, stages this insight (100–101). It shows a large drawing of a photo recovered from Bruce's secret stash of photos, dated "AUG 69" (the year blotted out), of their babysitter Roy that her father took in a hotel room he had arranged for when the boy was traveling with them on vacation without their mother (Alison the eldest was 8).[19] The photo of Roy's body as a vulnerable, yet cheesecake, spectacle is held in the twice-life-sized fingers of a left hand; it

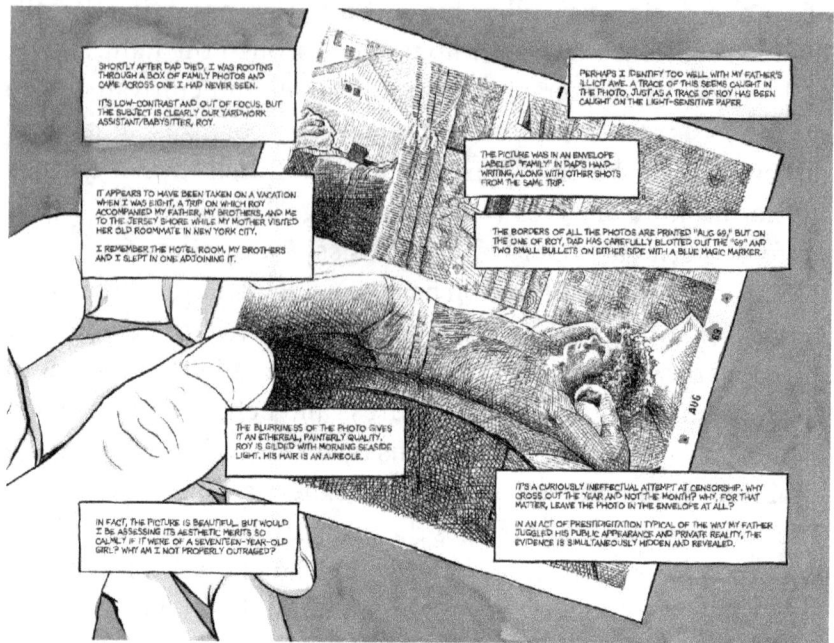

Figure 4. Excerpted from FUN HOME: A Family Tragicomic by Alison Bechdel (p. 100–101). Copyright © 2006 by Alison Bechdel. Reprinted by permission of Houghton Mifflin Publishing Company. All rights reserved.

reminds us of our complicity as viewers in this intimate glimpse, as our hand holding the book overlaps hers. In the photo a single young male body lies asleep on a bed with two pillows, his tousled head held between his upthrown arms, his torso, clad only in briefs, inclined toward the viewer (Figure 4). The drawn photo is surrounded by elongated dialogue tags that chronicle Bechdel's conflicted responses, acknowledging both her identification with her father's erotic desire for the aesthetic perfection of the boy's body, and her distanced critique as a sleuth of this evidence of his secret life.

These multiple responses are filtered through several autobiographical discourses: the memory of the occasion and their motel rooms by the Jersey shore; aesthetic appreciation for the "ethereal, painterly" quality of light with which Roy is "gilded" in the photograph (100); self-recrimination that she's not "properly outraged" at her father's pederastic desire; acknowledgement of her complicity in his "illicit awe" of the near-naked boy's beauty (101); detached assessment of her father's characteristic attempt to censor his possible sexual transgression by masking when the shot was taken; and recognition that her father's management of the contradictions of his public and private lives made him a magician in managing his double life (101). Thus she acts as a kind of detective, hunting the evidence of her father's secret life that was hidden in their everyday interactions, and rereading family photographs for evidence of his covert homosexuality. The apparent contradictions of his and her mother's apparently dutiful lives, like those of Swann and the Guermantes, begin to converge as Bechdel reimagines her father's life as a separate subject, rather than a relative, before she was born, imputing to him an intriguing gay subjectivity that she does not extend to her mother (102).

Telling the story of his repressed desire and associating it with her own coming out in 1980 and early experiences as a lesbian subjected to social humiliations, she bridges their generational divide and different lifestyles by asking herself, "Would I have had the guts to be one of those Eisenhower-era bitches? Or would I have married and sought succor from my high school students?" (108). This act of cross-generational empathy contextualizes her own coming of age in "a precocious feat of Proustian transposition" (113). Like life in the shadows à la Proust, the confusion occasioned by Alison's adolescent sexuality which impeded her desire to grow up as a boy, and her active disidentification as a child with the eroticized female body of "girlie" calendars (112), as well as the challenge of a big "phallic" snake the children encountered on a camping trip and were unable to kill (114–15), rewrite the conventional coming-out story. Not willing to appropriate either stereotypic position of normative gendered identity, Bechdel's fable argues for undoing gender binaries, seeing the serpent as a "vexingly ambiguous archetype" (116).

In its place, the narrative proposes a more fluid understanding of identification and desire, in which seeming oppositions are revealed to have always been convergent. In refusing a conventional coming out narrative of rebellion against strict paternal authority that opts for a pre-Oedipal fusion with the maternal, Bechdel bonds with her father's desire and revises her childhood yearning for erotic connection into a recognition of how she is like him.[20] That is, her story of coming to consciousness rewrites the feminist narrative of maternal bonding as a desire for fusion (for her the mother remains a shadowy figure), and ventures into the deep water of identification and desire across what become arbitrary boundaries of gender.

Bechdel's story about the meaning of Alison's childhood memories not only links her sense of her own sexuality to her father's secret gay side, it also produces a recognition about how their lives are linked over generations: "You could say that my father's end was my beginning. Or more precisely, that the end of his lie coincided with the beginning of my truth" (117). In depicting, through visual details of her father's dress, hair, gestures, and notebooks—as well as the series of young men in the house—the coming-out story that he, historically and temperamentally, was unable to tell, Bechdel interweaves his narrative with her own search for a partner, linking their desires. The story thus retrospectively offers Bruce an identity alternative to the one he has lived, based in rigid repression and fear of being branded as perverse and criminal (he is arrested for buying beer for a 13-year-old boy [161]). And Bechdel supplements the post-mortem coming-out narrative she authors for her father with an endearing origin story of her own sexuality, which tellingly occurs in a moment with her father.

In retrospect, Bechdel recalls that Alison's pivotal childhood moment of recognizing her lesbian identity occurred early, when she was about four or five. Lunching with her father at a truck-stop restaurant while he is on a business trip, she spots a "truck-driving bulldyke" with close-cropped hair in a checked flannel shirt (119, Figure 5). Recalling, "I recognized her with a surge of joy," the young Alison contrasts her own identification, presented as innate and "hard-wired," with her father's ongoing disapproval of her rejection of femininity (118). Her desire to recast her gender assignment is balanced by his discomfiture with the public exhibit of what he perceives as transgressive sexuality, and repeated throughout the chapter in cartoons that contrast his fastidiously dressed and combed presence with her rakish tomboy looks.

And yet, the chapter concludes, for all their tensions over her childhood refusal to conform to the stereotypic femininity required by her father's need to mask his own closeted homosexual desire and to preserve a public image of respectability, telling their story and juxtaposing cartoons of his feminized presence and her boyish recasting of it shows, in repeated near-mirror images, their genealogical and psychological bond. In Alison's refusal of compulsory heterosexuality as both a coming-of-age and coming-out story, Bechdel daringly rewrites features of that narrative to insist on her cross-gender identification with the repressed desire that underlay her father's overt heterosexual conformity.

Strikingly, late in Chapter 7, appropriately titled "The Antihero's Journey," there is a scene in which father and daughter attempt to reveal their coming-out stories to each other. The moment occurs after Alison has sent her parents her coming-out letter when she is back from college for the summer, and shortly before Bruce's death. The two-page sequence is the only time that Bechdel uses the square box-style of the traditional comic book, and she employs it for a tightly framed sequence of headshots depicting the dialogue between Alison and Bruce as they drive to see a movie (which she ironically refers to in Joycean terms as their "Ithaca" moment of shared aesthetic sensitivity [222]). The tightly framed two-shots of their profiles dramatize a moment of intimate disclosure. When Alison attempts to broach the subject of sexuality by noting that it was her father who gave her Colette's *Earthly Paradise* (a compilation of her autobiographical writings) to read at 14—with its passages of lesbian pleasure—he interrupts

Figure 5. Excerpted from FUN HOME: A Family Tragicomic by Alison Bechdel (p. 118). Copyright © 2006 by Alison Bechdel. Reprinted by permission of Houghton Mifflin Harcourt Publishing Company. All rights reserved.

and begins to tell her his own story of adolescent homosexual experience and his childhood desire to dress up as a girl, which she remarks paralleled her desire to dress as a boy. While the exchange of disclosures is brief and hardly celebratory (*Ulysses*, not the *Odyssey*, she notes wryly), it is as close as they come to a moment of shared coming-out stories. Might we see the graphic mode of three-box panels, four per page, as a kind of visual match for two central aspects of the lesbian coming-out story?[21] The focus on tight-framed intimate exchange parallels what Biddy Martin has defined as its parameters: the specific and intimate disclosure of originary experience to a sympathetic listener; and the circulation and publication of coming-out stories in activist magazines and journals (88–90). With its alternation of their "then-time" dialogue bubbles on white, and Bechdel's retrospective reflection in white type on a black background, the two pages on "our shared predilection" bracket a kind of breakthrough moment in sexual disclosure shared intergenerationally between father and daughter (rather than the more usual exchange with the same-sex parent) (222). In marking their homosexual bond, however tentative and brief it is, by creating a graphic analogue to the coming-out story, Bechdel enacts a complex homage that links Colette, Joyce, and lesbian coming-out stories while rewriting the analysis of how that desire is understood.

Photographic "Translation" and Graphic Intimacies

Bechdel's autographic act of drawing—and reading—family photos, her father's and her own, frames her autographic story as a quest to situate her own desire in a familial line that both "outs" and reclaims her father. Enacting a kind of Freudian "Nachträglichkeit"—recognition achieved in reflection after a traumatic event through reworking the story—Bechdel concludes Alison's coming-of-age chapter, "In the Shadow of Young Girls in Flower," with a meditation on photographic evidence that suggests how her autographic narration is rooted in acts of looking and seeing differently. On its last page (120), the story of coming of age as coming out is broken off as Alison reflects, in a metanarrative, on "what's lost in translation," by constructing an autographic dialogic of recognition and melancholic loss focused on a set of photos (120). Here, as with the centerfold at the chapter's middle, Bechdel presents a set of three drawn photos (one repeated) (Figure 6). The juxtaposed photos of her own and her father's bodies, his recovered from a box retrieved after his death, show each of them posing before a sympathetic photographer who may be the subject's lover. Each is cradled in one of Alison's near life-sized drawn hands, again implicating us as viewer-voyeurs of her intimate disclosure. These photos expunged from the family album become an occasion for probing the complex meanings of genealogical attachment as both transmission across generations and melancholy loss of primary relationship.

The drawn photo in the top frame, from her father's college days, depicts him in a woman's bathing suit as a convincing spectacle of femininity in drag. However much the occasion may have been a prank, his impersonation strikes Bechdel as "lissome, elegant," a persuasive act of gender-crossing (120). In the bottom panel, that photograph is behind two others held in her hands. The left is another drawn photo from her father's college days. Sunbathing in sunglasses, open-mouthed and limp-wristed in relaxation, he leans toward the camera, his bare chest and splayed legs a seeming gesture of invitation to the invisible photographer, whom the narrator speculates may have been his lover. The bottom drawn photo on the right shows Alison at the same age on a fire escape with a similar open-mouthed look and relaxed-wrist gesture, in a bathrobe that both "masculinizes" and covers the naked body beneath. She is also inclining toward the photographer, who was indeed her lover. The father-daughter affinity is reflected not only in their shared features, but in their parallel acts of cross-dressing against conventional norms of sexuality. Of these parallel "invitational" photos of father and daughter, the narrator observes: "It's about as close as a translation can get" (120).

Several things are striking here. First, to the casual viewer the resemblance of the two subjects may seem merely familial, but by "inhabiting" the photos through imagining her father's cross-dressing (with his gestures as well as bathing suit) and recalling her own body, Alison insists on the meaning of genealogical connection as a transmission of sexuality and desire in a way that both exceeds and precedes gender-specific binaries of "masculine" and "feminine." As visual evidence, the photos make the case for their shared same-sex orientation, and "prove" that he was fundamentally gay, despite his adult parental life, counteracting his official

Figure 6. Excerpted from FUN HOME: A Family Tragicomic by Alison Bechdel (p. 120). Copyright © 2006 by Alison Bechdel. Reprinted by permission of Houghton Mifflin Harcourt Publishing Company. All rights reserved.

heterosexual identity and complicating his motives for committing suicide. But in this photo-documentation of the coming-out script that her father refused to tell, we also observe Bechdel's "interested" act of looking at a resemblance that viewers may find less evident. Calling this genealogical mapping of bodies and desires a "translation," a vocabulary of words for a visual act, also recalls Bechdel's invocation of Proust as evidence in support of her father's gay legacy. Her situating of him as a Modernist artist-intellectual with whom she can empathically identify, despite their troubled history, creates a narrative afterlife that reclaims and memorializes him, while embedding a position for herself in the family story as both its creator and artistic flowering.

Figure 7. Excerpted from FUN HOME: A Family Tragicomic by Alison Bechdel (p. 1). Copyright © 2006 by Alison Bechdel. Reprinted by permission of Houghton Mifflin Harcourt Publishing Company. All rights reserved.

Artificer Paradises

The photo on the chapter-head for the first chapter of *Fun Home*, "Old Father, Old Artificer," is another drawing from a photo of a much younger Bruce Bechdel (Figure 7). Although there is no explanatory comment for the chapter-head photos, they invite our close looking. Here the title phrase is taken from Stephen Dedalus's entry at the end of Joyce's *Portrait of the Artist as a Young Man*, an autobiographical novel of coming to artistic consciousness that plays throughout the memoir.[22] Although the photo may not initially register on readers, after thinking about the stakes of photographic evidence in Chapter 4, we may return to look at Bruce with a new understanding of his vulnerable, bare-chested upper torso, heavy-lidded eyes, and tousled hair (all of which recall the photo of Roy) as he stands before the family house. This choice of an actual photo of her father, showing an erotic rather than conventionally dutiful parental image, has an almost androgynous uncanniness.[23] Although Bechdel would not have had to pose for this drawing, the thin body resembles drawings of Alison, so that it is possible for viewers to map her body onto his. We begin to *see* autographically how the daughter-narrator imaginatively inhabits her father by a cross-generational act of identification. Not only does she resemble him, but her drawing traces his photograph and merges his image with her own, in claiming his artistic and sexual legacy. If for Wordsworth the child is father to the man, here the daughter links her identity to performing an act of creative mourning for her dead father. By graphing and authoring the coming-out narrative he could not tell, Bechdel makes her father's story of private shame, "perversion," and early violent death into a happier story that enabled her own embrace of sexuality as their shared "erotic truth." Finally, this photo tells a story not of artificiality but of artifactual making, a memorializing disclosure that moves us in *Fun Home*'s snake-like recursive tale back to its beginning.

"Spiritual Paternity" at the Graphic Fault Line

The last page of *Fun Home* juxtaposes two panels on the page that require readers to situate ourselves imaginatively as viewers and reflect on our spectatorial positions (Figure 8). The top third is a full frontal close-up of a truck (Sunbeam Bread) seen from a low angle. It can only be the point of view of a subject about to be struck, annihilated, a terrifying view of impending death that is anxiety-producing to confront. The dialogue box superimposed across the grill refers to Icarus's fall, which Bechdel has just mused about, as a "what if" that conjoins her reflection on "spiritual paternity" (231) in Joyce (*Ulysses* had a better future than his children) and Icarus (if he'd had his father's inventiveness, could he have survived?) as modes of the antihero whom both her father (in a letter [230]) and Stephen Dedalus proclaim themselves to be. Although I cannot take up the many strands of "erotic truth" that Bechdel here brings into convergence, clearly the frame of the truck inexorably close and head-on suggests a brutal finality to life's creativity.

But that graphic is juxtaposed across a narrow gutter without words to the frame below it, double its size, in which the implacable finality of death is reinterpreted. It depicts a young Alison, drawn from behind, on the edge of a diving board, in mid-air over a pool, while her father, arms outstretched, waits to catch her when she jumps. It captures, as well, Alison's quest to come of age, come out, and come to truth about the mysteries of her father's life. And the graphic act of imagining the moment of her father's death, with its question of why he went back into the road after crossing it, is linked for teenaged Alison to her guilt that a letter to her parents announcing her coming out as a lesbian may have motivated the act as a suicide, prodding her to seek closure. Finally, the frame also recalls—and reverses—the Icarus-Daedalus myth, because Bechdel's retelling of the story of her father's life, for all its duplicities and shame, as intertwined with her own, enables her to "fly" as an artist and woman.

Figure 8. Excerpted from FUN HOME: A Family Tragicomic by Alison Bechdel (p. 232). Copyright © 2006 by Alison Bechdel. Reprinted by permission of Houghton Mifflin Harcourt Publishing Company. All rights reserved.

The conjunction of these opposed "tragic" and "comic" (happy ending) images is startling, and demands that viewers seek some kind of closure to resolve the paradox. Why does Bechdel reserve this set of frames for the memoir's final page, presented out of chronology from the story of her father's death (the focus of Chapter 2, "A Happy Death") and her own developmental narrative? Bechdel's ending offers readers an autographic perplex in the sense Whitlock has described: "Comics are not a mere hybrid of graphic arts and prose fiction, but a unique interpretation that transcends both, and emerge through the imaginative work of closure that readers are required to make between the panels on the page" ("Autographics" 968–69, referencing McCloud [92]). In this context we may also consider to what extent the moment referenced in the bottom panel is memory or fantasy. Little in the narrative suggests that Bruce, a meticulous, critical father (whom Alison rarely touched and recalls kissing on the arm only once—see 19) was, in her experience, as supportive as the drawing depicts.

Reading autographically suggests a possible closure, and a way to link the "tragic" top frame, in which the viewer graphically confronts a moment of deathly violence, to the bottom frame, in which we are invited to "stand behind" Alison. This final cartoon is a reversal of the camera's point of view on their positions in the drawn photograph that begins Chapter 7, "The Antihero's Journey"—the title recalling both *Portrait* and *Ulysses*, as well as many other novels referenced in *Fun Home*. Unlike the photo, it is a close-up, drawn from an angle that places the spectator on the diving board with young Alison, as she hovers before jumping. The drawing thus revisions the chapter's opening snapshot. In it, Bechdel's reverse-shot focus emphasizes her father's face and outstretched hands, perhaps conflating memory and fantasy, to make his paternal act one of tenderness and "spiritual" nurturance (just as the preceding pages, in which Bruce is leading Alison in the pool, depict him as a supportive teacher). And this final frame invites us to imaginatively accompany her leap—into life and sexuality, reversed and interpreted autographically. The frame's dialogue box about "tricky reverse narration" references the switch of both angles of view and gestural affect from the beginning drawn photo to the final frame of the book. It also captures the larger reversal of positions in which Bechdel meshes Bruce's history with Alison's as a transmission of sexual stories that impels her comics and enables her to become the author of their stories. Thus Bechdel's final cartoon of the family past is a deeply satisfying memorialization of her father's parental legacy. It suggests that the process of working through her own history, by narratively scripting the coming out that her father could not enact, and refusing to reject him as either "perverted" or failed, rescues him by showing his arms-out gesture of willingness to rescue her.

For Bechdel, as for another autographic self-maker, Charlotte Salomon, the last page of the narrative functions as a kind of signature.[24] This page's two graphic images can be related only by inhabiting both imagined spectatorial positions, and observing how their reversals complete the recursive circuit that repeatedly disrupts our reading of *Fun Home* "forward" in historical time. The reader's transversal of the network of the narrative becomes, if we attend to its autographic connections, an experience of how life is lived forwards but recognized backwards, as autobiographical consciousness.[25] That is, in some sense the autobiographical is inevitably a reworking of lived experience as filtered through memory, fantasy, and reflection across multiple sites of identity and processes of dis/identification. Thus narrative depends in a sense on the death of the past, even as the act of narrating revivifies it for the autobiographer. The narrating I may, in a familiar metaphor, come to voice, to instantiate a "newborn" subjectivity, as Bechdel does in the act of narrating a "dead" past. Such a narrative reminds us of the function of storytelling generally, as a process of retelling life experience of trauma and disappointment until the teller discovers some form of resolution that can both acknowledge pain and provide the closure of a happier ending.

The page's shocking conjunction of a moment of violent finality with one of creative birth situates their interlocked stories graphically across a narrow gutter that is both gap and suture: "His end was my beginning" (117).

Speaking Autographically

In a graphic memoir as densely intertextual as *Fun Home*, with its letters, diaries, maps, and citations from and readings of twentieth-century novels, how can the difference of the autographical be specified? As Sean Wilsey observed, Bechdel's writing, unlike that of most cartoon memoirists, is lucid, articulate, and full of "big words," addressing a new cosmopolitan readership able to move between "high" and "pop" forms. Does that make her text just an illustrated autobiography? If not, what can *Fun Home* tell us about the distinctiveness of autographics? My discussion suggests that *Fun Home* is narrated not through the linear chronology of a developmental story, but in a recursive pattern of returns and reversals punctuated by the rhythmic movement of self-questioning and self-commentary.[26] As we have seen, the story ends in its beginning through visual connections between photos and memory images; and it repeatedly casts back—to past events, to genealogical legacy, to classical myths of artistic and erotic creation—to interpret and rework the seeming "truth" of events. In finding an interpretive closure to the two apparently unrelated panels of the last page, Bechdel locates an autobiographical act of connecting experience and interpretation at the nexus of cartoons, pictures, and words. This act of self- and paternal creation through autographical narration is a story of relationship and legacy that depends on graphically embodying and enacting, not just telling, the family story.

How do we theorize this difference of autographics? Cartoonist Ariel Schrag remarked to Hillary Chute that the connection between autobiography and comics "has to do with *visualizing memory*. Every writer incorporates their past into their work, but that act becomes more specific when you're drawing" ("Gothic," my italics). As I have suggested, Bechdel, in the many drawn photos that punctuate *Fun Home*, probes the interplay between personal memory, a kind of subjectivity imaged in cartoons, and photography, an indexical form of documentary evidence (that is, referring to objects of sight, however misleadingly). And in her readings of photos—through both words and drawings—she undermines the claim of photographs to one kind of tacit authority, and opens them to interpretation that grants them a different kind of encoded subjectivity, a legacy of family history. If the autobiographical is a sustained act of reflecting on and shaping experience to discover and invent the patterned meanings in which subjectivity is inscribed, Bechdel's drawings of images render the visual world—photographs, objects, places, others, and herself—as a set of memory mirrors that are continuously shaped and refracted by self-engagement. In *Fun Home*, the signature or autograph of the autobiographical becomes an autographic juxtaposition discoverable in acts of looking, drawing, embodying, and comparing, in an ongoing spiral of reflection.

Discussing the importance of recent graphic memoirs such as Satrapi's *Persepolis* and Spiegelman's *In the Shadow of No Towers*, Whitlock notes their use of cartoon drawing to interrogate particular images (such as the veil or the World Trade towers) that are discursively fraught and embedded in complex histories, producing dissonance as readers must reflect on the otherness they present as such ("Autographics"; especially 974–77). In thinking about the kinds of closure autographics ask readers to resist, and to make, Whitlock argues, "The unique vocabulary and grammar of comics and cartoon drawing might produce an imaginative and ethical engagement with the proximity of the other" (978). While *Fun Home* is not primarily engaged with the contemporary global moment, it implicates readers in discerning its possible closure, and in learning to practice a radical critique of sexual politics and aesthetics.

Although I have not discussed how *Fun Home* extensively parallels the context of Watergate-era Nixonian politics to the climate of repression and "covert operations" in the Bechdel family home (as Jared Gardner's *Biography* essay explores), its politics of the personal, a foundational feminist perception, is writ large in two ways: its reframing of homosexuality across the generations and the sexes, and its situating of sexual desire as a struggle to assert bodies and pleasures in the face of an American history of pathologizing them. By interpreting her familial story as a narrative of middle-class American family life filtered through the social persecution of dissident artists in the later twentieth century, Bechdel graphs the personal as a site of struggle for liberation that has analogs in human rights battles being waged around the world, particularly for homosexuals and women. Bechdel uses her "autobiographical avatars" to induce readers to engage with "othering" practices that have habitually subjected homosexuals to dismissal and persecution as either perverse or diseased. Readers engaging with *Fun Home*'s "tricky" narrative sequence and multiple, disparate modes of self-inscription are brought, by its recursive autographic strategies, to question the social privileging of normative heterosexuality, as we take up its invitation to put ourselves empathically in its intimate picture. Holding *Fun Home*'s engaging pages in our hands, we may occupy unfamiliar reading positions and be brought to reinterpret initial assumptions, to weigh the apparent authority of archival evidence against the erotic truth of a repertoire of experiences. Its autographics stirs and persuades us to approach human histories and bodies in new and provocative ways, as through the pleasures of humor and cartoons we come to engage affectively and ethically with the complex, overlapping worlds *Fun Home* presents.

Notes

Author's Note: for illuminating conversations about *Fun Home* I am indebted to the expertise and generosity of Jared Gardner, who steered me to this project and offered insights about the comics; Gillian Whitlock for her perceptive and illuminating suggestions; Robyn Warhol, feminist narratologist par excellance; members of the Queer Studies Reading Group at Ohio State University, particularly Anne Langendorfer, Mary Thomas, and Cynthia Burack, who let me join their discussion of Bechdel's memoir; my Comparative Studies graduate seminar in Winter 2008 for fruitful discussions; and the Billy Ireland Cartoon Library & Museum at The Ohio State University for its resources and sponsorship of the academic conference on cartoons on October 25, 2007, at which I presented a draft of this essay.

1. The comic strips have been collected into several books, appearing every two years, with titles such as *Hot, Throbbing Dykes to Watch Out For*. The bi-weekly syndicated comic is now posted online at Bechdel's website and archive.
2. Caren Kaplan characterizes a range of combinatory autobiographical forms as "outlaw genre" practices because they transgress the law of genre and enact hybridized possibilities of narration. Melinda Luisa de Jesús points out that many contemporary ethnic American women's graphic narratives develop more specific versions of a "hybrid new identity" by using cartoons to emphasize the "striking visual contrast" between mother and daughter in the family, as in Lynda G. Barry's *One Hundred Demons* (5).
3. Chute and DeKoven, editors of an important special issue of *Modern Fiction Studies* on graphic narrative, observe that as a form it does not yet possess a critical apparatus; rather, in its "fundamental syntactical operation [of] the representation of time as space on the page," it is a hybrid form unlike the novel. They argue that graphic narrative is a multigeneric, mass culture art form in which verbal and visual narratives exist in tension. That is, the images do not simply illustrate the text, but move forward differently than the words with which they are interspersed (769).
4. *Second Life* is an example of "massively multiplayer online games" (MMORPGs). See the discussion by Tracy Wilson in the howstuffworks.com newsletter (2007) exploring the deep connection between the user and the avatar.
5. Miller trenchantly observes, "The challenge that faces autobiographers is to invent themselves despite the weight of their family history, and autobiographical singularity emerges in negotiations with this legacy" ("Entangled" 543). There is thus a relational aspect to nearly all life narratives. See Smith and Watson 8–13, 37–38.

6   See Michael Renov's discussion of domestic ethnography as autobiographical practice; it "constructs self-knowledge through recourse to the familial other" by a kind of participant observation that situates subject and practitioner intersubjectively (141–42).

7   Rocio G. Davis notes that "graphic narratives are highly effective künstlerroman [sic]... because the subjects of the autobiographical comics are, most often, graphic artists themselves" (269). In *Persepolis*, the autographic discussed by Davis, however, Satrapi does not focus on Marji's process of learning to draw as self-expression to the extent that Bechdel does.

8   De Jesús attends to cartoonist Lynda J. Barry's narrative, "The Aswang," in which a mythic Filipino vampire-monster becomes a figure for mother-daughter alienation and a way to think about her own choice of cartooning (12). I am indebted to de Jesús's concise history of developments in women's comics as part of what Bob Callahan, editor of *The New Comics Anthology*, called the "New Comics" (see 2–4).

9   Sidonie Smith and I have characterized the autobiographical interface as the space at which diverse media of visual and verbal self-construction intersect in registering the subjectivity of the maker, whether or not a traditional self-portrait is discernable (Watson and Smith 5–7).

10   Jared Gardner sees the "archival turn" ("Archive" 788) as distinctive of contemporary comics, noting that "archives are everywhere in the contemporary graphic novel... archives of the forgotten artifacts and ephemera of American popular culture" ("Archive" 787). Part of the pleasure for comic book readers and collectors, he argues, is this visual assemblage of drawn fragments of old comics and ephemera. Bechdel is an archiver of both family memorabilia and the larger history of Second Wave feminist texts, sayings, and styles.

11   In an interview with Hillary Chute, Bechdel acknowledged that her mother, after giving her letters and photos for *Fun Home* and initially finding the project amusing, changed her view of it: "She felt betrayed—quite justifiably so—that I was using things she'd told me in confidence about my father" (1006). But her mother, a "mixed-message person," also gave her a further box of letters between the parents (1007). She reiterated her mother's discomfort with the project at a lecture on October 29, 2007, at the Ninth Festival of Cartoon Art sponsored by the Cartoon Library, The Ohio State University, in Columbus, Ohio. In the Chute interview Bechdel acknowledged the ethical issue her project raised, stating "This memoir is in many ways a huge violation of my family" (1009). While that sense of betrayal may

remain for the family, *Fun Home* also serves as a bequest (to borrow Nancy K. Miller's term), specifically in memorializing her father after his death by contextualizing his covert pedophiliac acts, and identifying his desire with her own and with a long-repressed and persecuted history of homosexuality in the U.S.

12 Bechdel's fastidious attention to detail is evident not only in the careful drawing and coloring of the wallpaper, but in the concern she expressed to Hillary Chute that her drawing and coloring did not entirely capture the wallpaper, which she identified as William Morris's "Chrysanthemums": "I didn't get enough contrast in [the wallpaper]. I've since learned that there are eleven shades of green in the original—and I was only using five different shades" (1008).

13 For an extensive and erudite discussion of the climate of twentieth-century repression of homosexuality, see Jennifer Terry's *An American Obsession*, particularly the chapter on "The United States of Perversion."

14 Ken Plummer defines the coming-out story as a "Modernist tale" that proliferates in the later twentieth century. Its hallmarks are "a frustrated, thwarted and stigmatized desire for someone of one's own sex . . . it stumbles around childhood longings and youthful secrets; it interrogates itself, seeking 'causes' and 'histories' that might bring 'motives' and 'memories' into focus; it finds a crisis, a turning point, an epiphany; and then it enters a new world—a new identity, born again, metamorphosis, coming out" (52). For a brilliant discussion of genres and examples of American feminist coming-out stories, see Martin. For her, the coming-out story asserts a mimetic relationship between experience and writing, and centers its narrative on the declaration of sexuality as both discovered and always already there. Such narratives are also a quest for a language of feeling and desire that will "name their experience woman-identification" (88). Both Plummer and Martin, in emphasizing the narration of sexual identity, see it as a positional, rather than fully stable, identity.

15 At the "Graphic Narrative Conference" at The Ohio State University on October 25, 2007, narratologist David Herman gave an insightful talk on identity construction in graphic narratives that explored Bechdel's use of graphic tags as a means of disrupting the Bildungsroman's linear model of self-narration.

16 Sidonie Smith and I discuss "personal criticism" as an important autobiographical practice of writing the "I" that directs critical attention to the critic's praxis as a form of feminist pedagogy (see Smith and Watson 32–33, 36–37).

17 Bechdel observed to Chute in the interview that the photographs at the beginning of each chapter "feel particularly mythic to me, [they] carry a lot of meaning" (1009).

18 Bechdel glosses this chapter title as *À l'Ombre des Jeunes Filles en Fleurs*, a translation of the second volume of Proust's *In Search of Lost Time*. And the chapter offers an extended gloss upon Proust's oeuvre, noting how the apparently opposed paths, literal and metaphoric, of Swann and the Guermantes are revealed to "have always converged" in the course of the novels as a model of how its "vast network of transversals" works to undermine apparent binaries (102). Although Bechdel told Chute "I never actually read all of Proust; I just skimmed and took bits that I needed," using the novel as a metatext gives her a grid within which to map the apparent opposition and deep connection that she experienced with her father while growing up, and that forms the basis of their homosexual affinity ("Interview" 1005).

19 In the Chute interview, Bechdel asserts that "photographs really generated the book," discussing in particular this snapshot (1005) and calling it literally "the core of the book, the centerfold" (1006). She further states, "I felt this sort of posthumous bond with my father, like I shared this thing with him, like we were comrades" (1006).

20 On theorizing the matrilineal bond, see especially the work of Carol Gilligan and Nancy Chodorow, and the useful discussion of their studies by Susan Stanford Friedman.

21 My thanks to Sarah Carnahan in a graduate seminar at OSU, Winter 2008, for inquiring about the rationale for Bechdel's use of this highly conventional style of cartooning for this two-page sequence.

22 "[26 April] Welcome O life! I go to encounter for the millionth time the reality of experience and to forge in the smithy of my soul the uncreated conscience of my race. [27 April] Old father, old artificer, stand me now and ever in good stead" (253). Notably, although the words of the Joycean phrase are the first chapter title in *Fun Home*, only at the comic's end do we understand their full implications. Commenting on Bechdel's extensive use of Joyce's *Ulysses*, a book she was required to read in college but remembers resenting, Hillary Chute observes that Alison and her father "figure various Joycean characters," each occupying the position of Bloom and Stephen at various times; and Bechdel's observations on *Ulysses* come just before *Fun Home*'s final page, in which they also exchange the positions of Icarus and Daedalus in the myth ("Gothic" 4).

23 Bechdel showed this photo of her father Bruce during her talk on the book at the Ninth Festival of Cartoon Art at the Cartoon Library, The Ohio State University, on October 27, 2007.
24 See my discussion of the final painting of Charlotte Salomon's *Life or Theater?*, where the title of her work is inscribed across her back, which faces the viewer as the artist gazes out toward the Mediterranean, where she painted in exile. That visual inscription embodies her story in the artistic "I" she created as no verbal narrative could. I argue that "in merging her persona with the artist-autobiographer, making herself through the work, Salomon enacts the creation of [her] 'name'" (417). Like Bechdel, Salomon narrates a story of becoming the person who could inhabit, tell, and depict the story viewers have just encountered—in 789 non-consecutive pages, in Salomon's case.
25 Louis Menand's remark about biography as a form is suggestive: "All biographies are retrospective in the same sense. Though they read chronologically forward, they are composed essentially backward" (66). That is, the events that the subject became renowned for determine what the biographer selects to interpret as formative. A difference of autobiography from biography lies in the nature of the interpreter's recognition.
26 Hillary Chute also describes *Fun Home* as "recursive" ("Gothic" 2).

Works Cited

Barry, Lynda G. "The Aswant." Barry, *One Hundred Demons* 86–97.
———. *One Hundred Demons*. Seattle: Sasquatch, 2002.
Bechdel, Alison. *Fun Home: A Family Tragicomic*. Boston: Houghton Mifflin, 2006.
Callahan, Bob, ed. *The New Comics Anthology*. New York: Colliers, 1991.
Chodorow, Nancy. *The Reproduction of Mothering: Psychoanalysis and the Sociology of Gender*. Berkeley: University of California Press, 1978.
Chute, Hillary. "Gothic Revival: Old father, old artificer: Tracing the roots of Alison Bechdel's exhilarating new 'tragicomic,' *Fun Home*." *Village Voice* 11 July 2006. 17 Mar. 2008. Online ed. http://www.villagevoice.com/books/0628,chute,73800,10.htm.
———. "An Interview with Alison Bechdel." *Modern Fiction Studies* 52.4 (Winter 2006): 1004–13.
Chute, Hillary, and Marianne DeKoven. "Introduction: Graphic Narrative." *Modern Fiction Studies* 52.4 (Winter 2006): 767–82.

Davis, Rocío G. "A Graphic Self. Comics as Autobiography in Marjane Satrapi's *Persepolis*." *Prose Studies* 27.3 (2005): 264–79.

De Jesús, Melinda Luisa. "Of Monsters and Mothers: Filipina American Identity and Maternal Legacies in Lynda J. Barry's *One Hundred Demons*." *Meridians: feminism, race, transnationalism* 5.1 (2004): 1–26.

Doucet, Julie. *My Most Secret Desire*. 1995. Montreal: Drawn and Quarterly, 2004.

Friedman, Susan Stanford. "Women's Autobiographical Selves: Theory and Practice." *The Private Self*. Ed. Shari Benstock. Chapel Hill: University of North Carolina Press, 1988. 34–62.

Gardner, Jared. "Archives, Collectors, and the New Media Work of Comics." *Modern Fiction Studies* 52.4 (Winter 2006): 787–806.

———. "Autography's Biography, 1972–2007." *Biography* 31:1 (Winter 2008): 1–26.

Gilligan, Carol. *In a Different Voice: Psychological Theory and Women's Development*. Cambridge: Harvard University Press, 1982.

Herman, David. "Multimodal Storytelling: Identity Construction in Graphic Narratives." Conference paper. Academic conference on "Graphic Narrative." Blackwell Conference Center. The Ohio State University. Columbus, OH. 25 Oct. 2007.

Joyce, James. *A Portrait of the Artist as a Young Man*. 1916. New York: 1964.

Kaplan, Caren. "Resisting Autobiography: Out-Law Genres and Transnational Feminist Subjects." *De/Colonizing the Subject*. Ed. Sidonie Smith and Julia Watson. Minneapolis: University of Minnesota Press, 1992. 115–38.

Martin, Biddy. "Lesbian Identity and Autobiographical Differences." *Life/Lines*. Ed. Bella Brodzki and Celeste Schenck. Ithaca: Cornell University Press, 1988. 77–103.

McCloud, Scott. *Understanding Comics: The Invisible Art*. New York: Harper Perennial, 1994.

Menand, Louis. "Lives of Others." *The New Yorker*, 6 Aug. 2007: 64–66.

Miller, Nancy K. *Bequest and Betrayal: Memoir of a Parent's Death*. Bloomington: Indiana University Press, 2000.

———. "The Entangled Self: Genre Bondage in the Age of the Memoir." *PMLA* 122.2 (Mar. 2007): 537–48.

Olney, James. *Metaphors of Self: The Meaning of Autobiography*. Princeton: Princeton University Press, 1972.

Plummer, Ken. *Telling Sexual Stories*. London: Routledge, 1995.

Renov, Michael. "Domestic Ethnography and the Construction of the 'Other' Self." *Collecting Visible Evidence*. Ed. Jane M. Gaines and Renov. Minneapolis: University of Minnesota Press, 1999. 140–55.

Satrapi, Marjane. *Persepolis*. New York: Pantheon, 2003.
Smith, Sidonie, and Julia Watson. "Introduction: Situating Subjectivity in Women's Autobiographical Practices." *Women, Autobiography, Theory: A Reader*. Ed. Smith and Watson. Madison: University of Wisconsin Press, 1998. 3–52.
Terry, Jennifer. *An American Obsession: Science, Medicine, and Homosexuality in Modern American Society*. Chicago: University of Chicago Press, 1999.
Watson, Julia. "Charlotte Salomon's Memory Work in the 'Postscript' to *Life or Theater?*" *Signs*. Spec. issue on *Gender and Memory*. 28.1 (Autumn 2002): 409–420.
Watson, Julia, and Sidonie Smith. "Introduction: Mapping Women's Self-Representation at Visual/Narrative Interfaces." *Interfaces: Women, Autobiography, Image, Performance*. Ed. Smith and Watson. Ann Arbor: University of Michigan Press, 2002. 1–46.
Whitlock, "Autographics: The Seeing 'I' of the Comics." *Modern Fiction Studies* 52.4 (Winter 2006): 965–79.
———. *Soft Weapons: Autobiography in Transit*. Chicago: University of Chicago, 2007.
Wilsey, Sean. "The Things They Buried." Review of *Fun Home*, by Alison Bechdel. *The New York Times Book Review*, 18 June 2006. 17 Mar. 2008. Online ed. http://www.nytimes.com/2006.06/18/books/reviews/18wilsey.
Wilson, Tracy V. "How MMORPGs Works." *How Stuff Works*. 18 Mar. 2008. http://electronics.howstuffworks.com/mmorpg.htm.

12
RE-CITING, RE-SITING, AND RE-SIGHTING LIKENESS: READING THE FAMILY ARCHIVE IN DRUCILLA MODJESKA'S *POPPY* AND SALLY MORGAN'S *MY PLACE* (SMITH 1994)

To articulate the past historically does not mean to recognise it "the way it really was" (Ranke). It means to seize hold of a memory as it flashes up at a moment of danger.
            Walter Benjamin, No. VI, "Theses on the
                  Philosophy of History," *Illuminations*

Because the family photograph is a ritual of the domestic cult in which the family is both subject and object, because it expresses the celebratory sense which the family group gives to itself, and which it reinforces by giving it expression, the need for photographs and the need to take photographs (the internalization of the social function of this practice) are felt all the more intensely the more integrated the group and the more the group is captured at a moment of its highest integration.
                              Pierre Bourdieu, *Photography*

> *Those "happy," "serious," "loving," "miserable," but always passive visual moments which do exist, those moments which only show surface information about me, give no indication at all of the wider social, economic and political histories of our disgusting class-divided society. They are rendered invisible within my "family album."*
>
> Jo Spence, *Putting Myself in the Picture*

In the early decades of the twentieth century, the increasingly widespread availability of inexpensive and compact cameras enabled everyday families to record celebrations, rites of passage, familiar places, friends, and leisure activities. Such memorializing was, as Susan Sontag reminds us, "the earliest popular use of photography" (8). Within the fluid exigencies of everyday life, the click of cameras caught celluloid moments that registered familial identities, relationships, rituals, achievements, possessions, and social status for years and family members to come. Since then photographs have come to constitute one of the most important and portable components of a family's archive, offering up in discontinuous and sometimes powerfully haunting images traces of a family's experiential history.[1] For individual families, and for the larger culture, whose investment in ideologies of familiality is secured through the reproduction of individual family units, photography, as Pierre Bourdieu elaborates, "affirms the continuity and integration of the domestic group, and reaffirms it by giving it expression" (29).

Family photos are often thrown helter-skelter into shoeboxes or dresser drawers, a cluttered jumble of memorial moments out of place and out of chronology. Sometimes they are lovingly sorted out and catalogued, then gathered into fastidiously organized and documented family albums designed to leave to posterity an orchestrated family chronicle (Motz 63; Stokes 203). Most often, perhaps, they are stashed in drawers or boxes after being labeled with brief notes dating the photo, identifying place, naming people, in handwriting that may or may not be recognizable or legible.

In the hands of strangers, such collections become documentary evidence accumulated in historical archives and museums, there to be taken up by social and art historians or ethnologists. But in the hands of family members, photographs serve a variety of more personal functions. Called upon to confirm the family's "present unity from its past" (Bourdieu 31), they bind families together across generations, across geography, across differences in destinies, by providing records, however fragmented, of a mutual past for those who come in the future and occasions for the communal sharing of different but overlapping family narratives. In the process individual memory becomes social memory as private memories find narrative affiliation with the social memory accumulated in the family album (whether organized or disorganized).

But just how do perusals of photographs work to join people and their pasts? The figures in family photos may be easily identified. That, we say, is my grandmother. And that is my father. And that is me when I was five. They provide us with deceptively familiar visual likenesses, likenesses that reinforce for photographers and their subjects the "realism" of photographs. But, as Bourdieu notes, the capacity to see the family photograph "as the precise and objective reproduction of reality" derives from the social use of photography, a social use that "makes a selection, from the field of the possible uses of photography, structured according to the categories that organize the ordinary vision of the world" (77). In effect, we see and know our own family in the photographs as we are trained to see and know the cultural idea of familiality. As a result the photograph "becomes a sort of ideogram or allegory, as individual and circumstantial traits take second place" (Bourdieu 36). They take second place to what Marianne Hirsch terms "the gaze of 'familiality' that situates human subjects in the ideology, the mythology, of the family as institution" (114). This gaze materializes photographically in the formal conventions of family photographs—the postures aligned with roles, the relational attitudes asserted visually, the spatial arrangements, the settings, the ceremonial occasions snapped (see J. Hirsch).

Yet at the same time that family photographs have a patent familiarity, the images in the photographs are also provocatively unfamiliar. Issuing from an unrecoverable past, they enforce the gap between ourselves in the present and those figures of the past, the gap between ourselves now as we look and ourselves as we were formerly looked at. They are more like identity fragments, or rather disidentity fragments. And they are disidentity fragments sundered from the on-goingness of time. "The quick incision in the axis of time, that the photographic preservation of the second implies," claims Oddlaug Reiakvam, "creates discontinuity. The images are not responsible for 'before' or 'after' the constitutive moment of the photographic event" (40). The instantaneous moment (the smallest of time fragments) becomes a timeless image sundered from historical process. Thus photographs do not give up their stories easily, if at all. Marianne Hirsch describes this as the "ambiguity of the photographic image" (109). They tantalize us with their illusions of an exact copy, a likeness of someone, and with the story of that person and that place and time they seem to promise; but we are left to disentangle what the meaning of likeness is. In seeming to show us so much, they show us so little. Perhaps they show us only alignment in a set of photographic conventions that mask, as Marianne Hirsch argues, history, identity, and meaning.

If photographs themselves cannot be responsible for a before and after, for narrative meaning, people looking at the photographs can assume responsibility for constructing a before and after. Their memories stimulated by photographs, individuals can narrate stories through which family histories, in their citation and recitation, become family legends. Or since, as Jeremy Seabrook suggests, photographs "amplify biographies, even destinies" to the degree that they provide "a quickening of the sense of the importance of what has happened to those we care for" (172), family members can assume responsibility for eliciting narratives from other family members or for assembling a biographical narrative. Or they can take the images offered up in family photos and piece together their own histories within families. In this process family photographs become critical documents in the vexed practices of self-narrating.

In this essay I want to look at the ways in which the engagement with family photographs becomes an occasion to re-cite, re-site, and re-sight autobiograpical subjects and practices. Here I would recall the claim that Michel de Certeau makes about everyday life:

> Social life multiplies the gestures and modes of behavior (im)printed by narrative models; it ceasly [sic] reproduces and accumulates "copies" of stories. Our society has become a recited society, in three senses: it is defined by stories (récits, the fables constituted by our advertising and informational media), by citations of stories, and by the interminable recitation of stories. (186)

This citationality Judith Butler identifies as performativity, that is, "the power of discourse to produce effects through reiteration" (20). Family photographs function as an arena of citationality as they assemble the particular individuals gathered into the photographic field of vision through the cultural lens of the familial gaze. In reading family photographs, individuals recite the narratives given up by that gaze or re-cite the narrative as a particular and purposefully resisting affiliative look[2] that penetrates the mask of citationality. In this re-citation the autobiographer can re-site subjectivity, locating the "I" in a different narrative, a different history, a different filiality, a different look. And she can re-sight the image; that is, she can come to see and to know family history differently, using various sightlines of identity to destabilize other sightlines of identity.[3] Narratively engaging the otherness of and in the family photograph can become a means to examine, from within and without, the familial gaze and the history, culture, and models of identity that produce it.

I take up these issues as they affect two auto/biographical texts by Australian women: Drucilla Modjeska's *Poppy* and Sally

Morgan's *My Place*. From a comfortably middle-class family, Modjeska has the luxury of going to a rich pictorial archive where there are many images of her mother to consume as she writes her way to and through her mother's story. Sally Morgan, daughter in a working-class family, has no such pictorial luxuries to draw upon as she looks to solve certain puzzles of identity. For her there are few photographs, and the paucity of photos speaks volumes about her very real struggle to put together a narrative "life." However different their positions within contemporary Australian society and however divergent their life writing projects, these two women try to wrest usable meanings out of old photographs.

Drucilla Modjeska's *Poppy*: Like Wounded Mother, Like Daughter

> *Separation is my aim, yet ironically, through doing "mother-and-daughter work" I'm highlighting my mother: feeling, thinking, exchanging places with her; trying to disentangle myself, to take the useful bits, to re-evaluate those bits that continue to limit and distress me . . . and to let go.*
>
> Rosy Martin (214)

With the illness and eventual death of her mother, Drucilla Modjeska looks back across vast waters (separating her home in Sydney from her childhood home in England) toward her mother in order to recover from multiple losses—the first loss of the infant, the second of the adolescent who watches as her mother is institutionalized and her family dispersed through the subsequent divorce, the third loss of the adult immigrant, and the fourth loss of the bereaved daughter. Casting a dutiful eye on old photos she experiences how vast the gulf is between herself, a feminist and exile in Australia, and the mother who lived her life elsewhere (Whitlock 245). In anguish, she realizes that "I did not know her," realizes further that in not knowing her mother she "could not know myself" (5).

Intent on "knowing" her mother, the daughter seeks "evidence that would restore her to me" (12). On one wall of her writing room, she traces the family tree. The "names ... tethered by straight lines drawn in ink" provide her with one kind of evidence, one kind of knowledge about her mother, the knowledge of bloodlines and relationships that are "straightforward and unambiguous" (9). On another wall she pins snapshots from the archive of her suburban middle-class family life, another kind of evidence. But, she laments, "the photos themselves explain nothing," "make no sense." The figures in them become phantasms, "grotesque" and "swollen." There is nothing "straightforward and unambiguous" about these visual traces (9–10).

Scrutinizing family snapshots, the daughter concentrates on two photos in which "Poppy is not obscure, or obscured to me." In one her mother is a "vulnerable" and "self-conscious" but hopeful child of six with her future ahead. In this photo the daughter reads "the restless energy of hope." In the other, taken soon after Poppy's lover has died, her mother is an older woman, grieving yet "calm," not struggling. In both photos, brackets to the life lived in between hope and calm, her mother appears alone: child, old woman. The daughter triangulates these two photos with a third, typical of many other photographs in which Poppy is "embedded in the family. Hemmed in, surrounded" (10), obscured and obscuring. In fact, the first photo described in detail in the text is Poppy's wedding picture, one that captures her in that defining ritual of bourgeois life and in that defining set of relationships, expectations, opportunities designed to give her life as a woman its meaning and its demesne. The daughter describes how Poppy, who has given her daughter the photo during one of their last talks, reads in the photograph "the vanity she'd spent her life denying she'd inherited from" her mother (8). But the daughter looks at the wedding photos and sees there, not the vanity her mother sees, but "intention, it's not in her expression, not at all, but in the future that is prefigured by her body, and by the composition of the photos" (8). Arranged to both sides of her are all "the people who bordered her life, and would in the end prove impossible to escape" (8). In the middle is the new couple, flanked by the two families from which they have emerged to join in their own coupling; and the young woman of the couple is a mother who has willed herself into "an ordinary family" to "break the cycle of loss and sorrow she'd been born into." "If the photos make me sad," the daughter reflects, "it's not because what she wanted didn't happen, but because it did which confused the issue more thoroughly than any simple failure could" (9).

The casual residue of everyday life, the family snapshots "weigh" the daughter down with their "random images of a family past" (10); they hem her in just as her mother appears hemmed in by family life inside the frames of those photos. As she ponders them for what they reveal and conceal, she finds that the intransigent silences of images generate more questions than they seem to answer; multiply confusions; force contradictions. Even as they promise to provide documentary evidence about her mother's life, to deliver an image of her mother's past to her, they deliver primarily the sense of absence, loss, unfulfilled desire—loss of that earlier time, loss of the mother, loss of the "real" meaning of the life of the woman whose materiality is and isn't there before her, in the frame. If Modjeska begins her "life-writing" project[4] desiring to know her mother by piecing together through bits of evidence the "real" story, she discovers that she cannot get to any "real" story through family documents; she can only get to her version of an unrecoverable story.

Yet the very insufficiency of photographs to "make sense" and thereby function as an archive of the real becomes imaginatively productive for the daughter. In their intimate silences, the photos solicit imagination. And in this way photographic muteness allies with the muteness of Poppy herself, that other evidentiary source that the daughter tries to mine for meaning (when her mother is still alive). Questioning her mother about what she "really" thought, felt, did, the daughter is "unable to pin her down to a clear view of her own history" (10). Poppy in effect refuses to become a documentary source, will not give her daughter her version. She resists her daughter's will to pin her down or frame her up.

Poppy's persistent silence becomes a fascination for the daughter: "I am interested in the enigma, and therefore the power, of the silent feminine which I come up against time and again in this task" (24). But she comes to identify her mother's silence with a larger generational silence. "Born to Edwardian mothers, mothers to feminist daughters," writes the daughter, "Poppy's generation slips out in silence" (90). For the feminist daughter, herself struggling with the emotional residue of "independence," the enervating suspicion about familial constraints, and the pressure of undutifulness, Poppy needs to be released imaginatively as a subject of and in history instead of remaining a too familiar icon of the enduring, "wounded," sacrificial mother held in the psychological timelessness of a daughter's nostalgia, held as if in a single snapshot.

To release Poppy from the frame of the wounded mother, the daughter begins to turn a familial look to the family archive and to explore what the photos show and what they mask. In effect, she queries what Bourdieu describes as the "family function" of photographic practice, "the function conferred upon it by the family group, namely that of solemnizing and immortalizing the high points of family life, in short, of reinforcing the integration of the family group by resserting the sense that it has both of itself and of its unity" (19). The daughter reads the timeless ideogram of bourgeois familiality in early photographs in which "happy together at the side door of the cottage . . . . Richard and Poppy's bodies appear to move in unison" (36–37). Yet rereading later photos she discovers tensions cracking the conventional surface of the bourgeois idyll, those, for instance, in an election flyer photo from the late 50s:

> At first sight it is a happy family, conventionally arranged
> .... On closer examination you can see that Richard's cheeks
> are tight and that there is nothing other than the association
> of the sofa to link him with Poppy and Phoebe. Only he and
> I look at the camera. We flank a tableau of mother and child.
> May, on this occasion, strikes the discordant note, tied to
> neither father nor mother. The alarm is in her face. (69)

Reading the photograph against the grain of its conventions, the daughter sees the disjunction between the structural formality—designed to project condition and status, traditional values, stability, propositional relationships of husband to wife, parents to children, candidate to constituency—and the subtle, candid deviations from that formality that expose instability, contingency, emotional messiness, family discord. Underneath the posed surface of the family photos lies an unrepresentable story of mental instability, physical breakdown, institutionalization, shock treatment, separation, suicide threats, silence, recriminations, loneliness, divorce. "Get[ing] a grip on a picture of Poppy" (163) thus requires the daughter to find a way to understand her mother's nervous breakdown which, coming during the daughter's early adolescence, forces her own removal from her childhood home to a friend's house when her mother is committed to an institution. The breakdown brings divorce, brings the end of what seemed the fulfillment of Poppy's matrimonial intentionality. Such crises of the bourgeois family remain unphotographed, unimaged, unimagined, until the daughter finds the words through which to represent the formerly unspeakable.

Yet the story of Poppy's childhood, marriage, and nervous breakdown takes up only the first third of the narrative. For the daughter continues past the time of the wounded mother to imagine Poppy's life "as a woman" (90)[5] after the idyll of bourgeois family life comes to an end. She tracks how Poppy recovers, establishes new networks of friends, experiments with alternative living arrangements, goes to work counseling young working-class offenders, negotiates a long-term relationship with a Catholic priest, travels to India on a spiritual quest, dies of cancer; how her husband remarries and her daughters disperse around the globe. As she does so, she gives her mother to history and gives historical specificity to her mother's struggle as a woman in time, rejecting the timeless icon of sacrificing motherhood by forcing history back inside the frame: the history of wars and consumerism; of middle-class consolidation and the rising rate of divorce; of new state practices affecting the family; of treatments for mental breakdowns; of countercultural experimentations with relationships and engagements with spiritual alternatives; of restless emigration from one global location to another; of generational differences in opportunities available to women. Poppy's silence becomes not a spiteful gesture of maternal withholding but a gift of imaginative license, an imaginative license that sanctions another way of knowing. Released from the necessity of securing her mother's version of her own story, the daughter can fashion her own narrative.

But if this is the picture the daughter gets of her mother; there is also the manner of framing the picture that becomes paramount. And this too is generated from and in silence. The daughter imagines that in her breakdown her mother's "silence was a symptom and a cause" (83), a symptom of a specific historical condition: "The voice she needed hadn't been invented, or if it had, it hadn't been heard in the south of England" (83–84). The daughter assumes responsibility for inventing the voice of her mother, fabricating for her own narrative purposes imaginary diaries and letters written by her mother and by Marcus, her mother's lover, imagining how her mother might have put together for herself new meanings, outside relationships of familiality—a life of work, independence, travel, unpublicized love, faith. Imagining her mother speaking and desiring outside the familial context, the daughter re-sites her mother, releasing her from a singular snapshot. And she resists the temptation to fix her own familial look, to site her mother in a static identity.

Assuming the voice of her mother, the narrator "thinks toward" something she calls a "third voice" (151–152), a narrative mode braiding together what she describes as the father's tongue of academic learning, objectivity, and intellectual reflection upon the cultural meanings of her mother's story as a woman, and the mother's tongue of storytelling, a "blood and heart" tongue attentive to "the everyday, the unrecorded, the unsystematic . . . the ways of living that affected us quietly, their meanings accruing over years" (26). In the oscillations this third voice sets in motion, the daughter attempts to know the mother not through normative conventions of biography calling for final and authoritative interpretations of the meaning of a life—interpretations "straightforward and unambiguous"—but through an imaginary interpenetration of archival materials, actual and fictive—photographs and diaries, letters and pieces of personal conversations.

In knowing Poppy through this imaginative impersonation and the hybrid practice it engenders, Poppy "is given back to me" (139). And if in not knowing Poppy, she could not "know myself" (5), then in writing Poppy back into history, the daughter comes to know something of herself. While she describes her mother's story as "the safer ground of narrative" (192), and purposefully keeps her own secrets by not naming people and by not specifying relationships, the daughter nonetheless assembles her own narrative of loss, longing, and imaginative recovery of likeness as she pieces together a story of her mother. And as she releases Poppy from the ideogrammatic identity of wounded mother, she releases herself from the ideogrammatic identity of undutiful, rebellious, wounded daughter. For despite the geographical distance emigration to Australia placed between mother and daughter, perhaps even because of it, the daughter has been unable to escape her mother's gaze, a sign of "vanity" that links her to her mother and the vanity her mother read into the wedding photograph.

Introducing Poppy's trip to India with a journal entry in Poppy's voice, the narrator imagines the mother commenting on discarding her camera, and by discarding her camera, refusing the social function of family photographs:

> I've spent years lugging cameras and diaries around, she wrote as she was preparing to leave England, as if the possibility of confidences on paper makes the day real. I've never believed my life has happened unless I've had someone to tell it to: Nanny, Richard, Marcus, Jacob, the diary. As if they could hear the details of my life and reflect them back, whole and worthwhile. If there's no one to see me, I have doubted my existence. This is to be the journey I live for myself, without interference, and without scrutiny. (265)

The daughter too has lived within this vanity, imagining herself as the object of her mother's critical judgment. Contemplating her mother's death and then confronting it, the daughter finds herself with "no one to see me." Consequently she "doubt[s her own] existence." This may explain Modjeska's invocation of a phrase from Colette as the epigraph to the book: "To renounce the vanity of living under someone's gaze." If she can release her mother from ensnarement in her own familial gaze, as the daughter who sees Poppy as "wounded mother," she can also release herself from the internalization of her mother's critical familial look.

Conflating the narrative of her mother with her own narrative, Modjeska explores the way in which "the self is necessarily other to itself, but also . . . embedded in and constituted by multiple relations" (M. Hirsch 111). Perhaps this is why Modjeska names herself as narrating daughter "Lalage." "Lalage" becomes the imaginary projection of the narrating subject as other to itself. And perhaps in distancing the narrating subject, she distances herself from her investment in a fixated form of relationship. In this way the narrative bears affinities to what Philippe Lacoue-Labarthe describes as "allo-portrait" in an attempt to suggest the othering effects of self-portraiture (42). If the allo-portrait, as

Marianne Hirsch argues, "allows us to perceive and to acknowledge the otherness embedded in the self-portrait" (111), then we might think of Modjeska's text as allo-biography.

Thus while the daughter subjects the mother to her own knowledge-producing project, a potentially disempowering and silencing frame-up, she assumes what Caren Kaplan describes as "critical accountability" (119) by resisting the generic "truths" of biography "exposed in a single masculine climax" (Modjeska 26) and the evidentiary basis upon which they can be asserted. Impersonating her mother, the narrator calls attention to the constructedness of the biographical and the autobiographical process. Daughter and mother are mutually constitutive as one becomes the other becomes the one. In giving her narrator the name Lalage, Modjeska has already sited the narrator as patently other. In another layering of auto- and allo-biography, Lalage impersonates Poppy, yet again, as if in infinite regression, projecting the subject as the other. Yet she also cites the other as subject. Hers is a gesture of critical citationality.

The very process of imaginatively reconstructing the mother's story sutures the gap between the time of the photos and the moment of narration, between the lost mother and the narrating daughter. And the critical reading of photos functions as a suturing practice in which the biographical and the fictive, the autobiographical and the biographical join so that unstraightforward and ambiguous meanings persist. Unlike the family tree on the wall in her room, a form of knowledge about "kin and progeny" that remains finite and fixed, and unlike the photos from the family album, photos composing her mother through the familial gaze, her imaginative engagement with the material archive of her mother's life, including family photos, involves a form of knowing which is in flux, on-going, provisional, familially relational, a form of knowing in which time is multidimensional and the space of consciousness fluctuant.

Perhaps this is why Modjeska does not include any photographs within the text. She too has resisted framing herself and her mother in a series of conventional pictures. The only photograph to appear is on the paperback cover, and it pronounces itself as a frame-up of the conventional Madonna and child variety. For it is actually a photo of a photo of the mother and child, cropped uncomfortably, off-center, partially unreadable. Writing allo-biography displaces the constraining social function of the family album.

Sally Morgan's Cultural Location: Reciting Aboriginal Likeness

> *They took you away when I was twenty. Mr. Neville from the Aborigines Protection Board said it was the best thing. He said that black mothers like me weren't allowed to keep babies like you. He didn't want you brought up as one of our people. I didn't want to let you go but I didn't have any choice. That was the law.*
> Sally Morgan, "The Letter"

Modjeska's narrative engages the ways in which family photography functions as recitation of bourgeois familiality and bourgeois forms of biographical knowledge across the history of Australian immigration. With Sally Morgan's *My Place* we turn to the complex relationship of family photography to the history of familial relations in Australia's post/colonial contact zone.[6]

Part of the technological apparatus of Australian colonialism, photography was utilized by various colonial institutions, among them the church, the state, and anthropological research,[7] "to endorse and celebrate the establishment of the settlements" (King-Smith pamphlet) and to produce and circulate definitions of Aboriginality, document and police Aboriginal populations, and project their possible futures. In other words, photos became one means through which the formerly unknown, profoundly different and exotic other, could be catalogued, captioned, and domesticated within the frames of the colonizer's lens.[8] Not only were Aboriginal peoples fetishized in the national album; they were often infantilized, represented as unruly children, naive in their systems of belief, not yet emergent from a state of nature, still unclothed, unmannered, uneducated. To the degree, then, that they could be encouraged or made to grow out of their Aboriginality and assimilate into settler society by adopting the appearance, the identities, and the values of the colonizers, they could leave behind their "primitive" Aboriginality and become modern subjects of history. They could become part of the Australian national family. Family photos projected this alternative future for Aboriginal peoples, circulating images testifying to the desirability of modernization through "uplift." In this way photos registered the semiotics of identity formation and deformation, producing representations of the unassimilated and assimilated, the primitive and the modern.

Sally Morgan engages this history of the Australian family album in her corporative auto/biographical text, *My Place*, and in the "Family Album" appended to the 1989 "Illustrated" hardbound edition. Daughter and granddaughter of women of mixed Aboriginal and settler heritage, women who lived within systems designed to enforce assimilation by brutally separating children from mothers and kin, and who internalized the denigration of their Aboriginal heritage and the superiority of the white heritage, she discovers her mixed heritage only late in adolescence because mother and grandmother had purposefully kept it from her. "'It was only a little white lie,'" her mother tells her, then recognizes the "unintentional humour" (135). In her turn Morgan rebuts the little white lie with a narrative of Aboriginal identity recovered and revaluated.

Unlike Modjeska, Morgan does not come to familial knowledge as she writes—she knows about her Aboriginal heritage already. But through the process of writing, she reconstructs the experiential context of a childhood and adolescence lived in a family in which this suppressed history functioned as both enforceable silence and uncanny presence. She exposes as well the experiential effects of discourses of assimilation: the complicity of parents in maintaining ignorance, the strategies of passing, the need of people outside the family to fix identity, the behavioral manifestations of dissociation, the confusions of mother-daughter relationships, the psychological distance exacted as the price of forced separation, passing, and imposed ignorance. Simultaneously the narrative tracks the process through which the assimilated daughter/granddaughter understands "becoming black" (see Millech) as it records "a conscious process of reentry into a culture whose traces had repeatedly erupted in inexplicable ways . . . without ever adding up to anything coherent until she found out about her Aboriginal origins" (Longley 377).

Family photos are critical in Morgan's reconstruction of the extradiegetic search for family counter-history, as the photographable and the unphotographable become clues in her search for information. At one point she recalls how important the visits of her uncle Arthur became for her, one in particular during which Arthur brought along "some old photographs of Nan, taken in the nineteen twenties." Morgan comments that her grandmother "had always refused to allow any of us to take her photograph, so it was exciting to be able to see her as a young woman. Nan, however, was not impressed" (147). The implication here is that her grandmother has not wanted her likeness revealed and circulated in photos that would materialize her "difference" as an Aboriginal woman. For when people of mixed heritage pass as white, as Nan and Gladys do, and censor evidence of an Aboriginal heritage, then photographs threaten to undo that disidentification by revealing identities and histories that have been concealed. Morgan opens the next chapter with "Sally's" decision to write a family history. These fragments from Arthur's family archive arouse the daughter's desire for knowledge and inaugurate her historical re/search since they provide glimpses of a familial history unrecited for the next generation, glimpses of a puzzle in need of piecing. Imaginatively the narrator aligns the familial look directed at family photos, the will to know, and the writing of personal history.

This connection between writing/speaking and reading photos recurs when she describes how she used photos to try to solve the riddle of paternity (for both Daisy and Gladys) by looking for family likenesses (236–238). Standing her mother in front of the mirror she holds up one picture of a possible father, only to find no likeness. Then she holds up a picture of Howden Drake-Brockman, the white man for whom her grandmother worked as a domestic and whom they suspect is Daisy's father. "We both fell into silence," she writes, "'. . . he's the spitting image of you!'" (237). The photo of Drake-Brockman intimates familial genealogy, intimates also a profound secret of paternity denied, of rape and incest. This possible history cannot be written off the photographic image even if it has been written out of the white family history. Daisy goes to her grave with the secret of Gladys's father's identity[9]; but the granddaughter sees a likeness if she doesn't name the unspeakable. And she connects Gladys's shock at the paternity intimated in the photograph with her decision to speak, to tell her story, and in telling, to reconnect with a history suppressed and a heritage refused. The photos make imaginatively visible that which has been obscured in official family/national history.

As Bourdieu claims, the social function of family photographs is to provide evidence of the integration of the family. The presentation of family likeness, an affirmation of genealogy, is thus meant to register familial stability and legitimacy. In this scene, family photography begins, as it fulfills its social function, to unmask the instabilities in families, and in national family albums. In postcolonial locations such as Australia, family photos can thus become highly contested documents because disturbing questions arise about who's in whose family. In such radical contexts family histories are difficult to organize into family albums. For the everyday realities of life in the contact zone make the family album a potential site of suppressed as well as commonly told histories.

Yet in this context, photos also become critical means to establish Aboriginal kinship networks among those dispersed and dis/integrated. In reconstructing her search, Morgan describes how she uses old photographs as a "weapon" in her attempt to reassemble family. She says of her return to Corunna Downs to locate kin members that she went to meet people "armed with the photographs" which she showed them, hoping they would see likenesses and recognize relationship. Photographs become a way for her to situate her grandmother, mother, and herself in a kinship network, a network that expands the notion of family out of its constricted bourgeois domain. Traces of the past through which people can remember and reconnect with sundered parts of their history, the photos, an alternative to written records for people excluded from literacy (Cohen and Somerville xiv-xv), facilitate the recovery of family and kin in the context of the purposeful dispersal of families and in the personal context of her mother's and grandmother's dissociation from an Aboriginal past. It is this connection with and acknowledgment by a wider community of Aboriginal people in various communities, particularly Corunna Downs, that Morgan posits as evidence of her own identity as Aboriginal.

For Morgan, then, family photographs provide necessary evidence of another history suppressed, an alternative identity affirmed. But I want to look further at the ways in which the photos assembled in the Family Album of the Illustrated Edition can be read through and against the narrative of *My Place* as three scenes of familiality.

The first half of *My Place* is a rather conventionally autobiographical narrative—linear, chronologically organized, focalized on the narrating "I" as the center of consciousness, dependent upon various narrative discourses prevalent in white Australian culture. Detective story, spiritual journey, Bildungsroman, Aussie battler story, confessional, these form the cultural discourses of Morgan's "assimilated" education, her immersion in the literary conventions of the dominant culture. The first group of photos in the Illustrated Edition figure this assimilated subject. In the opening photo the young Morgan, sitting at a desk, looks up from her work, looks directly into the camera, smiles. The camera snaps the smiling, studious, emergent individual, the good assimilated child, an image reproduced in the other photos of the Milroy children. A photo of her mother and father presents a conventional bourgeois couple: Bill Milroy stands with his arm around his wife's waist, pulling Gladys toward him with protective firmness; Gladys leans into her husband in a gesture of pliant and smiling dependency. Together these several photos of children and parents fulfill the social function, enforcing the hegemony of white Australian culture, reciting assimilated familiality. What remains unphotographable, of course, is the father's violence, illness, and alcoholism; the mother's desperate hard work; and the grandmother's withdrawal from the world outside the home and her "strange" behaviors, all a part of Morgan's narrative. And then there is the photo of the Milroy children and their grandmother, in which Daisy's physical difference is simultaneously visible and invisible in the faces of her grandchildren. The image of the integrated family thus masks and unmasks the otherness within the family, the otherness within the individuals of the family.

The last photo in the first section of the album, a formal portrait of Morgan and her own husband, seems to play with this disjunction between formal ideogram and experiential history. In a thoroughly assimilated posture, Morgan and her husband pose formally as the young couple reciting the traditional relationships of bourgeois familiality. Yet while the pose is formal, the dress is hippie. In effect their presentation before the camera parodies the conventional bourgeois framing of the domestic couple. He keeps his hands in his pockets. She holds a dog in her lap, where a child would conventionally be placed. The dog, obviously uncomfortable in an unnatural position, strains within the parody. The camera registers a resistance to the assimilated lifestyle; but the form of resistance is historically specific to the early-seventies generation.

The woman who writes some ten years after this photo is snapped undermines the authority of assimilationist discourses in other ways. Detecting Aboriginality, confessing Aboriginality, battling for Aboriginality, educating oneself in Aboriginality, all these generic practices are counter-normative. Here the confession of Aboriginality is posited as something good; and the act of confessing it publicly becomes a political gesture in resistance to discourses of assimilation. It is a shape-changing assertion of difference within the genres assimilated children are taught to privilege, taught to smile upon.

If the first group of photos offers images of the atomic and assimilated family, the second group of photos in the family album provides glimpses of her mother and grandmother as children and young women amidst life on the sheep station of Corunna Downs. Including images of the colonial settler family, gathered not only from members of her own family but from the archive of the Drake-Brockman family and other libraries,[10] these photos of life on the sheep station can be read against the three personal testimonies that make up the second half of Morgan's text. For in the second half of the book, the writerly autobiographical narrative is interrupted as Morgan incorporates the collaborative life writing projects of Arthur, Gladys, and Daisy. The individualized focus attached to the western form of traditional autobiography is displaced by an orally based, collaborative, matrilineal project. To foreground their effects, I prefer to think of the three narratives not as oral histories but as ethnographic testimonies. Joining with members of her family in a solidarity forged across different histories and generations, Morgan facilitates the coming-into-history of Arthur, Gladys, and Daisy, who give testimony about the effects of colonial practices upon the lives of the colonized. Their narratives emerge out of equally heterogeneous discourses through which they identify themselves and understand their experiential histories. Here the ethnographic/testimonial "I," a collaborative "I" (mutually produced through the "I" of the oral speaker and the transcription of the ethnographer/daughter), does not "invite us to identify with it" because "we are too different" (Sommer 108). Instead it counters the daughter's more assimilated autobiographical "I," dramatizing the generational differences even as it asserts familial kinship.

Given the narratives of Arthur, Gladys, and Daisy, we can read the photos in the second familial context against the grain of bourgeois family ideology as a story of economic and sexual exploitation and familial denial. The photograph of the three men of the Drake-Brockman family functions as an ideogram of the patriarchal settler family: assured, proud, sturdy, affluent, powerful, authoritative. The frontal presentation signals solidity, stability, and timelessness. The conventional V-shape organization of the photo with the patriarch in the cup of the V and the two sons standing behind and to the side of him provide the visual image of a family tree, of orderly succession. Howden Drake-Brockman leans against his father's chair, asserting his identification with the bearded patriarch. The social stability of the settler community, and of official Australian national identity, is registered in this generational portrait of the *pater familias* and his successors.

The photos that follow this portrait provide more casual glimpses of life on the Drake-Brockman station, glimpses of functionaries, children, servants, including Morgan's grandmother. In several photos Daisy is aligned with other Aboriginal women, all family servants, who stand rigidly behind lounging men. Or she is photographed relating to the children as nursemaid. One photo seems idiosyncratic: Daisy lies on a bank of grass in what seems like a canned pose, her hand on the back of her head with her elbow thrown into the air. Here she is not dressed in the standard garb of servitude; here she is not relating to children or to whites, but only to the camera that glimpses her vitality and her sexuality. Finally, there are photos of Gladys and June Drake-Brockman (Howden's daughter) as babies and little girls; and two photos of Gladys as a girl at the orphanage and as a young woman.

In this assemblage of photos we get hints of a suppressed familiality. Children are not acknowledged as such, because their very existence testifies to fractures in the bourgeois settler family and to the practices of desire that breach the obviously unstable boundaries between cultural groups. Fathers are not identified, even if they remain palpably present. Children become mothers and mothers are separated from children and siblings separated from one another through state intervention and the official policies of assimilation.[11] The daughter/child is not recognized as family but kept on as a maid, an invisible domestic worker. And Gladys is not kept at home with her mother but sent to an orphanage where she can become "white."

Morgan's corporate narrative—autobiographical and testimonial—constitutes an alternative to the images gathered in the family album, a matrilineally-based narrative in which Aboriginal identification and history are spoken and reclaimed after long years of censorship and self-censorship. This counter album fills in gaps of the family album that cannot be assembled because family relations have not been acknowledged; because family members have been brutally separated; because heritage has been suppressed. Instead of photographs obsessively accumulated over time, here are subjects situated in their testimonial ethnographies as agents of counter-memory. Yet simultaneously this collection of snapshots works to hold together a family, some of whose members would not and will not be held together in relation, holds together complex histories of difference, identity, kinship, and disruption in the contact zone of settler and Aboriginal Australia.

Morgan's family album closes with a series of photos of the elders Morgan visited in Port Hedland, Marble Bar, and the Shaw river settlement. Incorporating photos of her Aboriginal kinship network she re-sites herself in a familial network broader than the nuclear family and more incorporating than the settler family. Documenting her relation to community, the photos function as a discursive site for the production and circulation of her identification with and through a specific notion of Aboriginality.

Historically, genres of photographs have produced "authentic" "aboriginality" in multiple registers—as a repertoire of "everyday" activities; a nostalgic reverie for a vanishing people; a catalog of the truly primitive (see Peterson). Ethnographers in particular, often complicit with certain colonialist practices, have drawn upon photography to present images of the pure and the impure, the authentic and the inauthentic. Morgan, piecing together her own history of becoming black out of the gaps in the family album, becomes the lay ethnographer, displacing and implicitly critiquing ethnography's expertise and its white lies. Through her narrative construction of a counter-family history and the alternative family album she assembles, Morgan posits her Aboriginality as an identity originating in her matrilineal heritage and socially confirmed in her identification with and acknowledgment by the community of Aboriginal people in Corunna Downs, her communal filiation. Yet the radically different experiential histories of Sally, Arthur, Gladys, and Daisy reveal that there is no pure or authentic position of Aboriginality as such; that the subjects of these narratives are multiply positioned, and that they make sense out of their past through narratives woven of discourses of class, gender, national identity, and generational differences, as well as discourses of Aboriginality.[12] And so in both the autobiographical mode and the testimonial mode, and in the documentary record of three different familialities, *My Place* historicizes Aboriginal identities and differences even as it posits a fixed Aboriginal identity. "Texts such as *My Place*," suggests Gareth Griffiths, "deny the myth of authenticity its authority over the subjected whilst simultaneously recognising the crucial importance of recovering a sense of difference and identity" (11). But, as the vigorous debate generated around the publication and broad distribution of *My Place* suggests, they also raise vexing questions about identity politics and about contested definitions of Aboriginality.[13]

As text and photographs document Morgan's Aboriginality, they simultaneously document her persisting assimilated otherness and the forms of autobiographical performativity she inherits with that otherness (see Attwood 1992; Michaels 44–46; Newman; Narogin 14). From the photos of the smiling "assimilated" child, across the album's divide of the history of settler families, to the "Aboriginal" woman smiling among her kin, Morgan remains both/and rather than either "white" or Aboriginal. The other always remains in the album.

Opening the Frame

The framing of every family photograph involves histories of photographic practices, their functions, production, and dissemination, as well as histories of families and their complex relationships to the larger culture. These histories coaslesce in every flash of light, every click of plastic. In this sense "this most private of collections is also thoroughly public" since "its meanings are social as well as personal" (Holland 3). Likewise, in every autobiographical utterance of an "I" lies a history of discourses of identity and truth-telling through which biographical and autobiographical lives materialize within specific cultural contexts. That is, the most personal of signifiers is saturated with public discourses.

Modjeska and Morgan write from very different cultural locations. Their families have radically different histories in Australia. Yet these women struggle to compose themselves auto/biographically out of family histories of dis/integration. And for both women, the pressure of the unspeakable, of the unknown and unknowable, is mediated by a complex engagement with the evidentiary surplus of family photographs. Taking up conventional images structured "to consolidate and perpetuate dominant familial myths and ideologies" (M. Hirsch 111), to provide evidence of integration, these women interrogate family histories and the histories of individuals within families. They interrogate as well the very ideologies of familiality that locate subjects in conventional poses, that solicit the unconscious performativity of subjects, and that negotiate the normative autobiographical recitations of identity. Focusing alternative likenesses and alternative narratives, Modjeska and Morgan use photographs as means to recontextualize the meanings generated in the familial gaze as it intersects the lived experience of a particular family member. Thus the autobiographically embedded incorporation of family photos becomes a semiotic component of identity formation in familiality, one that contributes to a posing and perhaps a certain solving of the mystery of identity as disidentification. Representations emerging from a "socially saturated" (Ruthrof 7) discursive site, the photos are re-sited in narratives engendered through other socially saturated discourses: for Modjeska the discourse of a critical feminism; for Morgan the discourses of individuality and Aboriginality.

In these disparate and hybrid texts, autobiographical subjects use the performativity of both family photography and autobiographical storytelling to dismantle their "construction in subordination" (Mouffe 382). Ultimately, as they turn affiliative critiques back upon the familial gaze, they turn the object/other in the photograph into the subject of a different kind of history. It is a shape-changing practice, one that moves the autobiographical subject back and forth across an unstable boundary: the intersubjective mutuality of mother/daughter; the in/authentic oscillation of assimilated individuality/ Aboriginality. Such visual/verbal autobiographical re-citations suggest the complex ways in which the auto/biographical subject becomes a continually negotiated site of identity and otherness.

Notes

1   Many theorists of photographic practices have elaborated this connection between photographic discourses and the history of the family in the industrial West. Sontag notes that widespread access to photographic technology occurred at the very historical moment when the extended family began to vanish (8-9). In the history of family photography can thus be read the formation and consolidation of an atomized nuclear family functioning as the central site of consumer culture and as the organizing center of personal identities and relationships. The reproduction of images of happy families through family snapshots continues to "reassure us of [the nuclear family's] solidity and cohesion" (Holland 1). And yet Jeremy Seabrook muses that, "as photography becomes a leisure pursuit, its function as a cohesive social

force is forfeited" (185). The excessive accumulation of disconnected images may signal a new technology of perception and a change in cultural notions of the human subject.

2 M. Hirsch describes "the familial look" as "an engagement in a particular form of relationship, mutually constitutive, mediated by the familial gaze but exceeding it through its subjective contingency" (114).

3 M. Hirsch describes this site of intervention by means of Jacques Lacan's third diagram schematizing perception and Kaja Silverman's reframing of Lacan's description through the exploration of the image/screen. "Subjects are constituted and differentiated in relation to a variety of screens—class, race, gender, sexuality, age, nationality, and familiality—and they can attempt to manipulate and modify the functions of the image/screen" (120).

4 For discussions of "life writing" as an alternative name for hybrid practices joining auto/biographical and fictive practices, see Neuman (333) and Whitlock (243).

5 The narrator uses this phrase in relationship to herself, as when she talks of "my life as a woman" (90).

6 I leave the slash in the term post/colonial to signal the on-going effects of colonial discourses and practices. The phrase "contact zone" comes from Pratt's *Imperial Eyes*.

7 For discussions of the uses of photography in anthropological research and ethnographies that attend to the practices in the Australian context, see Edwards.

8 The colonizers and the colonized became conscious of something identified as Aboriginality only after "discovery," conquest, and settlement, only after confrontations with otherness and with othering discourses through which difference was domesticated, on the one hand, and installed as superiority, on the other. See Attwood (1989), Rowse (esp. 83–103), and Reece.

9 Daisy remains silent to the end about certain experiences, refuses to speak—in a gesture of resistance to expectations of confession? or in continuing victimization? or in complicity with the moral standards of the dominant culture (Levy 227)? The daughter and her reader remain in a state of unknowing.

10 Morgan reveals to her reader that she used various archives during her search for information about her family. In entering the archives, she enters various institutions that have utilized the colonizing capacities of photography to position Aboriginal people in discourses of race, nation, and empire. But for Morgan the archive enables her to do other

cultural work. Taking up the materials produced by and in the archives, materials that have been used to write the settler history from which she wants to release the complexity of her family's narrative, she pieces together counter-histories.

11 Aboriginal children of mixed heritage presented the camera and various colonial institutions with evidence of the instability of official family life as they put the face on "illegitimate" alignments of desire in the contact zones of settler and Aboriginal cultures. Children of mixed settler and Aboriginal heritages became "problems" in need of a national solution. One solution was the forced removal of such children from their mothers and their resettlement in camps or orphanages where they were educated out of their Aboriginal heritage. An exhibit at the Araluen Gallery in Alice Springs, entitled "Between Two Worlds: The Commonwealth Government and the Removal of Aboriginal Children of Part-descent in the Northern Territory," documents, through archival photographs and texts, the motivation for and organization of such institutions and the effects of such deracination upon the children and the adults they became. Personal histories of children so removed have become important counter-histories to the official narratives of Australian settlement. See for instance, *Women of the Centre*.

12 Notions of Aboriginality have gone through complex transformations as individuals, communities, and generations of people respond to the ways in which specific contact zones exact articulations, negotiations, and/or denials of behaviors, practices, beliefs defined as and associated with Aboriginality.

13 There are radically different readings of Morgan's *My Place* circulating through Australian cultural studies communities and Aboriginal communities. See for instance, Attwood (1992), Huggins, and Griffith. Critiques from the cultural studies community question the grounds upon which Morgan, so assimilated into white Australian culture, posits what Attwood describes as an essentialist notion of Aboriginality as blood relation and communal recognition (1992).

For Aboriginal commentators the critique of Morgan questions the way in which she posits Aboriginality as an identity that need only be affirmed. Huggins, for instance, claims that Aboriginal identity is not only something fixed in "blood and spirit," and in various ways of perceiving, thinking, and organizing knowledge; but that it must be earned over a period of time in the everyday participation in Aboriginal community and politics, in "protocols and ethics," and that there is "an expectation that some recompense will be given back to our mob from those who have now become famous. . . ." She also objects to the text's "proposition that Aboriginality can be understood by all non-aboriginals . . . it reeks of whitewashing in the ultimate sense" (460–461). For others more closely related to Morgan there is criticism that her title page does not acknowledge corporate authorship, that she gathers the stories of her relatives under her name, in a gesture of assimilationist authority and authorship.

Works Cited

Attwood, Bain. *The Making of the Aborigines.* Sydney: Allen and Unwin, 1989.

———. "Portrait of an Aboriginal as an Artist: Sally Morgan and the Construction of Aboriginality." *Australian Historical Studies* 99 (October 1992): 302–318.

Barthes, Roland. *Camera Lucida.* Trans. Richard Howard. London: Fontana, 1984.

Benjamin, Walter. *Illuminations.* Trans. Harry Zohn. London: Fontana, 1970.

Bourdieu, Pierre, Luc Boltanski, Robert Castel, Jean-Claude Chamboredon and Dominique Schnapper. *Photography: A Middle-Brow Art.* Trans. Shaun Whiteside. Stanford: Stanford University Press, 1990.

Butler, Judith. *Bodies That Matter.* New York: Routledge, 1994.

Cohen, Patsy, and Somerville, Margaret. *Ingelba and the Five Matriarchs.* Sydney: Allen and Unwin, 1990.

De Certeau, Michel. *The Practice of Everyday Life.* Trans. Steven F. Rendall. Berkeley: University of California Press, 1984.

Edwards, Elizabeth. *Anthropology and Photography, 1860–1920.* New Haven: Yale University Press, 1992.

Griffith, Gareth. "The Myth of Authenticity: Representation, Discourse and Social Practice." Unpublished paper, 1994.

Hirsch, Marianne. *Family Photographs: Content, Meaning, and Effect.* New York: Oxford University Press, 1981.

Hirsch, Marianne. "Masking the Subject: Practicing Theory." *The Point of Theory: Practices of Cultural Analysis.* Ed. Mieke Bal and Inge Boer. New York: Continuum, 1994. 109–124.

Holland, Patricia. "History, Memory and the Family Album." *Family Snaps: The Meanings of Domestic Photography.* Ed. Jo Spence and Patricia Holland. London: Virago, 1991. 1–14.

Huggins, Jackie. "Always Was Always Will Be." *Australian Historical Studies* 99 (April 1993): 459–464.

Kaplan, Caren. "Resisting Autobiography: Out-Law Genres and Transnational Feminist Subjects." *De/Colonizing the Subject: The Politics of Gender in Women's Autobiography*. Ed. Sidonie Smith and Julia Watson. Minneapolis: University of Minnesota Press, 1992. 115–138.

King-Smith, Leah. *Patterns of Connection*. The Victorian Centre for Photography, April 4–May 3, 1992.

Lacoue-Labarthe, Philippe. *Portrait de l'artiste, en général*. Paris: Christian Bourgois, 1979.

Levy, Bronwen. "Now What's Erotic? Sexuality, Desire, and Australian Women's Writing." *Gender, Politics and Fiction: Twentieth Century Australian Women's Novels*. Ed. Carole Ferrier. St. Lucia: University of Queensland Press, 1992: 219–35.

Longley, Kateryna. "Autobiographical Storytelling by Australian Aboriginal Women." *De/Colonizing the Subject: The Politics of Gender in Women's Autobiography*. Ed. Sidonie Smith, and Julia Watson. Minneapolis: University of Minnesota Press, 1992. 370–384.

Martin, Rosy. "Unwind the Ties that Bind." *Family Snaps: The Meanings of Domestic Photography*. Ed. Jo Spence and Patricia Holland. London: Virago, 1991. 209–221.

Michaels, Eric. "Para-Ethnography." *Art & Text* 30 (September-November, 1988): 42–51.

Millech, Barbara "*My Place* as Feminist Auto/biography." Unpublished paper, 1994.

Modjeska, Drucilla. *Poppy*. Ringwood, Australia: McPhee Gribble, 1990.

Morgan, Sally. "The Letter." *Paperbark: A Collection of Black Australian Writings*. Ed. Jack David et. Al. St. Lucia: University of Queensland Press, 1990. 79–81.

Morgan, Sally. *My Place*. Fremantle: Fremantle Arts Centre Press, 1987.

Motz, Marilyn F. "Visual Autobiography: Photograph Albums of Turn-of-the-Century Midwestern Women." *American Quarterly* 41 (March 1989): 63–92.

Mouffe, Chantal. "Feminism, Citizenship, and Radical Democratic Politics." *Feminists Theorize the Political*. Ed. Judith Butler and Joan W. Scott. New York: Routledge, 1992. 369–384.

Narogin, Mudrooroo. *Writing from the Fringe: A Study of Modern Aboriginal Literature*. South Melbourne: Hyland House, 1990.

Neuman, Shirley. "Life Writing." *Literary History of Canada, Volume IV*. Ed. W. H. New. Toronto: Toronto UP, 1990. 333.

Newman, Joan. "Race, Gender and Identity: *My Place* as Autobiography." *Whose Place? A Study of Sally Morgan's "My Place."* Ed. Delys Bird and Ennis Haskell. Sydney: Angus & Robertson, 1992. 66–74.

Peterson, Nicholas. "The Popular Image." In *Seeing the First Australians*. Ed. Ian Donaldson and Tamsin Donaldson. Sydney: George Allen & Unwin, 1985. 164–180.

Pratt, Mary Louise. *Imperial Eyes: Travel Writing and Transculturation*. New York: Routledge, 1992.

Pring, Adele, ed. *Women of the Centre*. Apollo Bay, Australia: Pascoe Publishing Pty. Ltd., 1990.

Reece, R. H. W. "Inventing Aborigines." *Aboriginal History* 11 (1987): 14–23.

Reiakvam, Oddlaug. "Reframing the Family Photograph." *Journal of Popular Culture* 26 (Spring 1993). 39–67.

Rowse, Tim. *After Mabo: Interpreting Indigenous Traditions*. Melbourne: Melbourne University Press, 1993.

Ruthrof, Horst. *Pandora and Occam: On the Limits of Language and Literature*. Bloomington: Indiana University Press, 1992.

Seabrook, Jeremy. "My Life Is in That Box." *Family Snaps: The Meanings of Domestic Photography*. Ed. Jo Spence and Patricia Holland. London: Virago, 1991. 171–185.

Sommers, Doris. "'Not Just a Personal Story': Women's *Testimonios* and the Plural Self." *Life/Lines: Theorizing Women's Autobiography*. Ed. Bella Brodzki and Celeste Schenck. Ithaca: Cornell University Press, 1988. 107–130.

Sontag, Susan. *On Photography*. Ringwood: Penguin, 1979.

Spence, Jo. *Putting Myself in the Picture: A Political, Personal and Photographic Autobiography*. London: Camden Press, 1986.

Stokes, Philip. "The Family Photograph Album: So Great a Cloud of Witnesses." *The Portrait in Photography*. Ed. Graham Clarke. London: Reaktion Books, 1992. 193–205.

Tagg, John. *Grounds of Dispute: Art History, Cultural Politics and the Discursive Field*. London: Macmillan, 1992.

Whitlock, Gillian. "Graftworks: Australian Women's Writing 1970–90." *Gender, Politics and Fiction: Twentieth Century Australian Women's Novels*. Ed. Carole Ferrier. St. Lucia: University of Queensland Press, 1992. 236–258.

13
HUMAN RIGHTS AND COMICS: AUTOBIOGRAPHICAL AVATARS, CRISIS WITNESSING, AND TRANSNATIONAL RESCUE NETWORKS (SMITH 2011)

On any given day, graphic narration rides currents traversing the globe. Heterogeneous in their communities of origin and unpredictable in their routes to mass publics dispersed worldwide, diverse genres of graphic narration sometimes parallel, sometimes intersect, sometimes swerve in their travels to publics, archives, and markets here and there. There is, for instance, robust transnational traffic in national genres of comics, such as the long lineage of manga from Japan and *bande dessinée* from France and Belgium, including the Tintin series by Belgian cartoonist Hergé (Georges Prosper Remi). (An adaptation of one Tintin comic hit movie houses in 2011 as a Steven Spielberg film.[1]) Such traffic along "the transnational circuitries of images and narratives" becomes a means through which new global identities are constituted, dispersed communities constellated, and transnational political alliances or identifications forged.[2] Young people distributed across the globe, for instance, consume styles of comics as they consume friendships on social networking sites and display celebrity attachments through fashion, thereby producing strains of global youth culture through consuming habits and the rearrangements of desire those habits release.[3] Through these habits, young people constitute an identity for themselves as savants of global mass culture, hip readers of renegade visuality, and in-members of an emergent global sociality.

Graphic narration also rides the currents of the contemporary regime of human rights: the institutions, protocols, and routes of advocacy that draw attention to what Paul Farmer describes as the unequal "*distribution* of misery" around the globe, give form to the management of its attempted amelioration through discourses that "offer a universal and seemingly uncontested ethics of cross-cultural relations," and enjoin people to become activists in its service.[4] Rights advocates target genres of comics as part of the apparatuses of racist representation, state suppression, and the cultural conduits of degradation affecting marginalized groups and/or dissident voices. Equality Now, an NGO addressing the sources of structural violence against women, is currently engaged in a transnational campaign against Japanese comics called *hentai* that activists describe as celebrations of a normalized culture of rape exploiting women through pornographic degradation.[5] Activists have also critiqued the ways in which comics reproduce colonialist, racist, and anti-Semitic tropes of difference through crude visual stereotypes. Hergé's Tintin series, still popular after three-quarters of a century, has been analyzed for the way it represents blacks in "Tintin in America" and black Africans in "Tintin in the Congo," for instance.[6] Governments too are targeted for employing comic books to propagandize their version of political events, personages, or groups to a broad public, deploying the mass appeal of the comic book form to demonize those they consider "enemies of the state." In August 1999 the Chinese government released a comic book designed to "educate" the public about Falun Gong and its founder Li Hongzhi and to reframe the movement as subversive and Li as an enemy of the people.[7] For advocates for the rights of Falun Gong practitioners, the state in this instance traffics in propagandistic life writing.

At the same time that rights activists lodge charges against certain kinds of comics, they also exploit the capacities of the genre to affect transnational rights literacy and spur activism. As Gillian Whitlock observes so acutely, in times of crisis testimony about rights violations and claims for redress and reparation is negotiated through multilayered processes of producing, circulating, and reading crisis witnessing.[8] Crisis comics are one of these modes of witness to radical injury and harm. Rights advocates exploit the apparent simplicity and easy accessibility of the comic form to make rights discourse and politics legible to large and diverse audiences.[9] They educate readers in rights discourse, naming conditions as violations of universal rights and proposing agendas for change. They contribute to the global "social work" of producing and disseminating the subject positions of "victim," "perpetrator," and "rescuer" managed by the rights regime. They make public an archive of marginalization and suffering. They visualize representative subjects of particular forms of victimization. They project an agenda of rescue. Arraying boxes of witnessing, they narrativize and dramatize complex information at the same time that they intensify the affect of empathetic identification.

Official United Nations (UN) bodies publish material in comic book format, as did the World Health Organization (WHO) and the UN High Commissioner for Refugees (UNHCR) in comic books entitled *HIV/AIDS: Stand Up for Human Rights* (2003) and *HIV and AIDS: Human Rights for Everyone* (2006), developed to encourage recognition on the part of marginalized youth in the global south of their "universal right to health and dignity."[10] Government offices charged with rights literacy also use the comic book form. In celebration of the sixtieth anniversary of the Universal Declaration of Human Rights in 2008, the city of Bogota, Columbia, printed and distributed 1,200,000 comic books to educate citizens in rights discourse.[11] NGOs also use comics to reach audiences. Campaigns to combat the prison-industrial complex in the United States, for instance, reach a mass public through a widely available comic entitled "The Real Cost of Prisons," which presents information about the economics of contemporary punishment and incarceration in an accessible format. Well over one hundred thousand copies of "The Prison Town" (one of three comics included in "The Real Cost") have been printed; and many of those have been disseminated to inmates and their families, as well as prison reform activists.[12] The Office of the Americas for the Cause of Justice and Peace raises funds to distribute a comic book entitled "Addicted to War," chronicling the history of warfare in the United States, to secondary schools through the "Addicted to War Books-to-Schools Project."[13] In the Philippines, activists involved in the Coalition against Trafficking in Women produce comic books that gather, narrate, and illustrate the stories of women who have been in prostitution.[14] The various purposes of these comic books include building awareness, providing information, raising consciousness, soliciting identification, teaching an ethics of recognition, and garnering financial support.

In crisis comics the site of the autobiographical becomes the reader himself or herself. The syncopation of personal storytelling across media (language and image) and space/time (boxes and gutters) in graphic narration activates, as Jared Gardner argues of comics generally, readerly co-interpretation: "All comics are necessarily collaborative texts between the imagination of the author/artist and the imagination of the reader who must complete the narrative."[15] Some readers in crisis comics are addressed as those with the need to know their rights. These readers are the projected audience for such comics as the two previously mentioned, produced and circulated by the WHO and the UNHCR. Such readerships are enjoined to constitute themselves, by virtue of their reading, as subjects of human rights and individual agents of rights activism. In this way, their reading becomes a form of self-rescue as they enact the agency of producing rights knowledge. Other crisis comics address a cosmopolitan readership in developed countries. These readers are addressed as privileged, safe subjects to be enlightened about conditions elsewhere; and their reading rehearses a form of rescue of the other, through the invitation to empathetic identification and outrage. In both situations, genre can be thought of as social action, contributing to the "social work" of publicizing rights discourse, distributing rights identities, and interpellating the reader as a subject of rights activism.

The personal narration of crisis comics in the context of the regime of human rights and its management of injustice is constrained by the discourses, subject positions, protocols, institutions, and venues of rights activism.[16] Take as an example the incorporation of personal stories in NGO materials noted earlier. The NGO Campaign Against Trafficking of Women uses personal stories to intensify the lived reality of rights violations against women, to figure women as the victims of the violation of women's human rights, to put a human voice to suffering, and to appeal to empathetic readers who are solicited to join in the project of redress through identification across difference. Consider how the management of such scenes of witness involves a series of remediations that frame the story, the subject of rights, and the scenario of rescue. Representative women witness to their experiences in prostitution; their narrated lives are then remediated to become as-told-to life writing that is then visualized in a "third-person" hand of the graphic artist. There is an NGO that is functioning as a coaxer seeking the story, and a story of a particular kind. There may be an interviewer, a compiler, an editor, perhaps a translator, all of whom coproduce the form the life story will take and the experiential history that will be included and excluded. And there is a drawer who visualizes the story, distributing it in frames and gutters, figuring the avatar, attaching affect to the width of a line or the design of the page. Collectively, all these actors coproduce the personal story, reframing it as boxes of victimization. In addition, publishers and activists may attach paratexts to the life narrative that situate the stories and authenticate the narrative by providing the imprimatur of the professional activist and the bona fides of the organization attesting to the veracity of the witness. These aspects of the incorporation of personal stories in comic books for rights activism derive from the management of suffering and social justice and thus raise important questions about the relationship of boxes of witnessing to the commodification of contemporary life writing.

The example of the WHO and UNRCR comics about HIV/AIDS awareness among marginalized youth in the global south raises other issues related to activism comics. In their exploration of educational campaigns designed to circulate health information transnationally and the kinds of subjectivities those comics construct for readers, Hsuan L. Hsu and Martha Lincoln argue that the comic form employed by the WHO and the UNHCR in their series on HIV/AIDS manages the right to health and well-being in the global south as a universal right of the individual, and that, as a result of the focus on the individual as the locus of rights, the comics "neglect . . . the critical role of economic and social vulnerability in distributing health disparities unevenly around the globe."[17] In effect, the strategy of personalizing the experience of living with HIV/AIDS in comic book form occludes the structural inequalities that impact what the discourse of human rights defines as the universal right to health and well-being. Moreover, they argue, in the visualization of differences (the figures in the comics are given stereotyped racial, gender, and ethnic identities) the pandemic is decontextualized (the same comic books are translated into several languages and circulated broadly). Imaging bodily difference, the comics at once erase differences in local conditions on the ground and "recruit . . . racial and gender stereotypes to drive the plot and command the identification of readers."[18] Hsu and Lincoln then parse the racialized hierarchy of agency in this comic, noting that "readers are allowed to identify with the person who physically resembles them, yet simultaneously they are encouraged to identify with the person who speaks for them: the white male character, who dominates the cartoon's dialogue."[19] Comics such as the HIV/AIDS comics explored by Hsu and Lincoln paradoxically reproduce the universality of rights subjectivities through the transnational traffic in stereotype. The hypervisualized, seemingly unmarked white protagonist and the array of ready-made, stereotyped avatars of multicultural others surrounding him enacts the suspect pedagogical politics of the rights regime: the unmarked expert from the developed world teaching the "illiterate" subject of rights denied elsewhere around the globe how to assume the subject position of the universal individual and to take individual responsibility for making unsympathetic people better people.[20] In reaching for the identification of the reader with an avatar within the comic, the form reinforces the argument that rights activism is a matter of managing empathetic identification rather than targeting structural inequalities and formations of exploitation within and across nations.

I raise these issues about the way comics in human rights campaigns manage subjectivities not to deny the power of crisis comics to reach publics that might not otherwise be informed, come to consciousness, take action, and claim their experiences and identities as subjects of rights. I do so in order to provide a cautionary note about the impact of the regime of human rights, as the successor global regime to the cold war, on broadly accessible contemporary modes of personal narration and their commodification in global flows that do the work of rearranging histories, identities, and the politics of empathy. I do so as well to turn attention to other genres of crisis comics that, even if caught in the neoliberal politics of commodification, present alternative engagements with witnessing, memory, loss, and recovery in graphic form. For, at the same time that graphic narration in the mode of crisis comics circulates in the information economy of contemporary human rights activism, the genre of graphic memoirs, or "autographics," circulates as a register of remembering complex histories of violence—transnational, national, communal, familial, and personal.[21]

Joseph Slaughter explores how, over the course of two hundred years, human rights discourse and the literary bildungsroman have produced "mutually enabling fictions" that share "a common conceptual vocabulary, humanist social vision, and narrative grammar of free and full human personality development."[22] Slaughter reads the bildungsroman as the "novelistic wing of human rights," persuasively arguing that the two share a plot "for participation in the egalitarian imaginary of the new bourgeois nation-state, a plot for incorporation of previously marginalized people as democratic citizen-subjects."[23] We learn how to be subjects of rights through reading realist novels chronicling the education and development of an individual who achieves maturity and resolution in incorporation as a normative subject of the nation. Indeed, in this historical moment he argues, "the *Bildungsroman* remains the primary enabling fiction for and privileged genre of incorporation into an international 'reading public.'"[24] And writers across the globe committed to chronicling struggles for history, knowledge, and the status of the human in decolonizing and postcolonial societies and states read novels of incorporation and sometimes write novels of education that are indebted to, haunted by, and in conversation with the bildungsroman form. Deploying the form, they test its limits, open its ambiguities, reject its terms, and intervene in the violence of the state projects it secures through its fable of incorporation. Slaughter convincingly establishes a founding relationship between human rights discourse and this literary genre of modern citizenship and nation building, and then analyses the ways in which contemporary postcolonial bildungsromane "make legible the inequities of this egalitarian imaginary."[25]

As they witness to traumatic histories of marginalization and violence, graphic memoirs invoke, and riff on, conventions of this long-lived form of the bildungsroman. More particularly, they tell stories of the struggle to find an artistic practice sufficient for both telling and drawing complex stories of marginalization, traumatic loss, and remembering, thus working in the mode of *künstlerroman*, a variation of the bildungsroman that tells the story of coming-of-age as an artist. Adapting this persistent form in often-arresting ways, they unsettle readers with their combination of "high" subject and "low" or "mass" form associated with limited literacy, juvenilia, renegade outsiderness, or fantasy superheroism. Readers confronted a new kind of graphic memoir with the publication of Art Spiegelman's *Maus* in 1986, followed by *Maus II* in 1992. *Maus* dramatically altered the demography of the readership for "comics" and challenged reader expectations of the relationship of form and function, of the memoir as genre and the narration of stories of traumatic injury and harm. Ten years later in 2003, the publication (and subsequent translation) of Marjane Satrapi's *Persepolis* and later *Persepolis II*, continued to revolutionize graphic memoir, as it told the transnational narrative of coming-of-age during the Iranian Revolution. Then in 2006 Alison Bechdel's *Fun Home* mined the possibilities of graphic narration in a doubled coming-out story. Genocide, suicide, and the postmemory generation; revolution, state repression, and exile; suspected suicide and closeted sexuality: these are the experiential histories witnessed, histories that activate the obligation to tell/draw the story of the autobiographical subject as always entwined in the story of others.

"Graphic memoirs," writes Whitlock, now do the transnational and intersubjective work of "open[ing] up new and troubled spaces."[26] The sequential art of graphic memoir presents readers with boxes of memory, filled with images and words, arrayed across the gaps that are gutters, and linked through the self-referential "voiceover" that presents in turn narration, description, emotive reaction, meditation, or metacommentary on the process of remembering. Their hybridity encodes and routes meaning in multiple directions; their oscillations between conjunctive and competing modes of representation and storytelling (visual and textual) prompt new itineraries of "framing," "listening," and "feeling" through the visuality of the written and the discursivity of the depicted; their complexities and densities of language and pattern across frames and gutters energizes opportunities for metacommentary and complex recursiveness. Stories that seem to move forward, visually and narratively, constantly recycle earlier frames, motifs, incidents, characterizations; repetition abounds as acts of remembering engage the returns of inadequate modes and idioms of representation.[27]

Graphic memoirs that witness to histories of injury and harm often traffic in stereotypes and their unsettlement; but that trafficking eventuates in different politics of aesthetics than in such human rights comics as the HIV/AIDS ones previously explored. The condensed stylization of the visual components of graphic memoir, the two-dimensionality of the surface of the comic form, and the repetitive features of the autobiographical avatar in crisis comics align autographics with critiques of cultures of stereotype—of gender, sexuality, ethnicity, and nation—that energize structures of social marginalization, its scenes of violence and its complex, inexorable afterlives. Contemporary graphic memoirs that take on the sometimes hidden, sometimes hypervisible bodies and histories of those referenced in and through stereotypes at once put the question of difference in stylized frames and unsettle the commonplaces of cultural framing: Spiegelman unhinges readers with his casting of himself, his father, his mother, and other Jews as mice in *Maus* (the vermin of Nazi propaganda); Satrapi unsettles the West's stereotypes of the veil as emblematic of Muslim women's oppression and of Islamic nations as universally "backward" in *Persepolis*; and Bechdel disarms readers with her burrowing inside the psychic struggles of a father who would be labeled "pervert" in *Fun Home*. With all three, graphic memoir occasions an education in how to represent (for the artist) and how to interpret (for the reader) the taint of otherness attached to those who become objects against which routine violence is directed—by the West, by states, by society. These graphic memoirs in the mode of *Künstlerroman* mix media and meanings, unpack cultural stereotypes, play to the increasing visual literacy of a global community, and, refusing to situate their projects and their readings as calls for rescue, invite readers to collaborate in remembering alternative histories.

Whitlock observes that the accessibility and adaptability of graphic memoir, through its vocabulary and grammar, enables this genre of crisis comics to travel across cultures, despite the marks of national origin.[28] So, I conclude with reference to a new mode of crisis comics incorporating personal witnessing to catastrophic loss and disaster that may well gain momentum in riding the currents around the globe. We might call this "documentary crisis comics."

On August 24, 2009, the *New York Times* "Arts" section carried a review by George Gene Gustines of the publication of Josh Neufeld's "graphic novel" entitled *A.D.: New Orleans after the Deluge*.[29] In the weeks after the disastrous 2004 flood that devastated New Orleans and much of the southern coast of Mississippi, Neufeld had volunteered with the American Red Cross in the recovery effort. From New Orleans he blogged about what he encountered; and then self-published his blogs as "Katrina Came Calling" (2006). Subsequently, he located and interviewed a number of survivors about their experiences during and after the disaster. Chronicling the disaster and its afterlives, Neufeld entwined versions of six "lives" into *A.D.* The first iteration of the "novel" was published in serial form on Smith.com in 2007 through 2008. The online version included video and audiotapes of the interviews. "Publication" in this context came as an ensemble of genres—reportage, research, primary archival document, oral history, all remediated as graphic novel, the "novel form" of witness in which, he tells us in his *Times* interview, he took the novelist's license to edit witness stories and to combine features and parts of stories of his witnesses.[30] Neufeld also included on his site a message board where readers could offer their readings of *A.D.* Asked about the effect of this co-writing for the amazon.com site of *A.D.*, Neufeld responded: "I don't know if it's the future of journalism, but in my case, feedback of any kind is really important to me. And with a large-scale project like *A.D.*, doing it first on the web made creator–reader communication easy. Whether it was a New Orleanian reader correcting my pre-hurricane timeline (which I later amended) or one of the actual characters responding to his or her portrayal, I was grateful for the feedback. It was like having an entire community as my research and fact-checking team!"[31] For the recently printed version, published by Pantheon Graphic Novels, Neufeld expanded the story line to the afterlives of the hurricane and its displacements.

In its experimental form, *A.D.* joins other recent innovations in witness narrating, including Dave Eggers's *What Is the What* (2007), a fictionalized memoir of Valentino Achak Deng, survivor of the Sudanese civil war, and Tracy Kidder's *Strength of What Remains* (2009), a novelistic and quasi-ethnographic rendering of the story of Deogratias, Burundian survivor of civil war and the Rwandan genocide.[32] But where Eggers and Kidder narrate the story of the singular individual surviving radical injury and trauma, Neufeld innovatively disperses crisis witnessing across an ensemble of subject positions—primary witness, secondary witness, fictional composite witness, reporter, fact-checker, and reader. And in its multiple sites of witnessing—blog, online magazine, interactive blog, published text—*A.D.* locates crisis witnessing not in the printed book alone as the memoir commodity but in an ensemble of media through which the process of witnessing is collectively negotiated. To mediate the problematic aspects of his appropriation of other people's stories for his graphic novel, Neufeld evolved an interactive process of composition that engaged his subjects in editing and commentary; and he continued that collaboration in the tour marketing the book—some of the informants appeared with him at book signings when possible, as they did at the New Orleans launch on August 21, 2009.[33] Shuttling across genres, Neufeld drives graphic life writing witnessing to survival of a catastrophic event and the injustice of its aftermath in yet another direction, a hybrid mode of witnessing that calls itself a novel and conjoins journalism, oral history, and blogging.

In *Soft Weapons* Whitlock remarks that "autobiographical narrative is an agent in complex global dialogues and encounters and a way of thinking through the interdependencies of conceptions of self and other"; and she continues that "this personal and highly engaged way of grasping relations between the self and others is intrinsic to the transits of life narrative and the narrative imagination it engenders."[34] Human rights discourse and activist agendas pervade global dialogues and contemporary encounters across self-other circuits. In the global currents of rights politics, graphic witnessing to crises and to the crises of representing radical violence and harm contributes to the rearrangement of "opinion and emotion" related to histories of injustice, violent events, projects of remembering, and agendas for redress.[35] It is deployed instrumentally in specific campaigns to educate readers and constitute them as subjects of rights. But as previously noted, such instrumentalist uses of graphic life writing often operate through apparatuses of remediation and authentication management and thereby reproduce asymmetrical power relations across the divide of rescue politics in which there are those who know, teach, and manage and those who suffer and respond. These comics are sometimes designed to travel across global sites, as in the case of HIV/AIDS comic book campaign, carrying a message of individualist betterment, but the representative work that drawn avatars are given to do presents a universalized (stereotyped) difference unattached to the specificities of local conditions and histories.

Other modes of graphic witnessing enter such dialogues about survival, marginalization, and violent histories more obliquely, such as the graphic memoirs of Spiegelman, Satrapi, and Bechdel and the documentary graphic novel of Neufeld. These narratives exploit the possibilities the comic form provides for unsettling commonplace frames of difference, and they thematize issues of witnessing, remembering, and producing art in the time of a global commodification of suffering. Or, as in the case of Neufeld, they experiment with emergent opportunities for fracturing witnessing across multiple subjects through collective storytelling. However implicated such texts are in the "global commodification of cultural difference—the alterity industry," they model the hard work of rescuing dense, complicated stories of family, ethnic community, and nation rather than reproducing the rights agenda of rescuing "victims," or as Binyavanga Wainaina has satirically intoned, of "sav[ing] you from yourself."[36]

Notes

1. See Alison Leigh Cowan, "An Intrepid Cartoon Reporter, Bound for the Big Screen but Shut in a Library Vault," *New York Times*, August 20, 2009, A21.
2. Gillian Whitlock, *Soft Weapons: Autobiography in Transit* (Chicago: University of Chicago Press, 2006), 8.
3. The phrase "rearrangements of desires" comes from Gayatri Chakravorty Spivak in "Righting Wrongs," *The South Atlantic Quarterly* 103.2/3 (2004): 525.
4. Paul Farmer, *Pathologies of Power: Health, Human Rights, and the New War on the Poor* (Berkeley: University of California Press, 2003), 48 (italics in original); Whitlock, *Soft Weapons*, 13.
5. See update on this campaign at http://www.equalitynow.org/english/actions/action_3301_en.html (accessed August 10, 2009).
6. See, for instance, Hsuan L. Hsu and Martha Lincoln, "Health Media and Global Inequalities," *Daedalus* 138.2 (Spring 2009): 26.
7. See Seth Faison, "If It's a Comic Book, Why Is Nobody Laughing?" *New York Times*, August 17, 1999, repr. in "Beijing Journal," http://www.faluninfo.net/article/520/?cid=138 (accessed August 10, 2009).
8. Whitlock, *Soft Weapons*, 18.
9. In human rights campaigns, comic books are used to reach people who may have limited literacy and those who may absorb and process information in different ways than through standardized print venues. This latter point is presented in support of the work of graphic artists in campaigns for human rights on the Graphic Witness website: http://www.graphicwitness.org/ (accessed August 10, 2009).
10. *HIV/AIDS: Stand Up for Human Rights* (Geneva, Switzerland: World Health Organization, 2003); *HIV and AIDS: Human Rights for Everyone* (Geneva, Switzerland: World Health Organization, 2006); Hsu and Lincoln, "Health Media and Global Inequalities," 25.
11. See http:/www.unhcr.se/en/Publications/publ_index_en.html, the website for publications of the Office of the High Commissioner for Human Rights (accessed August 27, 2009).
12. See the Graphic Witness website linking people around "visual arts and social commentary": http://www.graphicwitness.org/ (accessed August 10, 2009).
13. See www.officeoftheamericas.org/addictedtowar_schools.html (accessed August 10, 2009).

14 See http://www.catwinternational.org/index.php (accessed August 10, 2009).
15 Jared Gardner, "Archives, Collectors, and the New Media Work of Comics," *Modern Fiction Studies* 52.4 (Winter 2006): 800.
16 See Kay Schaffer and Sidonie Smith, *Human Rights and Narrated Lives: The Ethics of Recognition* (New York: Palgrave, 2004), esp. chapter 2, for a discussion of the ways in which venues and formats for rights witnessing are constrained by the purposes, contexts, and politics of production and circulation.
17 Hsu and Lincoln, "Health Media and Global Inequalities," 21.
18 Ibid., 26.
19 Hsu and Lincoln argue that "encourag[ing] readers in the global south to identify with one of the diverse characters who physically resembles them . . . the comic [can] be exported without rescripting to address factors that shape the local epidemiology of AIDS" (25–26).
20 Ibid., 26.
21 See Gillian Whitlock, "Autographics: The Seeing 'I' of Comics," *Modern Fiction Studies* 52.4 (2006).
22 Joseph Slaughter, "Enabling Fictions and Novel Subjects: The *Bildungsroman* and International Human Rights" *Publications of the Modern Language Association* 121.5 (2006): 1407. See also *Human Rights, Inc.: The World Novel, Narrative Form, and International Law* (New York: Fordham University Press, 2007).
23 Slaughter, "Enabling Fictions and Novel Subjects," 1410.
24 Ibid., 1418.
25 Ibid.
26 Whitlock, "Autographics," 976.
27 For this brief discussion of features of comic narration, I am indebted to Hillary Chute and Marianne DeKoven, "Introduction: Graphic Narrative," *Modern Fiction Studies* 52.4 (Winter 2006): 767–82; Gardner, "Autography's Biography"; and Whitlock, "Autographics."
28 Whitlock, "Autographics," 969.
29 Josh Neufeld, *A.D.: New Orleans after the Deluge* (New York: Pantheon 2009).
30 George Gene Gustines, "Graphic Memoirs of Katrina's Ordeal," *New York Times*, August 24, 2009, C5.
31 "A Q&A with Josh Neufeld" on Amazon.com, http://www.amazon.com/D-New-Orleans-After-Deluge/dp/0307378144/ref=sr_1_1?ie=UTF8&s=books&qid=1251742183&sr=8-1 (accessed August 27, 2009).

32 See Dave Eggers, *What Is the What* (New York: Vintage, 2007); and Tracy Kidder, *Strength in What Remains* (New York: Random House, 2009).
33 See schedule for launch at http://antigravitymagazine.com/?p=530 (accessed August 27, 2009).
34 Whitlock, *Soft Weapons*, 11.
35 Ibid., 3.
36 Whitlock, 15; Binyavanga Wainaina, "Oxfamming the Whole Black World," *Mail and Guardian Online*, December 3, 2007, 23:59. http://mg.co.za/article/2007-12-03-oxfamming-the-whole-black-world (accessed August 1, 2010).

Part V
Women's Life Writing in America

14

INTRODUCTION: LIVING IN PUBLIC (2006)

From *Before They Could Vote: American Women's Autobiographical Writing, 1819—1919*

American women's autobiographical writing of the nineteenth and early twentieth centuries, other than slave narratives, suffragist tracts, and Civil War diaries, has received relatively little attention from literary critics and cultural historians. For literary and cultural critics, autobiographical writing has often been seen as a poor relation to the novel and to poetry, the genres in which American women writers created substantial bodies of work and about which significant bodies of scholarship have emerged. For their part, scholars of American women's history have read the autobiographical writings of nineteenth-century women primarily as documentary texts upon which to build careful descriptions of the nature of women's everyday lives and the gendered discourses through which everyday life was organized. In the first case, scholars approach women's autobiographical writing of the century as trivial or marginal to other literary forms. In the second case, scholars read women's autobiographical texts as primarily evidentiary. Neither approach to this rich and diverse field of cultural production does justice to the energy of specific women's texts and the complexity of diverse and changing practices of autobiographical writing in the nineteenth century. Assigning women's life writing to the zone of merely personal writing or reading it solely for its informational value skews our understanding of how widely women both wrote and read and how many imagined themselves as active agents within the context of public life.

Even the field of autobiography studies has been inattentive to much of American women's life writing.[1] *Before They Could Vote: American Women's Autobiographical Writing, 1819—1919* attempts to redress this inattention by presenting a collection of twenty-four personal narratives written or told by American women, some complete and some excerpted from longer works.[2] These women narrate lives of action, passion, and changing social relations throughout what we are calling the "forgotten" century in the United States, the decades between the early Federalist republic and the post-World War I inception of universal suffrage. We have selected writers from a broad range of regions, ages, ethnic backgrounds, and social and work locations in order to challenge two outmoded notions about women's personal writing in the nineteenth century: that there was a pervasive bifurcation of private and public spheres, a gendered world in which women were assigned to the home and imagined themselves through the affective prism of sentimentality and domestic femininity; and that women who went public with their personal stories were primarily white, middle-class women from the Northeast writing within and about their domestic domains.

This introduction discusses several concepts and themes that inform our selections and the ways they might be read: approaches to reading autobiographical discourses, autobiographical genres in this "century," public life and the woman writer, shifts in critical approaches to women's writing, and classroom uses and research prospects for women's life writing.

Reading the Autobiographical

Let us begin with a few theoretical remarks about autobiographical acts before turning to a consideration of women's participation in American autobiographical discourses.

Assuming her experiential history as a reference base and point of departure, an autobiographer represents her life story in order to share it with others. Her "experience" and the "memory" through which it is routed are already interpreted phenomena and thus at least once removed from any pure facticity. After all, autobiographers sometimes take liberty with that most elementary fact, the date of birth, choosing for themselves a more propitious moment or purposefully confusing the date. And memory is selective and untrustworthy. What truth we come to know in reading autobiography derives not from the facts of a life truly remembered, though they may be of interest if we can find them, but from the meanings the autobiographer assigns to and extracts from the representation of her life. She reads meaningful reality into her life and we read her reading. Because of the interpretive nature of any autobiographical act, then, the distinction between autobiographical narrative and fiction remains elusive. Autobiography is always a story in time interweaving historical fact and fiction.

The meanings the autobiographer reads into her life are historically and culturally contingent. Telling her story, she negotiates—sometimes with little, sometimes with discerning, self-consciousness—the cultures of subjectivity available to her, the discourses of identity circulating around her, and the narrative frames commonly used to tell stories. These identities and frames establish what goes into the text as part of an intelligible and official story, and what remains outside as unintelligible and unofficial excess—a kind of noise troubling conventional meanings. In effect, then, she reads her life through her readings of other life stories.

But discourses within the dominant culture are multiple, their calls to normative subjectivity often contradictory, their effects on a specific autobiographical subject unpredictable. And each specific autobiographical subject speaks not from a single location within the community but simultaneously, from multiple locations determined by gender, race, class, nationality, ethnicity, religion, and sexuality, among other markers of identity. Moreover non-dominant communities conserve their own alternative discourses of identity and modes of storytelling. They too circulate heterogeneous calls to subjectivity. Given this multiplicity of the "real," the autobiographical subject does not necessarily imitate prevailing cultural scripts in passive conformity. (And in fact, an imitation by a marginalized subject creates its own kind of noise in the system.) From her specific location within a complex experiential history she may quietly contest, critically adjust, or actively resist normative autobiographical meanings. The impact of her autobiographical mediation depends on the narrative adjustments she makes as she pursues her narrative act, her audience, the models available to her, and her social context and historical circumstances. Autobiographical practice, then, is neither static nor uniform.

Autobiographical Genres in the "Forgotten" Century and the History of American Autobiography

Our choice of time frame, 1819 to 1919, might seem unusual, bridging as it does two centuries. We have skewed this framing of the century in order to de-emphasize the centrality of the Civil War and to focus instead on multiple shifts in what constitute the territories and boundaries of the nation and thus the changing status of American Indians, African Americans, immigrants, and disenfranchised women as workers and writers. Ranging from the end of the early republic to the passage of the twentieth amendment to the Constitution in 1919 that enfranchised women, these narratives link a range of autobiographical genres to broad social transformations, geopolitical, economic, technological, social, and cultural. They offer opportunities to consider the forming, deforming, and reforming of identities in the dynamic context of American myths of identity and belonging. And they focus on what might be called the "forgotten" century for American women's life writing, a time whose myriad and diverse autobiographical forms have as yet not been carefully studied or organized as a canon.

As we have argued elsewhere, the autobiographical is not a single genre but a conceptual umbrella encompassing different forms that serve diverse audiences, purposes, and narrative strategies.³ Personal narratives are not merely transparent "accounts" of some past experience, or exact records of historical events in people's lives or the life of the nation. Rather, they are performances of self-narration through which the meanings of the past are produced for the occasions and social identities of the present and the future. Therefore, we cannot assume an unproblematic relationship between autobiographical remembering and the events of the past. Nor can we regard life narratives as merely private acts or acts marginal to literary and cultural production. These modes provide a forum for interrogating issues in gendered experience that change throughout the century: literacy and education; coming-of-age and the life cycle; the nature of work, marriage, and family; mobility and adventure; sexuality and experimentation with identity; and shifting notions of personal and collective identity.⁴

In sum, autobiographical modes are not static. Rather, they are changing, improvisatory, in motion, hybrid modes always in dialogue with the specificities of personal remembering and the cultural expectations generated by the contours of a life story. Autobiographical narratives are always compelled to satisfy certain cultural conventions, the forms, patterns, and rhetorical styles of stories tellable and intelligible at a particular historical moment. They are motivated by particular audiences, contexts of publication, consumption, and desires. And they are mediated by publication practices and venues, as well as editorial intermediaries and policies. Yet, however constrained, the modes of the autobiographical continue to be fluid and improvised, and thus malleable to the individual teller's understanding of her past and negotiation of her identity in the present.

Before commenting on autobiographical practices during this "forgotten century," we want to comment briefly on the relationship of gendered autobiographical discourses and "America." The history of "America" and the history of autobiographical practices are intimately connected. Autobiographical writing emerges as a compelling cultural activity in the West at approximately the same historical moment that European colonists and enslaved Africans began settling into the space described as "the New World," a world well known to its indigenous inhabitants. This New World, laid out in all its abundance before the colonists, invited ever-new opportunities for recreating self and community. America called for autobiographical subjects. Of course the earliest first-person written narratives were accounts of travel and travail through which male Europeans mapped their encounters with and projections of new geographies, peoples, experiences, and identities.

In the Puritan colonies, self scrutiny saturated the environment as what Daniel B. Shea calls "the ur-narrative of God's saving activity in time," a salvation history at once personal and communal that justified and sustained the beleaguered community (1991). In these close communities, soul searching and community building coincided. Individual lives affirmed and secured communal norms; those norms organized the spiritual lives of individuals, including the lives of women, for whom marriage was an economic necessity and public anonymity the mark of God-given femininity.

Despite the dutiful femininity expected of them in this Old World of gender relations, women left accounts of their lives. Autobiographical forms—the poetry of Anne Bradstreet (1612–1672), the captivity narrative of Mary Rowlandson (1682), the diaries of Sarah Kemble Knight (1704–1705) and Elizabeth House Trist (1783–1784), the journal of Esther Edwards Burr (1754–1757), the spiritual testimonies of Quakers Jane Hoskens (1771) and Elizabeth Ashbridge (1774)—provided ready and intimate vehicles through which colonial women simultaneously heeded the cultural call to feminize subjectivity and negotiated their personal and often eccentric responses to unsettling experiences. These are the autobiographical inscriptions of women undomesticated, if only temporarily, by captivity, by travel, or by ministry. Traversing new, often hostile, assuredly fluid environments, these undomesticated subjects end up disrupting communal constructions of femininity. Disputatious women, they adventure through a frontier of their own, reinventing femininity.

By the late eighteenth century heterogeneous autobiographical forms circulated through the vast space of what was becoming a new republic. These included conversion narratives, spiritual journals, adventure narratives, travel diaries, captivity narratives, sea adventures, gallows narratives (or criminal confessions), and slave narratives—all of which contributed powerful cultural myths and communal models of identity to a colony becoming a nation with its own incipient identity. The most influential of these personal narratives was *The Autobiography of Benjamin Franklin*, begun in 1771 but not published as a complete work until 1868. Through his adroit manipulation of the rhetoric of self-fashioning, Franklin creates an exemplary type of American subject: the national, communally-located self-made man, bourgeois, optimistic, flagrantly individualistic, and decidedly masculine. The legacy of his model American continued throughout the nineteenth century. But another autobiographical mode emerged, influenced by Romanticism and Transcendentalism, that celebrates an intensified, sometimes secularized, antinomianism in which the autobiographical I as creator of the world defies all provided frames and selves. In either mode the autobiographical subject assumes its participation in the making of an American history.

Not everyone in the nineteenth century, however, had equal access to the official status of the new republican subject or assumed equal access to the making of autobiography and, with autobiography, the making of history. The republican subject remained normatively white, male, and bourgeois, even in its rebellions. Its exclusions were manifold and manifest: bourgeois white women, Native Americans, slaves, former slaves, Mexican Americans, recent immigrants, and members of the working class. When such marginalized subjects turned to autobiographical writing, then, they brought to the official stories unofficial and eccentric histories.

Throughout the one hundred years from 1819 to 1919, women adopted and adapted a range of autobiographical forms to bring personal stories into print and public circulation. Certainly they turned to diaries, journals, and letters as convenient modes of self-inscription, as documented by a number of scholars (see Bloom, Bunkers, Buss, Culley, Gwin, Huff, Schlissel, Temple, Wink). Such genres were understood as properly feminine forms of the autobiographical for literate women during the nineteenth century. These sheltered scribblings were intimate, personal, and colloquial. They focused on the quotidian and were circulated within a vibrant private circuit of exchange among women, rather than the marketplace, as chronicled in Carroll Smith-Rosenberg's groundbreaking study *Disorderly Conduct: Visions of Gender in Victorian America*. There were, however, many more modes of the autobiographical to which they turned as they registered their forays into public worlds, and these additional forms were of interest to the expanding outlets for publication. These additional autobiographical genres included confession, captivity narrative, slave narrative, spiritual autobiography, travel narrative, coming-of-age story, collective autobiography, personal essay, ethnographic history, manifesto, immigrant narrative, as-told-to narrative, testimony, and oral witness.

For example, Mary Jemison's story of captivity takes up one of the most important genres of life writing in the nineteenth century. Other narratives unfold through plots common to their era. Mary Antin's narrative of immigrant assimilation to an idealized America tells a different story than does Zitkala-Ša's "Sketches," but immigration narratives inevitably identify tensions between American and ethnic discourses, as Betty Bergland notes (144). Yet some essayistic life writing is less well known and less commonly thought of as autobiographical, such as Fannie Barrier Williams's "The Club Movement Among Colored Women in America." What these disparate narratives have in common is their complication of the assumption that women's writing was confined to particular genres of the "personal." The spiritual autobiography of

Jarena Lee, for instance, not only documents an African American woman's public mission but also attests that the slave narrative was not the only genre of life writing taken up by African American women in the first half of the nineteenth century. Thus, such narratives turn the focus of women's writing from domesticity and the home to aspects of public life—work, travel, social movements, and political struggles.

Considering the hybrid and diverse modes of subjectivity in nineteenth-century women's life writing reveals how much these writers experiment with the cultural forms permeating private and public worlds. That is, they perform subjectivity in ways that undermine any simplistic binary opposition of public and private. And women's practices of autobiographical writing were multifaceted and wildly divergent. At different moments and in various regions, the audiences addressed and the modes used differed, depending upon the politics of publication, the desire of the public for narratives, and the social and cultural pressures for certain kinds of stories. Perhaps this very mobility and malleability of life writing accounts for why autobiographical practice flourished as an enabling means to articulate and reform subjectivity for many diversely located women. Life writing was restricted neither to middle-class women, nor to women of the northeast, nor to white women. Nor was it restricted to a dialogue sustained only between African American and white women. Life writing flourished during this century-long period as an enabling means of articulating and re-forming subjectivity, re-authoring a previously written self, or reflecting on the writer's professional roles for many kinds of women who were otherwise differently advantaged and situated (see Boardman, Lee, Ling, Namias).

Women's Life Writing and Print Culture

Over this century, women took up autobiographical genres for the multiple possibilities of subjectivity these forms made available. They used the existing media available through small and large publishers and in newspapers and magazines for the dissemination of their life stories to an American reading public. And it was not just the literati and the reasonably well-off, educated people of the northeastern states who participated in these thriving publication and circulation ventures. The poor, the vagrant, the criminal, the mobile, and women, too, became not only consumers of other people's writing but also tellers or producers of print culture in very public ways. In his exploration of the history of the book in nineteenth-century America, David D. Hall suggests that "several factors coalesced to bring about this transformation: new printing and paper making technologies that reduced the price of books, improvements in how books were marketed, a rapid increase in the rate of literacy, and a general speeding up of communication. With abundance came the introduction of new literary genres" (37). People began to recognize that writing one's story was not only an "American" thing to do; it brought social status, public recognition, and economic gain as well.

Autobiographical genres of self-narration multiplied. "A market economy, evangelical religion, and romanticism all encouraged people to think of themselves as free agents, characters in the making (and on the make) on the stage of their own devising," suggests Scott Casper (14). Personal stories could circulate far beyond the local community, materializing elsewhere as a commodity of self-locating. With the expansion of print culture, "a pamphlet," writes Ann Fabian, "created 'a memorial' more permanent than either the gossip of the street or the coverage of the press" (55). Autobiographical writing thus became a strategy for making one's way in the world, making the world attentive to one's passions, commitments, and goals, and making oneself as a world.

Casper points out that, for some people, life stories were the only capital readily available, a kind of personal property that could be turned into some modicum of profit for immediate return from audiences and readers. Those who were non-literate could dictate their stories to an intermediary or a publisher. The literate could write down their stories and either self-publish them or find a willing printer. Editors could publish the confessions of the non-literate, the renegade, the downtrodden, and the condemned. Travelers could produce chapbooks that focused on true-life adventures. Publishers increasingly directed their attention to "marginal figures who otherwise would not have survived in print: Indian captives, victims of shipwreck, eccentrics" (Casper 156). Accounts of criminal acts, a popular form of storytelling in America since the late seventeenth century (Fabian 52), became profitable publishing ventures for "printers, confessors, and some literate convicts" (51), and were peddled to an increasing working-class readership.[5] Exploring the kinds of narratives told by the poor, Fabian notes the importance of confessions of sinners and criminals, such as the narrative of the condemned Rose Butler that profited her editor rather than her, while still incorporating her narrative of her brief life.

Writing and publication histories are revealing for what they suggest about the political contexts and the emergent venues of life writing, as well as public responses to particular kinds of stories. What began as a rather brief narrative, such as Mary Jemison's "as-told-to" captivity narrative first published by James Seaver in 1824, was repeatedly reprinted and expanded with supporting materials to become a substantial book later in the century, including such materials as photographs, letters, and testimonials. What was written at one historical moment might be published at a much later moment. Frances Anne (Fanny) Kemble's *Journal of a Residence on a Georgia Plantation*, written in 1838 and 1839, did not appear in published form until 1863 when Kemble decided to go public with her reflections on the degraded life of the slave plantation to counter English support for the Confederacy during the Civil War. At the turn of the twentieth century, many narratives appeared originally in national magazines or newspapers, among them *The Independent*, *The Atlantic Monthly*, and *The Boston Globe*, and in local newspapers such as *The Butte Evening News*.

By the 1850s an increasing number of women began to make their living as writers—journalists, novelists, magazine writers (see Bauer and Gould, Kelley). Publishers recognized the money to be made by directing attention to the consumer public, especially middle-class women. With the market for print material expanded, middle-class white women could establish and sustain themselves as professional writers, along the lines that George Sand profitably did in France and George Eliot in England. Margaret Fuller, Lydia Sigourney, Sarah Orne Jewett, Lucy Larcom, Elizabeth Phelps, and Rebecca Harding Davis are among the nineteenth-century women who made their living as writers, something unheard of for women writers before Margaret Fuller.[6] Not restricted to domestic life, these women were publicly active and vocal. Their narratives, however, testify to the cultural pressures of official bourgeois femininity. In each narrative the autobiographical subject has to constitute femininity as well as national subjectivity and construct it in such a fashion as to legitimate her claim to narrative authority. By the early twentieth century, however, aspiring professional writers, such as Mary Antin or Mary Hunter Austin, could assert that her life story was simultaneously the making of the writer.

Writers sought to publish autobiographical narratives for a variety of purposes. The possibility of earning money from publishing one's life story, as noted above, could be very important, as it was for Adele Jewel, who helped support her family through reprintings of her brief life story of growing up as a deaf woman. In the case of Mary MacLane, the publication of her 1902 life narrative, originally titled *I Await the Devil's Coming*, led to national celebrity and public hunger for more of her spicy stories of life as a single woman. Important too was the possibility of modeling a transformed life. African American preacher Jarena Lee was motivated to write her life story as a way of calling others to God's purpose and validating her own "call." Sometimes the purpose was at once individual and collective. The ante-bellum speeches of abolitionist activists Sojourner Truth and Harriet Tubman referenced their own experience as representative of that of enslaved African women. The post-bellum narratives of Elizabeth Keckley, *Behind the Scenes; or Thirty Years a Slave, and Four Years in the White House* (1869) and Anna Julia Cooper, *A Voice from the South* (1892), shift the emphasis away from the horrors of slavery and the moral dilemma of the African American woman's sexual concubinage, to the representation of the African American woman as the independent self-supporting member of an emerging black bourgeoisie desirous of participating in the Franklinian myth of self-making (see Santamarina). Autobiographical narrative becomes a means to affirm the subject's identification with the mainstream values of American life, and to affirm it on behalf of the collectivity. This was the case at the dawn of the twentieth century when Booker T. Washington gathered essays and polemical writings in *A New Negro for a New Century*, including Fannie Barrier Williams's essay on the club movement, "The Colored Woman and Her Part in Race Regeneration" (1900).

For other writers the motivation for collecting life stories was linked to gathering alternative histories of cultures disappearing in the United States. Although there were indigenous forms of oral and pictographic personal narratives in Native American cultures (Hertha Dawn Sweet Wong 1992), only after contact with white Americans did written autobiography by Native American women emerge as a bicultural product, whether written alone or in collaboration with a white amanuensis/editor.[7] This communal identification is signaled in the titles of such narratives as Catherine Brown's *Memoirs of Catherine Brown, a Christian Indian of the Cherokee Nation* (1824) and Sarah Winnemucca's *Life Among the Paiutes: Their Wrongs and Claims* (1883). Yet the narrator weaves this alternative notion of communal subjectivity through narrative patterns inflected by the individualistic ethos of the dominant culture. Brown is influenced by Christian conversion narratives; Winnemucca may have been influenced as much by protest narratives as by traditional coup tales that establish communal stature (David Brumble, *American Indian Autobiography*, 1988). In these cultural contexts the ideologies of gender they engaged differentiate the narrative spheres of men and women.

The personal testimonies of nineteenth-century Mexican American women have only recently been recovered from various archives, primarily the archive of Western historian Hubert H. Bancroft, who collected over one hundred personal narratives (most in oral history form) of native Californians in the 1870s. In the late nineteenth century Bancroft hired assistants to collect oral histories of California pioneers and indigenes for his history of California, published from 1884 to 1890. One of the women Thomas Savage interviewed was Eulalia Pérez, whose testimony here marks a past that was being appropriated and suppressed by the national narrative of the new state of California. Perez's life narration provides a lively testimony countering the official history of an emergent nation. These women's personal narratives, according to Genaro M. Padilla, reveal common preoccupations: the affirmation of a distinct cultural heritage and a way of life forever changed by the Anglicization of California, the recording of the personal experiences of cultural disruption, and the braiding of domestic and social histories. But Padilla also notes that these women variously reflect upon and critique the gender arrangements deployed in the community and affirm their ability to find forms of empowerment in public life within the constraints of a patriarchal, racist society (*My History* 111).

Many autobiographical narratives of culturally eccentric subjects emerged through collaborative ventures. Often the narratives had to be authenticated by white patrons/editors who testified to their veracity and thereby legitimated the "life." In other cases the autobiographical occasion became entirely collaborative. White editors, whether amateur political activists or (later) professional anthropologists, collected the narrative, framed it, organized it, and in the process conformed both narrative mode and autobiographical subject to their ideological agenda. Nonetheless, autobiographical acts, even if collaborative, also became a medium of cultural critique and resistance. Women like Harriet Jacobs implicitly challenged the exclusionary bases upon which cultural notions of white feminine identity rested, bases implicating racial, ethnic, and class identifications. In the process these subjects reproduced different forms of femininity. They thereby undermined the assumed naturalness of sexual and racial differences, simultaneously affirming and troubling the meaning of American lives by turning their own specific lenses upon the process of forced Americanization.

By the early decades of the twentieth century, great masses swelled the populations of urban centers, including large numbers of immigrants who established ethnic communities in America's cities. Like African Americans, Native Americans, and Mexican Americans, these immigrants and their children struggled with hyphenated identities and the different histories determinative of those identities. Thus each group of immigrants and each generation of ethnic Americans confronted the dynamic tension between assimilation to a normative American identity that devalued cultural difference and the immigrant's allegiance to the culture of origin and its indigenous traditions, which continued over generations, as Sau-Ling Cynthia Wong's critique makes clear. Autobiographies of immigrant and ethnic women reveal how these tensions are exacerbated by multiple gender histories. Gender arrangements line up differently in different cultural contexts, their effects on women influenced by the intersection of generational position, class status, ethnic group, and racial identification. Autobiographers negotiate competing histories of normative femininity and, in those negotiations, make gender adjustments. The destabilizing possibilities of adjustments to and in a new land, to and in a multicultural identity, are evident in the succession of names Mary Antin adopts in her autobiography, *The Promised Land* (1912), as well as in the undoing and reinvention of identity in Lillian Wald's *The House on Henry Street* (1915) and Anzia Yezierska's *Children of Loneliness* (1923).

Women's Life Narratives in the Reconfiguration of American Studies

The reconfigured concept of the nineteenth-century United States as a nation with imperialist ambitions articulated by Amy Kaplan, Donald Pease, John Carlos Rowe, Robyn Wiegman, and others finds support in several narratives by women that attest to internal colonization (Fanny Kemble, Zitkala-Ša) and inequitable access for working class and non-white people (Lucy Larcom, Fannie Barrier Williams, the prostitute "Madeleine"). Several autobiographical narratives also suggest how seemingly disenfranchised women, such as Sarah Winnemucca and Eulalia Pérez, negotiated the boundary of the American nation transnationally. Notions of the dominance of the Eastern states—New England, mid-Atlantic, the South—are also challenged by the work of women writers publishing not just in private, daily forms but publicly throughout many regions of the nation: for instance, Mary Hunter Austin in California and the Southwest or Mary MacLane in the northern Rockies.

Compelling support for reconfiguring American studies as a site of comparative ethnic studies is also offered in the focus on ethnicity and class position in writers as diverse as African American preacher Jarena Lee and Russian Jewish immigrant Mary Antin, both of whom figure "Americanness" across multiple axes of identification. We have only to turn to Sui Sin Far's brief autobiographical essays to note how inadequate any single characterization of her ethnicity would be, or how her texts intervene in simplistic notions of ethnic identity formation by critiquing stereotypes of the Chinese in North America. Each of these reconfigurations of literary and cultural activity in the period between 1819 and 1919 redefines the nation as transnationally situated, a site of the colonization of some and the enfranchisement of others.

American literary culture becomes a marketplace of heterogeneous forms of writing and testimony through which seemingly marginal subjects exert their claims to a subjective agency not necessarily grounded in being of European descent, male, prosperous, or Christian. Most strikingly, perhaps, texts ranging from Rose Butler's public confession of arson in 1819 to Harriet Quimby's narrative of flight in 1912 contest an early dictum about gendered difference: that women's worlds in the nineteenth and early twentieth centuries constituted a separate sphere. Because this notion has been so pervasive in American literary studies and is implicitly challenged by many women's narratives, it requires further discussion.

The "Separate Spheres" argument, an orthodoxy of 1970s and 1980s theorizing of women's history in the United States, asserted a binary opposition between public and private spheres, with women situated in an increasingly privatized zone of domestic femininity and men active within the public zone organized according to masculine values, behaviors, attitudes, and practices.[8] As the essays in *No More Separate Spheres!* make clear, the separate spheres model was productive in the early stages of feminist theorizing of the historically specific construction of gender and gendered roles in nineteenth-century America.[9] It provided, as Linda Kerber notes, a "device" through which women's historians could explore the lives of nineteenth-century women and the social organization of gendered bodies, practices, and discourses (37). Although enabling as a framework for constructing the gendered differences of and in women's lives and cultural production, that model has become increasingly problematic for understanding the intersection of gender with other vectors of identity, including race, ethnicity, class, sexuality, and regional location. Separate spheres arguments universalize "woman," equate public powerlessness with the privatized virtues of pliant femininity, attach sentimentality to women and the feminine, depoliticize the home and family, and reproduce a rigid binary of private and public. In so doing, this bifurcated model belies the diversity and complexity of gendered lives.

For one thing the private sphere invoked through this schema tended to be a particular private sphere, one characterizing only particular households—the bourgeois households of the expanding white middle and upper classes. For millions of immigrants and for slaves—captive, escaped, and eventually "freed" by the Emancipation Proclamation—the household remained a space of labor commanded through slavery, indenture, and economic exigency. Then too, on the ever-moving western "frontier," the amorphous spheres of people's lives were constantly reconfigured and renegotiated through the demands of life on the prairies, in the mountains, and along the coasts. Finally, the intersection of gender with race, ethnicity, and sexuality suggests that feminized spaces could be spaces inhabited by men alone, and that within women's relationships the organization of gendered difference maps unequally across cultural locations. Indeed, as Amy Kaplan argues, in the age of Manifest Destiny, the 1830s through the 1850s, when U.S. boundaries were in continuing fluctuation, domesticity relied on and reproduced the contradictory logic of nationalist expansion. Far from being a "separate sphere," the domestic served as "an ambiguous third realm between the national and the foreign," and even women's texts dedicated to household management—such as those of Catherine V. Beecher and Sara Josepha Hale—inscribe the "racial underpinnings" shared by domestic and imperialist discourses (584).

A focus on autobiographical narratives written and/or published between 1819 and 1919 exposes the limitations of early feminist mappings of women's separate spheres. Women who wrote autobiographically came from regions as far-flung as New England and Mexican California, the Rocky Mountain west and the tenement streets of New York, the Georgia plantation and the Mojave Desert. They were not constrained in spaces understood problematically as "domestic." Certainly there are spaces of constraint exposed in these narratives, but they are diverse spaces of negotiation, both public and private. The brothel in Butte, Montana, for instance, is at once a place of labor, domesticity, and public entertainment. And the separate spheres that Zitkala-Ša negotiates are not those of feminized consumption and masculine labor but of the Lakota reservation and the Carlisle Indian School, with their differing political practices, ideas of education, and spiritual belief systems. Moreover these women are on the move, adventurous, and questing intellectually, spiritually, physically, and geographically. They emerge from a range of domestic spheres, though not idealized ones, to become agents in their worlds, making, mapping, negotiating, and sometimes changing those worlds.

The diversity of earlier women's autobiographical practices questions easy assumptions about what women were doing, during the century that led up to women's suffrage, that took them outside the home, and outside the imminent foreclosure of sentimental fiction's plots of marriage, childbirth, and/or death. Collectively such life writing challenges our assumptions about what characterized their pursuit of action and agency in public worlds, the worlds of labor (physical and intellectual) and professional work, the world of communities, and the worlds beyond the borders of the expanding nation. Even when these women reflect on domestic life in the home, they do so as accomplished writers, not simply recalling an early life but telling stories about coming of age as a process of encountering and negotiating constraints of gendered, sexual, and ethnic difference. Their narratives foreground the continually fluid, and at times migratory, social locations occupied by American women during the nineteenth and early twentieth centuries. They also expose the variety and the vagaries of becoming American and the gendered and racialized identities subsumed in the national narrative.

Conclusion

The autobiographical texts gathered in *Before They Could Vote* suggest a larger story, beginning with the 1819 as-told-to confession of nineteen-year-old Rose Butler, sentenced to death for alleged arson in a poor rooming house; to the transgressive narratives of women as disparate as the prostitute "Madeleine," the aviator

Harriet Quimby, the accomplished writer Sui Sin Far (Edith Maude Eaton), and the American Indian activist, author, and opera composer Zitkala-Ša in the early twentieth century. While theirs is no simple story of triumphant emergence onto a public stage, these women all intervened in the social, racial, and religious constraints that aimed to keep them fixed in domestic life, without, in most cases, renouncing the communities that sustained them and their activist commitments to important issues of their times. From Jarena Lee refusing to suppress her preaching in the African Methodist Episcopal Church, to Fanny Kemble protesting the wrongs of slavery on Butler Island, Georgia, to Sarah Winnemucca asserting the rights of the Paiute nation through her narrative of broken promises, to Eulalia Pérez telling a complex story of empowerment and compliance at the California mission, to the Massachusetts mill worker Lucy Larcom chronicling her humble beginnings and rise to literary eminence, to Fannie Barrier Williams's prominence in the African American middle-class in Chicago, these writers all tell stories of making their way in the multiple, changing public worlds of American life.

Yet few of these women became as famous in their own time as did writers Margaret Fuller, Sarah Orne Jewett, Mary Hunter Austin, Mary Antin, and Bryn Mawr College president M. Carey Thomas or activists Sojourner Truth and Harriet Tubman. Many have remained little known. The three brief testimonies published in *The Independent* describe the tensions of daily life between African American and white women in the aftermath of the Civil War and their changing sense of American public life. And a few "forgotten" writers such as Mary MacLane are included both for their piquant sense of the costs and pleasures of autobiographical writing and to introduce them to a wider public. Taken together, all these women, through their life narratives, produce a complex portrait of the challenges and costs of aspiring to self-affirming lives.

By collecting these narratives as *Before They Could Vote*, we argue against the tendency to overinvest in the notion of sentimental modes of cultural production in the nineteenth century, and call for a more nuanced understanding of the affective dimensions of writing in the myriad modes of the everyday. We dispute a reading of the "forgotten" century as predominantly a period of suffragist reform negotiated in domestic spheres prior to the Nineteenth Amendment and call for approaching this time as one generating heterogeneous narratives of activism and adventuring. We counter the tendency to approach this hundred-year span methodologically through the lens of a black-and-white binary of slavery versus freedom and to see its multicultural and transnational complexity. We assert that assimilation to an "American" identity was invariably complicated by the ambivalent relationship of women at multiple sites of immigration to the prospect of American citizenship. Finally, we hope that readers will take as much pleasure as we did in discovering some previously unknown autobiographical writers and texts.

The narratives of lesser-known women writers in *Before They Could Vote*, along with the diaries and journals of such self-conscious writers as Alice James and Louisa May Alcott, are a fascinating "pre-history" to reading lists that explore the "golden age" of Modernist women's narratives by such writers as Emma Goldman, Charlotte Perkins Gilman, Edith Wharton, Isadora Duncan, H.D., Ida B. Wells, Anzia Yezierska, Gertrude Stein, Zora Neale Hurston, and the later work of Mary Hunter Austin.

There are rich prospects for future research. New explorations of women's autobiographical cultures, contexts, genres, and rhetorical strategies might question prevailing understandings of the "canon" of nineteenth-century autobiographical writing employed by individuals and communities to negotiate national belonging and the organization of everyday life. How might lesser-known nineteenth-century women's narratives lead us to read core canonical American autobiographical texts such as those of Walt Whitman, Ralph Waldo Emerson, Henry David Thoreau, Frederick Douglass, Booker T. Washington, and Henry Adams differently? How might we understand the organization of gendered social systems and the socially constituted boundary between the zone of domesticity and the zone of public activity in the nineteenth century without recourse to a "separate spheres" model? How might attending to works by lesser known writers, as well as the little-known works of well-known writers such as Sarah Orne Jewett and Margaret Fuller, offer a more nuanced picture of the cultural meanings and uses of writing lives in the decades prior to suffrage? If the self-made man is a trope that informs many male autobiographical narratives of the time, from Frederick Douglass's to Edward Bok's, what complex terms and contingencies might inform the pressures on and impulses to self-making among "undomesticated" women? We leave it to readers to explore possible responses to these questions and to generate many others.

Notes

We thank Oxford University Press for permission to excerpt sections of Sidonie's essay on "Autobiography" from *The Oxford Companion to Women's Writing in the United States*.

1. In a 1991 essay on "Nineteenth-Century Autobiographies of Affiliation: The Case of Catharine Sedgwick and Lucy Larcom" in the influential collection *American Autobiography: Retrospect and Prospect*, Carol Holly acknowledged that her reading of these neglected texts was only a step toward the "comprehensive contextual study of "nineteenth-century autobiography by literary women, indeed by all nineteenth-century American women" (227).
2. Fewer than half (ten) of the women included in *Before They Could Vote* are subjects of entries in the encyclopedic *Oxford Companion to Women's Writing in the United States*, published in 1995 (edited by Cathy N. Davidson and Linda Wagner-Martin), suggesting that autobiographical narratives still may be seen as "sub-literary."
3. For an expanded discussion of the types and terms of autobiographical writing, including sixty genres of self-narrating, see our *Reading Autobiography*. See also the *Encyclopedia of Life Writing* edited by Margaretta Jolly.
4. As many of these women attest, becoming literate was critical to identity formation (Zagarri on literacy, 33, note 7). Acquisition of literacy

was a major achievement for Zitkala-Ša, Sarah Winnemucca, and Sui Sin Far, among others. In *Learning to Stand and Speak: Women, Education, and Public Life in America's Republic* Mary Kelley explores how women's lives were reshaped through female academies and seminaries.

5   Such personal stories were seen to give "authentic voice" to those confessing and, as Fabian points out, to persuade readers to accept their truth as authoritative, despite the fact that they were often lurid and sensationalized narratives designed to capture their audiences through titillation and revelation. Sometimes the authenticity was fictional, but powerful and compelling nonetheless, as in the case of certain Barbary Coast narratives presented as women's adventures of being captured by pirates but written by men (see Baepler, cited in Fabian 52).

6   Lawrence Buell points out that Sigourney's *Letters of Life* (1866) was "the first full-dress autobiography written by an American author of either sex whose primary vocation was creative writing" (60).

7   The narrator constitutes her self as an autobiographical subject through what Arnold Krupat calls a synecdochic sense of self "where narration of personal history is more nearly marked by the individual's sense of himself [sic] in relation to collective social units or groupings" (xx).

8   See Linda Kerber' s essay on feminist scholarship of the nineteenth century, especially the work of Barbara Welter in *The Cult of True Womanhood* and Aileen Kraditor on the notion of the cult of domesticity. See also Frances Cogan's alternative of Real Womanhood. These critiques help us see how the notion of women's constitutive domesticity was "a normative ideal [*for white women*] rather than a description of reality" (Zagarri 33, our interpellation).

9   For critiques of the separate spheres argument, see Dana Nelson and Cathy N. Davidson and Jessamyn Hatcher.

Works Cited

Albertine, Susan. "Industrialization." In *The Oxford Companion to Women's Writing in the United States*, edited by Cathy N. Davidson, Linda Wagner-Martin, and Elizabeth Ammons, 421–23. New York: Oxford University Press, 1995.

Ammons, Elizabeth. *Conflicting Stories: American Women Writers at the Turn into the Twentieth Century.* New York: Oxford University Press, 1991.

Andrews, William L. *To Tell a Free Story: The First Century of Afro-American Autobiography, 1760–1865.* Urbana: University of Illinois Press, 1986.

Andrews, William L., et al., eds. *Sisters of the Spirit: Three Black Women's Autobiographies of the Nineteenth Century.* Bloomington: Indiana University Press, 1986.

Anonymous. (Negro Nurse) "More Slavery at the South." *The Independent* 72 (January 25, 1912): 196–200.

———. [Northern Woman] "Observations of the Southern Race Feeling." *The Independent* 56 (March 17, 1904): 594–99.

———. [Southern Colored Woman] "The Race Problem-An Autobiography." *The Independent* 56 (March 17, 1904): 586–89.

———. [Southern White Woman] "Experiences of the Race Problem." *The Independent* 56 (March 17, 1904): 590–94.

Antin, Mary. *The Promised Land.* Boston: Houghton Mifflin, 1912.

Austin, Mary Hunter. *Earth Horizon: Autobiography.* Boston: Houghton Mifflin, 1932.

———. *The Land of Little Rain.* Boston: Houghton Mifflin, 1903.

Baepler, Paul, ed. *White Slaves, African Masters: An Anthology of American Barbary Captivity Narratives.* Chicago: University of Chicago Press, 1999.

Bataille, Gretchen M., and Kathleen M. Sands. *American Indian Women Telling Their Lives.* Lincoln: University of Nebraska Press, 1984.

Bauer, Dale M., and Philip Gould. *The Cambridge Companion to Nineteenth-Century American Women's Writing.* Cambridge and New York: Cambridge University Press, 2001.

Bergland, Betty. "Postmodernism and the Autobiographical Subject: Reconstructing the 'Other.'" In *Autobiography and Postmodernism*, edited by Kathleen Ashley, Leigh Gilmore, and Gerald Peters, 130–66. Amherst: University of Massachusetts Press, 1994.

Bloom, Lynn Z. "I Write for Myself and Strangers": Private Diaries as Public Documents. In *Inscribing the Daily: Critical Essays on Women's Diaries*, edited by Suzanne L. Bunkers and Cynthia A. Huff, 23–37. Amherst: University of Massachusetts Press, 1996.

Boardman, Kathleen and Gioia Woods, eds. *Western Subjects: Autobiographical Writing in the North American West.* Salt Lake City: University of Utah Press, 2004.

Boyle, Eleanor, ed. *The Terrific Kemble: A Victorian Self-Portrait from the Writings of Fanny Kemble.* London: H. Hamilton, 1978.

Brumble, H. David. *American Indian Autobiography.* Berkeley: University of California Press, 1988.

Buell, Lawrence. "Autobiography in the American Renaissance." In *American Autobiography: Retrospect and Prospect*, edited by Paul John Eakin, 47–69. Madison: University of Wisconsin Press, 1991.

Bunkers, Suzanne L., ed. *Diaries of Girls and Women: A Midwestern American Sampler*. Madison: University of Wisconsin Press, 2001.

Bunkers, Suzanne L., and Cynthia Anne Huff, eds. *Inscribing the Daily: Critical Essays on Women's Diaries*. Amherst: University of Massachusetts Press, 1996.

Bush, Laura L. *Faithful Transgressions in the American West: Six Twentieth-Century Mormon Women's Autobiographical Acts*. Logan: Utah State University Press, 2004.

Buss, Helen M. *Mapping Our Selves: Canadian Women's Autobiography*. Montreal: McGill-Queen's University Press, 1993.

———. *Repossessing the World: Reading Memoirs by Contemporary Women*. Waterloo, Ontario: Wilfrid Laurier University Press, 2002.

Buss, Helen M., and Marlene Kadar, eds. *Working in Women's Archives: Researching Women's Private Literature and Archival Documents*. Waterloo, Ontario: Wilfrid Laurier University Press, 2001.

Butler, Rose. *An Authentic Statement of the Case and Conduct of Rose Butler, who was tried, convicted, and executed for the crime of arson*. New York: Broderick and Ritter, 1819.

Carlisle, Marcia. "Introduction." In *Madeleine: An Autobiography*, by "Madeleine," v-xxviii. New York: Persea Books, 198.

Cary, Richard. "Introduction." In *The Uncollected Short Stories of Sarah Orne Jewett*, edited by Richard Cary, iii-xviii. Waterville, ME: Colby College Press, 1971.

Casper, Scott E. *Constructing American Lives: Biography and Culture in Nineteenth-Century America*. Chapel Hill: University of North Carolina Press, 1999.

Cogan, Frances. *All-American Girl: The Ideal of Real Womanhood in Mid-Nineteenth-Century America*. Athens: University of Georgia Press, 1989.

Culley, Margo, ed. *American Women's Autobiography: Fea(s)ts of Memory*. Madison: University of Wisconsin Press, 1992.

Culley, Margo. *A Day at a Time: The Diary Literature of American Women from 1764 to the Present*. New York: Feminist Press at the City University of New York, 1985.

Davidson, Cathy N., and Jessamyn Hatcher. "Introduction." In *No More Separate Spheres!: A Next Wave American Studies Reader*, edited by Cathy N. Davidson and Jessamyn Hatcher, 7-26. Durham, NC: Duke University Press, 2002.

Davidson, Cathy N., Linda Wagner-Martin, and Elizabeth Ammons, eds. *The Oxford Companion to Women's Writing in the United States.* New York: Oxford University Press, 1995.

Derounian-Stodola, Kathryn Zabelle. "Captivity and the Literary Imagination." In *The Cambridge Companion to Nineteenth-Century American Women's Writing,* edited by Dale M. Bauer and Philip Gould, 105–121. Cambridge and New York: Cambridge University Press, 2001.

———, ed. *Women's Indian Captivity Narratives.* New York: Penguin Books, 1998.

Dobkin, Marjorie Housepian, ed. *The Making of a Feminist: Early Journals and Letters of M. Carey Thomas.* Kent, Ohio: Kent State University Press, 1979.

Douglass-Chin, Richard J. *Preacher Woman Sings the Blues: The Autobiographies of Nineteenth-Century African American Evangelists.* Columbia: University of Missouri Press, 2001.

Eakin, Paul John, ed. *American Autobiography: Retrospect and Prospect.* Madison: University of Wisconsin Press, 1991.

Encyclopedia of Life Writing, edited by Margaretta Jolly. London and Chicago: Fitzroy Dearborn, 2001.

Fabian, Ann. *The Unvarnished Truth: Personal Narratives in Nineteenth-Century America.* Berkeley: University of California Press, 2000.

Faderman, Lillian. *Surpassing the Love of Men: Romantic Friendship and Love between Women from the Renaissance to the Present.* New York: Morrow, 1981.

Far, Sui Sin. "Leaves from the Mental Portfolio of an Eurasian." *The Independent* (January 21, 1909): 125–32.

———. "Sui Sin Far, the Half Chinese Writer, Tells of Her Career." *Boston Globe,* (May 5, 1912, morning edition): 31.126.

Fisher, Dexter. *The Third Woman: Minority Women Writers of the United States.* Boston: Houghton Mifflin, 1980.

Fuller, Margaret, et al. *Memoirs of Margaret Fuller Ossoli.* Boston: Phillips, Sampson and Co., 1852.

———. *The Portable Margaret Fuller,* edited by Mary Kelley. New York: Penguin Books, 1994.

———. Furnas, J. C. *Fanny Kemble: Leading Lady of the Nineteenth-Century Stage: A Biography.* New York: Dial Press, 1982.

Graulich, Melody, and Elizabeth Klimasmith, eds. *Exploring Lost Borders: Critical Essays on Mary Austin.* Reno: University of Nevada Press, 1999.

Hall, David D. *Cultures of Print: Essays in the History of the Book.* Amherst: University of Massachusetts Press, 1996.

Halverson, Cathryn. *Maverick Autobiographies: Women Writers and the American West, 1900–1936*. Madison: University of Wisconsin Press, 2004.

Haywood, Chanta M. *Prophesying Daughters: Black Women Preachers and the Word, 1823–1913*. Columbia: University of Missouri Press, 2003.

Holly, Carol. "Nineteenth-Century Autobiographies of Affiliation: The Case of Catharine Sedgwick and Lucy Larcom." In *American Autobiography: Retrospect and Prospect*, edited by Paul John Eakin, 216–34. Madison: University of Wisconsin Press, 1991.

Horowitz, Helen Lefkowitz. *The Power and Passion of M. Carey Thomas*. New York: Alfred A. Knopf, 1994.

Huff, Cynthia. "Textual Boundaries: Space in Nineteenth-Century Women's Manuscript Diaries." In *Inscribing the Daily: Critical Essays on Women's Diaries*, edited by Suzanne L. Bunkers and Cynthia Anne Huff, 123–38. Amherst: University of Massachusetts Press, 1996.

Humez, Jean M. *Harriet Tubman: The Life and the Life Stories*. Madison: University of Wisconsin Press, 2003.

Jemison, Mary. *A Narrative of the Life of Mrs. Mary Jemison*. Edited by James E. Seaver. 1824. Ann Arbor, Mich.: Allegany Press, 1967.

Jewel, Adele M. "A Brief Narrative of the Life of Mrs. Adele M. Jewel." Ann Arbor, Mich.: Dr. Chase's Steam Printing House, 1869.

Jewett, Sarah Orne. "Looking Back on Girlhood," *Youth's Companion* 65 (January 7, 1892): 5–6.

Kaplan, Amy. "Manifest Domesticity." *American Literature*, 70, no. 3 (Sept, 1998): 581–606.

Kelley, Mary. *Empire of Reason: Women, Education, and Public Life*. Chapel Hill, North Carolina: University of North Carolina Press, 2006.

———. "Introduction." In *The Portable Margaret Fuller*, edited by Mary Kelley, ix–xxxiv. New York: Penguin Books, 1994.

———. *Private Woman, Public Stage: Literary Domesticity in Nineteenth-Century America*. 1984. Chapel Hill: University of North Carolina Press, 2002.

Kemble, Fanny. *Journal of a Residence on a Georgian Plantation in 1838–1839*. New York: Harper & Brothers, 1863.

———. *The Terrific Kemble: A Victorian Self-Portrait from the Writings of Fanny Kemble*, edited by Eleanor Boyle. London: H. Hamilton, 1978.

Kerber, Linda K. "Separate Spheres, Female Worlds, Woman's Place: The Rhetoric of Women's History." In *No More Separate Spheres!: A Next Wave American Studies Reader*, edited by Cathy N. Davidson and Jessamyn Hatcher, 29–65. Durham, N.C.: Duke University Press, 2002.

Kilcup, Karen L., and Thomas S. Edwards, eds. *Jewett and Her Contemporaries: Reshaping the Canon*. Gainesville: University of Florida Press, 1999.

Kolodny, Annette. "Inventing a Feminist Discourse: Rhetoric and Resistance in Margaret Fuller's *Woman in the Nineteenth Century*." In *Reclaiming Rhetorica: Women in the Rhetorical Tradition*, edited by Andrea A. Lunsford, 137–66. Pittsburgh: University of Pittsburgh Press, 1995.

———. *The Land before Her: Fantasy and Experience of the American Frontiers, 1630–1860*. Chapel Hill: University of North Carolina Press, 1984.

Kraditor, Aileen S. *Up from the Pedestal: Selected Writings in the History of American Feminism*. Chicago: Quadrangle Books, 1968.

Krentz, Christopher. "Introduction." In *A Mighty Change: An Anthology of Deaf American Writing, 1816–1864*, edited by Christopher Krentz, xi–xxxiii. Washington, DC: Gallaudet University Press, 2000.

Krupat, Arnold. "Native American Autobiography and the Synecdochic Self." In *American Autobiography: Retrospect and Prospect*, edited by Paul John Eakin, 171–94. Madison: University of Wisconsin Press, 1991.

Larcom, Lucy. "Beginning to Work." In *A New England Girlhood: Outlined from Memory*. New York: Houghton Mifflin; Cambridge: Riverside Press, 1889.

Lee, Jarena. *The Life and Religious Experience of Jarena Lee, a Colored Lady, Giving an Account of Her Call to Preach the Gospel*. 1836. Cincinnati: Printed and Published for the Author, 1839.

Lee, Rachel C. *The Americas of Asian American Literature: Gendered Fictions of Nation and Transnation*. Princeton: Princeton University Press, 1999.

———. "Journalistic Representations of Asian Americans and Literary Responses, 1910–1920." In *An Interethnic Companion to Asian American Literature*, edited by King-Kok Cheung, 249–73. New York: Cambridge University Press, 1997.

Ling, Amy. *Between Worlds: Women Writers of Chinese Ancestry*. New York: Pergamon Press, 1990.

———. "Creating One's Self: The Eaton Sisters." In *Reading the Literatures of Asian America*, edited by Shirley Geok-lin Lim and Amy Ling, 305–18. Philadelphia: Temple University Press, 1992.

MacLane, Mary. "Mary MacLane Meets the Vampire on the Isle of Treacherous Delights." *Butte Evening News*, March 27, 1910.

———. *Tender Darkness: A Mary MacLane Anthology*. Edited by Elisabeth Pruitt. Belmont, CA: Abernathy and Brown, 1993.

———. *The Story of Mary MacLane*. 1902. Helena, MT: Riverbend, 2002.

"Madeleine." *Madeleine: An Autobiography*. 1919; New York: Persea Books, 1986. 206–239.

Mobley, Marilyn Sanders. *Folk Roots and Mythic Wings in Sarah Orne Jewett and Toni Morrison: The Cultural Function of Narrative*. Baton Rouge: Louisiana State University Press, 1991.

Myerson, Joel. *Critical Essays on Margaret Fuller.* Boston: G. K. Hall, 1980.

Namias, June. *White Captives: Gender and Ethnicity on the American Frontier.* Chapel Hill: University of North Carolina Press, 1993.

Nelson, Dana D. "Representative/Democracy: Presidents, Democratic Management, and the Unfinished Business of Male Sentimentalism." In *No More Separate Spheres!: A Next Wave American Studies Reader*, edited by Cathy N. Davidson and Jessamyn Hatcher, 325–54. Durham, N.C.: Duke University Press, 2002.

———. "Women in Public." In *The Cambridge Companion to Nineteenth-Century American Women's Writing*, edited by Dale M. Bauer and Philip Gould, 38–68. Cambridge: Cambridge University Press, 2001.

Padilla, Genaro M. *My History, Not Yours: The Formation of Mexican American Autobiography*. Madison: University of Wisconsin Press, 1993.

Painter, Nell Irvin. *Sojourner Truth: A Life, a Symbol.* New York: W. W. Norton and Company, 1996.

Peake McDonald, Cornelia. *A Woman's Civil War: A Diary with Reminiscences of the War from March 1862.* Edited by Minrose C. Gwin. Madison: University of Wisconsin Press, 1992.

Pease, Donald E. *Visionary Compacts: American Renaissance Writings in Cultural Context.* Madison: University of Wisconsin Press, 1987.

Pérez, Eulalia. "An Old Woman and Her Recollections." In *Three Memoirs of Mexican California. As recorded in 1877 by Thomas Savage*. Edited and translated by Vivian C. Fisher, 74–82. Berkeley: Friends of the Bancroft Library, University of California at Berkeley, 1988.

Pierce, Yolanda. "African-American Women's Spiritual Narratives." In *The Cambridge Companion to Nineteenth-Century American Women's Writing*, edited by Dale M. Bauer and Philip Gould, 244–61. Cambridge: Cambridge University Press, 2001.

Pruitt, Elisabeth, ed. *Tender Darkness: A Mary MacLane Anthology.* Belmont, Calif.: Abernathy & Brown, 1993.

Quimby, Harriet. "How I Made My First Big Flight Abroad: My Flight Across the English Channel." *Fly Magazine*. Leslie-Judge Co., June 1912.

Rowe, John Carlos. *Literary Culture and U.S. Imperialism: From the Revolution to World War II.* New York: Oxford University Press, 2000.

Ruoff, A. LaVonne Brown. *American Indian Literatures: An Introduction, Bibliographic Review, and Selected Bibliography.* New York: Modern Language Association of America, 1990.

Rupp, Leila. *A Desired Past: A Short History of Same-Sex Love in America.* Chicago: University of Chicago Press, 1999.

Sánchez, Rosaura. *Telling Identities: The California Testimonios.* Minneapolis: University of Minnesota Press, 1995.

Santamarina, Xiomara. *Belabored Professions: Narratives of African American Working Womanhood.* Chapel Hill: University of North Carolina Press, 2005.

Schlissel, Lillian. *Women's Diaries of the Westward Journey.* New York: Schocken Books, 1982.

Schlissel, Lillian, Vicki Ruiz, and Janice J. Monk. *Western Women: Their Land, Their Lives.* Albuquerque: University of New Mexico Press, 1988.

Scott, John Anthony. *Fanny Kemble's America.* New York: Crowell, 1973.

Seaver, James E., ed. *A Narrative of the Life of Mrs. Mary Jemison.* 1824. Ann Arbor, Mich.: Allegany Press, 1997.

Shea, Daniel B. "The Prehistory of American Autobiography." In *American Autobiography: Retrospect and Prospect,* edited by Paul John Eakin, 25–46. Madison: University of Wisconsin Press, 1991.

Sherman, Sarah Way. *Sarah Orne Jewett: An American Persephone.* Hanover: University of New Hampshire/University Press of New England, 1989.

Smith, Sidonie. *Moving Lives: Twentieth-Century Women's Travel Writing.* Minneapolis: University of Minnesota Press, 2001.

———. "Cheesecake, Nymphs, and 'We the People': Un/ National Subjects About 1900." *Prose Studies: History, Theory, Criticism* 17.1(1994): 120–40.

Smith, Sidonie, and Julia Watson. *Reading Autobiography: A Guide for Interpreting Life Narratives.* Minneapolis: University of Minnesota Press, 2001. Second and expanded edition 2010.

———. "Situating Subjectivity in Women's Autobiographical Practices." In *Women, Autobiography, Theory,* edited by Sidonie Smith and Julia Watson, 3–54. Madison: University of Wisconsin Press, 1998.

———, eds. *Women, Autobiography, Theory.* Madison: University of Wisconsin Press, 1998.

Smith-Rosenberg, Carroll. *Disorderly Conduct: Visions of Gender in Victorian America.* New York: Alfred A. Knopf, 1985.

———. "The Female World of Love and Ritual: Relations between Women in Nineteenth-Century America." In *Women's America: Refocusing the Past,* edited by Linda K. Kerber and Jane Sherron De Hart, 168–82. New York: Oxford University Press, 2000.

Stewart, Jeffrey C. "Introduction." In *Narrative of Sojourner Truth: A Bondswoman of Olden Time, With a History of Her Labors and Correspondence Drawn from Her "Book of Life,"* by Olive Gilbert, xxxiii-xlvii. New York: Oxford University Press, 1991.

Temple, Judy Nolte. "Fragments as Diary: Theoretical Implications of the *Dreams and Visions* of 'Baby Doe' Tabor." In *Inscribing the Daily: Critical Essays on Women's Diaries*, edited by Suzanne L. Bunkers and Cynthia Anne Huff, 72–85. Amherst: University of Massachusetts Press, 1996.

Thomas, M. Carey. *The Making of a Feminist: Early Journals and Letters of M. Carey Thomas*. Edited by Marjorie Housepian Dobkin, 90–93, 116–19, 124, 130–35. Kent, Ohio: Kent State University Press, 1979.

Truth, Sojourner. Speech at the Akron Women's Rights Convention. *Anti-Slavery Bugle*, June 21, 1851. In *Narrative of Sojourner Truth*, edited by Margaret Washington, 117–18. New York: Vintage Books, 1993.

Tubman, Harriet. "Testimony." 1855. In *A North-Side View of Slavery. The Refugee: or the Narratives of Fugitive Slaves in Canada. Related by Themselves, with an Account of the History and Condition of the Colored Population of Upper Canada*, edited by Benjamin Drew, 30. Boston: John P. Jewett and Company, 1856.

Washington, Booker T., Norman Barton Wood, and Fannie Barrier Williams. *A New Negro for a New Century: An Accurate and Up-to-Date Record of the Upward Struggles of the Negro Race. The Spanish-American War, Causes of It; Vivid Descriptions of Fierce Battles; Superb Heroism and Daring Deeds of the Negro Soldier . . . Education, Industrial Schools, Colleges, Universities and Their Relationship to the Race Problem*. Chicago: American Publishing House, 1900.

Watson, Julia. "Bringing Mary MacLane Back Home: Western Autobiographical Writing and the Anxiety of Place." In *Western Subjects: Autobiographical Writing in the North American West*, edited by Kathleen Boardman and Gioia Woods, 216–46. Salt Lake City: University of UtahPress, 2004.

Welter, Barbara. "The Cult of True Womanhood: 1820–1860." *American Quarterly* 18.2 (1966): 151–74.

White-Parks, Annette. *Sui Sin Far/Edith Maude Eaton: A Literary Biography*. Urbana: University of Illinois Press, 1995.

Wiegman, Robyn. *American Anatomies: Theorizing Race and Gender*. New Americanists. Durham, N.C.: Duke University Press, 1995.

Williams, Fannie Barrier. *The New Woman of Color: The Collected Writings of Fannie Barrier Williams, 1893–1918*. Edited by Mary Jo Deegan. DeKalb: Northern Illinois University Press, 2002.

Wink, Amy. *She Left Nothing in Particular: The Autobiographical Legacy of Nineteenth-Century Women's Diaries*. Knoxville: University of Tennessee Press, 2001.

Winnemucca (Hopkins), Sarah. *Life Among the Piutes: Their Wrongs and Claims*. Edited by Mrs. Horace Mann. 1883. Reno: University of Nevada Press, 1994.

Wong, Hertha Dawn. *Sending My Heart Back across the Years: Tradition and Innovation in Native American Autobiography.* New York: Oxford University Press, 1992.

Wong, Sau-ling Cynthia. "Immigrant Autobiography: Some Questions of Definition and Approach." In *American Autobiography: Retrospect and Prospect,* edited by Paul John Eakin, 142–70. Madison: University of Wisconsin Press, 1991.

Xiao-Huang-Yin. "Between the East and the West: Sui Sin Far—the First Chinese American Woman Writer." *Arizona Quarterly* 7 (1991): 49–84.

Zagarri, Rosemarie. "The Postcolonial Culture of Early American Women's Writing." In *The Cambridge Companion to Nineteenth-Century American Women's Writing,* edited by Dale M. Bauer and Philip Gould, 19–37. Cambridge: Cambridge University Press, 2001.

Zanjani, Sally Springmeyer. *Sarah Winnemucca.* Lincoln: University of Nebraska Press, 2001.

Zitkala-Ša (Gertrude Simmons Bonnin). *Dreams and Thunder: Stories, Poems, and the Sundance Opera.* Edited by P. Jane Hafen. Lincoln: University of Nebraska Press, 2001.

———. "Impressions of an Indian Childhood." *The Atlantic Monthly* 85.507 (January 1900): 37–47.

———. "An Indian Teacher among Indians." *The Atlantic Monthly* 85.509 (March 1900): 381–86.

———. "The School Days of an Indian Girl." *The Atlantic Monthly* 85.508 (February 1900): 185–94.

———. "Why I am a Pagan." *The Atlantic Monthly* 90.542 (December 1902): 801–803.

15

CHEESECAKE, NYMPHS, AND "WE THE PEOPLE": UN/NATIONAL SUBJECTS ABOUT 1900 (SMITH 1994)

The new American showed his parentage proudly; he was the child of steam and the brother of the dynamo, and already, within less than thirty years, this mass of mixed humanities, brought together by steam, was squeezed and welded into approach to shape; a product of so much mechanical power, and bearing no distinctive marks but that of its pressure. The new American, like the new European, was the servant of the powerhouse, as the European of the twelfth century was the servant of the Church, and the features would follow the parentage.[1]

      Henry Adams, *The Education of Henry Adams*

After almost a century of indigenous resistance movements of many kinds, of labor, of civil and women's rights, of gay rights, the desirability and credibility of a "melting pot" America has been challenged. Discourses promoting more inclusive capacities of co-incorporation, commonly referred to as multiculturalism,[2] vie with the older discourses of assimilation. Thus the energetic articulations of discrete and multiple nationalisms by members of various minoritized communities within the United States destabilize any facile bases upon which a national unity might be predicated as they promote affiliations with transnational diasporic communities. Further, the reach of multinational capital and the globalization of culture erode any comfortable understanding of national and cultural borders. And the continuing movements of large numbers of people across national borders, not as tourists but as refugees or migrants searching for new homes and futures, continue to confuse the relationship of the spaces bodies inhabit and the national identity those bodies are allotted.[3] At such a moment it might be interesting to look back to the early twentieth century to the narratives through which "Americans" negotiated their multicultural and national identities in the last decade of another century.

About 1900, then, in "America." The Civil War had effectively enhanced the costs of union in the national mythology. Settlers had pressed across the great plains and on into the vast spaces of the West all the way to the Pacific Ocean, joining one side of the continent to the other through rails and people's everyday lives. Leaders such as Teddy Roosevelt began to press national interests around the globe, for instance, in Cuba and the Philippines. And in their myriad communities Americans engaged the wrenching transformation from a largely agrarian to a modem industrialized and urban society. Several churning conditions were at work: the murder of President McKinley by a disgruntled anarchist; the agitations of emerging labor unions seeking redress of their grievances against the large industrialists and America's self-made millionaires; the general economic stresses of the 1890s; the long and vigorous campaigns for women's suffrage; and the mass migrations of African-Americans from the South, immigrants from Europe and Asia, and poor farmers from rural areas to the sprawling urban areas in which they were teemed in tenements with few municipal structures able to cope with the numbers and the pressures on city services. All of these factors threatened the stabilities of the emergent national power by insinuating into the national scene myriad unsettled forces.

At the turn of the century in America the discourses of democratic liberalism had to draw heterogeneous subjects away from diverse kinds of identitarian politics to a consensus implied in the nation's founding documents, particularly in the resounding phrase "We the People." In the face of the centrifugal forces of "sectarian" identifications—of race, ethnicity, religious affiliation, geographical origin, class, and so on, something called an "American" had to take shape communally, had to be forged in the midst of diverse contingent realities and histories. Thus the various schemes of "Americanization" in the last decades of the nineteenth and early decades of the twentieth centuries sought to "reform," in two senses of the word, those people discursively designated as not-quite-American in the national landscape: the new migrants, emigrating African-Americans, "quaint" and "vanishing" Native Americans. The metaphor through which the country understood the process by which diverse inhabitants became a part of the corporate "nation" called America was the "melting pot" and its desired effect was "assimilation." To be truly an American one had to assimilate by becoming a normative American subject, adopting the values, behaviors, dress, and point of view of the Anglo-American middle-class, and shedding differences of language, cultural outlook, dress, and demeanor. Yet however compelling the call to an inclusive consensus at moments of crisis, the realities of everyday life revealed the persistence of an exclusionary politics of Americanism. About 1900 the everyday lives of Native Americans, African-Americans, immigrants, and bourgeois (white) women—sites of differential otherness within the United States—became grounds of struggle over definitions of Americanness. And those struggles were evidenced in autobiographical narratives.

If what Terry Eagleton terms the "impossible irony" of nationalism has the effect of "canceling the particularity of an individual life into collective anonymity,"[4] then how are we to understand the relationship of the national subject and autobiography? Autobiographical narrative is specific to an individual and his or her precise experiential history. Yet autobiographical narrative is also a vehicle through which an individual life emerges out of collective anonymity to enact the complex relationship of collective identity to particularity. In the recitation of an individual life, the collective national mythology is relived and re-"lived." The making of Americans gains credibility, becomes a believable story, in the many recitations of the making of Americans.[5] Concomitantly, the assembling of an autobiographical narrative becomes one potent means for persons to assemble themselves as Americans, and thus to believe themselves to be Americans. In this way people participate in a corporate consensus about the proper "national" subject and by implication about the improper or unnational subject.

Yet this very affirmation, this believability, affirms as well the constructedness of national identity and renders fluid the grounds upon which that identity rests. For, the diverse locations from which persons write themselves as Americans exact complex negotiations that disturb the genealogy, the history, and the normative identity through which the discourses of nationalism coalesce. They signal the persistence of pockets of the unnational within the national community, pockets of disidentification that are themselves not congruent, or easily differentiated, or easily collapsed together. If it is, as Sneja Gunew notes, "the 'extravagance' of migrants, their extra-territorial nature which demands that they be controlled,"[6] it is also that same extravagance that forces the continual renegotiation of the terms of national identity by those who claim status as national subjects. People newly inhabiting the national territory have been inhabitants elsewhere, and their histories remain part of their terms of identification. There are those as well, Native Americans and African-Americans, for instance, whose indigenous "extravagance" vis-à-vis myths of national identity brings consciousness of disidentifications with the national consensus and its corporate "We the People."

In the following discussion I look at Mary Antin's *The Promised Land: The Autobiography of a Russian Immigrant* (first published in serial form in the *Atlantic Monthly* in 1911 and 1912, then published as a book in 1912) and the autobiographical sketches Zitkala-Ša published in the *Atlantic Monthly* in 1900 and 1902. Both women share a habitation, the ground of America. But their location vis-à-vis an American national identity is another matter altogether, for they are differently aligned with and in the discourses of nationalism. For both, however, it is precisely their incommensurability with the imaginary ideal of the American national identity that occasions a narrative. How, then, do they write their Americanness into their narratives? In other words, how do they believe themselves to be American? How do unsettling histories as differences insinuate themselves as traces of the unnational in these narratives? And how do these two women, who could not even be "citizens" of the nation, claim a national identity despite their ex-corporation from the body politic? How does the belated "I" become the "we" of "we the People"?

Mary Antin and Her Promised Land

> America is the youngest of the nations, and inherits all that went before in history. And I am the youngest of America's children, and into my hands is given all her priceless heritage. (364)

In her narrative of Americanization, revealingly entitled *The Promised Land*, Mary Antin insists again and again throughout the text that she "must bear witness" to the successful assimilation of immigrants.[7] Hers, she asserts, is a representative story. The urgency of her prose and her project derives from the political context in which she wrote. In the early decades of the twentieth century the vast numbers of immigrants landing in the United States were seen as a destabilizing force in national life, especially since urbanization and industrialization meant that the accumulation of immigrants into overpopulated and underserved urban areas became an inescapable reality of American cities. With the closing of "the frontier," immigrants could no longer fan out across a vast space onto cheap land, their differences diluted in the distances separating farm from farm, neighbor from neighbor. In urban slums they remained "huddled masses." If they were yearning to be free, the nation was yearning for them to be assimilated. Unassimilable immigrants—those who could not be dissociated from their sectarian identifications and remade into bourgeois Americans, those whose differences refused to disappear—were represented as the dirty, crude, uneducated mass of aliens corrupting the health of the nation. Ironically, as Antin was writing *The Promised Land*, the forty-two-volume Dillingham Commission report to Congress warned that "immigrants then entering the country from Eastern and Southern Europe were different from, and inferior to, their predecessors from the North and West."[8]

Anti-immigrant discourses were part of what Lee Quinby describes as "the logic of apocalypse"[9] that permeated national debates and everyday life in the early part of the twentieth century: the avowal of pending national doom with the increase of unnational subjects in the national midst (their languages, foods, habits, behaviors all were taken as signs of this un-Americanness) and the concomitant call for restoring old verities, "traditional" social alignments, for shoring up national boundaries and identities. They were also inflected with discourses of race, ethnicity, and class. Gunew notes that in the nineteenth and early twentieth centuries "ethnicity" was associated etymologically with socially constituted behaviors and characteristics of self-presentation while "race" was associated with essential biological difference among human types.[10] Understood as racial, identities could not be changed; understood as ethnic, identities could be changed. But class status confused notions of race and ethnicity because often the construction of unassimilable difference was as much a product of class identifications and markers as it was of markers of "race." In the midst of this debate *The Promised Land* promised that even the child of "the greasy alien on the street" (182), so denigrated by middle-class Americans, could become a clean and proper national subject.[11]

Having herself become a clean and proper American subject, Antin structures her immigrant story in terms of a popular conversion model of radical discontinuity between an old world and a new.[12] In the first part of this divided text, she presents life lived in Russia as backward, insular, sectarian. A Jew, she cannot join the nation, cannot assume a national identity, since Jewish and Russian are mutually exclusive categories of identification. Antin situates the old Jewish *shtetl* as a place of habitation outside the nation, an unnational space always vulnerable to the exertions of power of the Russian state. Thus it functions as a settlement or reservation of difference. Living outside the nation but subject to its violent attacks upon "aliens" in its midst, the Jews in the *shtetl* remain subject as well to traditional religion, superstition, and the customs determining social organization and personal destiny. Precisely because it cannot be a part of history and nation, the *shtetl* is an oasis in time, frozen in the medieval past in its repetitions of "antiquated" conventions, inelastic customs, patriarchal constraints. For Antin the sign of this backwardness is the way in which the *shtetl* maintains femininity as a constitutive constraint. Her dissatisfaction with the old way of life, a critical dissatisfaction that organizes the first part of her narrative, is a dissatisfaction with the way in which the medieval organization of life in the *shtetl* denied education and intellectual inquiry to women. In the *shtetl*, "every girl hoped to be a wife. A girl was born for no other purpose." As a result "a girl's real schoolroom was her mother's kitchen" (34). Arrival in America breaks the constraints of the antiquated cultural and communal life of Maryuska and provides her with a new start, a new identity, a new name, a new destiny as the "American" Mary Antin.

Thus the second half of the narrative becomes a kind of Bildungsroman as Antin traces her entry into and progress through the American education system, including the informal education of the settlement house. Throughout, she presents herself as a model pupil–quickly fluent in English, hardworking, ambitious, independent, meritorious. To become modern is to become educated; to become educated is to become American.

And to become educated is to participate in what Gunew terms "new inflections of the feminine,"[13] to escape the sectarian and medieval organization of femininity in Russia. Antin measures her Americanization through the gap that opens between her cultural location as a woman and her sister's cultural location as a woman. "A long girlhood, a free choice in marriage, and a brimful womanhood," she claims, "are the precious rights of an American woman" (277). A degraded femininity saturates the cultural location left behind; a different and "freer" femininity becomes her right in America.

Access to public education thus becomes the primary means through which this immigrant subject is reformed as a national subject who understands herself to be free of constitutive constraints, free to choose her future. In this way America's national heritage is delivered into her "hands," evidenced by the radically diverse discourses of national identity through which Antin writes her narrative of Americanization. For instance, there is her self-presentation as a daughter of Ben Franklin, self-starting, self-disciplined, optimistic, progressive. Claiming for herself autonomous individualism, she is indeed the confident "self-made man." In one chapter she even becomes that descendant of Ben, the Horatio Alger hero, as she describes her entrepreneurial venture of selling newspapers. Through persistence, drive, and the good fortune always a part of the Alger Ur-story, the narrator presents the young Antin managing to make some money with the help of an avuncular benefactor, a businessman who recognizes her merit and her potential. There is also the heritage of Emersonian individualism, the profound faith in her own destiny and the transcendental belief in the joining of the spiritual and material universes. And there is the effusive Whitmanesque prose, optimistically celebrating American democracy through the discourse of rights and celebrating as well the expansiveness, the beauty, even the mystical dimension of the human soul at one with the forces of the natural world. It is as if Antin takes up Whitman's call to "sing myself."

Becoming American, Antin puts herself in the subject position of the male hero; all the discourses through which she assembles her "life" are masculinist: those of Ben Franklin, Horatio Alger, Ralph Waldo Emerson, Walt Whitman. Yet imagining herself and her experiential history through masculinist discourses is not tantamount to imagining herself as a man. It is that, as an American "girl," it is her "right" to be able to imagine herself through this legacy. She assumes as her right the privilege of inhabiting the national narrative and its national voices. Yet paradoxically, as Kirsten Wasson notes, it is the "strategies of transgression" Antin locates in her childhood resistances to "filiopiety"—that is, to the discourses of the Talmudic fathers—that enable the "American" Antin to cross-identify.[14]

In *The Promised Land*, Antin re-cites the story of Americanization. Being American comes not from longevity in habitation, or from any fixed grounds of identification such as race or ethnicity. Being American is the willed act of becoming American by imagining herself in the national identity of the free and autonomous individual. As the assimilated immigrant woman, Antin becomes the most American of Americans, the "true" American. As she urgently declares, it is the acceptance of America and the American national identity through which the immigrant is "naturalized." The narrative of American national identity is not merely a nostalgic myth about some former national glory. In 1912 Antin reassures her readers that the narrative of national identity remains recitable; that it can be believed because it can be recited. The performativity of national identity remains intact because it remains assumable by a discrete individual, even assumable by someone, a woman, who cannot claim citizenship in this nation.

But I want to look again at *The Promised Land*, look to the ways the story of assimilation is disrupted by the site of the unnational, even in this most celebratory recitation of Americanization. Reconstructing her childhood in Polotzk, the older narrator confronts the distance of the split subject: her childhood self seems almost too distant to recover. In this context she suggests that her most vivid memories are memories of food and eating, and most particularly of her mother's Polotzk cheesecake: "Why, I can dream away a half-hour on the immortal flavor of those thick cheese cakes we used to have on Saturday night." The memory of the cheesecake evokes an extended description of taste and smell, the ambience of the occasion, its distinctness: "You have nothing in your cupboard to give the pastry its notable flavor. It takes history to make such a cake." Intriguingly, Antin is pleased it remains discrete as memory: "Glad am I that my mother, in her assiduous imitation of everything American, has forgotten the secrets of Polotzk cookery." And since, she admits, "I am no cook," the daughter has not learned its "secrets" either (90–91). In fact, she has not eaten Polotzk cheesecake since coming to America, some "fifteen" years earlier.

Cultural identities inhere in the preparation and rituals surrounding food, as Antin remarks early in the narrative (16). Food sustains cultural integrity and community as that identity is digested on a daily basis. And specific foods have their importance in the imagining of community as metaphors of national identity—"American as apple pie," we might say. This intense memory of the Polotzk cheesecake thus becomes the site of the un-American, the unnational, the unassimilated, the undigested. "Do you think," she writes, "all your imported spices, all your scientific blending and manipulating, could produce so fragrant a morsel as that which I have on my tongue as I write?" (91). Antin persists in writing the unnational in her subsequent recipe: "Polotzk cheese cake, as I now know it, has in it the flavor of daisies and clover picked on the Vall; the sweetness of Dvina water; the richness of newly turned earth which I moulded with bare feet and hands; the ripeness of red cherries bought by the dipperful in the marketplace; the fragrance of all my childhood's summers" (91). This is a recipe of sensuality, of taste, smell, touch, of pleasure; and it interrupts the agenda of the narrative of Americanization with the whiff of the repressed, the return to the mother of childhood, the imaginative return to the motherland (even if not a national motherland).

The memory of the cheesecake becomes a conduit to Antin's past, a residual trace of childhood, of Russia, of her mother's identification with the old way of life, and of the spectacles of femininity she left behind. For, rituals around food preparation and consumption are also part of the everyday practices through which gender differences are culturally reproduced.[15] In claiming she is "not a cook," Antin asserts her assimilation of a new womanhood in America. Hers has been the production of intellectual fare. Paradoxically, then, it is precisely the desire for assimilation and the assertion of new womanhood that maintains the discreteness of the unnational, the unassimilable. The cheesecake has not been translated into an American recipe. If it had been reproduced and consumed in America it would have been displaced, translated, digested, eventually eliminated as difference. Untranslatable, it cannot be assimilated. The intense memory of the cheesecake is memory of the unassimilated, the trace of difference not made over into the same. As she lingers in the absorbing memories of childhood, Antin slows down the pace of the narrative, disrupts the linearity of this narrative of Americanization, disrupts the representation of life in the Pale as constraining and oppressive.

If America as "the promised land" overwrites the old Jewish *shtetl* and the Jewish heritage as "the promised land," then the memory of the Polotzk cheesecake intimates what must be forgotten as disruptive of national identification in order for the narrative of nationalism to succeed. In this passage Antin simultaneously remembers and affirms the means of forgetting the Polotzk cheesecake. The very writing of a narrative of Americanization returns the autobiographical subject to that which has had to be forgotten, the residue of pleasure identified with the unassimilated mother and her old spectacles of femininity in the Jewish *shtetl*.[16]

But there are other pockets of the unnational in Antin's narrative. In the second half of the text the counternarrative is of another kind. Although Antin claims her narrative is representative of the immigrant experience, there is another narrative of the immigrant experience exposed through gaps in her narrative of Americanization. The narrative of life in Boston is a narrative of spiraling movement downward into more and more abject poverty. Her father, she acknowledges in passing, becomes increasingly sullen and bitter; and her sister remains embedded in Old-World customs and gender alignments. Theirs are unnational fates, fates that signal the discontinuity marked by the slash of the habitation/nation system. While Antin's is an act of imaginative identification made possible through education, theirs is a failure of imagination made inevitable through the heritage of the old habitation and the social inequalities in the new habitation. "In later years," she writes of her father, "a new-born pessimism, fathered by his perception that in America, too, some things needed mending, threw him to the opposite extreme of opinion, crying that nothing in the American scheme of society or government was worth tinkering" (217). Antin may overwrite this narrative of class division, economic insecurity, and disidentification with her optimistic discourse of meritocracy (she becomes a kind of pet to her wealthy schoolmates because they recognize her intelligence and eagerness to assimilate) and national bounty ("Money in America was plentiful" [297]) but she cannot entirely suppress it. In order for her narrative of successful assimilation to be credited, the narratives of failure must be tucked away in its recesses. Her very success is measured by failures as she contrasts her achievements with her sister's embeddedness in the old femininity.

A third location of the unnational comes after the closure of the text proper. A glossary of words and definitions (Yiddish, Hebrew, Russian, German) is appended to the text. If incorporating foreign words into the body of the text interrupts the flow of English as the mono-language of assimilation, appending a glossary functions as a way to contain those traces of difference, that mother tongue. The foreign words of the mother tongue are translated into English, their difference mediated by the authoritative structure of the glossary with its rules of pronunciation, its notation of derivation, its definitions, all apparati of Anglo-American linguistic dominance. All these structures effect a standardization, and effectively a denial of the otherness of the language. Yet the inclusion of the glossary also disrupts the monolingualism of the text, insisting on the foreignness of the language, even if that place of foreignness, that place of necessary translation, is marginalized at the back of the text. The language is at once the digested and undigested otherness of the assimilated American immigrant.

Finally, in those passages permeated by the discourse of Emersonian transcendentalism and, with it, one resonant strand of nationalist ideology, Antin claims that she was always already an American.

> The doors opened to me because I had a right to be within. My patent of nobility was the longing for the abundance of life with which I was endowed at birth. . . . Given health and standing-room, I should have worked out my salvation even on a desert island. Being set down in the garden of America, where opportunity waits on ambition, I was bound to make my days a triumphal march toward my goal. (335)

Similarly, she earlier announces, "I had been pursuing a single adventure since the beginning of the world" (296). Antin was an "American" long before she came to America and she would have been "American" wherever she landed. Neither time nor place makes an American of her. By implication, the "American" is not necessarily a national subject. The "American" is the autonomous, free "individual," the universal human subject. And yet it is precisely in becoming American that Antin imagines herself as unfettered by contingencies of time, space, ethnicity, and gender.

It is this imaginary ideal of the universal subject lifted out of constitutive constraints that Antin celebrates in her closing chapter. And yet tucked into this closure is a strange and haunting statement. She opens the chapter entitled "Heritage" with a concern about the "proper stopping place" (359) for an autobiographical narrative written by someone rather young. She has brought her narrative up to "the college gates" and suggests that what comes after would be "repetition" (359), or might better be "left to the imagination" (360). She then concludes this opening paragraph with the following: "The rest of my outward adventures you may read in any volume of American feminine statistics" (360). But in an earlier passage in which she expresses some concern about being able to remember her initial response to America, Antin notes, "the individual, we know, is a creature unknown to the statistician, whereas I undertook to give the personal view of everything" (181). In effect, her story stops when she becomes a mere feminine statistic, when she loses her individuality in the repetitive spectacles of femininity, wifehood, and motherhood. Such repetitive spectacles are precisely some of the repetitive spectacles that support the identifications of American manhood.

Zitkala-Ša and the Iron Routine of Americanization

> These sad memories rise above those of smoothly grinding school days. Perhaps my Indian nature is the moaning wind which stirs them now for their present record. But, however tempestuous this is within me, it comes out as the low voice of a curiously colored seashell, which is only for those ears that are bent with compassion to hear it.[17]

Antin's migration took her from the Pale of Russia west to Boston and Americanization, as her divided narrative tracks her journey from a suffocating way of life that would constrain her future as a woman to her rebirth and growth into a new American identity. Zitkala-Ša's migration moved her east from the plains of the Yankton-Sioux reservation in South Dakota to the missionary schools of Indiana, then further East to teach in a missionary school, and finally back again to reservations in the west.[18] In the four autobiographical sketches she published in installments in *Atlantic Monthly* in 1900 and 1902, Zitkala-Ša works to suture the radical discontinuities between her Sioux and her assimilated American identities. Having been educated as a subject of the Doctrine of Assimilation that functioned as the official policy of the Bureau of Indian Affairs at the turn of the twentieth century, Zitkala-Ša uses her sketches to disrupt the "iron discipline" of the civilizing mission and its denigration of indigenous Americans by critiquing its effects and by positing what Julia V. Emberley describes as "different cultural diacritica"[19] that provide alternative models of identity and systems of values.

Unlike Antin, Zitkala-Ša reconstructs her childhood on the reservation, that site of the unnational—or rather of a contesting notion of communalism—as an idyll of belonging, freedom, spiritual oneness with the community and with nature. Her childhood self is full of "wild freedom and overflowing spirits": "It was as if I were the activity, and my hands and feet were only experiments for my spirit to work upon" (415). In brief yet eloquent sketches, she presents her mother and the elders as living teachers who pass on traditional Sioux knowledge through the rituals of everyday life (for instance, bead work and its practical aesthetics), through their "respect" for the integrity of the child (424), and through the reinforcement of the mutually sustaining relationship between humans and the natural world.

But, Zitkala-Ša confesses, this Edenic childhood comes to an end when she chooses to follow the missionaries who, as participants in official governmental policies of assimilation, recruit children from the reservation. Having been told that the exotic "red apples" of the palefaces grow plentifully in the east, the young girl of eight desires to go east to the missionary school. And since, as the older narrator informs the reader, her mother understands the importance of education in the "paleface" culture, she allows her daughter to go to "the land of the red apples." In this inversion of the Biblical narrative, Zitkala-Ša turns Christian mythology against itself, positioning the missionaries as seductive devils who tempt the child with fruit itself, rather than the promise of knowledge—"it was not yet an ambition for Letters that was stirring me" (430).

But Zitkala-Ša here confesses her own complicity in the civilizing mission: she presents herself as desiring the red apples. The civilizing mission and its agenda of Americanization succeeded to the extent that it stimulated desire in the Indian subject for symbolic apples, the education that would make her over into an American. In this way the desire and the consequent internalization of a normative national identity is experienced as freely chosen.

The second set of sketches tracks the violent interventions in cultural identities and behaviors that come with education for Americanization. This process begins with the train ride east to Indiana. With the invention of the steam engine, trains became both the literal and figurative engines of modernity, integral to western industrialization, urbanization, the expansion of commercial and communications networks, capital accumulation and commodity distribution, indigenous colonization, and settlement. They also became engines for discourses of modernity, providing the material basis and the cultural sign for the reach of enlightenment philosophies, which included certainty in the superiority of western cultures, "enthusiasm for technology as an agent of social change,"[20] and belief in the moral utility of the civilizing mission that would bring enlightenment to the less civilized. Rumbling powerfully along its miles of tracks, tracks carved boldly out of rugged and intransigent terrain, the train signaled Euro-American dominance, rationalism, discipline, and mastery over nature itself. The railroad was the engine of nationalism, enabling expansion and communication across a vast continent, the mass migration of settlers, the resettling of Native American tribes onto reservations, and a divinely sanctioned manifest destiny.

Zitkala-Ša associates her fall from grace with this engine of progress when she describes her experience of being "watched" by palefaces who "riveted their glassy blue eyes upon us" (433). In the train compartment, traveling among "Americans," the child becomes "Indian," her diminished status mirrored back in the gaze of the palefaces. In this moment of transition from the reservation to the school she becomes conscious of and embarrassed by her cultural difference in America. As she pursues her critique of the mission education of "Indians," Zitkala-Ša invokes and ironizes the metaphor of the train as an engine of enlightenment and progress: "It was next to impossible to leave the iron routine after the civilizing machine had once begun its day's buzzing" (442). It is through the iron routine of the iron law of the great white father that the Indian girl would be reformed into an assimilated American girl. Missionary education becomes the process through which a threateningly unnational subject is disassociated from "Indian" spectacles of femininity and identified through Anglo-American spectacles of femininity. Upon arriving at the Indian school she recalls noticing that the girls, dressed in American clothing, "seemed not to care that they were even more immodestly dressed than I, in their tightly fitting clothes" (436). These are the clothes that she herself dons as the "authorities" make her over into a properly dressed and properly behaving American girl. Cutting her hair, the teachers effectively strip her of her symbolic power: "Among our people, short hair was worn by mourners, and shingled hair by cowards!" (437). Threatening her with stories of the revenge of the devil, they frighten her into nightmare, rendering her even more incapable of action. Punishing her for making angels in the snow, they break her bodily contact with the earth. The education of Zitkala-Ša becomes an education in disempowered femininity—in docility, fearfulness, inactivity, domesticity.

The narrator characterizes herself as rebellious in the face of such enforced conformity to a degraded femininity: she tries to escape having her hair shorn; she pencils out the devil's eyes in the book of Biblical stories; she mashes turnips until the pot cracks. But as her description of the four years spent back in Pine Ridge indicates, the process of transformation had taken hold of its subject. She finds herself "in the heart of chaos," the chaos of being a neither/nor subject: "I was neither a wee girl nor a tall one; neither a wild Indian nor a tame one" (444). Her alienation from her community and its alternative cultural diacritica is evident in her behavior. She recklessly rides a pony and pursues a coyote merely for fright value (444); she fails to appreciate the concern of the elders (445); she betrays her suffering before her mother (446); she yearns to join the older Americanized Indians; and she disobeys her mother's wish that she not continue her education (447).

The second set of sketches concludes with Zitkala-Ša's recollection of her participation in a statewide oratory contest among college students in Indiana (448–9). She describes how she sits "before that vast ocean of eyes" directed toward her. Before her waves "a large white flag, with a drawing of a most forlorn Indian girl on it" and on the flag is writing "that ridiculed the college which was represented by a 'squaw.'". Having participated in a state competition, having, that is, participated in a combative ritual of white culture as an assimilated student, Zitkala-Ša sees reflected back to her in the gaze of the audience the representation of difference that marks her as a "squaw," the denigrated Indian woman. For all her Americanization through the "iron routine" of the education system, for all her incorporation in the field of the "white" flag, for all her presence before the audience as "the same," she remains the "forlorn Indian girl" to them. In the eyes of the "barbarians" in the audience she remains the unassimilated and powerless other, the surface of her Indian body a mark of difference unassimilable to her competitive performance as an American.

In fact the young woman has successfully competed against the "paleface," using his own tool—the competitive speech contest–to defeat him. In her competence, fierceness, and competitiveness, she enacts a different femininity, deconstructing before their very eyes their specular representations of her as the denigrated "squaw." "The white flag dropped out of sight, and the hands which furled it hung limp in defeat," she writes. The hands go limp, the flag folds. The palefaces are disempowered, emasculated, because the image of the other is a figment of their own imaginary. It is they who become forlorn in her remembering because she has destabilized "race" as a defining categorization of human potential. She presents them with a posture of defiance—she stares back "fiercely" with her teeth set "hard." And when she wins one of the two prizes awarded, she notes that "the evil spirit laughed within me."

Yet Zitkala-Ša does not reconstruct this moment as a moment of triumph. Rather, she describes herself then as isolated and lonely: "The taste of victory did not satisfy a hunger in my heart. In my mind I saw my mother far away on the Western plains, and she was holding a charge against me." Ironically, with the alienation of being not-quite-white and not-quite not-white, Zitkala-Ša presents herself as "a most forlorn Indian girl" against a "white" field. To win this triumphant achievement of assimilation into white culture, the younger girl has sacrificed her mother (whom she defied to continue her education), her mother tongue, and her mother culture. The older narrator leaves her younger self alone at the end of this scene, inside her room, enclosed in a competitive individualism, a product of education for assimilation.

The third set of sketches considers the price she pays emotionally and physically as she continues to serve the paleface missionaries by teaching in the Carlisle Indian School in Pennsylvania. At the new school, she recalls, her boss only sees her as "the little Indian girl" (451) in her frailty. When he sends her west to recruit new students for the school he describes her as an animal sent "loose to pasture" (452). Even as an educated, assimilated American woman, Zitkala-Ša is infantilized, diminished, dehumanized. On the reservation, to which she returns to recruit a new generation of students, she finds white encroachment, increasing economic impoverishment, white retribution for political action, her mother's impotent defiance. Returning east she becomes outraged by the way in which the self-interest of the white teachers supersedes considerations of qualification and effectiveness. Enraged by the unjust treatment of indigenous peoples, yet alienated from traditional communal sources of meaning, Zitkala-Ša describes herself at the time as "the petrified Indian woman of whom my mother used to tell me" (458). Cold and unfeeling, she is in effect dead.

Inverting the normative paradigm of Christian conversion narratives so central to the civilizing mission and to the nationalist discourses subsuming that mission, Zitkala-Ša traces her descent into the death-in-life of enlightenment and progress through Christianization or, as she elsewhere describes it, the "long-lasting death [that] lies beneath this semblance of civilization" (459). The benefits of education for Americanization have not delivered empowering individualism to her. They have, rather, served to de-individualize her. The very conformity and uniformity exacted in the organized rows and seats of the schoolroom "bound my individuality like a mummy for burial" (443). They have precipitated her "fall" into alienated subjectivity, her abjection of the other within, the other she became through the concentrated gaze of the "glassy blue eyes." Education for assimilation has left her isolated, ineffective, unfeeling—petrified, in several senses. Yet, continuing with the conversion paradigm, Zitkala-Ša announces that she experienced a new birth when she reestablished hope that she could "flash a zigzag lightning across the heavens" (458) and rage in powerful complaint. Having resigned from her teaching position, she has begun to prepare for "a new way to solve the problem of my inner self" (458). (In the first years of the century Zitkala-Ša published her sketches, several short stories later published as *American Indian Stories*, and *Old Indian Legends* [1901]. After 1902 she became, along with her husband Raymond T. Bonnin, a community activist.[21])

If the sketchily linear direction of Zitkala-Ša's narrative traces the journey from an idyllic but interrupted childhood into alienated maturity, the final sketch provides a return of sorts, a manifesto in the form of a brief explanation of her embrace of "paganism" as a preferable mode of being in the world. Her return to Sioux beliefs enables her to recover "a child's eager eye" (459), to become "a wee child toddling in a wonder world" (462). In her purposeful assertion of an alternative system of values, Zitkala-Ša reestablishes her identification with nature and with an alternative "national" community. Yet this is not a nostalgic or romanticized return. Zitkala-Ša recognizes that the very culture from which she had been sundered at the age of eight had already been radically altered in its confrontation with the palefaces and that it would not be the same culture to which she returns. Even her mother, a former figure of resistance, has become Christian, has been made over and pacified. But that cultural standpoint provides her with a point of reference through which she can mount a searing critique of the effects of the civilizing mission and its agenda of Americanization, a critique through which she can realize "this dream of vent for a long-pent consciousness" (458).

Through her autobiographical sketches Zitkala-Ša remembers what has been forgotten in order for Americanization to take effect: both the pleasures and promise of the unnational way of life overwritten through Americanization and the pains of the process of Americanization. In this way memory functions as countermemory to national narratives. But she cannot get back to that which has been lost outside the discourses of assimilation, outside the very process of losing. Even as this memory work registers resistance to the national mission of pacification and assimilation, Zitkala-Ša's text registers the inescapable mark of Americanization. For the very context of her understanding of her past and its meaning in her autobiographical narrative is inflected throughout with the education that has Americanized her. The language of the paleface is precisely the language of her self-constitution as an unnational subject. Describing a moment of childhood freedom, she writes: "We shouted and whooped in the chase; laughing and calling to one another, we were like little sportive nymphs on that Dakota sea of rolling green" (421). This language of nymphs and rolling green seas is the stuff of English poetry. She is figuring, through the images of the dominant culture, the very difference of her Indian childhood. Later, describing the visit of the missionaries who recruit her effectively, she summarizes: "Alas! they came, they saw, and they conquered!" (430), echoing the Latin lessons of college. Her critique of the colonial oppression of the dominant culture is rendered in the canonical discourses of the conqueror.

Zitkala-Ša's autobiographical narrative resists certain normative conventions of the genre—it is fragmented rather than unified and coherent, a sketch, not a finished product; it concludes in concealment—she withholds information about how she solves "the problem of my inner self" (458)—rather than revealing it. Even so, in its constitutive deformations her narrative participates in the autobiographical tradition in America and its privileging of the autonomous individual. This "I" of autobiographical utterance, as the authors of *The Empire Writes Back* argue, stands for "the independent 'individual' whose social inflection is one of the strongest trace marks left by Europeanization on the postcolonial world"[22] and Americanization in the indigenous colonization of the United States. Publication itself registers the degree of distance between the already Americanized subject and any pre-lapsarian or "authentic" traditional subject.

The Zitkala-Ša of the narrative is both/and—the national and the unnational subject. She unmakes herself as an American of conformity and docility, even as she can never entirely escape having been remade as American. She writes herself through western discourses to the traditionally based but historically adapted beliefs of the Sioux Indians. She critiques the civilizing mission from inside the effects of that mission. She inveighs against Americanization to other Americans, having already become American. Her resistance narrative, an act through which she would assert her sense of her own individuality against the cultural expectations of docility and industriousness, through which she would assert the viability of alternative spiritual values against a denigrating Christianity hostile to Indian difference, is precisely the durable legacy of her American education and its myth of radical individualism.

Conclusion, Exclusion, Inclusion

> [Antin] has developed an irritating habit of describing herself and her people as Americans, in distinction from such folks as Edith and me, who have been here for three hundred years.[23]

> All that Zitkala-Ša has in the way of literary ability and culture she owes to the good people, who, from time to time, have taken her into their homes and hearts and given her aid. Yet not a word of gratitude or allusion to such kindness on the part of her friends has ever escaped her in any line of anything she has written for the public. By this course she injures herself and harms the educational work in progress for the race from which she sprang.[24]

Antin and Zitkala-Ša are among those Homi K. Bhabha calls the "overlooked in the double sense of social surveillance and psychic disavowal and, at the same time, overdetermined, psychically projected, made stereotypical and symptomatic."[25] The "squaw" and the daughter of "the greasy alien in the street" are cultural projections of unnational subjects. But while they share a certain location of the unnational in America about 1900, they are very differently positioned as "Indian" and "immigrant" subjects of and in America.

In the final sketch Zitkala-Ša writes from the literal site of the reservation to which she has returned. But this return is not a return to the disempowered place of the denigrated "squaw." By means of the discourse of radical individualism, she has displaced the founding discourse of the civilizing mission, the very mission of modernity through which she was educated into her split consciousness. Even as she has been made an "Indian" through education for democracy, that sign of modernity, she has penetrated this defining arena of American national identity. If the authority of the discourse of national identity derives from its abstract generality, it is that very generality that generates the time lag through which Zitkala-Ša queries its ethics and its effects upon those it would reform. Perhaps this is what she learns from what Bhabha calls "that split consciousness" which follows the recognition that "the reinvention of the self and the remaking of the social are strictly out of joint."[26]

What I understand Zitkala-Ša to have come to recognize as she assembled painful memories of loneliness and alienation is the dominant culture's intractable response to what they see as her "belatedness" as a Sioux woman.[27] That is, for all her Americanization Zitkala-Ša confronts the radical gap between the discourse of liberal humanism founding the civilizing education for Americanization and the "quotidian conversation and comments" that "reveal the cultural supremacy and racial typology upon which the universalism of Man is founded."[28] In a modernist autobiographical project, Zitkala-Ša uses the legacy of modernist authority to critique the project of national identity as conformity and sameness rather than radical equality. And she slows down, if only in one life, the future thrust of the civilizing mission, by discrediting progress from within modernity and its discourses. She turns cultural literacy into cultural critique. Speaking as a subject of the racist imaginary from inside normative discourses, Zitkala-Ša forces those discourses to deliver up their violent effects.

Mary Antin writes out of a different history of oppression. She comes from a place in which Jews could not participate officially in national life and national narratives due to virulent anti-Semitism that defined them as racially other. Part of the Hebrew diaspora, they were represented as always alien, always unnational subjects, often as a disease undermining the health of the nation. In this context the Jewish community secured its borders of difference and strained to maintain traditional beliefs, including its own systems of difference. In the old country, racial, ethnic, and gender identities were fixed as essential. Coming to America, Antin becomes an exceptional child of American education, "the prodigy" of "the greasy alien in the street," of which her family, her teachers, her friends, and the school officials are proud. Having successfully become American, Antin comes to understand gender, race, and ethnicity as contingent human markers. As an immigrant from Europe Antin can come to act, talk, imagine, and look like a middle-class American. She can be educated out of her differences of language, behaviors, religion, ethnicity, even race itself without a remainder of physical difference, the difference marked on a body like that of Zitkala-Ša. Antin does not presume her belatedness because, as a migrant from eastern Europe, she can assimilate almost seamlessly into an American identity, a seamless passage blocked to Zitkala-Ša. In fact, Antin presumes, paradoxically, her timeliness and her timelessness.

Gunew suggests that the extravagance of the everyday lives of migrants is not as threatening to the body politic when individualized, especially when it is materialized in autobiographical narratives published through mainstream publishers. The masses of lives that remain untold in the discourses of national identity may be much more distressing to a national consensus.[29] But even those like Antin, who do publicize their celebrative narrative of Americanization, can pose significant challenges to the corporate We the People. "Among many kinds of interrogation," notes Gunew, "the migrant voice can alert readers (secure in either cultural or linguistic certainties) to the arbitrary nature of place, that the motherland or fatherland amounts to an imaginary territory perilously shored up by conventions which may melt away on close scrutiny.[30] In imagining herself as American, Antin imagines herself as always having been American (despite her return to the realm of the statistic). In that imagining she intimates a certain unhinging of the habitation from the nation, a certain spatial disjunction, a certain deterritorialization of the national imaginary.

In assembling narratives directed at mainstream Americans comfortable in their national identification and uncritical in their support of assimilationist policies, Antin and Zitkala-Ša negotiate in complex ways the imperatives of remembering and forgetting as they struggle to align the autobiographical "I" with and against the corporate "We the People." Both women force memories and recover forgettings through the sieves of inclusions and exclusions constitutive of this "We the People." Their texts become enunciatory sites rife with the tensions between the identifications of this corporate "We" and the disidentifications of individual histories out of national time and out of national place. In this way Antin and Zitkala-Ša test the negotiability of the historically specific communal consensus about national identity prevalent about 1900.

Notes

1 Henry Adams, *The Education of Henry Adams*, 1918. (Boston: Houghton Mifflin, 1973), 466.
2 There are many different discourses of multiculturalism; and so it is important to look carefully at what is being promoted as multicultural, how the term is deployed in specific arguments about culture, or race relations, or the politics of difference, or the political correctness debates, and whose purposes the discourse is promoting. For a discussion of multiculturalism in a comparative context, see Sneja Gunew, "Multicultural Multiplicities: US, Canada, Australia," in *Meanjin* 3 (Spring 1993): 447–61.

 See also, *Debating PC: The Controversy over Political Correctness on College Campuses*, ed. Paul Berman (New York: Laurel, 1992); and *Beyond PC: Toward a Politics of Understanding*, ed. Patricia Aufderheide (Minneapolis: Graywolf Press, 1992).
3 Eve Rosofsky Sedgwick has defined this grafting of corporate identification to geographical locale as the "'habitation/nation system'"—"the set of discursive and institutional arrangements that mediate between the physical fact that each person inhabits, at a given time, a particular geographical space, and the far more abstract, sometimes even apparently unrelated organization of what has emerged since the late seventeenth century as her/his national identity," in *Nationalisms and Sexualities*, ed. Andrew Parker, Mary Russo, Doris Sommer, Patricia Yaeger (New York: Routledge, 1992), 239.
4 Terry Eagleton, "Nationalism: Irony and Commitment," in *Nationalism, Colonialism, and Literature* (Minneapolis: University of Minnesota Press, 1990), 23.

5   "To make people believe," suggests Michel de Certeau, "is to make them act. But by a curious circularity, the ability to make people act—to write and machine bodies—is precisely what makes people believe. Because the law is already applied with and on bodies, 'incarnated' in physical practices, it can accredit itself and make people believe that it speaks in the name of the 'real.' It makes itself believable by saying: 'This text has been dictated for you by Reality itself.'" In *The Practice of Everyday Life*, trans. Steven F. Rendall (Berkeley: University of California Press, 1984), 148.

6   Sneja Gunew, "Migrant Women Writers: Who's on Whose Margins," in *Gender, Politics and Fiction: Twentieth-Century Australian Women's Novels*, ed. Carole Ferrier (St. Lucia: University of Queensland Press, 1992), 176.

7   Mary Antin, *The Promised Land*, 1912. (Princeton: Princeton University Press, 1985), 269; also 87–8, 181, 198, 214, 242, 271, 287, 325, 357.

8   Oscar Handlin, "Foreword" to *The Promised Land*, vi.

9   See Lee Quinby, *Anti-Apocalypse: Exercises in Genealogical Criticism* (Minneapolis: University of Minnesota Press, 1994), esp. chapter 4 on Henry Adams and the New Man.

10 Sneja Gunew, "Feminism and the Politics of Irreducible Differences: Multiculturalism/Ethnicity/Race," in *Feminism and the Politics of Difference*, ed. Sneja Gunew and Anna Yeatman (Sydney: Allen and Unwin, 1993), 8-10.

11 See, for instance, Thomas J. Archdeacon's discussion of anti-Semitic discourses at the turn of the century, in *Becoming American: An Ethnic History* (New York: Free Press-Macmillan, 1983), 158–62.

12 For an excellent discussion of Antin's use and disruption of the conversion narrative, see Kirsten Wasson, "A Geography of Conversion: Dialogical Boundaries of Self in Antin's *Promised Land*," in *Autobiography and Postmodernism*, ed. Kathleen Ashley, Leigh Gilmore, Gerald Peters (Amherst: University of Massachusetts Press, 1994), 167–85.

13 Gunew, "Feminism," 12.

14 Wasson, "A Geography of Conversion," 175—6.

15 See Susan Bordo, *The Unbearable Weight: Feminism, Western Culture, and the Body* (Berkeley: Univ. of California Press, 1993), esp. Chapter 3.

16 See Christopher Miller, in *Nation and Narration*, ed. Homi Bhabha (New York: Routledge, 1992): "In order for a unit to arise and take on the condition of nationhood, it is necessary for all the individuals within it to remember certain things and forget certain things; to remember what brings them together and forget what could tear them apart. The problem is of course in deciding whom and what to 'forget.'" (62).

17 Zitkala-Ša (Gertrude Bonnin), "The School Days of an Indian Girl," in *Classic American Autobiographies*, ed. William L. Andrews (New York: Mentor, 1992), 443.
18 For a brief survey of the life of Zitkala-Ša, see Dexter Fisher, "Zitkala-Ša: The Evolution of a Writer," *American Indian Quarterly* 5 (1979): 229–38.
19 Judith V. Emberley, *Thresholds of Difference: Feminist Critique, Native Women's Writings, Postcolonial Theory* (Toronto: University of Toronto Press, 1993), 141.
20 Michael Adas, *Machines as the Measure of Men: Science, Technology, and Ideologies of Western Dominance* (Ithaca: Cornell University Press, 1989), 230.
21 For further details, see Fisher, "Zitkala-Ša."
22 Bill Ashcroft, Gareth Griffiths, and Helen Tiffin, *The Empire Writes Back: Theory and Practice in Post-Colonial Literatures* (London: Routledge, 1989), 114.
23 Barrett Wendell, *Barrett Wendell and His Letters*, ed. M.A. DeWolfe Howe (Boston: *Atlantic Monthly*, 1928), 282. Quoted in Mary Dearborn, *Pocahontas's Daughters: Gender and Ethnicity in American Culture* (New York: Oxford University Press, 1986), 222. Wendell was one of Antin's mentors during her years in the American education system.
24 Review in *The Red Man and His Helper*, 12 April 1901, Carlisle, Pennsylvania. Quoted in Fisher, "Zitkala-Ša," 230.
25 Homi K. Bhabha, *The Location of Culture* (New York: Routledge, 1994), p. 236.
26 Ibid., 244.
27 And by this I am invoking Bhabha's rereading of Franz Fanon's "The Fact of Blackness" in *The Location of Culture*, 236–8.
28 Bhabha, *The Location of Culture*, 237.
29 Gunew, "Migrant Women Writers," 175.
30 Ibid., 173.

16

Strategic Autoethnography and American Ethnicity Debates: The Metrics of Authenticity in *When I Was Puerto Rican*.[1] (Watson 2013)

> If I'm not Puerto Rican enough and in my eyes Puerto Rico is not Puerto Rican the way it was Puerto Rican before, then what is Puerto Rican?
>
> Esmeralda Santiago (in Hernandez, 163)

As my epigraph suggests, the question of what constitutes the "ethnic" and who can successfully "transculturate" and embody that ethnicity is vexed, nowhere more, I would suggest, than in diasporan women's life writing. While some memoirists—Ken Bugul, Michelle Cliff—have avoided controversy by casting their autobiographical narratives as fiction, and others—such as Maryse Condé—have separated stories of their past from the cosmopolitan subjects they have become, those life writers seeking to narrate their pasts from a present location may encounter ethnic essentialist bias in the reception of their narratives. In response to the outpouring of memoirs published in the US by writers born outside its shores over the last two decades, critics have sought to valorize narratives that assert positive and progressive models of ethnic essence for emergent hybrid subjects telling stories that can inspire the postcolonial creation of a national imaginary in their homelands. But "positive models" are insufficient to the complexities of experience that many diasporan writers seek to narrate and to the process of becoming the authors who can tell—and market—those stories. In this essay I argue that asserting ethnicity depends on two things: establishing a set of metrics that authenticate the narrator's authority as an eyewitness observer to the originary culture; and creating an illusion that a seamless process of "transculturation" has occurred. And I ask the reader's patience in what may seem like a tendentious, many-pronged discussion of contexts, as specifying these allows me to set up the terms for a new way of reading diasporan women's memoirs.

Challenging essentialist expectations, José L. Torres-Padilla asserts that ethnicity is a construction—"ethnogenesis" or "the semiotic process of producing signs that create or recreate ethnicity" (186–7). "Ethnicity" is produced in response to a "felt rhetorical need" that emerges from "direct engagement with the new geographical site" (192) to which the writer has migrated. That is, textual representations of ethnic identity differ with the "elsewhere" site from which they are generated, the historical moment, and the experiencing subject producing them; ethnicity cannot be a shared, static essence representing a nation. Particularly for diasporan women writers, the valences around ethnicity are charged. These subjects confront the bind of narrating themselves as legible through repressive myths of female domesticity in their countries of origin, and as critics of asymmetrical gender arrangements. The tension between myths of ethnic essence and diasporan stories is particularly evident in women's narratives of displacement from an originary "home" to multicultural locations in the continental United States.

One narrative that shows how fraught the reception politics of ethno-autobiographical practice in postcolonial environments may become is *When I Was Puerto Rican* (WPR), Esmeralda Santiago's first autobiographical narrative. WPR has been a focus of impassioned debate since its publication by a mainstream press in the United States in 1994.[2] A staple of high school and university reading lists, it is a fast-moving and spirited narration by Santiago's childhood avatar Negi, a poor young woman who struggles to come of age in various locations—rural and urban spaces on the island, a Brooklyn barrio, and a multicultural school.[3] Her family's immigration to New York, on what I, for convenience, call the American mainland, when she was thirteen enabled her to reflect, as an adult, on how leaving her place of birth made her a "hybrid" American subject, but also enabled her education and status as an author.

As the *"Was"* in Santiago's title suggests, the other side of migration and hybridity is an experience of lost belonging. But the verb's past tense has generated a critical debate: Can such a hybrid subject narrate her early experience "authentically"? If she successfully transculturates, is she still "ethnic," or a sell-out to the dominant American culture? This issue is acute in the case of Puerto Rico because of its special status as an island existing as a "free associated state" (Estado Libre Asocuado), without full rights in a neocolonial relationship to the mainland.[4] Its ambiguous status has fueled a quest over decades to find narratives of identity and origin for the many immigrants (nearly 50% of all Puerto Ricans) now living on the mainland, what critic Raquel Romberg terms the fantasy of a "national ethnic essentialism" without nation status (1).

Some critics have questioned whether Santiago's autobiographical story can be representative of Puerto Rican experience and identity when the island-born author's assimilation to mainland middle-class identity betrays the poor working-class women from whom she came. The sharpest criticism has come from feminists who assert that Santiago is a class-traitor for disavowing ethnicity in her narrative's title and for her success as a writer.[5] The implication is that, because of education and authorship, Santiago cannot "authentically" represent "brown-and-down" Puerto Rican women faced with the issues of large families headed by unmarried women, sexual promiscuity, and harsh patriarchal rule (Sánchez-González 160). But, as a form of ethnic essentialism, this critique tends to allegorize "positive models" without addressing the complexity of becoming an educated, marketable writer.

For her part, Santiago, who left Puerto Rico at thirteen in 1961, has responded that she did not intend to represent contemporary island culture, but to focus on an earlier mid-century moment after the American neocolonial project "Operation Bootstrap," begun in the 1940s, instituted programs to make the island a site for production and consumption of American goods and protect its sizable military bases. At the same time, she legitimates her story by depicting the island ways of Boricua (the precolonial name for Puerto Rico): the island's colorful folklore, food, tropical spaces, and, ambivalently, its asymmetrical gendered roles, long seen as its defining machismo. That is, Santiago defends *WPR* as both a counter-narrative to official histories of the island and a record of a pre-consumerist kind of ethnic culture now vanished from an island where McDonald's and Subway fast-food restaurants abound. As my epigraph suggests, her double claim asks that *WPR* be read in dialogue with critiques of ethnicity, even as she asserts a privileged relationship to it.

In thinking about how diasporan subjects exist in a complex relationship to ethnic essentialism, it is also important to consider the problematics of location. Once in the US, as Torres-Padilla notes, a Spanish-speaking immigrant writer shifts from being a national to an ethnic subject, identified within the dominant white culture as a "Hispanic" or Latina "other," neither fully of her national origin nor of dominant white America; rather she becomes hybrid and hyphenated (182). And the situation is aggravated for Puerto Ricans whom, because they cannot claim nation-state status, Juan Flores has characterized wryly as "off the hyphen" or "lowercase" subjects (181 and Ch. 8, *passim*). The question that emerges is important for life writing generally: How can a memoir represent the experience and recollection of "home" without essentializing a myth of national—or in the case of Puerto Rico, subordinated non-nation—identity, yet evoke a sense of shared community for diasporan readers?

Part of Santiago's response is to turn to an expansion of the ethnos: she narrates an autoethnographic story about self-transculturation to a mainland location of hybrid identity. In approaching her narrative from this interpretive standpoint we can observe its strategic features and elaborate *WPR*'s uneasy relationship to a myth of ethnic origin that it both propounds as a mythic memory and relativizes, the moment of ethnogenesis.[6] To situate Santiago's act of strategically essentialist storytelling and the responses it has provoked, I will frame it within several autobiographical contexts: life writing, ethnography, autoethnographic transculturation, and internal and external metrics of authenticity. Using these contexts reframes the question of essentialism by focusing on how diasporan narrators seek to validate their performances as transcultural subjects.[7]

First, as an act of life writing, *WPR* employs different discursive strategies than the novel.[8] Reading the text as autobiographical addresses issues central to women's life writing: differences of the past-time experiencing I's childhood story from the reflexive narration of the adult I; the non-transparency of experience; the performance of identity for multiple, situated publics; the centrality of the body as site and sign of truth claims about history, politics and cultural struggles; and the multiple collaborators in coaxing, producing, circulating, and, not least, reading and commenting on the narrative.[9]

Second, *WPR* can helpfully be situated in the context of critiques of ethnography initiated in the 1980s by anthropologists such as Clifford Geertz, James Clifford, and George Marcus, and the feminist deconstruction of Western privilege posed by Trinh T. Minh-ha. Those critiques probingly questioned the transparency of ethnographic accounts, arguing that images of the other "are constituted . . . in specific historical relations of dominance and dialogue" (Clifford 23, cited in Conquergood 182) and that ethnographic writing acquires its authority through employing rhetorical strategies. That is, the "experience" claimed in an ethnography must be read as a construction achieved by tactics that assert the interviewer's authority, such as "insider" status with an informant group and extensive fieldwork as an eyewitness in a culture remote from the interviewer's own. Poststructuralist critiques of ethnography suggest how life writing by diasporan and postcolonial autobiographers (who, though not professional ethnographers, are no longer "innocent" informants but observers of cultural practices) might be resituated from essentialist debates about fidelity to a homeland to the use of rhetorical strategies for claiming ethnic belonging.

Santiago, for example, takes up the call to narrate the ethnos by creating a child narrator who is attentive to the social and cultural details of the various locations in which she grew up; as an insider to Puerto Rican culture able to translate it to diasporan and metropolitan outsiders, she narrates a counter-ethnography. Indeed, *WPR* is, in its first two-thirds, almost a textbook performance of autoethnographic storytelling.[10] It describes settings, cultural practices, and social relations that the child narrator asserts are "authentic," thereby authorizing herself as a storyteller, despite her limited vantage point as young and uneducated. Yet such claims to authenticity are strategic. As Clifford Geertz asserted,

> The capacity to persuade readers . . . that what they are reading is an authentic account by someone personally acquainted with how life proceeds in some place, at some time, among some group, is the basis upon which anything else ethnography seeks to do . . . finally rests (143–4).

That is, the ascription of the "real" or "true" to a place is a rhetorical act that seeks consensus about the reliability of the narrator on a version of the past.

The present-time Santiago who narrates *WPR* is no longer located in the ethnos at her memoir's heart. Rather she has shifted to a subject position of privilege as a Harvard-educated author, as the last chapter of her memoir details. *WPR*'s claim to ethnic belonging, then, engages with what Mary Louise Pratt has discussed as processes of transculturation from the place of origin to a dramatically different world by a subject able to appropriate colonial tactics in a contact zone of encounter (7). In a similar vein Françoise Lionnet helpfully theorizes the narration of such subjects as an act of *métissage* or the braiding of languages and discourses to assert subjectivity.[11] Reading Santiago's narrative autoethnographically, as both a situated story about the past and a meditation on self-transculturation, resituates it, and leads us to question how authenticity is produced as a truth effect, taking account of how the child narrated I is positioned by an older narrating I.

Thus, while the claim of diasporan subjects in memoir to be "self-translators"—linguistically, geographically, culturally, and positionally—may seem an unproblematic fantasy about relationship to a place of origin, focusing on how narrators achieve such effects shifts our attention to the rhetoric of authenticity.[12] For, autoethnographic narrators claiming to be self-transculturators face two issues: they have to account both for their literariness, and for how the language of writing is related to the language of remembered experience. The trenchant question raised by Juan Flores, "In what language do we remember?", is an ambiguity at the heart of autoethnographic performance (56). Flores notes that language is both "an abundant reservoir of expressive codes with which to relate (to) the past" [and] "the locus of contention over issues of identity and community" (57). Similarly, Mary Besemeres discusses doing "ethnographic work" between two or more languages and urges that this aspect of "hybrid" narratives be theorized as "reflexive" ethnography, or autoethnography ("Ethnographic" 219).[13] Santiago's childhood is both literally and metaphorically a "translation," as she only became fluent in

English, the language in which *WPR* was written, after coming to the American mainland. But if we probe its rhetoric of autoethnographic authenticity, both the achievement and the problem of her assertion become evident. When the autobiographer performs as an ethnographic insider-observer, I would suggest, readers must attend to the apparent seamlessness of the narrated child "I"'s performance and investigate what conjunction of strategies has produced it.[14] In the doubled and troubled narration of *WPR*, autoethnographic narration is linked to several metrics that produce the effects of "authenticity."

Internal Metrics of Authenticity in Ethnic Narratives

Just as poststructuralist critiques raise fundamental questions about "authenticity" in ethnography, the twenty-first century proliferation of hoax memoirs adds to the climate of mistrust around "authenticity" or similar claims to "local" knowledge.[15] Instead of weighing the accuracy of claims that a local narrator makes about the "truth" of past experience, we might consider the stakes of making such claims, which rely on memories, individual and collective, that, however potent, are partial and contestable, and ask: which metrics of authenticity *internal* to a narrative position its teller as an authoritative subject?[16] And what do interested others, such as editors and presses, local and international readers, and critics (including what Sidonie Smith and I call "suspicious readers" on internet blogs) contribute in shaping the text through *external* metrics? Exploring these questions may clarify how narrating "I"s establish their authority to speak as "authentic" subjects and which rhetorical acts underwrite assertions of "authenticity."

Santiago's protagonist Negi, the child narrated "I," is a participant-observer who uses a continuous past tense to tell her story, documenting her experience of Puerto Rico, but also at times misperceiving because her innocent telling, in stories or dialogue, reports political and social truths that she cannot yet understand.[17] That is, she makes specifics of mid-century Puerto

Rico legible, but also exposes it as a site of patriarchal *machismo* that can be brutally repressive of girls and women. Negi's narration includes the following strategies to make the complex cultural world of the island available to readers.

1. Self-authorization as a representative insider-outsider subject
The autoethnographic narrator, as a participant-observer "I," communicates a seemingly unmediated experience of culture by asserting the authority to speak on behalf of self and others. In framing her child narrated "I"'s story, Santiago layers authoritative voices from a cultural tradition with her own adult narration to "authenticate" the history and culture of Puerto Rico and make it credible to diasporan readers. Her framing Prologue and Epilogue, couched in the present tense of the adult narrator, describe the challenge of capturing the sensory particulars of island experience in English translation and the everyday world to which she has transculturated herself. The "Prologue: How to Eat a Guava" is a "how-to" for readers engaging her narrative. Locating herself in a Shop & Save grocery store in New York, Santiago invites readers—implicitly, metropolitan and diasporan subjects—to imagine the sensuous texture of island life her story will describe by following detailed instructions for consuming its characteristic fruit. Readers are invited to experience the guava through every sense—touch, sight, smell, sound (of eating), and, above all, taste, while avoiding the seeds that could "end up in the crevices between your teeth" (3). As a synecdoche of Puerto Rico, the guava conjures the years of plentiful rain when the fruit was especially succulent, as well as other times when the impatient children ate it green and sour, puckering at its acid grittiness. Metatextually the guava is the fruit of knowledge of an irreducibly different tropical world. But this epiphany also evokes a memory of separation for the narrator, the guava she ate on the day she left Puerto Rico as an adolescent. By the end of the passage the fragrant guava, in the sweetness of memory, has become emblematic of Santiago's childhood. The narrator's "authenticity" as a representative Puerto Rican is

thereby asserted: she embodies knowledge of the island's sensory richness that those born on the mainland, even Boricuan descendants, cannot access.

What passes for a guava in New York—a green and hard import "under the harsh fluorescent lights of the exotic fruit display"—cannot produce substitute knowledge. Instead the narrator turns to "the apples and pears of my adulthood . . . predictable and bittersweet" (4)—and the Western-Biblical fruit of knowledge—contrasting Puerto Rico, a site of commingled senses, with her urban regime of routinized consumption. But of course, the exotic sensuousness of her guava memory is precisely what the rhetoric of the Prologue seeks to produce, to secure Santiago's insider status as an only apparently removed "local" in whom experiential island knowledge is embodied.

Similarly, in *WPR*'s "Epilogue: One of These Days" the narrative flashes forward to Esmeralda, Santiago's somewhat older narrator ten years after her graduation from the Manhattan Performing Arts High School to which she, against all odds, was accepted—and where her "up by the bootstraps" climb commenced. From the perspective of a Harvard University scholarship student, she recalls returning to the school and "the skinny brown girl with the curled hair, wool jumper, and lively hands" called Negi that she was then (269). The Harvard student is sufficiently aligned with the elegant teacher who conducted the audition and subsequently became her mentor that they can joke and laugh together. Esmeralda remarks on her own "chutzpah," Yiddish for brashness, using the lingo of a different ethnic group. In bracketing her story with these frame moments, Santiago attempts to legitimate how Negi, the island child, could become the writer able to tell her story while remaining essentially connected to her sensuous homeland. Speaking *of* her experience, she attempts to speak representatively *as* Puerto Rican and to invite its diasporan communities to identify. But this rhetorical move generated the tensions reflected in critical debates about whether she can speak *for* the island's citizenry.

2. The "you-are-there" immediacy of the eyewitness narrator

Characteristically, autoethnographic memoirs set up their narrators as participant-observers able to transport readers to an indigenous culture and awaken them to its difference from their metropolitan worlds. To do this, narrators become linguistic glossers and translators, speaking as first-hand actors conversant with the particulars of their worlds and performing acts of what Mary Besemeres terms the "language migrant's self-translation" (*Translating* 275). The local concepts they construct serve as what William Boelhower has called a "cultural encyclopedia" that references in sensory detail the remembered world of previous encounter (110) in terms accessible to outsiders.[18] And the thick description they produce seeks the sensory effect that Trinh T. Minh-ha references: "The speech is seen, heard, smelled, tasted, and touched" (121). The effect of unmediated encounter with a different culture that readers may experience depends on the narrated "I"'s ability to place them in the setting and evoke that "you are there" quality.

To reference the particulars of growing up on the island, *WPR* uses over a hundred Spanish terms for foods, material items, and social roles that, it implies, are both untranslatably specific and necessary to a sensory knowledge of Puerto Rico. (I discuss the appended glossary of terms in External Metrics.) Such local vernacular further communicates the narrator's authenticity and helps outsider readers, whether tourists or emigrants, navigate her world. A central act of translation involves the culture of food that bonds Puerto Ricans. Readers are introduced to the staples of everyday cuisine, some in such detail that they could serve as recipes or menu guides: *asopao*, "delicious, thick with rice and chunks of chicken, cubed potatoes, green olives, and capers" (48, 220); *Morcillas*, roasted or fried spiced black sausages (273); the popular *sancocho* or vegetable stew (90 and 274); *pasteles* made of "plantains, green bananas, yautías, and yucca" that readers learn how to prepare (273); and coconut-milk delicacies like *arroz con dulce*, *tembleque*, and *coquito* (161 and 271–4). As a linguistic and cultural local expert, Negi, the narrated I, incorporates these dishes as moments of vicarious encounter that underscore her eyewitness status.

Similarly, personal names both characterize people and convey intimate detail. The name of Santiago's childhood narrator, "Negi," a term for a dark-skinned person, is glossed by her mother: "[W]hen you were little you were so black, my mother said you were a *negrita*" (13). Negi asserts that this name lacks the negative connotations she will later learn are attached to "Negro" and cognates for African Americans on the mainland to racialize them and other ethnic groups.[19] Other family members are categorized by the degree of curl in their hair and their skin color: Delsa is "nutty brown," Papi more "sun ripened," Norma "rust colored," Marni "pink." One of Negi's teachers, Miss Jimenez, has a freckled, "café con leché" complexion (63). As a naïve narrator Negi describes these skin differences without reflecting on the hierarchy of color they imply in Puerto Rico's braided African, Spanish, and indigenous Taíno culture or as marking the family's low place in a colonially inflected social hierarchy. Her mother's rationale for dual names, however, both acknowledges that official hierarchy and resists internalizing its logic of a color spectrum, while Negi's assertion that "We all have our official names, and then our nicknames, which are like secrets that only the people who love us use" invites readers to the intimacy of the family (14).

3. Myths of origin and the politics of (re)constructing a national imaginary

In postcolonial contexts, stories of originary identity and its violation by colonial invasion and persecution of indigenous groups, and the continuation of practices of domination as neocolonial "regulation," can assert a suppressed counterhistory of the lost rights of the subordinated. References to imagined origin as a primordial paradise may suggest an alternative vision of the nation as they summon local and diasporan subjects to recall their suppressed past as a potential site of political emancipation. Although Santiago avoids a direct political call for emancipation of the "affiliated" status of Puerto Rico, *WPR* refers to a mythic past that Negi has internalized and contrasts it to the coming of US government agents. The myth is set up in *WPR*'s epigraph from a poem by earlier Puerto Rican poet Luis Lloréns Torres, printed in both Spanish and English, that imagines the "*bohío*," or little shack, on the hill as a presence awakening to the morning's sensuous richness. In this pastoral praise "home" is a lushly idealized origin that the island's descendants inherit; it romanticizes the island as a place of primordial abundance and a timeless moment of innocence. The myth encompasses the pre-colonial Taíno of Borinquen, who in fact succumbed rapidly to disease soon after encounter with the genocidal practices of Spanish explorers. It also suggests that European and African peoples who passed through the island were naturalized, suturing Puerto Rican belonging as an identity with a different origin from that of mainland Americans. The specificity of being Puerto Rican, then, is not just a geographic, but a mythic, heritage conferring authenticity, as Negi's description of their version of the childhood Indians-and-Cowboys game as "Caribs and Spaniards" suggests (184).

Negi, by contrast, critiques the neocolonial relationship of Puerto Rico to the mainland when the uneducated family and village encounter American aid personnel and tease out the meanings of "imperialism." With its Operation Bootstrap policy, the United States sought to make the island both an efficient producer of American goods and source of military personnel, and a consumer market, after the island's inhabitants were "converted" to the norms of middle-class white America: marriage and monogamy; an emphasis on conspicuous consumption and deferred gratification through a regulated work week; and the Northern food pyramid of what to eat and cultivate, ignoring the island's lush vegetation and local food culture.

In a chapter ironically titled "The American Invasion of Macún" a half-century after the first US invasion in 1898, Negi describes a scene while the family lives as *jíbaros* to whom an American representative, sweating in dress-shirt and tie and speaking bad Castilian Spanish incomprehensible to the village, introduces the North American food chart, with its broccoli and iceberg lettuce, apples and pears—all unavailable on the island—that betrays his ignorance of Puerto Rican food culture. The sack of groceries provided each family is full of unfamiliar processed foods—peanut butter, cornflakes, and canned fruits—that they don't know how to use. Similarly, the lecture on sanitation emphasizing lice and tapeworms (the *solitaría*, which subsequently infects Negi) signals, in humorously critical scenes, the US government's view of Puerto Ricans as primitive, dirty, and ignorant—without culture, except as hosts to parasites (64–8). Negi poses telling questions to her father about the difference of "politics" from an English word she hears, "polio" (71). In response Papi defines an imperialist in words comprehensible even to an eight-year-old: "They expect us to do things their way, even in our country," framing the relationship between the mainland US and its "associated state" as colonial (73). From Negi's stance of childish innocence, the ignorance and arrogance of US aid personnel and the effects of their policies are juxtaposed to the vulnerability to manipulation the villagers have—but also their skill in creative survival.

This episode implies another kind of transculturation, suggesting how the local culture, at least in rural settings, learned economic survival through flexible adaptation. Conversely, metropolitan and diasporan readers are implicitly positioned as economic and cultural outsiders in need of education about the failures of an arrogant American policy based on ignorance of Puerto Rico's richly diverse culture. To the dominant nation state, the origin and the contemporary moment of island culture are illegible, while Papi's counter-rhetoric suggests a counterhistory for a national imaginary.

4. The mapping of social subjects—role as class

Social roles are explicated as another kind of naming practice that serves to map distinctions in status. Negi's stories of her family's relocation from San Juan to the village of Macún, then back to urban areas, clarify how subject positions were asymmetrically classed and gendered in mid-century Puerto Rico, building up a complex cultural map. The family, initially poor urban dwellers, leave the city in economic desperation, to become "*jíbaros*," a collective name for "Rural Puerto Rican with distinctive dialect and customs" (273). It is a learned social role, and their performance a "how-to" that comically glosses the process. Negi, as a four-year-old, learns to be a *jíbara*. Her initiation occurs when, on touching the hot corrugated-metal sheets of their new house on stilts sunk in red clay, she burns her hand. The components of their rural life are recited in ethnographic detail: the *bohío* house is a boxlike shack (12); they listen to traditional folk music with "The Day Breaker's Club" on the radio; she learns how to steal the hen's eggs and gets covered with termites from the logs she brings in. These vividly detailed stories situate the family as *jíbaros* living by their wits and sharing simple pleasures that, Negi asserts, define a pastoral island life before extensive contact with northern *gringos*.

5. Bonds and binds of gendered and sexed bodies

Autoethnographic narrators, particularly women, often focus on how traditional patriarchal arrangements requiring marriage and the performance of dutiful domesticity constrain their agency in personal and social settings. In *WPR* when the family shifts from being "poor but happy" rural *Jíbaros* to return to the city, crucial differences of gendered, religious, and sexual practice (coded as ubiquitous heterosexuality, despite San Juan's longstanding homosexual communities) emerge. As an adolescent, Negi becomes an acute observer of the struggles of the working-class poor in the El Mangle district, notorious for its rough housing and unsanitary open sewers. Negi's stories cluster around the gendered body—her mother's and her own—as a site where cultural norms and strictures are legible, and disclose how forms of *machismo* are regulatory mechanisms to enforce female domesticity. The constraints of femininity become evident as Negi is sometimes sexually victimized, at other times punished for her transgressive sexual curiosity.

As with other aspects of authorizing her authenticity, Negi organizes her narration around Spanish terms about gendered difference. A key one is *"jamona,"* a Spanish word for "ham" but also a derogatory term for a woman when "she's too old to get married" (89). Her father asserts that adult relations privilege men, while women should fear the status of *jamona* as meaning "no one wants her" (90). The oppressive side of male power also becomes clear to Negi as Mami weeps in the night for the man with whom she had a half-dozen children but never formally married, and who is often away on trysts with other women: "a woman alone, even if ugly, could not suffer as much as my beautiful mother did" (104). Discussions between Negi and Mami also illumine how women seek to negotiate gender asymmetry, as Negi learns Spanish words for concepts to keep men in line. Mami asserts that libertines such as Papi "were always up to one *pocavergüenza* or another" ("shameless act" 92), which makes them in the eyes of women *sinvergüenza* ("shameless" 274). But in this male-dominated world, tolerating "shameless actions" (274) can bond dutiful women together only in a community of suffering, divided by the binary logic of *machismo* into mothers and whores, or "*Putas* . . . who lived in luxury in the city on the money that *sinvergüenza* husbands did not bring home" (29).

Machismo is also reinforced through social media—in newspaper articles of men shooting their wives in crimes of passion, in romantic soap operas on the radio portraying women's suffering over men's dalliances, and in melodramatic jukebox songs of lost love. As an autoethnographer, Santiago notes how the media form social subjects: Negi develops fantasies of romantic love and nurtures a dream of fulfillment (155) at odds with the love-hate relationship of her parents' violence in a pre-birth-control world. But Negi is presented as able to resist internalizing Puerto Rican social norms because she is, comically, too intemperate to perform femininity. In school she is singled out for "my wildness, my loud voice, and large gestures" as an unruly *jíbara* (39). In the country she helps her father build things, learns to fight and hunt with the boys, and participates in sexual explorations (116). Because her mother and the children leave the island when she is thirteen, Negi eludes the working-class woman's fate of being trapped into early wedlock and childbirth, and is rescued by migrating—at least into other dilemmas. Similarly, the family's lack of religious involvement protects her from the gendered norm of feminine self-denial religiously enforced through Catholicism. Thus the asymmetrically gendered social world that she narrates is one she can elude.

6. Models and mentors for the autoethnographic "I"

While autoethnographic narrators often describe characters as social types and models of behavior that represent potential selves, such models can be ambivalent. Negi develops a complex relationship to her parents as she discovers that qualities she admires in each may require her subordination to them. Negi's mother, determined to work outside the home, breaks the unwritten taboo of gendered labor by getting a job in a factory in the country, and leaves the other children with Negi as a surrogate mother (122). When Negi refuses to nurture them, her mother says she is lazy and "had failed in [her] duty as a female, as a sister, as the eldest" (125). Negi, by performing domesticity poorly (she is responsible for her youngest brother's serious foot injury), resists the gendered imperative of female caretaking. She also becomes suspicious of the "beauty" norm, viewing Mami, with her carefully groomed and "accessible beauty," as not just "a woman desired by many," but a kind of "public property" with numerous children that she doesn't want to emulate (190).

Her father's mentoring of Negi is complex, in part because of her apparent Oedipal attachment: "I wanted nothing more than for Papi to go on losing people he loved so that he'd always turn to me, so that I alone could bring him comfort" (28). Negi identifies with the poetic and intellectual sensitivity that her father, despite his brutality to her mother, displays toward her for her writing and oral performance. Protective of her intelligence, he takes her out of her new school in San Juan where Sra. Leona, the teacher, "treated me like I had a disease" because she daydreams (150–1). But their romantic bond is abruptly severed when Mami takes the children to New York and inaugurates a new life, as the intricate story of gendered relations mutates into a different form (discussed below). In the Puerto Rico Negi describes, where religious, cultural, and class norms depend on containing female sexuality, negotiating her performance as a social insider is challenging because of pressures from all sides to remain subordinate. As the adolescent Negi discovers that her parents are ambivalent role models, the limits of autoethnographic narration for telling a complex story become evident.

7. Folkloric practices and rituals around liminal states

The folkloric dimension of *WPR* as autoethnography, embedded in particulars, emerges around Negi's experience of rituals that mark cultural boundaries and, in turn, offer readers access to the liminal or uncanny borderlands of her insider knowledge. Although the family does not attend church and rarely engages in formal religion, everyday life is saturated with folkloric practices, such as those of the Three Kings festival. Unofficial religious culture clusters around the *botanica*,[20] which Negi narrates as a place that both reveals and conceals mysteries. In describing her encounter with Nicasia, a *curandera* or healer, Negi incorporates details of everyday spirituality in a liminal space that both entices and scares her.[21] When she is called on to close the eyes of a dead baby and help its soul "fly up to Heaven," (143) assured by the *curandera* that a "powerful spirit [is] protecting you" (146), she approaches the white-draped coffin. But the event is demystified as Negi's encounter with the clammy corpse leaves her feeling that "death was stuck to me" (147), a "cold and oily" feeling she cannot shake (149). In telling of Negi's "underworld" encounter and fear of contamination by the unquiet dead, Santiago suggests another limit of autoethnographic knowledge even as she signals secret spaces of folk culture.

The Limits of Autoethnographic "Authenticity"
In *WPR*'s first ten chapters, the eyewitness narration of the child Negi creates an ethnographically dense world. 1950s Puerto Rico emerges as a complex and diverse "norm," while the United States mainland is represented as an obtuse yet dominant "elsewhere" with a neocolonial mission. Readers must negotiate the practices and values of this world through cultural and linguistic immersion, and are provided with terms and concepts for "translating" the encounter to their diasporan or metropolitan experience. Cumulatively, the metrics of authenticity in Santiago's story enable her narrator to project the "truth effects" of autoethnographic encounter as a qualified insider. But this story of mid-century life in Puerto Rico is juxtaposed, in the last three chapters of *WPR*, to a different one occasioned by the family's move to the mainland, where the impossibility of seamless transculturation becomes evident. There, autoethnographic narration confronts a fundamental problem: it cannot account for either how the insider child became a skilled and educated adult able to tell her experiential story; or how the story gained recognition and was published. That is, the family's migration from the island to New York is not just an experiential crisis; it is also a narrative one. In *WPR*'s last three chapters Negi's performance as an autoethnographer is thwarted both by a new world she cannot comprehend and by the adolescent narrator's growing awareness of the complexity of ethnic, gender, and class identifications. These factors exert pressure on her to tell a different kind of story, which in turn requires a narrative template that can account for her self-transculturation as a writer able to tell and publish her story.

Telling Coming-of-age Stories

The imbrication of the child's story with the adult narrator's reflection on her coming of age is a staple of life writing but a complex negotiation, particularly for diasporan writers who grow up without privileged access to education. The conventional "Western" genres of such narration—the *Künstlerroman* and *Bildungsroman*—in their emphasis on self-reflection, seem to undercut an unmediated account of the "authentically" ethnic. But as narrators who migrate from a postcolonial origin to a metropolitan culture encounter new demands, they often fashion different versions of themselves through these templates. For Santiago, accounting for how she became able to tell her story in English and link her insider perspective as a working-class Puerto Rican to the worldly one of the Harvard graduate-narrator of the Prologue and Epilogue requires that she employ these genres.

The *Künstlerroman* or story of becoming an artist depicts how the narrated I pursued a writing vocation that would enable her to script the remembered world of childhood. Regarded as a Western trope about inborn—usually male—artistic exceptionality, for diasporan women it requires a doubled story. Throughout *WPR* Negi refers to herself as an emergent artist, showing how she developed the introspection to reflect on her experience and develop an interior consciousness, even as she performs as autoethnographer. Three kinds of stories about self-creation contribute to this formation. First, Negi suggests that the stimulus to become a reflective subject was initiated in dialogues with and thoughts of her adored, if negligent, father. Papi, despite being uneducated and frustrated, has "a vision of himself as a poet" (176). He introduces her to a romantic notion of "soul," not as a religious construct but as "the part of a person that feels" and that takes up writing (54). Second, Negi experiences moments of introspection, alone or in school, when she discovers she can imaginatively engage with this emergent self: "I walked beside myself. It was my soul wandering" (54). She splits herself in self-observation that turns inward as well as outward: "I sent the part of me that could fly outside the window to the *flamboyant* tree" (139). Third, Negi projects this imaginative subjectivity into her performances as a storyteller after the family arrives in Brooklyn. There she describes how, to counter pervasive racialized stereotypes of Puerto Ricans as hypersexual and disreputable, she created new familial bonds by telling fairy tales in which her "sisters and brothers . . . no matter how big the odds, always triumphed and always went on to live happily ever after" (235–6). Ultimately the account of how her poetic impulses produced her story is telescoped in the parable of eating the guava, the moment of self-reflexivity with which the narrative begins.

The parallel genre of the *Bildungsroman*, which traces how education and upward mobility produce the citizen, is also in tension with the insider's autoethnographic account because it discloses how the "authentic" insider had to gain access to a different world, which she stands outside, to acquire the education to tell her story. This aspect of *WPR* emerges in its strikingly different final three chapters, after the family migration. These chapters, which concern Negi's experiences after her mother leaves the children's father, who says he no longer loves her (208), and resettles them in Brooklyn, may clarify what disconcerted those critics who wanted to read *WPR* as an exemplary ethnic story. No formal internal break signals the momentous transition from Puerto Rico to New York across an ocean, languages, and cultures. But the last sentences of Chapter 10 foreshadow it:

> For me, the person I was becoming when we left was erased, and another one was created. The Puerto Rican *jíbara* who longed for the green quiet of a tropical afternoon was to become a hybrid who would never forgive the uprooting (209).

Santiago's emphasis on "hybrid" signals how her claim of island belonging will be complicated as the meanings of being "Puerto

Rican" shift on the mainland and the impossibility of autoethnographic narration emerges.

Migration to the US is a complicated story—it signals liberation and deliverance for Negi, but embeds the rest of her family in a Latino barrio in Brooklyn's Bedford-Stuyvesant. Negi registers surprise that the streets of New York are not "paved with gold," not even "bright and cheerful, clean, lively," but "dark and forbidding, empty, hard" (218), teeming with the daily violence of *"gente mala"* (252). In encounters with New York's multiple cultures her ability to navigate the environment no longer suffices because she speaks only Spanish and Spanglish (258), and lacks a conceptual grid to interpret the differences of ethnic groups she now encounters: orthodox Jewish men with long sidelocks, kosher delis, Italian pizza parlors, and the people she calls *"morenos,"* African Americans who "walked with a jaunty hop that made them look as if they were dancing down the street . . . and didn't like Puerto Ricans" who represented economic competition for scarce jobs (225). Negi also tries to categorize her Graham Avenue school world, describing the girls and boys of each ethnic group by clothing, hairstyles, habits, and place in the social hierarchy; but her understanding is insufficient to interpret their cultural interactions and find her own place. Crucially she discovers that "Puerto Rican" is not a unitary identity but one that depends on place of birth and socialization. The Brooklyn Puerto Ricans, who often spoke no Spanish, saw the island as "backward and mosquito-ridden," while other newly arrived Puerto Ricans "stuck together in suspicious little groups" (230). She is reluctant to identify with either, and unnerved by the racialized violence among the ethnically defined street gangs that segmented Brooklyn.

Negi is also inaugurated into a different and problematic sense of femininity on the mainland, as familial and gender relations are recoded in puzzling ways. In the reconstituted family, women assert more dominant roles, but at a cost. When the family discovers that Papi had married another woman after they left, Negi feels betrayed but observes, "Mami became ... both mother and father to us. We could count on her in a way we had never been able to count on Papi" (245). But the maternal-headed household is not economically viable: the American social services network redefines Mami as a "welfare mother" (250), unmarried, now with seven children. The new "family" consists of an alcoholic aunt, Tata, and her unemployed friend Don Julío, who seem to have internalized mainland stereotypes of Puerto Ricans, as well as various cousins who are street-smart but ignorant of their island heritage (205).

In this puzzling urban world where the meanings of being "Puerto Rican" shift, Negi's confident autoethnographic narration of cultural and linguistic specifics falters. "Puerto Rican" becomes both a negative stereotype and an identity subsumed in "Hispanic." To distinguish Negi from these others, Santiago turns to the *Bildungsroman* as a story of assimilation to mainland values and flight from the past. In this American version of the genre subjects understands themselves as displaced, linguistically incompetent outsiders who, by hard work, can pull themselves up by the bootstraps and find the American dream, as life writing texts from Benjamin Franklin to Edward Bok, Sui Sin Far, and Mary Antin, depict. Initially speaking only Spanglish, Negi studies the dictionary, goes daily to the library to teach herself English, and eventually reverses her school status as "learning-disabled." Recoding her island experience, she chafes that "being in Brooklyn was not a new life but a continuation of the old one ... everything had changed but nothing had changed" (247). Negi's need to seek new opportunities for education and upward mobility thus leads her to shift from ethnic identification to an individual-focused exceptionalism.

In her personal aspiration Negi begins to disidentify with transnational forms of Hispanic identification on the mainland. As translator for her mother at the welfare office, she watches how other Hispanics insist they are Puerto Rican to collect benefits (as members of the United States), and cites one's remark: "These *gringos* don't know the difference anyway. To them we're all spiks"

(250). Observing Hispanic women, she perceives as welfare-cheaters, Negi notes, "it reflected badly on us" (252). She becomes unsentimentally adamant about leaving the neighborhood, where "every man was a potential rapist, and every dark doorway was a potential hiding place for someone waiting to hurt me" (253). In fleeing the threat of violence, Negi also wants to escape the prospect of her own fertility, as threatening as her neighborhood to her ambition, and her unmotivated extended family. "It was on those tense walks home from school that I decided I had to get out of Brooklyn . . . How can people live like this?" (260). She further distances herself from the neighborhood by refusing to go to an academic high school and, instead, opts to audition for New York's famed Performing Arts High School as an actress (259). Her mother's prescient remark, "You'll be exposed to a different class of people," suggests Negi's motivation. Tellingly, at her audition, Negi succeeds, despite her broken English, by miming a scene as if she were enacting one of the family stories she told at home (265). Everything changes as she "transculturates" her sense of exceptionality in a meteoric rise at Performing Arts and, thereafter, as a scholarship student at Harvard, from which Santiago in fact graduated with highest honors.

Crucially, the narrative breaks off here, and is framed by the Epilogue, which, as I discussed, looks back from the perspective of the adult narrator on Negi's transformation into Esmeralda, the woman who escaped the *barrio* for education and literary success.[22] As the *Bildungsroman* of the final chapters suggests, for the immigrant aspiring to the American dream, the multicultural neighborhood's working-class inhabitants become legible only as menacing shadows. What are we to make of this dramatic shift in narrative mode as Negi abandons autoethnographic narration in favor of staging herself as the exemplary citizen of the *Bildungsroman*? It is illuminating to turn to how Santiago's story gained the attention of a publisher, and how the politics of publishing "authentic" accounts of ethnic subjects produced this bundling of the child's autoethnographic story and the adolescent's coming-of-age narrative.

External Metrics of Authenticity

On her website, years after *WPR* was published, Santiago noted that her original text was to a significant extent organized and shaped by its first editor at the educational publishing house, Addison-Wesley, in 1993. She describes how she was "discovered" by Merloyd Lawrence, who had her own imprint at the press. Santiago states:

> [T]he first draft of the book was much longer than the finished work, and it was in two parts, When I Was Puerto Rican—about my early years on the island—and My American Life—about my adolescence and young womanhood. After editing, the book was much shorter. (FAQs)

While the website makes no reference to an available original manuscript or editor's notes, the account suggests a collaborative dimension in organizing *WPR* into a legibly ethnic narrative.

Additionally, several paratextual materials that are typically introduced in the editing process shape *WPR*'s effect as an "authentic" Puerto Rican autoethnography.[23] *WPR* includes several kinds of paratexts or added materials: The 103 Spanish terms for foods and customs Negi uses are listed in a glossary with a pronunciation guide for non-Spanish speakers. A Puerto Rican proverb in both Spanish and English prefaces each chapter to wryly underscore its "lesson." The text's epigraph-poem, by poet Luis Lloréns Torres, praises the island as the Boricuan "home" and natural paradise. Additionally, the framing Prologue and Epilogue narrated in the present tense by the adult Santiago serve as a paratext signaling one way that autobiographical narrators—with the help of invested others such as editors—authorize their stories.

Although these paratexts may seem "natural" when reading, they authorize the story as "authentic."

Furthermore, the epitexts used in marketing *WPR* are striking. Its covers have fluctuated between photographs of a young Santiago (or a girl who resembles her) superimposed on a sunny gold background and a painting of a *bohío* house surrounded by *jíbaras* in vivid orange, rose, and palm-green (whose artist is not identified). The moment of its publication in the early nineties was a time when, as Juan Flores observes, mass-market publishers began constructing "Latino literature" as "an attractive marketing rubric" for inclusion in the American multicultural canon (169). It is hardly surprising, then, that these epitexts emphasize *WPR*'s autoethnographic dimension, just as its narrative template changes dramatically in the last chapters to produce a legibly "happy" account of an assimilated individual.

Telling Conflicting Stories

Santiago's bifurcated story is troubling unless we recognize the dramatic shift in narrative templates in the last three chapters of the memoir about life in Brooklyn. The assimilationist narrative following Santiago's engaging autoethnographic story of coming of age on the island is a strategic translation of genres—from autoethnography to *Bildungsroman*—produced in editorial collaboration to conform the narrative to the desires of metropolitan and diasporan audiences for upbeat endings and to account for the author's remarkable literacy. To regard *WPR* as a single coherent narrative ignores two things: the gap between island and mainland contexts of identity, and the multiple genres that contend in *WPR*, which its engaging voice seeks to finesse. The metrics of authenticity that the first part of *WPR* sets up are unsustainable in the mainland setting of hybrid identities to which the adult Santiago belongs both too much and too little. Negi, the consummate performer of roles—as *jíbara*, family mediator, interrogator of gendered and classed positions, and, in New York, translator and actress—is an identity compressing the several subject positions through which Santiago moves. Only from the distance of the mainland and the gap of educated, middle-class fluency in English, can she place her cultural world in relation to the manifestly other world of the island, to reflect on its language, worldview, and habitus and narrate her own ethnogenesis.[24]

As Santiago's narrative shows, ethnic memoirists develop counter-ethnographic accounts by incorporating their insider experiences as alternative histories. Reading their memoirs not as essentialist witnessing but as strategic autoethnography helpfully recasts the "stuck" question of whether narratives such as Santiago's are representative cultural models or assimilationist "sellouts." Autoethnography, as a tactical process, both strategically asserts a collective *ethnos* or social group replacing the bios of the individual life, and employs metrics that signal the narrator's double position as cultural insider and literate, reflexive outsider. Rather than a failed narrative performance, then, WPR is an exemplary narrative about two things: how autoethnographic narration depends on metrics that authenticate the narrator's authority as an eyewitness observer embedded in cultural detail; and how a seamless process of "transculturation" that renders that experience transparently from a different location, at a later moment and in a different language, is a necessary illusion of both the genre and its marketing. For diasporan women life writers who confront gender and class asymmetries that make education, linguistic competency, and access to public life challenging, negotiating these competing requirements is a complex agenda that might be acclaimed as much for the fissures it exposes in life writing as for the achieved "identities" readers want to proclaim.

Notes

1 I am grateful to Sidonie Smith for helpful suggestions while this essay was in process, and to the Friedrich Meinecke Institute at the Free University, Berlin, for the occasion to present it and the numerous questions generated.

2   The narrative was first published by the educational publishing house Addison-Wesley in 1993, then in 1994 bought by Viking, a subsidiary of Random House, which fueled its wide circulation in paperback.
3   A few parent groups in Virginia and California challenged *WPR*'s place in high school libraries as too "sexually explicit."
4   After the United States wrested Puerto Rico from Spain in 1898 and made it an island colony, it was given American citizenship in 1917 and declared a "free associated state" in 1952; but while its citizens have US passports and serve in its military, they do not have governmental self-determination.
5   Torres-Padilla discusses island feminists' disparagement of *WPR* for disavowing collective efforts and accepting a market desire for stories of subaltern women subordinated to colonial paternalism (182). Sánchez-González is also critical of *WPR* as validating mainland agendas at the expense of island women (160).
6   Enrique Morales-Diaz also asserts that Santiago as narrator "speaks on behalf of a group or community" (138). He draws on John Beverley's well-known criteria for *testimonio* and attends to how Santiago redirects the female gaze from abjection to assertion.
7   James Clifford's observation that "participant-observation obliges its practitioners to experience, at a bodily as well as an intellectual level, the vicissitudes of translation" nicely captures Santiago's challenge in approaching her readers (24).
8   Lisa Sánchez-González reads *WPR* as a novel about a protagonist interested only in saving her own life (158). She pronounces it a "failed allegory" undermining its own authority and unable to speak "progressively and productively for the community" because, as a "willfully assimilating exile," Santiago is self-subverting (159). To the contrary, I argue that attending to the autobiographical templates Santiago employs shows that *WPR* is neither allegorical nor failed.
9   See *Reading Autobiography* for extended discussion of these issues, particularly in Chapters 2 and 3.
10 Carmen S. Rivera alludes to ethnographer Oscar Lewis' 1965 *La Vida: A Puerto Rican Family in the Culture of Poverty*, criticizing its focus on the "sordid aspects of the lives of Puerto Ricans," particularly prostitution (26, Note 5). Lewis may, however, be interesting as an *editorial* intertext.
11 The concepts of the contact zone and processes of transculturation, derived from critiques of ethnography, were used by Pratt in *Imperial Eyes*. Published a few years earlier, Lionnet's study developed the

concept of *métissage* as the braiding of disparate, discordant Western and indigenous idioms into Creolités.

12 Some critics have seen such autobiographical texts as "tourist guides" for diasporan and metropolitan readers (Sau-Ling Wong on *The Woman Warrior*); some as ethnic passing (Browder, *Slippery Characters*); and others as assimilationist narratives refusing to acknowledge the narrating I's privileged position, as the debate around Santiago suggests.

13 Although I use "strategic autoethnography" here, I have argued for the term "counter-ethnography" elsewhere, because it signals that life writings call ethnographic practices into question even as they appropriate ethnographic features. See my discussion of *In the Land of the Grasshopper Song* for an extended theoretical statement.

14 Not all diasporan women's coming-of-age narratives are autoethnographic. Luisita Lopez-Torregrosa's memoir, *The Noise of Infinite Longing: A Memoir of Family—and an Island*, detailing her Puerto Rican childhood, for example, is ambivalent about San Juan as "a place of dreams still" (282); but she does not engage metrics of authenticity, instead insisting on the radical particularity of her memories and her untranslatable present identity.

15 This anxiety, as Laura Browder argues, has shadowed ethnic memoirs in settler nations such as Australia, Canada, and the United States since their inception.

16 Sidonie Smith and I have developed what we call the "metrics of authenticity." These effects are "produced internally at the intersection of the [subject's] singular experiential history and the shared communal discourses and narrative rhetorics through which that experiential history unfolds, as well as externally through the production, marketing and circulation of . . . narratives for transnational publics." We discuss how several metrics about the truth claims of testimony are taken up in human rights witnessing by survivors of violence, including: the you-are-there sense of immediacy; the invocation of rights discourse; affirmation of the duty to narrate a collective story; the normative shape of victim experience and identity; and the ethno-documentation of cultural specificity. (See "Witness or False Witness?"). I have adapted these metrics to categories of autoethnographic subject formation.

17 James Phelan's discussion of Frank McCourt's *Angela's Ashes* assesses how autobiographical narrative adjudicates differences between a child's experience narrated in a historical past tense that seems to issue from that moment of childhood experience and the adult narrator's version and re-evaluation of events, the one the reader will identify with

and learn from (72). Child-narrated narrative, because of its "hypermimetic quality," is constructed in ways it does not acknowledge, with the authorial "I" contributing a shape the child cannot acknowledge: filling in lapses in memory, constructing characters and dialogue, foregrounding some events while suppressing others, to *make* a story.

18 Cited in Torres-Padilla, 192.
19 Rivera notes that *Negra* and *Negrita* are considered terms of endearment in Puerto Rico and not necessarily reflective of skin color. But Negi's adolescence in New York has influenced how the adult narrator comes to understand her name (26, note 9).
20 A *botanica* is a boutique selling herbs and icons for curing physical and spiritual malaise.
21 Raquel Romberg, in describing Puerto Rican spiritual practices both on the island and in the diaspora, argues that *brujería*, which she translates as "witchcraft" and its practitioners, *brujos*, "witch-healers," changed from a traditional folk religion in mid-century to "a dynamic transnational arena of ritual experimentation," a set of practices that now are "cosmopolitan and eclectic," linked to the nationalist project of creating a consolidated, essentialized Puerto Rican identity linked to evangelical Christianity as an entrepreneurial activity. See *Witchcraft and Welfare*.
22 The sequel to this narrative is *Almost a Woman* (1997), which explores Santiago's teenaged experience. One review states that it "continues the riveting chronicle of her emergence from the barrios of Brooklyn to the theaters of Manhattan" (*Amazon*). The third installment of this serial autobiography, *The Turkish Lover* (2004), focuses on Santiago's adulthood and the abusive man who dominated her life for seven years, qualifying the American dream optimistically narrated in *When I Was Puerto Rican*.
23 See *Reading Autobiography*, 99 and 248, for discussion of paratexts and epitexts.
24 Santiago later translated WPR into Spanish in a version that, according to critic Guillermo Irizarry, has grammatical errors, prose infelicities, and "linguistic interferences," which correspond to its "lack of internal coherence" (5).

References

Besemeres, Mary. "The Ethnographic Work of Cross-Cultural Memoir." *a/b: Auto/Biography Studies* 25.2 (2010): 219–30.

———. *Translating One's Self: Language and Selfhood in Cross-Cultural Autobiography*. Oxford: Peter Lang, 2002.

Boelhower, William. *Through a Glass Darkly: Ethnic Semiosis in American Literature.* New York: Oxford University Press, 1987.

Browder, Laura. *Slippery Characters. Ethnic Impersonators and American Identities.* Chapel Hill, NC: University of North Carolina Press, 2000.

Clifford, James. *Predicament of Culture.* Cambridge: Harvard University Press, 1988.

Conquergood, Dwight. "Rethinking Ethnography: Towards a Critical Cultural Politics." *Communication Monographs* 58 (1991): 179–94.

Echano, Marta Vizcaya. "'Somewhere between Puerto Rico and New York': The Representation of Individual and Collective Identities in Esmeralda Santiago's *When I Was Puerto Rican* and *Almost a Woman*." *Prose Studies* 26.1–2 (2003): 112–30.

Flores, Juan. *From Bomba to Hip-Hop. Puerto Rican Culture and Latino Identity.* New York: Columbia University Press, 2000.

Geertz, Clifford. *Works and Lives: The Anthropologist as Author.* Stanford: Stanford University Press, 1988.

Sánchez-González, Lisa. *Boricua Literature. A Literary History of the Puerto Rican Diaspora.* New York: New York University Press, 2001.

Hernández, Carmen Dolores. *Interviews with Writers.* Westport, CT: Praeger, 1997.

Irizarry, Guillermo. "Travelling Textualities and Phantasmagoric Originals: A Reading of Translation in Three Recent Spanish-Caribbean Narratives." 19 October 2011 www.lehman.cuny.edu/ciberletras/v04/Irizarry.html.

Lionnet, Françoise. *Autobiographical Voices: Race, Gender, Self-Portraiture.* Ithaca, NY: Cornell University Press, 1989.

López-Torregrosa, Luisita. *The Noise of Infinite Longing.* New York: HarperCollins, 2004.

Morales-Diaz, Enrique. "Catching Glimpses: Appropriating the Female Gaze in Esmeralda Santiago's Autobiographical Writing." *CENTRO: American Me: A Study of Contemporary Chicano/a Autobiography* XIV.2 (2002): 131–47.

Minh-ha, Trinh T. *Woman, Native, Other: Writing Postcoloniality and Feminism.* Bloomington: Indiana University Press, 1989.

Phelan, James. *Living to Tell about It. A Rhetoric and Ethics of Character Narration.* Ithaca and London: Cornell University Press, 2002.

Pratt, Mary Louise. *Imperial Eyes: Travel and Transculturation.* London: Routledge, 1992.

Rivera, Carmen S. *Kissing the Mango Tree: Puerto Rican Women Rewriting American Literature.* Houston: Arte Publico Press, 2002.

Romberg, Raquel. "At the Intersection of Consumerism and Tradition: Spirits and Witches in Modern Puerto Rico." Paper given at the "Cultural Circulations" conference, The Ohio State University, Jan. 29, 2005.

———. *Witchcraft and Welfare: Spiritual Capital and the Business of Magic in Modern Puerto Rico* Austin: University of Texas Press, 2003.

Santiago, Esmeralda. *When I Was Puerto Rican.* NY: Addison-Wesley, 1993. NY: Random House, 1994.

———. "Frequently Asked Questions" (FAQs). 25 Oct. 2005 www.esmeraldasantaigo.com/FAQ/faq.html.

Smith, Sidonie, and Julia Watson. *Reading Autobiography: A Guide for Interpreting Life Narratives.* Minneapolis: University of Minnesota Press, 2nd expanded edition, 2010.

Smith, Sidonie, and Julia Watson. "Witness or False Witness? Metrics of Authenticity, Collective I-Formations, and the Ethic of Verification in First-Person Testimony." *Biography* 35:4 (Fall 2012): 590–627.

Torres-Padilla, José L. "When 'I' Became Ethnic: Ethnogenesis and Three Early Puerto Rican Diaspora Writers." *CENTRO* XIV.2 (2002): 181–97.

Watson, Julia. "'As Gay and as Indian as They Chose': Collaboration and Counter-Ethnography in *In the Land of the Grasshopper Song.*" *Biography* 31.3 (2008): 397–428.

Wong, Sau-Ling. "Autobiography as Guided Chinatown Tour? Maxine Hong Kingston's *The Woman Warrior* and the Chinese-American Autobiographical Controversy." *Multicultural Autobiography.* Ed. James Robert Payne. Knoxville, TN: University of Tennessee Press, 1992. 248–79.

17

"America's Exhibit A": Hillary Rodham Clinton's *Living History* and the Genres of Authenticity (Smith 2012)

Does she have the stuff to come on "Hardball"... into the belly of the beast?
    Chris Matthews to Howard Fineman, MSNBC (2000)

In this terrain, women are held up simultaneously to often deeply contradictory standards—could Clinton, a girl, really be commander in chief? Or was she too tough and unladylike for the job?
    Susan Douglas, *Enlightened Sexism* (269–70).

As the old canard goes: A year is a millennium in politics. So what the candidate line-up will look like in 2016 is far from predictable. But for many politicos, the expectation is that Hillary Rodham Clinton will make a second run for the Democratic nomination and then for the White House. She will be 69 in 2016, not the oldest candidate; Ronald Reagan was 69 when elected. She'll have her experience as Secretary of State in the Obama administration, international bona fides, and security credibility that expand her claims to formidable expertise. Chances are she will have written another book, this one on foreign policy. Clinton's 2003 best-selling autobiography *Living History* will more than likely be reissued sometime before the campaign begins in earnest. It will most likely enter the *New York Times* best-seller list for a second time.

Given this possible future for Clinton's autobiography, I want to return to *Living History* to meditate on the political uses of autobiography in the gendered arena of American presidential politics.[1] *Living History* earned big bucks. Its audio book version won an Emmy. The book tour, interviews, and reviews that followed put Clinton in contact with a national audience of celebrity fans and potential voters that the aspiring presidential candidate would recruit into "Hillaryland."[2] Translations of the book, including the Chinese version,[3] turned her autobiography into a global bestseller.

As prologue to a campaign for the presidential nomination, *Living History* sought to do the social work of convincing the voting public that a woman could assume national leadership. Not that Hillary Clinton was the first woman to launch a presidential bid in the United States. Margaret Chase Smith, a Congresswoman and Senator from Maine, made a bid for the Republican nomination in 1964, losing out to Barry Goldwater; and Shirley Chisholm, Congresswoman from the 12th District of New York, made a bid for the Democratic nomination, the first by an African American, in 1972. But Clinton was the first former First Lady to position herself for a presidential run and the first woman with national and global celebrity status to establish a viable plan for pursuing and gaining the nomination. The "Hillary" of *Living History*, then, would translate celebrity aura into active support, skepticism into investment, and do so by performing a convincing political persona. But how would this woman, this feminist professional, former First Lady, and duly-elected senator, craft the story of representative American-ness in the hyper-masculinized genre of the aspiring candidate's autobiography? And how would she perform the intimacy that secures the claim to authenticity in this highly mediated form?

Mobilizing the "Authentic" Political Persona

Before pursuing these questions, let me comment briefly on the social action of the contemporary candidate autobiography. A corporate production, candidacy in late capitalism is crafted, packaged, marketed, displayed, polled, and sold. The presidential candidate must perform as a celebrity, sustain celebrity appeal, and successfully navigate the shoals of celebrity culture.[4] In this densely mediated environment, the political persona is ever more deftly and promiscuously imaged, voiced, choreographed, and networked.[5] Central to the political utility of the persona is the "life story," the story that does the political work of securing the symbolic relationship between person and political system (Corner 398), at once individualizing the candidate and projecting the candidate as the embodiment of represivity, to use Dana Nelson's term (325 "Representative/ Democracy"). The aspiring candidate wants to get a book written, get it out, get it read, and get it on the *New York Times* best-seller list. Its very shelf life registers its power to compel voter support. In the first decades of the twenty-first century, memoir culture, celebrity culture, and presidential politics converge to convert a life story into money, message, and conduit for affective attachment that circulates through what Lauren Berlant defines as the intimate public sphere (see *Queen* 1–24).

Contemporary candidate autobiography would seem to be highly managed and instrumental, and thus inauthentic. But in politics, convincing authenticity is the coin of the realm. How exactly is an aura of authenticity produced in the utilitarian, commodified form of political autobiography? Autobiographical discourse itself promises a kind of authenticity. The "narrating 'I'" functions as the "voice" of the politician seeking to capture the attention of the reader sitting at home, in a coffee house, on the beach.[6] In its address to the imagined interlocutor, the narrating

"I" promises to draw the reader into the zone of familiarity, identification, and affective attachment, thereby overcoming, if only for a moment and illusorily, the sense of remoteness between voter and candidate.

But there are other metrics of authenticity at the intersection of the singular history and shared discourses. Generic intelligibility, by which I mean a species or template of storytelling that is recognizable to an audience, is certainly one of the most important in producing the aura of authenticity. Modes of autobiographical narration reproduce intelligible subject positions, plots, tropes, and rhetorics of self-representation. Doing so, they project a "reality" effect of the sincere or "real" person behind the political persona. "We elect our leaders," observes Laura Kipnis, "because they've made themselves legible to us as a collective mirror"; in this way they "embody the appropriate collective story" (317). Kipnis's observation zeroes in on the importance of generic mode to the aura of authenticity attached to a candidate's story.

It is to the authenticity effects of generic intelligibility in Clinton's *Living History* that I now turn. What is fundamentally at stake in this book that would launch a thousand voters is how to find the right story—the right stuff—for the narrating "I" to tell. The "I" of *Living History* has to mobilize autobiographical narration to do the social work of launching a presidential bid by a feminist woman by offering the public access to the "real" "Hillary," whose claims to political power are legitimate. This challenge involves negotiating a masculine subject position, projecting for "the people" what Nelson describes as critical to producing the aura of constitutional "presidentialism"—a "concentrated and purified experience of representation in the executive body of the president—the concrete correlative for national manhood" (333).[7] Equally challenging, the narrating "I" brings to this autobiographical project multiple histories: she is at once a feminist and a former First Lady, in themselves potentially contradictory subject positions and, certainly, historically non-presidential subject positions.

In this context, it is important to recall that Hillary Clinton's autobiography is a corporate project. The narrating "I" of *Living History* is the collective endeavor of Clinton herself, her three ghost writers, and the editor(s) involved in its publication. Ghostwritten certainly does not surprise—ghostwriting of political memoirs is the norm, as in Theodore Sorenson's ghost-writing of John F. Kennedy's *Profiles in Courage* and, more recently, Mark Salter's co-authorship of John McCain's *Faith of My Fathers: A Family Memoir* (1999). The corporate ghostwriting in *Living History*, however, exposes the postmodern bureaucratization of a candidacy, its standardization, packaging, and test marketing.

This ensemble of actors producing *Living History* as the aspiring presidential candidate's official autobiography actually mobilizes a constellation of generic modes and autobiographical discourses, all of which produce their different authenticity effects. In following the diverse strands and entanglements of the different generic modes, we begin to understand how the published autobiography produces—or not—the authenticity effect of a *real Hillary*, the convincing persona that is always at stake in the political field.

The case of Hillary Clinton's *Living History* and its "management" of "being American" (Berlant *Queen* 25) captures what's at stake in the political arena for the feminist who would be president. Clinton's very public narrative is routed through several generic modes—modernist Bildungsroman, feminist Bildungsroman, First Lady memoir, buddy narrative, and war memoir—and it forestalls routing through another mode, the celebrity confession. In exploring the authenticity effects of these generic modes and tracking the intimations of inauthenticity inherent in their contradictory subject positions and rhetorics, we can assess how the heterogeneous, sometimes conflicting, genres of life writing expose the difficulty of successfully managing political and politicized gender. In what follows, we can observe how it takes a "village" of genres to make, and unmake, the "real" "Hillary."

Modernist Bildungsroman

Living History seems a robustly modernist autobiography, characterized by its retrospective narrative trajectory, its developmental, autonomous narrated "I," and its narrative grammar of modernity as a telos of freedom and progress. In this it reproduces a highly intelligible mode of political memoir in which, Margaret Henderson notes, "individualistic narrators use linearity and realism to recount their lives, the seemingly authoritative mode with which to make the self cohere, produce verisimilitude, and construct the historical record" (169). This generic mode is the mode of the traditional Bildungsroman, whose history extends back to the late eighteenth century. Indeed *Living History* can be read as a coming-of-age story of education and a journey of subjective incorporation as a normative national subject. In *The Queen of America Goes to Washington: Essays on Sex and Citizenship*, Lauren Berlant calls this the "infantile citizen form," "a political subjectivity based on the suppression of critical knowledge and a resulting contraction of citizenship to something smaller than agency: patriotic inclination, default social membership, or the simple possession of a normal national character" (27). The infantile citizen's Ur-narrative, according to Berlant, "casts his [sic] pilgrimage to Washington as a life-structuring project that began in childhood" (*Queen* 37). The first paragraph of *Living History* announces the trope of the defining national fable:

> I wasn't born a first lady or a senator. I wasn't born a Democrat. I wasn't born a lawyer or an advocate for women's rights and human rights. I wasn't born a wife or mother. I was born an American in the middle of the twentieth century, a fortunate time and place. (1)

Living History reproduces what Joseph Slaughter describes in another context as the tautological/teleological structure of

Bildungsroman; that is, it "situate[s] the human personality both before and after the process of incorporation" (26). The narrating "I" of the autobiography is the *elected* senator who tells the story of becoming what she was from the beginning, in *Living History*'s case the essential American subject. As such, the narrator acts as guarantor of the First Lady's "enfranchisement" (Slaughter 20) as a bona fide and electable candidate.

For the aspiring presidential candidate, then, the modernist Bildungsroman form reproduces the realness norms naturalizing American national identity. Through the performative act of life writing, the narrating "I" of *Living History* registers the characterological features of modernist subjectivity, among them free will, intelligence, mastery, entrepreneurial autonomy, and ambition. This reiteration of the national fable of individualist self-making secures the symbolic relationship between person and nation (Corner 398). As Philip Holden observes, the social project of modernist self-narrating involves projecting the legitimacy of power by suturing the story of the individual to the story of the nation, projecting as it does so the coherence of both national subject and nation.[8]

Yet, the modernist autobiography of the political leader has been a masculinist mode of Bildungsroman, conjoining the phallic agent of narration, the linearity of progressive time, and the symbolic narrated "I." The realness norms producing the authenticity effect of American identity for the aspiring presidential candidate are effects of the masculinist tropes of phallic leadership. The constraint of the modernist mode of Bildungsroman is to position the woman who would be president in a constitutively masculine subject position, to position her, in effect, as an inauthentically gendered presidential aspirant.

Feminist Bildungsroman

In this light, let us return to the opening paragraph to reread the subsequent sentences:

> I was free to make choices unavailable to past generations of women in my own country and inconceivable to many women in the world today. I came of age on the crest of tumultuous social change and took part in the political battles fought over the meaning of America and its role in the world. (1)

Here the narrator positions herself as a historical figure in what Berlant terms the "crisis of the national future"—the struggle of those historically excluded from full citizenship to claim full, rather than partial, citizenship in a collective founded on the "abstract principles of democratic nationality" (*Queen* 18). This self-positioning introduces a variant generic mode into *Living History*, the feminist Bildungsroman. The "arrival" in a Senate seat for the former First Lady is the culmination of the feminist fable of the struggle for full citizenship, the arrival in "Washington City" as a senator. We observe the voice and form of feminist Bildungsroman when the narrator tells us what it was like to be "a woman"—in a Seven Sisters college, in the antiwar movement, in law school, in the campaign, in the governor's mansion, in the law firm, in the White House, and on the senatorial campaign trail. We hear it also when Clinton parses her discomforts with gendered roles, her negotiations of gender bias, and her analysis of gender ideology in action. This "Hillary" is positioned as generational symbol, "America's Exhibit A" (141), the embodiment of the future of America's second-wave feminism and of "America" itself.

The feminist Bildungsroman produces its authenticity effects by condensing the Ur-story of second-wave feminism. Clinton's narrative is the generational auto/biography of women fighting for equality in the workplace and in national politics for some thirty years, of women competing in the world despite formidable obstacles, accumulating success and power as entrepreneurial feminists, projecting themselves as individualist agents of change. Its claim to authenticity is an effect of its triumphalist plot of achievement against the odds and its tacit acknowledgment that most women have to work far harder than men to get respect, that women cannot just "be" charismatic political personalities. "America's Exhibit A" reiterates the individualist plot of development and possessive masculinity of liberal feminism.

The mobilization of feminist Bildungsroman in *Living History* exposes the realness norms pervading and defining modernist autobiography as masculinist norms. And it strips the normative narrative that is the nation's privileged fable of American political identity of its gendered features, contesting the gendered content of the viable political persona. Doing so, it would remake the nation as more fully inclusive, women's citizenship as full rather than partial, and "Hillary" as a real candidate. And yet, the liberal feminist move to resituate the narrator from the subject of modernist Bildungsroman to the subject of feminist Bildungsroman does not necessarily promise full generic citizenship. What Margaret Henderson observes of the feminist Bildungsroman form in the autobiographies of Robin Morgan and Betty Friedan illuminates the difficulty of claiming legitimate or "real" political power through a revisionary mode: "In liberal feminist fashion, they modify rather than transform the genre, which forms an uncanny parallel to the limited concessions granted by the social order of late capitalism to accommodate feminist demands" (171).

Further, even as *Living History* presents a paradigmatic story invoking legacies of 1970s liberal feminist discourse, two specters haunt the grammar of the feminist Bildungsroman. First is the specter of what radio pundit Rush Limbaugh calls a "feminazi," the woman too strident, humorless, power-hungry, and threatening to elect to lead the nation. This alternative version of the real "Hillary" had long circulated in hostile media that portrayed her as a lying, cold-hearted "bitch," a scandalous persona. We sense this ghost every time the narrator makes a joke and pokes fun at herself. Second is the specter of the feminist who failed to assert her agency to sever a relationship that had been the source of betrayal and public humiliation. If the first specter is the specter of too much feminism, the second is the specter of too little. The contradiction undermines Clinton's claim to the authenticity of her femininity and the authenticity of her feminism.

First Lady Memoir

Living History also has to be read as a First Lady memoir, that mode of life writing Shawn J. Parry-Giles, and Diane M. Blair describe as an intractably gendered genre in American political life.[9] This generic mode is by definition a narrative of a gendered "role," of heteronormative coupling, feminine subject positions, and feminized fables of identity that attach both narrated and narrating "I"s to another whose history as president compels the wife's version as the summation of her identity. It is a genre out of "women's culture," identified with affect and mission. As such, it is a genre that reproduces the gendered privatization of politics (Berlant, *Female Complaint* xii). It is also a haunted genre, inflected as it is by the cultural anxieties surrounding the role itself, a non-elective, non-Constitutional post that troubles the notion of legitimate power in a representative democracy. The role of First Lady in the "First Heteronormative Relation" is a role without a warrant. Or rather, its warrant is to maintain the integrity of the zone of presidential politics as phallic ground.

Hillary Clinton was not the first activist and politically savvy advisor in the role; for instance, recall Eleanor Roosevelt and Lady Bird Johnson. She was, however, the first avowedly feminist woman in the White House; and her version of the genre is one of role discomfort. Of the 1992 presidential campaign, the narrating "I" observes: "I had worked full-time during my marriage to Bill and valued the independence and identity that work provided. Now I was solely 'the wife,' an odd experience for me" (111). Further on, she describes how, after 1994, she was convinced by advisors that she "could advance the Clinton agenda through symbolic action" (265).[10] The story of the First Wife is the story of how the narrated "I" rerouted herself through feminized sentimentalism's symbolic script of indirect influence through activism on behalf of women and children.[11] That subject position is also performed by the narrating "I" through *Living History*'s tracking of the story of romance, marriage, and motherhood, and its maternalist advocacy on behalf of Bill Clinton's presidency and of the Constitution itself.

In telling the story of this gendered role, which she describes as "an ideal—and largely mythical—concept of American womanhood" (119), the narrator of *Living History* interrupts the grammar of the liberal feminist Bildungsroman. If the mode of feminist Bildungsroman unfolds through a triumphalist plot of self-making, in this mode the narrator tells of constant failure, failure either to fit or escape sentimentality's role. The First Lady mode becomes one of role abjection, to invoke a Kristevan concept. It exposes the ways in which she is an inappropriate subject who is clumsily or uncomfortably feminized, as the serial recourse and references to unsuccessful hairstyles metonymically suggest.

The negotiations of the First Lady memoir form fail to produce a determinable ground upon which to authenticate a political persona. In political terms, this is the genre, and the abject subject position from which Clinton must extract herself if she is to position herself for a run for the presidency and make a claim for legitimate power. The paradox of generic mode here is that, in the very narration of her history as First Lady, the narrating "I" reproduces the "realness" norms of femininity *and* renders "Hillary" inauthentically feminine.

Buddy Narrative

To manage the political persona of the woman who would be president, the narrator of *Living History* reconfigures the First Lady memoir as the "buddy" narrative of the First Partnership. Through the buddy narrative the narrator shifts from the subject position of wife to that of sidekick. This is yet another of *Living History*'s generic modes.

Bill and Hillary Clinton presented themselves to the nation as the First Buddyship. (Interestingly, they named their White House dog "Buddy.") After they arrived at the White House and during their eight years in residence, the Clintons packaged their relationship to the American public as a working relationship, and a new kind of First Marriage. Loren Glass observed at the time that

> [I]nsofar as the vision of the 'professional couple' is a focus-group-driven product of the Clinton administration's professional media team, it is a product of itself: "professionalism" is both the manufactured image and the working reality of the Clinton White House. Even their personal relationship is increasingly characterized as pragmatic and professional; their marriage seems to be a "working" relationship, in both senses of the term (par. 32).

A "dual-career" marriage in the White House required media management because it so predictably drew fire for its rescripting and disruption of gendered roles and affects. Clinton wore her pantsuits; Bill emoted for the public and the electorate. "Bill and Hillary"—or "Billary" as they were sometimes called—as a presidential package deal confused the norms of the First Couple's heteronormativity in ways that unsettled public/private binaries, the idioms of patriarchally organized relations, and the gendered politics of leadership. In the First Buddyship, affect and agency became fungible features of presidential leadership.

This fungibility persists in the rhetorical moves of Clinton's *Living History*. The narrating "I" of the First Professional Couple places herself at the center of presidential politics, as in this passage where she bemoans the failure of the Clinton health care initiative: "Someday we will fix the system. When we do, it will be the result of more than fifty years of efforts by Harry Truman, Richard Nixon, Jimmy Carter and Bill and me. Yes, I'm still glad we tried" (249). The slippage of the initial "we" of the American people as a collective to the second "we" of "Bill and me" registers Clinton's self-figuration as co-president during the "Clinton years." Consider as well the passage where she tells of the presidential visit to Jordan and Israel in October 1994: "Heading back home, I believed I was leaving Israel another step closer to peace and security" (254). In such gestures the narrator of *Living History* inserts herself rhetorically in the subject position of co-equal partner in the phallic arena of presidential leadership. The narrator of *Living History* mobilizes the power of rhetoric to intimate that she has already been a "real" president, already inhabited the subject position and exercised the phallic leadership attached to political leadership—in reality and in the pronouns of narration. This is authenticity by pronominal location.

The positing of the subject position of co-president in her version of the buddy narrative, however, reinforces "Hillary's" uncomfortable feminization as First Lady, thereby undermining the authenticity effect of her self-performance as dutiful wife. It also leaves Clinton open to charges of unseemly and opportunistic self-aggrandizement, demonstrated by the attacks on her credibility by Republicans, among them Dick Morris, who rewrites her narrative as *Rewriting History*. But it is not only Clinton's frenzied antagonists who make trouble for her buddy story. The Buddy did as well. Bill Clinton penned his own presidential memoir. When *My Life* appeared in 2004, dutifully delayed for a year until his wife's book appeared, his life story only energized opposition research. The book to retrieve his presidency and himself from the scandals of the Clinton years effectively marginalizes his wife's book, and undermines the credibility of her claims to the First Buddyship, as it was bound to do. In a certain way, Bill's narrative puts "Hillary" back in place and reminds the public that he will not go gently.[12] In one more way, the recourse to the generic mode of Buddy narrative undermines the credibility and sincerity of candidate "Hillary."

Celebrity Confession

Here we come to the management of a generic mode that haunts *Living History*, which is suppressed in the corporate voice of the narrating "I" and emerges in traces only—the mode of celebrity confession. Written in the wake of the President's very public adultery, *Living History* is dogged by Bill Clinton's sex acts and indiscretions. With the publication of *The Starr Report* in 1998, the "president's privates," as Glass notes, had become the "vital center of public discussion in the United States and the world" (par. 2) and the White House had become a theater of capacious desire. Glass goes on to argue that "Clinton's apparent inability to restrain his libido, to keep his dick in his pants, constantly reminds us of the human penis behind the official phallus. This repeated thrusting of the pornographic penis into a public realm organized around the symbolic phallus indicates a crisis in the patriarchal structure of authority that has traditionally undergirded the American public sphere" (par. 5, 3/22). Hillary Clinton's intimacy with the president's privates became a public affair in all senses of the word. That spectacular scandal had consumed the celebrity tabloids as well as national news media. Indeed, the coverage of the scandal, the Starr Report, and the impeachment turned the mainstream news organizations into touts for pornographic representations and pleasures, moral outrage, and crusader zeal.

Reviews of the book indicate that for many, finding out what Hillary would say and how she would say it drove readers to purchase and consume *Living History*.[13] The public, pundits, and politicos had struggled to script "Hillary's" reaction, predicament, and emotions, parsing every gesture, look, behavior, and statement. In the remediations of Hillary's predicament and response, her celebrity, initially attached to her position as First Lady, intensified. With the publication of her story, readers hoped for a first-hand account of what "Hillary" really felt about her husband's philandering and her public humiliation. Readers and reviewers read for the mode of celebrity confession, the revelation of the gritty details of betrayal, humiliation, and rage. As Susan Douglas so vividly captures in *Enlightened Sexism*, celebrity culture "is a world governed first and foremost by emotional ties" (247). It is driven by the desire for intimacy with one's fantasy projections, and what agency it provides comes from the persistent belief that pain and suffering are universally experienced and the agency to exercise feel-good adulation, intense identification, and moralizing judgment.

The ensemble of actors composing *Living History* certainly anticipated that readers would buy Clinton's autobiography to read as a confession. But confessional mode is not a presidential mode. It is not surprising, then, that the narrating "I" of *Living History* manages the history of humiliation by refusing the narrative of individualizing and privatizing sentimentality with its promise of titillation and the pleasures attached to witnessing another's debasement. The narrator says next to nothing about how it felt to endure her husband's philandering and its aftermath. She acknowledges celebrity gossip culture and second-wave feminist judgment:

> After all that has happened since, I'm often asked why Bill and I have stayed together. It's not a question I welcome, but given the public nature of our lives, it's one I know will be asked again and again. . . . All I know is that no one understands me better and no one can make me laugh the way Bill does. Even after all these years, he is still the most interesting, energizing and fully alive person I have ever met (75).

This is the extent of her "confessional." This "Hillary" reveals only what is minimally necessary to come across as credibly human.

The narrator of *Living History* might have mobilized more sympathy by playing to the tropes of celebrity confession, emoting for a public nurtured on narratives of debasement, personal pain, and overwrought emotion. She might have brokered her celebrity to capture sympathy and admiration as the wronged woman. But to take up the subject position of wronged wife would be to keep Bill's penis in the story and, with it, the identification of political leadership with the phallus, however much the exposure of the president's penis as a topic for circulation, satire, and constitutional crisis undermines the invisibility of the political economy of phallic power, as Glass suggests. Moreover, to succumb to the reader's desire for intimate details of unhappiness, rage, shame, and humiliation would be to depoliticize the presidential aspirant, to keep her in her place, the place of the wounded heart. For the woman who would be president, the place of sentiment is not perceived as a place of performative capaciousness, of the president's soft body; rather, it is the "natural" place of femininity.

And yet, there is a downside for the presidential aspirant in managing the public humiliation of the Lewinsky scandal by eschewing the mode of celebrity confession. Scandals of love found and lost animate and preoccupy celebrity culture, saturating the public sphere with larger-than-life dramas of (most often) philandering men and wronged women. In such dramas celebrities are fully sexualized and sensualized beings, appearing to the public as untouchable icons of libidinal attraction or melodramatic icons of emotional excess in affective transactions around humiliation and shame (see Rubenstein 222-3). Protecting her "privacy" by refusing the subject position of a sexualized celebrity icon, the narrator of *Living History* reinforces the media images and representations of "Hillary" as non-sexual, too "manly" and self-controlled to be an object of desire to whom potential supporters can affectively be attached. Such attachment, too, is a coin of the realm in celebrity politics. Moreover, as Janice M. Irvine observes, the "popular notion of authenticity that casts feelings as expressive of a core, moral self" is powerful in celebrity culture (3). The stoic constraint of the narrative voice and failure to disclose wounded feelings combine to project a "cold," withholding "Hillary" rather than an emotionally spontaneous, or "real" Hillary.[14]

War Memoir

The narrator of *Living History* refuses the mode of confession with its allure of intimate revelations and "confidences" (Bauman 34), instead mobilizing the survivor narrative, a public genre mobilized for the collective action of redressing wrongs and the wrongs of rights denied. This, the fifth of the generic modes that *Living History* incorporates (not counting celebrity confession, which it suppresses) can be observed in the narrator's mobilization of warrior discourse to ground the narrative grammar of the survivor story. *Living History*'s narrator takes up the subject position of the battle-scarred woman warrior, the subject under assault; but the assaults are not inflicted by a philandering husband (though she concedes them) and the perpetrator is not Bill Clinton. Wrongs are wrought by political opponents and the perpetrator is the Republican party, with its media touts. The narrator represents herself as having survived the assault on everything she ever did; the assault on her past, as lived and remembered, which, she tells the reader, is an "archeological dig" for opposition research (105). The assaults are several: on her character—her integrity, motivations, morals, ambition; on her identity; and on her gendered humanity as insufficiently maternal, insufficiently feeling, given to irrational anger. Such assaults contest the "realness" and authenticity of Clinton's gendered person, identity, and history. In the discourse of Clinton's war memoir, the terms of reference are "enemies," "battles," "victories." "This was all-out political war," the narrator says of Troopergate (209). In the chapter entitled "Soldiering On," she describes wearing "armor" that "thickened over the years" (443). The factional "battles" over health-care reform were "the front lines" (230): "We soon learned that nothing was off-limits in this war and that the other side was far better armed with the tools of political battle" (230). Through generic adaptability, the domestic battle of the sexes (the afterlife of the Lewinsky scandal) recedes before a national battle between the Right and the Center Left, the Republican and Democratic agendas for the nation.

As First Lady the narrator didn't have her finger on the button; she hadn't ordered the armed forces to the field; but she mobilizes the discourse of warfare as a proxy for performing the defining acts of a presidency. She provides evidence to her readers that she has honed the idioms of muscular masculinity associated with presidential power, that she can exercise the discipline of phallic leadership. The "real" "Hillary" in this script is not the emoting, debased wife. The presidential aspirant is not looking to secure the bond with her public, with potential voters, around domesticated pain and suffering. She is looking to secure a bond around the figure of the warrior, stoical and single-minded, who soldiers on and fights for the country as an agent of the nation's muscular defense as she assures her readers of her self-control by means of the performance of stoic self-discipline. The survivor hones the hard presidential body, promising the electorate protection, safety, and ruthless, firm certitude (see Nelson *Bad* 6).[15]

And yet, the rhetoric of bellicosity deployed in the performance of phallic self-command undermines the intimacy of intersubjective exchange with readers seeking the authentic "Hillary" behind the carefully composed mask. For the woman who would be president, the competing demands for what Nelson terms the "hard" and "soft" bodies of phallic leadership—the former "offer[ing] us a strong guarantee for national boundaries and self-identity" and the latter "hold[ing] out for us sensations of democratic recognition for our individuality and equalitarian exchange" ("Representative/Democracy" 334)—cannot be so easily negotiated. On one hand, the political persona can appear too feminine to be president; on the other, she can appear too masculine to be president.

Conclusion: How to Be "Hillary"

The claim to power in the political field derives in large part from the projection of an ordered identity and a knowable, authentic self (Mansfield 80). The "Hillary" of *Living History* would perform that certainty. The iconic image on the front cover of the book certainly does its paratextual work in that direction, consolidating the fractured subject positions captured in snapshots on the back cover into the unified image of self-knowing self-sufficiency.[16] On the back cover "Hillary" is dispersed into a pastiche of frames positioning the Senator and former First Lady in her multiple roles, most particularly those of "First Lady." The family album situates Clinton in gendered familial roles and in generational identities, and in her ascriptive roles as daughter, wife, mother, First Lady. The "Hillarys" of the back cover present a woman interpellated in heterogeneous subject positions, while the front cover projects a singular iconic image of the celebrity. This is a figure sans "background," sans relationship. The hair that has often been so unruly is almost perfectly coiffed. The eyes sparkle. The mouth smiles. This "Hillary's" chin rests on her hands in a gesture of assured self-confidence and self-support. The eyes are marked with age lines, enough to project experience, but not too many to foreground aging. The cheeks are marked by smile lines, intimating the ludic break-up of a gendered mask. The cover gives us an iconic figure of a powerful woman, staring directly at the reader, unafraid of public scrutiny. It announces everything: I'm here. I'm together. I'm "like steel tempered in fire" (Clinton 393). In this celebrity photograph Clinton's pose and image are of enigmatic and glamorized "self-sufficiency" (see Rubenstein 206–7). Nothing mediates this phallic presentation of Clinton. Here is the inaugural gesture of legitimate political power of the successful candidate, leaving behind the illegitimate political power identified with presidential spouses.

But you can't always read a book by its cover. On the one hand, all these generic modes promise some grounds of authenticity upon which the candidate can project her bona fides of character, competence, readiness, and legitimacy for presidential leadership. On the other hand, the contradictions set in motion through the autobiography by the cacophony of generic modes expose the instability of the subject positions those modes would fix and the unity of political persona the presidential aspirant would consolidate for her reader: the subject positions of American individualist, second-wave feminist, First Lady, buddy, war hero, as well as the subject position of wronged wife the narrative would erase and the gendered identities—feminine, feminist, masculine—of being "ambiguously gendered" (Rubenstein 209). This restlessness of generic modes also opens up the suspicion that it is impossible to locate the "real" Hillary or find any ground of authenticity in this political persona, except the "Exhibit A" of ambition.

Situating herself as "America's Exhibit A," the narrator of *Living History* invokes legal discourse, her professional *lingua franca*, and thereby situates her addressee as adjudicator of her authenticity, with judgment as the end of the reading. Has this woman projected a convincing performance of the capacity for presidential leadership? This question can be recast as a question of genre. Has she convinced us that she has, not the "right stuff," but the right generic mode of gendered identity to be president?

Readers indeed weighed in on the book and on the "real" Hillary. Readings, of course, can be neither predicted nor contained, however much an ensemble of actors works to project authenticity in the candidate narrative. In the arena of presidential politics, readers bring their political ideologies, myths of national identity, desired repertoire of traits, and grounds of judgment to an evolving assessment of the politician and his or her personal fable. Those supportive of her bid for the presidency found the "real" Hillary in the second-wave-feminist warrior woman. They could dismiss the recourse to feminine subject positions and feminized plots as obligatory for the feminist who would be president. Others found the "real" Hillary elsewhere. For some of them, *Living History* gave us the corporately produced faux-authenticity of the test-marketed "Hillary," the prized political commodity of contemporary political cultures. For her detractors, the "real" Hillary remained a scandal. That was the message of Morris's *Rewriting History* and its front cover. Featured on the cover is a "cut-up" of Clinton. Her mouth in close-up appears in the top half of the cover, her eyes in close-up on the bottom half. The mouth signifies on multiple levels: as the danger zone or sprung trap of authenticity's appearance; as the site of female seduction; as the "other" feminine mouth she didn't have, the brightly soft one of Monica; as the origin of lying and subterfuge; as the *vagina dentata*, or toothed vagina. The mismatch pathologizes Clinton as an untrustworthy congenital liar and demonizes her as monstrous woman, at once too feminine (in her wiliness) and not feminine enough (in her lack of sexual attraction). The dismembered "Hillary" here becomes the personification of scandal, the scandal of illegitimate, corrupting power whose name is "woman." It isn't just that Hillary Clinton lived through the scandal of the Clinton presidency. Her image is rebranded as a scandal, indeed the scandal of the feminine as disorderly and deceptive (see Mansfield 95).

Public judgments proliferated in the news, on talk radio, and on the internet: feminist warrior; shrewd politician; scandalous self-fabricator. The public weighed the evidence: too much femininity, too little femininity, too much feminism, too little feminism, too much muscular masculinity, too little phallic authority, too hot-tempered, too coldly calculating. Too soft. Too hard. Too indeterminate. Too inauthentic. The performativity of genre that courses through *Living History* intersects the cultural politics of authenticity in the era of "enlightened sexism," with its enduring "double standards" of judgment (see Douglas epigraph).

In the end, Clinton's very conventional campaign autobiography refracts thirty years of feminist activism and its discontents. The aspiring candidate and her entourage in "Hillaryland" manage her "brand" as a legitimate political persona; and yet her autobiography keeps "woman" in circulation as "a political category" not yet fully incorporated in the political system as legitimate political subject (see Berlant *Queen* 36). Reading her autobiography, we witness the instability of the grounds of a woman's gendered identity in the last enclave of phallic exclusivity in American political life. We "brand" her as a particular kind of woman.

This corporate and public branding will go on and intensify, especially if, or when, Hillary Clinton makes another run for the presidential nomination in 2016. As my opening noted, Clinton most likely will have written another book by then. The narrator of this next book, the (perhaps former) Secretary of State in the Obama administration, will also be a corporately produced persona of a would-be president. But what will that "Hillary" be? And how will we read the book?

Notes

1 I am indebted to Ben Belado, Beth Davila, and Hannah Dickinson for surveying and summarizing recent work on presidential politics and for tracking reviews and commentary on Clinton's *Living History*.
2 The term "Hillaryland" became the nickname for the section of the 1992 presidential campaign headquarters in Little Rock where Hillary Clinton's staff organized her activities. "The name stuck," she writes in *Living History* (115).
3 The Chinese translation caused an uproar around the Chinese government's act of censorship. The section in which Clinton describes her participation in and speech before the women delegates of the 1995 United Nations Beijing Conference on Women had been deleted.
4 "Celebrity politics," argue Darrell M. West and John Orman, "fit the needs of a new media that focused on human features, not detailed substance" (10). This is not to argue that celebrity is new to presidential politics. In the two-hundred-plus span of American presidential politics, candidates for the presidency have often been celebrities of a kind, men who earned recognition for various achievements or exploits such as Ulysses S. Grant, Theodore Roosevelt, and Dwight Eisenhower.
5 Tracking changes in the presentation of political personas in a succession of mediascapes, John R. Corner describes the contemporary moment of political performance as one characterized by the "degree of self-conscious strategy attending its planning and performance, the intensity of its interaction with media systems and the degree to which certain personal qualities" are "seen not merely to enhance but to *underwrite* political values" (387).
6 James Phelan, pointing to the "synesthesia of narrative voice," suggests that "as we see words on a page we can hear sounds" (Phelan "Voice" 2). And Julia Watson and I note, in the revised edition of *Reading Autobiography*, that "voice as an attribute of the narrating 'I' . . . is a metaphor for the reader's felt experience of the narrator's personhood,

and a marker of the relationship between a narrating 'I' and his or her experiential history.... Although the text unfolds through an ensemble of voices, we as readers ascribe a distinct voice to that ensemble, with a way of organizing experience, a rhetoric of address, a particular register of affect, and an ideological inflection that is attached to the subject's history" (79–80).

7   In "Representative/Democracy," Nelson explores the implications of the Constitution's production of the presidential system of government, one that locates "representivity's logic and desires" (326) in the figure and body of the president as synecdoche for the nation. "This presidential institutionalization of representative democracy," she argues, "offered a reassuringly hierarchicalized substitute for the messiness of local interaction: a rationally stratified structure, the atomization of factional interests through electoral distance, and (eventually) the ritual release of democratic energy in the form of elections" (333).

8   Over the last fifty years, as Philip Holden has observed, national leaders have produced a succession of such modernist narratives, especially national leaders of movements for decolonization who were identified or elected as "fathers" of the nation. Through a temporality of modernist, progressive linearity, an individualist fable of agentic heroism, and a realist aesthetics, these narratives join the story of "the growth of the individual" to "the growth of national consciousness and, frequently proleptically, the achievement of an independent nation-state" (5).

9   Parry-Giles and Blair explore how First Ladies, through their speech acts such as books and public addresses, have projected themselves into the public arena of the nation's political life. And after they have left the White House, former First Ladies have sometimes written autobiographies through which they add their "take" on the presidency of their husbands (565–599). Eleanor Roosevelt, Nancy Reagan, Barbara Bush, and Clinton all wrote books while residing in the White House; many wrote newspaper columns and delivered speeches at large public events, often events related to themes to which they have dedicated their attention: beautiful America for Ladybird Johnson, literacy for Laura Bush, childhood obesity for Michelle Obama.

10 As First Lady, Clinton wrote *It Takes a Village*. Parry-Giles and Blair remark that such an act is "part of the rhetorical performance of the role, illustrating the commitment to the history of the institution as well as the adherence to lingering republican motherhood values" (576). She wrote a children's book in 1998 entitled *Dear Socks, Dear Buddy: Kids' Letters to the First Pets*.

11 The First Lady genre also projects her identification with a community of women and the terms of their identification with her as a professional woman. In this genre, the narrator connects herself laterally to other First Ladies around the world and claims that her advocacy on behalf of women and children connects her to a larger transnational community of women fighting for women's human rights. She describes the culmination of this activist commitment as her "triumphant" speech to the 1995 United Nations Conference on Women in Beijing. Clinton's advocacy for women's human rights enacts a liberal feminist transnationalism: intervention on the part of a Western feminist to "rescue" Third World women from Third World men.

12 As Stephanie Liu perceptively observes in her reading of Bill Clinton's autobiography in this special issue of *ALH* on "Presidential Memoir," he is pursing his own ghosts. In his search for the secret parental past of his father, Bill Clinton produces a narrative of addiction and multiple personalities.

13 Reviews of Clinton's *Living History* were, as could be expected, mixed. After the book's role in Clinton's potential presidential candidacy, the story of her response to the Lewinsky scandal is the most commonly addressed topic. There were two general patterns for the treatment of the Monica Lewinsky scandal in the reviews: 1) reproducing excerpts of the passages dealing with Lewinsky and Clinton's reaction, with very little attention to the rest of the book, or 2) chastising Clinton for not providing any new information and commenting on how relatively minor a role the Lewinsky scandal plays in the larger narrative. This second mode also tended to express skepticism about Clinton's sincerity and/or honesty. Next to Clinton's presidential aspirations, the scandal and her response to it in the book was the most frequently addressed topic.

14 In her brilliant analysis of Clinton's "comeback" in the 2000 senatorial campaign, Diane Rubenstein explores how Clinton is re-sexualized through her "listening tour" around New York during which she manages spontaneous laughter and cozy beer-drinking.

15 On the two bodies of the president, Nelson writes: "Americans have come to expect two somewhat contradictory symbolic roles from the president. In one aspect, Americans look for a sense of democratic connection and recognition—a heart-warming unity delivered by the 'soft' president who can 'feel our pain.' In the other, Americans look for an avenging protector, a steely sense of safety that comes through the toughness of the 'hard' and unforgiving president" (*Bad for Democracy* 6).

16 Exploring newspaper accounts of Clinton's 2000 campaign that present Clinton as an enigma, Diane Rubenstein ponders the celebrity fascination with Clinton that resides in her projection of "that originary narcissism of childhood": "While still not as fully affirmative as Nietzsche's 'Dionysian' subject, she does not suffer from *ressentiment* and appears to have little need for male desire in order to please or desire herself" (207).

Works Cited

Bauman, Zygmunt. *Liquid Love: On the Frailty of Human Bonds*. Cambridge, GB: Polity Press, 2003. Print.

Berlant, Lauren. *The Queen of America Goes to Washington City: Essays on Sex and Citizenship*. Durham: Duke University Press, 1997. Print.

Clinton, Hillary Rodham. *Dear Socks, Dear Buddy: Kids' Letters to the First Pets*. New York: Simon & Schuster, 1998. Print.

———. *It Takes a Village and Other Lessons Children Teach Us*. New York: Simon & Schuster, 1996. Print.

———. *Living History*. New York: Simon & Schuster, 2003. Print.

Corner, John R. "Mediated Persona and Political Culture: Dimensions of Structure and Process." *European Journal of Cultural Studies* 3.3 (2000): 386–402. Print.

Douglas, Susan. *Enlightened Sexism: The Seductive Message that Feminism's Work Is Done*. New York: Henry Holt & Co., 2010. Print.

Glass, Loren. "Publicizing the President's Privates." *Postmodern Culture* 9.3 (1999): N.pag. Web. 23 June 2010.

Henderson, Margaret. "The Feminine Mystique of Individualism is Powerful: Two American Feminist Memoirs in Postfeminist Times. *a/b:Auto/Biography Studies* 23.2 (Winter 2008): 165–84. Print.

Holden, Philip. *Autobiography and Decolonization: Modernity, Masculinity, and the Nation State*. Madison: University of Wisconsin Press, 2008. Print.

Irvine, Janice. M. "Transient Feelings: Sex Panics and the Politics of Emotions." *GLQ* 14.1 (2007): 1–40. Print.

Kipnis, Laura. "Adultery." *Critical Inquiry* 24 (Winter 1998): 289–327. Print.

Mansfield, Nick. *Subjectivity: Theories of the Self From Freud to Haraway*. New York: New York University Press, 2000. Print.

Morris, Dick. *Rewriting History*. New York: ReaganBooks, 2004. Print.

Nelson, Dana. *Bad for Democracy: How the Presidency Undermines the Power of the People*. Minneapolis: University of Minnesota Press, 2008. Print.

Nelson, Dana. "Representative/Democracy: Presidents, Democratic Management, and the Unfinished Business of Male Sentimentalism." *No More Separate Spheres!: A Next Wave American Studies Reader*. Ed. Cathy N. Davison and Jessamyn Hatcher. Durham: Duke University Press, 2002. 325–354. Print.

Parry-Giles, Shawn J., and Diane M. Blair. "The Rise of the Rhetorical First Lady: Politics, Gender Ideology, and Women's Voice, 1789–2002." *Rhetoric & Public Affairs* 5.4 (2002): 565–599. Print.

Phelan, James. "Voice; or Authors, Narrators and Audiences." In *Teaching Narrative Theory*. Eds James Phelan, Brian McHale, and David Herman. New York: Modern Languages Association, 2010. Print.

Rubenstein, Diane. *This Is Not a President: Sense, Nonsense, and the American Political Imaginary*. New York: New York University Press, 2008. Print.

Slaughter, Joseph. *Human Rights, Inc.: The World Novel, Narrative Form, and International Law*. New York: Fordham University Press, 2007. Print.

Smith, Sidonie and Julia Watson. *Reading Autobiography: A Guide to Interpreting Life Narratives*. 2nd Revised Edition. Minneapolis: University of Minnesota Press, 2010. Print.

Part VI
Global Circuits, Political Formations

18

Introduction: De/Colonization and the Politics of Discourse (1992)

From *De/Colonizing the Subject: The Politics of Gender in Women's Autobiography*

Is [autobiography] the model for imperializing the consciousness of colonized peoples, replacing their collective potential for resistance with a cult of individuality and even loneliness? Or is it a medium of resistance and counterdiscourse, the legitimate space for producing that excess which throws doubt on the coherence and power of an exclusive historiography?
                Doris Sommer, "'Not Just a Personal Story':
                Women's *Testimonios* and the Plural Self"[1]

Authors' Note: *For this "Introduction" only, we have retained a discussion of the essays included in the collection. The issues raised in particular essays signal larger debates about the self-representation of "subaltern" subjects, the narrative pressure generated by negotiating between local and imposed national languages, and the afterlife of colonial practices in various regions of the world that remain of larger interest.*

The Colonial Subject

Decolonization, of course, refers literally to the actual political processes set in motion in various geographical locations before and during this century. Colonies established under European domination achieved independent statehood, sometimes through peaceful and sometimes through violent struggle. But decolonization remains a problematic notion, a potential disenchantment. Colonial relationships persist today—in Northern Ireland, on the West Bank in Israel, in South Africa, in many other parts of the world. Indigenous colonialisms characterize the relationships among peoples in many countries. Moreover, as communication networks shuttle information instantly around the globe and multinational corporations reorganize the flow of labor, capital, and control across national borders, a process of neocolonization seems to render the earlier achievement of autonomous nationhood almost irrelevant to the circulation of goods, money, and culture.

Yet if we must constantly probe the reach, contradictory strategies, and contested achievements of *decolonization*, we must also probe the reach of the term *colonization*. So widespread has become the practice of weaving the word *colonization* through various critiques of the subject of Western humanism and the politics of representation that the word now seems to signify a universalized descriptor of subjectivity. From a Foucauldian theoretical perspective all "I"s are sites where the generalized operations of power press ineluctably on the subject. From a Lacanian perspective everyone is subjected to and "colonized" by the Law of the Father. In the vogue of a materialist postmodernity, all "I"s, subject to the cultural field of multiple determinations, are colonized through irresistible interpellations. In the midst of this theoretical quagmire, Gayatri Spivak's provocative query, "Can the subaltern speak?" needs to be opened out.[2] Can any subject speak? Or is every subject "spoken for" and thus "colonized" by processes constitutive of "the human condition," from the psychological and biological to the economic, political, and discursive?

We have difficulty with such a comprehensive invocation of the concept of colonization, and for a variety of reasons. If decolonization holds out the promise of a change in subjects, so universalized a notion of colonization forecloses that possibility. Because no one can escape the realm of "the subjected," because decolonization remains a utopian dream, no one set of political actions assumes legitimacy, efficacy, or a prompt utility. The colonized subject is effectively stripped of agency.

Furthermore, however compelling and sophisticated this critique of the subject may be, it is a central instance of the universalizing agenda of Western theorizing that erases the subject's heterogeneity as well as its agency. This agenda has become increasingly apparent in feminist theories that hypostasize a universally colonized "woman" universally subjected to "patriarchal" oppression. As theorists such as bell hooks, Elizabeth V. Spelman, and Spivak, among others, insist, privileging the oppression of gender over and above other oppressions effectively erases the complex and often contradictory positionings of the subject. The axes of the subject's identifications and experiences are multiple, because locations in gender, class, race, ethnicity, and sexuality complicate one another, and not merely additively, as Spelman so effectively argues.[3] Nor do different vectors of identification and experience overlap neatly or entirely. One cannot easily sever, separate out, or subsume under one another the strands of multiple determinations. For instance, colonial regimes needed and global economies continue to need "classes" as well as "races" in order to achieve their goals. And class identifications call particular women to specific psychological and cultural itineraries that may collide and/or converge with itineraries of race and nation.

Nor can one be oblivious to the precise location in which the subject is situated. Attention to specific locations leads Spivak to insist that "the situation of the subject(s) of post-modern neo-colonialism must be rigorously distinguished from the situation of immigrants, who are still caught in some way within structures of 'colonial' subject production; and, especially, from the historical problem of ethnic oppression on First World soil."[4]

Moreover, just as there are various colonialisms or systems of domination operative historically, there are various patriarchies operative historically, not one universal "patriarchy." There are various positions of men toward patriarchy, not just an equivalence among them. As Carolyn Kay Steedman emphasizes in her analysis of the autobiographical storytelling of her working-class mother, her father was neither the patriarch of Lacan's Law of the Father nor the uncontested and powerful figure at the center of socioeconomic, political, and cultural regimes; he was, like her mother, an outlaw.[5] As there are various positions of specific men (for instance, those enjoying the benefits of hegemonic power, those suffering under the domination of others) to colonial environments, there are differences in the relationships of specific women to those men. Thus domination has different meanings and implications for the "wife," "daughter," and "independent woman" of the colonizer and for the "wife," "daughter," and "independent woman" of the colonized.

Insistence on an undifferentiated (read normatively white) global "sisterhood" of oppressed women empties the subject of all its "colorfulness"[6] by "colonizing under the sign of the same those differences that might otherwise call that totalizing concept into question."[7] Since there are always, as Chandra Talpade Mohanty reminds us, "*political* implications of *analytic* strategies and principles,"[8] we need to resist the tendency of Western theorizing to install another colonial regime, albeit now a discursive regime that works to contain "colorfulness" inside a Western theoretical territory.

Finally, as scholars of colonialism and imperialism have argued recently, the avant garde taking up of the terms *colonization* and *decolonization* by "First World" theorists intent on dislodging the certitudes of the old subject of Western humanism does an injustice to, and effectively occludes, very real colonial practices in specific geographical locations and historical periods.

Although the universally colonized "woman" might be a limiting concept, a concept of colonization too carefully circumscribed, too narrowly applied to specific historical processes and geographical venues, also has its limitations. Certainly the work of historians, sociologists, political theorists, anthropologists, and literary critics must be grounded in the locales and temporalities of specific colonial, postcolonial, and neocolonial experiences. But there has been more colonizing going on in the world than that which took place under the obvious colonial authorities, say, the British Raj or the French and British Protectorates. And there have been, as cultural critics point out, colonies within colonies, oppressions within oppressions. While attention to specific colonial regimes helps us resist certain totalizing tendencies in our theories, thinking broadly about the constitutive nature of subjectivity and precisely about the differential deployments of gendered subjectivity helps us tease out complex and entangled strands of oppression and domination. To this end, for instance, feminist theorists have sometimes invoked theories of gendered subjectivity, sometimes histories of gendered social practices and behaviors, to critique postcolonial theorizing that maintains a masculinist bias by failing to factor issues of gender and sexuality into discussions of colonialist discourses and colonial practices.

It is not the intent of this volume to assert the universalized colonization of the human subject or the universalized colonization of "woman." Rather the intent here is to offer explorations grounded in specific locations of colonialism and its legacies: for instance, colonial Kenya, India, Indochina/Vietnam. Our selection of essays takes as a guiding definition the one used by Chandra Talpade Mohanty when she argues that "however sophisticated or problematical its use as an explanatory construct, colonization almost invariably implies a relation of structural domination, and a suppression—often violent—of the heterogeneity of the subject(s) in question."[9] And so, other essays open out the discussion of colonial practices and decolonizing strategies by looking at autobiographical subjects in such diverse contexts as post-reservation Native American culture, the Australian outback, pre- and postbellum American slavery, and compressed urban environments in Western countries.

The subject in question is called variously *the colonial subject, the dominated object,* and *the marginalized subject.* Acknowledging the significant distinctions among these phrases, we note here that, for the sake of brevity, we will use throughout our discussion the phrase *the colonial subject.* We note also that the writing/language that emanates from the position of the colonial subject is variously called the *discourse of the margins, minority discourse,* and *postcolonial discourse.* Whatever the label, that subject and that writing emanate from what Abdul R. JanMohamed and David Lloyd call a position of damage, one in which "the cultural formations, languages, the diverse modes of identity of the 'minoritized peoples' are irreversibly affected, if not eradicated, by the effects of their material deracination from the historically developed social and economic structures in terms of which alone they 'made sense.'"[10] And so, the essays in this collection, in their different ways, ask what autobiographical processes are set in motion when this subject struggles toward voice, history, and a future.

The Autobiographical Subject

The very notion of "autobiography" itself requires at least three perspectival adjustments. The first involves historicizing Western practices. Although the genres of life writing in the West emerge in Antiquity, the term *autobiography* is a post-Enlightenment coinage. Yet the word and the practice invoke a particular genealogy, resonant ideology, and discursive imperative. Powering and defining centers, margins, boundaries, and grounds of action in the West, traditional "autobiography" has been implicated in a specific notion of "selfhood." This Enlightenment "self," ontologically identical to other "I"s, sees its destiny in a teleological narrative enshrining the "individual" and "his" uniqueness.[11] Autobiography also entwines the definition of the human being in a web of privileged characteristics. Despite their myriad differences of place, time, histories, economies, and cultural identifications, all "I"s are rational, agentive, unitary. Thus the "I" becomes "Man," putatively a marker of the universal human subject whose essence remains outside the vagaries of history, effectually what Spivak has termed the "straight white Christian man of property,"[12] whose identity is deeply embedded in a specific history of privilege.

Since Western autobiography rests upon the shared belief in a commonsense identification of one individual with another, all "I"s are potentially interesting autobiographers. And yet, not all are "I"s. Where Western eyes see Man as a unique individual rather than a member of a collectivity, of race or nation, of sex or sexual preference, Western eyes see the colonized as an amorphous, generalized collectivity. The colonized "other" disappears into an anonymous, opaque collectivity of undifferentiated bodies. In this way, argues Rey Chow, "Man (hence Europe) . . . hails the world into being . . . in such a way as to mark [the non-European world] off from European consciousness or universality."[13] Moreover, heterogeneous "others" are collapsed and fashioned into an essentialized "other" whose "I" has no access to a privatized but privileged individuality.[14]

Thus the politics of this "I" have been the politics of centripetal consolidation and centrifugal domination. The cultural dominance of the West effectively enables this "Man" to *"make a meaning stick,"*[15] to make *his* meaning stick. The impact of this epistemological franchise on the matter of meaning has ramifications for the perpetuation of relations of dominance. As Deborah Cameron argues, "Meaning can be deployed to sustain domination" in that "it can *reify* domination by presenting as eternal and natural what is in fact historical and transitory."[16] Erasing historical contingency in service to a universalized humanism, the Man without history contains and silences the heterogeneity of subject peoples.

Western autobiography colludes in this cultural mythmaking. One of the narratives that brings this Man into being, it functions as an exclusionary genre against which the utterances of other subjects are measured and misread. While inviting all subjects to participate in its practices, it provides the constraining template or the generic "law" against which those subjects and their diverse forms of self-narrative are judged and found wanting. In order to unstick both this Man and his meanings, we need to adjust, to reframe, our understanding of both traditional and counter-traditional autobiographical practices.

The second adjustment requires that we consider the flexibilities of generic boundaries. In fact, we need to consider, with Ralph Cohen, how "classifications," including generic ones, "are empirical, not logical"; that is, how they are historical assumptions constructed by authors, audiences, and critics in order to serve communicative and aesthetic purposes.[17] And, we would add, political purposes. If that is so, autobiographical writing is at this historical moment a "genre of choice," for authors, audiences, and critics. Autobiographical writing surrounds us, but the more it surrounds us, the more it defies generic stabilization, the more its laws are broken, the more it drifts toward other practices, the more formerly "out-law" practices drift into its domain.[18] While popular practitioners carry on the old autobiographical tradition, other practitioners play with forms that challenge us to recognize their experiments in subjectivity and account for their exclusion from "high" literature.

The third adjustment will require more time to accomplish. What has been designated as Western autobiography is only one form of "life writing." There are other modes of life story-telling, both oral and written, to be recognized, other genealogies of life storytelling to be chronicled, other explorations of traditions, current and past, to be factored into the making and unmaking of autobiographical subjects in a global environment.[19]

Alternative and Diverse Autobiographical Practices

Decolonization is always a multidimensional process rather than a homogeneous achievement. And it involves the deformation/

reformation of identity. That is why we have chosen to foreground the slash in the word *de/colonization*. The slash symbolizes the exchange between the processes of colonization and decolonization and the issues inherent in the process of neocolonization. Given the colonial, postcolonial, and neocolonial locales in which a writer produces an autobiographical text, what, then, does the speaker make of the autobiographical "I"? And what strategies drive, what meanings emerge from, what uses define her autobiographical project?

The autobiographical occasion (whether performance or text) becomes a site at which cultural ideologies intersect and dissect one another, in contradiction, consonance, and adjacency. Thus the site is rife with diverse potentials, some of which we would like to suggest here, some of which the essays that follow explore in more detail. Take the mimetic potential of autobiographical practice. On the one hand, the very taking-up of the autobiographical transports the colonial subject into the territory of the "universal" subject and thus promises a culturally empowered subjectivity. Participation in, through re/presentation of, privileged narratives can secure cultural recognition for the subject. On the other hand, entry into the territory of traditional autobiography implicates the speaker in a potentially recuperative performance, one that might reproduce and re/present the colonizer's figure in negation.[20] For, to write "autobiography" is partially to enter into the contractual and discursive domain of universal "Man," whom Rey Chow calls the "dominating subject."[21] Entering the terrain of autobiography, the colonized subject can get stuck in *"his* meaning." The processes of self-decolonization may get bogged down as the autobiographical subject reframes herself through neocolonizing metaphors.

Yet autobiographical practices can be productive in that process as the subject, articulating problems of identity and identification, struggles against coercive calls to a "universal humanity."[22] For the marginalized woman, autobiographical language may serve as a coinage that purchases entry into the social and discursive economy.[23] To enter into language is to press back against total inscription in dominating structures, against the disarticulation of that spectral other that Chow calls the "dominated object."[24] Precisely because she is subject to "incommensurable solicitations and heterogeneous social practices,"[25] the autobiographical speaker can resist the processes of negation. Deploying autobiographical practices that go against the grain, she may constitute an "I" that becomes a place of creative and, by implication, political intervention. "The colonized," argue Chandra T. Mohanty and Satya P. Mohanty, "are not just the object of the colonizer's discourses, but the agents of a conflicted history, inhabiting and transforming a complex social and cultural world."[26] If, with Judith Butler, we think of agency as "located within the possibility of a variation on th[e] repetition" of certain "rule-bound discourse[s],"[27] and if we think of discourses of identity as heterogeneous even in their seeming hegemony, then we make a space in autobiographical practices for the agency of the autobiographical subject.

In this space, too, the autobiographical speaker may authorize an alternative way of knowing, filtered through what Barbara Harlow describes as specific "conditions of observation"[28] and others refer to as "experience." Averring the integrity of her perspective on identity, experience, and politics, the autobiographical subject may offer up what Nancy Hartsock calls a "standpoint epistemology": "an account of the world as seen from the margins, an account which can expose the falseness of the view from the top and can transform the margins as well as the center . . . an account of the world which treats our perspectives not as subjugated or disruptive knowledges, but as primary and constitutive of a different world."[29] Thus both self-representation and self-presentation have the potential to intervene in the comfortable alignments of power relationships, relationships "controlled by conditioned ways of seeing."[30] They also have the potential to celebrate through counter-valorization another way of seeing, one unsanctioned, even unsuspected, in the dominant cultural surround. And shifts in vision can herald social change, even the creation of new worlds, since, as Arif Dirlik argues, "culture is not only a way of seeing the world, but also a way of making and changing it."[31]

Also in this alternative space, narrative itineraries may take different paths. For the colonial subject, the process of coming to writing is an articulation *through* interrogation, a charting of the conditions that have historically placed her identity under erasure. Consequently, her narratives do not necessarily fall into a privatized itinerary, the journey toward something, the personal struggle toward God, the entry into society of the Bildungsroman, the confessional mode, and the like. Such Western modes both define and collusively maintain the narrow range of narrative paradigms, holding the politicized dimension of identity and self, as of cultural consciousness, in abeyance. Such modes secure the "individual" rather than the collective character of self-representation. Yet even if the colonial subject does mime certain traditional patterns, she does so with a difference. She thus exposes their gaps and incongruities, wrenches their meanings, calls their authority into question,[32] for "illegitimate" speakers have a way of exposing the instability of forms.

As many of the essays acknowledge, the colonial subject inhabits a politicized rather than privatized space of narrative. Political realities cannot be evaded in the constitution of identity. In fact, attention to them can become a source of subversive power, as Harlow claims in her essay on women's prison writings: "In the same way that institutions of power ... are subverted by the demand on the part of dispossessed groups for an access to history, power, and resources, so too are the narrative paradigms and their textual authority being transformed by the historical and literary articulation of those demands."[33] Attention to the politics of identity can also become a source of hybrid forms, what Kaplan calls "out-law" genres, and what others explore as counterhegemonic narratives: ideographic selfhood, ethnography, collective self-storytelling.

As a process and a product of decolonization, autobiographical writing has the potential to "transform spectators crushed with their inessentiality into privileged actors," to foster "the veritable creation of new [wo]men," to quote, with a shift in emphasis, the revolutionary Frantz Fanon.[34] Thus autobiographical performances, drawing upon exogenous and indigenous cultural practices, signal the heterogeneity of the subject and her narrative itinerary. In resistance to the panoptic figuration of an anonymous object unified as cultural representative, the autobiographical speaker may "dissolve," as David Lloyd suggests, "the canonical form of Man back into the different bodies which it has sought to absorb."[35] But the power of cultural forms to recolonize peoples cannot be underestimated. As all of this suggests, the relationship of the colonial subject to autobiographical inscription is indeed troubled.

The Essays

We offer here our contribution to the debates about autobiographical practices, politics, and gender in the global environment. We have tried to gather essays that range broadly around the world, from North to South, from the Americas to Africa to Australia. There are essays on women in historically colonial, transitional, and currently postcolonial environments; essays from various borders of marginality; essays on women writing from diverse class positions; essays exploring the authors' positions in systems of oppression and their impact on the relationship between the author and the essay's subject; essays exploring the complicities of authors in colonizing practices. From multiple perspectives we hope through this volume to investigate the heteronomous meanings of the "colonial subject" and to explore autobiography as a potential site of decolonization.

We do not claim to present here a representative sampling of women's autobiographies of colonization and decolonization, nor do we claim to offer a "history" of such autobiographical practices. We believe that no definitive history could be collected and written at this time. Both the parameters of colonization and the texts of women's coming to voice are in flux, with narratives still being "discovered" and produced, reprinted and translated, and otherwise brought into circulation. Nor can "academic" women necessarily measure the power of an autobiography to "speak" to readers either within a culture or transnationally. Our selections need to be understood as in every sense exemplary, and clustered in some areas at the expense of others.

For example, the Indian subcontinent, with its history of British colonization, is the only area of Asia explored in depth here. Yet the autobiographical practices discussed—of British women under the Raj, of Kamala Das, of Indira Gandhi as semiotic sign—offer illuminating instances of the numerous and complex ways that women's self-representational practices both display and interrogate moments of this specific colonial heritage. British women in mid-nineteenth-century India, as Nancy Paxton shows, both participate in the Empire's colonization of the bodies and subjectivity of the Indian populace and experience their own marginality within a gendered society that places them in proximity to, and sometimes in communication with, the silences of Indian women. By exploring the conjunction of technologies of gender and of imperialism in these texts, Paxton discovers points of exposure, those textual moments in which the constitution of the imperial 'I' confronts the destabilizing impacts of embodiedness. Shirley Geok-lin Lim discusses how Kamala Das explores the cultural imperatives that have defined her as a silent, dutiful postcolonial daughter. The insufficiency of available cultural discourses for Das to write her embodied sensuality leads her to unavoidably transgressive self-assertion. Lim explores how this negotiation of Indian female sexuality involves Das in an epistemological confrontation with patriarchal society. Gita Rajan discusses Indira Gandhi as a semiotic text of postliberation India to be deciphered against Western cultural modes of subjectivity. In Gandhi's self-presentation, the subaltern is figured; but over successive historical moments, she both ensnares and undoes her subaltern status. Reading Gandhi, Rajan rereads both her own culture and the influential Indian critic, Gayatri Spivak, in order to rewrite the possibility of agency as/for Indian women. In this triangulated reflection on Indian de/colonization, Paxton, Lim, and Rajan are not primarily interested in defining colonizers and colonized, but in observing the operations that complicate distinctions between colonizer and colonized. In each case politics operates as a move from a private, unwritten history to an articulation that can become transformative and, in the rare case of Indira Gandhi, formative as collective political history.

The task of representing the range and specificity of women's identities in the United States and North America has been daunting. We have made choices and left gaps for others to fill. The most notable gap is in Chicana autobiography, where both a first-person literature by such writers as Cherríe Moraga, Gloria Anzaldúa, and Sandra Cisneros and critical work by such emerging literary critics as Ramón Saldívar and Sonia Saldívar thrives in book-length works that cannot be glossed briefly. But an exploration of how the appropriation of Chicano culture can be read through its cookbooks is mapped in Anne Goldman's essay. Recipes for exoticization, hybridization, and normalization can be found in the remaking of Mexican food for mainstream American consumption, as can recipes for the distortion and erasure of indigenous cultures. As Goldman suggests, the Western reader has to begin by reading the effacement that the practices of the dominant culture have exercised upon ethnic identities in the name of authenticating them. But she also proposes, in her subsequent reading of the cookbook narratives of Cleofas Jaramillo and Fabiola Cabeza de Baca, how the colonized subject can resist cultural appropriation through her own authenticating of autobiographical recipes. Debra A. Castillo also explores how indigenous North American culture is literally colonized and its collective autobiographical inscription effaced. Tracing the migration of identity and the Western claim to ownership of the apparatuses of identity in Rosario Castellanos's autobiographical writing, Castillo marks the disruption of language between a Mexican child of Spanish descent and her Indian nursemaid, who cannot lay claim to identity in verbal terms but is only the "ashes without a face" of centuries of colonization.

Other essays look to the problem of the subject in the African American community. In his essay on the narratives of ex-slaves, William L. Andrews focuses on the difference in discursive strategies employed by Harriet Jacobs, who, writing prior to the Civil War, invokes the moral discourse of true womanhood, and Elizabeth Keckley, who, writing just a few crucial years later, employs the discourse of economic materialism. This difference speaks not just of a historical shift in the formation of the African American woman's cultural identity, but also of the variety and specificity of responses to oppression and of the bind of needing both to internalize and to resist/rewrite discursive strategies as the condition of writing the female subject into literary identity. Andrews points up the instability of borders separating colonization and decolonization, and refocuses our attention from a unitary agenda of liberation to the problematic of the subject speaking the master's discourse if she is to speak at all.

In a similar vein, Claudine Raynaud considers Zora Neale Hurston's *Dust Tracks on a Road* as a discursively manipulated text. Hurston's autobiography was, if not colonized, censored by both her editor and herself as they struggled in the margins of the draft over the kind of subject that would be acceptable to her predominantly white audience. Working with previously unexamined manuscripts, Raynaud notes editorial excisions and interpolations in various hands and considers both their origins and the resulting differences in the voices of a text that has been read as Hurston's "authoritative" autobiography. If Raynaud looks for the "noise" in the margins of the drafts of Hurston's text, Françoise Lionnet theorizes the relationship between noise and the resistance of *métissage*. If autobiographical texts are reams of pages to be inscribed and excised, they are also voices—many voices in tension and in play. In examining the autobiographical writings of Jamaican-born American resident Michelle Cliff, Lionnet focuses on the patois of native dialect and the metaphors of mangoes and maroons in order to foreground Cliff's strategies for writing the narrative of difference through the inimical discourses of standard English and First World autobiographical paradigms.

Native American ethnicities may also be read against the dominating culture's penchant for stereotyping and classifying. The essays by Janice Gould and Greg Sarris are autobiographical essays about autobiography. Each writer insists on framing "autobiography" as a problematical model of storytelling that not only silences Native Americans but fails to account for differently told and differently heard stories. Gould explores the dilemma of being fixed through racist categorizations and the uncertainties of cultural identification she confronts as a Maidu mixed-blood. Yet, she identifies herself with a large and growing group of mixed-blood Native American writers who tell stories of difficult negotiations of cultural mixing, loss of homeland and tribal family, locations in urban landscapes where the particulars of difference are neither seen nor prized. Sarris's autobiographical account of Mabel McKay's appearance before a class of literature students at Stanford University is a double narrative of McKay's unmaking of fictions of identity and her making, in a basket, of a figure of collective self-reference that is concretely located yet resistant to conventional Western modes of interpretation. Refusing to be contained in the lecture hall of the "mainline" institution, McKay unsettles her audience and challenges Sarris himself by telling stories that defy their understanding and classifying.

In another look at indigenous peoples, Kateryna Olijnyk Longley discusses the autobiographical narratives of aboriginal women in Australia whose identities are culturally under erasure and yet specifically oral, generational, and tribal. For Aborigines, as for many Native Americans, coming to writing and autobiographical inscription coincided with or resulted from oppression and genocidal acculturations. As Longley suggests, Aboriginal stories thus allude to an empowered past irretrievable outside collective narrative and a resulting sense of identity caught between flux and flight.

There is assuredly much in European autobiography to lure us: for instance, the engendering of the imperial subject in First World autobiography or the complexities of historical consciousness and the tensions of ethnicities and nationalisms in an increasingly "unified" Europe. We choose, however, to look at texts in which European women are placed in specific colonial locations. Marguerite Duras's best-seller *The Lover*, as Suzanne Chester argues, positions the problems of de/colonization precisely at the slash. In this veiled autobiography personal history is written by and read through French colonial domination of Southeast Asia. The interplay of its subject's complex positionings with respect to gender, class, and race creates a tension of discourses through which oppressor and oppressed constantly change places. For European women in colonial locations, identity becomes a nomadic fiction. In discussing the autobiographical narratives of Isak Dinesen and Beryl Markham, two white women writing of life in colonial Kenya, Sidonie Smith explores the relationship of gender to the narrative politics that emerge in a specific colonial environment. However divergent their narrative strategies, both Markham and Dinesen make and remake themselves as "African." Between Africa as the maternal goddess in Dinesen's nostalgic dream and Africa as the wild space of Markham's masculinist adventuring, different metaphorical scenarios play out the complicities and resistances of "colonial" narrative practices.

The two essays on texts by Middle Eastern women explore the representation of childhood in part to foreground identity formation through practices of postcolonial education. Both discussions gesture toward the diversity of identity formations, ethnic heritages, and political configurations "orientalized" under the sign of the Middle East. In recovering the serialized autobiography of Egyptian feminist and educator Nabawiyya Musa from archives in Cairo, Margot Badran discovers a model of middle-class Egyptian "feminism" antinomial to the privileged and Europeanized feminism of Huda Sha'rawi, the only other pre-contemporary Egyptian woman autobiographer extensively discussed in the West to date. Badran reads a self-decolonizing strategy in Musa's refusal of a model childhood, and her insistence on a childhood characterized by a series of rebellions that prepared her to oppose the Egyptian ideology of colonial womanhood in championing educational reforms. During a Palestinian winter, Janet Varner Gunn writes autobiographically of discovering her impatience with the imperialist presumption underlying Western idealization of the individual. In this setting she reads the reification of romantic individualism idealized in Annie Dillard's *An American Childhood* against the unromantic realities of childhood and the "conscientization" of identity in the autobiography of Palestinian "terrorist" Leila Khaled. Gunn explores how Khaled's education prepares her to question individualist values and to redefine identity as collective, history as mission, and education as practice. Reframing her own poetics of experience as a politics, Gunn asks if Western autobiographical writings, including her own, can avoid being acts of expropriation.

The essays by Lee Quinby, John Beverley, Caren Kaplan, and Carole Boyce Davies, in different ways, theorize the collection's focus on women's autobiography, inquiring into claims about subject formation that make such writing both persuasive and suspect. These mappings of the territorialization and transgression of autobiographical theory offer a mirror for reading these essays against First World accounts of autobiography and its canon. Quinby uses *The Woman Warrior* to develop a Foucauldian analysis of how the female subject of autobiography is formed at the intersection of two discourses of power, the systems of alliance and sexuality, that are deployed to maintain the daughter's silence and marginalization. Quinby argues for reading Hong Kingston's narrative as "memoirs," promoting the new subjectivity of ideographic selfhood, rather than as autobiography, because she considers autobiography's totalizing and normalizing of the subject to be implicated in modern power structures. In an influential essay published three years ago and reprinted here with a new postscript, John Beverley discusses *testimonio* as an embryonic form of collective autobiographical witnessing that gives voice to the struggles of oppressed peoples against neo- and postcolonial exploitation. *Testimonio* has to be seen, Beverley argues, as an alternative to autobiography, an essentially conservative humanistic mode. A narrative urge to communicate the personal as political becomes, in *testimonio*, an affirmation of the marginalized speaking subject and her experience of the real. In *I, Rigoberta Menchú* Beverley finds conscious resistance to "a humanist ideology of the literary." The subject of *testimonio* narrates more than she authors, in the Western sense, her subalternity, and thus destabilizes the reader's world.

Caren Kaplan both builds on and resituates Beverley's analysis of *testimonio* as a form of anti-humanistic, collective witnessing in her notion of out-law genres of autobiography. She sees as problematic autobiography's fixation on stable—read nationally identified—subjects at a time when identities are nomadic, national borders are being redefined, and the parameters invoked in naming women's differences are shown to be part of the instrumentality for maintaining those differences. Kaplan proposes, in this transitional surround, reframing autobiographical practice through "out-law" genres. Refusing to contain collaborative life stories in traditional autobiographical frameworks, Carole Boyce Davies discusses the ways in which this "crossover genre" becomes a form for the empowerment of women formerly silenced. Elaborating the degree and the form of editorial intervention in three forms of collaborative life storytelling, she considers the complex dynamic between the speaking subject and the "interpreter" in projects that transform oral histories into written texts.

Finally, Julia Watson considers "sexual decolonization" as a notion within Western feminism that appears problematic when read in the context of neocolonial and postcolonial women's writing. Generally invoked in critiques of a universalized patriarchy, sexual decolonization requires an oppositional framework that reifies sexual difference. But autobiographies both lesbian and feminist have now begun to critique oppositional notions of gender for their complicity in maintaining heterosexist hegemony. In Audre Lorde's "biomythography," Adrienne Rich's irreducibly split self-representation, and Jo Spence's phototherapy, Watson finds autobiographical practices that deconstruct hierarchical sexual difference while contesting sexual identity as a sufficient index of colonized status.

These introductory remarks suggest possible ways to stimulate debate around the key concepts we have been addressing: *colonization, decolonization, authorship, authenticity, agency, subjectivity, individuality, location, resistance, collusion*. But our intent is less to fix the relationships than to provoke connections. Individual readers will make and remake this dialogue to fit their different interests.

We do want, however, to call into question Western literary practices and theorizing. It does us no good, it does literary practice no good, to take up critical definitions, typologies, reading practices, and thematics forged in the west through the engagement with canonical Western texts and to read texts from various global locations through those lenses. Different texts from different locales require us to develop different theories and practices of reading, what we might call "standpoint" reading practices. Such practices call all of us, positioned specifically in our own locales, both to engage the autobiographical practices of colonial subjects and to critique our own points of observation.[36]

Finally, despite the location of production, we hope that our collection signifies a collectivity of people working in a global environment, positioned in different personal and theoretical locations. We hope, then, that we gesture toward what Kaplan calls "transnational" perspectives rather than enshrining neo-imperialist scriptures on the politics of autobiographical practices. We have worked to resist an easy and imperialist universalization of experience in order to recognize, salute, and give validity to positions of difference and to affinities rather than prescriptive identifications. We do not want to appropriate in a too-easy gesture of imperial identification, or to romanticize in a fantasy of feminist homogeneity, or to silence by a telescoping act of interpretation the multiple and specific voices of the postcolonial autobiographical texts here invoked.

Notes

1. Doris Sommer, "'Not just a Personal Story': Women's *Testimonios* and the Plural Self'" in *Life/Lines: Theorizing Women's Autobiography*, ed. Bella Brodzki and Celeste Schenck (Ithaca, N.Y.: Cornell University Press, 1988), 111.
2. Gayatri Chakravorty Spivak, "Can the Subaltern Speak? Speculations on Widow Sacrifice," in *Marxism and the Interpretation of Culture*, ed. Cary Nelson and Lawrence Grossberg (Urbana: University of Illinois Press, 1988), 271–313. This provocative essay has generated various contestatory theoretical stances on the "voice" of the subaltern.
3. Elizabeth V. Spelman, *Inessential Woman: Problems of Exclusion in Feminist Thought* (Boston: Beacon, 1988); see especially chapter 5.
4. Gayatri Chakravorty Spivak, "The Political Economy of Women as Seen by a Literary Critic," in *Coming to Terms: Feminism, Theory, Politics*, ed. Elizabeth Weed (New York: Routledge, 1989), 226.
5. Carolyn Kay Steedman, *Landscape for a Good Woman: A Story of Two Lives* (New Brunswick, N.J.: Rutgers University Press, 1987), 65–82.
6. For a provocative analysis of the struggle of "the universal human subject" with all the "colorful" around it, see Peter Stallybrass and Allon White, *The Politics and Poetics of Transgression* (Ithaca, N.Y.: Cornell University Press, 1986), 199.
7. Judith Butler, *Gender Trouble: Feminism and the Subversion of Identity* (New York: Routledge, 1990), 13.
8. Chandra Talpade Mohanty, "Under Western Eyes: Feminist Scholarship and Colonial Discourses," *Boundary* 2, 12 (1984): 336. See also Ketu H. Katrak, "Decolonizing Culture: Toward a Theory for Postcolonial Women's Texts," *Modern Fiction Studies* 35 (Spring 1989): 158–60.
9. Mohanty, "Under Western Eyes," 336.
10. Abdul R. JanMohamed and David Lloyd, "Introduction," *Cultural Critique* 6 (Spring 1987): 8–9.
11. David Lloyd argues that the concept of a universal human subject soliciting common identification "inaugurates a universal history of development which always contains the realization of individual autonomy within a narrative so exclusive that it becomes the legitimation of an

irreducible heteronomy," with the result that "the path by which social identity is formed is the one which leads back from differentiation to identification with an imperial Man whose destiny is always the same." "Genet's Genealogy: European Minorities and the Ends of the Canon," *Cultural Critique* 6 (Spring 1987): 85.

12 Gayatri Chakravorty Spivak, *Harper's Magazine* (September 1989), 52.

13 Rey Chow, "'It's you and not me': Domination and 'Othering' in Theorizing the 'Third World,'" in *Coming to Terms: Feminism, Theory, Politics*, ed. Elizabeth Weed (New York: Routledge, 1989), 158.

14 As JanMohamed and Lloyd argue, "Minority individuals are always treated and forced to experience themselves generically." "Introduction," 10.

15 John B. Thompson, *Studies in the Theory of Ideology* (Cambridge: Polity, 1984), 132. Deborah Cameron quotes this passage in her comparative analysis of various feminist language theories, "What Is the Nature of Women's Oppression in Language?" *Oxford Literary Review* 8 (1986): 84.

16 Cameron, "What Is the Nature," 83.

17 Ralph Cohen, "History and Genre," *New Literary History* 17 (Winter 1986): 210.

18 See Marjorie Perloff, "Introduction," in *Postmodern Genres*, ed. Marjorie Perloff (Norman: University of Oklahoma Press, 1988), 7.

19 On Arabic autobiographical traditions see, for instance, Leila Ahmed, "Between Two Worlds: The Formation of a Turn-of-the-Century Egyptian Feminist," in *Life/Lines: Theorizing Women's Autobiography*, ed. Bella Brodzki and Celeste Schenck (Ithaca, N.Y.: Cornell University Press, 1988), 154–74. On traditions of life writing in Japan, see Chizuko Yonamine, "'Self in a Tenth-Century Japanese Autobiography" (paper presented at the conference "New Approaches to Biography: Challenges from Critical Theory," University of Southern California, 19–21 October 1990).

20 See Abdul R. JanMohamed, "Negating the Negation as a Form of Affirmation in Minority Discourse: The Construction of Richard Wright as Subject," *Cultural Critique* 7 (Fall 1987): 246–47.

21 Chow, "It's you," 157.

22 "The most crucial aspect of resisting the hegemony," suggests JanMohamed, "consists in struggling against its attempt to form one's subjectivity, for it is through the construction of the minority subject that the dominant culture can elicit the individual's own help in his/her oppression." JanMohamed, 246–47.

23 For a discussion of the relation between hegemonic domination and human agency, see Benita Parry, "Problems in Current Theories of

Colonial Discourse," *Oxford Literary Review* 9 (1987): 27–58. Parry suggests that certain strands of deconstructive practice that take their cue from Derridean deconstruction produce "a theory assigning an absolute power to the hegemonic discourse in constituting and disarticulating the native." Thus from one point of view, the subaltern does not, cannot, "talk back" to the "metropolis." Critiquing Spivak's theory, Parry suggests that "the story of colonialism which she reconstructs is of an interactive process where the European agent in consolidating the imperialist Sovereign Self, induces the native to collude in its own subject(ed) formation as other and voiceless. Thus while protesting at the obliteration of the native's subject position in the text of imperialism, Spivak in her project gives no speaking part to the colonized" (p. 35).

24 Chow, "It's you," 157.
25 Parry, "Problems in Current Theories," 43–44.
26 Chandra T. Mohanty and Satya P. Mohanty, "Contradictions of Colonialism," *Women's Review of Books* 7 (March 1990), 19.
27 "To understand identity as a *practice*, and as a signifying practice," suggests Butler, "is to understand culturally intelligible subjects as the resulting effect of a rule-bound discourse that inserts itself in the pervasive and mundane signifying acts of linguistic life." *Gender Trouble*, 145. See also Paul Smith, who argues that "a person is not simply an *actor* who follows ideological scripts, but is also an *agent* who reads them in order to insert him/herself into them or not." *Discerning the Subject* (Minneapolis: University of Minnesota Press, 1988), xxxiv–xxxv.
28 Barbara Harlow, "Introduction," in *The Colonial Harem*, Malek Alloula (Minneapolis: University of Minnesota Press, 1986), xxii.
29 Nancy Hartsock, "Foucault on Power: A Theory for Women?" in *Feminism! Postmodernism*, ed. Linda J. Nicholson (New York: Routledge, 1990), 171.
30 Arif Dirlik. "Culturalism as Hegemonic Ideology and Liberating Practice," *Cultural Critique* 6 (Spring 1987): 14.
31 Dirlik, "Culturalism as Hegemonic Ideology," 14. 'Recalling culture in its double meaning," suggests Dirlik, "both as a 'way of seeing' and as a way of making the world, remains the historical subject (or agent) to his dialectical temporality which, Jameson has suggested, decenters him from his privileged position in history . . . in other words, there is the possibility of a truly liberating practice which can exist only as a possibility and which must take as its premise the denial of a center to the social process and of a predestined direction to history" (49).

32 Homi Bhabha, "Of Mimicry and Man: The Ambivalence of Colonial Discourse," *October* 28 (1984): 125–33. See also Parry's critique of Bhabha's concept of mimicry/hybridity. She argues that, unlike Spivak, Bhabha makes a space for the articulation of the subaltern or minoritized speaker: "A narrative which delivers the colonized from its discursive status as the illegitimate and refractory foil of Europe, into a position of 'hybridity' from which it is able to circumvent, challenge and refuse colonial authority, has no place for a totalizing notion of epistemic violence. Nor does the conflictual economy of the colonialist text allow for the unimpeded operation of discursive aggression." "Problems in Current Theories," 42.

33 Barbara Harlow, "From the Women's Prison: Third World Women's Narratives of Prison," *Feminist Studies* 12 (Fall 1986): 502—3.

34 Frantz Fanon, *The Wretched of the Earth* (1961), trans. Constance Farrington (New York: Grove Press, 1963), 36.

35 Lloyd, "Genet's Genealogy," 185.

36 Spivak warns that academic scholars must engage the texts of the other through knowledge of the language of the other. "Political Economy," 228.

19
MEMORY, NARRATIVE, AND THE DISCOURSES OF IDENTITY IN *ABENG* AND *NO TELEPHONE TO HEAVEN* (SMITH 1999)

(Because part of me is a girl and part of me is a woman speaking to her.)[1]

Time is not linear. All things are happening at the same time. The past, the present, and the future coexist.[2]

I and Jamaica is who I am. No matter how far I travel—how deep the ambivalence I feel about ever returning. And Jamaica is a place in which we/they/I connect and disconnect—change place.
(LLB 76)

In an essay on "out-law genres," Caren Kaplan persuasively argues that "the popularity of the concept of autobiography in contemporary studies and practices of Western culture does not obviate the troubling legacy of this complicated genre."[3] In the theoretical debates around the meaning of "post" in postcoloniality and the relationship of "posts" to one another, "autobiography" has become a most vexed term, genre, and orientation to knowledge because autobiographical modes have been recognized (and misrecognized) as western cartographies of the subject. Autobiography's legacy has been particularly troubling because of its identification with the western romance of individualism. As the authors of *The Empire Writes Back* argue, the "I" of bourgeois autobiography announces "the independent 'individual' whose social inflection is one of the strongest trace marks left by Europeanization on the postcolonial world."[4] In the master narratives of modernity, the autobiographical "I" has functioned as a culturally forceful enunciatory site of the autonomous, free, rational, unified individual or "self." This "self" assumes itself as universal human subject, a subject of undividedness.

Now, it may be that the "I" of bourgeois individualism has dominated the autobiographical landscape of modernity, that "autobiography" and modernity assume one another. But there are histories of diverse modes of personal referentiality in the West, and elsewhere than the West, as recent scholarship has attested—for instance, a precolonial Islamic tradition among intellectuals, a tradition of women's personal writing in Heian Japan, a tradition of pictographs of the Plains Indians in the United States. Therefore I have to remind myself to be careful about making general statements about the homogeneity of modes of self-referentiality in the West and about the western purchase on autobiographical narrative. Personally referential narrative is not, ipso facto, western. It is a much deployed genre (or rather collection of related forms) in the West. It has been and continues to be identified with the western romance of individualism. But saying so only reveals the ways in which the forms of personal writing we call "autobiography" or "memoir" are historically specific and culturally contingent modes of self-referentiality.

If the autobiographical mode is durably a legacy of "capitalist modernity" (the phrase Aijaz Ahmad prefers[5]), then what are de/colonizing subjects[6] to make of such practices and such publicity. If to take up the autobiographical mode is to take up certain discourses of selfhood and truth-telling, what are the performative liabilities and possibilities? For autobiographical narrative has been taken up by those who, as Homi K. Bhabha notes, have been "'overlooked'—in the double sense of social surveillance and psychic disavowal—and, at the same time, overdetermined—psychically projected, made stereotypical and symptomatic."[7]

And here is the source of contention among cultural critics. Some, with Audre Lorde, would argue that "the master's tools will never dismantle the master's house."[8] To write autobiography is to conform one's experiential history to modernist discourses of identity, the very discourses through which one has been overlooked and overdetermined. It is performativity as denial of difference. From this point of view, taking up autobiographical narrative in its traditional project is tantamount to choosing to collaborate in one's own subjection by making oneself over in the image of the oppressor. It is to reiterate a culturally normative subject position and to become intelligible within the terms of the dominant culture. It is to affirm through recitation the ontological authority of the norm, to naturalize the norm that is only constituted as ontological in its recitations.

To resist the cultural authority of this bourgeois individual, cultural critics sometimes call for a return to more "authentic" modes of storytelling, "traditional" or "native" practices whose integrity is measured by the degree to which they can be said to originate in a time before the colonization of mind and memory. Cautious about the implications of this call to an origin (outside the history of the last several centuries), others would attend to the traces of alternative practices, the traces of otherness held in cultural memory, albeit unthinkable and unmemorable outside the history of colonialism.

For if recourse to an autobiographical "I" is not a sign of empowerment forged through the unproblematized authority of personal experience, neither is it necessarily a sign of complicity in the forces of oppression. The effects of autobiographical recitation cannot be too quickly assessed in what Iain Chambers calls "this complex, asymmetrical, structuring of the field of power."[9] To take possession of the autobiographical "I" in a cultural context in which that "I" is normative, is at once to be possessed by cultural norms and to become culturally intelligible. To write as an "I" is to claim a subject position privileged in the discourses of modernity. Thus the wresting of an individual narrative can be seen as a necessary point of departure for liberatory practices.[10] Assembling an experiential history can function as counter-memory, a means to re-narrativize the past and to break the silences of official history. As Bhabha suggests, there can be menace in mimicry, the re-siting of an unauthorized subject in the authoritative "I" position such that the recitation is rendered not-quite the same and not-quite different.[11] In such re-siting, issues of authenticity and inauthenticity trouble the sutures of self-representation. And when Joan Borsa claims that "one can take on master texts without subscribing to them, without reproducing their meaning," she gestures toward the disruptive capacities of recitation.[12]

Autobiographical practices can be taken up as occasions to critique dominant discourses of identity and truth-telling by rendering the "I" unstable, shifting, provisional, troubled by and in its identifications. Further, the autobiographical subject is multiple, "the articulation of an ensemble of subject positions, corresponding to the multiplicity of social relations in which it is inscribed."[13] Since the autobiographical "I" as a marker of the subject is neither fully rational, unified in a coherent identity, nor transparent to itself, its recitations are multiply productive of identifications and disidentifications, riven by suturings and fracturings. Further, autobiographical discourses, like the discourses of modernity generally, are not unified but heterogeneous and contradictory in their effects. The autobiographical subject who would resist certain discourses of selfhood by means of the deconstruction of constitutive constraint "is itself enabled, if not produced, by such norms."[14] Narratively occupying the "I" can become a means to interrogate, from within and without, history, memory, culture, and power. It can also become a means for "establishing" what Judith V. Emberley describes as "different cultural diacritics"[15] that promote alternative terms of identity and systems of value. Such resisting autobiographical practices can be ones that introduce some kind of crisis (some incommensurability) into this too believable field of history by "mak[ing] visible the laws and limits of [a normative] system of representation."[16] A narrating subject, culturally cathected as a self-consolidating other, can deploy the performativity of autobiographical storytelling to struggle with and against his/her "construct[ion] in subordination."[17]

1. Remembering

Rectangles remembering an event she would never know of.[18]

The autobiographical "I," then, is a site of specific emplacements (to use Linda Warley's term) and the vagaries of mobility simultaneously. As Chandra Talpade Mohanty emphasizes in her discussion of writing and resistance, "resistance is encoded in the practices of remembering against the grain of 'public' or hegemonic history, of locating the silences and the struggle to assert knowledge which is outside the parameters of the dominant."[19] All of this is a way of saying that the "I" as an enunciatory site is a point of convergence of autobiographical politics and the politics of memory. There are, of course, different kinds of memory. Generic event memory (or habit memory or implicit memory) is the kind of memory that comes into play in the "things happen this way" sense. (How we negotiate a grocery store, for instance, or swim.) There is eidetic memory—the memory of images so prominent in childhood, the memory that seems to make of childhood recollection a different order from adult remembering. And there is episodic memory that involves, according to the psychologist Katherine Nelson, "conscious recollection of previous experiences" that are "remarkable."[20] Episodic memories become narrativized through "mental constructs which people use to make sense out of experience."[21]

Now I want to note three characteristics of narrative memory. First of all, narrative remembering functions as a medium of symbolic interaction. It is an occasion of exchange and an effect of social exchange. In her essay on the psychological and social origins of autobiographical memory, Nelson suggests that narrative memories "become valued in their own right--not because they predict the future and guide present action, but because they are shareable with others and thus serve a social solidarity function."[22]

Second, remembering is emplaced. Narrative memories are attached to places; and places become personally and communally meaningful through memories and the social context of remembering. Paul Connerton, in his study *How Societies Remember*, claims:

> We conserve our recollections by referring them to the material milieu that surrounds us. It is to our social spaces—those which we occupy, which we frequently retrace with our steps, where we always have access, which at each moment we are capable of mentally reconstructing—that we must turn our attention, if our memories are to reappear.[23]

Thus remembering flows from and returns to material sites and practices. Objects, buildings, views, gestures, rituals, etc., stimulate the processes of remembering as if our memories lie expectantly within them, only awaiting our attention for retrieval.

Third, embodiedness is critical to the recovery of memory (of and through emotion), since embodiment, memory, and subjectivity join in an autobiographical system. There must be a body in the memory. That is, there must be a subject who knows and owns the images coming from the external world and the memories invoked in interaction with the world; there must be memories through which the subject continually reconstructs notions of identity produced in symbolic exchange with the world; and the subject must understand herself as located in a body continually present to itself through "background body states and emotional states,"[24] states that are also changing with exchanges in the world.

Memory is embodied in another cultural sense as well. Historical memory is embodied in the very subjects that are its sites of remembering. These rememberings emerge through bodily gestures and presentations, through bodily emplacement within spaces of memory. Connerton goes so far as to suggest that the past itself inheres in "habitual memory sedimented in the body."[25]

These sedimentations of memory are effects of the cultural possibilities of remembering. For the cultural past produces "artificial memory," a term I take from the neuroscientist Stephen Rose.[26] By "artificial" I mean to foreground the interpretive effects of past events carried into the future through various symbolic modes of remembering. In his study of "lieux de mémoire," Pierre Nora differentiates what he calls the History with a capital H from "real memory." By real memory he means "life, borne by living societies founded in its name." Continually in process, "open to the dialectic of remembering and forgetting," "real memory" functions as "a bond tying us to the eternal present." Memory surrounding the remember, memory in process, memory as a continually renegotiated ground of social interaction, this "real memory" is social and unviolated. History, on the other hand, is an artificial form of remembering composed of "sifted and sorted historical traces . . . of mediation, of distance"; it is "the reconstruction, always problematic and incomplete, of what is no longer."[27] But I would argue with Nora's schematization and suggest that what he calls real memory is artificial as well.

For Nora "lieux de mémoire" "originate with the sense that there is no spontaneous memory" and so, in order to keep the traces of memory, we must create sites of memory—such as museums, festivals, anniversaries, etc. He argues that "without commemorative vigilance, history would soon sweep them away."[28] "Lieux de mémoire" are sites where memory "crystallizes and secretes itself" in ways that are fixed, stable, instrumental.[29] Such sites are "bastions" upon which "we buttress our identities"; but, according to Nora, "if what they defeated were not threatened, there would be no need to build them."[30]

Personal remembering, then, unfolds in and enfolds itself within the context of competing and contradictory artificial rememberings, since as things happen to people they learn what memory narratives to share, what memories to forget. This is the embodied politics of remembering. Toni Morrison and bell hooks have invoked this politics in their phrase "rememory." More recently Ian Hacking has articulated a theory of "memoropolitics" that has attended the emergence of the sciences of memory in the late nineteenth century and the predominance of the sciences of memory in the twentieth century. "Memoro-politics," which he triangulates with Michel Foucault's two poles of anatomo- and bio-politics—the politics of the human body and the politics of the human population—is "a politics of the secret, of the forgotten event that can be turned, if only by strange flashbacks, into something monumental."[31] Hacking identifies this politics of the secret as the displacement in the late nineteenth century of the politics of the soul. "There could be no sciences of the soul. So there came to be a science of memory."[32] Nora, addressing the politics of the buried past from a slightly different angle, suggests that "one of the costs of the historical metamorphosis of memory has been a wholesale preoccupation with the individual psychology of remembering."[33]

We might, then, speak of the de/colonization of memory as an effect of memoro-politics. The de/colonizing subject is a subject of an overwriting and overdetermining official history (artificial memory). The politics of the secret is the politics of the psychic trauma of de/colonization, of the disavowal of difference. The secret is the secret of the virtual subjection of the post/colonial subject as the embodiment of the past of colonialism. As Harry/Harriet says to Clare Savage in Michelle Cliff's *No Telephone to Heaven*: "But we are the past here.... A peculiar past. For we have taken the master's past as our own. That is the danger."[34]

Harry/Harriet's attention to the embodiment of memory provides an entree to my discussion of autobiographical remembering in Cliff's *Abeng* and *No Telephone to Heaven*, paired texts entwining autobiographical and fictive features in a coming-of-age story linked to untold, and oral, narratives of Jamaican colonization and resistance. In an effort to tease out the implications of Cliff's politics of memory, I want to look at two sites of autobiographical remembering in each of the novels.

2. Plantation Genealogy

The pattern on the wallpaper was only a small glimpse of the background against which this part of her family had once existed. These images surrounded them as they sat in their parlor. The danger to Clare was that the background could slide so easily into the foreground (A 24–25)

In an early scene in *Abeng*, the third-person narrator places the protagonist "Clare Savage"—a version of the author's younger self—in a scene in which Clare's father, Boy Savage, takes his daughter to visit the remains of his ancestral plantation. The narrator emphasizes the father's pride in his family genealogy, a mode of autobiographical emplacement. This genealogy secures Boy's paternal pedigree, his descent through the father, grandfather, and great-grandfather. I use the term "pedigree" here purposefully since genealogical guides, as Julia Watson remarks, refer to "pedigree" as "the validated evidence documenting ancestral identity, transactions, and events."[35] Proud of his pedigree, Boy would make Clare his own daughter (a daughter not of woman born, in effect) by inserting her psychically in that pedigree. He would make her his own, the embodiment of his past carried into the future, by attaching her to the space sacralized in his memory museum, the old Savage plantation.[36]

For Boy, autobiographical memory is "embodied" in this site that serves as a "lieu de mémoire." Walking through the dilapidated remains of Judge Savage's once grand plantation, through the rooms in ruins, rooms fading with the faded wallpaper, Boy works to keep his pedigree intact by populating this imaginative diorama with shades of ancestors from the past. Even if the building is in ruins, its ruins become a romanticized trace, reaffirming "the old values of hierarchy and origin"[37] and with them the certainties of border cleavages. This scene of historical reenactment is necessary to Boy's certitude of identity since it provides him with a story of origins. This pedigree fixes an individual in a family tree and roots the family tree in a specific sociocultural location. That is, "it installs particular families in the privileged world of those who can trace their origins and attest to the coherence of their stock."[38]

As Boy guides Clare through certain spaces on the plantation, he reproduces an imaginative homestead for his memories. But his homestead is the great house of the plantation. Thus the return to the plantation most precisely is an embodied mnemonic device for remembering himself as "white." For the pedigree that Boy claims as his means of self-locating functions to erase the other histories embodied in the ruins of the plantation, the histories of the middle passage, the slave quarters, the politics and economics of slavery, the rape of slave women, the violent passage from slavery to emancipation, and the continuing legacies of colonialism. Pedigree can only be sustained through the forgetting of trauma and the traumatic forgetting of the maternal line. Boy would forget the name of the mother, write her out of history, render her invisible, as the traumatic events in the slave quarters are rendered invisible on the old plantation. The matronym is subsumed under the patronym, its genealogical traces erased through the privileges of pedigree. Boy's genealogical device, a product of modernity, tries to keep the secrets of the past at bay, and the biggest secret is that the dispossessed have no genealogical claims to make.[39]

Boy's act of claiming genealogical pedigree, which "values origin, stock, race, blood, in an increasingly heterogeneous world," serves to "establish 'descent' where it is most in question."[40] In owning a pedigree, Boy believes in his own self-possession. Tracing his genealogical origins thus becomes a means to suture the multiple origins in his past, to suture his fragmented subjectivity through the apparent seamlessness of identification. But the need to secure pedigree signals self-losing. For pedigree can only be sustained through the forgetting of the otherness within and the refusal of the incomplete, the absent, the ungraspable, the spectral. The ruined foundation upon which Boy would erect his identity "disturbs what was previously considered immobile; it fragments what was thought unified; it shows the heterogeneity of what was imagined as consistent with itself."[41]

The narrator of *Abeng* refuses pedigree as a productive mode of autobiographical emplacement. As one who knows, the narrator puts the plantation under a new description, revealing the indeterminacy of the past.[42] She makes only too clear that pedigree is a means of reproducing class privilege, racism, patriarchal and heterosexual norms. She exposes the ironies in the Savage genealogy, which is literally a narrative of patrilineal degeneration and profligacy rather than progress, and of genealogical mixing rather than purity. She also fills the narrative space with her research into the history of the slave trade and the history of emancipation. That is, she contains Boy's remembering in her counter-memory. And she populates the plantation with those figures erased in Boy's genealogy and imagines their various forms of resistance. Thus she assigns vitality and agency to the slaves.

Finally, the narrator refuses the postcolonial suture, exploring the neo-imperial practices of real estate developers who continue to exploit the natural and human resources of Jamaica. The plantation has become "Paradise Plantation," seducing tourists to relocate in this tropical Eden, siting their homes of wealth upon the grasses of the slave quarters without having found an archeological dig necessary. The history of slavery has become evacuated of its palpable materiality as it serves as a romantic backdrop to the expansion of First-World wealth into the "islands" of desire and the nostalgia of the exotic. The old plantation is now a commodified tourist attraction, a site of staged authenticity.[43] Pedigreed remembering has degenerated into a prop for touristic pleasure. As such it provides only a distorting and disempowering relationship to the past, as Dean

MacCannell says of tourist attractions in historical locations: "[T]hey are reminders of our break with the past and with tradition, even our own tradition."[44]

Autobiographical pedigree cannot serve emancipatory purposes. The Savages, writes the narrator, "relinquish[ed] responsibility for their lives" (A 29). When Boy returns in *No Telephone to Heaven* he has left Jamaica behind for the United States, where he camouflages himself as "white," practicing the arts of passing and the homely arts of painting plates with his "family crest" and other reproductions of the old plantation. In America he reproduces an imaginary homeland that gives him a pedigree through which he camouflages his heterogeneous inheritance.

3. Diary

> *I would never have thought to keep a diary without having read [Anne Frank]. She gave me permission to write, and to use writing as a way of survival. My diary kept me separate from my family, just as hers helped her to maintain her identity in a very claustrophobic situation.*[45]

> *Don't tell outsiders anything real about yourself. Don't reveal our secrets to them. Don't make us seem foolish, or oppressed. Write it quickly before someone catches you. Before you catch yourself.* (LLB 16)

Clare Savage drifts between her father's fierce allegiance to genealogical pedigree and her mother's haunting remoteness, her palpable autobiographical silence. While her Afro-Saxon[46] father extols the history and virtues of the English and participates in the denigration of the African cultural heritage and the people who are dark of body, her mother, even as she identifies emotionally with the poor and dark of body, represents them as victims, powerless ones who require feeding and sympathy, the helping hands of the privileged class. The narrator of *Abeng* recognizes Clare's struggle with pedigree and mournful benevolence as a struggle with her own fragmentation.

That Clare becomes a diary writer is critical to her negotiation of this confounded fragmentation.[47] And the way she comes to diary writing is critical to the narrator's engagement with the politics of autobiographical memory. Clare reads *The Diary of Anne Frank* at the same time that a schoolmate dies suddenly. Because of the conspiracy of silence surrounding that death (at the school, in her family, in the community), Claudia Lewis ceases to exist, cannot be remembered. By contrast, Anne Frank and her death at an early age remain unforgettable in the world: "But Anne most certainly had been there. She had left behind evidence of her life" (A 69).

Reading the diary and establishing intimacy with Anne, Clare is transported elsewhere, to another time and space, and in that elsewhere she is imaginatively released to articulate questions about oppression, suffering, victimization, ethics, heroism, and God's beneficence. The evidence of the diary is the trace or countermemory of the past that prompts Clare to direct urgent questions to her father. It is through her undutiful persistence that she glimpses the inadequacies of Boy's explanations, as well as those of the teachers at her school. She glimpses, that is, the inadequacy of official history. In reaching to understand how Anne, a young girl much like herself, could have been incarcerated and then exterminated, Clare "reaches," the narrator tells us, "without knowing it, for an explanation of her own life" (A 72). Thus the tracings of this other space and time get read back into Clare's autobiographical memory; and in that remembering she seeks to rescue herself in the refractions of another's experience and subjectivity.

Clare purchases her first diary after viewing the film version of *The Diary of Anne Frank*. With its lock and key, this diary becomes Clare's eccentric hiding place, a repository in which she records her secret thoughts, experiences, feelings, those traces of misidentification. The lock and key keep the secrets, and the secret self struggling with identity, desire, and the differences within, "safe" from betrayal (*LLB* 107). Thus, within the safety of this eccentric space, the young girl begins the process of self-authoring by "rewriting the stories that already exist about her since by seeking to publicize herself she is violating an important cultural construction of her femininity as passive or hidden."[48]

Interestingly, Clare cannot address her diary, as Anne Frank addressed hers, to "Kitty." "Kitty" was Anne Frank's imaginary friend, a friend she adapted from a Dutch series for young girls, *Joop ter Heul* (by Cissy van Marxveldt), as she compensated for her loss of everyday friendships. "Kitty" became for the incarcerated teenager an ideal reader: "the friend for whom I have waited so long."[49] To "Kitty" Anne could disgorge "all kinds of things that lie buried deep in my heart."[50] Clare, like Anne, desires a relationship with a perfect friend, an interlocutor of the secret heart, but it cannot be with "Kitty," which is the name of her mother, because her relationship with her mother is so troubled and unsatisfying. Thus, the narrator tells us, Clare "did not know what to call it" (*A* 80).

The diary as an autobiographical mode is both productive and limited in terms of a politics of decolonization. On the one hand, the diary leaves a testamentary trace of the everyday lives of the silenced, the dispossessed, the overwritten and overdetermined. In this way it registers the claim of the authority of experience by providing Clare with an alternative space for self-exploration in the midst of the family and the culture that constricts her self-imagining. Diary keeping, on the other hand, grounds the writing subject in the continuous present of the quotidian, a particularly efficacious temporal milieu for a young girl subject to her father's investments in the past and in the long genealogical narrative. And in fact, the final scene of the novel finds Clare recording in her diary the secrets of her first menstruation, her coming to embodied femininity. She sits alone in her exile, policed by the racist Miss Beatrice, separated by her parents from her only friend Zoe, her body aching from the onslaught of menses; but she writes, bringing into words the secrets that others would cover with their conspiracy of silence. Her diary provides her an alternative forum for remembering what must be forgotten within the regimes of truth surrounding her.

Moreover, in the diary she becomes a subject being brought into being through a surfeit of "I"s. As Valerie Raoul notes in her discussion of the *journal intime*, "the '*intimiste*' performs a triple self-projection, performing more-or-less simultaneously all three functions: author, character and reader of the text.... The specular and speculative narcissistic nature of the act of diary-writing enables the Self to be simultaneously desiring and desired, watching and watched, inside and outside, judging and judged."[51] The surfeit constitutes a stay against the forces of annihilation, an accumulation in the memory museum of consciousness.[52]

Yet, significantly, the narrator of *Abeng* never gives the reader a glimpse of the diary. It remains an unspoken text within the text. And the last line of the novel refuses the authority of experience by rendering it as "not knowing": "She was not ready to understand her dream. She had no idea that everyone we dream about we are" (A 166). Thus the narrator, at the same time that she emphasizes the necessity of diary writing as a medium of self-authorization, resists the authority of the self-referential "I" of diary. For the recourse to an unqualified authority of experience is itself problematic. It certainly functions as a point of departure for self-understanding and cultural critique; but it must remain a point of departure rather than a fixed site. For "experience," as Joan W. Scott cautions, "is at once always already an interpretation and is in need of interpretation."[53]

Diary is itself a self-referential practice with a history and certain effects. As a ledger of deposits in a memory bank, diary-keeping can function to reinforce the commodification of identity through consumer capitalism.[54] "Experience" then becomes so much capital to be accumulated, stored, packaged, and the self so accumulated rendered other to itself. Further, diary-keeping can function as a medium of self-regulation, for even as it encourages the unsilencing of the secret it maintains the necessity of secrecy. It keeps the secret in its certain space. In his consideration of Foucault's cartographic metaphors, Rob Shields suggests that "spatial control is an essential constituent of modem technologies of discipline and power. Discipline ... requires a specific enclosure of space."[55] The diary becomes a cultural space where young girls survey themselves on the way to adulthood. Finally, diary-keeping promotes the privatization of experience, and with privatization that belief in a unique self that even as it is uncovered must be kept under lock and key. Promoting an individualist practice of identity, it may forestall more complex and contextualized notions of identity and agency.

The narrator leaves us at the end of *Abeng* with a diary-writing Clare who doesn't know. The figure here is a figure of qualified promise. On the one hand, Clare has unconsciously learned to question if not to resist her father's fierce autobiographical pedigree through her own autobiographical project. On the other hand, she has only limited self-knowledge and as yet no politics of remembering. Clare may dream of healing herself—through her healing of the otherness (Zoe) within—by suturing the "wound" with cool and damp moss. But she doesn't yet know that she is dreaming about her own desire for self-suturing. She hasn't yet formulated a politics of the secret through which to resist the memoro-politics of the secret that is implicated in colonialism's legacies.

4. Autobiographical Bildungsroman

The fiction had tricked her. Drawn her in so that she became Jane. (NTH 116)

In the second of the two Clare Savage novels, Cliff continues her investigations of the politics of personal remembering, exploring Clare Savage's life after she leaves Jamaica. I look next at two sites of remembering in *No Telephone to Heaven*, the first of which is Clare's reading of Charlotte Brontë's *Jane Eyre*, a female Bildungsroman written as retrospective autobiography.

As Thomas Cartelli notes, Clare succumbs to the call of Brontë's autobiographical narrator at the very moment she is most seduced by the call of the metropolitan center (*NTH* 90), when she is living in London in camouflage, passing as normatively "white."[56] Jane's personalism, her intimate address to her reader, seduces Clare into identification with the romance of (female) individualism. "The fiction had tricked her. Drawn her in so that she became Jane" (NTH 116). This "becoming Jane" forces a particular kind of remembering in Clare Savage, a remembering through which she conforms her experiential history to the individualist tropes of the "mother" country and sutures the differences.

Jane's autobiographical project becomes the cultural mode through which she (Jane/her reader Clare) constitutes herself as a free, unified, rational, self-regulating subject, the bourgeois individual. As I have argued elsewhere, autobiographical storytelling emerged as one compelling means of constituting bourgeois subjects and thereby regulating both bodies and minds.[57] It also situated that subject in "historical time"—"natural, homogeneous, secular calendrical time," the time underwriting the master narrative of development and progress.[58] Becoming Jane would keep Clare a "modern" young woman.

Identification with Jane, however, is only the first response to Clare's reading of female *Bildung*:

> Comforted for a time, she came to. Then, with a sharpness, reprimanded herself. No, she told herself. No, she could not be Jane. Small and pale. English. No, she paused. No, my girl, try Bertha. Wild-maned Bertha. . . . Yes, Bertha was closer to the mark. Captive. Ragôut. Mixture. Confused. Jamaican. Caliban. Carib. Cannibal. Cimarron. All Bertha. All Clare. (*NTH* 116)

The identification with Brontë's protagonist is an unconscious process, the product of the suturing capacities of the autobiographical mode. But Clare "comes to" and, in coming to, she resists the self-suturing of "English" autobiographical paradigms. For this bourgeois "I" who speaks so earnestly in *Jane Eyre* is an "I" not only with attitude but with a politics, a politics that rests upon the "unquestioned ideology of imperialist axiomatics."[59] Jane becomes a female individualist who, as Gayatri Spivak argues, moves from a position of marginality, of a family outside the Law, to a position of centrality, a family in the Law. She does so through the mediation of Bertha Mason, the figure who "render[s] indeterminate the boundary between human and animal," thus simultaneously diminishing "her entitlement under the spirit if not the letter of the Law"[60] and justifying Jane's assumption of active agency as a civilizing agent for Rochester. The liminal figure of Bertha is integral to the self-regulatory pressure of Jane's *Bildung*. Jane moves inside the Law as Bertha is excised from the Law.

The figure of Bertha functions as a mnemonic device for remembering "the axiomatics of imperialism,"[61] most precisely the axiomatics of the civilizing mission. The novel form itself is implicated in what Mary Louise Pratt describes as the "mother country's" "obsessive need to present and represent its peripheries and its others continually to itself."[62] Through the figure of Bertha, the reader mis/remembers the Caribbean woman as the lure of wealth and the corruption of unchecked desire and mis/remembers the white woman as the civilized subject of modernity and progress.

Clare's identification with Jane signals the mis/recognition of herself as a universal "white" woman. Her shift in identification to Bertha exposes the cultural construction of whiteness as universal norm. That shift also signals her attentiveness to traces within herself of the excluded other, and inarticulate difference. For Bertha has no narrative voice. She speaks only through animal sounds, laughter, fire, and the disorderliness of her body and her clothes. She is rupture, the tear in order and the self-disciplining effects of traditional autobiography. Clare's shift in identification from Jane to the exotic, crazy woman from Jamaica undoes her mnemonic strategies of remembering—her obsessive recitation of the succession of kings and queens of England to maintain stability in her life through recourse to History. "Bertha" functions as a site of remembering with a difference, remembering as difference. In "coming to," then, Clare reroutes her reading against the grain of the personalism of autobiographical narrative (female *Bildung*). In the memoro-politics of de/colonizing autobiographical practices, she becomes the secret within.

5. The Grandmother's Homestead

> *And in the presence of this knowledge the historians plant, weed, hoe, raise houses, sew, and wash—and continue their investigations: into the one-shot contraceptive; the slow deaths of their children; the closing up of vulvas and the cutting-out of tongues. By opening the sutures, applying laundry soap and brown sugar, they draw out the poisons and purify the wounds. And maintain vigilance to lessen the possibility of reinfection.*[63]

"Coming to," Clare Savage returns to the place from which she has fled. Her journey, the journey that forms the narrative spine of *No Telephone to Heaven*, takes her to an adopted land (the United States); then to the imperial motherland (England); then to Europe where she drifts with Robby, the African American Vietnam vet suffering the literal and figurative wounds of multiple traumas. Fragmented, drifting, passing but psychically emptied by her own camouflage, Clare returns to Jamaica and to her grandmother's homestead. But despite this description of narrative movement, the structure of time in *No Telephone to Heaven* is not the autobiographical time of modernity and canonical Bildungsroman—not linear, unfolding, progressive, and sutured. This novel enfolds time as remembering itself does. The present wraps itself around the past as the past unwraps and rewraps itself around the present, its future. In the present (of time and of narration) the past constantly materializes in and as memory. And the remembering subject is herself the embodiment of the past.

This remembering is a kind of living memory, the living memory that Clare must wrest from the remains of her grandmother's homestead. But the homestead is an inheritance in ruins, for the site of living memories has surrendered to the ruination of neglect in service to "progress" and "modernity," to patriarchal and imperial histories that erase the spatial memory of an unofficial and forgotten past. This is the past her father would have her forget: her mixed racial heritage, her maternal genealogy, the subjugated knowledges of women—the knowledge of resistance to oppression and economic exploitation, women's empowerment and agency. In claiming her grandmother's legacy, she remembers what has been forgotten and dedicates the land to the community of resistors. Its disorder becomes camouflage, covering another order, to resist.

In fact, it is the old women with their alternative knowledges who bear the brunt of the forces of violence—physical and epistemological in the novel. The latter part of the narrative and the imagination of Christopher and Clare (linked as they are) are haunted by the old women from the nursing home consumed by fire. The old women of Jamaica are literally consumed in an oven of obliteration. They are consigned to the fires of figurative obliteration as well. Clare's mother remembers from her childhood how the schoolteacher, educating his pupils for the modern nation state of Jamaica, "warned them about false knowledge. That which was held in the minds and memories of old women" (*NTH* 69). The narrator, however, associates old women with the everyday materialization of living memory in practices, behaviors, languages, healings.

Actively remembering, Clare begins to undo pedigree and *Bildung* in resistance to the imperatives of forgetting upon which identity is grounded. In her final moments she crawls under her grandmother's house to find there her mother's childhood toys and books. It is as if she has come upon sacred relics, physical manifestations of an excluded otherness[64] through which she re/members herself as the buried past. This is the kind of remembering Nora would describe as memory "affective and magical."[65] Here is memory emplaced, embodied, transformative. But these relics are guarded by the scorpion she has to squash in order to touch this past. The retrieval of the hidden past is dangerous. Remembering otherwise is dangerous. This is, after all, Clare's last act of remembering.

Conclusion: The Narrator

> *It is not individuals who have experience, but subjects who are constituted through experience.... Experience in this definition*

then becomes not the origin of our explanation, . . . but rather that which we seek to explain, that about which knowledge is produced.[66]

Counter-memory is a way of remembering and forgetting that starts with the local, the immediate, and the personal. Unlike historical narratives that begin with the totality of human existence and then locate specific actions and events within that totality, counter-memory starts with the particular and the specific and then builds outward toward a total story. Counter-memory looks to the past for the hidden histories of those excluded from dominant narratives. But unlike mythical narratives that seek to detach events and actions from the fabric of any larger history, counter-memory demands revision of existing histories by supplying new perspectives about the past. Counter-memory embodies aspects of myth and aspects of history, but it retains an enduring suspicion of both categories. Counter-memory focuses on localized experiences with oppression, using them to reframe and re-focus dominant narratives purporting to represent universal experience.[67]

Kaplan reminds us that it is part of the imperializing effects of western academic scholarship to define autobiography, as Georges Gusdorf does, as a western genre and to identify its western modes and characteristics as generically determinative. To loosen this hold on modernist autobiographies, Kaplan calls for reading strategies resistant to the privileging of the twins of modernity, individualism and nationalism, in order to see beyond the limits, or to see within the limits other practices and their possibilities.[68]

There is a sense in which *Abeng* and *No Telephone to Heaven* can be read as veiled autobiography. Cliff herself has noted the autobiographical content of her first two novels. But what does it mean for Cliff to write autobiographically, but not as autobiography? In resisting the autobiographical "I" Cliff resists one of the most consequential trace marks of Europeanization on the colonial subject. Yet hers is not a wholesale refusal of autobiographical remembering since she creates narrators deeply invested in assessing the effects of various modes of self-narrating. Imagining a younger version of herself requires her to cross over to the other in herself via a politics of memory. And she does so through what George Lipsitz defines as counter-memory, remembering that "combin[es] linear history and orally transmitted popular memory" in order to subject linear history to "the standard of collective memory and desire."[69]

The narrators' voices in these novels are intensely autobiographical. They call attention to themselves as narrators, refusing to suture the edges of their representations. And they call attention to the process of narrating, breaking the memories reproduced in conventional tropes and topoi through various rhetorical strategies. The narrator of *No Telephone to Heaven*, for instance, challenges angrily certain narrative norms in several ways:

1) She disrupts the desire for continuous history and with it the myth of "progress" by resisting linear, teleological time. Shifting from one narrative time to another, without offering comfortable segues to the reader, she makes of time and thus of remembering a universe of folds. In such a universe acts of remembering are unsuturings as well as suturings, unmakings and remakings of the past.
2) She shifts linguistic registers, familiar as she is with standard English and with patois—what Edward Kamau Brathwaite terms "submerged" or "nation language." Thus linguistic continuity is frayed by the heteroglossia of Creolité.
3) She routes her politics of remembering England's master narratives (for instance, *Jane Eyre* and *The Tempest*) through the readings of other West Indian writers, most prominently Jean Rhys. In this way she attests to her own "mastery" of the canon (the genres of official memory, autobiography among them) and claims her affiliation with a community of mis/rememberers.

Through this politics of remembering, the narrator of *No Telephone to Heaven*, like the "historians" described in the epigraph to this section, clips the sutures of official memories that function to seal the frayed edges of the traumatic past; for these sutures bind infected and infecting representations.

Through her narrators, then, Cliff dismembers the universal subject of bourgeois individualism, the traditional autobiographical "I." And she strains against the psychologization of memory implicit in certain modes of autobiography because remembering the past is not merely personal but consequentially social and political. Cliff refuses as well any recourse to an "authentic" and "essential" subject outside the legacy of colonial history. Thus she rejects what Aijaz Ahmad describes as "the ideational logic of this cultural differentialism" which "privilege[s] self-representation over all other kinds of representation and ... treat[s] self-representation as a moment of absolute authenticity, as if between the self and its representation there could be no moment of bad faith or false consciousness."[70]

With her politics of remembering Cliff achieves an alternative notion of the past than the past of "progress" or the nostalgic past of identity essentialists. In this sense she shares with Ella Shohat a notion of the subjugated past "not as a static fetishized phase to be literally reproduced, but as fragmented sets of narrated memories and experiences on the basis of which to mobilize contemporary communities."[71] Further, she complicates the utility of recourse to a fixed identity, to any "true" self beneath the history of rememberings, as she poses identity, according to Judith Raiskin, as "at once shifting and strategic and psychically 'real.'"[72] Through her narrators Cliff disrupts the autobiographical imperative at the same time that she affirms autobiographical memory as the grounds for a critique of experience.

Ultimately, Cliff turns away from the freedom to choose an identity (a politics of individualism) to a power to choose an identity by remembering differently (a resistance politics).[73] Self-locating, whatever its limitations, is necessary to this memoro-politics. To resist autobiographical practices *tout court* would mean to be possessed by an oppositional logic that is one of the most disabling legacies of post/colonialism. To fold autobiographical practices into an imaginative engagement with the politics of experience, to do and undo autobiographies through the mobius strip of history and collective myth, is to "open up," as Jennifer Drake observes for art activisms generally, "routes to action beyond reaction."[74]

Notes

1. Michelle Cliff, *The Land of Look Behind* (Ithaca, NY: Firebrand Books, 1985) 105. All further references are to this edition and will be given in the text preceded by *LLB*.
2. Opal Palmer Adisa, "Journey into Speech—A Writer between Two Worlds: An Interview with Michelle Cliff," *African American Review* 28.2 (Summer 1994): 273–81; 280.
3. Caren Kaplan, "Resisting Autobiography: Out-Law Genres and Transnational Feminist Studies." *De/Colonizing the Subject: The Politics of Gender in Women's Autobiography*, ed. Sidonie Smith and Julia Watson (Minneapolis: University of Minnesota Press, 1992) 115–38; 116.
4. Bill Ashcroft, Gareth Griffiths, and Helen Tiffin, *The Empire Writes Back: Theory and Practice in Post-Colonial Literatures* (London: Routledge, 1989) 114.
5. Aijaz Ahmad, "The Politics of Literary Postcoloniality," *Race & Class* 36.3 (1995): 1-20; 7.
6. There are a variety of terms used to designate subjects struggling with the legacies of imperialist ideologies and their construction of difference in subordination: "marginalized," "minoritized," "postcolonial." I have invoked the term "de/colonizing subject" to signal the condition of mobility, the ongoing process of crossing back and forth along that slash that both sutures and divides the experience of subjection and the claims of agency and resistance.
7. Homi K. Bhabha, *The Location of Culture* (New York: Routledge, 1994) 236.
8. Audre Lorde, "The Master's Tools Will Never Dismantle the Master's House" (1979), *Sister Outsider: Essays and Speeches* (Trumansburg, NY: The Crossing Press Feminist Series, 1984) 110–13; 112.
9. Iain Chambers, *Migrancy, Culture, Identity* (London: Routledge, 1994) 79.
10. *The Empire Writes Back*, 84.
11. Homi Bhabha, "Of Mimicry and Men: The Ambivalence of Colonial Discourse," *October* 28 (1984): 125–33.

12 Joan Borsa, "Towards a Politics of Location: Rethinking Marginality," *Canadian Women Studies* 11 (1990): 36-39; 39.
13 Chantal Mouffe, "Feminism, Citizenship, and Radical Democratic Politics," *Feminists Theorize the Political*, eds. Judith Butler and Joan W. Scott (New York: Routledge, 1992) 369-84; 376.
14 Judith Butler, *Bodies That Matter: On the Discursive Limits of "Sex"* (New York: Routledge, 1993) 15.
15 Judith V. Emberley, *Thresholds of Difference: Feminist Critique, Native Women's Writings, Postcolonial Theory* (Toronto: University of Toronto Press, 1993) 141. Emberley is drawing upon the work of Paul Tennant, "Native Indian Political Organization in British Columbia, 1900-1969: A Response to Internal Colonialism," *BC Studies* 55 (Autumn 1982): 3-49, who in turn is invoking a phrase of Fredric Barth's (qtd. in Tennant 7).
16 Dipesh Chakrabarty, "Marx after Marxism: History, Subalternity and Difference," *Meanjean* 3 (Spring 1993): 421-34; 433. Chakrabarty describes history as "this gift of modernity to many peoples" (433).
17 Mouffe 382. The phrase is from Mouffe's discussion of the project of feminism: "Feminism, for me, is the struggle for the equality of women. But this should not be understood as a struggle for realizing the equality of a definable empirical group with a common essence and identity, women, but rather as a struggle against the multiple forms in which the category 'woman' is constructed in subordination" (382).
18 Michelle Cliff, *Abeng* (1984; New York: Dutton, 1990). All further references are to this edition and will be given in the text preceded by *A*.
19 Chandra Talpade Mohanty, "Cartographies of Struggle: Third World Women and the Politics of Feminism," *Third World Women and the Politics of Feminism*, ed. Chandra Talpade Mohanty, Ann Russo, and Lourdes Torres (Bloomington, IN: Indiana University Press, 1991) 1-47; 38-39.
20 Katherine Nelson, "The Psychological and Social Origins of Autobiographical Memory," *Psychological Science* 4.1 (Jan. 1993): 7-14; 7.
21 Bessel A. Van der Kolk and Onno Van der Hart, "The Intrusive Past: The Flexibility of Memory and the Engraving of Trauma," *Trauma: Explorations in Memory*, ed. Cathy Caruth (Baltimore, MD: Johns Hopkins University Press, 1995) 158-82; 160.
22 Nelson, 12. Nelson proposes that this ability to understand narrative memory structures, which are part of cultural and familial narrative practices, occurs in the late pre-school years. Children learn how to remember and what to remember and how to tell about their memories.

23 Paul Connerton, *How Societies Remember* (Cambridge: Cambridge University Press, 1989) 37. I am indebted to Linda Warley for pointing me to the Connerton discussion of memory. Linda Warley, "Locating Subjects: Contemporary Canadian and Australian Autobiography," Diss. University of Alberta, Fall 1994.

24 Antonio R. Damasio, *Descartes' Error: Emotion, Reason, and the Human Brain* (New York: G.P. Putnam's Sons, 1994) 239.

25 Connerton 102.

26 Stephen Rose, *The Making of Memory: From Molecules to Mind* (New York: Doubleday, 1992) 326.

27 Pierre Nora, "Between Memory and History: Les Lieux de Mémoire," *History and Memory in African-American History* (New York: Oxford UP, 1994) 284–300; 285.

28 Nora 289.

29 Nora 284.

30 Nora 289.

31 Michel Foucault, *Language, Counter-Memory, Practice: Selected Essays and Interviews*, trans. Sherry Simon, ed. Donald Bouchard (Ithaca, NY: Cornell University Press, 1980) 214.

32 Ian Hacking, *Rewriting the Soul: Multiple Personality and the Sciences of Memory* (Princeton: Princeton University Press, 1995) 214.

33 Nora 292.

34 Michelle Cliff, *No Telephone to Heaven* (New York: Dutton, 1987) 127. All further references are to this edition and will be given in the text preceded by *NTH*.

35 Julia Watson, "Ordering the Family: Genealogy as Autobiographical Pedigree," *Getting a life: Everyday Uses of Autobiography*, ed. Sidonie Smith and Julia Watson (Minneapolis: University of Minnesota Press, 1996) 297–323; 297.

36 As Judith Raiskin observes, Cliff's choice of the last name "Savage" to mark Boy's patronym ironically undermines his belief in his privilege and his "whiteness." "Inverts and Hybrids: Lesbian Rewritings of Sexual and Racial Identities," *The Lesbian Postmodern*, ed. Laura Doan (New York: Columbia University Press, 1994) 156–72; 164.

37 Watson 298.

38 Watson 299.

39 "Ambivalent when not silent about the historically dispossessed . . . and invisible (women, rootless adventurers, orphans, the adopted), genealogical narrative, in graphing the history of some, defaces many others" (Watson 299).

40 Watson 298–99.

41 Michel Foucault, "Nietzsche, Genealogy, History," *The Foucault Reader*, ed. Paul Rabinow (New York: Pantheon Books, 1984) 82.

42 "The indeterminacy of the past" and "the past under a new description" are phrases I take from Hacking's discussion of the ways in which the remembering subject creates an altered history of the past.

43 See Dean MacCannell, *The Tourist: A New Theory of the Leisure Class* (Berkeley, CA: University of California Press, 1989) 91-108.

44 MacCannell 83.

45 Michelle Cliff, in Judith Raiskin, "The Art of History: An Interview with Michelle Cliff," *The Kenyon Review* 15.1 (Winter 1993): 57-71; 68.

46 This is the phrase Cliff uses in *The Land of Look Behind*.

47 In interviews Cliff recalls a painful childhood memory in which her parents seek out her diary, break its lock, and humiliate her by reading it aloud in front of her. "That incident really shut me down as a writer" ("Journey into Speech" 274).

48 Linda Anderson, "At the Threshold of the Self: Women and Autobiography," *Women's Writing: A Challenge to Theory*, ed. Moira Monteith (Brighton: Harvester, 1986) 54-71; 59.

49 Anne Frank, *The Diary of Anne Frank: The Critical Edition*, ed. David Barnouw and Gerrold van der Stroom, trans. Arnold J. Pomerans and B. M. Mooyaart-Doubleday (New York: Doubleday, 1989) text-b, 6/20/42, 181.

50 *The Diary of Anne Frank* 6/20/42, 180.

51 Valerie Raoul, "Women and Diaries: Gender and Genre," *Mosaic* 22.3 (1989): 57-65; 60.

52 See Raoul for a discussion of the diary as "inventory, a sort of memory bank in which one makes deposits, ensuring that nothing is lost, and creating a reserve which may be drawn on later, with interest" (61).

53 Joan W. Scott, "Experience," *Feminists Theorize the Political*, ed. Judith Butler and Joan W. Scott (New York: Routledge, 1992) 22-40; 39.

54 Raoul 61.

55 Rob Shields, *Places on the Margin: Alternative Geographies of Modernity* (New York: Routledge, 1991) 39. I am indebted to Christine Bucher for bringing this passage to my attention. Cf. Chris Prentice, "The Interplay of Place and Placelessness in the Subject of Post-Colonial Fiction," *SPAN: Journal of the South Pacific Association for Commonwealth Literature and Language Studies* 31 (January 1991): 63-84.

56 Thomas Cartelli, "After *The Tempest*: Shakespeare, Postcoloniality, and Michelle Cliff's New, New World Miranda," *Contemporary Literature* 36 (Spring 1995): 82-102.

57 Sidonie Smith, "Performativity, Autobiographical Practice, Resistance," *a/b: Auto/Biography Studies* 10.1 (Spring 1995): 17-33; 19.

58 Chakrabarty 431.
59 Gayatri Spivak, "'Three Women's Texts and a Critique of Imperialism," *Feminisms: An Anthology of Literary Theory and Criticism*, ed. Robyn R. Warhol and Diane Price Herndl (New Brunswick, NJ: Rutgers University Press; 1991) 798–814; 802.
60 Spivak 803.
61 Spivak 801.
62 Mary Louise Pratt, *Imperial Eyes: Travel Writing and Transculturation* (New York: Routledge, 1992) 6.
63 Michelle Cliff, *Claiming an Identity They Taught Me to Despise* (Watertown, MA: Persephone Press, 1980) 30–31.
64 I am indebted to Rhonda Knight for suggesting to me this connection between sacred relic and excluded otherness.
65 Nora 285.
66 Scott, "Experience" 25–26.
67 George Lipsitz, "Myth, History, and Counter-Memory," *Politics and the Muse: Studies in the Politics of Recent American Fiction*, ed. Adam J. Sorkin (Bowling Green, OH: Bowling Green University Press, 1989) 161–78;162.
68 Kaplan, "Resisting Autobiography" 115–38.
69 Lipsitz 174. Lipsitz differentiates his concept of counter-memory from that of Foucault, for whom counter-memory "must record the singularity of events outside of any monotonous finality" (139). For Lipsitz Foucault's take on counter-memory of details and accidents is too pessimistic to sustain an emancipatory rhetoric of memory.
70 Ahmad 16.
71 Ella Shohat, "Notes on the 'Post-Colonial,"' *Social Text* 31–32 (Spring 1992): 99–114; 109.
72 Raiskin, "Inverts and Hybrids" 167.
73 I am indebted to Jennifer Drake for refining this distinction between the freedom to choose and the power to choose (205).
74 Jennifer Drake, "Art Activism America: Cultural Hybridity and Representation," (Dissertation, Binghamton University, June 1996) 32.

20

NARRATIVES AND RIGHTS: *ZLATA'S DIARY* AND THE CIRCULATION OF STORIES OF SUFFERING ETHNICITY (SMITH 2006)

At this historical moment, the human rights regime is the primary global project for managing injustice and immiseration around the world (Farmer 49), and life stories are at once ground and grist of rights work, rights instrumentalities, and rights politics. This conjunction of life narration, broadly defined, and contemporary human rights activisms, is indeed, as Kay Schaffer and I argue in *Human Rights and Narrated Lives: The Ethics of Recognition*, a productive and problematic yoking of the decidedly intimate with the global.[1] Since the language of human rights is the contemporary *lingua franca* for addressing the problem of suffering (Ignatieff 7), the attachment of personal storytelling to the discourse and the institutions of the human rights regime enables survivors of and witnesses to injury and harm to make their grievances public and to draw attention to specific environments of suffering around the world. At the same time, this yoking of personal narrative and international rights politics affects the kinds of life stories and the narrative subject positions that can gain a global audience.

Take, for instance, the post-Cold War resurgence of ethnic nationalism, with the attendant reorganization of politics in Eastern Europe, that has set large numbers of people in motion—into refugee camps, resettlement programs, and diasporic communities in receiving nations such as the United States. Under violent assault, displaced, haunted by traumatic memories, members of ethnic communities turn to life storytelling to extend global recognition of the violence unleashed against people on the basis of their ethnic identification. Their acts of narration emerge out of local contexts of rights violations. But to the extent that local movements "go international," these witnesses participate through their storytelling in global processes that create a climate for the intelligibility, reception, and recognition of new stories about ethnicity under assault. Gillian Whitlock calls this breakthrough to public attention a "discursive threshold" (144).

Through their stories of ethnic suffering, witnesses expose the violence inflicted by those pursuing the project of ethnic nationalism as a goal of state formation. They also reveal the complexities and conundrums involved in telling stories of ethnic difference and grievance through frameworks and institutions founded on the concept of abstract universality. For many witnesses, the embeddedness of stories of ethnic suffering in the discourses, institutions, and practices of the human rights regime provides the previously unheard and invisible a narrative framework, a context and occasion, an audience, and a subject position from which to makes claims. And yet, in order to circulate their stories within the global circuits of the human rights regime and bring crises of violence and suffering to a larger public, witnesses give their stories over to journalists, publishers, publicity agents, marketers, and rights activists whose framings of personal narratives participate in the commodification of suffering, the reification of the universalized subject position of innocent victim, and the displacement of historical complexity by the feel-good opportunities of empathetic identification.

This case of personal storytelling in the regime of human rights suggests how it is that life narration reproduces, is animated by, and contributes to a paradox at the heart of human rights discourse and practice: the uneasy enfolding of the universal in the ethnic particular. Elicited, framed, produced, circulated, and received within the contemporary regime of human rights, the life story of ethnic suffering at once ennobles an authentic (and sentimentalized) voice of suffering and depersonalizes that voice precisely because of the commodification of suffering in the global flows of the human rights regime. Emerging from a local site of ethnic struggle, the story enters the Western-dominated global circuits through which it can lose its local specificity. It can reach global audiences far from its point of origin, there to be interpreted and reproduced in unpredictable ways, some of which might universalize suffering and elide difference.

In this essay, I cannot possibly do justice to the complexities of the conjunction of life storytelling and the contemporary regime of human rights as that conjunction captures and complicates transnational ethnic formations and the remembering of suffering at this historical moment. What I can do here is to locate one published narrative of besieged ethnicity in Eastern Europe that circulated in the United States, Zlata Filipović's *Zlata's Diary: A Child's Life in Sarajevo*, and elucidate some of the contradictory effects of the commodification of narratives of suffering ethnicity through a rights regime that attaches abstract universality to ethnic difference under assault. I do so in order to assess what we might learn about the mobilization and globalization of personal stories of ethnic suffering in a human rights regime that serves as one of the central "managers" of ethnicity today.[2]

Zlata's Diary and the Ethics of Ethnic Identities

Reflecting on the dynamic relay between the ethnic, the national, and the diasporic, Ien Ang notes that "the rise of militant, separatist neo-nationalisms in Eastern Europe and elsewhere in the world signals an intensification of the appeal of ethnic absolutism and exclusionism which underpin the homeland myth, and which is based on the fantasy of a complete juncture of 'where you're from' and 'where you're at'" (34). She notes, as have Bruce Robbins and Elsa Stamatopoulou, the power of "the principle of nationalist universalism," or what she describes as "the fantasmatic vision of a new world order consisting of hundreds of self-contained, self-identical nations" (Ang 34; Robbins and Stamatopoulou 425). The struggle to enforce this new world order was dramatically and traumatically witnessed in the events in the former Yugoslavia in the 1990s. In the midst of the "new Europe," the people of the former Yugoslavia found themselves the subjects of salient ethnicities.

In the wake of President Tito's death and the loss of Soviet hegemony in Eastern Europe, the former Yugoslavia fractured into ethnic and (tenuously) multi-ethnic states. Croatia and Slovenia declared independence in 1991. In early March, 1992, the government of Bosnia-Herzegovina held a referendum on independence from the Yugoslav federation (dominated by Serbia), which was boycotted by the Bosnian Serbs. The Bosnian parliament declared independence on April 5, 1992. Before official recognition of the decision by the European Community on April 6, however, wars for ethnic dominance and hegemony erupted in Bosnia. Secessionist Serb paramilitaries armed and launched their bid to gain control of the new country for annexation to the Republic of Serbia. Immediately, the city of Sarajevo came under siege, one that would last until a cease-fire went into effect in late 1995. Inhabitants of the mountain-surrounded, multi-ethnic city of Sarajevo, which had gained the world's attention when it hosted the international athletes and spectators of the 1984 Olympic Games, found themselves trapped inside the blockaded city, forced to organize their everyday lives so as to evade sniper bullets and mortar attacks and to find scarce food and medical supplies. Bosnian Serb paramilitaries, supported by Slobodan Milošević in the Republic of Serbia, pursued a policy of genocide ("ethnic cleansing") for which they have now been held accountable in the international war crimes trials at The Hague. By early 1994 the United Nations reported that some 10,000 people had lost their lives or gone missing, among them 1,500 children; another 56,000 had been wounded, including 15,000 children.³ Eventually, the international community intervened, taking action against the besieging Serbs. As the Serbian paramilitaries lost ground, peace negotiations gained momentum. In October 1995, the United Nations brokered a cease-fire in Bosnia; in December the Dayton Accords were signed, establishing the blueprint for post-war stability, which would involve two autonomous governmental entities, the Federation of Bosnia and Herzegovina (or the Muslim-Croat Federation) and the Republika Srpska. In late February 1996 the Bosnian government declared the siege of Sarajevo officially over.

Throughout the four-year siege, journalists assigned to Sarajevo reported on the realities of life lived under siege, the deaths of noncombatants, and the devastation of the city and its infrastructure. They brought their stories of the siege to an international public. Yet foreign journalists were not the only ones to provide stories of ethnic cleansing and ethnicity under assault to the wider world. Zlatko Dizdarević's *Sarajevo: A War Journal* (1993) chronicled the early years of the siege. Then in late 1993 another personal story reached an international audience, this one the diary of a young girl.

For a two-year period from September 1991 to October 1993, the young Zlata Filipović kept a diary in which she recorded her everyday life in an increasingly besieged Sarajevo. Through her diaristic record of that everyday life, the young Bosnian-Croat described, and sometimes reflected upon, the disintegration of a cosmopolitan way of life and the gradual disruption and degradation of middle class familiality through the war of ethnic nationalisms and the genocidal assault of Bosnian Serb paramilitaries. In the summer of 1993, Zlata shared her diary with her teacher, who subsequently found a publisher in Sarajevo. Through the sponsorship of the International Centre for Peace, UNICEF originally published the diary in Croatian. With the recognition of the diary in Bosnia, Zlata became a "celebrity" victim, labeled "the young Anne Frank" of Sarejevo. Recognizing the affective appeal and power of personalizing the story of the siege through its refraction in the eyes of the young girl, international journalists covering the war turned their attention to "Zlata's story."

Several months after its publication in Sarajevo, a French photographer took a copy of *Zlata's Diary* to Paris where Le Robert Laffont-Fixot made a successful bid to become its French publisher. Le Robert Laffont-Fixot also provided the money and means to fly Zlata and her family from Sarajevo to Paris just before Christmas of 1993. In early 1994 the French translation of the diary appeared as *Journal de Zlata*. In this instance, life writing functioned as a means of life saving. The material diary became a commodity through which a life's sheer survival and betterment could be exchanged. Zlata's diary writing gained her and her family escape from snipers and the bombs of the siege and enabled her to start a new life in Paris (and subsequently Ireland).

From Paris the diary traveled to New York City, where it was auctioned off in a sale conducted by its French publisher. With a bid of $560,000, Viking Penguin (a subsidiary of Penguin Books) won the rights to publish *Zlata's Diary: A Child's Life in Sarajevo* and brought it out in March 1994. After publication in the United States, the diary reached an ever-widening mass audience. Irene Webb of International Creative Management subsequently bought the rights to represent the book in any movie deal. As reported in the *New York Times*, January 19, 1994, Webb announced: "It's like the 'Diary of Anne Frank,' but with a happy ending" (Lyall C20). Upon publication, the English language version of the diary circulated broadly within the United States, becoming "an extraordinary national best seller," according to the book cover. Eventually it moved into the social studies curriculum in the nation's public schools. As one website announces: "Zlata's diary brings Sarajevo home as no news report ever could" (*The Unsung Heroes of Dialogue*).

In the years after the diary's publication, Zlata became a "spokeschild" for the conditions of ethnic genocide and displacement in the former Yugoslavia, appearing through the auspices of the United Nations as an ambassador speaking on behalf of the children of

Bosnia. International attention brought increased interest in the conditions in the former Yugoslavia and, after the cessation of fighting, in the rights of the child internationally. In 1995 Zlata appeared as a special guest at the 1995 Children's World Peace Festival in San Francisco. The attention garnered by the diary and its circulation within the United States and Europe produced an aura-effect around Zlata herself, elevating her and legitimating her as a "universal" voice of the child suffering from human rights abuses. Since those years, Zlata has continued as an activist on behalf of the human rights of children, helping to launch UNICEF reports on the impact of armed conflict on children. Her diary continues to be highlighted as suggested reading on websites mounted by activists working on behalf of the UN Convention on the Rights of the Child. During the summer of 2004, a stage version of *Zlata's Diary*, produced by Communicado Productions, toured Scotland. Though no longer a child, Zlata continues to speak on behalf of besieged childhood from her home in Dublin.

Reflections on This Story of Suffering Ethnicity

Inter-ethnic appeals and the production of collective memory

Through the publication of the diary in the west, "Zlata" becomes a marketable archetype of the suffering victim of ethnic nationalism in extremis. The publication of her story of lost childhood, of innocence under assault, is meant to lend immediacy to calls for intervention on the part of the international community in the ethnic war in Bosnia and the organized acts of genocide carried out in service to nationalist myths and the nationalist "fantasy of a utopic space to be occupied by all those who suffered 'the same' violence at the hands of the enemy" (Wilson 16).[4] And yet, the case of *Zlata's Diary* suggests how interethnic the appeal to ethnicity under assault becomes.

Within *Zlata's Diary* and within its zones of circulation and reception, Jewish ethnicity comes to underwrite the aura of suffering of a largely unmarked Croatian ethnicity. Here is an instance in which one ethnicity gets attached to another ethnicity globalized in world memory through a particular mode of life writing, the child's diary. Zlata herself invokes the comparison to Anne Frank early in her *Diary*. Like Anne Frank she chooses a name for her diary. Writing on Monday, March 30, 1992, she opens her entry with "Hey, Diary! You know what I think? Since Anne Frank called her diary Kitty, maybe I could give you a name too" (27). In all subsequent entries Zlata addresses the diary as "Mimmy," projecting an affectionate and interested interlocutor and keeper of her secrets. Moreover, already in 1993 in Sarajevo, Zlata, at thirteen, was called "the young Anne Frank" (Di Giovanni, v). The identification of Zlata's story with the story of Anne Frank, its modeling upon the earlier text, its adoption of the earlier diarist's mode of address to an interlocutor: all these features suggest the way in which the "authenticity" of this contemporary girl, this "Zlata," derives from the earlier editing and marketing of "Anne Frank" as a figure of universalized innocence and heroic suffering whose celebrity can be borrowed in making claims about the struggle against racial violence and ethnic cleansing.

In Zlata's self-positioning in her diary as a modern-day Anne Frank and in the marketing of "Zlata" as a new "Anne Frank," both narrator and marketer assume the global resonance of the iconic figure of Anne Frank, assume that "Anne Frank" will be collectively remembered as having been tragically lost in the Holocaust. The affective appeal of the Sarajevan girl's story of lost childhood becomes intelligible to a broad educated readership through the global aftereffects of collective world memory of another "ethnic" girl's narrative of lost girlhood and lost life. The haunting remains of "Anne Frank," and the aura of the Holocaust as paradigmatic event of twentieth-century genocide, attaches itself to this "child's" narrative as Zlata and her publishers attach her story to that of Anne Frank, who has, through her widely read *Diary*, as the website for the Anne Frank Foundation states, "become a worldwide symbol representing all victims of racism, anti-Semitism and fascism. She stands for victims who lived at the same time as she did just as much as for the victims of today. The foremost message contained in her *Diary* sets out to combat all forms of racism and anti-Semitism" (Anne Frank Foundation). In this instance, Jewish ethnicity functions as an ethnicity of reference in the globalization of the human rights regime.

This aspect of the production and circulation of *Zlata's Diary* within the regime of human rights points to ethnic remembering and storytelling as an historical effect of transethnic comparisons; an inter-ethnic energy distributed across unevenly remembered events in world memory. The forces of globalization, Clifford Bob notes, offer victims and activists responding to ethnic violence "symbols of oppression and repertoires of contention" through which to organize and project their local grievances in an international arena (134). Brent Edwards argues that "the level of the international is accessed unevenly by subjects with different historical relations to the nation" (7). I would adapt his argument to make the point that the level of the transnational is accessed unevenly by ethnic subjects with different historical relations to the global circuits of world memory.

The Depoliticization of a Globalized Ethnic Suffering

In her critique of the sentimentalization of suffering, Karyn Ball has called for the comparative study of traumatic histories in order, she writes, "to forge links among traumatic histories that would raise Americans' historical consciousness and promote their sense of civic responsibility" (15). Ball's is a call for comparative studies of histories of suffering, necessary to complicating any one model of traumatic remembering, any one paradigm for understanding witness testimony, and any singular model of possibilities for recovery and recognition. In one sense we might read *Zlata's Diary* as pursuing, at once consciously and unwittingly, what Ball describes as a "strategy of comparison in order to forge links among traumatic histories" by yoking "Zlata" and "Anne Frank." Here is a strategy of comparison in action. And yet, this strategy of comparison from the ground up, as it were, and through the perspective of an adolescent immersed in a globalized popular culture, may not so much illuminate the incommensurable differences and the specificities of ethnic histories as it would effect the flattening of history through an appeal to empathetic, de-politicized sentimentality.

As a text commanding response and responsible action, *Zlata's Diary* is represented and marketed in ways that sentimentalize the suffering Bosnian-Croat subject by lifting that subject outside history and politics. The commodification of stories of ethnic suffering obscures the complex politics of historical events, stylizes the story to suit an educated international audience familiar with narratives of individual triumph over adversity, evokes emotive responses trained on the feel-good qualities of successful resolution, and often universalizes the story of suffering so as to erase incommensurable differences and the horror of violence. The commodification of the young girl's diary gives us a version of the story of "Anne Frank"—but with a happy ending.

Yet there is more to the relationship established between the contemporary Zlata and the 1940s Anne Frank. The forces of commodification have framed the earlier diary as well. In successive decades since its initial publication, *The Diary of Anne Frank* has been edited and interpreted, re-edited and re-interpreted, marketed and circulated, to give some of its audiences an "Americanized" "Anne Frank" situated not in a determinative ethnicity but as an adolescent subject inspiring hope and promise "for everyone." As an early reviewer of the stage version of the *Diary* wrote in 1955, "Anne Frank is a Little Orphan Annie brought into vibrant life" (*New York Daily News* 6 October 1955, qtd. in Rosenfeld). Alvin H. Rosenfeld suggests that the early version of the diary and the 1955 stage play based on the diary, as adapted by Goodrich and Hackett, present "an image of Anne Frank that would be widely acceptable to large numbers of people in the postwar period . . . one characterized by such irrepressible hope and tenacious optimism as to overcome any final sense of a cruel end" (251-2). He further elaborates how the play and its reviews erase the haunting marks of ethnic difference, eliding references to the Jewishness of the Frank family and playing up the figure of the "universal" teenager struggling with her own adolescence and hopeful about the future. The Jewish particularities of the Anne Frank who lived in the attic and died in Bergen-Belsen are suppressed in order to broadcast a story of universal inspiration. Made into a story that "speaks" to "everyone" about what Hanno Loewy points to as "the personalized world of family experience" (156), *The Diary of Anne Frank* becomes a story that can no longer speak of ethnic difference. The iconic "Anne Frank" becomes an abstract universal "detached from her own vivid sense of herself as a Jew" (Rosenfeld 257). Rosenfeld defines Anne Frank as a "contemporary cultural icon" (244), whose name is so well-known that "[t]o the world at large" the 1.5 million children who perished in the Holocaust "all bear one name—that of Anne Frank" (243).[5] "Anne Frank" has become the child that died in the genocidal Holocaust.

The production, circulation, and reception of Zlata's story of ethnicity under assault as "the deepest truth about the Bosnia situation" has had the effect of "leech[ing]," according to David Rieff, "the Bosnian tragedy of its complexity" (32). If the category of the ethnic, and the global visibility and saliency of particular ethnic identifications, are historical effects of a modernity founded on the articulation of universal categories of abstract equality (see Kazanjian 4–27), then the trackings of ethnicities enfolded in one another at once create a superfluity of the particularities of difference and cancel differences through the abstract equality (a universalism) of those who share suffering. The figure of the child commodified in the global flows of the rights regime and its management of ethnicity becomes the sentimental public face of ethnic trauma and the violence of ethnic nationalism, the essentialized figure of the community's "victim" and its victimization. To put it another way, "Zlata," with her invocation of "Anne Frank," becomes a universalized category, ethnicity's besieged child.

The Remains of Ethnic Suffering

The commodification of ethnic suffering also contributes to the ethnic as a site of sentimental attachment. For members of communities experiencing contemporary displacement, ethnicity can function as a trace of continuity across rupture; and stories of ethnic suffering can offer occasions for constituting the remembered past as a resource for understanding identities in the social present (Eller). When *Zlata's Diary* enters into circuits of consumption in the United States and western Europe—through the purchase of publishing and film rights—the narrative begins to circulate in venues where it can be invoked as a marker of Croatian ethnicity under assault, or a lost Bosnian cosmopolitanism, thereby sustaining nationalist narratives of suffering and loss so often central to the imagination of the ethnic as a site of sentimental attachment. Because reading narratives of suffering and loss is not only "a profoundly personal act, belonging to a psychological sphere, but . . . also the effect of inhabiting various cultural spaces" (Bennett and Kennedy 7), published narratives such as this diary produce an archive of memories of "ethnicity." The story might thereby set in motion new releases of affective energies (Guattari 36); and those energies can be put to use in the social struggles over competing rememberings of "Bosnia" and its wars of ethnic nationalisms. This story can become a part of the cultural stories, the reservoir of collective memory upon which ethnic nationalism is both founded and sustained.

For some, then, *Zlata's Diary* participates in the production and circulation of new collective memories (for members of the diasporan Croation community in the United States, for instance), offering a future site of melancholy, what David Eng and David Kazanjian define as the "psychic and material practices of loss and its remains" (5). It puts in play residual glimpses of the past as remembered tradition of interethnic community or ethnic grievance. Contributing to "a contemporary landscape of memory" (Bennett and Kennedy 8) through which future subjects may negotiate their ethnic attachments and pasts, the personal diary may underwrite future historical grievances. This narrative of loss told through the voice of the "innocent" child becomes a site of melancholy which "creates a realm of traces open to signification, a hermeneutic domain of what remains of loss" (Eng and Kazanjian 4). The child becomes the sentimental public figure of ethnic trauma.

The Universalized Innocence of Ethnic Appeals

The marketing of Zlata as a victim/commentator on suffering ethnicity presents the young girl in the subject position of unassailable innocent. As Kay Schaffer and I note in *Human Rights and Narrated Lives*, some survivors of human rights abuses are more easily equated with the subject position of victim than others. The child is, as Hughes D'aeth suggests in his discussion of the film *Rabbit-Proof Fence* (2002), easily the most accessible and readily believable of victim identities. In the context of human rights campaigns, life narrators are expected to take up the subject position of "innocent" victims; and they are expected to be able to occupy that position with moral authority. And yet, the person whose rights are violated cannot always be assumed to occupy the subject position of innocent victim. The marketing of sentimental suffering, especially through a child's-eye narrative viewpoint and the trope of childhood lost, obscures the permeability of the categories of victim and perpetrator, and obscures the relationship of perpetrator to beneficiary. Such stories reinforce the differentiated identities of ethnic victim and ethnic perpetrator, reinforce rather than confuse the moral alignment of innocence and victimization. Begging the question of innocence in childhood, we might say that in human rights discourse and campaigns "the child" is given to speak for the better part of "ourselves," the better part of human nature, the better part of our community. Rieff, in his critique of *Zlata's Diary*, assails the way in which the child is made to speak wisdom, to be positioned as the voice of knowledge (33).[6]

The "innocence" effect is produced through Zlata's self-conscious invocation of the trope of lost childhood and her shifting terms of reference. Within her diary, Zlata is self-conscious about the importance of her narrative, its possible attraction to others.

She even writes about becoming a "personality" after the initial publication of the diary. And once interest is expressed in her diary, she begins to reflect on the situation in Sarajevo in rather poignant ways. Zlata's self-consciousness about her celebrity and her recognition of her role as representative child of Sarajevo emphasizing the tragedy of "lost childhood" (a discourse that comes from the journalists and advocates who take up her story) undoes the truth effect of "innocent child" and the "child's-eye view" otherwise produced through the diary. Already, within the production of the diary, the politics of commodified sentimentality are evident.

The innocence effect is also reinforced through the packaging of *Zlata's Diary* and the paratextual use of photographs that visualize the young girl's story as a sentimentalized drama of lost childhood. One photograph in particular captures "innocence" and the "production of innocence" at the same time. There is a photo of Zlata in bed, framed by the caption: "Zlata, who loves books, reads by candlelight." To capture the picture for mass distribution through global media, the candlelight has to be photographed; photographed, it is overwhelmed and rendered inauthentic by the light from the flash of the bulb. Through such visuals, the authenticity of sentimental childhood is at once produced and exposed as artificial, as the reviewer for *Newsweek* noted (27). My point here is not that the diary is "inauthentic" or "suspect" as witness testimony; it is, rather, that the commercialization of the diary and its immersion in what Lauren Berlant has described as "sentimental politics," here a politics of the ethical (soliciting response and responsibility across social divides), obscures the difficult politics of histories of difference and violence. We see here the modernist project of producing the authority of universalized innocence.

Saving Whose Child?

The paratextual apparatus of the "introduction" to the diary invites the reader to act in response to this child witness and her story. In her Preface, journalist Janine Di Giovanni orients the reader to the text to come, prompting the reader to adopt an activist stance. She writes: "Zlata kept a careful record of the chilling events—the deaths, the mutilations, the sufferings. When we read her diaries, we think of desperation, of confusion and of innocence lost, because a child should not be seeing, should not be living with this kind of horror. Her tragedy becomes our tragedy because we know what is happening in Sarajevo. And still, we do not act" (xii). Di Giovanni establishes a reading praxis that foregrounds the figure of the innocent child and the trope of innocence lost, orienting a global middle-class readership to the "representative" story of all the suffering children of Sarajevo.

Di Giovanni assumes an adult audience implicated, as surrogate parents, in this tragedy. The journalist can address these readers as passive bystanders to massive human suffering. For the journalist introducing the narrative to the Western reader, the point is to spur an affect of shame. Here, as elsewhere in the era of humanitarianism and human rights, images of children and lost childhoods are invoked to shame individuals, communities, nations, and that imagined "international community" into action. Those images become invitations to rescue. And the reader is addressed as the universal parent, called to respond as the parent of all children. The diary and its paratexts shift the register of appeal from the particularity of the ethnic subject under duress to the universal abstraction of the child of human rights. But the appeal of "the child" in need of saving is that the child is everybody's child and thus nobody's specific child in a specific location.

There is yet another large audience for Zlata's diary, other young people in classrooms in Europe and the United States. An "innocent" victim of and witness to ethnicity besieged, Zlata writes from her location within a middle-class family. And her diary is marketed to a broad middle-class readership educated about, familiar with, and prepared to respond to stories of childhood suffering. The published version includes a cast of family characters and a photo album, with images of the wholesome, open-faced, smiling Zlata, a figure of the innocent child tugging on the sympathies of the reader. The home is middle-class and the occasions of the photos are birthday parties and family outings. The photo album appeals to western readers—both adults and children, presenting a home and a family the educated reader can imagine inhabiting.

Throughout the diary, Zlata's citation of global popular culture resonates in its references with the lives of young people in western Europe and the United States. The constant citation of a global popular culture (a popular culture whose primary, though by no means whole, point of reference is the United States) situates the subject of the diary in a non-differentiated space of consumer adolescence and global youth culture. In this, Zlata is "representative" of a commodified and "universal" adolescent subject knowledgeable about and attentive to the products, icons, celebrities, and self-descriptions of the global marketplace. As she interweaves comments on the common references of global youth culture and the trope of childhood lost, Zlata assumes the subject position of the universal middle-class child anxious about childhood itself.[7]

The international community looked on, watched the war in Bosnia on nightly news, and failed to take decisive action to intervene in the early years of the siege. *Zlata's Diary* made, and continues to make, good reading in the social studies courses of U.S. and European classrooms. But as Thomas Keenan argues so persuasively in his exploration of the mutually constituting intersection of endless images of suffering and political inaction, "images, information, and knowledge will never guarantee any outcome, nor will they force or drive any action. They are, in that sense, like weapons or words: a condition, but not a sufficient one" (114). And yet Zlata herself gained stature as a spokesperson for the UN's covenant on the rights of the child. She and her story continue to spur occasions for children from around the world to connect through organized and online activities. In this, Zlata and her diary have participated in and contributed to a new arena of human rights activism.

We can, however, turn the argument around once again. Lisa Makman has observed that children themselves have now become the crusading upholders of the rights of the child to a childhood perceived by increasing numbers of people in industrialized democracies as under assault. Makman tracks recent UN discourse about "the world's children" and attributes this focus on childhood under assault to cultural anxieties, circulating in the mainstream media in the United States, about the "ero[sion]" of a "universal" innocent childhood due to the influences of new technologies and global media (289, 291) Through the commodification of stories of ethnic suffering and the sentimentalized "channels of affective identification and empathy" (Berlant 53), ethnicity's besieged child is becoming the universally besieged child of a universally besieged childhood.

Conclusion

As a marker of identity and difference, ethnicity is an effect of modernity rather than a residue from the past prior to modernity. Ethnicity, Jack David Eller suggests, is "a radical appropriation and application of otherness to the practical domain" (1997). Thus, modernity involves what Rey Chow describes as "the systematic *codification and management of ethnicity*" (11). The contemporary regime of human rights is a primary site for this project of codification and management. In human rights campaigns targeted on ethnic rights in the midst of ethnic nationalism in extremis, ethnicity has to be "managed" as immobile difference through a modernist fiction of a totalizing ethnicity (a definitive inside to a collectivity) under assault from an outside (see Chow). Moreover, human rights discourse and campaigns are responses to, and in turn engage in, the production of salient ethnicities and ethnicities of reference.

This case study of *Zlata's Diary* and the problematics of ethnic suffering exposes the "logical contradictions" and "epistemic paradoxes" (Kadir 14) enfolded within and enfolding the production, circulation, and reception of personal narratives in the regime of human rights. Abstract universality and ethnic difference are both "mythographic reductions" at once underwriting, energizing, and reconfiguring the human rights regime. Through the pathways and byways of global circuits localized and local circuits globalized, the tensions binding abstract universality and ethnic difference release energies that reconnect, diverge, and converge around the international community's struggle with injustice and suffering. I have used *Zlata's Diary* to reflect on the circuits of ethnicity as sentimental politics in the regime of human rights. And so, let me conclude with some observations about the conjunction of the human rights regime and narrations of suffering ethnicity.

Narratives enlisted in and attached to human rights campaigns participate in the articulation of a history of suffering and loss attached to ethnic identity and the articulation of communal fictions of ethnicity (imaginings and grievances). Narratives of suffering and loss bind communities sharing some common "ethnic" past (of language, culture, defining events), across their local, national, and diasporic differences at the same time that they appeal to others who do not share that ethnic marker. They provide historical information, intergenerational communication, rallying cries, sites of healing. They offer a means to claim rights and demand redress and also to claim a shared past and shared tradition. They ignite an affective charge attached to identity under assault, project a figure of the victim for political mobilization, and serve as a means of shaming the nation and the international community into acknowledging and redressing claims. Because they are so critical to the contemporary regime of human rights, stories such as that presented in *Zlata's Diary* become cultural capital, for individuals and for ethnic communities. Sometimes the publication and circulation of a specific narrative becomes a "focusing event" (Bob, 136, citing Kingdon, 99–100) that galvanizes international attention and action, as was the case with Rigoberta Menchú's *I, Rigoberta Menchú: An Indian Woman in Guatemala* (1984), which gained recognition for the situation of Guatemala's indigenous community in its struggle against a repressive state.[8]

Emanating from local settings that are inflected by and inflect the global, life stories are taken up in a host of formal and informal, material and symbolic, sites and networks where they undergo further transformations. In effect, narratives of suffering such as *Zlata's Diary* are produced, circulated, and received within an intricate, uneven, and overlapping set of spheres: the local, the national, the regional, the global. They also travel within overlapping, uneven, and intersecting zones of ethnic identification and affiliation: the diasporic, the transethnic; the national ethnic; and the local ethnic—all heterogeneous zones of identification and historical tracings that are differently located, differently accessed. Moreover, such stories unfold through and enfold overlapping, uneven, and contradictory appeals to ethnic singularity and abstract universality at once.

Finally, commodified narratives of suffering ethnicity enter a global field saturated with multiple modes of appeal and cues to interpretation. They reach for readers/viewers/the public, calling that public into definition (as a middle-class public of parents and children; as an ethnic public of dispersed Bosnian-Croat refugees). As with all such appeals, suggests Thomas Keenan, "the public is the possibility of being a target and of being missed" (108).

Notes

I am indebted to Kay Schaffer for her comments on certain aspects of the framing and marketing of *Zlata's Diary*. I am indebted to Laurie McNeill for conversation about Anne Frank's diary. I am also indebted to John Cords and Elspeth Healey for their research assistance.

1 In our study, we look expansively at the multiple sites of personal storytelling attached to human rights campaigns: published life narratives; fact-finding in the field; handbooks and websites; nationally-based human rights commissions; human rights commission reports; collections of testimonies; stories in the media; and the scattered everyday venues through which narratives circulate.
2 See Chow on the management of ethnicity (11).

3 See the *Final Report* of the United Nations Commission of Experts established pursuant to Security Council resolution 780 (1992) submitted May 27 (United Nations, 1994).
4 Wilson here cites the work of Glenn Bowman and his discussion of the ways in which "the narrating of past mass violations plays a constitutive role in the formation of all nationalisms" (qtd. Wilson 16). Wilson does not give a reference for the Bowman paper.
5 As Rosenfeld makes clear, "Anne Frank" is remembered differently in different communities at different historical moments. After analyzing the Americanization of "Anne Frank," he goes on to explore the reception of the diary by Germans and by Jewish writers and intellectuals and concludes that "in both Germany and Israel one finds a common history marked by a common symbol but shaped by very different motives and yielding diverse interpretations of the past" (277).
6 Rieff also indicts the way she is made to speak as a commentator on behalf of Bosnian innocence. Comparing the versions of the diary published in Paris and in the United States and the interpolations added to the Viking Penguin edition, he notes the addition of references to political events and critiques of the leaders and their antics (33-4).
7 Stuart Hall has cautioned that cultural formations may work in contradictory ways. There is at once the force of homogenization and universalization across national and ethnic differences through appeals to global mass culture. There is also the incorporation and reflection back through global mass culture of the specific context of ethnic difference and its histories of suffering (Hall 32). I may be overstating the former case here.
8 For a discussion of the publication and reception of Menchú's narrative, see Smith and Schaffer (29-31) and the essays in Arias.

Works Cited

Ang, Ien. *On Not Speaking Chinese: Living between Asia and the West.* London: Routledge, 2001.

Anne Frank Foundation. *Responsibilities of the Anne Frank-Fonds.* Available: www.annefrank.ch/content/default.htm (accessed September 15, 2004).

Arias, Arturo, ed. *The Rigoberta Menchú Controversy;* with a response by David Stoll. Minneapolis and London: University of Minnesota Press, 2001.

Ball, Karyn. "Trauma and Its Institutional Destinies." *Cultural Critique* 46. Fall (2000): 1-44.

Bennett, Jill, and Rosanne Kennedy. *World Memory: Personal Trajectories in Global Time.* London: Palgrave, 2003.

Berlant, Lauren. "The Subject of True Feeling: Pain, Privacy, and Politics." *Cultural Pluralism, Identity Politics, and the Law*. Eds. Austin Sasat and Thomas R. Kearns. Ann Arbor: University of Michigan Press, 1999. 49–84.

Bob, Clifford. "Globalization and the Social Construction of Human Rights Campaigns." *Globalization and Human Rights*. Ed. Alison Brysk. Berkeley: University of California Press, 2002. 133–47.

"Child of War: The Diary of Zlata Filopović." *Newsweek*, February 28, 1994, 24–27.

Chow, Rey. "Introduction: On Chineseness as a Theoretical Problem." *Boundary 2*, 25.3 (1998): 1–24.

Di Giovanni, Janine. "Introduction." *Zlata's Diary: A Child's Life in Sarajevo*. New York and London: Penguin, 1994. v-xiv.

Dizdarević, Zlatko. *Sarajevo: A War Journal*. Trans. Anselm Hollo. New York: Fromm International, 1993.

Edwards, Brent. *The Practice of Diaspora: Literature, Translation, and the Rise of Black Internationalism*. Cambridge: Harvard UP, 2003.

Eller, Jack David. "Ethnicity, Culture, and 'the Past.'" *Michigan Quarterly Review* 36.4 (1997): 552–601.

Eng, David L., and David Kazanjian. *Loss: The Politics of Mourning*. Berkeley: University of California, 2003.

Farmer, Paul. *Pathologies of Power: Health, Human Rights, and the New War on the Poor*. Berkeley: University of California Press, 2003.

Filipović, Zlata. *Zlata's Diary: A Child's Life in Sarajevo*. New York and London: Penguin, 1994.

Guattari, Félix. *The Three Ecologies*. Trans. Ian Pindar, and Paul Sutton. London: Athlone, 2000.

Hall, Stuart. "The Local and the Global: Globalization and Ethnicity." *Culture, Globalization, and the World-System: Contemporary Conditions for the Representation of Identity*. Ed. Anthony D. King. Minneapolis: University of Minnesota, 1997.

Hughes D'aeth, Tony. "Which Rabbit-Proof Fence? Empathy, Assimilation, Hollywood." Sept. 2002. *Australian Humanities Review*. Available: http://www.lib.latrobe.edu.au/AHR/archive/Issue-September-2002/hughesdaeth.htm. 4 June 2003.

Ignatieff, Michael. *Human Rights as Politics and Idolatry*. Princeton: Princeton University Press, 2001.

Kadir, Djelal. "Introduction: America and Its Studies." *PMLA* 118.1 (2003): 9–24.

Kazanjian, David. *The Colonizing Trick: National Culture and Imperial Citizenship in Early America*. Minneapolis: University of Minnesota, 2003.

Keenan, Thomas. "Publicity and Indifference (Sarajevo on Television)." *PMLA* 117.1 (2002): 104–16.

Kingdon, John. *Agendas, Alternatives, and Public Policies*. New York: HarperCollins, 1984, 2d ed.

Loewy, Hanno. "Saving the Child: The 'Universalisation' of Anne Frank." Trans. Russell West. *Marginal Voices, Marginal Forms: Diaries in European Literature and History*. Ed. Langford, Rachael, and Russell West. Amsterdam: Rodopi, 1999, 156–74.

Lyall, Sarah. "Auction of a War Diary." *New York Times* January 19, 1994, sec. C: 20+.

Makman, Lisa Hermine. "Child Crusaders: The Literature of Global Childhood." *The Lion and the Unicorn* 26 (2002): 287–304.

Menchú, Rigoberta. *I, Rigoberta Menchú: An Indian Woman in Guatemala* (1983). Ed. Elisabeth Burgos-Debray, trans. Ann Wright. London and New York: Verso, 1984.

Rieff, David. "Youth and Consequences: *Zlata's Diary: A Child's Life in Sarajevo*." *The New Republic* March 28, 1994: 31–35.

Robbins, Bruce, and Elsa Stamatopoulou. "Reflections on Culture and Cultural Rights." *The South Atlantic Quarterly* 103.2/3 (2004): 419–34.

Rosenfeld, Alvin H. "Popularization and Memory: The Case of Anne Frank." *Lessons and Legacies: The Meaning of the Holocaust in a Changing World*. Ed. Peter Hayes. Evanston: Northwestern University Press, 1991. 243–78.

Schaffer, Kay and Sidonie Smith. *Human Rights and Narrated Lives: The Ethics of Recognition*. New York: Palgrave Macmillan, 2004.

United Nations. *Final Report of the United Nations Commission of Experts*. 1994. http://www.ess.uwe.ac.uk/comexpert/ANX/VI-01.htm#I.C. Accessed August 15 2004.

The Unsung Heroes of Dialogue. Available: www.un.org/Dialogue/heroes.htm. Accessed February 10, 2004.

Whitlock, Gillian. *The Intimate Empire: Reading Women's Autobiography*. London: Cassell, 2000.

Wilson, Richard A. "The Sizwe Will Not Go Away: The Truth and Reconciliation Commission, Human Rights and Nation-Building in South Africa." *African Studies* 55.2 (1996): 1–20.

21

PARSUA BASHI'S *NYLON ROAD*: THE VISUAL DIALOGICS OF WITNESSING IN IRANIAN WOMEN'S GRAPHIC MEMOIR (WATSON 2016)

[A] *political battle... is taking place in part through the medium of the visual image.*

Judith Butler (827)

Many memoirs by diasporic women in the generations after the 1979 Iranian Revolution and the founding of the Islamic Republic attracted international attention for their accounts of navigating the contradictions of Iran's strict fundamentalist regime. These transnational narratives of upheaval and its aftermath, usually narrated by subjects now living in the West, are often situated by feminist critics within a liberal-humanist framework. Through this framework memoirs such as Azar Nafisi's *Reading Lolita in Tehran* are read as "written for the West," observes Madhi Tourage, because they are taken up by a global readership seeking validation of Enlightenment values.[1] Gillian Whitlock, expanding on this notion of readership, argues that Nafisi's performance of literary authority in her memoir was undoubtedly an ethical act of defying Islamic fundamentalism in Iran at a key moment, but one vulnerable to becoming a "soft weapon." That is, Nafisi's account of reading Western literature and her story of emigration could be wielded, after the events of 9/11, in a marketing campaign for Western intervention in the Middle East when her "ideas [found] a brand" and she became a kind of "commodity" (21–2).

Responding to the global framing of diasporic memoirs, Nima Naghibi calls for a more nuanced reading practice with "a critical diasporic cultural politics [that] focuses on a creative tension between the home and the host country, interrogating the concept of the nation-state, and celebrating a border space that facilitates fluid cultural identities." And she calls for rethinking the narration of the Islamic Revolution in numerous memoirs as a space of "both rupture and possibility, positioning diasporic Iranian women writers as key witnesses to testimonial narratives of loss and suffering" (154). Naghibi's call raises many interesting questions, two of which I will take up: What kinds of representational strategies might make life narratives more resistant to exploitation by campaigns announcing a message of "freedom" and "liberation," and thereby enable a comparative critical cultural politics? And, which autobiographical media offer the affordances to effectively link the personal and the political in ways that promote the telling of stories of crisis and trauma, on the one hand, and of innovative possibility, on the other, as they summon readers to map the "creative tensions" that they set up?

Telling a coming-of-age story set in revolutionary-era Iran, Marjane Satrapi's graphic memoirs, which exploit the multimodal potential of comics to represent tensions between rupture and possibility, have been resoundingly successful. In *Persepolis*, Satrapi innovatively links the protagonist's and her family's experiences of suffering, trauma, and catastrophe to the secret pleasures and riotous good times they experienced, despite all, in revolutionary-era Iran, as well as the trials of becoming an artist in the era of the Islamic Republic. A landmark of graphic inscription and visual storytelling, *Persepolis* was originally published in French in four short volumes, rapidly translated into two English volumes, and made into a feature film that Satrapi drew, wrote, and co-directed, all widely distributed in the Global North. Her appearances on the lecture circuit and TV talk shows in the US and Europe made her a recognized and engaging spokesperson for democracy and women's rights, even as her comics' criticism of the fundamentalist regime made them unavailable in Iran. And Satrapi's elegant stylizations, in black-and-white squared-off figures that capture the contradictions of personal experience in single frames, evoking both German Expressionist woodcuts and the carved iconography of Persepolis, the capital of ancient Persia, are both revelatory and moving. As Hillary L. Chute observes, *Persepolis*' "exploration of extremity" takes place predominantly in the private sphere, but it represents memory and testimony in ways that make Iran's traumatic history legible and politically charged (*Graphic*, 135). Marji's "acts of verbal-visual witnessing" retrace events of the Revolution and its aftermath in order to recover what has been effaced by war (163), making *Persepolis* exemplary of how graphic narratives "reconstruct and repeat in order to counteract" (173). Further, the linkage of young Marji's struggles with sexuality to the traumatic histories of family members and neighbors related in the two volumes of *Persepolis* link its graphic exploration of the personal to a critique of norms of "morality."

Nima Naghibi and Andrew O'Malley similarly observe that *Persepolis* "upsets the easy categories and distinctions that it appears to endorse: between the secular West and the threateningly religious East; between the oppressed and liberated woman (i.e., veiled and unveiled); between domestic and political/public" (245). In so doing, it becomes "a forceful and interventionary response to the current anti-Iranian and anti-Muslim sentiment in the West" (245). They further contend that the ability of *Persepolis* to render young Marji's volatile and changing responses, while simultaneously conveying conflicting perspectives on an issue, hinders viewers from jumping to quick judgments, even as its striking visual imagery elicits empathic responses that overcome Western stereotypes about Muslim women. And yet, Naghibi and O'Malley observe that even *Persepolis* has often been read through a Western humanist filter focused on engaging personal details, such as teenaged Marji's touching costume of jeans jacket, Michael Jackson button, and hijab in *Persepolis I* (131), while ignoring its sharp critique of British and American oil-driven foreign policy and anti-Muslim propaganda.

Assuredly the combination of anguish about the revolution's undermining of a distinguished Persian history and grief at the loss of family members and friends to the regime's persecution makes *Persepolis* a moving and important intervention. It is notable, however, that Satrapi migrated to France in 1993 (and spent the mid-eighties in Vienna during her high-school education), although she affirms her identity as Iranian.² In my view these details do not threaten Satrapi's credibility as a compellingly acute narrator. Nonetheless, it is important to note that she has remade herself as a cosmopolitan diasporic subject. Naghibi acknowledges that disputes around "authenticity" abound in discussions of memoirs by Iranian writers who left in the early post-Revolution years and express nostalgia for the pre-revolutionary past. Those who left have been called "the Iranians of the imagination," as distinguished from "those who stayed behind and suffered through the war and the policies of the Islamic Republic" and want to claim that they are "the 'real' Iranians" (152). While Naghibi does not subscribe to this binary distinction, she observes that "the question of authenticity continues to haunt debates and discussions in the diasporic Iranian community," a tension that Sidonie Smith and I have also explored for other kinds of witness narratives (Note 11, 188–9).³

But Satrapi's is not the only graphic memoir to have tracked how the experience of the Revolution and the Islamic Republic affected both micro- and macro-Iranian histories. Parsua Bashi published her graphic memoir, *Nylon Road*, in a European language, German, in 2006, while she was living as a migrant (her preferred term) in Zürich; it was subsequently translated into English a year later, as well as into Spanish. As I will discuss, its innovative style of visual and verbal dialogics accomplishes two things: it is a tough yet engaging antidote to narratives of nostalgia and victimage, and its dialogical style actively resists appropriation to a liberal humanist point of view. Like Satrapi, Bashi as a girl and young woman identified with socialist-leftist ideological positions and criticized the excesses and abuses of the Revolution and its repressive aftermath. But because Bashi, born three years before Satrapi, did not leave Iran until 2004 (at age 37), her account of living there for decades offers an extended window on the upheaval of revolution and the fundamentalist regime that suggests how ideological shifts threaten, and texture the processes of, memory itself. Both artists generate imaginatively diverse images of their protagonists' growing up as the flux of events plunges them into near-constant change and generates shifting self-definitions. But while Satrapi's story, in both its images and discursive locations, is an evolutionary narrative of becoming a politically aware artist, Bashi's comic is an open-ended dialogic. In *Nylon Road*'s plot the narrator engages serially, and non-chronologically, with eleven sharply contrasted younger "ghost" selves that were shed and "forgotten" after her migration and by whom she is "awakened" to the diversity of her former beliefs and positions, although she is by no means reconverted to any of their stances.[4]

Interestingly, Bashi's innovative use of these avatars places them on the scene of past events in a way similar to how eyewitnesses are positioned, although they are not of course genuine eyewitnesses but visual fictions called up from memory. The eyewitness holds a special status in narrative accounts. The attestation "I was there" makes a unique bid for readers' attention and empathy. In Gillian Whitlock's phrase, the eyewitness serves as a "conduit and a receptor," as "the reporter cultivates moral empathy by a subjective eyewitness account that responds to trauma performatively" (156). As Hillary L. Chute compellingly demonstrates, the affordances of comics enable them to play a particular kind of role in witnessing: the act of "being a witness to oneself" in Chute's term (*Disaster*, 29) can, as it does in testimony, "visually incarnate[e]" the witness to trauma and "express the simultaneity of traumatic temporality and the doubled view of the witness as inhabiting the present and the past" (206).

Of course, a diasporic witness to her former experience of a repressive regime is incapable of literally being an "eyewitness" because migration is the necessary precondition for narrating a story of vulnerability, flight, and presumed relief. Only an on-the-scene journalist or observer can claim eyewitness status for on-site narrating in war or crisis. But some diasporic memoirists are in a stronger position than others to profess as surrogate eyewitnesses to the experience of national upheaval and oppression. In comics Joe Sacco has intriguingly explored this status, as Chute notes, by marshaling an exhaustive repertoire of documentary evidence to supplement what the memory of others or his own absence from the scene cannot reliably supply, as he does in *Footnotes in Gaza*. Bashi's embodied former selves similarly exert pressure, variously expressed, to compel *Nylon Road*'s narrator to constantly negotiate with her memories as embodied subjects who are in "creative tension" with her migrant self and not resolvable into a coherent post-migration identity.

Bashi's strategy of positioning her eleven embodied past selves on site, rather than having her memories recalled by a continuous child narrated I (although she does not reference official archives), dramatizes the narrating "I"'s personal past in the context of shifting events and ideological alignments that her past selves responded to quite differently over the decades in the flux of experience. Her rhetorical tactics and visual tropes for situating self-presentation, while not the "objective" approach of documentary testimony, provide a prismatically multi-sited account of her pre-migration past that contextualizes her post-migration experience differently than that of other diasporic women writers' memoirs, conferring an experiential authority closer to that accorded the eyewitness.

The rhetorical strategy of imagined eyewitnessing also lets Bashi powerfully assert her position. She documents the significant abuses that, as a young woman, she underwent during the early days of the

Republic that exemplify its repressiveness (a severe whipping by the Islamic Court, loss of most of her family and friends through emigration, and loss of custody of her child in a divorce trial); this catalog of humiliations and losses, however, is not defined as *all* that it meant to stay in Iran and work for change after the Revolution. Simultaneously, Bashi can extend her critique to the excesses of neoliberal capitalism, as embodied in her experience in Zürich but visible globally in both practices toward, and media representations of, women. This aspect of her dialogical representation has two effects: it undermines the West's claim to ethical superiority, and it underscores the tendency to represent Islamic women as abject others without distinguishing among the histories and practices of various nations and periods. Bashi's dialogical structure in *Nylon Road*'s sustained montage of past selves ultimately becomes a means of foregrounding the limits placed on women globally by conservative politics, be they "democratic," "socialist," or "religious-fundamentalist."

In sum, Bashi's graphic memoir, with its exponential multiplying of the figure of the drawn and narrated past self, is a challengingly dialogical "read," and one explicitly resistant to being framed in liberal-humanist terms. Yet it has not enjoyed much success in English and is not well-known in either Anglophone nations or Iran, where copies are prohibited from circulating officially.[5] Despite *Nylon Road*'s neglect by English-language readers of comics and life narrative, in my view it merits attention as a case study in how a feminist diasporic graphic memoirist can improvise an innovative visual and verbal strategy for navigating both national politics and global cultural relations.[6]

I. The Search for "Me" in *Nylon Road*

Parsua Bashi is well-positioned to narrate her story. Born into a middle-class family with three children in 1966, over a decade before the Revolution, she refused her parents' urging that she migrate—unlike most of her family and friends—after the establishment of the Islamic Republic. Instead, she studied art at the

University of Tehran when it reopened in 1983 and became a successful, award-winning graphic designer. Bashi encountered difficulties in her personal life, however, after marrying at 23 to escape the pressures the Republic exerted on unmarried women fraternizing with men in public, for which she was sentenced to a severe whipping. She and her husband had a daughter, but she soon found him oppressively dominating and sought a divorce. When the punitive divorce court assigned custody of her daughter to the father, she grieved but eventually was "struck by Cupid's arrow" in 2002 and left Iran in April 2004 for German-speaking Switzerland, although she did not know German, to live in Zürich with Nathanael Su, a well-known jazz musician of Swiss and Cameroonian parentage, whom she married (6, top right).[7] *Nylon Road* originated as a comic whose struggling protagonist has discovered the difficulty of remaking herself abroad, in her thirties, and resuming her artistic career. There she began work on a book of comic drawings.

Parsua Bashi wrote me that her idea of making the comic arose when she experienced "a Vacuum space between my past in Iran and my new life in Zürich" that spurred her to begin "a kind of daily sessions to write about my past, and draw some little pictures only to show to some friends" (Personal Correspondence, 28 Nov. 2015, subsequently referred to as PC). *Nylon Road* thus originated as a form of self-therapy with sketches that Bashi developed into a graphic memoir in collaboration with a translator and editor from Kein & Aber Publishing Company in Zürich. It was awarded the "Cultural Worlds in Switzerland" prize by Pro Helvetica, the Arts Council of Switzerland. Bashi's journey was, however, no one-way trajectory. In 2009, three years after the memoir's publication, she left Zürich and returned to Tehran, where she continues to live, working as a successful graphic designer. She has written other books in Persian that have been translated into German and published.[8] Her return and reintegration are remarkable in light of the focus of *Nylon Road* on the protagonist's discontent with—and sharp criticism of—life in Iran after the Revolution, although speculation on this two-way transit is beyond my inquiry.

As noted above, *Nylon Road* conducts its coming-of-age story as a conversation among versions or avatars of Parsua at various ages that, she says, "came from a real emotional/psychological situation that I was in at the time of writing this book. I had not any model in my mind. In fact I did not even have a concrete plan to write and draw a comic book" (PC).[9] This dialogical set-up of conversations enables her to interrogate notions of identity coherence for subjects caught in conflicting concepts of home, history, and memory amid the ideological perspectives of fundamentalist post-revolutionary Iran, the capitalist Global North, and—less frequently mentioned in Iranian diasporic memoir—the socialism associated with the former Soviet Union. The memoir thus serves as an act of transnational witnessing to Bashi's own experience of double displacement, and resists any final resolution other than the artistic satisfaction of visually and verbally representing her condition.

Both Bashi's creation of an autographic, *Nylon Road*, and her return to Iran three years later, prompt us to read her comic through a doubly "binocular" lens, in Marianne Hirsch's term. That is, its shifts across the gutters of the page suggest Parsua's ambivalence at different historical moments about her location and position (1213). *Nylon Road* serves simultaneously as a dissident history of the Revolution and the Islamic Republic, and a critique of Western consumerism and commodity capitalism that the narrator finds definitive of Swiss and, more generally, Western values; and Parsua, its protagonist, finds no border space, other than on the page of her memoir of double loss. Yet *Nylon Road*'s weighing of the difficulties and costs of migration and resettlement against the experience of repression, violence, and misogyny it identifies as realities of post-revolutionary Iran finds no full resolution. In its treatment of the individual and collective trauma occasioned differently by the Republic and by migration, it belongs to the genre of life writing that Sidonie Smith has termed "crisis comics,"[10] although, unlike most such comics, *Nylon Road* does not include an appeal for readers to bear witness to suffering or contribute to an agency aiding the artist. Rather, its tough yet funny interrogation of the complicity of the world's nations—including Iran and the Islamic Middle East, Europe and the Americas, and the former Soviet socialist bloc—critiques how all of them in different ways conform their citizens to repressive ideologies that discourage independent thinking.

II. The Varied Reception of *Nylon Road*

Nylon Road has had little success in gaining traction in North America, in contrast to its reception in the German-speaking world,[11] where it has attracted a substantial, appreciative readership. With translation into Spanish, it also won readers in Spain. But despite its rapid translation into English (2007), *Nylon Road* is a graphic memoir that, even in this age of comics' popularity, remains almost unknown even among life-writing scholars. The varied reception of *Nylon Road* might be attributed to both the contrasting publishing strategies of its Swiss and American publishers and its differential reception by critics in Europe and North America. The original German edition of the comic was marketed as a kind of double-edged sword—a memoir simultaneously critical of the Islamic Republic and Western neoliberalism that was welcomed in European reviews as a witty and probing intervention into cultural politics. In the *Süddeutsche Zeitung*, a leading German newspaper, Simon Poelchau characterized *Nylon Road* as a thoughtful dialogue among several different embodiments of Parsua about the excesses of both Iran and the West, noting, for example, her sharp quip that in Zürich she enjoys gourmet dining while Iranians are starving under Western-imposed sanctions.[12] In the online journal *Migrazine*, Olivera Stajić observed *Nylon Road*'s substantive interrogation of Islamic fundamentalism and Western feminists' easy rejection of its critique of the limits of their positions.[13] Clearly *Nylon Road* was heralded as a serious contribution to debates about both the place of post-Revolution Iran in global politics and a comic sharply aware of discrepancies between Western humanist ideology and its economic and cultural practices.[14]

In English-language journalism and scholarship, however, *Nylon Road* received little critical attention. An anonymous review in the *Toronto Globe and Mail*—one of the few newspapers to cover it—was, in my view, a cranky misreading: "There's a lot of anger here, not only that of the mullahs and their minions, but that of Bashi, appalled at how more than 2,000 years of Persian history and culture had been lost in the dark backward abyss of religious fanaticism." Online, Jonathan Liu's review in *Wired* was less than informative: "What [*Nylon Road*] really reveals is how little the two cultures really know about each other, let alone being able to understand and sympathize with each other." These reviews offer little insight into the complexity of *Nylon Road*; there are to date, no critical essays on it in English, to my knowledge.[15]

A comparison of the two versions of the cover of *Nylon Road* suggests a possible reason for its lack of impact in North America. The original illustration used for the German and Spanish covers, which does not appear elsewhere in the comic, captures Bashi's dilemma as a diasporic subject caught between conflicting national and political identities (Figure 1). On it, Parsua, the narrating "I", sits in a full-frontal, cross-legged position, gazing at the viewer as she draws on a sketchpad. Each of her stocking-clad legs is inscribed, one with Persian characters, the other with Roman-alphabet letters and numerals.[16] The nylon stockings serve as both a signifier of feminine fashion and a marker of Bashi's uneasy location between opposed cultural and linguistic worlds along, not the silk road of ancient discovery, but the "nylon road" of women's contemporary transnational transmission of image, fashion, and sexuality. As an adult migrant to Switzerland, Parsua is literally situated at a crossroads of conflicting ideological, religious, and social views between the two worlds, Iranian-Muslim and Western-secular, that she inhabits. The iconic image captures her dilemma—how to make this gendered, cultural, religious, and linguistic transition without losing all that she has been and known—and expresses it through the binocular optic of a fashion statement embodying that tension.

Figure 1. Front cover, German edition. Reprinted by permission of Kein & Aber AG, and Parsua Bashi. All rights reserved.

In contrast, the cover of the English-language edition chosen by the British-American publisher, St. Martin's Press, reproduces a frame in the comic depicting a child-woman emerging from a line of shadowy, veiled female figures who are submerged in dark shrouds (Figure 2).

Figure 2. Front cover, English edition. Reprinted by permission of St. Martin's Griffin, and Parsua Bashi. All rights reserved.

She is barefoot, slumped in dejection, and wears only a slip of a dress as she stands on the round surface of the globe against a vaguely Zoroastrian planetary background.[17] While this pose characterizes an initial moment of abjection after the narrating "I"'s migration to Zürich, her helpless appearance is untypical. And the difference in affect between the two covers is striking: The original Swiss cover suggests the ironic self-representation of an acknowledged transnational artist, while the English-language one depicts a dislocated refugee as global victim, which was not Bashi's situation; rather, she left Iran voluntarily for a romantic interest.

Additionally, each version of *Nylon Road* has a different subtitle. For the original text in German it is simply *eine graphische Novelle*, "A Graphic Novel." The English version, however, is subtitled *A Graphic Memoir of Coming of Age in Iran*, affixed next to Parsua's feet on the "road of life." This subtitle places Bashi's comic within the Bildungsroman tradition of education as accommodation to Western norms and values, which counter the history of Parsua's transits that complicates and even subverts that tradition. Paratextually, the cover of the English version makes a bid for readers' sympathy with an apparently hapless victim, while the German original invites the viewer's engagement with a savvy and elegant bicultural artist. The English cover thus stylizes the comic as a "soft weapon," to use Whitlock's phrase, in the American "war on terror," a representation of Bashi's position at odds with both the comic's original cover and the narrative that unfolds in it.

Interestingly, Bashi expressed to me her concern about the different covers used to market her graphic memoir: "[T]he German version of my book is entirely my work from *a* to *z*. The cover design and the layout of the book is [sic] mine as well. My publisher Mr. Haag trusted me totally and . . . having worked as a graphic designer for a long time helped me to make the book have a proper look . . . [But] for the English version the publisher wanted to change the cover design with one of the panels of the book. Honestly talking, I do not like either their choice of the drawing nor the layout. . . . I did not have any authorization in the publisher's visual or literal preference" (PC).[18] That is, Bashi's artistic agency was undermined in the English-language publisher's design and cover of the book. While these differences in cover choice may seem slight, they are linked to larger distinctions about the circulation of Bashi's graphic memoir and the receptivity of Western and diasporic audiences to what I call its dialogical conversations.[19] What is going on between the covers of *Nylon Road* that its American publisher modified and that Western readers in North America missed?[20]

III. Reading and Viewing the Dialogics of *Nylon Road*

In working out a graphic mode to represent her psychic and political struggles, Bashi uses a fluid line reminiscent of contemporary magazine illustration and visual techniques drawn from portraiture to create a style of self-representation that I term a visual dialogic (and discuss in more detail in this essay's last section). Her drawings represent encounters between her narrating and embodied past "I"s as confrontations, often by shifting the positions of the I's within the frame to signal which of the opposed points of view is being defended. Bashi described her process of composing the comic as it moved from what Hillary L. Chute calls hand-drawn "marks" to final form, writing me: "First I draw quick pencil sketches on paper, then draw them again in a final form by ink on paper, scanned the in outlined versions, and colored them in computer by a drawing software. For each panel 3 versions. The bubbles with the text was the last layer" (PC). That is, the "I" who appears in each chapter as both narrator (in rectangular boxes above the frames) and speaker (in text bubbles of dialogue) is embodied in a kind of visual "language" that organizes multiple, fragmented moments of remembered experience. While *Nylon Road*'s graphics have a different, more cartoon-like "look" than the boldly beautiful images of *Persepolis*, they conduct innovative experimentations. Within the limits that Bashi set for herself of outlined figures and a two-color scheme (terracotta, gray, black, and white), the comic frames and pages explore a gamut of visual self-representation that also serves as a collage of witnessing to four decades of history.

It is challenging, but rewarding, to closely map the contrapuntal narrative shuttles that *Nylon Road* navigates between Parsua's life in Tehran from the early 1970s till 2004 and her life thereafter as an Iranian migrant in Zürich. The comic consists of twelve unnumbered chapters, each separated by an untitled page with a small cartoon pulled from a detail in the text. Each chapter returns to the frame story, in which Parsua is situated in her present location, Zürich, and engages with a self from her past life in Tehran. Readers thus shift continuously between the dramatically different contexts of past upheavals and the apparent serenity and stability of Switzerland. Bashi's narrative logic presents her selves, at different ages, as eyewitnesses to their historical moments. And each past self conducts an increasingly contentious dialogue with the narrating "I", demanding an account of who she has become in her present life.

The eleven avatars confronting Parsua in various chapters are distinguished by their ages, clothing, and hairstyles, as well as the hijab or headscarf worn by adult Parsuas in Iran. This visible evidence strengthens our sense of *Nylon Road*'s "binocular" view of the Iranian Islamic Republic as the narrator's dialogue with her increasingly adversarial former I's—presented associatively rather than in chronological sequence—brings competing truth claims into view along with their divergent appearances. Teenaged Parsua is ideologically invested in Marxism: her young adult self is stunned by changes that are introduced with the Khomeini regime; a later one becomes an active resister, first against the post-Revolutionary fundamentalist government and then, in Europe, against the excesses of neoliberalism and the ubiquity of racial prejudice. Both a verbal and a visual dialogic, these conversations juxtapose various Parsuas' earlier dissident views on the Iranian Revolution and the subsequent Islamic Republic to the narrating "I"s as a montage for the experience of historical flux. Although *Nylon Road* does not draw on intergenerational memory (unlike Satrapi's memoir and many others), its assemblage of decades of remembered experience during and after the Revolution enables Parsua's selves to perform a novel kind of "eyewitnessing" to events after many Iranians had emigrated. Thus Bashi's strategy of giving voice to her distinct former selves, rather than simply recalling memories, situates her narrating "I" as engaging with the gap between her former embodied positions and her new migrant consciousness.

The way that Bashi strategically lays out her contending "I"s on the page confers an authority on her past selves that, because of the dominance of the image in graphic memoir, makes the effect of *Nylon Road* unlike the linear thrust of written autobiography, with its privileging of the authority of the present-tense narrator and, thereby, the Bildungsroman's teleological view of life. The past selves of Parsua, varied with the age and position of the avatar and responding to one another's assertions and styles as they narrate moments of growing up in Iran, are contrapuntal figures rather than the evolutionary self characteristic of the Bildungsroman; as such, they position the narrating "I" as a fractured and provisional, rather than consolidated, identity. The comic's reworking of the traditional Bildungsroman format allows Bashi to present a persona who is a mature and accomplished woman at home but an innocent abroad, insufficiently prepared for the cosmopolitan world of Zürich, even as she sees beyond its complacent materialism.

In sum, unlike the quest for integration of past and present selves that transforms a social outsider into an enfranchised citizen in the Bildungsroman, Bashi's narrative undercuts that plot in two ways. Recollection is depicted as an involuntary, experiential process summoned by embodiments who are radically different from the present-time narrating "I" at the same time that they "know" her. And memory shifts from being a merely personal function as it focuses on public events that foreground the differing customs and values of the Islamic Republic from the secular West, represented in Zürich. *Nylon Road* thus wages an ideological debate through the power of images as much as the presentation of contending political positions, even as it deconstructs the binaristic stereotype of "Islam versus the West" as an inadequate framework for the complexity of women's lives in the shifting gender politics of both post-Revolutionary Iran and Western Europe. In what follows, I deal with *Nylon Road*'s dense, rich chapters at length.

The frame story that begins Chapter One introduces the narrating "I" in a half-page panel depicting her in a blouse and pants, with uncovered long hair and folded arms, gazing calmly at the viewer as she presents herself as a 37-year-old woman who left Tehran in April 2004, two years earlier, after falling in love (a story she omits).

Parsua begins by disclosing her expectation that, after emigration, she would become not just another immigrant, but someone able to engage in "real life" in her "new society" (8). Subsequent frames detail her struggle to learn both German and Swiss-German dialect, find a job appropriate to her graphic-design skills, and develop a social circle. But the difficult process of cultural and linguistic assimilation leaves her feeling discouraged and displaced. Parsua sums up her dilemma: "I started to feel like a useless asshole" (Figure 3).

In the panel four images depicting her as idle and disgruntled occupy a single visual plane, a style that Bashi develops further in subsequent chapters. This moment of self-recognition in frustration becomes the spur to her self-reflection.

While the narrator stands brushing her teeth, "a happy-go-lucky little girl" of 6 appears in shorts and sandals holding flowers and toys. Recognizing this grinning apparition by her birthmark, the narrator, stunned, asks, "How could I have forgotten me?" (15). Parsua-6 responds, "The only reason I'm here is because you called." She goes on to tell Parsua that the adult woman is out of touch with herself—"I was the one who had lost contact"—and

Figure 3. From *Nylon Road* (p. 12) by Parsua Bashi. Reprinted by permission of Kein & Aber AG, and Parsua Bashi. All rights reserved.

informs her that there are "more of us waiting to see you," establishing the narrative convention of visits by past selves that anchors *Nylon Road*'s plot. When Parsua responds, "I simply could not deny my past. I had to remember the days I had spent with them—with myself," what might seem a Western cliché of getting in touch with "the child within" inaugurates an urgent autobiographical quest (18, bottom half). The encounters that ensue trace the narrator's engagements with the eleven former selves who appear, in non-chronological order, at ages 6, 13, 16, 18, 19, 21, 23, 29, 33, 35, and 36. Disclosing her unhappiness as a dislocated migrant, Parsua identifies the moment as a turning point and awakening: "I was alone, hopeless, desperate, and apparently unable to deal with the situation. . . . They were here to remind me that what I am now is the result of their lives" (18). Parsua's quest then moves toward increasingly tense encounters with the historical moments that her former selves experienced and the extreme ideological points of view, from the perspective of her newly Westernized persona, that they espoused.

Unlike the search for unequivocal rescue from the Islamic Republic that many Iranian diasporic memoirs recount, as Chapter One goes on, Parsua begins to regard her migration to Zürich as producing a traumatic gap in her life that becomes visible on reflection. The revelation—"I saw my entire life in a flash"—is drawn as "MY LIFE!", a jagged-topped building of concrete blocks that have broken apart the edifice of a formerly coherent self (19, top left). But in a close-up portrait, the next frame reveals the other side of that moment, a simultaneous "ENLIGHTENMENT" or "Aha" awareness, with literal light bulbs in Parsua's eyes. She is awakened to the kind of double consciousness that stirs a desire to examine her past—and inaugurate her story (19, top right).

Bashi wrote to me about this moment: "The Idea of having conversation with myself came from a real emotional/psychological situation that I was in at the time of writing this book . . . I really had these conversations with myself, since I was mainly alone and had time," in the "Vacuum space" that she experienced between her Iranian past and new life in Switzerland (PC). The felt space, depicted as a gap between parts of the building, is echoed in the gutter between the two frames that juxtapose "The interruption" and "ENLIGHTENMENT," which both occur as Parsua feels that her life became "absurd and meaningless" (19 top left). As Hillary L. Chute observes, "the gutter [is] . . . the figuration of a psychic order outside of the realm of symbolization, a space that refuses to resolve the interplay of elements of absence and presence" (*Disaster*, 35). This unresolved, traumatic space marks the narrator's awakening to autobiographical consciousness as a difference that produces rupture rather than consolidating an edifice of the self.

In this crisis of self-reflection, while Parsua listens to the radio, the second avatar appears in her 16-year-old self from 1982, situated during the Iran-Iraq war and in the wake of the Cultural Revolutionary Council's installation of a rigidly fundamentalist

Islamic system. Parsua-16, steeped in that milieu, voices a critique of the "relaxed" European view of the world reflected in feel-good broadcasts, while in Iran "other people are dealing with shit" such as mandatory prayer in school and the conscription of all 18-year-old men for the war (24). In Bashi's depiction this moment is a collision of two versions of herself, differently embodied in Parsua's long hair and blouse and the veiled garment of the patriotic teenager sternly admonishing her. As they stroll together in Zürich, they glimpse a hippie Western woman who has appropriated a prayer shawl to wear as a skirt. She appalls Parsua-16 because she has no idea that the shawl is traditionally used as a head-covering by a range of Middle Eastern people, from Palestinians to militant fundamentalists, and would disregard her as a "foreigner" (25). In the ensuing argument between Parsua's two selves, each makes points about perceptions of Islam, dramatized on the page by their shifting body language, gestures, and dominant or subordinate placement in the visual dialogic.

During Parsua's reflection in Chapter Three on whether she is "homesick" for her "hometown" or has just forgotten the violence of Iran's past in nostalgia, her 18-year-old self of 1984, the fourth year of the Iran-Iraq war, appears in pants and a ponytail to narrate the painful personal realities of those years (28). It is a litany of losses: the brother she felt close to was smuggled to Turkey to avoid the army, and many of her family and friends left for Europe or North America, trips that turned into a kind of permanent emigration that was "seriously tearing families apart, some forever" (30). Eventually "none of our family or friends were left," except for her parents, yet Parsua-18 seeks to remain true to her ideal of what the nation, which once was Persia, could again be (33). As narrator, Parsua sums up the conflicted feelings expressed in debates with her friends and family, asking whether it was worse to abandon her native land—"I was young [but] strictly against emigration" (32, middle) and leave it to "a bunch of mediocre midgets" (32, bottom), or to feel "abandoned" in not leaving a place that, in the view of many, had betrayed its Persian history (33, top right). Despite the urging of even her parents, Parsua-18 remains staunch in her determination to study fine arts at Tehran University. Responding to her avatar's question about the most difficult part of migration, Parsua acknowledges that she felt more in exile at home—"most homesick in my own hometown" (35). At the same time in her adopted new land she is virtually speechless without her mother tongue, as she confronts the difficulty of successfully integrating into the complexity of Swiss-German society (34, bottom). The experience of crisis in Iran has "vaccinated [her] against" homesickness; after a life of it in Tehran, she is without a "home" anywhere (35, bottom).

Parsua's notion of her self-sufficiency is next challenged by her 23-year-old self (in 1989) who calls on her to recall a moment when the revolutionary guards were busily rounding up what she calls "THE USUAL SUSPECTS"—political activists, boys and girls together, journalists and artists, writers and intellectuals, monarchists, dealers of music cassettes and alcohol, "bad hejabs"—for alleged crimes in appearance, ideas, or expression (Figure 4).

In Tehran, Parsua-23, lonely without her friends, develops an inexplicable crush on a male artist colleague who is drawn as portly and invasive, enveloping her in a sea of words (45, panel, second row). When she is caught walking on the street with a male classmate by a Pasdar (member of the Revolutionary Guard) who challenges them for associating in public, she defiantly responds that such acts are not prohibited by Sharia law. For this retort she is sent to the Islamic Court and sentenced to a whipping of seventy lashes (44). Summing up her response to this painful moment, the narrating "I" recognizes that her sense of citizenship was violated in Iran: "I felt enormously ashamed to be part of such a society" (44).

Depressed and humiliated, she turns to her boyfriend, despite their differences. When he asserts that he will "protect her"—"I'll make a PERFECT woman out of you"—she agrees to be married and, three months later, discovers she is pregnant (45). Although

Figure 4. From *Nylon Road* (p. 42) by Parsua Bashi. Reprinted by permission of Kein & Aber AG, and Parsua Bashi. All rights reserved.

Parsua now regrets her "stupid decision" to wed this tyrant and the impact it had on the daughter she gave birth to, she consoles her younger self for the bitter experience. As narrator, she goes on to observe how the limiting laws of religious fundamentalism lead young people into bad marriages in Iran; conversely, in Europe, people can get to know each other before marriage (47). Finally, both Parsuas resolve their quarrel by admitting that young people can make mistakes anywhere, as both Middle Eastern and Western European nations exert forms of domination over their citizens. And yet, the details that emerge of her sheltered life despite supportive parents, the brutal punishment she received in the Islamic court, and her subsequent coercion into marriage, stand as an indictment of how the Republic's excesses caused damage to her personal life.

This critique of personal life is extended, in Chapter Five, to a critique of political conservatism in both the Middle East and Euro-American nations. In Zürich Parsua's encounter with a passionately pro-Persian Iranian-migrant woman forms a pedagogical moment in the comic that is aimed as much at expatriates as Western readers. When this other woman, speaks as "we PERSIANS" and denounces Arabs as "CAMEL RIDERS," the four-page spread juxtaposes icons of Persian culture, displaying the splendors of the empire before the Arabs arrived that she enumerates, with an ever-closer focus on her screaming mouth. But Parsua's response, as a cosmopolitan subject, is pained: "I was so embarrassed" (54), she confesses, as she denounces the woman as "a chauvinist racist" (55), uneasy with the nostalgia of the pro-Persia diasporic woman, reminiscent of the "Iranians of the imagination" to whom Naghibi refers.[21]

In response, "one of my most patriotic selves" appears, the 35-year-old woman of 2001, a few years before Bashi migrated. Initially the two Parsuas argue about their justifications of the Islamic Republic and the "West," their upper and lower positions within the frame alternating as each makes her argument. "Patriotic" Parsua-35, committed to the relative freedom of pre-Revolutionary Iran, denounces Islamic fundamentalism and proclaims, in angry profiles, the excesses of Muslim leaders as "terrorists" who subject their own citizens to cruelty. In response Parsua challenges her former self's view as "poisoned by rage" for claiming that the Islamic Republic's imposition of religion is at fault for all Iran's woes, not least because Islam has been merged with Iranian culture for 1,400 years (56–7). Their dispute, captured in a montage of close-up profiles of the two women sparring, induces Parsua to regard fundamentalisms as "simply for political purposes," "propaganda . . . based on those false clichés" that use avowals of a "sacred mission" to hide their "dictatorial regime" (58). The narrating "I" acerbically retorts to her avatar, that, while the fundamentalist Islamic Republic makes laws mandating the veiling of women and prohibiting alcohol, the West deports Middle Easterners as terrorists and, in France, condemns head-scarf-wearing as a religious symbol at the same time that it condones right-wing Aryan-nation protests and starting wars in Iraq and Afghanistan. The so-called "holy war" of fundamentalism thus links right-wing conservatives in East and West like "a double-sided blade" in which they use mutual hatred to impose undemocratic limitations on their citizens' rights, a point on which her two selves, despite their different dress and locations, ultimately concur in the chapter's last frame, a moment of shared insight (Figure 5).

The chapter's process, then, does not suggest that Parsua "reconverts" from her Westernized tastes to Iran-nostalgia;

Figure 5. From *Nylon Road* (p. 61) by Parsua Bashi. Reprinted by permission of Kein & Aber AG, and Parsua Bashi. All rights reserved.

rather it produces a recognition of repressive practices that underlie the ideologies of both the Islamic Republic and Western neoliberalism. As the final frame concludes, conservative propaganda in Iran, by shoring up the theocentric Iranian regime's claim of a "holy war," masks real issues of poverty, hunger, unemployment, and censorship of speech, enabling the dictatorship to mystify its power as religion (57). In parallel fashion, the West resists acknowledging how its own media reports can fuel attacks by immigration police and right-wing groups directed at Muslims (59–61). Thus Parsua's response, in her dialogue with "patriotic" Parsua-35, structurally links Islamic fundamentalism with its seeming opposite, the West's claim of liberatory humanism.

Chapter Six takes up narrating Parsua's encounter with her divorced 29-year-old "mother-self," who lost custody of her daughter because she asked for a divorce from her jealous and possessive husband (65). Yet when weeping Parsua-29 recounts her sad story, Parsua rebukes her for refusing to recognize that she had a need to survive, despite her pain about the personal loss of her daughter and the political loss of her homeland (66). Parsua the narrator talks back to her newly divorced self about how the bitter loss of her child to her husband fueled not only her grief, but her critique of Iranian custody laws favoring the husband as a "religious" policy. And she draws a political conclusion that her younger self couldn't see, namely how "religion" masks the Islamic Republic's underlying "political purposes," in frames of the prejudicial court process that caricature the judge and lawyer. The narrative rehearses Parsua-29's testimony to the judge as a set of drawn memory-moments about her "paranoid" husband's jealousy as he forbids her to see others, including her own mother, slaps her for "flirting," and takes the television away from their child (70). While her testimony is useless because, as a housebound woman she had no witnesses, the drawings form a powerful indictment of a sexist and corrupt judicial process. A meta-drawing of objects incorporated in each frame for three pages represents Justice as a blindfolded woman in floor-length coat and veil holding a sword and balance scales in increasingly precarious fashion. When the judge assigns the child to her father, saying "True Muslim women live their lives with husbands even if they get beaten every day," the scales topple (69).

Parsua-29 summarizes the social and professional rejection she experienced in a "JUST DIVORCED" composite drawing that itemizes aspects of her pariah status in Iran, including the many men who offer help privately in exchange for sex. Parsua urges her former self to let go of her victimage as "a poisonous habit of begging for sympathy," drawn as the coat of pain and sorrow the she can only flush down the toilet at the chapter's end. She then reminds her 29-year-old self of the leap she took to become independent and considers her question about whether more progressive societies exist (72). Their conversation becomes an occasion for a feminist critique of the treatment of women, as Parsua notes that, on the one hand, Iranian women had the vote earlier than their Swiss counterparts (enfranchised in 1972); yet, on the other, in Iran women earn 30% less for the same jobs (72). Ultimately, "women all over the world are struggling for their rights. Some more, some less . . ." (72). Thus the narrating "I"s personal encounter with Parsua-29's beliefs and position serves as an act of consciousness-raising that exposes socio-political contradictions globally. Her younger self's dejected reaction, understandable and brave at one moment, is modified, by the end of their dialogue to enable change and growth as she moves beyond it. That is, in this passionate dialogue one self's point of view does not negate the other's, but, in dialogical fashion, can lead to self-forgiveness and insight, if not the end of personal pain about loss (74). In confronting each other's different values as they debate the cost of fidelity to one's native land versus the experience of a more tolerant society at the cost of losing a homeland, the drawn narrated and narrating "I"s reconcile—though the memory of losing her child is drawn as a knife that still stabs Parsua to the heart (74).

The next former self to confront Parsua is her most recent, the 36-year-old who owned a graphic design studio in Tehran. Europeanized Parsua introduces her as an embarrassing, "almost arrogant" and "loud" feminist (76). But Parsua-36 provocatively extends the comic's critique of the West, pointing out how even the figures of accomplished Western writers and artists are used as a "consumer product" in advertising campaigns, "selling the female body in public" (Figures 6–1 and 6–2).

Her sweeping condemnation further asserts that, at the same time in Iran, brave women defending human rights were imprisoned and even killed, events that Western media sensationalized by representing them as victims in burqa (which are not worn in Iran), among the many ways in which the Western designers of book covers display gross ignorance of Middle Eastern cultures. Yet the narrator's encounter with "loud" feminist Parsua-36 not only exposes excesses in both Western and Eastern worlds; it also reminds the narrator of the ignorance of citizens of both the global North and South about each other's cultures: "I learned that not knowing is not a sin. Not knowing and yet being prejudiced is where the problem starts" (79). Although a didactic "lesson," her point seems apropos, not least for the English version and reception of *Nylon Road* itself.

Parsua's avatars can be harshly critical of the narrator's seemingly "free" and comfortable status in Zürich, none more so than the 21-year-old Parsua of 1987 in Chapter Eight who appears on the scene to narrate her years of privation during the Iraq-Iran war. The urgent voice of Parsua's younger self compels the narrating "I" to reflect on the greedy myopia of the Swiss gourmet dinners she now enjoys and her new friends' preoccupation with vacations and consumer luxuries—like the truffle oil that she tries for the first time in Zürich (84, 88). Parsua reflects on the limits of her past self's memory, which could not know that in the nineties some things got better in Iran under its fifth president, Khatami (1997–2005)—although repression and human rights abuses

Figure 6.1. Parsua Bashi, Sketch for *Nylon Road*, published by permission of the artist.

Figure 6.2. From *Nylon Road* (p. 77) by Parsua Bashi. Reprinted by permission of Kein & Aber AG, and Parsua Bashi. All rights reserved.

intensified thereafter. This lack of perspective, she implies, is shared by both emigrants and Westerners (Figure 7).²²

At the same time Parsua-21 recalls contradictory aspects of wartime life in Iran. On the one hand, food was rationed and oil poured into plastic bags, while in Europe even chocolate is elaborately packaged; there were ration coupons and long waiting lines in markets; and the lack of cosmetics made hygiene a struggle. On the other hand, there was the solidarity of family life for the middle-class families like hers who sewed their own clothes modeled on pre-revolutionary catalogs; took photos to document both war and propaganda; held "exhibitions" of their paintings and photos, watched banned movies, and made live music inside the walls of their homes; and had endless private conversations about the harsh realities of life that generated a kind of everyday intimacy that Parsua finds rare in the commodity-obsessed Swiss world (86–92). To Parsua-21, Europeans are "sissies" (92), unlike the leftists who stayed in Iran and "dealt with the hardship" of everyday life (93). There are of course exceptions in both settings, people who crawl out

Figure 7. From *Nylon Road* (p. 85) by Parsua Bashi. Reprinted by permission of Kein & Aber AG, and Parsua Bashi. All rights reserved.

of what Bashi depicts as European cocoon pods to help others struggling in the developing world (93). As the ongoing dialogue with her former selves makes clear, the claim that either the Islamic Republic or a Western nation is the superior one can be challenged by countervailing evidence. By the chapter's end Swiss Parsua comes to acknowledge that she survives in her new social world, as in the old, by acts of forgetting and normalizing the burden of accumulated memories.

Reminded repeatedly by her former selves of repressive realities that marked post-revolutionary life in Iran, Parsua remains aware that nostalgia for the past is a form of false consciousness—in what is perhaps a textual barb directed at earlier emigrants. This is also borne out in Chapter Nine, which charts how young Parsua-19's study of graphic design at Tehran University in 1985, after the universities reopened, was hindered by "conditions where nothing was allowed to be seen or heard" in the aftermath of the revolution's "explosion of light" depicted on a propaganda poster to ironic effect next to a sign proclaiming "OUR UNIVERSITIES ARE MAN-MAKING FACTORIES," both of which evoke scorn in Parsua-19 (98). She goes on to narrate the widespread censorship that fine-arts librarians exercised on viewing books about Western artists—such as Egon Schiele, with his provocative naked bodies—that are lined up in her office, and Western design journals. Equally obnoxious were the severe punishments that violating rules on fraternizing with male students or bringing in materials from other countries could occasion. But as Parsua-19 narrates this tale of the universities' repressive stifling as the "new normal," she also details the innovative kinds of resistance that it spurred. The chapter's drawings of posters, books, magazines, and videos, as well as the caricature of the library's monstrously "fat, spinsterly, old virgin" (97) and malevolent director, texture its narrated memories as both vivid and tough, driven by the students' shared determination to learn about a wider world of arts and cultures in the West and subvert their supervisors, often at personal cost.

As *Nylon Road* expands its critique toward broader political and ideological targets, the narrating "I"'s harshest critic emerges in the pigtailed teenaged self of Chapter Ten. Parsua-13 speaks from the position of the heady moment in 1979, just after the Iranian Revolution began, when she chose, among the available versions of leftist theory, to identify as a Marxist-Leninist and immersed herself in its prescribed reading of Marxist classics (103–05). But Parsua, as narrator, ironically mocks the teenager's study of party tenets, texts, and mandated practices of group "self-criticizing" (106) and body-building as "A teenage fashion just like any other," comparable to the fad—and pain—of getting a tattoo (109). From Parsua-13's perspective, however, Europeans are superficial. They can be split into the bourgeoisie and the proletariat, the latter with no access to agency, their personal styles reflecting gendered and classed forms of oppression. As a rejoinder Bashi's full-page drawing suggests that the teenager's study of "dialectical materialism" was useful in getting her own way in the family—in the name of "rights," in a family scene where competing viewpoints were tolerated as her father listens to the BBC World Service on the radio (108). But while Parsua-13 rejects seeing the martyred youth of Iran in 1981 as following a "fad," Parsua the narrator defends her view in a startling way: she compares the fate of the youth in Iran to the ways that capitalism conforms young women to styles of dress and behavior that also repress individual expression, a form of what Marcuse termed "repressive tolerance."[23] In the narrator's view political positions are inevitably compromised because they are embedded in the ideologies of specific regimes and political moments.

Parsua-13 also offers a novel defense of her point of view in this debate, visualizing a fantasy of young women costumed in different garb to display capitalist, religious-fundamentalist, and socialist modes of conforming girls to three kinds of ideological "cults" (Figure 8). Each kind of costuming produces consumers who suffer the disciplinary effects of their interpellation in the unquestioning adherence that governments demand. Parsua

Figure 8. From *Nylon Road* (p. 110) by Parsua Bashi. Reprinted by permission of Kein & Aber AG, and Parsua Bashi. All rights reserved.

sums up this critique of "the power of wealth" to shape political belief in her contrast of three kinds of regimes, as embodied in their leaders: "fashionista" capitalism crowns designer Karl Lagerfeld; the Islamic Republic honors the Ayatollah; and Soviet-style socialism heralds Stalin—all with wads of money in their hands (112). While Parsua-13's Marxist self cannot be reconciled to the narrator's critique by an offer of ice cream, Parsua concludes the chapter with a powerful insight: despite her selves' bickering about positions, a "lost childhood" was the price of her early fervor during the Revolution (112). Interestingly, Chapter Ten suggests how deeply Bashi, as a teenager, was steeped in dialectical materialism, training that surely contributed to *Nylon Road*'s dialogical structuring and use of visual counterpoint.

The most provocative avatar of all steps up in Chapter Eleven: Parsua's 33-year-old self, now a graphic designer who has been awarded her first prize (117). She is interested in Western fashion but becomes angry when the narrating "I" shows her a spread in *Vogue* entitled "Colonial Girl," featuring "Calcutta Cat" and "Delhi Doll," derived from women's garb in colonial India (116). While contemporary Parsua defends free expression, tolerance, and the celebration of difference as practices enshrined in the West, Parsua-33, a tough and self-assured urbanite, searingly critiques the cynicism of the global fashion industry sustained by colonial and racist practices that emerged with the Enlightenment and the modern nation-state. Fashion magazines, Parsua-33 alleges, "make a profit from their own crimes of history by pretending that colonialism was just an aesthetic phenomenon" (116). Disgusted at the fascination the narrating "I" exhibits for Western consumerist fashion, however, this younger self alleges that the narrating "I" is blind to how cynically the West levels and commodifies history as a fashion statement.

When the narrating "I" contrasts the freedom of artists to criticize politicians in Europe with the fundamentalism that constrains artists in Iran, Parsua-33 begins to taunt her about the manipulative tactics of Western advertising. À la layouts in the fashion pages of *Vogue* or *Elle,* this younger self visualizes a fantasy depicting fashion lines of "Sweet Slaves," complete with manacles and chains (121); "Hot 9/11" with models wearing Twin-Towers-explosion T-shirts; and models with shaved heads and Holocaust-camp shirts. As the two Parsuas' heated debate about the conundrum of "free" speech continues, Parsua-33 argues that the Eurocentric West ignores taboos on trivializing genocidal acts that are Indian-, African-, or Asian-related even as it valorizes Eurocentric events (123).

Their debate, located at what Spiegelman called the "intersection of personal and world-historical events," focuses the narrator on the blind spots of belief systems, all of which construct an "other" and set limits to the critique of their own histories (Spiegelman, *In the Shadow,* unpaged). But at the end of their dialogue Parsua remains stymied, like the narrating "I" at the crossroads depicted on *Nylon Road*'s original cover, between the clashing systems of different cultures and traditions. Finally, reconciliation with her last self is impossible. When Parsua as narrator poses the irresolvable conundrum of freedom and censorship that—for her—constrains the exercise of democratic freedom in societies in various ways, Parsua-33 responds, "Why bother writing a book? Why not just shut up? . . . your theories are BULLSHIT!" (124). In a witty graphic metalepsis, Bashi captures the chapter's lack of closure with the narrating "I" jumping out of the comic page on which she is drawn jumping out of the page, chided by finger-pointing Parsua-33 (124). Completing the spectrum of attitudes of her former selves, some of them echoed more widely in their social milieu, Bashi represents Parsua as at an impasse—and yet, her narrative of the challenges that both post-revolutionary Iran and the "civilized" West pose has unfolded in specific and compelling detail.

Nylon Road's brief final Chapter Twelve consists of facing pages that juxtapose alternate views of Parsua the narrator. On the left side, in nine close-up portraits, Parsua is visualized full-face, smoking and pondering how to conclude her story in a way that is funny and provides closure but is not "paranoid," "two-faced," or "simply crazy" (126). The rejoinder on the witty right page is a self-portrait in which seven of her collective younger selves, led by the six-year-old, orchestrate an end to her abyss of self-reflection by holding aloft a banner reading "The End." A picture within the picture, this group of little figures surrounds a self-portrait of Parsua the narrator that is clipped onto on the bookshelf in her study. Below it her drawing hand appears in profile, at rest and holding the pencil for Bashi's comics drawings (Figure 9).

A metaleptic gesture familiar in autographics and other forms of self-portraiture, from Dürer and Parmigianino through Van Gogh and Kollwitz, this last panel emphasizes the recursive nature of graphic storytelling. (See further discussion of the graphic in the "Toolbox" below.) That is, Bashi represents herself as an artist-maker performatively. In this binocular structure, the narrating "I" of the comic is revealed as a projection of the agent who has drawn, written, organized, and edited her memoir, as the hand drawn by her invisible hand signifies. Further, as the drawing suggests, Parsua is as much an effect of her former selves as she is a speaking subject—and thus still a subject in transit. In true dialogical fashion this visual and narrative self-examination cannot be resolved into the coherent, consolidated self as public citizen of the Western Bildungsroman. Rather she remains an open possibility at the nexus of memory and narration. Far from serving as an authoritative visual and textual life story about either belonging in, or migrancy from, Iran, *Nylon Road* presents an "I" who **both** asserts her role in directing the narrative and is unmasked as a constructed fiction by her past. Assembled at the expense of acknowledging and incorporating—but struggling in creative tension with—past "forgotten" versions of herself, she remains a locus of competing claims about the "truth" of her experience.

In sum, throughout *Nylon Road*, Bashi uses conversations with her former selves to set up and intensify a dialogical structure of interrogation that is both personal and political. Neither her present-time "I," nor any of her past selves, emerges as "right," the

Figure 9. From *Nylon Road* (p. 127) by Parsua Bashi. Reprinted by permission of Kein & Aber AG, and Parsua Bashi. All rights reserved.

victor in this clash of views. But through the lens of graphic memoir the succession of encounters serves to problematize questions of identity and belonging for the narrating "I" as a migrant subject in Zürich. Both the roles of leftist Iranian resister in the Islamic Republic and liberated Euro-migrant trouble her. In that sense *Nylon Road* is a story of the narrator's inadequacy to construct a coherent identity either at home or in Europe; both versions are inadequate, inauthentic from the other's point of view. Yet, as in many transnational narratives, *Nylon Road*'s confession of unease with residing in either past or present social identities bares an in-between space that is generative of its graphic dialogism. Parsua's determination to be neither nostalgic nor in denial about her past experience in Iran sets up a colloquy of selves in a debate about whether to invest in any prevailing political ideology—even as one is inescapably interpellated by those informing the location one inhabits.

Thus *Nylon Road* poses issues for both readers of the Iranian diaspora and those in the West. At the same time that *Nylon Road* acknowledges—in often funny and sometimes harrowing detail—the post-revolutionary excesses and blind spots of the Islamic Republic, it also suggests that neither Western market capitalism nor Soviet-style socialism can adequately redress forms of prejudice toward outsiders and violence toward women. And it resists, through its dialogical structure, the binary logic of much testimonial memoir in which the West serves as the locus of rescue for Middle Eastern emigrants. In Bashi's dynamic and ever-incomplete project of self-invention, Parsua's multiple, unresolved selves signal that the consolidation of a transnational identification occurs at the cost of letting go of memory in order to belong. Particularly in light of Bashi's 2009 return to Iran, her ironic rendering of violent repression in the Islamic Republic of Iran, compulsory conformity under Soviet socialism, and materialist excess in the name of tolerance in the West, leaves readers with provocative questions about whether any "elsewhere" can serve as a locus of adequate rescue for democratic values. Forming a moving target of self-representation, the dialogical narrative organization of *Nylon Road* offers a view of self-construction that, in the act of reconstructing memory through situated witnesses embodying particular standpoints, links the personal inextricably to the shifting global currents and contexts that texture it.

IV: A Toolbox for Reading the Drawn Autographic Witness

Autographics offers unique resources for representing the contradictions of multiply inflected subjectivity as a mosaic of self-reflection in ways that verbal narration cannot fully capture. Because Bashi was primarily a graphic designer rather than a comics artist, she had to devise a set of visual codes for representing the psychological complexity of her process of engaging memory as an unhappy diasporic subject caught between dramatically different worlds. In my view she sought visual means that would both stylize the appearances and attitudes of her past selves at significant ages and correspond to key moments in pre-and post-revolutionary Iranian history. These embodied former selves, necessarily repressed in her post-migration life, cumulatively pressure Parsua's recognition of contradictions of her experience. Bashi's efforts to visually encode autobiographical reflection about her conflicted position as a remarried Iranian woman artist in Zürich are worth further consideration. What is her vocabulary of visual tactics and tropes, and is this repertoire shared with other autobiographical comics?

By asking this, I am implying that the question of *how* comics represent the autobiographical is a complex one. Drawing pictures that resemble the artist making the comic is not a display of self-reflexivity, nor is simply including fragments from memory archives such as letters, diaries, or photographs. Rather, depicting an autobiographical act of self-reflexivity requires an artist-author to devise a narrative "mirror" that she can turn back on herself. After Parsua's initial question, "How could I have forgotten me?" (15), the eleven selves that appear enable her to stage encounters in which neither the narrating "I" nor her many past selves can claim to be the authoritative version of her own, or Iran's, past. Instead, the encounters staged between present and past versions of herself as they discuss, and often dispute, the meaning of experience, produce a dialogical narrative that proceeds by recursive twists and turns.[24] The dialogue that *Nylon Road* conducts among Parsuas is both interior—about the shifting meaning of the past depending on one's location—and public, linked to Iran's history. It presents the narrating "I", a Europeanized cosmopolite in Zürich but also a migrant, as both insider and outsider in a critique of women's experience that is ideologically charged in ways not adequately reflected by global media.

The set of terms I propose parses the autographic strategies Bashi employs in drawing Parsua in relation to her embodied past selves in *Nylon Road*. This vocabulary of visual distinctions can be seen as a kind of "toolbox" for autographic representation, and may offer rubrics for thinking about visual tropes in graphic memoir more generally.

The **processual "I"** shows the narrating "I" as a developmental aggregate, the culmination of a series of past selves at different moments that are lined up behind her, for example, on the bottom of page 18, which is also used as the cover of the English edition of *Nylon Road* (see Figure 2). This stylization depicts identity as a chronological process that proceeds in a linear, organically developmental fashion toward consolidating a present I.

The **conflictual "I"**, by contrast, represents the narrating "I" as a product of disparate and competing identifications—as on the cover of the original German edition and its Spanish translation (see Figure 1). There, each of Parsua's crossed legs is clad in a nylon stocking covered with characters and word fragments in a different alphabet, and the contrast of Persian and Roman scripts locates her at a crossroads between her Iranian legacy and the Greco-Roman heritage of democracy and capitalism. So clad, she embodies the conflict of ideologies and cultures that she has experienced—in the humorous form of pantyhose.

The indexical "I" signals meta-level reflexivity in embedding one or more visual replications of the narrated I in a particular box or panel. Thus, a photograph or drawing of a past "I" can serve as a mirror-avatar for the narrating "I", but also heighten the contrast between past and present I's. For example, Bashi incorporates a portrait of her younger self from a photo album, "Tehran Autumn, 1989," as a sweet-faced girl in a hijab who was not allowed to show affection to her boyfriend in public under the laws of the Islamic Republic, in contrast to the free expression of couples the narrating "I" observes in Zürich (38). Satrapi similarly uses many portraits of her younger self as visual icons in photographs, paintings, or mirrors within the frame, particularly in *Persepolis I*.

The dialogical "I" can be visualized in various ways. Within a frame Bashi often creates a multifaceted self-portrait by juxtaposing several heads or bodies of the narrator to depict different-aged selves as in conversation with one another. For example, when Parsua, reflecting on her migrant status, describes herself as a "useless asshole," Bashi places four free-floating drawings of herself at loose ends within a single box (12, bottom; see Figure 3). The drawing externalizes her self-critical interior monologue as a set of faces that are set alongside, but not literally "speaking" to, one another on the same visual plane. Rather than being developmental, these self-portraits of the unsettled, unresolved narrator represent her as a set of discontinuous, dissonant personae.

But dialogism can also be signaled in a succession of boxes that juxtapose past and present I's in conversation, sometimes using filmic techniques of positioning one disputant at the top of the frame and switching her location to a bottom corner as the other responds. In some text-rich panels Bashi focuses on talking heads in profile or three-quarter view as they trade views on an issue such as artistic freedom.

The interpellated "I" is presented through a multi-panel box or page that embodies different belief systems in the appearances and attitudes of young women. For example, Bashi draws a girl wearing differing costumes to depict a contrast of global ideologies—Western neoliberalism, Islamic fundamentalism, and socialist utilitarianism (110; see Figure 8). Her costuming literally fashions the personae inhabiting them as a kind of interpellation conforming young woman to identities as, variously, "consumer," "sheep," and "comrade" whose performances are mandated by powerful interests that enforce membership in a national "cult" (she acknowledges Islamic fundamentalism as a particularly repressive one). For each figure, the instructions are the same: "Wear this . . . Read this . . . Be like this . . . Good, you fit"(110). Bashi turns this criticism on herself as well, stylizing Parsua-13 as trying on seven styles of radical resistance circulating in Iran in the seventies before she opts to become a "Marxist-Leninist" (103).

The recursive "I" can be presented by visual self-reference, and is a frequently-used convention of self-portraiture in both painting and cartooning. In it a portrait of the narrating "I" includes the maker's hand, either in the act of drawing or in repose, as a reference to the artist's body drawing the comic outside the frame. In suggesting that a self-image must be drawn by another invisible hand, a drawing of the artist's hand is an example of what narrative theory terms "metalepsis"; such images create a *mise-en-abîme* or recursive circuit of self-representation. (Recall the famous M. C. Escher graphic of "Drawing Hands.") Such cartoonists as Alison Bechdel and Art Spiegelman employ this trope as a visual signature. For example, a famous full-page box depicts

Art, the artist drawing *Maus*, as he sits atop a heap of corpses in the shadow of a Holocaust watchtower (*Maus II*, 41). Bashi's final full-page box similarly depicts the drawn narrating "I" in a picture surrounded by little drawings of seven earlier selves who, as an ensemble, surround the present-time narrator as if she is their creation. (127; see Figure 9 and related discussion in III). They present Bashi's narrating "I" as recursive, a performative construct produced at the nexus of the disparate histories of her past selves. Yet the drawn hand of the artist, visible below this group self-portrait around Parsua, also unmasks Bashi as the maker of *Nylon Road*'s visual dialogics.

In sum, Bashi productively exploits the affordances of graphic memoir for self-presentation by employing visual tropes that represent self-relationship in encounters among her various selves across disparate times and places. As Chimamanda Ngozi Adichie has asserted for written narrative, the depictions of a self in migration across locations, histories, and ideologies, cannot be "just a single story."[25] Bashi's multiple apparitions in the selves of memory require a repertoire of visual tropes, on dazzling display in *Nylon Road*.

V. Conclusion

Narratives structured as debates about the position of the autobiographical subject vis-à-vis her own and national history, whether written or in the visual-verbal form of graphic memoir, can be challenging to follow. Publishing in 2006, Bashi used an open-ended dialogical structure to depict her relationship to her homeland, Iran, and her post-migration life in Switzerland, ensuring that, while *Nylon Road* was written in the West, it is decidedly not "written for the West." The comic provocatively suggests that, for transnational subjects, questions of audience and allegiance may be so fraught with ambivalence that the authority of any single version of an experiential history is troubled.

As a kind of feminist counter-comic, *Nylon Road* thus critiques not only the severe strictures that its narrating "I", Parsua, experienced and that were imposed on women under the Islamic Republic, but also those implicit within the "repressive tolerance" of Western consumer capitalism that she encountered as an expatriate in Zürich. As a collective trope for the variation and embeddedness of memory, Bashi's eleven avatars, in dialogue with her rather than static portraits frozen in memory, both innovatively juxtapose diverse ideological perspectives on the past and trouble nostalgic versions of it. Its intricate charting of how reawakening memory activates the narrating "I"'s questions about identity is a bracing tonic to a rose-colored glasses view of either home or adopted nation.

At a time when the publication of memoirs critical of the Islamic Republic is impossible in Iran, *Nylon Road*'s summoning of the past in the form of active narrators enables the airing of a range of controversial issues and a spectrum of standpoints on them. Bashi's graphic representation of Parsua as a collection of ideologically diverse past selves probes stereotypes about the "looks" and beliefs of women, Iranian, European, and globally. As *Nylon Road*'s Chinese-box procession of encounters frame its protagonist at the crossroads of clashing past experiences, it redirects the Bildungroman's conventional claim of new-made immigrant identity to a different self-recognition, "What I am now is the result of their lives" (18).

Bashi's interrogative, non-omniscient stance toward her own past thus shapes a comic that, in its mix of humor and biting satire, is critical of both human rights abuses in Iran and commodity capitalism in the West. As *Nylon Road* invites reader-viewers to acknowledge divergent experiential histories by engaging its debates across religious fundamentalist, Soviet-style socialist, and neoliberal capitalist positions, its alternative story of belonging, diaspora, and the creation of transnational identity productively challenges other memoirs of Iran's recent tumultuous history even as it demonstrates the stakes of self-representation.

Notes

With thanks to Carol DeBoer-Langworthy and *Lifewriting Annual* for encouraging this essay; to Lisa Mühlemann of Kein & Aber Press, Zürich, for facilitating the use of images from *Nylon Road*; and to Nathanael Su for helpful steering. I am, above all, grateful to Parsua Bashi for her generous responses to my queries and helpful information about several aspects of *Nylon Road*'s inception, process, and reception. Errors of fact or interpretation, no doubt inevitable for a Western scholar of life narrative of the Iranian diaspora, are entirely my own.

1. Touragi extends his critique to memoirs by writers remaining in Iran such as *Iran Awakening: One Woman's Journey to Reclaim Her Life and Country* by 2003 Nobel Peace Prize laureate Shirin Ebadi.
2. Over a decade ago Satrapi insisted that her identity is as an Iranian woman. See the interview by the Asia Society http://asiasociety.org/marjane-satrapi-i-will-always-be-iranian.
3. See Smith and Watson, "Witness or False Witness?", which traces the indeterminacy of claims to ethnic or ideological belonging in several contemporary life narratives, while observing the importance of testimonies for creating communities of affiliation.
4. I call this process a dialogical one, drawing on Bakhtin's concept in *The Dialogic Imagination* for an ongoing process of exchange with no final resolution. The dialogic is unlike a Hegelian dialectic in which thesis and antithesis confront each other and, in tension, generate a new synthesis that moves toward closure. Parsua's encounters with her former selves conduct a continuing dialogue as a chain of exchanges that remains unresolved at the comic's end. (See Bahktin, especially 292–4).
5. While Iranian film is beyond the purview of this essay, several filmmakers such as Abbas Kiriostami, Jafar Panahi, Asghar Farhadi, and Samira Makhmalbaf have provocatively represented contradictions between fundamentalist tenets and everyday life in contemporary Iran, raising troubling questions from within the nation. In another register, the film, video, and photographic works of artist Shirin Neshat stunningly documents the contradictions of Iranian and other Middle Eastern women's lives in transnational settings.
6. As Naghibi observes, "some narratives of the regime may languish in obscurity, unsuccessful in their attempts to claim willing witnesses" (155) if they fail to establish an "empathic engagement" (158) with readers.

7   To reference citations from *Nylon Road* I use the page number, followed by the location of the image on the page when one is referenced.
8   Bashi's more recent books include: Parsua Bashi with Martin Walker: *Persische Kontraste* (Persian Contrasts), Zürich: Walkwerk, 2008; and Parsua Bashi: *Briefe aus Teheran* (Letters from Tehran), Kein & Aber Verlag, 2010, translated from Persian by Suzanne Baghestani.
9   Although the convention in life narrative is to use the first name of the author for the narrated I and the last name for the narrating "I", in *Nylon Road* the complexity of having eleven former selves engage in dialogue with the narrator makes this impractical. I therefore use "Parsua" to refer to the narrating "I" and add, after the name of each former self, her age to make their differently situated positions and points of view clear. It is also crucial to distinguish both the narrated I's and the narrating "I" from the flesh-and-blood author Bashi, who draws, writes, organizes and edits the comic, not least because she is referred to as the maker on its last page, with the drawn artist's hand invoking the invisible hand that drew it.
10 Smith describes the crisis comic as a mode of "witness to radical injury and harm" that addresses readers variously as "those with the need to know their rights," "individual agents of rights activism" who can "rescue themselves," and "privileged readers to be enlightened about conditions elsewhere" (62–4). Bashi's intended audience includes both privileged readers in the global North and those of the Iranian diaspora who are interested in the interplay of rescue and alienation in their own experience of migration.
11 As of early 2016 Kein & Aber has sold about 3,000 copies of *Nylon Road*, and the Spanish translation has sold about 1,000. Information from Lisa Mühlemann, Head, Rights and Licenses, Kein & Aber AG, Zürich.
12 Simon Poelchau in the *Süddeutsche Zeitung*, aptly observes: "Despite her criticism of the fundamentalist regime of the mullahs, Bashi resists damning Islam as such. In her opinion those in power use religion as an ideological weapon to legitimate their authoritarian politics." (My translation of: "Bei aller Kritik an dem fundamentalistischen Regime der Mullahs unterlässt Bashi es aber, den Islam als solches zu verdammen. Ihrer Meinung nach benutzen die Machthaber im Iran die Religion als ideologische Waffe, um ihre autoritäre Politik zu legitimieren.")
13 Stajić states, "In addition to the pure narrative [Bashi] also visually depicts some fundamental debates of modern society: How far should freedom of opinion go? Isn't criticism of Islam at times counterproductive? And how fully do women in the West really lead independently empowered lives?" (My translation of: "Abseits des bloßen Narrativs

bebildert sie auch einige Grundsatzdebatten der modernen Gesellschaft: Wie weit darf Meinungsfreiheit gehen? Ist Islamkritik manchmal nicht auch kontraproduktiv? Und inwieweit führen die Frauen im Westen tatsächlich ein selbstbestimmtes Leben?") Olivera Stajić, "Dialog mit dem Ich." 2010/2. http://www.migrazine.at/artikel/dialog-mit-dem-ich Accessed 8-24-2016.

14 Parsua Bashi wrote the following to me about the reception of *Nylon Road* in media for Iranian audiences: "There were three Persian press reviews, a couple of interviews and some more reviews in some Iranian Blogs: BBC Persian website, Radio Zamenh website, Radio Farda (VOA Persian radio branch in Prague) and some others that I have not recall (*sic*) now, and yes they were definitely have been read (*sic*) by Iranians inside Iran. But as you might know all the mentioned websites are filtered (blocked) by Iranian Gov., so we could say they were read by Iranians unofficially" (PC). Ordering books published elsewhere through websites is also impossible because online money transfer outside the country is not allowed.

15 The only scholarly attention *Nylon Road* has received in English in North America that I am aware of is in two conference papers that I presented at international conferences: "Graphic Memories of Revolution: Women on the Verge in the Middle East," Session on Transnational Comics, Modern Language Association Convention, Jan. 10, 2014; and "Graphic Memoir as Visual How-To: Bashi's *Nylon Road*," International Auto/Biography Association Conference, Banff, Alberta, Canada, May 30, 2014.

16 Afsaneh Rezaei, a PhD Student in the Department of Comparative Studies at The Ohio State University, advised me that the lettering on the right stocking leg "is likely Persian" (though the words she discerned could mean something in either Persian or Arabic), noting "There are a couple of instances where I think I can see the letter گ, which is only in the Persian alphabet. And the date and location printed right under her elbow say Zurich 1385/خیروز ۱۳۸۵—the number referring to a year in the Persian calendar (1385, would be 2006/2007)." She added that another student thought it resembled "the Persian calligraphy practice 'Siah Mashgh'/سیاه مشق—just writing the same words or letter over and over to perfect their calligraphic forms."

17 The cover design is by Lisa Marie Pompilio under the St. Martin's Griffin imprint in New York. The visual convention of self-representation as a processual figure emerging over time from past selves was

memorably used in Charlotte Salomon's brilliantly drawn-and-painted page of herself included as the last page of *Life? or Theatre?*, where she represents herself as emerging from her childhood and schoolgirl selves in over two-dozen figures in jumpers, culminating in her then-present self in a bathing suit on the French Mediterranean in 1941 as an "arrived" artist.

18 The Kein & Aber original text is on a heavy-stock paperback in an 8″ by 11″ format with generous margins. The English-language version from St. Martin's Press is a smaller paperback, about 6″ x 9″ with a quarter-inch margin on each side. Otherwise the pagination and materials included are identical, with of course different front and back matter on publication.

19 *Nylon Road*'s translation into colloquial English is, in my view, well done, faithful to the original German yet fresh and funny.

20 Admittedly, Bashi articulated and published her comic at a moment in Zürich when she was free to air her discontent with both the intolerance of the Iranian regime and the consumerism of Switzerland, without danger to herself. But a careful reading of the comic's critique of "repressive tolerance" undercuts any easy binary in which the West emerges as a "freer" or more liberated location able to integrate Parsua and remake her migrant self as a Western citizen.

21 Naghibi's study focuses on exceptions to nostalgic memoir-writing but notes that it is typical of many memoirists: "Diasporic Iranian writers are in fact keenly aware of the object of their nostalgic longing: their homeland, Iran" (9).

22 See, for example, the op-ed by Maziar Bahari, "A Humane Voice for a Cruel Regime," which tracks the jailing and torture of journalists and diplomats during the reign of supreme leader Khamenei.

23 "Repressive tolerance" is not Bashi's term, but one coined by Herbert Marcuse for the paradoxical condition of modern neoliberal societies; I use it as a shorthand way to link Bashi's critique of Western consumer capitalism to the longstanding Frankfurt School analysis of neoliberalism. Marcuse asserts, "Tolerance is extended to policies, conditions, and modes of behavior which should not be tolerated because they are impeding, if not destroying, the chances of creating an existence without fear and misery.... Tolerance is turned from an active into a passive state, from practice to non-practice" (95).

24 Many graphic memoirists have depicted themselves at various ages by employing avatars, visual personae, to represent past experiences and inner conflicts on the page. For example, Spiegelman used drawn mouse

attributes and different clothing to mark the various ages of his younger self, the child Art. Famously, in conversation with his therapist in *Maus II*, Art is drawn as a child-mouse, creating a reflexive narrative about himself at ages back to infancy. Similarly, Phoebe Glockner, in *Diary of a Teenage Girl*, and Lynda Barry, in *One Hundred Demons*, use visual juxtapositions of present and past selves at various ages as a structuring principle. The effect is to trouble notions of memory as chronological and coherent by introducing discordant elements of a personal past that undercut "official" stories about the coherence of the I's identity. Similarly, the contending claims of narrated I's at various ages saturate Alison Bechdel's *Fun Home: A Family Tragicomic*, particularly when the narrating "I" confronts the diary, photos, and other artifacts of her younger self. As in these examples, the encounters of Parsua with eleven past selves at different ages show how memory, in any given moment, is incomplete and fallible.

25 Nigerian novelist Chimamande Ngozi Adichie's TED Talk of October 7, 2009, "The Danger of a Single Story," is an important and helpful statement about how the experience of multiple locations and cultures reshapes one's notions of identity, making any single version of it a partial and inadequate account.

Works Cited

Adichie, Chimamanda Ngozi. TED Talk, October 7, 2009, "The Danger of a Single Story." https://www.youtube.com/watch?v=D9Ihs241zeg, accessed January 4, 2016.

Bahari, Maziar. "Opinion: A Humane Voice for a Cruel Regime." *New York Times*, September 25, 2016, SR 4.

Bakhtin, Mikhail. *The Dialogic Imagination*. Austin: University of Texas Press, 1981.

Bashi, Parsua. Personal correspondence—Interview with Julia Watson, November 28, 2015, unpublished message.

———. *Nylon Road: A Graphic Memoir of Coming of Age in Iran*. (Zürich: Kein & Aber AG, 2006.) Editing/translation by Teresa Go, Miriam Wiesel. New York: St. Martin's Griffin, 2009.

Butler, Judith. "Photography, War, Outrage." *PMLA* 120:3 (May 2005), 822–27.

Chute, Hillary L. *Graphic Women: Life Narrative and Contemporary Comics*. New York: Columbia University Press, 2010.

———. *Disaster Drawn: Visual Witness, Comics, and Documentary Form.* Cambridge, MA and London: The Belknap Press of Harvard University Press, 2016.

Ebadi, Shirin, with Azadeh Moaveni. *Iran Awakening: One Woman's Journey to Reclaim Her Life and Country.* New York: Random House, 2007.

Hirsch, Marianne. "Editor's Column: Collateral Damage." *PMLA* 119. 5 (October 2004), 1209–15.

Liu, Jonathan H. "The Geekly Reader. Review: *Nylon Road.*" November 3, 2009. http://www.wired.com/2009/11/the-geekly-reader-nylon-road/ Accessed December 31, 2015.

Marcuse, Herbert. "Repressive Tolerance." In Robert Paul Wolff, Barrington Moore, Jr., and Herbert Marcuse, *A Critique of Pure Tolerance* (Boston: Beacon Press, 1969), pp. 95–137. http://www.marcuse.org/herbert/pubs/60spubs/65repressivetolerance.htm. Accessed September 13, 2016.

Nafisi, Azar. *Reading Lolita in Tehran. A Memoir in Books.* New York: Random House, 2003.

Naghibi, Nima. *Women Write Iran: Nostalgia and Human Rights from the Diaspora.* Minneapolis: University of Minnesota Press, 2016.

———. and Andrew O'Malley. "Estranging the Familiar: 'East' and 'West' in Satrapi's *Persepolis*." English Studies in Canada, 31.2–3 (June/September 2005). https://ejournals.library.ualberta.ca/index.php/ESC/article/viewFile/25086/18593 Accessed August 30, 2016.

Poelchau, Simon. "Textmarker: *Nylon Road.*" 1–30–2007. Munich: *Süddeutsche Zeitung.* http://jetzt.sueddeutsche.de/texte/anzeigen/357415/Textmarker-Nylon-Road. Accessed December 31, 2015.

"Quick Reads": *Globe and Mail*, Toronto, Aug. 13, 2011: R18. Cited in *Biography*, 34: 4, 852.

Sacco, Joe. *Footnotes in Gaza.* London: Jonathan Cape, Random House, 2009.

Satrapi, Marjane. *Persepolis: The Story of a Childhood* (2000), trans. Mattias Ripa and Blake Ferris. New York: Pantheon, 2003.

Smith, Sidonie. "Human Rights and Comics: Autobiographical Avatars, Crisis Witnessing, and Transnational Rescue Networks." In *Graphic Subjects: Critical Essays on Autobiography and Graphic Novels*, ed. Michael A. Chaney. Madison: University of Wisconsin Press, 2011, 61–72.

Smith, Sidonie, and Julia Watson. "Witness or False Witness? Metrics of Authenticity, I-Formations, and the Ethic of Verification in Testimony." *Biography*, 35:4 (Fall 2012), 590–626.

Spiegelman, Art. *In the Shadow of No Towers.* NewYork: Viking Press, 2004.

———. *Maus II: A Survivor's Tale: And Here My Troubles Began*. New York: Pantheon Books, 1991.

Stajić, Olivera. "Dialog mit dem Ich." 2010/2. http://www.migrazine.at/artikel/dialog-mit-dem-ich. Accessed August 24, 2016.

Tourage, Mahdi. "Review Essay: Written for the West: Reading Three Iranian Women's Memoirs." https://www.google.com/#q=Review+Essay+Written+for+the+West:+Reading+Three+Iranian+Women's+Memoirs. Accessed December 21, 2015.

Whitlock, Gillian. *Soft Weapons: Autobiography in Transit*. Chicago: University of Chicago Press, 2007.

Sidonie Smith is Mary Fair Croushore Professor of the Humanities, Professor of English and Women's Studies, and Director of the Institute for the Humanities at the University of Michigan. She is a past-President of the Modern Language Association of America (2010). Her most recent book is *Manifesto for the Humanities: Transforming Doctoral Education in Good Enough Times* (2015). She is author of *A Poetics of Women's Autobiography* (1987) and *Subjectivity, Identity, and the Body* (1993), as well as numerous essays. With Kay Schaffer, she co-authored *Human Rights and Narrated Lives* (2004). With Julia Watson, she co-authored *Reading Autobiography: A Guide for Interpreting Life Narratives* (2001; expanded edition 2010).

Julia Watson is Professor Emerita of Comparative Studies, a former Associate Dean of Arts and Sciences, and a Core Faculty member of Project Narrative at The Ohio State University. With Sidonie Smith she co-authored *Reading Autobiography: A Guide for Interpreting Life Narratives* (extended edition, 2010), co-edited five collections, and published several essays. Among her many essays the most recent are on women's visual diaries and on voice in Patti Smith's *Just Kids*.

www.ingramcontent.com/pod-product-compliance
Lightning Source LLC
Chambersburg PA
CBHW061701300426
44115CB00014B/2523